# Rothmans Rugby Yearbook 1978-79

## (INCORPORATING PLAYFAIR RUGBY ANNUAL)

Editor: **Vivian Jenkins**

D1386278

Macdonald and Jane's, London

Editing and design by Graeme Wright
Photographs supplied by Colin Elsey/Colorsport

Published by The Queen Anne Press Division
Macdonald and Jane's Publishers Ltd
Paulton House, 8 Shepherdess Walk, London N1 7LW

Filmset, printed and bound by Cox & Wyman Ltd,
London, Fakenham and Reading

# CONTENTS

# FOREWORD
# FROM ROTHMANS OF PALL MALL

It was in 1972 that Rothmans of Pall Mall first introduced the *Rothmans Rugby Yearbook*, and we said in the foreword to that first issue: 'We are sure that this new publication will go on to score a success similar to the one achieved by the companion yearbook for soccer.'

Brave words perhaps, but the prediction has been well justified, and we go into this, our seventh edition, confident in the knowledge that the book has become an integral part of rugby literature. Confident, but not complacent, and we hope that readers will find this issue even more comprehensive than those which have preceded it in facts, figures, features, and photographs about the game.

The past year again has been one of triumph for Wales, and that triumph is recorded in the yearbook alongside the other triumphs and failures of the season.

It is gratifying to us to see that the *Rothmans Rugby Yearbook* has become the authoritative reference work for the game. We like to think that it does the same job for rugby that *Wisden* does for cricket, and the *Rothmans Football Yearbook* does for soccer. One of the joys of rugby is that pleasure comes not only from playing or watching the game, but also from reading about it, discussing it, and indulging in friendly arguments about who really is the best.

We hope that the *Rothmans Rugby Yearbook* not only provides the facts and figures to set the discussions rolling, but also several hundred pages of pleasurable reading.

# MESSAGE FROM THE CHAIRMAN OF THE INTERNATIONAL BOARD

I am confident I express the feelings of rugby players, administrators and supporters throughout the world when I claim that we are all a little richer with the publication of the 1978–79 *Rothmans Rugby Yearbook*. Congratulations to all concerned, and especially that true rugby man of many parts, Vivian Jenkins.

The game is – and has been always – in a continuing state of change. Thus it is essential for the International Board to keep itself fully informed on trends, problems and attitudes, and to identify precisely the needs of players and the game itself. It poses a considerable challenge.

Naturally the laws of the game must come under careful examination in concept and technical detail on a continuing basis. So must amateurism, the very cornerstone of Rugby Union football.

Then there is the explosive growth of the code throughout the world. Fresh demands for assistance and guidance could well be made on the Board and its member Unions. Meanwhile the Board is delighted to welcome France to its membership. There is no doubt that the unique flair of the French for the game will now be reflected on the world administrative front also.

Every year is a good year for rugby, and I am sure that 1978–79 will prove no exception. I hope that everyone connected with the game will continue to enrich their lives by a sustained involvement at all levels.

R C Stuart   *New Zealand RU, 1978*

# EDITORIAL PREFACE

This, the seventh issue of the *Rothmans Rugby Yearbook*, should at least start out with blessing from on high. The number seven has always had a special significance, not least in biblical lore. There were, for instance, Seven Champions of Christendom. They included, happily, St George, St Andrew, St Patrick, St David and St Denis of France. The patron saints of Spain and Italy were also involved; so one day, who knows, we may yet see the *tournoi des cinq nations* becoming a *tournoi des sept*. The yearbook, with an eye to the future, pays due homage to them all!

Meanwhile we have done our best to do justice to the ups-and-downs of a particularly eventful rugby year. The failure, marginally, of the Lions in New Zealand, the Grand Slam successes of Wales, the near-misses of their opponents – all these make different reading, according to one's special allegiance. The moving finger, perforce, can only record.

Meanwhile our Player of the Year, lauded in a special article by his distinguished fellow-countryman Tony Lewis, is Gareth Edwards. A case of piling Ossa on Pelion, perhaps, in view of his manifold achievements, but we felt he stood out alone. Andy Irvine might have been a contender, after his feats in New Zealand, but injury checked his full flowering thereafter. Cliff Morgan – than whom few have better symbolised the spirit of the game – writes on the subject of amateurism and those who would challenge it. Christopher Wordsworth, of *The Observer*, salutes the coming All Blacks.

Finally my thanks to Michael Nimmo, Graeme Wright and all those who have assisted in the preparation of the yearbook. Betty Gray, who did the fair-copying, has laboured longest of all. The judgment, now, is yours.

## ADVISORY PANEL

R H G Weighill CBE DFC *Secretary Rugby Football Union*
J Law OBE *Secretary/Treasurer Scottish Rugby Football Union*
R FitzGerald *Secretary/Treasurer Irish Rugby Football Union*
W H Clement MC TD *Secretary Welsh Rugby Football Union*
V J W M Lawrence *Hon Secretary Four Home Unions' Tours Committee*
J A Prodger *Carreras Rothmans Limited*

# REVIEW OF THE YEAR

**The Editor**

8  The two main happenings, within the scope of the Yearbook, were the Lions' tour of New Zealand, with its disappointing outcome from the touring team's point of view, and the International Championship, which automatically takes pride of place in UK affairs.

Of the Lions' tour almost everything has already been said. Thousands of words have been written on the subject, with a flurry of books from various authors – most of them critical of the team's management and captaincy, as well as the off-field behaviour of some of the players. It is a hard fact of life that nothing succeeds like success, and that failure inevitably produces a search for scapegoats. 'The vulgar', it was opined as long ago as 1640, 'keep no account of your hits, but only of your misses.' The Lions have had their full share of castigation. Perhaps it is kinder, at this distance, to look for some of the redeeming features.

At least our forwards showed they have made a remarkable advance since the days when the All Blacks' packs carried all before them. In Andy Irvine at full-back, too, we had the outstanding runner of the tour, on either side. Some of his tries were sheer magic. There is no point in speculating, now, on what would have happened had Gareth Edwards been available, or if the weather had not been so foul, the tour so long, and so on. Excuses, however valid, can profit no one. The bleak fact remains that the All Blacks won the series, albeit by a whisker – and they probably needed to even more than the Lions did. After their defeats by John Dawes's team in 1971 and their fruitless expedition to South Africa in 1976, it looked as though New Zealand's rugby was on the decline. That, in the wider sense, could hardly have benefited world rugby. But it was a comfort to hear no less a person than Bob Stuart, captain of the 1953–54 All Blacks in Britain and this year's chairman of the International Board, saying in London during the course of his visit, 'You should have beaten us'. It does not help, but at least it applies some salve to the wound.

What we should be doing now is digesting the lessons of the tour, for future purposes. One remedy has already been applied. It has been laid down, at long last, that no Lions' tour, in future, shall be of more than 18 matches. This should make the top players more readily available, and make it easier for them, when on tour, to produce their best form. In this connection it was interesting to read the comments of Peter Whiting, the former All Black forward, in an interview in *Rugby World*. He complained, in his own turn, of the demands being made on New Zealand's players. These have accelerated greatly since South Africa's virtual exclusion from the international sphere, and as a result the All Blacks are due to tour here this season – and the next, and the next. It gives added force to Whiting's remarks. It is worth remembering, too, when complaining about demands on our own players, that it can cut both ways. Yet I wonder, should the All Blacks fall by the wayside this winter, whether our own spectators will take this into account.

In the Championship, last season, almost everything went Wales's way. A third Triple Crown in succession, the Grand Slam for the second time in three seasons, and a third outright Championship in four years make one wonder what there is left for them to achieve. John Dawes, their coach, made no bones about his feelings. 'The results speak for themselves', he said. 'This team deserves to be recognised as one of the greatest of all time.' Some of these opponents who lost to Wales might not altogether agree.

England, beaten by the odd penalty goal in five at Twickenham, were level until eight minutes from the end. There were those who maintained – and still do – that the last penalty goal was for a 'non-offence'. Ireland, again, gave Wales a real fright before going down 20–16 at Lansdowne Road. France, at Cardiff, sadly missed Jean-Pierre Romeu, their champion goal-kicker. Dropped earlier in the season, after France's defeat by the All Blacks in Paris, he had retired from international rugby. Wales's victories, in short, were hard-earned; but the team certainly never knew when they were beaten, and their capacity to fight back in the closing stages of a hard-fought match was a tribute to their endurance and will-to-win. Gareth Edwards, our Rothmans Player of the Year, was their guiding star, but Phil Bennett, their captain, at fly-half, also made a decisive contribution. His 25 points took his total for Wales to 166, thus furthering his own national record, and if his 44 points for the Lions, in eight international appearances, are taken into account he has now beaten Don Clarke's world record as well. The famous New Zealand full-back scored 207 points in his 31 international appearances. Bennett has now reached 210 in 37, with more, very probably, to come. That, and the Welsh team's successes, ought to be some consolation to Bennett for his setbacks on the Lions' tour.

France, although Championship runners-up, had a somewhat disappointing season. After beating the All Blacks 18–13

9

at Toulouse, but then losing to them 15–3 in Paris, they decided to change their style of play. Jacques Fouroux, who had led them to the Grand Slam the previous season, and Romeu were dropped in favour of a pair of half-backs, Gallion and Viviès, who were meant to institute a running rather than a kicking game. It worked well enough in the case of Gallion, who scored a try in all of his first three matches; but Viviès kicked almost as much as Romeu had done before him. Worse still, he was in nothing like the same class as a goal-kicker. Aguirre, at full-back, also fell short in this respect. France, nevertheless, beat England in Paris and then, after hair-breadth wins against Scotland and Ireland, came to Cardiff with the Grand Slam again within their grasp. This time their goal-kicking reached its nadir: had they succeeded with only two or three out of six missed penalty attempts, after taking an early lead of 7–0, they could well have won. Instead, they missed their chances and Wales, with every man contributing in a typical fighting rally, came back to win and round off their historic year.

With the 'differential penalty', as yet, only marginally introduced, goal-kicking still rules the roost in the Championship and in the game generally. Without the penalty goals of Bennett and Fenwick, and the dropped goals of Fenwick and Edwards, would Wales, I wonder, have been hailed as the 'greatest team ever'? Yet no one can belittle the champions on that account, for until the laws are changed the goal-kickers will remain supreme.

England had another encouraging season, with two wins and two defeats. Their pack, led by a new captain, Bill Beaumont, who won plaudits all round, was equal to almost every demand made on it, but behind the scrum there were still question marks at half-back and in the centre. Even here, though, there was some improvement. John Horton, at fly-half, and Dodge, in the centre, did well enough to deserve an extended trial this season. Caplan, at full-back, was also a decided gain.

England, with a new emphasis being laid on their 'B' and Under 23 teams, are building up a line of progression which should serve them well in future years. The signs are beginning to show already, and should gain further impetus. More debatable was the system of regional and divisional matches initiated by the 1976–77 president, Dickie Jeeps. The idea was no doubt good from the national point of view, but the clubs were not happy about being deprived of their players so often. For instance, Peter Squires, the England wing, made only two appearances for his club, Harrogate, before Christmas. This season the regional and divisional matches are being held over, owing to the impact of the Argentinian and New Zealand tours, and I dare say the clubs would not mind if such an arrangement became permanent.

Ireland won only one of their matches, against Scotland, but there were signs that under a new coach, Noel Murphy, they will become a real force before long. They lost only narrowly to Wales and France, by four points and a point respectively, and gave England a hard match at Twickenham. The advent of a new fly-half, Tony Ward, of Garryowen, was their most encouraging sign of all. He scored 38 points, to equal the Championship record, and his general play was on a par with his goal-kicking. Mike Gibson, picked this time as a wing, took his total of caps to 65 to set a new world record for an individual country. At 35 he looked as good as ever. A remarkable man!

Scotland, I fear, were 'whitewashed' for the first time in 10 years. Yet they could have drawn with Ireland if they had taken an easy penalty-goal opportunity in the final minute. Instead, Doug Morgan, their captain, elected for a tap-kick, and possible try, but the gamble failed. Injuries to key players, and some odd quirks of selection did not help the Scottish cause.

In the Southern Hemisphere the Lions' tour of New Zealand obviously took pride of place. The All Blacks' success gave them what seemed a much-needed boost, and there were signs, happily, that back play has again begun to play a part in their scheme of things. Yet there is little doubt that the Lions themselves contributed most to their own undoing. South Africa, still struggling to find a formula for their re-admission to the international arena, had little to occupy them except their own domestic affairs; but a visit from a World Invitation XV, captained by Willie John McBride, on a programme of three matches, at least enabled them to see some of the top players from the rest of the globe. In the 'international' at Pretoria the Springboks won 45–24, and awarded 'caps'; but it was a hollow victory, in a way. The touring team was very much a 'scratch' combination and had little time to prepare.

In Australia, again, it was a comparatively uneventful season, with no major international matches, although by now Wales's short tour there will have filled in some of the gaps. The main item of note in Australia itself was the advance of Queensland in inter-state affairs. They beat New South Wales twice and were generally rated the best side in the country. The success of the brilliant Wallaby Schoolboys on their tour of Britain was the brightest omen of all for Australia's rugby future.

Tours by New Zealand to France, Scotland to the Far East, France to Argentina, and England Under 23 to Canada helped to fill in the rugby picture round the world, but possibly the most exciting new development was the first visit to England by a team representing the USA. They won only two of their six matches, and were comprehensively beaten 37–11 by an England XV at Twickenham; but it was good to see them there at all. It could lead to a whole new world of rugby in the next decade.

The Eagles, as they were termed, made friends wherever they went, both on and off the field, and the only shadow – a long one indeed – fell when the tour was over. Craig Sweeney, their captain, who had been an outstanding leader in every respect, died of a heart attack after a training session in California. He was only 32. A tragic loss.

On the laws front, the International Board made no changes of any major consequence, though there are hints we may see an extension of the 'differential penalty' once the Southern Hemisphere countries have seen more of it in action. However, there is disquiet in many quarters about the effect the new definition of the tackle is having on mauls and rucks. 'Sacks on the mill', as they term these jumbles of bodies in New Zealand, have become a commonplace, and the game badly needs tidying up in this respect.

In England, the anomalies of the 'merit table' method of qualifying for the John Player Cup competition may yet lead to limited national leagues, on Scottish lines. The RFU sent out a circular to their clubs to find out their views. On a wider scale, the effects of sponsorship became more and more apparent in the game. I recall the late Sir William Ramsay, who was in at the beginning of it all, saying 'I feel that all will be well as long as we can control the funds at Union level'. This, alas, does not always seem to be happening, and the game is suffering a marked sea-change as a result. A tightening-up in this respect is needed. Yet at grass-roots level the game remains much as it always was. The coming season, one hopes, will produce as much good fun and companionship as ever.

# ROTHMANS PLAYER OF THE YEAR – GARETH EDWARDS

**Tony Lewis** *The Sunday Telegraph*

Most sporting careers have a nasty habit of running into snags before the *Boys' Own* ending materialises. Not so with Gareth Edwards. The 1977–78 rugby season arrived and he began gently as usual; but he was not wholly deaf to the cawing critics who reckoned that he did not play often enough for Cardiff; that Brynmor Williams was a better player; and that he was overweight and uncaring. By the end of the season he had done much to help hand them a third successive Triple Crown, as well as the Grand Slam, on a plate and everyone was chirping 'The Greatest'.

Edwards had won 49 Welsh caps before the season started and John Dawes, particularly, had spent much time persuading him to keep going for the magic fiftieth. No Welsh player had achieved it before. Yet months earlier Edwards had doubted his own will to take on another season, and highly as he prized the British Lions' jersey he did not go to New Zealand in the summer of 1977. Rest was the only cure for a player who had scarcely been off the international field from 1967. His caps had been won successively, and that itself, especially in the scrum-half position, was a near miracle of physical endurance. The lure of 50 caps, however, was irresistible, and rightly so. None of his past honours, from the cherished OBE to his freedom to fish the Teifi, had dulled his schoolboy's relish for great deeds.

How many times back in Colbren Square, Gwaun-cae-Gurwen, had he dived over for the winning try against 'England', grazing his knees on the concrete pitch; then being called in for tea by his Mam, and scoffing it before sneaking back out in semi-darkness to make the vital conversion? How often had Bill Samuel, his schoolteacher in Pontardawe, laid down in sergeant-major style the great plans for him? Samuel trained him hard as an athlete, gymnast, cricketer, footballer, and as a rugby player, at first at centre-threequarter. 'We've a regular scrum-half already', he had boomed at the young man. 'You'd better try centre.' Even the Welsh Secondary Schools were to say as much to Gareth. They once picked him as a centre against the Yorkshire Schools, but the game was snowed off.

Bill Samuel it was who directed a flood of written correspondence in the direction of Millfield School. The headmaster, its founder, R J O ('Boss') Meyer, was so taken with the persistence of the man that he agreed to interview the object of

*Strength and balance, flair and courage – Gareth Edwards displayed them all against England at Twickenham where he won his fiftieth successive cap for Wales and further extended his own world record for appearances by a scrum-half.*

his devoted instruction; i.e. G O Edwards. Meyer truthfully thought that Samuel was either exaggerating beyond all conniving, or that he had on his hands one of the most talented sportsmen in the world. It says much for the judgment of both that they were proved right. Samuel instilled ambition in Gareth as only someone facing up daily to the modest horizons of Welsh valley life could: Meyer made him believe that sporting talent was something precious, to be given air and opportunity. 15

So much did Gareth owe to his two schools that it is not surprising that the twinkle of the boy with the new rugger boots for Christmas has never left him. Fifty Welsh caps – could he ever have aspired to such an unimaginable goal? Yet on 4 February 1978 he was allowed the privilege of leading Phil Bennett's Welsh side on to the field at Twickenham. That was it. He was, by now, more than a mere player; he was the talisman without which a Welsh side was never complete.

There was some fortune that day in the way Wales won by 9 points to 6. Bennett kicked three penalty goals, Hignell two, though the Englishman shaved the posts with other attempts. However, Wales squeezed England back for most of the second half as Edwards kicked mercilessly for position. Kicking was just about the only option for the half-backs in the mud and rain, and diagonally he sent kicks spinning towards the corner flags, right and left. His pack gave him time, and on one occasion, on the English 22-metre line, he stood back to drive a low skimming kick to the corner, a gain of 21 metres, precisely. Almost an academic exercise! It eventually wore England down.

At Cardiff Scotland took a lead. Doug Morgan kicked a penalty goal. If that surprised most spectators, no one in the world was shaken by the Welsh response. Close to the Scots' line the Welsh scrummage took a precious heel against the head. Up in the press box I felt like writing about the impending try even before it had happened. 'Edwards goes to the blind side, dummies, dips his shoulder, waggles his hips, and dives through a brave tackle to score.' So it was. From close-quarters he has nearly always been unstoppable. The words of Bill Samuel often came back to him on the field. 'Boy, be a good gymnast. Scrum-half is to do with strength, but more important, it's balance.' This is surely why Gareth Edwards can get in his pass or his kick or can score tries when opponents are actually hanging on to him. One leg on the ground is enough if you have the physique and sense of equilibrium. Later in this 22–14 victory Edwards cheekily turned play to the two metres of blindside ground available to send Derek Quinnell careering in for a long-range try. From start to finish, too, he demonstrated how pin-point kicking from scrum-half can sway the modern game.

So Wales were on their way to a third successive Triple Crown; but they were also setting off in the direction of Ireland, where such vaunted hopes had notoriously gone agley before. Gareth knew that better than anyone. In 1968 Wales, led by John Dawes, went down 9–6 in a welter of orange peel, apple cores, and bottles. Edwards had been awarded a dropped goal which only the referee had adjudged over the bar and between the posts. In 1970 Edwards led Wales across for the big prize. Ireland tossed Wales and their Crown back into the Irish Sea. Edwards had his only disastrous game for Wales. The Triple Crown next beckoned from over the water in 1974. Edwards was captain once more and Wales just managed a 9–9 draw. It was just as well he could swim, and had an instinct for survival.

This last time, in 1978, it was hardly a different experience on the field. Ireland were Murphy-motivated. It was desperately hard and none too clean. Edwards recalls even his old touring friend Slattery flailing his boot past his nose. ' "C'mon Slatts", I said.' Slattery offered a glazed 'Sorry, Gar', but the battle raged on.

Wales led, Ireland caught them up 13–13, and caused utter confusion in the Welsh team. As Edwards steadied them, Fenwick proved his temperament by kicking his long penalty-chances. The Welsh players have since told how Gareth chatted them through their badly shaken spell, cajoled them with a slap on the backside, and chided J P R Williams for being upset by the crowd. He kept his calm and his kicking won precious ground; the menace of the Irish forwards was blunted for vital spells. Finally Edwards broke wide from a set-piece on the right. He ignored the promises of scissors and dummy scissors by Bennett and Gravell, instead spinning a pass high over a head to Fenwick, who flipped the ball on to J J Williams, who scored the try. It was the turning point, and Edwards, yet again, had played a vital part in it.

Selecting one player from a fine team which won all the prizes is unfair, but it is forgivable in this case, even in the eyes of his team-mates. Wales went on to beat France 16–7 for the Grand Slam, with Edwards again demonstrating how much he had perfected his blend of anticipation, timing, and experience. He dropped a goal, sent kicks sizzling upfield a good 55 metres to touch from quite narrow angles. His running was controlled. The ball in his hands meant a safe service for Bennett and on his boot trouble for France. To cap everything it was Edwards's run, ducking and weaving past defenders from all of 30 metres,

16

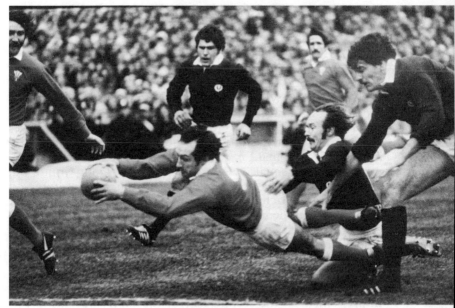

*A typical Edwards blind-side try set Wales on the path to victory over Scotland at Cardiff and took his total in international matches to 20, the Welsh record.*

that set up the position for Bennett's second try, which settled the match.

'There was a time years ago', he admits, 'when I stood for the Welsh anthem "Hen Wlad Fy Nhadau", cried, and ran around as a demented patriot for the first 20 minutes. Now I can look around and take in the atmosphere slowly. Once I used to worry about my pass; it was awful. Now I know that the boys want control as well as flair. I can pass, I can run, and I can kick; it is just a question of when to do what.'

I recall writing before that match against France, moved by the knowledge that I might well be witnessing Gareth Edwards's last appearance in a Welsh jersey. 'If Barry John's talent became verbal magic after his brief career, Gareth has become the living legend, there to behold, time after time, before our very eyes – hard as Welsh slate, quixotic as a wink across the bar. How else could he possibly leave us but with a Grand Slam?'

How else, indeed? – and how he lived up to our hopes. 'Gareth the Great' – the cap certainly fits, and not only Welshmen, I feel, will be happy to acclaim him as Player of the Year.

# BRITISH ISLES TO NEW ZEALAND AND FIJI 1977

**John Brooks** *The Christchurch Press*

In 1971, John Dawes was a prominent figure in one of the two most successful rugby sides to have visited New Zealand – the other being the 1937 Springbok team led by Philip Nel. Dawes was a shrewd captain and an admirable ball-distributor at centre in the 1971 combination, which was superbly coached by Carwyn James and equally well managed by Dr Doug Smith, but unfortunately he seemed to have left the blueprint at home on his journey as coach in 1977. New Zealand won the series 3–1, and there were dented reputations in the visiting camp.

Neither Dawes nor the manager, George Burrell, cut very convincing figures. Both made some astonishing statements, and Dawes seemed to have difficulty in establishing his best XV or in working out a purposeful pattern of play. Eventually the emergence of Terry Cobner as a pack leader produced a marked improvement in the second half of the tour, and during this period the pack shoved all opposition willy-nilly about the field, including the All Blacks.

In the backs, in contrast, there were substantial problems and, considering the slim margin between triumph and defeat in the fourth international, ·the presence of Gareth Edwards, J P R Williams, and Gerald Davies might have made all the difference. The outstanding individual was Andy Irvine, whose brilliant attacking from full-back was a feature of the tour. The fact that he topped the try-scoring from his specialist position – scoring five tries against King Country/Wanganui and 11 in all – spoke volumes for his ability with the ball in hand. At fly-half, Phil Bennett, the captain, appeared to lose concentration and confidence towards the end of the tour and kicked away too much possession.

No praise is too high for the forwards. Graham Price was outstanding at tight-head prop, and consistently fine performances came from Duggan, Brown, Cotton, and Wheeler, with the replacement lock, Bill Beaumont, emerging as an ideal partner for Brown.

The Lions were seen in action by 730,000 spectators who paid more than $NZ2m, but the tour was not one of the great ones. Certainly the visitors dropped only one game – to NZ Universities – outside the internationals, but with a few exceptions they did not rate as an entertaining side. Continuous rain and muddy pitches were another bugbear. The last straw was to be plunged into the steam-heat of Suva and go down to Pio Tikoisuva and his ebullient Fijians.

## THE TOURING PARTY

**Captain** P Bennett  **Manager** G Burrell (Scotland)
**Assistant Manager** S J Dawes (Wales)

### FULL-BACKS
**A R Irvine** (Heriot's FP & Scotland)
**B H Hay** (Boroughmuir & Scotland)

### THREEQUARTERS
**P J Squires** (Harrogate & England)
**H E Rees** (Neath & Wales 'B')
**J J Williams** (Llanelli & Wales)
**G L Evans** (Newport & Wales)
**C M H Gibson** (North of Ireland FC & Ireland)
**S P Fenwick** (Bridgend & Wales)
**D H Burcher** (Newport & Wales)
**I R McGeechan** (Headingley & Scotland)

### HALF-BACKS
**P Bennett** (Llanelli & Wales)
**J D Bevan** (Aberavon & Wales)
**D W Morgan** (Stewart's Melville FP & Scotland)
**D B Williams** (Cardiff & Wales 'B')
***A D Lewis** (Cambridge U & London Welsh)

### FORWARDS
**W P Duggan** (Blackrock Coll & Ireland)
**J Squire** (Newport & Wales)
**T J Cobner** (Pontypool & Wales)
**T P Evans** (Swansea & Wales)
**A Neary** (Broughton Park & England)
**D L Quinnell** (Llanelli & Wales)
**G L Brown** (West of Scotland & Scotland)
**N E Horton** (Moseley & England)
**A J Martin** (Aberavon & Wales)
**M I Keane** (Lansdowne & Ireland)
***W B Beaumont** (Fylde & England)
**F E Cotton** (Sale & England)
**P A Orr** (Old Wesley & Ireland)
**G Price** (Pontypool & Wales)
**C Williams** (Aberavon & Wales)
***A G Faulkner** (Pontypool & Wales)
**R W Windsor** (Pontypool & Wales)
**P J Wheeler** (Leicester & England)

*Replacement during tour*

## TOUR RECORD

**All matches**   Played 26 Won 21 Lost 4 Drawn 1 Points for 607 Against 320
**In New Zealand**  Played 25 Won 21 Lost 3 Drawn 1 Points for 586 Against 295
**In Fiji**    Played 1 Lost 1 Points for 21 Against 25

## MATCH DETAILS

| 1977 | OPPONENTS | VENUE | RESULT |
| --- | --- | --- | --- |
| 18 May | Wairarapa–Bush | Masterton | W 41–13 |
| 21 May | Hawke's Bay | Napier | W 13–11 |
| 25 May | Poverty Bay–East Coast | Gisborne | W 25–6 |
| 28 May | Taranaki | New Plymouth | W 21–13 |
| 1 June | King Country–Wanganui | Taumarunui | W 60–9 |
| 4 June | Manawatu–Horowhenua | Palmerston North | W 18–12 |
| 8 June | Otago | Dunedin | W 12–7 |
| 11 June | Southland | Invercargill | W 20–12 |
| 14 June | NZ Universities | Christchurch | L 9–21 |
| 18 June | NEW ZEALAND | Wellington | L 12–16 |
| 22 June | S & Mid-Canterbury–N Otago | Timaru | W 45–6 |
| 25 June | Canterbury | Christchurch | W 14–13 |
| 29 June | West Coast–Buller | Westport | W 45–0 |
| 2 July | Wellington | Wellington | W 13–6 |

| 5 July | Marlborough–Nelson Bays | Blenheim | W 40–23 |
| 9 July | NEW ZEALAND | Christchurch | W 13–9 |
| 13 July | NZ Maoris | Auckland | W 22–19 |
| 16 July | Waikato | Hamilton | W 18–13 |
| 20 July | NZ Juniors | Wellington | W 19–9 |
| 23 July | Auckland | Auckland | W 34–15 |
| 30 July | NEW ZEALAND | Dunedin | L 7–19 |
| 3 August | Counties–Thames Valley | Pukekohe | W 35–10 |
| 6 August | North Auckland | Whangarei | W 18–7 |
| 9 August | Bay of Plenty | Rotorua | W 23–16 |
| 13 August | NEW ZEALAND | Auckland | L 9–10 |
| 16 August | Fiji | Suva | L 21–25 |

## APPEARANCES AND SCORERS

(New Zealand only)

| | App* | T | C | PG | DG | Pts | | App* | T | C | PG | DG | Pts |
|---|---|---|---|---|---|---|---|---|---|---|---|---|---|
| Bennett | 14 | 2 | 13 | 26 | – | 112 | Martin | 13 | – | – | 2 | – | 6 |
| Morgan | 15 | 3 | 16 | 18 | – | 98 | Bevan | 11 | 1 | – | – | – | 4 |
| Irvine | 18 | 11 | 8 | 9 | – | 87 | Brown | 14 | 1 | – | – | – | 4 |
| J J Williams | 14 | 10 | – | – | – | 40 | Beaumont | 9 | 1 | – | – | – | 4 |
| Rees | 12 | 7 | – | – | – | 28 | Orr | 12 | 1 | – | – | – | 4 |
| Squires | 9 | 6 | – | – | – | 24 | C Williams | 9 | 1 | – | – | – | 4 |
| Gibson | 11 | 2 | 2 | 4 | – | 24 | Wheeler | 13 | 1 | – | – | – | 4 |
| G L Evans | 17 | 6 | – | – | – | 24 | Windsor | 13 | 1 | – | – | – | 4 |
| Hay | 11 | 5 | – | – | – | 20 | Cotton | 16 | – | – | – | – | 0 |
| Burcher | 14 | 4 | – | – | – | 16 | Price | 14 | – | – | – | – | 0 |
| Fenwick | 12 | 1 | 1 | 3 | – | 15 | T P Evans | 13 | – | – | – | – | 0 |
| McGeechan | 15 | 3 | – | – | – | 12 | Neary | 13 | – | – | – | – | 0 |
| D B Williams | 12 | 3 | – | – | – | 12 | Keane | 12 | – | – | – | – | 0 |
| Squire | 14 | 3 | – | – | – | 12 | Horton | 4 | – | – | – | – | 0 |
| Cobner | 11 | 3 | – | – | – | 12 | Faulkner | 2 | – | – | – | – | 0 |
| Duggan | 15 | 2 | – | – | – | 8 | Lewis | 2 | – | – | – | – | 0 |
| Quinnell | 14 | 2 | – | – | – | 8 | | | | | | | |

*Includes appearances as replacements. Irvine was a replacement four times, Orr three times, McGeechan, D B Williams, Morgan and Squire twice each, and G L Evans, Duggan, Quinnell, Neary, Martin, Keane, C Williams, and J J Williams once each. One of McGeechan's appearances as a replacement and one of Morgan's were in the third international match.

In the match against Fiji the touring team's scorers were: Tries: Bennett, Beaumont, Burcher Conversions: Bennett (3)   Penalty Goal: Bennett. This brought Bennett's total of points for the tour to 125. Irvine made his 19th appearance of the tour, at full-back, G L Evans his 18th, McGeechan his 16th, and Burcher, Bennett, Squire, Price, and Brown their 15th, the last-named coming on as a replacement.

### International matches

| | App | T | C | PG | DG | Pts | | App | T | C | PG | DG | Pts |
|---|---|---|---|---|---|---|---|---|---|---|---|---|---|
| Bennett | 4 | – | – | 6 | – | 18 | J J Williams | 3 | 1 | – | – | – | 4 |
| Morgan | *2 | 1 | 1 | 1 | – | 9 | Duggan | 4 | 1 | – | – | – | 4 |
| Irvine | 4 | – | – | 2 | – | 6 | | | | | | | |

*Once as a replacement. Other appearances were: Four times – Fenwick, Price, McGeechan (once as a replacement); Three times – G L Evans, D B Williams, Cobner, Brown, Cotton, Wheeler, Beaumont; Twice – Quinnell; Once – Rees, Squires, Burcher, Squire, T P Evans, Martin, Keane, Windsor, Orr, Neary.

**TOTALS** (In New Zealand)
**All matches**
For:       80T 40C 62PG 586 Pts
Against: 29T 13C 46PG 5DG 295 Pts

**International matches**
For:       3T 1C 8PG 41 Pts
Against: 6T 3C 7PG 1DG 54 Pts

### MATCH 1   18 May, Masterton

**Wairarapa–Bush 13** (1G 1PG 1T)   **British Isles XV 41** (3G 1PG 5T)          21
**Wairarapa–Bush:** N F Kjestrup; S Paton, B B Patrick, H T Huriwai, K England;
A J O'Neill, B H Herangi; *No 8* N D Taylor; *Second Row* P C Mahoney,
P J Guscott, B W Clarke, I F Turley; *Front Row* W N Rowlands (*capt*),
G K McGlashan, N P Sargent   *Replacement* J Darlington for Clarke (57 mins)
**Scorers** *Tries:* McGlashan, Paton   *Conversion:* Kjestrup   *Penalty Goal:* Kjestrup
**British Isles XV:** Hay; Squires, McGeechan, Burcher, J J Williams; Bennett (*capt*),
D B Williams; *No 8* Quinnell; *Second Row* T P Evans, Keane, Horton, Cobner;
*Front Row* Price, Wheeler, Orr   *Replacements* Duggan for Horton (30 mins), Irvine
for Hay (55 mins)
**Scorers** *Tries:* J J Williams (3), Cobner (2), Burcher (2), Squires   *Conversions:*
Bennett (3)   *Penalty Goal:* Bennett
**Referee** A R Taylor (Canterbury)

### MATCH 2   21 May, Napier

**Hawke's Bay 11** (1PG 2T)   **British Isles XV 13** (3PG 1T)
**Hawke's Bay:** M Tocker; P J Durham, R F Allen, R P Bremner, K Taylor;
H J Paewai, D S McCarroll; *No 8* J P Ryan; *Second Row* J Paraha, M J McCool,
R L Stuart (*capt*), T J Carter; *Front Row* B R Dunstan, I G Grant, J M O'Connor
*Replacement* W Nixon for Bremner (30 mins)
**Scorers** *Tries:* Stuart, Taylor   *Penalty Goal:* Tocker
**British Isles XV:** Irvine, J J Williams, Gibson, Fenwick, G L Evans; Bevan,
Morgan; *No 8* Duggan; *Second Row* Neary, Brown, Martin, Quinnell; *Front Row*
Cotton (*capt*), Windsor, C Williams
**Scorers** *Try:* Irvine   *Penalty Goals:* Fenwick (3)
**Referee** W Adlam (Wanganui)

### MATCH 3   25 May, Gisborne

**Poverty Bay–East Coast 6** (2PG)   **British Isles XV 25** (2G 3PG 1T)
**Poverty Bay–East Coast:** W Isaac; J V Walter, B H Sherriff, R M Parkinson,
G F Torrie; G W Thompson, S Donald; *No 8* L G Knight; *Second Row* R Falcon,
B Cameron, C N Kirkpatrick, I A Kirkpatrick (*capt*); *Front Row* R A Newlands,
G W Allen, W E McFarlane   *Replacement* L Rickard for Sherriff (25 mins)
**Scorer** *Penalty Goals:* Isaac (2)
**British Isles XV:** Hay; Squires, Gibson, McGeechan (*capt*), G L Evans; Bevan,
Morgan; *No 8* Duggan; *Second Row* T P Evans, Keane, Martin, Neary; *Front Row*
Cotton, Windsor, C Williams   *Replacement* Irvine for Hay (45 mins)
**Scorers** *Tries:* G L Evans, McGeechan (2)   *Conversions:* Morgan (2)   *Penalty Goals:*
Morgan (3)
**Referee** M G Farnworth (Auckland)

### MATCH 4   28 May, New Plymouth

**Taranaki 13** (2DG 1PG 1T)   **British Isles XV 21** (2G 3PG)
**Taranaki:** S G Davison; A C Brown, R P Wharehoka, B E Gladding,
J M O'Sullivan; P Martin, D S Loveridge; *No 8* M C Carey; *Second Row*
R J Fraser, J M Thwaites, I M Eliason, G N K Mourie (*capt*); *Front Row*
R B McEldowney, F K O'Carroll, J T McEldowney   *Replacement* P J Fleming for
Loveridge (62 mins)

**Scorers** *Try:* O'Sullivan  *Dropped Goals:* Martin (2)  *Penalty Goal:* Martin
**British Isles XV:** Irvine; J J Williams, Fenwick, Burcher, G L Evans; Bennett
(*capt*), D B Williams; *No 8* Quinnell; *Second Row* Cobner, Brown, Horton, T P
Evans; *Front Row* Price, Wheeler, Orr
**Scorers** *Tries:* J J Williams, Irvine  *Conversions:* Irvine, Bennett  *Penalty Goals:*
Irvine (2), Bennett
**Referee** P A McDavitt (Wellington)

## MATCH 5  1 June, Taumarunui

**King Country–Wanganui 9** (1G 1PG)  **British Isles XV 60** (8G 3T)
**King Country–Wanganui:** F W Hill; B W Donovan, M R Murray,
W M Osborne, R J Murray; C P Howard, N W Pye; *No 8* J W Tarrant; *Second
Row* A D Middleton, G J Coleman, G D Mitchison, R B Stafford (*capt*); *Front Row*
G T Lethborg, G Potaka, R B Donaldson  *Replacement* R Snowdon for Middleton
(60 mins)
**Scorers** *Try:* Snowdon  *Conversion:* Hill  *Penalty Goal:* Hill
**British Isles XV:** Irvine; Squires, Fenwick, McGeechan, J J Williams; Bennett
(*capt*), Morgan; *No 8* Quinnell; *Second Row* Neary, Martin, Keane, Squire; *Front
Row* Cotton, Wheeler, Orr  *Replacements* D B Williams for Morgan (30 mins),
G L Evans for McGeechan (74 mins)
**Scorers** *Tries:* Irvine (5), J J Williams (2), D B Williams, Bennett, Squire, Quinnell
*Conversions:* Bennett (8)
**Referee** J Walker (Otago)

## MATCH 6  4 June, Palmerston North

**Manawatu–Horowhenua 12** (1DG 3PG)  **British Isles XV 18** (1G 3T)
**Manawatu–Horowhenua:** A C Innes; K W Granger, D L Rollerson (*capt*),
M D Nutting, M G Watts; D C Morris, M W Donaldson; *No 8* G H Old; *Second
Row* L R Robinson, J K Loveday, J A Callesen, K A Eveleigh; *Front Row*
K K Lambert, J D Easton, P C Harris  *Replacements* P Broederlow for Morris (52
mins), G A Knight for Loveday (74 mins)
**Scorers** *Dropped Goal:* Morris  *Penalty Goals:* Rollerson (3)
**British Isles XV:** Hay; G L Evans, Fenwick, Burcher, Squires; Bevan,
D B Williams; *No 8* Duggan; *Second Row* Cobner (*capt*), Keane, Horton, Squire;
*Front Row* Price, Windsor, C Williams  *Replacement* Quinnell for Cobner (14 mins)
**Scorers** *Tries:* C Williams, D B Williams, Fenwick, Hay  *Conversion:* Fenwick
**Referee** T F Doocey (Canterbury)

## MATCH 7  8 June, Dunedin

**Otago 7** (1PG 1T)  **British Isles XV 12** (4PG)
**Otago:** B W Wilson; R Gibson, G W Bennetts, D V Colling, J S Colling;
J L Jaffray, T J Burcher; *No 8* M W R Jaffray (*capt*); *Second Row* R A Roy, G A
Seear, W Graham, R M Smith; *Front Row* L A Clark, K C Bloxham, R O'Connell
*Replacement* S Thomson for Bennetts (25 mins)
**Scorer** *Try:* Wilson  *Penalty Goal:* Wilson
**British Isles XV:** Irvine; Rees, Burcher, Gibson, J J Williams; Bennett (*capt*)
D B Williams; *No 8* Duggan; *Second Row* Squire, Horton, Martin, T P Evans; *Front
Row* Price, Wheeler, Cotton  *Replacement* Keane for Horton (35 mins)
**Scorer** *Penalty Goals:* Bennett (4)
**Referee** B Duffy (Taranaki)

## MATCH 8  11 June, Invercargill

**Southland 12** (4PG)  **British Isles XV 20** (1G 2PG 2T)
**Southland:** J J Gardiner; E D McLellan, W Boynton, S Pokere, S O'Donnell;
B J McKechnie, D O J Shanks; *No 8* A A McGregor; *Second Row* N R Anderson,

M J Leach, F J Oliver (*capt*), L M Rutledge; *Front Row* D R Saunders, B R Lamb, P R Butt
**Scorer** *Penalty Goals:* McKechnie (4)
**British Isles XV:** Hay; Rees, Gibson, McGeechan, G L Evans; Bennett (*capt*), D B Williams; *No 8* Duggan; *Second Row* Squire, Brown, Martin, T P Evans; *Front Row* Price, Windsor, Orr  *Replacement* Irvine for Hay (half-time)
**Scorers** *Tries:* G L Evans, Rees, Gibson  *Conversion:* Irvine  *Penalty Goals:* Martin (2)
**Referee** J P G Pring (Auckland)

23

### MATCH 9   14 June, Christchurch

**NZ Universities 21** (1G 5PG)   **British Isles XV 9** (1G 1PG)
**NZ Universities:** M D Heffernan; R F S Scott, D T Fouhy, D L Rollerson (*capt*), R S Hawkins; P A Macfie, M J T Romans; *No 8* G W Elvin; *Second Row* D N Thorn, W Graham, G J Brown, R C Scott; *Front Row* P T Oliver, D A Syms, G P Denholm
**Scorers** *Try:* Macfie  *Conversion:* Rollerson  *Penalty Goals:* Rollerson (3), Heffernan (2)
**British Isles XV:** Hay; Squires, McGeechan (*capt*), Burcher, Rees; Bevan, Morgan; *No 8* Quinnell; *Second Row* Squire, Brown, Keane, Neary; *Front Row* Cotton, Wheeler, C Williams  *Replacements* Martin for Brown (55 mins), Orr for Keane (65 mins)
**Scorers** *Try:* Quinnell  *Conversion:* Morgan  *Penalty Goal:* Morgan
**Referee** K H Lynch (Poverty Bay)

## MATCH 10   18 June, Wellington     1st International

# NEW ZEALAND 16 (2G 1T)
# BRITISH ISLES 12 (4PG)

In this crucial first match of the international series the lead changed hands five times. All the points were scored in an exciting first half, with the decisive score, a try by Grant Batty for New Zealand, coming two minutes before half-time, when the Lions were attacking and a try seemed in prospect. Trevor Evans was put down by a hard tackle by Bruce Robertson, and his lobbed pass to mass support on his right was intercepted by Batty. Although he had 60 yards to run and his legs were unsound, the New Zealand left wing had too much start, even for the fast-pursuing Irvine who just failed to prevent the try. It was a disaster for the Lions, but Batty deserved the ovation he was given. The Lions, later, termed it the 'twelve-points try'.

The All Blacks, with a capacity crowd of 45,000 present, were off-side in the first line-out, and Irvine kicked a superb goal from 55 metres down-wind. Within a minute or two New Zealand hit back with a typical try by Going. Receiving possession from a ruck 10 metres out, he shaped to pass first right and then left, only to find Duncan Robertson and Batty covered. Instead he decided to run on his own and ducked under Bennett and Duggan to score, though the kick failed.

The Lions' captain suffered a bruised chest in this incident, but stayed on the field and kicked penalty goals in the nineteenth and twenty-fifth minutes to put his side 9–4 ahead. Then it was the All Blacks' turn again. A penalty kick by Bryan Williams was held up by the wind as it descended near the posts, and Johnstone fastened on to the ball in a scramble before diving over to score. Williams converted easily.

A minute later Going offended at a scrum and Bennett kicked his third penalty goal, for the Lions to lead 12–10. Finally, just before the interval, came Batty's dramatic try. Williams converted and the All Blacks maintained their four points lead throughout the second half on a cold, bleak Wellington day.

**NEW ZEALAND:** C P Farrell (Auckland); B G Williams (Auckland), W M Osborne (Wanganui), B J Robertson (Counties), G B Batty (Bay of Plenty); D J Robertson (Otago), S M Going (North Auckland); *No 8* L G Knight (Poverty Bay); *Second Row* K A Eveleigh (Manawatu), F J Oliver (Southland), A M Haden (Auckland), I A Kirkpatrick (Poverty Bay); *Front Row* K K Lambert (Manawatu), R W Norton (Canterbury) *(capt)*, B R Johnstone (Auckland)
**Scorers** *Tries:* Going, Johnstone, Batty *Conversions:* Williams (2)
**BRITISH ISLES:** Irvine; Squires, McGeechan, Fenwick, J J Williams; Bennett *(capt)*, D B Williams; *No 8* Duggan; *Second Row* Cobner, Keane, Martin, T P Evans; *Front Row* Price, Windsor, Orr
**Scorers** *Penalty Goals:* Irvine, Bennett (3)
**Referee** P A McDavitt (Wellington)

## MATCH 11    22 June, Timaru

**South/Mid-Canterbury–N Otago 6** (2PG)    **British Isles XV 45** (6G 3PG)
**South/Mid-Canterbury–N Otago:** D A Nicol; I D Palmer, A J Grieve, W J Cooper, A M McLaren; A M Goddard, P C Williams; *No 8* R H King; *Second Row* N E Glass, J C Ross, W J Anderson *(capt)*, P J Grant; *Front Row* G Prendergast, R D Sloper, B L Higginson
**Scorer** *Penalty Goals:* Nicol (2)
**British Isles XV:** Irvine; Rees, Gibson, G L Evans, J J Williams; McGeechan, Morgan; *No 8* Quinnell; *Second Row* Cobner *(capt)*, Beaumont, Martin, Neary; *Front Row* Cotton, Wheeler, C Williams
**Scorers** *Tries:* Rees (2), Irvine, G Evans, Wheeler, J J Williams *Conversions:* Irvine (6) *Penalty Goals:* Irvine (3)
**Referee** B Williams (West Coast)

## MATCH 12    25 June, Christchurch

**Canterbury 13** (1G 1PG 1T)    **British Isles XV 14** (2PG 2T)
**Canterbury:** M D Heffernan; R F S Scott, A C R Jefferd, M R McEwan, S C M Cartwright; O D Bruce, L J Davis; *No 8* D M Thompson; *Second Row* A J Wyllie *(capt)*, V E Stewart, G Higginson, J K Phillips; *Front Row* W K Bush, R W Norton, J C Ashworth *Replacement* S I Purdon for Wyllie (61 min)
**Scorers** *Tries:* Jefferd, Ashworth *Conversion:* Heffernan *Penalty Goal:* Heffernan
**British Isles XV:** Irvine; J J Williams, Fenwick, Burcher, G L Evans: Bevan, Morgan; *No 8* Duggan; *Second Row* Cobner *(capt)*, Brown, Martin, T P Evans; *Front Row* Cotton, Windsor, Orr *Replacement* Squire for T P Evans (53 mins)
**Scorers** *Tries:* G L Evans, J J Williams *Penalty Goals:* Irvine (2)
**Referee** D H Millar (Otago)

## MATCH 13  29 June, Westport

**West Coast–Buller 0  British Isles XV 45** (4G 3PG 3T)
**West Coast–Buller:** R P Mumm; P A Teen, B Davidson, B R Morgan,
A M Mundy; A Ireland, J G Gilbert; *No 8* B McGuire; *Second Row* J D N Sullivan,
M M Sinclair, J L Lee (*capt*), N M J Roberts; *Front Row* R J Banks, R J Mitchell,
J A Steffens
**British Isles XV:** Hay; Squires, Burcher, Gibson, Rees; Bevan, Morgan; *No 8*
Squire; *Second Row* T P Evans (*capt*), Beaumont, Keane, Neary; *Front Row* Cotton,
Windsor, C Williams
**Scorers** *Tries:* Squires (2), Squire, Morgan, Keane, Bevan, Hay  *Conversions:*
Morgan (4)  *Penalty Goals:* Morgan (3)
**Referee** G L Harrison (Wellington)

## MATCH 14  2 July, Wellington

**Wellington 6** (2PG)  **British Isles XV 13** (3PG 1T)
**Wellington:** C J Currie; B G Fraser, L G May, R S Cleland, W G Procter;
J P Dougan, D J Henderson; *No 8* A R Leslie (*capt*); *Second Row* P B Quinn,
J K Fleming, B F Gardner, M G Stevens; *Front Row* A E Keown, F B H Walker,
K L Phelan
**Scorer** *Penalty Goals:* Cleland (2)
**British Isles XV:** Irvine; J J Williams, Fenwick, McGeechan, G L Evans; Bennett
(*capt*), D B Williams; *No 8* Quinnell; *Second Row* Neary, Brown, Martin, Cobner;
*Front Row* Price, Wheeler, Cotton
**Scorers** *Try:* Cobner  *Penalty Goals:* Bennett (3)
**Referee** C P Gregan (Waikato)

## MATCH 15  5 July, Blenheim

**Marlborough–Nelson Bays 23** (5PG 2T)  **British Isles XV 40** (4G 4PG 1T)
**Marlborough–Nelson Bays:** R E Gordon; B W Hunter, G Rogers,
S W P Marfell, B R Ford; J Speedy, P J Baker; *No 8* B A Kenny; *Second Row*
D W Neal, T J Julian (*capt*), M G West, M J Best; *Front Row* J W Baryluk,
K G Sutherland, G R Paki Paki
**Scorers** *Tries:* Rogers (2)  *Penalty Goals:* Marfell (5)
**British Isles XV:** Hay; Squires, Gibson, Burcher, Rees; Bevan, Morgan; *No 8*
Squire; *Second Row* T P Evans (*capt*), Beaumont, Brown, Quinnell; *Front Row*
Price, Windsor, C Williams  *Replacements* Orr for Price (38 mins), D B Williams
for Morgan (46 mins)
**Scorers** *Tries:* Burcher, Hay, Rees, D B Williams, Brown  *Conversions:* Gibson (2),
Morgan (2)  *Penalty Goals:* Gibson (2), Morgan (2)
**Referee** N B Whittaker (Manawatu)

# MATCH 16  9 July, Christchurch  2nd International

# NEW ZEALAND 9 (3PG)
# BRITISH ISLES 13 (3PG 1T)

With five changes in the pack, as well as one in the backs, the
Lions were a much different team from that of the first international, and the cohesion and spirit displayed by the forwards
decided the issue. None the less, it took a fine try by J J Williams
to put the icing on the cake. The All Blacks had lost Lambert
through illness and Bruce Robertson through injury; then Batty

hobbled off the training field and announced his retirement. But better goal-kicking could still have won them the match.

In the opening minutes Williams missed a penalty attempt for the All Blacks; Bennett was more reliable when the Lions had a similar scoring chance. The Lions' captain then made a good run from deep inside his own half and punted on. Farrell failed against the rolling ball, the Lions surged on, and eventually the ball reached J J Williams, who dummied through the cover superbly to score. Before half-time Bryan Williams kicked two penalty goals for New Zealand, and Bennett two for the Lions, who led 13–6 at the interval. One of the tourists' penalties was the result of a late tackle on Bennett by Eveleigh, which led to some hostile exchanges.

In the second half the home crowd could hardly believe their eyes when Bryan Williams missed a 'sitter' of a penalty attempt from in front of the posts. He made belated amends with a penalty goal 10 minutes from the end, but a final bid to reverse the result failed when Lyn Jaffray lost control of the ball near the posts, and Gareth Evans touched down for a 'minor'. The All Blacks, who pressed furiously in the closing stages, came desperately close to snatching the match out of the fire, but justice would not have been served had the Lions lost after their earlier excellent efforts.

A crowd of 50,000 watched the game, played on a heavy, muddy surface. Isolated outbreaks of violence, the worst caused by the late charge on Bennett, did nothing for Rugby.

**NEW ZEALAND:** C P Farrell (Auckland); B G Williams (Auckland), J L Jaffray (Otago) W M Osborne (Wanganui), N M Taylor (Bay of Plenty); O D Bruce (Canterbury), S M Going (North Auckland); *No 8* L G Knight (Poverty Bay); *Second Row* K A Eveleigh (Manawatu), F J Oliver (Southland), A M Haden (Auckland), I A Kirkpatrick (Poverty Bay); *Front Row* W K Bush (Canterbury), R W Norton (Canterbury) (*capt*), B R Johnstone (Auckland)
**Scorer** *Penalty Goals:* Williams (3)
**BRITISH ISLES:** Irvine; J J Williams, Fenwick, McGeechan, G L Evans; Bennett (*capt*), D B Williams; *No 8* Duggan; *Second Row* Quinnell, Beaumont, Brown, Cobner; *Front Row* Price, Wheeler, Cotton
**Scorers** *Try:* J J Williams *Penalty Goals:* Bennett (3)
**Referee** B Duffy (Taranaki)

### MATCH 17   13 July, Auckland

**NZ Maoris 19** (2G 1PG 1T)   **British Isles XV 22** (2PG 4T)
**NZ Maoris:** H K Whiu; G W Skipper, E J T Stokes, W M Osborne, D A Haynes; E Dunn, S M Going; *No 8* M G West; *Second Row* T J Waaka, R J Lockwood, V E Stewart, T J Carter; *Front Row* L Toki, R W Norton (*capt*), W K Bush
*Replacement* P B Quinn for West (60 mins)
**Scorers** *Tries:* Going (2), Osborne *Conversions:* Whiu (2) *Penalty Goal:* Whiu
**British Isles XV:** Hay; Squires, Gibson, Burcher, J J Williams; Bevan, Morgan; *No 8* Duggan; *Second Row* T P Evans (*capt*), Keane, Martin, Neary; *Front Row*

Cotton, Windsor, Orr  *Replacements* C Williams for Cotton (15 mins), Squire for Duggan (half-time)
**Scorers** *Tries:* Orr, Squires (2), Gibson  *Penalty Goals:* Gibson (2)
**Referee** J P G Pring (Auckland)

## MATCH 18  16 July, Hamilton

**Waikato 13** (1G 1PG 1T)  **British Isles XV 18** (2PG 3T)
**Waikato:** T Irwin; A L Clark, C L Fawcett, L Hohaia, J W O'Rourke; D R McGlashan, K M Greene *(capt)*; *No 8* R G Myers; *Second Row* I J Lockie, R J Lockwood, J C Sisley, P G Anderson; *Front Row* G L Irwin, J P Bennett, D L Olsen
**Scorers** *Tries:* Lockwood, T Irwin  *Conversion:* T Irwin  *Penalty Goal:* T Irwin
**British Isles XV:** Irvine; Rees, Burcher, McGeechan, G L Evans; Bennett *(capt)*, D B Williams; *No 8* Quinnell; *Second Row* Squire, Beaumont, Brown, Cobner; *Front Row* Windsor, Wheeler, C Williams  *Replacements* Orr for C Williams (45 mins), Morgan for D B Williams (78 mins)
**Scorers** *Tries:* Rees (2), Irvine  *Penalty Goals:* Bennett (2)
**Referee** B Dawson (Southland)

## MATCH 19  20 July, Wellington

**NZ Juniors 9** (1G 1PG)  **British Isles XV 19** (2G 1PG 1T)
**NZ Juniors:** B W Wilson (Otago); M G Watts (Manawatu), D T Fouhy (Wellington), S Pokere (Southland), D A Haynes (North Auckland); M K Sisam (Auckland) *(capt)*, M W Donaldson (Manawatu); *No 8* G W Elvin (Otago); *Second Row* J D Sullivan (West Coast), W Graham (Otago), W A Craig (Auckland), G J W Rich (Auckland); *Front Row* R C Ketels (Counties), G J Collins (Canterbury), M I Pervan (Auckland)  *Replacement* A J Dawson (Counties) for Sullivan (15 mins)
**Scorers** *Try:* Pokere  *Conversion:* Wilson  *Penalty Goal:* Wilson
**British Isles XV:** Hay; Rees, McGeechan, Gibson, G L Evans; Bevan, Morgan; *No 8* Squire; *Second Row* T P Evans *(capt)*, Keane, Martin, Neary; *Front Row* Cotton, Windsor, Orr  *Replacement* J J Williams for Gibson (11 mins)
**Scorers** *Tries:* Windsor, Rees, Squire  *Conversions:* Morgan (2)  *Penalty Goal:* Morgan
**Referee** M G Farnworth (Auckland)

## MATCH 20  23 July, Auckland

**Auckland 15** (1G 3PG)  **British Isles XV 34** (1G 4PG 4T)
**Auckland:** C P Farrell; B G Williams, T M Twigden, P J Parlane, T G Morrison; P M Richards, B M Gemmell; *No 8* G J W Rich; *Second Row* B G Ashworth, A M Haden, B Munro, D N Thorn; *Front Row* B R Johnstone *(capt)*, A B Hathaway, S L Watt  *Replacement* G P Denholm for Watt (60 mins)
**Scorers** *Try:* Williams  *Conversion:* Parlane  *Penalty Goals:* Williams, Watt (2)
**British Isles XV:** Irvine; J J Williams, Burcher, Fenwick, G L Evans; Bennett *(capt)*, Morgan; *No 8* Duggan; *Second Row* Quinnell, Beaumont, Brown, Neary; *Front Row* Price, Wheeler, Cotton
**Scorers** *Tries:* Irvine (2), J J Williams, Bennett, Duggan  *Conversion:* Morgan  *Penalty Goals:* Morgan (4)
**Referee** D H Millar (Otago)

## MATCH 21  30 July, Dunedin  3rd International

### NEW ZEALAND 19 (1G 1DG 2PG 1T)
### BRITISH ISLES 7 (1PG 1T)

28

The All Blacks' selectors dropped six members of their losing team in the second international – including Going, who was replaced at scrum-half by another veteran, the 34-year-old Lyn Davis, whose understanding with his Canterbury colleague Bruce improved the All Black backline. But the most impressive newcomer was Bevan Wilson, the 21-year-old Otago fullback. His steadiness under the high ball and safe kicking were just what the All Blacks needed.

One wonders whether the Lions' forwards were on speaking terms with their backs after the match. The pack won possession from the set-pieces and delivered it with copybook control, only for the backs to fritter the advantage away.

The All Blacks' first score came after only 47 seconds, Kirkpatrick going over for a try after a chip-kick by Robertson. Wilson converted to make it 6–0. Duggan then crossed for an unconverted try for the Lions after picking up a loose ball on the blind side of a scrum, and in the tenth minute Haden replied with a similar effort for the All Blacks. This made it 10–4 to New Zealand at half-time.

For a quarter of an hour afterwards, the Lions were on top but missed two kickable penalty attempts. Then Irvine and Wilson put over penalty goals for their respective sides, Wilson following with another for New Zealand to put them 16–7 ahead. In the final minute Robertson dropped a goal for the All Blacks to round off the scoring, and even though the home team deserved their win, the margin rather flattered them. The crowd, 34,000, was disappointingly small.

**NEW ZEALAND:** B W Wilson (Otago); B G Williams (Auckland), B J Robertson (Counties), W M Osborne (Wanganui), B R Ford (Marlborough); O D Bruce (Canterbury), L J Davis (Canterbury) *No 8* L G Knight (Poverty Bay); *Second Row* I A Kirkpatrick (Poverty Bay), F J Oliver (Southland), A M Haden (Auckland), G N K Mourie (Taranaki); *Front Row* W K Bush (Canterbury), R W Norton (Canterbury) *(capt)*, J T McEldowney (Taranaki)
**Scorers** *Tries:* Kirkpatrick, Haden  *Conversion:* Wilson  *Dropped Goal:* Robertson *Penalty Goals:* Wilson (2)
**BRITISH ISLES:** Irvine; J J Williams, Fenwick, Burcher, G L Evans; Bennett *(capt)*, D B Williams; *No 8* Duggan; *Second Row* Quinnell, Beaumont, Brown, Cobner; *Front Row* Price, Wheeler, Cotton  *Replacements* McGeechan for J J Williams (32 mins), Morgan for D B Williams (50 mins)
**Scorers** *Try:* Duggan  *Penalty Goal:* Irvine
**Referee** D H Millar (Otago)

### MATCH 22  3 August, Pukekohe

**Counties–Thames Valley 10** (1G 1T)  **British Isles XV 35** (3G 3PG 2T)

**Counties–Thames Valley:** R N Lendrum; D G McMillan, B J Robertson, B C Duggan, H P Milner; G K Taylor, M M Codlin; *No 8* A J Dawson; *Second Row* R H Craig, P Clotworthy, J Rawiri, H J Hadbraken; *Front Row* J E Spiers, A G Dalton (*capt*), L J Hughes
**Scorers** *Tries:* McMillan, Lendrum *Conversion:* Lendrum
**British Isles XV:** Hay; Rees, Gibson, Burcher, G L Evans; Bevan, Morgan; *No 8* Squire; *Second Row* Neary (*capt*), Keane, Martin, T P Evans; *Front Row* Price, Windsor, Faulkner
**Scorers** *Tries:* Morgan, G L Evans (2), Hay (2) *Conversions:* Morgan (3) *Penalty Goals:* Morgan (3)
**Referee** P A McDavitt (Wellington)

### MATCH 23  6 August, Whangarei

**North Auckland 7** (1PG 1T)  **British Isles XV 18** (1G 4PG)
**North Auckland:** M J Gunson; L A Roberts, C Going, J E Morgan, D A Haynes; E Dunn, S M Going (*capt*); *No 8* H K Sowman; *Second Row* I Phillips, H H Macdonald, B Holmes, T J Waaka; *Front Row* W R Neville, P H Sloane, C D'Arcy
**Scorers** *Try:* Haynes *Penalty Goal:* Gunson
**British Isles XV:** Irvine; Rees, Fenwick, McGeechan, G L Evans; Bennett (*capt*), Lewis; *No 8* Duggan; *Second Row* Cobner, Beaumont, Brown, Quinnell; *Front Row* Cotton, Wheeler, Orr *Replacement* Neary for Cobner (65 mins)
**Scorers** *Try:* McGeechan *Conversion:* Bennett *Penalty Goals:* Bennett (4)
**Referee** J Walker (Otago)

### MATCH 24  9 August, Rotorua

**Bay of Plenty 16** (1DG 3PG 1T)  **British Isles XV 23** (5PG 2T)
**Bay of Plenty:** G D Rowlands (*capt*); G E Moore, E J T Stokes, N M Taylor, J T Kamizona; L J Brake, T R Davis; *No 8* T M Connor; *Second Row* D A Matuschka, W M Jones, J B Spry, A M McNaughton; *Front Row* L Keepa, R J Doughty, J R Helmbright *Replacements* R D Moon for Taylor (60 mins), A Compton for Kamizona (65 mins)
**Scorers** *Try:* Taylor *Dropped Goal:* Brake *Penalty Goals:* Rowlands (3)
**British Isles XV:** Hay; Rees, Gibson, Burcher, Bennett (*capt*); Bevan, Lewis; *No 8* Duggan; *Second Row* T P Evans, Keane, Brown, Squire; *Front Row* Price, Windsor, Faulkner *Replacements* McGeechan for Gibson (30 mins), Irvine for Hay (70 mins)
**Scorers** *Tries:* Rees, Burcher *Penalty Goals:* Bennett (5)
**Referee** N Thomas (Manawatu)

## MATCH 25  13 August, Auckland  4th International

# NEW ZEALAND 10 (2PG 1T)
# BRITISH ISLES 9 (1G 1PG)

Remorseless pressure by the Lions' forwards, stubborn All Blacks' defence, and a spectacular try in the second minute of injury time which gave New Zealand the series were the high-spots of this final match. The decisive score came when the Lions were still leading 9–6. Bennett failed to find touch with a clearing kick whereupon Osborne, who fielded, kicked high in return and sprinted hard to tackle Fenwick, the catcher, in possession. The Lions' centre passed to Wheeler, who was put down by Mourie, and the ball popped loose into the grateful

*Typical of the appalling ground conditions that bedevilled the 1977 Lions in New Zealand were those at Athletic Park, Wellington, when they played, and defeated, the NZ Juniors.*

hands of Knight, who ran some 20 metres to score. The goal-kick, which failed, mattered not, and a photograph showing Knight on the ground with the ball and Bennett standing beside him, head bowed and hands on knees, told the story of the match – and the series.

The Lions' forwards, on a warm day, were even better than in the third international. Price played magnificently at prop and Neary took advantage of the Lions' momentum to disrupt the All Blacks' back play. In the line-outs Brown and Beaumont were in command, and several times the Lions poured through gaps to start powerful attacks. Yet so much pressure could again produce only one try. This was scored, following a break from loose play, by scrum-half Morgan, whose conversion and penalty goal gave his side a 9–3 lead at half-time. Wilson had kicked a penalty goal for the All Blacks.

In the second half, Wilson succeeded with another penalty goal attempt, but Morgan missed twice. His second failure, when the Lions were leading 9–6, proved crucial, for it came only five minutes from the end when another three points would almost certainly have decided the match. Instead, the All Blacks came back with Knight's try; to the delight of the all-ticket 58,000 crowd. It was the Lions' final frustration.

**NEW ZEALAND:** B W Wilson (Otago); B G Williams (Auckland), W M Osborne (Wanganui), B J Robertson (Counties), B R Ford (Marlborough); O D Bruce (Canterbury), L J Davis (Canterbury); *No 8* L G Knight (Poverty Bay); *Second Row* I A Kirkpatrick (Poverty Bay), A M Haden (Auckland), F J Oliver (Southland), G N K Mourie (Taranaki); *Front Row* K K Lambert (Manawatu), R W Norton (Canterbury) *(capt)*, J T McEldowney (Taranaki) *Replacements* N M Taylor (Bay of Plenty) for Ford (45 mins), W K Bush (Canterbury) for McEldowney (61 mins)
**Scorers** *Try:* Knight  *Penalty Goals:* Wilson (2)
**BRITISH ISLES:** Irvine; Rees, Fenwick, McGeechan, G L Evans; Bennett *(capt)*, Morgan; *No 8* Duggan; *Second Row* Neary, Beaumont, Brown, Squire; *Front Row* Price, Wheeler, Cotton
**Scorer** *Try:* Morgan  *Conversion:* Morgan  *Penalty Goal:* Morgan
**Referee** D H Millar (Otago)

## MATCH 26  16 August, Suva

**Fiji 25** (1G 1DG 4T)  **British Isles XV 21** (3G 1PG)
**Fiji:** K Musunamasi; J Kuinikoro, O Ratu, S Nasave, W Gavidi; P Tikoisuva *(capt)*, S Viriviri; *No 8* V Ratudradra; *Second Row* R Qariniqio, I Tuisese, I Taoba, V Narasia; *Front Row* N Ratudina, A Racika, J Rauto
**Scorers** *Tries:* Narasia (2), Kuinikoro, Racika (2)  *Conversion:* Racika  *Dropped Goal:* Tikoisuva
**British Isles XV:** Irvine; Bennett *(capt)*, McGeechan, Burcher, G L Evans; Bevan, Lewis; *No 8* Squire; *Second Row* Neary, Beaumont, Martin, T P Evans; *Front Row* Price, Windsor, Faulkner  *Replacement* Brown for T P Evans (70 mins)
**Scorers** *Tries:* Bennett, Beaumont, Burcher  *Conversions:* Bennett (3)  *Penalty Goal:* Bennett
**Referee** S Koroi (Suva)

# NEW ZEALAND TO ITALY AND FRANCE 1977

**Bob Donahue** *Agence France Presse*

Having won the Lions series, New Zealand brought a reorgan-
ised squad to France where they drew an 'unofficial world
championship' series. They lost the first international but won
the second, emphatically, in Paris. The young New Zealanders
went home heads high, leaving the French somewhat bemused.

The All Blacks were the better running side throughout their
eight-match tour, their 45–3 win at Brive in the opening match
cementing their *esprit de corps* and exciting French observers. To
a French public weary of 10-man victories, Graham Mourie's
team presented a 15-man attacking game, based on control of
loose possession and quick transmission to strong threequarters. They supported and covered well, tackled hard, and
always tried to keep the ball alive. Of their 30 tries in France
(with only four against) their backs scored 20. As the New
Zealand coach Jack Gleeson had expected, his men held,
wheeled, and spoiled to sufficient effect at the scrum. Line-outs
were decisive in the internationals, with New Zealand turning
the tables after Toulouse. Spirit, tactical flair, and fitness won
for the All Blacks in Paris.

An early injury cost the touring team their place-kicker and
only full-back, Bevan Wilson. In addition Bryan Williams,
Brian Ford, and John Black were also unavailable for the second
international. The French had to do without Bastiat and Rives
in the back row in both internationals, as well as Averous and
Harize on the wings. One should record, too, that the international matches were notable for the quality of the refereeing,
and that the weather, for the time of the year, was the warmest
in South-Western France in 50 years.

On the way to this, their first special tour to France, New
Zealand had paid a first visit to Italy, meeting an Italian second
XV containing two South Africans and a French scrum-half
(the national side were in Warsaw that day for a European
championship match). The score was even, 6–6, at half-time
and the All Blacks led by only a point, 10–9, five minutes from
the end. Their 17–9 win must have come as something of a
relief, with 'jet-lag' no doubt still affecting their performance.

The Padua result did nothing to dampen French confidence,
already fuelled by reports of unconvincing All Black play in the
Lions series. The extent and decisive manner of the touring
team's victory four days later in Brive came as a shock to many,

for the scratch side in Brive looked by no means the weakest of the six assembled by France's selectors. Later, regional spirit stiffened the opposition, but it was the internationals that really mattered, and in that respect the drawn series was something of an anti-climax.

## THE TOURING PARTY

**Captain** G N K Mourie   **Manager** R M Don   **Assistant Manager** J Gleeson

| FULL-BACK | FORWARDS |
|---|---|
| **B W Wilson** (Otago) | **G N K Mourie** (Taranaki) |
| **THREEQUARTERS** | **K A Eveleigh** (Manawatu) |
| **B G Williams** (Auckland) | **L G Knight** (Poverty Bay) |
| **B R Ford** (Marlborough) | **G A Seear** (Otago) |
| **B J Robertson** (Counties) | **R G Myers** (Waikato) |
| **S S Wilson** (Wellington) | **R L Stuart** (Hawke's Bay) |
| **N M Taylor** (Bay of Plenty) | **F J Oliver** (Southland) |
| **W M Osborne** (Wanganui) | **A M Haden** (Auckland) |
| ***B Hegarty** (Wellington & Biarritz) | **G A Knight** (Manawatu) |
| **HALF-BACKS** | **B R Johnstone** (Auckland) |
| **O D Bruce** (Canterbury) | **J C Ashworth** (Canterbury) |
| **B J McKechnie** (Southland) | **J T McEldowney** (Taranaki) |
| **M W Donaldson** (Manawatu) | **A G Dalton** (Counties) |
| **K M Greene** (Waikato) | **J E Black** (Canterbury) |

*Replacement during tour*

## TOUR RECORD

| | |
|---|---|
| **All matches** | Played 9 Won 8 Lost 1 Points for 216 Against 86 |
| **In Italy** | Played 1 Won 1 Points for 17 Against 9 |
| **In France** | Played 8 Won 7 Lost 1 Points for 199 Against 77 |
| **International matches** | Played 2 Won 1 Lost 1 Points for 28 Against 21 |

## MATCH DETAILS

| 1977 | OPPONENTS | VENUE | RESULT |
|---|---|---|---|
| 22 October | Italy XV | Padua | W 17–9 |
| 26 October | French Selection | Brive | W 45–3 |
| 29 October | French Selection (South-East) | Lyon | W 12–10 |
| 1 November | French Selection (Languedoc) | Perpignan | W 12–6 |
| 5 November | French Selection (South-West) | Agen | W 34–12 |
| 8 November | French Selection (South-West) | Bayonne | W 38–22 |
| 11 November | FRANCE | Toulouse | L 13–18 |
| 15 November | French Selection | Angoulême | W 30–3 |
| 19 November | FRANCE | Paris | W 15–3 |

## APPEARANCES AND SCORERS

### All matches

| | App* | T | C | PG | DG | Pts |
|---|---|---|---|---|---|---|
| McKechnie | 6 | – | 8 | 6 | 3 | 43 |
| Williams | 6 | 4 | – | 4 | – | 28 |
| Taylor | 7 | 4 | 2 | – | 1 | 23 |
| Ford | 6 | 4 | – | – | – | 16 |
| Mourie | 7 | 4 | – | – | – | 16 |
| S Wilson | 7 | 4 | – | – | – | 16 |
| Bruce | 6 | 2 | – | 1 | 1 | 14 |
| Seear | 6 | 1 | 2 | 2 | – | 14 |
| L G Knight | 7 | 3 | – | – | – | 12 |
| Osborne | 8 | 2 | – | – | – | 8 |
| Myers | 4 | 1 | – | – | – | 4 |
| Eveleigh | 5 | 1 | – | – | – | 4 |
| Donaldson | 5 | 1 | – | – | – | 4 |
| Stuart | 6 | 1 | – | – | – | 4 |
| Johnstone | 7 | 1 | – | – | – | 4 |
| B Wilson | 3 | – | – | 1 | – | 3 |
| Robertson | 8 | – | – | – | 1 | 3 |
| Haden | 9 | – | – | – | – | 0 |
| Oliver | 5 | – | – | – | – | 0 |
| G A Knight | 5 | – | – | – | – | 0 |
| Dalton | 5 | – | – | – | – | 0 |
| Greene | 4 | – | – | – | – | 0 |
| Black | 4 | – | – | – | – | 0 |
| Ashworth | 4 | – | – | – | – | 0 |
| McEldowney | 2 | – | – | – | – | 0 |
| Hegarty | 0 | – | – | – | – | 0 |

34

*Includes appearances as replacements. Stuart and Osborne were replacements twice each, and Mourie, Eveleigh, and Robertson once each. Stuart's and Osborne's appearances as replacements included one each in an international match.

### International matches

| | App* | T | C | PG | DG | Pts |
|---|---|---|---|---|---|---|
| McKechnie | 2 | – | 1 | 2 | 1 | 11 |
| Williams | 1 | 1 | – | 1 | – | 7 |
| S Wilson | 2 | 1 | – | – | – | 4 |
| Seear | 2 | – | – | 1 | – | 3 |
| Robertson | 2 | – | – | – | 1 | 3 |

### TOTALS

**All matches**
For:     33T 12C 14PG 6DG 216 Pts
Against: 5T  3C 16PG 4DG  86 Pts

**International matches**
For     2T 1C 4PG 2DG 28 Pts
Against: 1T 1C 4PG 1DG 21 Pts

### MATCH 1   22 October, Padua

**Italy XV 9** (1G 1PG)   **New Zealanders 17** (1G 1PG 2T)
**Italy XV** *Try:* L Francescato  *Conversion:* Zuin  *Penalty Goal:* Zuin
**New Zealanders** *Tries:* Mourie (2), Ford  *Conversion:* McKechnie  *Penalty Goal:* McKechnie

### MATCH 2   26 October, Brive

**French Selection 3** (1PG)   **New Zealanders 45** (2G 2DG 1PG 6T)
**French Selection** *Penalty Goal:* Gabernet
**New Zealanders** *Tries:* L Knight (3), Taylor, Bruce, Osborne, Mourie, Seear
*Conversions:* Taylor (2)  *Dropped Goals:* Bruce, Taylor  *Penalty Goal:* Williams

### MATCH 3   29 October, Lyon

**French Selection 10** (2PG 1T)   **New Zealanders 12** (3T)
**French Selection** *Try:* Ferrou  *Penalty Goals:* Pommier (2)
**New Zealanders** *Tries:* Ford (2), Williams

### MATCH 4   1 November, Perpignan

**French Selection 6** (1DG 1PG)   **New Zealanders 12** (1G 2DG)
**French Selection** *Dropped Goal:* Lopez  *Penalty Goal:* Lopez

**New Zealanders** *Try:* S Wilson   *Conversion:* McKechnie   *Dropped Goals:* McKechnie (2)

#### MATCH 5   5 November, Agen

**French Selection 12** (2DG 2PG)   **New Zealanders 34** (2G 2PG 4T)
**French Selection** *Dropped Goals:* Viviès, Mazas   *Penalty Goals:* Viviès (2)
**New Zealanders** *Tries:* Taylor (3), Johnstone, S Wilson, Donaldson   *Conversions:* Seear (2)   *Penalty Goals:* Seear, Bruce

#### MATCH 6   8 November, Bayonne

**French Selection 22** (1G 4PG 1T)   **New Zealanders 38** (2G 6PG 2T)
**French Selection** *Tries:* Bilbao, Clemente   *Conversion:* Uthurriscq   *Penalty Goals:* Uthurriscq (4)
**New Zealanders** *Tries:* Williams (2), Mourie, Ford   *Conversions:* McKechnie (2)
*Penalty Goals:* McKechnie (3), Williams (2), B Wilson

## MATCH 7   11 November, Toulouse   1st International

### FRANCE 18 (1G 1DG 3PG)
### NEW ZEALAND 13 (1DG 2PG 1T)

The All Blacks fielded six new caps – McKechnie, Stuart Wilson, Donaldson, Seear, Gary Knight, and Black. The forwards totalled only 18 caps between them, and it was Mourie's first full international as captain. McKechnie, chosen for the tour as a fly-half, but held to be the team's best goal-kicker after Bevan Wilson's injury, made a difficult début out of position at full-back. The All Blacks were not expected to win, yet they almost did, and the lessons learnt were to prove more than sufficient in Paris. At Toulouse the French looked slow, and they admitted afterwards that they had little cause to boast.

McKechnie put over a penalty goal for New Zealand in the first minute, but then Romeu began the punting that was quickly to sap his confidence and swing a match which the All Black forwards arguably deserved to draw. The New Zealand full-back fielded and punted indifferently, and he missed two penalties close to the posts. Bryan Williams also failed with three out of four penalty attempts, while Bruce muffed a simple drop-kick which would have put the All Blacks in the lead nine minutes from the end.

In the nineteenth minute, following a high punt by Romeu, came a try by Paparemborde, his seventh against International Board countries. The fly-half converted and was on his way to making history in the second half with a dropped goal and three penalty goals, taking his total of points in internationals to 136 – three more than the record set up by Pierre Villepreux in 1972. New Zealand drew level with a dropped goal by Robertson, and two minutes from half-time France's captain Jacques

Fouroux, palpably off-form, passed to no one for Taylor to intercept and run 36 metres before putting in a short kick which Robertson snapped up from a favourable bounce. The centre in turn slipped the ball out to Williams, who crossed for an unconverted try on the right. This put New Zealand 10–6 ahead at half-time, and shortly afterwards Williams made it 13–6 with a thumping penalty goal from 40 metres. Thereafter, however, Romeu took over with his dropped goal and three penalty goals, and New Zealand lost a match they could well have won. Bryan Williams's thirty-first international match ended sadly when he was carried off near the end with a dislocated femur.

France won the line-outs that mattered, but were surprised to be only marginally stronger in the scrum. And if both packs carried aggression beyond the legal limits, New Zealand learnt that France were not as formidable as they had been reputed to be.

**FRANCE:** J-M Aguirre (Bagnères); D Bustaffa (Carcassonne), R Bertranne (Bagnères), F Sangalli (Narbonne), G Novès (Toulouse); J-P Romeu (Montferrand), J Fouroux (Auch) (*capt*); *No 8* A Guilbert (Toulon); *Second Row* J-C Skréla (Toulouse), M Palmié (Béziers), J-F Imbernon (Perpignan), J-L Joinel (Brive); *Front Row* R Paparemborde (Pau), A Paco (Béziers), G Cholley (Castres)
**Scorers** *Try:* Paparemborde  *Conversion:* Romeu  *Dropped Goal:* Romeu  *Penalty Goals:* Romeu (3)
**NEW ZEALAND:** McKechnie; Williams, Robertson, Taylor, S Wilson; Bruce, Donaldson; *No 8* Seear; *Second Row* Mourie (*capt*), Oliver, Haden, L G Knight; *Front Row* G A Knight, Black, Johnstone  *Replacements* Stuart for G Knight (60 mins), Osborne for Williams (76 mins)
**Scorers** *Try:* Williams  *Dropped Goal:* Robertson  *Penalty Goals:* McKechnie, Williams
**Referee:** J R West (Ireland)

**MATCH 8   15 November, Angoulême**

**French Selection 3** (1PG)   **New Zealanders 30** (3G 3T)
**French Selection** *Penalty Goal:* Haget
**New Zealanders** *Tries:* S Wilson, Stuart, Eveleigh, Myers, Bruce, Osborne
*Conversions:* McKechnie (3)

## MATCH 9   19 November, Paris (Parc des Princes)
## 2nd International

**FRANCE 3** (1PG)   **NEW ZEALAND 15** (1G 1DG 2PG)
Again France were favoured to win, but the All Blacks rose to the occasion magnificently and had much the better of things both behind and in the scrum. Their forwards excelled themselves, and their backs were in command, both as defenders and attackers. It was the first time France had been beaten at Parc des Princes without scoring a try. Skréla and Paco stood out in front, the new wings, Bustaffa and Noves, looked promising

*Gary Seear, the Otago No 8 – one of the All Blacks' big successes in the second international at Parc des Princes. Outstanding in general play, he also kicked an enormous penalty goal.*

enough, but their centres were unreliable. Rives and Bastiat were much missed. On this showing New Zealand had many of the makings of greatness, but France looked on the decline.

In the ninth minute, after Romeu had failed with a kickable penalty and Seear had burst 20 metres from a French throw-in, New Zealand's full-back, McKechnie, skidded cricket-style into a catch from a desperate French clearance kick, sprang to his feet, and dropped a superb goal from near touch. He then kicked a penalty goal, whereas Romeu failed with a drop-kick attempt for France. In these early stages the All Blacks defended stubbornly whenever France attacked, and they gave timely wing-support to McKechnie under the high ball. After 30 minutes Seear kicked a huge penalty goal for New Zealand and France were nine points down, but a penalty goal by Romeu made it 9–3 at the interval.

In contrast to what had happened at Toulouse, the All Blacks went on to win 60 per cent of the line-out possession. Donaldson and Bruce outmanoeuvred the French halves, and the visiting flankers brought down the open-side wings time and again. In Toulouse, chanting French supporters had demanded the replacement of Fouroux; now the Paris crowd cheered the All Blacks when they scored the game's only try. A quick throw-in from Mourie to Lawrie Knight in the first minute of the second half caught the French threequarters out of position and Robertson capped a brilliant tour by putting Stuart Wilson over on the left. McKechnie, whose eight points and general play represented a considerable comeback, converted, and the All Blacks, from then on, never looked like being headed.

38

**FRANCE:** J-M Aguirre (Bagnères); D Bustaffa (Carcassonne), R Bertranne (Bagnères), F Sangalli (Narbonne), G Novès (Toulouse); J-P Romeu (Montferrand), J Fouroux (Auch) (*capt*); *No 8* A Guilbert (Toulon); *Second Row* J-C Skréla (Toulouse), M Palmié (Béziers), J-F Imbernon (Perpignan), J Gasc (Graulhet); *Front Row* R Paparemborde (Pau), A Paco (Béziers), G Cholley (Castres)
**Scorer** *Penalty Goal:* Romeu
**NEW ZEALAND:** McKechnie; Taylor, Robertson, Osborne, S Wilson; Bruce, Donaldson; *No 8* Seear; *Second Row* Mourie (*capt*), Oliver, Haden, L Knight; *Front Row* G Knight, Dalton, Johnstone
**Scorers** *Try:* S Wilson *Conversion:* McKechnie *Dropped Goal:* McKechnie *Penalty Goals:* McKechnie, Seear
**Referee** C G P Thomas (Wales)

# SCOTLAND TO FAR EAST 1977

Scotland's aim on their tour to the Far East was not so much to confront their Thai, Hong Kong, and Japanese hosts with the full international squad as to bring on some of the younger Scottish aspirants. Of the 25 players in the party, no fewer than 12 were uncapped at the time of the tour. Yet the Scots, captained by Mike Biggar, the London Scottish international flank forward, still ran up some overwhelming scores. They won all five games, scored 307 points, conceded only six tries, and finished off with a 74–9 win against the Japanese national side in Tokyo. It was the second highest score of the tour, surpassed only by the 82–3 win against Thailand in the opening match – the first occasion a national team from the British Isles had played in Bangkok.

Of the touring team's points, 63 came from the boot of Colin Mair, the uncapped West of Scotland full-back, who converted 17 of the 21 tries scored in the two Tokyo matches. Bill Gammell, Edinburgh Wanderers' international wing, was next in the scoring list with 40 points, all from tries, including four in the match against Japan. One of the five uncapped forwards, Gordon Dickson, scored seven tries, three of them in the Bangkok game.

In the international, the smaller, lighter Japanese put up a good fight for the first 40 minutes, as the interval score of 15–3 indicated; but in the second half the Scots began to dominate up front. As in the previous games, their powerful forward thrusts sapped the strength of the opposition. Scrum-half Laidlaw impressed with his accurate service and penetrative running, Renwick with his electrifying bursts, and Gammell with his powerful finishing. It was only in the closing stages, when the Scots appeared to be in complete command, that Japan were able to break away and score a try through their wing Ujino.

Peter Hughes, the English referee, accompanied the party and took charge of the last two games.

## THE TOURING PARTY

**Captain** M A Biggar   **Manager** T Pearson
**Assistant Manager** G W Thomson   **Player/coach** N A MacEwan

### FULL-BACKS

A E Kennedy (Watsonians)          C D R Mair (West of Scotland)

40

*Mike Biggar, the London Scottish wing-forward (with headband), captained Scotland on their tour of the Far East.*

| THREEQUARTERS | FORWARDS |
|---|---|
| **L G Dick** (Swansea) | **D S M MacDonald** (London Scottish) |
| **W B B Gammell** (Edinburgh Wanderers) | **W S Watson** (Boroughmuir) |
| | **M A Biggar** (London Scottish) |
| **R A Moffat** (Melrose) | **G Dickson** (Gala) |
| **A G Cranston** (Hawick) | **J M Berthinussen** (Gala) |
| **J M Renwick** (Hawick) | **A J Tomes** (Hawick) |
| **K W Robertson** (Melrose) | **I A Barnes** (Hawick) |
| HALF-BACKS | **J McLauchlan** (Jordanhill) |
| **J Y Rutherford** (Selkirk) | **G M McGuinness** (West of Scotland) |
| **R Wilson** (London Scottish) | **R F Cunningham** (Gala) |
| **M J T Hurst** (Jordanhill) | **C D Fisher** (Waterloo) |
| **R J Laidlaw** (Jedforest) | **C T Deans** (Hawick) |

## TOUR RECORD

Played 5   Won 5   Points for 307   Against 47

## MATCH DETAILS

| 1977 | OPPONENTS | VENUE | RESULT |
|---|---|---|---|
| 4 September | Thailand | Bangkok | W 82–3 |
| 7 September | Hong Kong | Hong Kong | W 42–6 |
| 12 September | Waseda & Meiji Universities (Past & Present) | Tokyo | W 59–13 |
| 15 September | Japanese Selection | Osaka | W 50–16 |
| 18 September | JAPAN | Tokyo | W 74–9 |

## MATCH 1   4 September, Bangkok

**Thailand 3** (1PG)   **Scottish XV 82** (10G 1PG 1DG 4T)
**Thailand** *Penalty Goal:* J Polprasert
**Scottish XV** *Tries:* Dickson (3), Dick (2), Moffat (2), Renwick (2), Biggar, Barnes, Cranston, Laidlaw, MacDonald   *Conversions:* Mair (10)   *Penalty Goal:* Mair   *Dropped Goal:* Rutherford

## MATCH 2   7 September, Hong Kong

**Hong Kong 6** (2PG)   **Scottish XV 42** (4G 2PG 3T)
**Hong Kong** *Penalty Goals:* M Darke (2)
**Scottish XV** *Tries:* Fisher (2), Gammell (2), Biggar, McLauchlan, Renwick   *Conversions:* Mair (4)   *Penalty Goals:* Mair (2)

## MATCH 3   12 September, Tokyo

**Waseda & Meiji Universities (Past & Present) 13** (3PG 1T)   **Scottish XV 59** (8G 1PG 2T)
**Waseda & Meiji** *Try:* M Fujiwara   *Penalty Goals:* Y Matsuo (3)
**Scottish XV** *Tries:* Dickson (2), Gammell (2), Moffat (2), Biggar, Laidlaw, McGuinness, Robertson   *Conversions:* Mair (8)   *Penalty Goal:* Mair

## MATCH 4   15 September, Osaka

**Japanese Selection 16** (4T)   **Scottish XV 50** (7G 2T)
**Japanese Selection** *Tries:* K Aruga, H Kodama, F Oyama, T Kudo
**Scottish XV** *Tries:* Gammell (2), Rutherford (2), MacEwan, Cranston, Dick, Dickson, Renwick   *Conversions:* Mair (7)

## MATCH 5   18 September, Tokyo

**JAPAN 9** (1G 1PG)   **SCOTTISH XV 74** (9G 4PG 2T)
**JAPAN:** S Tanaka; H Ujino, M Yoshida, S Mori, M Fujiwara; Y Matsuo, J Matsumoto; *No 8* H Ogasawara; *Second Row* H Akama, N Kumagai, K Segawa, I Kobayashi; *Front Row* T Yasui, T Takada (*capt*), T Hatakeyama
**Scorers** *Try:* Ujino   *Conversion:* S Tanaka   *Penalty Goal:* Matsuo
**SCOTTISH XV:** Mair; Gammell, Renwick, Cranston, Dick; Wilson, Laidlaw; *No 8* MacDonald; *Second Row* Dickson, Tomes, Barnes, Biggar (*capt*); *Front Row* Cunningham, Deans, McLauchlan
**Scorers** *Tries:* Gammell (4), Laidlaw (2), Cranston, Dickson, Moffat, McGuinness, Wilson   *Conversions:* Mair (9)   *Penalty Goals:* Mair (4)
**Referee** P E Hughes (England)

# FRANCE TO ARGENTINA 1977

**Hugh E Mackern** *El Grafico*, Buenos Aires

The fifth French tour to Argentina in June 1977 was far from a happy one. The touring team won all but one of their matches comfortably, but except at odd moments their rugby was not attractive to watch and there was far too much rough and bad-tempered play in practically every match. The outstanding player was Jean-Pierre Rives, who again proved himself to be a top-class wing-forward, with Skréla not far behind; but the other forwards relied more on physical strength and intimidation than on skill. The backs scored some brilliant tries in the opening match but were given few chances in the two internationals against Argentina. In these, France played safety-first '10-man rugby' with Jean-Pierre Romeu kicking continually from fly-half.

In the first international these tactics proved successful, for the dominance of the French pack in the scrums and line-outs enabled Romeu to build up a decisive lead with four penalty goals and a dropped goal. It was only then that the touring team attempted to run the ball, and their backs added two good tries. France were unquestionably the better team, but the result would have been much closer but for poor place-kicking by Argentina.

The second match, in which France failed to beat Argentina for the first time in history, was an exciting but unpleasant encounter. It might easily have ended in a free fight but for strict refereeing by Mr Quittenton, of England, who awarded 37 penalties. Consequently the game was a purely physical clash in which little real rugby was played. A French newspaper summed up the outcome admirably in a heading which read 'Aguirre 18, Porta 18, Rugby 0'.

The Argentine forwards held their own well this time and the home side led 9–0 at half-time thanks to three penalty goals by Porta. By the middle of the second half, however, Aguirre had put France on level terms with three superb kicks from near or behind the half-way line, and thereafter he and Porta kicked penalty goals alternately, the last two coming in injury time. A draw was a fair result but Argentina were slightly more enterprising and might have won.

Argentina sadly missed three of their outstanding backs. Sansot and Etchegaray were injured before the tour, and Travaglini was not available because of family problems.

# THE TOURING PARTY

**Captain** J Fouroux   **Manager** P Alamercery   **Assistant Manager** J Desclaux

| FULL-BACKS | FORWARDS |
|---|---|
| **J-M Aguirre** (Bagnères) | **J-P Rives** (Toulouse) |
| **M Droitecourt** (Montferrand) | **J-C Skréla** (Toulouse) |
| THREEQUARTERS | **A Guilbert** (Toulon) |
| **J-L Averous** (La Voulte) | **R Petrissans** (Bayonne) |
| **R Bertranne** (Bagnères) | **J-L Joinel** (Brive) |
| **F Sangalli** (Narbonne) | **J-F Imbernon** (Perpignan) |
| **D Bustaffa** (Carcassonne) | ***M Palmié** (Béziers) |
| **G Novès** (Toulouse) | **M Sappa** (Nice) |
| **J-M Etchenique** (Biarritz) | **E August** (Mimizan) |
| **J-M Mazas** (Narbonne) | **G Cholley** (Castres) |
| HALF-BACKS | **R Paparemborde** (Pau) |
| **J-P Romeu** (Montferrand) | **A Vaquerin** (Béziers) |
| **A Caussade** (Lourdes) | **P Dospital** (Bayonne) |
| **J Fouroux** (Auch) | **Y Brunet** (Perpignan) |
| **J Gallion** (Toulon) | **C Swierczynski** (Bègles) |

43

*Replacement during tour*

# TOUR RECORD

Played 7   Won 6   Drawn 1   Points for 192   Against 53

# MATCH DETAILS

| 1977 | OPPONENTS | VENUE | RESULT |
|---|---|---|---|
| 11 June | Buenos Aires Selection | Buenos Aires | W 38–4 |
| 15 June | Interior Selection | Salta | W 28–12 |
| 18 June | Combined Clubs XV | Buenos Aires | W 23–6 |
| 22 June | Cuyo RU | Mendoza | W 25–4 |
| 25 June | ARGENTINA | Buenos Aires | W 26–3 |
| 28 June | Santa Fé RU | Paraná | W 34–6 |
| 2 July | ARGENTINA | Buenos Aires | D 18–18 |

### MATCH 1   11 June, Buenos Aires

**Buenos Aires Selection 4** (1T)   **French XV 38** (5G 2T)
**Buenos Aires** *Try:* McCall
**French XV** *Tries:* Droitecourt, Aguirre (2), Averous, Mazas, Brunet, Bertranne
*Conversions:* Aguirre (5)

### MATCH 2   15 June, Salta

**Interior Selection 12** (4PG)   **French XV 28** (2G 1DG 3PG 1T)
**Interior Selection** *Penalty Goals:* Guarrochena (4)
**French XV** *Tries:* Petrissans, Paparemborde, Joinel   *Conversions:* Romeu (2)
*Dropped Goal:* Romeu   *Penalty Goals:* Romeu (3)

### MATCH 3   18 June, Buenos Aires

**Combined Clubs XV 6** (1G)   **French XV 23** (2G 1PG 2T)
**Combined Clubs XV** *Try:* Wust   *Conversion:* Lago
**French XV** *Tries:* Gallion, Rives, Novès, Averous   *Conversions:* Aguirre,
Caussade   *Penalty Goal:* Aguirre

**MATCH 4   22 June, Mendoza**

**Cuyo RU 4** (1T)   **French XV 25** (3G 1PG 1T)
**Cuyo** *Try:* Morales
**French XV** *Tries:* Aguirre (2), Guilbert, Swierczynski   *Conversions:* Romeu (3)
*Penalty Goal:* Romeu

**MATCH 5   25 June, Buenos Aires**                                **1st International**

**ARGENTINA 3** (1PG)   **FRANCE 26** (1DG 5PG 2T)
**ARGENTINA:** M Alonso (Club Atlético San Isidro); D Beccar Varela (CA San
Isidro), G Beccar Varela (CA San Isidro), A Cappelletti (Banco Nación),
J Gauweloose (Club Universitario, Buenos Aires); H Porta (Banco Nación) *(capt)*,
R Castagna (CA Rosario); *No 8* R Mastai (C Universitario, B A); *Second Row*
H Mazzini (Champagnat), J J Fernández (Deportiva Francesa), E N Branca
(Curupayti), J Carracedo (San Isidro Club); *Front Row* M Carluccio (Deportiva
Francesa), J Braceras (Alumni), F Insua (San Isidro Club)   *Replacement* F Bustillo
(C Universitario, B A) for Carluccio (79 mins)
**Scorer** *Penalty Goal:* Porta
**FRANCE:** Aguirre; Bustaffa, Bertranne, Sangalli, Averous; Romeu, Fouroux
*(capt)*; *No 8* Guilbert; *Second Row* Rives, Imbernon, Palmié, Skréla; *Front Row*
Cholley, Brunet, Paparemborde
**Scorers** *Tries:* Bustaffa, Bertranne   *Dropped Goal:* Romeu   *Penalty Goals:* Romeu
(4), Aguirre
**Referee** R C Quittenton (England)

**MATCH 6   28 June, Paraná**

**Santa Fé RU 6** (2PG)   **French XV 34** (2G 1DG 1PG 4T)
**Santa Fé** *Penalty Goals:* Quevedo (2)
**French XV** *Tries:* Bertranne (2), Petrissans, Caussade, Bustaffa, Swierczynski
*Conversions:* Droitecourt (2)   *Dropped Goal:* Caussade   *Penalty Goal:* Droitecourt

**MATCH 7   2 July, Buenos Aires**                                **2nd International**

**ARGENTINA 18** (6PG)   **FRANCE 18** (6PG)
**ARGENTINA:** M Alonso (CA San Isidro); D Beccar Varela (CA San Isidro),
G Beccar Varela (CA San Isidro), A Cappelletti (Banco Nación), J Gauweloose
(C Universitario, B A); H Porta (Banco Nación) *(capt)*, T R Landajo (Pueyrredon);
*No 8* R Sanz (Regatas Bella Vista); *Second Row* H Mazzini (Champagnat),
J J Fernández (Deportiva Francesa), E N Branca (Curupaytí), J Carracedo (San
Isidro Club); *Front Row* M Carluccio (Deportiva Francesa), J Costante (CA
Rosario), F Insua (San Isidro Club)   *Replacements* F Bustillo (C Universitario, B A)
for Carluccio (55 mins), R Mastai (C Universitario, B A) for Branca (65 mins)
**Scorer** *Penalty Goals:* Porta (6)
**FRANCE:** Aguirre; Bustaffa, Bertranne, Sangalli, Droitecourt; Romeu, Fouroux
*(capt)*; *No 8* Guilbert; *Second Row* Rives, Imbernon, Palmié, Skréla; *Front Row*
Vaquerin, Swierczynski, Cholley
**Scorer** *Penalty Goals:* Aguirre (6)
**Referee** R C Quittenton (England)

# USA TO ENGLAND 1977

The first visit by a representative USA team to England since their national Union was formed in 1975 fulfilled at least two of their manager's aims. Mr Ken Wood, who was in charge of the party, said on arrival in London: 'We hope to win our games, play some attractive rugby, and make a great many friends.' This last they wholly achieved. Mr Wood himself, the captain Craig Sweeney, and the team generally were extremely popular wherever they went. On the field, they played the game hard, but without viciousness and with much entertaining running; off it, they made themselves most agreeable to their hosts. They did not win all their games, it is true. They lost four of the six, but one of the defeats, against Cornwall, was by only a point, and there were those who felt they should have won. A 50–50 record would have been no bad outcome, seeing that some of the players had met for the first time only on the 'plane.

Physically their forwards were built to take on any in the world. Craig Sweeney, the captain, at lock, who died tragically soon after the tour, was 6ft 5in tall and weighed 17st 9lb, and one of the flankers, Andrews, stood 6ft 5in. So did Fraumann, at No 8, who tipped the scales at 16st 11lb; and indeed it was he who turned out to be the outstanding forward in the party. His line-out play, and speed about the field, marked him out, while – like others of his team-mates – he sometimes made use of the American football one-handed torpedo-pass, over vast distances, to the delight and astonishment of those who had not seen it before. This was something from which British rugby could learn.

Behind the scrum the Americans had plenty of individual ability, with Bordley, Jablonski, Halliday, and Duncanson often impressing; but it was in collective skills that the backs as a whole fell short. The forwards scrummaged well, and often held their own in the line-outs. At mauling and rucking they still had a good deal to learn, but improved as the tour wore on.

After an encouraging win against Civil Service in their first match, they were disappointed at losing to Cornwall. Then came disaster, 33–6, in the mud at Coventry, and honourable defeat, 12–18, against England's champion club, Gosforth. Finally a heartening win, 20–18, over the University at Cambridge led up to the high-point of the tour, the match against the England XV at Twickenham. Here the visitors were only 9–3 down at half-time, but thereafter their limitations were exposed. They lost 37–11, but the cheers they received at the end from a crowd of 15,000 must have been considerable compensation for their English-born coach, Dennis Storer. He has laboured long and hard in the cause of American rugby, and the day may yet come...!

46

## THE TOURING PARTY

**Captain** C B Sweeney  **Manager** H K Wood Jr (Maryland)
**Assistant Manager** D Storer (South California)

| FULL-BACK | FORWARDS |
|---|---|
| D Jablonski (Santa Monica) | W G Fraumann (Chicago Lions) |
| THREEQUARTERS | J Lombard (Chuckanut Bay) |
| R J Duncanson III (UCLA) | G B Haley (BATS) |
| R C Freed (Wisconsin) | C H Culpepper (Roanoke, Virginia) |
| M Liscovitz (Monmouth, New Jersey) | B F Andrews (Santa Monica) |
| | G G Kelleher (Santa Monica) |
| J M Conroy (Washington) | G S Brackett (Boston) |
| G W Schneeweis (Santa Monica) | C B Sweeney (Santa Monica) |
| M R Halliday (Palmer Coll, Iowa) | R J Ederle (Scioto Valley, Ohio) |
| D Wack (Amherst Coll, New England) | E N Parthmore (Ohio State Univ) |
| | J T Hanson (San Francisco) |
| HALF-BACKS | J G Lopez (Fort Wayne, Indiana) |
| S W Gray (UCLA) | R M Ording (XO Club, Cal) |
| R M Bordley (Washington) | (UCLA – University of California, |
| S Kelso (University of Iowa) | Los Angeles; BATS – Bay Area |
| T Scott (UCLA) | Touring Side; XO – Ex-Olympic) |

## TOUR RECORD

Played 6   Won 2   Lost 4   Points for 75   Against 124

## MATCH DETAILS

| 1977 | OPPONENTS | VENUE | RESULT |
|---|---|---|---|
| 28 September | Civil Service | Gloucester | W 15–6 |
| 1 October | Cornwall | Camborne | L 11–12 |
| 5 October | Coventry | Coventry | L 6–33 |
| 8 October | Gosforth | Gosforth | L 12–18 |
| 12 October | Cambridge University | Cambridge | W 20–18 |
| 15 October | AN ENGLAND XV | Twickenham | L 11–37 |

**MATCH 1   28 September, Gloucester**

**Civil Service 6** (2PG)   **USA XV 15** (1G 3PG)
**Civil Service:** P Hatfield (Old Modernians); C Wilding (Fylde), M Triggs (Bridgend), P Maney (Headingley), W McNicholl (Boroughmuir); M Gosling (Cardiff), M Weir (Fylde); *No 8* L Connor (Waterloo); *Second Row* H Jenkins (Llanelli), J Piggott (Liverpool), J Kempin (Leicester), D Drew (Penzance Newlyn) *(capt)*; *Front Row* H Hopkins (Swansea), M Davidson (Blaydon), W Dickenson (Richmond)

**Scorer** *Penalty Goals:* Gosling (2)
**USA XV:** Jablonski; Duncanson, Halliday, Schneeweis, Liscovitz; Gray, Kelso;
*No 8* Fraumann; *Second Row* Lombard, Kelleher, Sweeney (*capt*), Haley; *Front Row*
Ederle, Lopez, Parthmore
**Scorers** *Try:* Halliday  *Conversion:* Jablonski  *Penalty Goals:* Jablonski (3)
**Referee** R C Quittenton (Sussex)

## MATCH 2   1 October, Camborne

**Cornwall 12** (4PG)   **USA XV 11** (1PG 2T)
**Cornwall:** P J Winnan (Penryn); B S Trevenski (Falmouth), M J Triggs
(Bridgend), J S Cocking (St Ives), B J Wills (Camborne); B J Jenkin (Hayle),
D Mungles (Hayle); *No 8* R G Corin (St Ives); *Second Row* P J Hendy (St Ives),
C J Durrant (Camborne), M Doney (Hayle), R Spurrell (Plymouth Albion); *Front*
*Row* T A Pryor (Redruth) (*capt*), J Trevorrow (St Ives), R G Tomkin (Camborne)
*Replacements* D Corin (St Ives) for Hendy (37 mins), T Perkins (Plymouth Albion)
for Wills (51 mins)
**Scorer** *Penalty Goals:* Winnan (4)
**USA XV:** Jablonski; Freed, Schneeweis, Conroy, Halliday; Bordley, Scott; *No 8*
Fraumann; *Second Row* Culpepper, Sweeney (*capt*), Brackett, Andrews; *Front Row*
Parthmore, Hanson, Ording  *Replacement* Liscovitz for Halliday (30 mins)
**Scorers** *Tries:* Halliday, Liscovitz  *Penalty Goal:* Jablonski
**Referee** W L Prideaux (North Midlands)

## MATCH 3   5 October, Coventry

**Coventry 33** (2G 2DG 1PG 3T)   **USA XV 6** (2PG)
**Coventry:** P A Rossborough (*capt*); S Maisey, G W Evans, D J Duckham,
P S Preece; T S K Aitchison, P Lander; *No 8* B F Ninnes; *Second Row* G Robbins,
N Bakewell, I R Darnell, S Oliver; *Front Row* T Dingley, C T Weston,
J M Broderick
**Scorers** *Tries:* Maisey (2), Ninnes, Evans, Broderick  *Conversions:* Rossborough,
Aitchison  *Dropped Goals:* Aitchison (2)  *Penalty Goal:* Aitchison
**USA XV:** Bordley; Duncanson, Schneeweis, Wack, Liscovitz; Gray, Kelso; *No 8*
Fraumann; *Second Row* Haley, Sweeney (*capt*), Kelleher, Lombard; *Front Row*
Ederle, Hanson, Ording
**Scorer** *Penalty Goals:* Kelso (2)
**Referee** P E Hughes (Lancashire)

## MATCH 4   8 October, Gosforth

**Gosforth 18** (2PG 3T)   **USA XV 12** (1G 2PG)
**Gosforth:** B Patrick; S J Archer, H E Patrick, J K Britton, J S Gustard;
R W Breakey, M Young (*capt*); *No 8* P J Dixon; *Second Row* D Robinson,
J Hedley, T C Roberts, I Richardson; *Front Row* A Johnson, D F Madsen, C White
**Scorers** *Tries:* Gustard, Roberts, Archer  *Penalty Goals:* Young (2)
**USA XV:** Jablonski; Conroy, Wack, Halliday, Liscovitz; Bordley, Kelso; *No 8*
Fraumann; *Second Row* Culpepper, Sweeney (*capt*), Brackett, Andrews; *Front Row*
Parthmore, Hanson, Ording  *Replacement* Lopez for Hanson (50 mins)
**Scorers** *Try:* Culpepper  *Conversion:* Jablonski  *Penalty Goals:* Jablonski (2)
**Referee** W K Burrell (Scotland)

## MATCH 5   11 October, Cambridge

**Cambridge University 18** (3G)   **USA XV 20** (2G 2T)
**Cambridge University:** I R Metcalfe (King Edward's, Birmingham, & St
Catharine's); M W O'Callaghan (Christchurch Boys HS, NZ, & Emmanuel),
M K Fosh (Harrow & Magdalene), I A Greig (Queen's Coll, Queenstown, SA, &
Downing), P W G Parker (Collyers GS & St Catharine's); M Parr (St Joseph's,

Blackpool, & Trinity Hall), J S Davies (Christ Coll, Brecon, & St John's); *No 8* E T Butler (Monmouth & Fitzwilliam) (*capt*); *Second Row* P N Hosthuis (King William's, IOM, & St John's), N R M Heath (Solihull & Downing), L Browne (Belfast Royal Acad & St Catharine's), A Mitchell (Clifton & Magdalene); *Front Row* R J Brooman (Merchant Taylors, Northwood, & Trinity), K S Geoghegan (Gonzalo, Dublin, & King's), P A V Shaw (Queen Elizabeth GS, Wakefield, & Downing)

**Scorers** *Tries:* O'Callaghan (2), Parr *Conversions:* Parker (3)

**USA XV:** Bordley; Duncanson, Schneeweis, Halliday, Jablonski; Gray, Scott; *No 8* Fraumann; *Second Row* Culpepper, Sweeney (*capt*), Brackett, Andrews; *Front Row* Ederle, Lopez, Parthmore *Replacement* Lombard for Andrews (half-time)

**Scorers** *Tries:* Duncanson (2), Jablonski (2) *Conversions:* Jablonski (2)

**Referee** M H Titcomb (Gloucestershire)

## MATCH 6   15 October, Twickenham

**ENGLAND XV 37** (5G 1PG 1T)   **USA 11** (1PG 2T)

**ENGLAND XV:** W H Hare (Leicester); J Carleton (Orrell), P W Dodge (Leicester), N R French (Wasps), D M Wyatt (Bedford); J P Horton (Bath), D J Carfoot (Waterloo); *No 8* N D Mantell (Rosslyn Park); *Second Row* P J Dixon (Gosforth), W B Beaumont (Fylde) (*capt*), J P Scott (Rosslyn Park), M Rafter (Bristol); *Front Row* J A H Bell (Middlesbrough), G N J Cox (Moseley), B G Nelmes (Cardiff)

**Scorers** *Tries:* Wyatt (4), Scott, Carleton *Conversions:* Hare (5) *Penalty Goal:* Hare

**USA:** Bordley; Duncanson, Halliday, Schneeweis, Liscovitz; Gray, Kelso; *No 8* Fraumann; *Second Row* Culpepper, Sweeney (*capt*), Brackett, Lombard; *Front Row* Ording, Hanson, Parthmore

**Scorers** *Tries:* Kelso, Duncanson *Penalty Goal:* Halliday

**Referee** C G P Thomas (Wales)

*Prior to their tour of England the USA had played Canada at Vancouver on 21 May 1977, with the following result:*

**Canada 17** (1G 1PG 2T)   **USA 6** (2PG)

**Canada:** G Gonis (Calgary Irish); S McTavish (UBC Old Boys), A Bauer (Edmonton Leprechauns), J Greig (UBC), M Dandy (Toronto Nomads); J Billingsley (UBC), P Wiley (UBC) (*capt*); *No 8* R Hindson (UBC); *Second Row* A Foster (Calgary Irish), H de Goede (James Bay), D Eburne (UBC), W Collins (UBC); *Front Row* M Eckardt (James Bay), M Luke (St John's), C Walt (James Bay)

(Note: UBC – University of British Columbia)

**Scorers** *Tries:* Bauer, Greig, de Goede *Conversion:* Gonis *Penalty Goal:* Hindson

**USA:** D Jablonski (Santa Monica); D Guest (BATS), D Stephenson (Santa Monica), D Wack (Amherst), M Liscovitz (Monmouth); R Bordley (Washington, DC), S Kelso (Univ of Iowa); *No 8* T Selfridge (Schenectady); *Second Row* T Klein (BATS), C Sweeney (Santa Monica) (*capt*), R Causey (Baton Rouge), J Lombard (Chuckanut Bay); *Front Row* M Sherlock (Old Blues), J Hanson (San Francisco), B Henderson (Wichita)

(Note: BATS – Bay Area Touring Side)

**Scorer** *Penalty Goals:* Jablonski (2)

**Referee** J Curnow (British Columbia)

# ENGLAND UNDER 23 TO CANADA 1977

This was the first overseas tour by an England Under 23 team, and they won all their six matches, including the two 'internationals' against All-Canada. Only twice was the team in danger of defeat – in the first match, against the British Columbia President's XV, when the players were still suffering from 'jet-lag', and in the last match but one, against an unfancied but most committed Ontario team. In the three most important matches, against British Columbia and Canada, twice, the team played extremely well and won convincingly.

Superiority by their forwards in the line-out and at mauling comprised the touring team's main strength. The Canadian teams could not match their technique in this respect, and regularly lost possession. Behind the scrum the touring team's backs never quite realised their full potential, showing too little variation in attack, though in defence they tackled admirably. Their goal-kicking, too, was of a high standard.

In the first match against Canada, at Ottawa, in dry and hot conditions, the Under 23 team dominated the first half to lead 20–0 at half-time. From then on they fell away, and Canada came back extremely well to close the gap to 26–13. In the second 'international' played in an airless stadium at Toronto with the temperature in the 80s, Canada had the better of the first half and forced the visitors into many errors. In the second half the Under 23 team played exceptionally well and scored three tries before going on to win 29–9.

The Canadians, who a month earlier had won their first international against the USA, were naturally disappointed at these results, but from the England point of view the tour had been well worthwhile. The players benefited from the experience gained, and some, notably Scott, the captain, Sorrell, Dodge, and Bell looked set for higher honours in the future. Scott and Dodge, indeed, won their first senior caps for England shortly afterwards.

## THE TOURING PARTY

**Captain** J P Scott   **Manager** D P Rogers   **Assistant Manager** P D Briggs

| FULL-BACKS | THREEQUARTERS |
| --- | --- |
| **D P Sorrell** (Bristol) | **J Carleton** (Orrell) |
| **D R Boyd** (West Hartlepool) | **R Mogg** (Gloucester) |

**THREEQUARTERS** (*cont*)

**C W Lambert** (Harlequins)

**A M Bond** (Broughton Park)

**P W Dodge** (Leicester)

**J F Thornton** (Rosslyn Park)

**HALF-BACKS**

**J A Palmer** (Bath)

**I Ball** (Waterloo)

**N P Coombes** (Plymouth)

**D J Carfoot** (Waterloo)

**FORWARDS**

**R J Doubleday** (Bristol)

**G N J Cox** (Moseley)

**R Tabern** (Waterloo)

**J A H Bell** (Middlesbrough)

**S P Redfern** (Leicester)

**S B Boyle** (Gloucester)

**N J Pomphrey** (Bristol)

**J P Scott** (Rosslyn Park)

**N D Mantell** (Rosslyn Park)

**P J Sherratt** (Nottingham)

**T W Jones** (Blackheath)

**N C B Turner** (Rosslyn Park)

**D H Cooke** (Harlequins)

50

## TOUR RECORD

Played 6   Won 6   Points for 147   Against 63

## MATCH DETAILS

| 1977 | OPPONENTS | VENUE | RESULT |
|------|-----------|-------|--------|
| 25 May | British Columbia Pres XV | Vancouver | W 16–7 |
| 28 May | British Columbia | Victoria | W 44–21 |
| 31 May | Alberta | Calgary | W 16–7 |
| 4 June | CANADA | Ottawa | W 26–13 |
| 7 June | Ontario | Brantford | W 16–6 |
| 11 June | CANADA | Toronto | W 29–9 |

### MATCH 1   25 May, Vancouver

**British Columbia President's XV 7** (1PG 1T)
**England Under 23 XV 16** (1DG 3PG 1T)
**British Columbia President's XV** *Try:* Zischka  *Penalty Goal:* White
**England Under 23 XV** *Try:* Lambert  *Dropped Goal:* Ball  *Penalty Goals:* Ball (3)

### MATCH 2   28 May, Victoria

**British Columbia 21** (2G 3PG)   **England Under 23 XV 44** (4G 4PG 2T)
**British Columbia** *Tries:* Logan *and penalty try*  *Conversions:* Wiley (2)  *Penalty Goals:* Wiley (2), White
**England Under 23 XV** *Tries:* Mantell (2), Carleton, Sorrell, Mogg, Boyle
*Conversions:* Sorrell (4)  *Penalty Goals:* Sorrell (4)

### MATCH 3   31 May, Calgary

**Alberta 7** (1DG 1T)   **England Under 23 XV 16** (4PG 1T)
**Alberta** *Try:* Pieschel  *Dropped Goal:* Thomson
**England Under 23 XV** *Try:* Ball  *Penalty Goals:* Ball (4)

### MATCH 4   4 June, Ottawa

**CANADA 13** (1G 1DG 1T)   **ENGLAND UNDER 23 26** (6PG 2T)
**CANADA:** G Gonis (Calgary Irish); M Dandy (Toronto Nomads), D Whyte
(University of British Columbia), A Bauer (Edmonton Leprechauns), S McTavish
(UBC Old Boys); G Hirayama (UBC), P Wiley (UBC) (*capt*); *No 8* R Hindson
(UBC); *Second Row* H De Goede (James Bay), D Eburne (UBC), B Collins (UBC),

A Foster (Calgary Irish); *Front Row* M Eckardt (James Bay), M Luke (St John's), C Walt (James Bay)
**Scorers** *Tries:* Gonis, Whyte *Conversion:* Wiley *Dropped Goal:* Whyte
**ENGLAND UNDER 23:** Sorrell; Carleton, Bond, Dodge, Mogg; Palmer, Carfoot; *No 8* Mantell; *Second Row* Pomphrey, Scott (*capt*), Boyle, Cooke; *Front Row* Bell, Cox, Doubleday *Replacement* Ball for Sorrell (60 mins)
**Scorers** *Tries:* Ball, Bond *Penalty Goals:* Ball (2), Sorrell (4)
**Referee** J Marr (Ontario)

51

### MATCH 5   7 June, Brantford

**Ontario 6** (2PG)   **England Under 23 XV 16** (4PG 1T)
**Ontario** *Penalty Goals:* Spence (2)
**England Under 23 XV** *Try:* Tabern *Penalty Goals:* Ball (4)

### MATCH 6   11 June, Toronto

**CANADA 9** (3PG)   **ENGLAND UNDER 23 29** (2G 3PG 2T)
**CANADA:** G Gonis (Calgary Irish); M Dandy (Toronto Nomads), D Whyte (UBC), R Greig (UBC), S McTavish (UBC Old Boys); G Hirayama (UBC), P Wiley (UBC) (*capt*); *No 8* D Edburne (UBC); *Second Row* H De Goede (James Bay), R Hindson (UBC), G Grant (University of Victoria), A Foster (Calgary Irish); *Front Row* M Eckardt (James Bay), M Luke (St John's), C Walt (James Bay)
**Scorers** *Penalty Goals:* Hindson (2), Wiley
**ENGLAND UNDER 23:** Sorrell; Carleton, Bond, Dodge, Mogg; Palmer, Carfoot; *No 8* Mantell; *Second Row* Pomphrey, Scott (*capt*), Boyle, Cooke; *Front Row* Bell, Cox, Doubleday
**Scorers** *Tries:* Bond, Cooke, Mantell, Mogg *Conversions:* Sorrell (2) *Penalty Goals:* Sorrell (3)
**Referee** G Jones (Alberta)

*As a sequel to their tour, England Under 23 played France Under 23 at Orrell on 1 October 1977, with the following result:*

**England Under 23 10** (2PG 1T)   **France Under 23 3** (1PG)
**England Under 23:** D P Sorrell (Bristol); J Carleton (Orrell), P W Dodge (Leicester), D Shorrock (Fylde), R R Mogg (Gloucester); J A Palmer (Bath), N P Coombes (Plymouth Albion); *No 8* N Jeavons (Moseley); *Second Row* P Polledri (Bristol), N J Pomphrey (Bristol), J P Scott (Rosslyn Park) (*capt*), D H Cooke (Harlequins); *Front Row* J A H Bell (Middlesbrough), R Tabern (Fylde), R J Doubleday (Bristol) *Replacement* D R Boyd (Hartlepool Rovers) for Sorrell (60 mins)
**Scorers** *Try:* Bell *Penalty Goals:* Sorrell (2)
**France Under 23:** S Bianco (Biarritz); J-M Rancoule (Lourdes), T Merlos (Lavelanet), P Laferrere (Mont-de-Marsan), L Bilbao (St Jean-de-Luz); B Viviès (Agen), J Gallion (Toulon) (*capt*); *No 8* J-P Beraud (Biarritz); *Second Row* E Buchet (Nice), J-M Salvage (Mazamet), J-C Galan (Montauban), J Gratton (Auch); *Front Row* G Raynaud (Narbonne), B Herrero (Nice), M Colomine (Narbonne)
**Scorer** *Penalty Goal:* Viviès
**Referee** C Norling (Wales)

NOTE: *Further details of matches played by England Under 23 in 1977–78 can be found on page 65.*

# THE INTERNATIONAL CHAMPIONSHIP 1977–78

It was Wales's *annus mirabilis*, beyond all doubt. They won the Triple Crown for the third year in succession – something no country had done before – and for the 15th time in all, to go one ahead of England. They brought off their second Grand Slam in the same period, their eighth in all, one more than England's seven. Finally their outright Championship win, their third in four seasons, was their 20th in all, again the greatest number.

They have not been beaten in a Championship match at Cardiff since 23 March 1968, when they lost to France – a run of 20 such matches without defeat (though New Zealand beat them there in 1972). One can only hail a great side, with Phil Bennett, the captain, Gareth Edwards, Gerald Davies and J P R Williams the long-serving heroes in a team of abounding talent. The reception they were given at 10 Downing Street by a Prime Minister representing a Cardiff constituency was no less than they deserved.

The final table read:

|  | P | W | D | L | F | A | Pts |
|---|---|---|---|---|---|---|---|
| **Wales** | 4 | 4 | 0 | 0 | 67 | 43 | 8 |
| **France** | 4 | 3 | 0 | 1 | 51 | 47 | 6 |
| **England** | 4 | 2 | 0 | 2 | 42 | 33 | 4 |
| **Ireland** | 4 | 1 | 0 | 3 | 46 | 54 | 2 |
| **Scotland** | 4 | 0 | 0 | 4 | 39 | 68 | 0 |

France, the runners-up, might even have ended as champions if they had taken their goal-kicking chances at Cardiff. There they missed six penalty goal attempts, four of them from relatively easy positions. They must have regretted their decision to drop Jean-Pierre Romeu in favour of a new fly-half who had less goal-kicking potential.

England ended in mid-table, which was a fair reflection of their standing. They found an admirable new captain in Beaumont, and highly promising newcomers in Dodge and Caplan. The pack, too, was always a considerable force.

Ireland, with only one victory, could well have had more. They gave Wales a fright in Dublin, and ran France to a point in Paris, in a match, on a frost-bound ground, which should never have been played. Ward, their new fly-half, and Noel Murphy, in his first season as national coach, deserved a better outcome to their efforts.

Scotland, 'whitewashed' for the first time in ten years, were not helped by injuries to some of their leading players, notably Gordon Brown; but selectorial errors and mistakes in captaincy also added to their woes. A shake-up in both connections would not be out of place.

53

## 21 January, Paris (Parc des Princes)
**France 15** (2G 1PG)   **England 6** (2DG)

England had not won in Paris since 1964 but gave France a hard game, and but for some untimely injuries might have run them much closer. In the 30th minute, when the visitors were leading 3–0, they lost Andy Maxwell, their Headingley centre, with a knee injury which sadly brought his international career to an end. Peter Dixon, at wing-forward, had to leave the field at the same time with a sprung collar-bone. It meant that England's supply of replacements had been used up, and when Cowling, the Leicester prop, dislocated a shoulder early in the second half he insisted on continuing, in spite of intense pain. He deserved a medal of some kind. Propping with a dislocated shoulder against a French pack must be the ultimate in agony.

France, nevertheless, had the invention and flair behind the scrum and it brought them the tries that mattered. Jerome Gallion, a young successor to the long-established Fouroux at scrum-half, made a brilliant debut.

At half-time England, in spite of their injuries, were 6–3 ahead. Old, at fly-half, had dropped two well-taken goals, with a penalty goal by Aguirre sandwiched in between. After 16 minutes of the second half Gallion made a break on the blind side for France. From the ensuing ruck the ball was worked quickly to Averous, who, with the aid of an overlap, scored near the posts. Aguirre converted, and France then produced their killer punch.

Gallion, fed by Cholley from a line-out, ducked inside Burton and the injured Cowling before racing 25 metres, at wing-threequarter speed, for a superlative try. Aguirre again converted and England, from then on, were no longer in the hunt.

**France:** J-M Aguirre (Bagnères); J-F Gourdon (Bagnères), R Bertranne (Bagnères), C Belascain (Bayonne), J-L Averous (La Voulte); B Viviès (Agen), J Gallion (Toulon); *No 8* J-P Bastiat (Dax) *(capt)*; *Second Row* J-P Rives (Toulouse), J-F Imbernon (Perpignan), M Palmié (Béziers), J-C Skréla (Toulouse); *Front Row* R Paparemborde (Pau), A Paco (Béziers), G Cholley (Castres)
**Scorers** *Tries:* Averous, Gallion   *Conversions:* Aguirre (2)   *Penalty Goal:* Aguirre
**England:** W H Hare (Leicester); P J Squires (Harrogate), B J Corless (Moseley),

A W Maxwell (Headingley), M A C Slemen (Liverpool); A G B Old (Sheffield), M Young (Gosforth); *No 8* J P Scott (Rosslyn Park); *Second Row* P J Dixon (Gosforth), W B Beaumont (Fylde) (*capt*), N E Horton (Toulouse), M Rafter (Bristol); *Front Row* M A Burton (Gloucester), P J Wheeler (Leicester), R J Cowling (Leicester)   *Replacements* C P Kent (Rosslyn Park) for Maxwell (34 mins), A Neary (Broughton Park) for Dixon (34 mins)
**Scorer** *Dropped Goals:* Old (2)
**Referee** N R Sanson (Scotland)

### 21 January, Dublin
### Ireland 12 (1G 2PG)   Scotland 9 (3PG)

Ireland deserved their win, if only because they scored a try, but Scotland could well have forced a draw. In the closing minute, with the home team leading 12–9, the Scots were awarded a penalty kick only 10 metres from the Irish line and 15 metres in from touch. Morgan, the visiting captain, who had already kicked three penalty goals, could easily have added a fourth; but he chose instead to take a tap-kick, with the object of setting up a try. But the Irish defence closed in with the same finality as it had throughout the game, and the move was snuffed out.

'Brave but mad' was how Noel Murphy, the Ireland coach, described Morgan's effort. The player himself said, 'I play to win, and felt I had to go for a try rather than draw with a penalty'. His coach and selectors backed him, though the latter had already incurred criticism by picking Andy Irvine on the wing, instead of at full-back.

As a result, Ireland gained their first win in the Championship after six consecutive defeats, and owed much to the sensible play and goal-kicking of their new fly-half Tony Ward. He and Morgan alternated with successful penalty attempts to make it 6–6 just before half-time, when Ireland scored their all-important try. McKinney had come on as a replacement for the injured O'Driscoll, and within two minutes of his arrival he took a pass from Slattery behind a Scottish 5-metres scrum and dived over to score. Scotland had heeled the ball and lost it, which gave Slattery his chance. Ward converted and Ireland crossed over 12–6 ahead.

The Scots now had the wind in their favour and did a lot of pressing in the second half; but their only score was a third penalty goal by Morgan – a good one, from 35 metres. It was not enough, and there will be many an argument about whether or not Morgan should have gone for that fourth penalty goal in the crucial closing seconds.

In this match 'Sandy' Carmichael, the Scotland prop, won his 50th cap – the first player from his country to do so.

**Ireland:** A H Ensor (Wanderers); T O Grace (St Mary's Coll), A R McKibbin (London Irish & Instonians), P P McNaughton (Greystones), A C McLennan (Wanderers); A J P Ward (Garryowen), J J Moloney (St Mary's Coll) (*capt*); *No 8* W P Duggan (Blackrock Coll); *Second Row* J B O'Driscoll (London Irish), M I Keane (Lansdowne), D E Spring (Dublin U), J F Slattery (Blackrock Coll); *Front Row* M P Fitzpatrick (Wanderers), P C Whelan (Garryowen), P A Orr (Old Wesley) *Replacements* S A McKinney (Dungannon) for O'Driscoll (39 mins), L A Moloney (Garryowen) for Ensor (67 mins)
**Scorers** *Try:* McKinney  *Conversion:* Ward  *Penalty Goals:* Ward (2)
**Scotland:** B H Hay (Boroughmuir); A R Irvine (Heriot's FP), J M Renwick (Hawick), I R McGeechan (Headingley), D Shedden (West of Scotland); R Wilson, (London Scottish), D W Morgan (Stewart's Melville FP) (*capt*); *No 8* D S M MacDonald (West of Scotland); *Second Row* M A Biggar (London Scottish), A J Tomes (Hawick), A F McHarg (London Scottish), C B Hegarty (Hawick); *Front Row* A B Carmichael (West of Scotland), D F Madsen (Gosforth), J McLauchlan (Jordanhill)
**Scorer** *Penalty Goals:* Morgan (3)
**Referee** P E Hughes (England)

# 4 February, Twickenham
## England 6 (2PG)  Wales 9 (3PG)

On one of the wettest international match days ever seen at Twickenham, with the car parks almost awash, neither side could score a try and the outcome was decided by penalty goals. Phil Bennett kicked three in four attempts for Wales, and Hignell only two in six attempts for England. It made the final difference. Yet some of Hignell's misses were very narrow ones, and the result could easily have gone the other way.

In the first half the England forwards, with the wind at their backs, had much the better of things, but in the second half it was the Welsh forwards' turn. In the last 20 minutes they were well on top and the England line was under continual pressure. When two boxers end up level on points the one who is the aggressor at the end usually gets the verdict. To that extent Wales just about deserved their win.

Neither back-line came into the picture in the foul conditions, but Gareth Edwards, in his 50th international for Wales, played an all-important part, more particularly in the second half. Time and again he pinned England to their own line with perfectly judged kicks to the corners. One huge effort of his, from 65 metres, set up the position from which Wales mounted their closing attacks. England's forwards, well led by Beaumont, fought back to the end, but their backs, apart from Squires on the right wing, posed few threats.

At half-time England were leading 6–3. Hignell kicked his first penalty goal in the eighth minute; Bennett equalised for Wales two minutes later; then Hignell put his side ahead with his second effort, a quarter of an hour before half-time.

Bennett's equaliser came three minutes after the interval and his winning kick, from the England 22 line, only eight minutes from the end. This was after the newly capped wing-forward Mordell – who later disputed the decision – had been penalised for handling in a ruck.

**England:** A J Hignell (Cambridge U); P J Squires (Harrogate), B J Corless (Moseley), P W Dodge (Leicester), M A C Slemen (Liverpool); J P Horton (Bath), M Young (Gosforth); *No 8* J P Scott (Rosslyn Park); *Second Row* R J Mordell (Rosslyn Park), W B Beaumont (Fylde) *(capt)*, N E Horton (Toulouse), M Rafter (Bristol); *Front Row* M A Burton (Gloucester), P J Wheeler (Leicester), B G Nelmes (Cardiff)
**Scorer** *Penalty Goals:* Hignell (2)
**Wales:** J P R Williams (Bridgend); T G R Davies (Cardiff), R W R Gravell (Llanelli), S P Fenwick (Bridgend), J J Williams (Llanelli); P Bennett (Llanelli) *(capt)*, G O Edwards (Cardiff); *No 8* D L Quinnell (Llanelli); *Second Row* J Squire (Newport), A J Martin (Aberavon), G A D Wheel (Swansea), T J Cobner (Pontypool); *Front Row* G Price (Pontypool), R W Windsor (Pontypool), A G Faulkner (Pontypool)
**Scorer** *Penalty Goals:* Bennett (3)
**Referee** N R Sanson (Scotland)

### 4 February, Murrayfield
### Scotland 16 (1G 1DG 1PG 1T)   France 19 (1G 3PG 1T)

Scotland, in teeming rain, gave France an extremely hard match, and could justly claim at the end that luck had not exactly favoured them. At one stage, late in the first half, they were leading 13–0, and France appeared to be at sixes and sevens. But Irvine had injured his shoulder when scoring Scotland's second try, and was off the field, leaving his side a man short, when France hit back with the first of theirs. Gallion put up a high kick from a line-out to the Scottish in-goal, where Hegarty, pulled out of the pack in the absence of Irvine, attempted to field it. Alas for Scotland, the wet ball slipped through his arms to the ground, and Gallion, in hot pursuit, dived on it to score. It was the turning point, and France, 13–4 down at half-time, gradually fought back to win a most exciting match.

Morgan opened the scoring for Scotland with a penalty goal in the tenth minute, after which Shedden and Irvine scored spectacular tries, the second converted by Morgan. Shedden charged down a delayed clearing kick by his opposite number Gourdon and chased the ball over the line to score. Irvine followed up a long kick upfield by Morgan, hacked on over the line and then beat an obstructing Gourdon in the race for the ball.

Sadly Irvine landed on the point of his left shoulder in scoring the try and after receiving treatment had to leave the field for good early in the second half. Shedden, who was concussed shortly afterwards, was another casualty. Cranston and Hogg were the replacements, with Hay moving to full-back.

France, now, embarked on their recovery. Aguirre kicked a penalty goal and then Haget, showing exceptional pace for a lock, powered his way to a try which Aguirre converted. That made it 13–13. Thereafter two penalty goals by Aguirre for France and a dropped goal by Morgan for Scotland made up the balance of the scoring. The French protested about Morgan's effort – from an indirect free-kick – because he did not 'tap' the ball first. But the referee failed to spot the omission, and to that extent Scotland, too, had their slice of luck.

**Scotland:** A R Irvine (Heriot's FP); B H Hay (Boroughmuir), J M Renwick (Hawick), I R McGeechan (Headingley), D Shedden (West of Scotland); R Wilson (London Scottish), D W Morgan (Stewart's Melville FP) *(capt)*; *No 8* G Y Mackie (Highland); *Second Row* M A Biggar (London Scottish), A J Tomes (Hawick), A F McHarg (London Scottish), C B Hegarty (Hawick); *Front Row* N E K Pender (Hawick) C T Deans (Hawick), J McLauchlan (Jordanhill) *Replacements* A G Cranston (Hawick) for Irvine (42 mins), C G Hogg (Boroughmuir) for Shedden (57 mins)
**Scorers** *Tries:* Shedden, Irvine *Conversion:* Morgan *Dropped Goal:* Morgan *Penalty Goal:* Morgan
**France:** J-M Aguirre (Bagnères); J-F Gourdon (Bagnères), R Bertranne (Bagnères), C Belascain (Bayonne), J-L Averous (La Voulte); B Viviès (Agen), J Gallion (Toulon); *No 8* J-P Bastiat (Dax) *(capt)*; *Second Row* J-P Rives (Toulouse), F Haget (Biarritz), M Palmié (Béziers), J-C Skréla (Toulouse); *Front Row* R Paparemborde (Pau), A Paco (Béziers), G Cholley (Castres)
**Scorers** *Tries:* Gallion, Haget *Conversion:* Aguirre *Penalty Goals:* Aguirre (3)
**Referee** C G P Thomas (Wales)

## 18 February, Cardiff
## Wales 22 (1DG 1PG 4T)    Scotland 14 (2PG 2T)

On a bitterly cold day Scotland failed to take full advantage of a strong wind in their favour in the first half and were a point behind, 8–7, at the interval. Wales then had a purple patch in which they scored 14 points in the next 15 minutes, and at 22–7 the game seemed as good as over. But Scotland came back spiritedly, and by the end had narrowed the margin to eight points.

Morgan opened the scoring with a 30 metres penalty goal for Scotland, but Gareth Edwards replied with a typical try for Wales – his 20th such effort – when he burst over from short range to score. Bennett failed to convert, and before half-time Renwick – after a superb Scottish movement capped by the centre's split-second finishing sidestep – and Gravell had scored unconverted tries for their respective sides.

In the first minute after the interval Bennett dropped a goal for Wales, after which there came in quick succession a try by Fenwick, picking up a rolling ball after J J Williams had been brought down a few yards out, a penalty goal by Bennett, from 35 metres, and a try by Quinnell, who handed off two Scottish forwards in a storming run from well outside the visitors' 22. Neither try was converted, and Wales, at that point, seemed to ease off.

58   Scotland, in contrast, launched a series of attacks and after Morgan had kicked an easy penalty goal, a tap-kick from an indirect free-kick set up a position from which Tomes crossed for a try. Morgan converted, and Scotland had registered their biggest score at Cardiff. At the end, however, it was Wales who were doing the attacking, and they always seemed to have something in reserve.

**Wales:** J P R Williams (Bridgend); T G R Davies (Cardiff), R W R Gravell (Llanelli), S P Fenwick (Bridgend) J J Williams (Llanelli); P Bennett (Llanelli) (*capt*), G O Edwards (Cardiff); *No 8* D L Quinnell (Llanelli); *Second Row* J Squires (Newport), A J Martin (Aberavon), G A D Wheel (Swansea), T J Cobner (Pontypool); *Front Row* G Price (Pontypool), R W Windsor (Pontypool), A G Faulkner (Pontypool)
**Scorers** *Tries:* Edwards, Gravell, Fenwick, Quinnell   *Dropped Goal:* Bennett
*Penalty Goal:* Bennett
**Scotland:** B H Hay (Boroughmuir); W B B Gammell (West of Scotland), J M Renwick (Hawick), A G Cranston (Hawick), D Shedden (West of Scotland); I R McGeechan (Headingley), D W Morgan (Stewart's Melville FP) (*capt*); *No 8* D S M MacDonald (West of Scotland); *Second Row* M A Biggar (London Scottish), A F McHarg (London Scottish), A J Tomes (Hawick), C B Hegarty (Hawick); *Front Row* N E K Pender (Hawick), C T Deans (Hawick), J McLauchlan (Jordanhill)   *Replacement* C G Hogg (Boroughmuir) for Shedden (8 mins)
**Scorers** *Tries:* Renwick, Tomes   *Penalty Goals:* Morgan (2)
**Referee** J R West (Ireland)

## 18 February, Paris
## France 10 (2PG 1T)   Ireland 9 (3PG)

Most people thought that the frozen pitch at Parc des Princes was unfit for play, but the French Federation overruled the objections of the players, the referee and Irish committeemen and decided that the match should go on. It was their right, as the 'visited Union', but normal play was almost impossible under the conditions. Players had the utmost difficulty in retaining their balance on the frozen surface, and the referee said afterwards 'It was a miracle no one was seriously hurt'.

All-out scrummaging was inhibited by the forwards' failure to gain a stud-hold, and the game became largely a matter of quick-witted exploitation of the bouncing ball. In this respect Ireland, in the early stages, fared rather better than France; but in the second half the home team began to exert ferocious pressure, and it needed exceptional defence by Ireland to keep them out. Duggan, at one stage, seemed to be playing half the

French team on his own. Ward, too, made an outstanding contribution with his goal-kicking. He succeeded with three penalty attempts out of three. Aguirre, for France, was far less reliable, missing with five attempts from around 35 metres; but he kicked the two that mattered, one from 50 metres, to add to the only try of the match, by Gallion.

This came in the 25th minute, to open the scoring, and was a gem of its kind. Bastiat took out the Irish loose forwards round the blind side of a scrum and slipped the ball to Gallion, who ran clean through from 30 metres without a hand being laid on him. Here again the frozen surface did not help the Irish defenders. Ensor, at full-back, who had a fine game otherwise, was unable to turn in time to challenge the French scrum–half, whose try was his third in his first three internationals. Aguirre's conversion attempt rebounded from a post, but thereafter he and Ward kicked penalty goals alternately until half-time, when France led 10–6. The only score in the second half was a third penalty goal by Ward. Gibson, chosen for the first time as a wing, was making his 63rd appearance for Ireland, to equal McBride's record. He looked as sharp and committed as ever.

**France:** J-M Aguirre (Bagnères); L Bilbao (St Jean-de-Luz), R Bertranne (Bagnères), C Belascain (Bayonne), J-L Averous (La Voulte); B Viviès (Agen), J Gallion (Toulon); *No 8* J-P Bastiat (Dax) *(capt)*; *Second Row* J-P Rives (Toulouse), F Haget (Biarritz), M Palmié (Béziers), J-C Skréla (Toulouse); *Front Row* R Paparemborde (Pau), A Paco (Béziers), G Cholley (Castres)
**Scorers** *Try:* Gallion  *Penalty Goals:* Aguirre (2)
**Ireland:** A H Ensor (Wanderers); C M H Gibson (North of Ireland FC), A R McKibbin (London Irish and Instonians), P P McNaughton (Greystones), A C McLennan (Wanderers); A J P Ward (Garryowen), J J Moloney (St Mary's Coll) *(capt)*; *No 8* W P Duggan (Blackrock Coll); *Second Row* S A McKinney (Dungannon), M I Keane (Lansdowne), H W Steele (Ballymena), J F Slattery (Blackrock Coll); *Front Row* E M J Byrne (Blackrock Coll), P C Whelan (Garryowen), P A Orr (Old Wesley)
**Scorer** *Penalty Goals:* Ward (3)
**Referee** C G P Thomas (Wales)

## 4 March, Murrayfield
## Scotland 0   England 15 (2G 1PG)

England retained the Calcutta Cup with their first win at Murrayfield for a decade, and scored their first tries in five matches. The last one had been against Ireland at Lansdowne Road the previous season. The return of Cotton and Dixon, who had been injured and forced to withdraw from the match against Wales, stiffened the England pack considerably and it was the work of the forwards, splendidly led by Beaumont, that really decided the match. Also Scotland, 9–0 down at half-time, threw away what chance they had by kicking too much in the second half, instead of running the ball with the object of bringing in Irvine, their key attacker, from full-back. Caplan, who had been brought in to win his first cap for England at full-back after a late withdrawal by Hignell, made a notable debut, and just missed scoring a try in the second minute – ample evidence, if such were needed, of his readiness to join in running attack.

60    England's first score, even though they had a brisk wind in their favour, was delayed until the 31st minute of the first half. Slemen, who had a thoroughly good game, began it with a run down the left, after which the ball moved towards the right via Wheeler, Nelmes, Dixon and Beaumont to Squires, who cut inside two opponents for a try near the posts. Young converted, and six minutes later Dodge kicked a huge penalty goal from 50 metres, at an angle, to give England a bigger lead at half-time than had begun to look likely.

Scotland had the wind behind them in the second period, but Breakey, who had come in as a new cap to replace the injured McGeechan – the original choice – at fly half, continually kicked away possession with high punts upfield and little was seen of Irvine. If the fly-half had moved the ball to his backs, as he had shown himself well capable of doing in the earlier stages, it might have been a different story. Instead the only score of the second half came from England – a try by Nelmes, converted by Young, after a run by Dodge.

**Scotland:** A R Irvine (Heriot's FP); W B B Gammell (Edinburgh Wanderers), J M Renwick (Hawick), A G Cranston (Hawick), B H Hay (Boroughmuir); R W Breakey (Gosforth), D W Morgan (Stewart's Melville FP) (*capt*); *No 8* D S M MacDonald (West of Scotland); *Second Row* M A Biggar (London Scottish), A J Tomes (Hawick), D Gray (West of Scotland), C B Hegarty (Hawick); *Front Row* N E K Pender (Hawick), C T Deans (Hawick), J McLauchlan (Jordanhill)
**England:** D W N Caplan (Headingley); P J Squires (Harrogate), B J Corless (Moseley), P A Dodge (Leicester), M A C Slemen (Liverpool); J P Horton (Bath), M Young (Gosforth); *No 8* J P Scott (Rosslyn Park); *Second Row* P J Dixon (Gosforth), W B Beaumont (Fylde) (*capt*), M J Colclough (Angoulême), M Rafter (Bristol); *Front Row* F E Cotton (Sale), P J Wheeler (Leicester), B G Nelmes (Cardiff)
**Scorers** *Tries:* Squires, Nelmes   *Conversions:* Young (2)   *Penalty Goal:* Dodge
**Referee** J R West (Ireland)

## 4 March, Dublin
### Ireland 16 (1DG 3PG 1T)   Wales 20 (4PG 2T)

Wales, with an unchanged team, succeeded in their quest for a record-breaking third successive Triple Crown, but were given plenty of shocks in a magnificent match.

Ireland, 13–3 down after half an hour, pulled back to 13–13 in the next 20 minutes and held Wales to the same score until seven minutes from the end. It meant that the result was still very much in the balance, with the Irish forwards going berserk and Keane, at lock, playing the game of his life. But Wales still had some all-important shots in their locker. A try by J J Williams and penalty goal by Fenwick took them to 20–13 before Ireland, defiant to the end, scored a last penalty goal in the dying minutes. It was not enough, but Wales had been shaken by the fury of the Irish pack. It said much for Bennett and his team that they were able to recover their poise and win.

Fenwick, who scored 16 of his side's points, kicked two penalty goals, from 50 and 40 metres, in the first twelve minutes and added a third, in reply to one by Ward for Ireland, halfway through the half. Fenwick then crossed for the first Welsh try, unconverted, after being fed by Price from a ruck, and Ward kicked his second penalty goal for Ireland. At half-time the score was 13–6 to Wales.

Shortly afterwards Ward dropped a goal from a tap-kick and then put in a high punt which led to Ireland's try. J P R Williams, harassed behind his own line, sliced his intended clearing kick and Moloney dived on the ball to score. That made it 13–13. Play then swayed this way and that until Gareth Edwards, who had done much to steady the Welsh side, sparked off the move which led to the winners' second try. The scrum-half lofted a high overhead pass to Fenwick, who sent out a similar one to J J Williams, for the latter to race over and break the log-jam. Fenwick's subsequent fourth penalty goal and Ward's third for Ireland rounded off the proceedings.

Mike Gibson was making his 64th appearance for Ireland, a new world record for an individual country, and was always a threat. His worst moment came when he was late-tackled by J P R Williams – a lapse which had the crowd booing the Welsh full-back for the rest of the game.

**Ireland:** A H Ensor (Wanderers); C M H Gibson (North of Ireland FC), A R McKibbin (London Irish and Instonians), P P McNaughton (Greystones), A C McLennan (Wanderers); A J P Ward (Garryowen), J J Moloney (St Mary's Coll) (*capt*); *No 8* W P Duggan (Blackrock Coll); *Second Row* S A McKinney (Dungannon), M I Keane (Lansdowne), H W Steele (Ballymena), J F Slattery (Blackrock Coll); *Front Row* E M J Byrne (Blackrock Coll), P C Whelan (Garryowen), P A Orr (Old Wesley)
**Scorers** *Try:* Moloney  *Dropped Goal:* Ward  *Penalty Goals:* Ward (3)
**Wales:** J P R Williams (Bridgend); T G R Davies (Cardiff), R W R Gravell (Llanelli), S P Fenwick (Bridgend), J J Williams (Llanelli); P Bennett (Llanelli) (*capt*), G O Edwards (Cardiff); *No 8* D L Quinnell (Llanelli); *Second Row* J Squire (Newport), A J Martin (Aberavon), G A D Wheel (Swansea), T J Cobner (Pontypool); *Front Row* G Price (Pontypool), R W Windsor (Pontypool), A G Faulkner (Pontypool)
**Scorers** *Tries:* Fenwick, J J Williams  *Penalty Goals:* Fenwick (4)
**Referee** G Domercq (France)

## 18 March, Twickenham
## England 15 (2G 1PG)   Ireland 9 (1DG 2PG)

England had not beaten Ireland at Twickenham since 1970, but this time they made no mistake. Their forwards gradually gained the upper hand, more particularly in the mauls and rucks, and Ireland failed to reproduce the fire they had shown against Wales in Dublin. But the scores were still level, 9–9, when Slemen scored a match-winning try for England in the second half. Young's conversion from wide out meant that Ireland had to score twice to win, but even one such effort proved beyond them.

Ireland started with the wind in their favour, but England scored first when Dixon forced his way over for a try after a blind-side break by Horton, with Colclough in support. Young converted and England led 6–0 at half-time. Shortly afterwards Ward kicked a penalty goal for Ireland and followed it with a neat dropped goal from in front of the England posts. Young restored England's lead with a penalty goal, the result of 'trampling' by the Irish forwards, but Ward was soon back in the picture with a penalty goal for Ireland after Gibson – his side's outstanding back – had been tackled from behind, without the ball, by Slemen.

The England wing made ample amends, however, when he came across the field from the blind side to support an England passing movement, and swerved outside Squires on the far right to take the final pass and race over, at impressive speed, for a try wide out. Young converted with a fine kick.

Ward's nine points for Ireland took his total for the Championship to 38. This equalled the joint record held previously by Hosen, of England, and Bennett, of Wales, and set the seal on a remarkable first season in the national side by the Irish fly-half.

**England:** D W N Caplan (Headingley); P J Squires (Harrogate), P W Dodge (Leicester), B J Corless (Moseley), M A C Slemen (Liverpool); J P Horton (Bath), M Young (Gosforth); *No 8* J P Scott (Rosslyn Park); *Second Row* P J Dixon (Gosforth), W B Beaumont (Fylde) (*capt*), M Colclough (Angoulême), M J Rafter (Bristol); *Front Row* F E Cotton (Sale), P J Wheeler (Leicester), B G Nelmes (Cardiff)
**Scorers** *Tries:* Dixon, Slemen   *Conversions:* Young (2)   *Penalty Goal:* Young
**Ireland:** A H Ensor (Wanderers); C M H Gibson (North of Ireland FC), A R McKibbin (London Irish and Instonians), P P McNaughton (Greystones), A C McLennan (Wanderers); A J P Ward (Garryowen), J J Moloney (St Mary's Coll) (*capt*); *No 8* W P Duggan (Blackrock Coll); *Second Row* S A McKinney (Dungannon), H W Steele (Ballymena), M I Keane (Lansdowne), J F Slattery (Blackrock Coll); *Front Row* E M J Byrne (Blackrock Coll), P C Whelan (Garryowen), P A Orr (Old Wesley)
**Scorer** *Dropped Goal:* Ward   *Penalty Goals:* Ward (2)
**Referee** F Palmade (France)

62

## 18 March, Cardiff
**Wales 16** (1G 2DG 1T)   **France 7** (1DG 1T)

Everything had pointed to this match being the decisive one of the Championship, and so it turned out. With both sides bidding for the Grand Slam after three previous victories, it was a thrilling struggle, played to the limits of physical endeavour. Wales won in the end largely by dint of a purple patch of 13 points in eight minutes near the end of the first half.

Key factors in the Welsh win were a masterly display by Gareth Edwards at scrum-half, a hardly less commanding one by Bennett at fly-half – he scored both his side's tries – a notable performance by Martin in the line-out and the success of the Welsh loose forwards in snuffing out the threat of their opposite numbers and of Gallion at scrum-half.

France, playing down-wind on a sunny but cold day, did the early attacking and were almost over twice before Skréla, in the 20th minute, burrowed through a maul for his side's only try. Aguirre could not convert, but shortly afterwards Viviès dropped a goal from a tap-kick to increase the lead.

Then came Wales's dramatic reply. First Bennett, in the 30th minute, side-stepped two opponents on the short side for a try which he himself converted. Next Edwards, in the 36th minute, dropped a vitally important goal, from 30 metres. Finally Edwards, yet again, in the 38th minute, sparked off the movement which led to Wales's second try.

It was from Edwards's long touch-kick and diagonal run in subsequent loose play that J. J. Williams, on the right wing, was able to pick up the scrum-half's difficult final pass and return the ball inwards, overhead and one-handed, to Bennett, who scored. The conversion attempt failed, but France, from then on, were struggling. The only score in a gruelling second half was a dropped goal by Fenwick for Wales in injury time.

**Wales:** J P R Williams (Bridgend); J J Williams (Llanelli), R W R Gravell (Llanelli), S P Fenwick (Bridgend), G L Evans (Newport); P Bennett (Llanelli) (*capt*), G O Edwards (Cardiff); *No 8* D L Quinnell (Llanelli); *Second Row* J Squire (Newport), A J Martin (Aberavon), G A D Wheel (Swansea), T J Cobner (Pontypool); *Front Row* G Price (Pontypool), R W Windsor (Pontypool), A G Faulkner (Pontypool)
**Scorers** *Tries:* Bennett (2)   *Conversion:* Bennett   *Dropped Goals:* Edwards, Fenwick
**France:** J-M Aguirre (Bagnères); D Bustaffa (Carcassonne), R Bertranne (Bagnères), C Belascain (Bayonne), G Novès (Toulouse); B Viviès (Agen), J Gallion (Toulon); *No 8* J-P Bastiat (Dax) (*capt*); *Second Row* J-C Skréla (Toulouse), F Haget (Biarritz), M Palmié (Béziers), J-P Rives (Toulouse); *Front Row* R Paparemborde (Pau), A Paco (Béziers), G Cholley (Castres)
**Scorers** *Try:* Skréla   *Dropped Goal:* Viviès
**Referee** A Welsby (England)

# 'B' INTERNATIONALS 1977–78

### 3 December, Murrayfield
### Scotland 'B' 3 (1PG)   Ireland 'B' 7 (1T 1PG)

**Scotland 'B':** C D R Mair (West of Scotland); T D Dunlop (West of Scotland), R W Breakey (Gosforth), H M Burnett (Heriot's FP) *(capt)*, A W Blackwood (Stewart's Melville FP); J Y Rutherford (Selkirk), R J Laidlaw (Jedforest); *No 8* G Dickson (Gala); *Second Row* D J McLeod (Hawick), D Gray (West of Scotland), D J M Smith (Glasgow High), A A Stewart (London Scottish); *Front Row* H Campbell (Jordanhill), C T Deans (Hawick), J N Burnett (Heriot's FP) *Replacement* W D Aitchison (Highland) for Mair (29 mins)
**Scorer** *Penalty Goal:* Mair
**Ireland 'B':** S N G Ennis (Clontarf); S D Dobbin (CIYMS), P P McNaughton (Greystones), A W Irwin (Queen's Univ, Belfast), M C Finn (UC, Cork); A J P Ward (Garryowen), C S Patterson (Instonians); *No 8* D Spring (Dublin U); *Second Row* A J McLean (Ballymena), E J O'Rafferty (Wanderers), C M McCarthy (UC Cork and Coventry), C C Tucker (Shannon); *Front Row* M P Fitzpatrick (Wanderers), C F Fitzgerald (St Mary's Coll) *(capt)*, G A J McLoughlin (Shannon)
**Scorers** *Try:* Patterson   *Penalty Goal:* Ward
**Referee** M Messan (France)

### 11 December, Nantes
### France 'B' 15 (1PG 3T)   Wales 'B' 3 (1PG)

**France 'B':** C Delage (Brive); L Bilbao (St-Jean-de-Luz), P Merlos (Lavelenet), R Lafferrere (Mont-de-Marsan), B Anne (Bourgoin); B Viviès (Agen), M Beraud (Biarritz) *(capt)*; *No 8* J Cristina (Montferrand); *Second Row* P Coulais (Toulon), J-M Alliou (Toulon), A Maleig (Oloron), R Petrissans (Bayonne); *Front Row* B Forrestier (Biarritz), P Dintrans (Tarbes), J Lees (Oloron)   *Replacement* M Terrain (Lourdes) for Coulais (70 mins)
**Scorers** *Tries:* Bilbao, Christina, Anne   *Penalty Goal:* Viviès
**Wales 'B':** I Walsh (Pontypridd); H E Rees (Neath), M K Swain (Moseley) *(capt)*, A Donovan (St Paul's Coll, Cheltenham and Swansea), R Ellis-Jones (London Welsh); D Richards (Swansea), D B Williams (Newport); *No 8* E T Butler (Cambridge U and Pontypool); *Second Row* J Manfield (London Welsh), J Perkins (Pontypool), B G Clegg (Swansea), S Lane (Cardiff); *Front row* G Howls (Ebbw Vale), A Phillips (Cardiff), J Richardson (Aberavon)   *Replacements* G Evans (Maesteg) for Richards (34 mins), C Davis (Newbridge) for Lane (38 mins)
**Scorer** *Penalty Goal:* Evans
**Referee** A Welsby (England)

### 19 March, Le Havre
### France 'B' 11 (1PG 2T)   Scotland 'B' 3 (1PG)

**France 'B':** C Delage (Brive); P Mesny (Grenoble), M Duffranc (Tyrosse), P Lafferrere (Mont-de-Marsan), B Anne (Bourgoin); J Servien.(Romans), M Beraud (Biarritz) *(capt)*; *No 8* J Cristina (Montferrand); *Second Row* R Petrissans (Bayonne), A Maleig (Oloron), J-M Alliou (Toulon), P Coulais (Toulon); *Front*

*Row* B Forrestier (Biarritz), P Dintrans (Tarbes), J Lees (Oloron)
**Scorers** *Tries:* Coulais, Lafferrere   *Penalty Goal:* Servien
**Scotland 'B':** J F Brown (Ayr); K W Robertson (Melrose), A P Friell (London
Scottish), B G Halliday (Boroughmuir), A G Dougall (Jordanhill); J Y Rutherford
(Selkirk), R J Laidlaw (Jedforest); *No 8* G Dickson (Gala); *Second Row* D J McLeod
(Hawick), I K Lambie (Watsonians), G M Watson (Boroughmuir), J R Dixon
(Jordanhill) *(capt)*; *Front Row* N A Rowan (Boroughmuir), K G Lawrie (Gala),
G M McGuinness (West of Scotland)
**Scorer** *Penalty Goal:* Brown
**Referee** M Prideaux (England)

## 7 May, Constanta
## Rumania 'B' 12 (1G 2PG)   England 'B' 13 (1G 1PG 1T)

**Rumania 'B':** S Podarescu (Grivita); A Marin (Grivita), M Holban (Farul),
V Benedek (Politehnica), J Peter (Timisuara Univ); M Marghescu (Dynamo),
V Ion (Farul); *No 8* F Constantin (Farul); *Second Row* I Podaru (Farul), I Urdea
(Farul), D Musat (Farul), P Bors (Dynamo) *(capt)*; *Front Row* F Ionita (Farul),
E Grigore (Farul), I Bucan (Politehnica)   *Replacement* D Teleasa (Steaua) for Marin
(46 mins)
**Scorers** *Try:* Ion   *Conversion:* Podarescu   *Penalty Goals:* Podarescu (2)
**England 'B':** K M Bushell (Harlequins); R Demming (Bedford), R Jardine
(Gloucester), A M Bond (Sale), R R Mogg (Gloucester); L J Cusworth (Moseley),
C J Gifford (Moseley); *No 8* J L Butler (Gosforth); *Second Row* M L Baker
(Bristol), S Boyle (Gloucester), J H Fidler (Gloucester), S R Johnson (Leicester);
*Front Row* T A Pryor (Redruth) *(capt)*, J A G D Raphael (Bective Rangers),
C White (Gosforth)   *Replacement* N J Pomphrey (Bristol) for Johnson (78 mins)
**Scorers** *Tries:* Demming, Mogg   *Conversion:* Bushell   *Penalty Goal:* Bushell
**Referee** T Witting (Rumania)

*On 3 May the same England 'B' team had beaten Bucharest 22–3 at Bucharest.*

# ENGLAND UNDER 23 1977–78

*For details of England Under 23 v France Under 23 at Orrell on 1
October, see page 51.*

*For details of England Under 23 v France Under 23 at Orrell on 1
October, see page 51.*

## 12 April, Wilmslow
## England Under 23 13 (1G 1PG 1T)   English Students 17 (1G 1PG 2T)

**England Under 23:** D P Sorrell (Bristol); P E Bignell (Northampton), M Burke
(Waterloo), M K Fosh (Cambridge U), J Lane (Bristol); J Palmer (Bath), I G Peck
(Bedford); *No 8* J P Scott (Rosslyn Park) *(capt)*; *Second Row* N J Pomphrey
(Bristol), P D Jackson (Harlequins), A Jasczak (Saracens), D H Cooke (Harlequins);
*Front Row* J A Bell (Gosforth), M A Howe (Bedford), P V Boulding (Bedford)
*Replacements* P Cue (Bristol) for Sorrell (25 mins), J Leigh (Bristol) for Burke (30
mins)
**Scorers** *Tries:* Palmer, Bignell   *Conversion:* Cue   *Penalty Goal:* Cue
**English Students:** T V D Woodman (Liverpool Poly); J D Bassnet
(Wolverhampton Poly), C R Woodward (Loughborough Students),

A G T Harrower (Madeley Coll), P Asquith (London U); I Wilkins (St Paul's, Cheltenham), M R Conner (Loughborough); *No 8* P J Ackford (Kent U); *Second Row* R Montgomery (Kingston Poly), S Bainbridge (Alsager Coll), N Williams (Bristol Poly), T J Allchurch (Durham U) *(capt)*; *Front Row* S P Wilkes (W Midlands), A Wolstenholme (St Luke's, Exeter), R J Doubleday (RAC, Cirencester)
**Scorers** *Tries:* Wilkins, Woodward, Harrower *Conversion:* Wilkins *Penalty Goal:* Wilkins
**Referee** K Lockerbie (Northumberland)

66

## 6 May, Hilversum
## Holland 3 (1PG)  England Under 23 24 (1G 2PG 3T)

**Holland:** T Oortwijn (The Hague) *(capt)*; W Peperkamp (Castricum), P Overakker (Delft), C Schröder (Hilversum), A Michel (Amsterdam); C Zwitser (Amsterdam), V Triebert (The Hague); *No 8* D Altink (Leyden); *Second Row* P Peereboom (KCT), J Dudink (Amsterdam), K Huysman (Utrecht), P Paul (KCT); *Front Row* C Koemans (Leyden), J Schaap (The Hague), W Rijsdam (Leyden)
**Scorer** *Penalty Goal:* Oortwijn
**England Under 23:** W M Rose (Leicester); J D Bassnet (New Brighton), P W Dodge (Leicester) *(capt)*, C R Woodward (Harlequins), J Carleton (Orrell); N J Preston (Richmond), I G Peck (Bedford); *No 8* S Gorvett (Bristol); *Second Row* P J Polledri (Bristol), S Bainbridge (Gosforth), P D Jackson (Harlequins), D H Cooke (Harlequins); *Front Row* J A Bell (Gosforth), S Brain (Moseley), R J Doubleday (Bristol)
*Replacement* P J Ackford (Plymouth Albion) for Gorvett (49 mins)
**Scorers** *Tries:* Bassnet, Woodward, Bell, Carleton *Conversion:* Rose *Penalty Goals:* Rose (2)
**Referee** L Prideaux (North Midlands)

# NATIONAL TRIAL MATCHES 1977–78

## ENGLAND

## 7 January, Twickenham
## England 15 (5PG)  The Rest 15 (1G 3PG)

**England:** D W N Caplan (Headingley); P J Squires (Harrogate), B J Corless (Moseley), C P Kent (Rosslyn Park), J Carleton (Orrell); A G B Old (Sheffield), M Young (Gosforth); *No 8* E Bignell (Blackheath); *Second Row* P J Dixon (Gosforth), W B Beaumont (Fylde) *(capt)*, N E Horton (Toulouse), M Rafter (Bristol); *Front Row* W H Greaves (Moseley), P J Wheeler (Leicester), R J Cowling (Leicester) *Replacement* D P Sorrell (Bristol) for Caplan (59 mins)
**Scorer** *Penalty Goals:* Old (5)
**The Rest:** W H Hare (Leicester); R Demming (Bedford), P W Dodge (Leicester), A W Maxwell (Headingley), M A C Slemen (Liverpool); J P Horton (Bath), C J Gifford (Moseley); *No 8* J P Scott (Rosslyn Park); *Second Row* R J Mordell (Rosslyn Park), R Field (Moseley), M Colclough (Angoulême), A Neary (Broughton Park) *(capt)*; *Front Row* T Pryor (Redruth), J A G D Raphael (Bective Rangers), B G Nelmes (Cardiff)
**Scorers** *Try:* Carleton *Conversion:* Hare *Penalty Goals:* Hare (3)
*(Carleton changed places with Demming, of The Rest, at half-time. Kent, in the centre,*

*and Bignell, at No 8, were also demoted from the England side, with Dodge and Scott moving up to take their places.)*
**Referee** R C Quittenton (Sussex)

## SCOTLAND

### 7 January, Murrayfield
### Blues 18 (1G 4PG)   Whites 20 (1G 2PG 2T)

**Blues:** A R Irvine (Heriot's FP); W B B Gammell (Edinburgh Wanderers), J M Renwick (Hawick), A G Cranston (Hawick), B H Hay (Boroughmuir); I R McGeechan (Headingley), D W Morgan (Stewart's Melville FP); *No 8* D S M MacDonald (West of Scotland); *Second Row* A K Brewster (Stewart's Melville FP), I A Barnes (Hawick), A J Tomes (Hawick), M A Biggar (London Scottish) (*capt*); *Front Row* A B Carmichael (West of Scotland), C T Deans (Hawick), J McLauchlan (Jordanhill) *Replacement* A J Campbell (Hawick) for Barnes (47 mins)
**Scorers** *Try:* Cranston  *Conversion:* Morgan  *Penalty Goals:* Morgan (4)
**Whites:** J F Brown (Ayr); D Shedden (West of Scotland), C G Hogg (Boroughmuir) (*capt*), A P Friell (London Scottish), A G Dougall (Jordanhill); R Wilson (London Scottish), R J Laidlaw (Jedforest); *No 8* G Y Mackie (Highland); *Second Row* C B Hegarty (Hawick), D Gray (West of Scotland), W S Watson (Boroughmuir), S R G Pratt (London Scottish); *Front Row* N E K Pender (Hawick), D F Madsen (Gosforth), J Aitken (Gala) *Replacement* A R Grant (London Scottish) for Brown (79 mins)
**Scorers** *Tries:* Hogg (2), Shedden  *Conversion:* Brown  *Penalty Goals:* Brown (2)
**Referee** A M Hosie (Hillhead)

## IRELAND

### 7 January, Dublin (Lansdowne Road)
### Whites 13 (3 PG 1T)   Blues 21 (1G 5PG)

**Whites:** L A Moloney (Garryowen); T O Grace (St Mary's Coll), A R McKibbin (London Irish and Instonians), P P McNaughton (Greystones), J P Dennison (Garryowen); A J P Ward (Garryowen), J C Robbie (Cambridge University); *No 8* D E Spring (Dublin University); *Second Row* H W Steele (Ballymena), M I Keane (Lansdowne), W P Duggan (Blackrock Coll), J F Slattery (Blackrock Coll) (*capt*); *Front Row* E M J Byrne (Blackrock Coll), P C Whelan (Garryowen), P A Orr (Old Wesley)
**Scorers** *Try:* Grace  *Penalty Goals:* Ward (3)
**Blues:** A H Ensor (Wanderers); D Dobbin (CIYMS), M Finn (UC Cork), V Cosgrave (Wanderers), J Miles (Malone); M A Quinn (Lansdowne), C Patterson (Instonians); *No 8* J O'Driscoll (London Irish); *Second Row* A McLean (Ballymena), E O'Rafferty (Wanderers), L Galvin (Athlone), S A McKinney (Dungannon) (*capt*); *Front Row* M P Fitzpatrick (Wanderers), C F FitzGerald (St Mary's Coll), G A J McLoughlin (Shannon) *Replacement* J J Moloney (St Mary's Coll) for Patterson (half-time)
**Scorers** *Try:* Patterson  *Conversion:* Quinn  *Penalty Goals:* Quinn (5)
**Referee** D I H Burnett (Leinster)

## WALES

### 21 January, Cardiff
### Probables 24 (4PG 3T)    Possibles 3 (1PG)

**Probables:** J P R Williams (Bridgend); T G R Davies (Cardiff), R W Gravell (Llanelli), S P Fenwick (Bridgend), G L Evans (Newport); P Bennett (Llanelli) (*capt*), G O Edwards (Cardiff); *No 8* D L Quinnell (Llanelli); *Second Row* J Squire (Newport), A J Martin (Aberavon), G A D Wheel (Swansea), J Manfield (London Welsh); *Front Row* G Price (Pontypool), M Watkins (Cardiff), A G Faulkner (Pontypool)   *Replacement* B Gregory (Pontypool) for Quinnell (62 mins)
**Scorers** *Tries:* Davies (2), Williams   *Penalty Goals:* Bennett (4)
**Possibles:** C J Webber (Newport); E H Rees (Neath), M J Swain (Moseley), D H Burcher (Newport), R Ellis-Jones (London Welsh); J D Bevan (Aberavon) (*capt*), D B Williams (Newport); *No 8* C Davis (Newbridge); *Second Row* G Williams (Bridgend), B G Clegg (Swansea), J Perkins (Pontypool), M Shellard (Pontypridd); *Front Row* J Dixon (Abertillery), A G Phillips (Cardiff), J Dale (Newport)   *Replacements* A D Lewis (London Welsh) for Williams (half-time), R Moriarty (Swansea) for Clegg (55 mins), A J Donovan (Swansea) for Webber (56 mins)
**Scorer** *Penalty Goal:* Webber
**Referee** C G P Thomas (Tonteg)

# RESULTS OF INTERNATIONAL MATCHES (*up to 30 April 1978*)

*Years for Five Nations' matches are for the second half of the season: e.g. 1972 means season 1971–72. Years for matches against touring teams from the Southern Hemisphere refer to the actual year of the match.*

*Points-scoring was first introduced in 1886, when an International Board was formed by Scotland, Ireland, and Wales. Points-values varied between countries until 1890, when England agreed to join the Board, and uniform values were adopted. The table below shows points-values from the 1890–91 season onwards.*

| Northern Hemisphere seasons | Try | Conversion | Penalty goal | Dropped goal | Goal from mark |
|---|---|---|---|---|---|
| 1890–91 | 1 | 2 | 2 | 3 | 3 |
| 1891–92 to 1892–93 | 2 | 3 | 3 | 4 | 4 |
| 1893–94 to 1904–05 | 3 | 2 | 3 | 4 | 4 |
| 1905–06 to 1947–48 | 3 | 2 | 3 | 4 | 3 |
| 1948–49 to 1970–71 | 3 | 2 | 3 | 3 | 3 |
| 1971–72 to | 4 | 2 | 3 | 3 | 3 |

## ENGLAND v SCOTLAND
**Played 94   England won 45, Scotland won 35, Drawn 14**

1871 Raeburn Place (Edinburgh)
**Scotland** 1G 1T to 1T

1872 The Oval (London)
**England** 2G 2T to 1G

1873 Glasgow
**Drawn** no score

1874 The Oval
**England** 1G to 1T

1875 Raeburn Place
**Drawn** no score

1876 The Oval
**England** 1G 1T to 0

1877 Raeburn Place
**Scotland** 1G to 0

1878 The Oval
**Drawn** no score

1879 Raeburn Place
**Drawn** 1G each

1880 Manchester
**England** 2G 3T to 1G

1881 Raeburn Place
**Drawn** 1G 1T each

1882 Manchester
**Scotland** 2T to 0

1883 Raeburn Place
**England** 2T to 1T

1884 Blackheath (London)
**England** 1G to 1T

1885 No Match

1886 Raeburn Place
**Drawn** no score

1887 Manchester
**Drawn** 1T each

1888 No Match

1889 No Match

1890 Raeburn Place
**England** 1G 1T to 0

1891 Richmond (London)
**Scotland** 3G (9) to 1G (3)

1892 Raeburn Place
**England** 1G (5) to 0

1893 Leeds
**Scotland** 2DG (8) to 0

1894 Raeburn Place
**Scotland** 2T (6) to 0

1895 Richmond
**Scotland** 1PG 1T (6) to 1PG (3)

1896 Glasgow
**Scotland** 1G 2T (11) to 0

1897 Manchester
**England** 1G 1DG 1T (12) to 1T (3)

1898 Powderhall (Edinburgh)
**Drawn** 1T (3) each

1899 Blackheath
**Scotland** 1G (5) to 0

70

1900 Inverleith (Edinburgh)
**Drawn** no score

1901 Blackheath
**Scotland** 3G 1T (18) to 1T (3)

1902 Inverleith
**England** 2T (6) to 1T (3)

1903 Richmond
**Scotland** 1DG 2T (10) to 2T (6)

1904 Inverleith
**Scotland** 2T (6) to 1T (3)

1905 Richmond
**Scotland** 1G 1T (8) to 0

1906 Inverleith
**England** 3T (9) to 1T (3)

1907 Blackheath
**Scotland** 1G 1T (8) to 1T (3)

1908 Inverleith
**Scotland** 1G 2DG 1T (16) to 2G (10)

1909 Richmond
**Scotland** 3G 1T (18) to 1G 1T (8)

1910 Inverleith
**England** 1G 3T (14) to 1G (5)

1911 Twickenham
**England** 2G 1T (13) to 1G 1T (8)

1912 Inverleith
**Scotland** 1G 1T (8) to 1T (3)

1913 Twickenham
**England** 1T (3) to 0

1914 Inverleith
**England** 2G 2T (16) to 1G 1DG 2T (15)

1920 Twickenham
**England** 2G 1T (13) to 1DG (4)

1921 Inverleith
**England** 3G 1T (18) to 0

1922 Twickenham
**England** 1G 2T (11) to 1G (5)

1923 Inverleith
**England** 1G 1T (8) to 2T (6)

1924 Twickenham
**England** 3G 1DG (19) to 0

1925 Murrayfield
**Scotland** 2G 1DG (14)
to 1G 1PG 1T (11)

1926 Twickenham
**Scotland** 2G 1DG 1T (17) to 3T (9)

1927 Murrayfield
**Scotland** 1G 1DG 4T (21)
to 2G 1PG (13)

1928 Twickenham
**England** 2T (6) to 0

1929 Murrayfield
**Scotland** 4T (12) to 2T (6)

1930 Twickenham
**Drawn** no score

1931 Murrayfield
**Scotland** 5G 1T (28) to 2G 1PG 2T (19)

1932 Twickenham
**England** 2G 2T (16) to 1T (3)

1933 Murrayfield
**Scotland** 1T (3) to 0

1934 Twickenham
**England** 2T (6) to 1T (3)

1935 Murrayfield
**Scotland** 2G (10) to 1DG 1T (7)

1936 Twickenham
**England** 3T (9) to 1G 1PG (8)

1937 Murrayfield
**England** 2T (6) to 1PG (3)

1938 Twickenham
**Scotland** 2PG 5T (21)
to 1DG 3PG 1T (16)

1939 Murrayfield
**England** 3PG (9) to 2T (6)

1947 Twickenham
**England** 4G 1DG (24) to 1G (5)

1948 Murrayfield
**Scotland** 2T (6) to 1PG (3)

1949 Twickenham
**England** 2G 3T (19) to 1PG (3)

1950 Murrayfield
**Scotland** 2G 1T (13) to 1G 1PG 1T (11)

1951 Twickenham
**England** 1G (5) to 1T (3)

1952 Murrayfield
**England** 2G 1DG 2T (19) to 1T (3)

1953 Twickenham
**England** 4G 2T (26) to 1G 1T (8)

1954 Murrayfield
**England** 2G 1T (13) to 1T (3)

1955 Twickenham
**England** 1PG 2T (9) to 1PG 1T (6)

1956 Murrayfield
**England** 1G 2PG (11) to 1PG 1T (6)

1957 Twickenham
**England** 2G 1PG 1T (16) to 1PG (3)

1958 Murrayfield
**Drawn** 1PG (3) each

1959 Twickenham
**Drawn** 1PG (3) each

1960 Murrayfield
**England** 3G 1DG 1PG (21)
to 3PG 1T (12)

1961 Twickenham
**England** 1PG 1T (6) to 0

1962 Murrayfield
**Drawn** 1PG (3) each

1963 Twickenham
**England** 2G (10) to 1G 1DG (8)

1964 Murrayfield
**Scotland** 3G (15) to 1PG 1T (6)

1965 Twickenham
**Drawn** England 1T (3) Scotland 1DG (3)

1966 Murrayfield
**Scotland** 1PG 1T (6) to 1DG (3)

1967 Twickenham
**England** 3G 2PG 1DG 1T (27)
to 1G 2PG 1T (14)

1968 Murrayfield
**England** 1G 1PG (8) to 1PG 1DG (6)

1969 Twickenham
**England** 1G 1T (8) to 1PG (3)

1970 Murrayfield
**Scotland** 1G 2PG 1T (14) to 1G (5)

1971 Twickenham
**Scotland** 2G 1DG 1T (16)
to 3PG 2T (15)

*1971 Murrayfield
**Scotland** 4G 1PG 1T (26)
to 1PG 1DG (6)

1972 Murrayfield
**Scotland** 4PG 1DG 2T (23) to 3PG (9)

1973 Twickenham
**England** 2G 2T (20) to 1G 1PG 1T (13)

1974 Murrayfield
**Scotland** 1G 2PG 1T (16)
to 1DG 1PG 2T (14)

1975 Twickenham
**England** 1PG 1T (7) to 2PG (6)

1976 Murrayfield
**Scotland** 2G 2PG 1T (22)
to 1G 2PG (12)

1977 Twickenham
**England** 2G 2PG 2T (26) to 2PG (6)

1978 Murrayfield
**England** 2G 1PG (15) to 0

*Special Centenary match – non-championship*

71

# ENGLAND v IRELAND
**Played 90   England won 51, Ireland won 31, Drawn 8**

1875 The Oval (London)
**England** 2G 1T to 0

1876 Dublin
**England** 1G 1T to 0

1877 The Oval
**England** 2G 2T to 0

1878 Dublin
**England** 2G 1T to 0

1879 The Oval
**England** 3G 2T to 0

1880 Dublin
**England** 1G 1T to 1T

1881 Manchester
**England** 2G 2T to 0

1882 Dublin
**Drawn** 2T each

1883 Manchester
**England** 1G 3T to 1T

1884 Dublin
**England** 1G to 0

1885 Manchester
**England** 2T to 1T

1886 Dublin
**England** 1T to 0

1887 Dublin
**Ireland** 2G to 0

1888 No Match

1889 No Match

1890 Blackheath (London)
**England** 3T to 0

1891 Dublin
**England** 2G 3T (9) to 0

1892 Manchester
**England** 1G 1T (7) to 0

1893 Dublin
**England** 2T (4) to 0

1894 Blackheath
**Ireland** 1DG 1T (7) to 1G (5)

1895 Dublin
**England** 2T (6) to 1T (3)

1896 Leeds
**Ireland** 2G (10) to 1DG (4)

1897 Dublin
**Ireland** 1DG 3T (13) to 2PG 1T (9)

1898 Richmond (London)
**Ireland** 1PG 2T (9) to 1PG 1T (6)

1899 Dublin
**Ireland** 1PG 1T (6) to 0

1900 Richmond
**England** 1G 1DG 2T (15) to 1DG (4)

1901 Dublin
**Ireland** 2G (10) to 1PG 1T (6)

1902 Leicester
**England** 2T (6) to 1T (3)

1903 Dublin
**Ireland** 1PG 1T (6) to 0

1904 Blackheath
**England** 2G 3T (19) to 0

1905 Cork
**Ireland** 1G 4T (17) to 1T (3)

1906 Leicester
**Ireland** 2G 2T (16) to 2T (6)

1907 Dublin
**Ireland** 1G 1GM 3T (17) to 1PG 2T (9)

72

1908 Richmond
**England** 2G 1T (13) to 1PG (3)

1909 Dublin
**England** 1G 2T (11) to 1G (5)

1910 Twickenham
**Drawn** no score

1911 Dublin
**Ireland** 1T (3) to 0

1912 Twickenham
**England** 5T (15) to 0

1913 Dublin
**England** 1PG 4T (15) to 1DG (4)

1914 Twickenham
**England** 1G 4T (17) to 1G 1DG 1T (12)

1920 Dublin
**England** 1G 3T (14) to 1G 1PG 1T (11)

1921 Twickenham
**England** 1G 1DG 2T (15) to 0

1922 Dublin
**England** 4T (12) to 1T (3)

1923 Leicester
**England** 2G 1DG 3T (23) to 1G (5)

1924 Belfast
**England** 1G 3T (14) to 1T (3)

1925 Twickenham
**Drawn** 2T (6) each

1926 Dublin
**Ireland** 2G 1PG 2T (19) to 3G (15)

1927 Twickenham
**England** 1G 1T (8) to 1PG 1T (6)

1928 Dublin
**England** 1DG 1T (7) to 2T (6)

1929 Twickenham
**Ireland** 2T (6) to 1G (5)

1930 Dublin
**Ireland** 1DG (4) to 1T (3)

1931 Twickenham
**Ireland** 1PG 1T (6) to 1G (5)

1932 Dublin
**England** 1G 2PG (11) to 1G 1PG (8)

1933 Twickenham
**England** 1G 4T (17) to 1PG 1T (6)

1934 Dublin
**England** 2G 1T (13) to 1T (3)

1935 Twickenham
**England** 1G 3PG (14) to 1T (3)

1936 Dublin
**Ireland** 2T (6) to 1T (3)

1937 Twickenham
**England** 1PG 2T (9) to 1G 1T (8)

1938 Dublin
**England** 6G 1PG 1T (36) to 1G 3T (14)

1939 Twickenham
**Ireland** 1G (5) to 0

1947 Dublin
**Ireland** 2G 1PG 3T (22) to 0

1948 Twickenham
**Ireland** 1G 2T (11) to 2G (10)

1949 Dublin
**Ireland** 1G 2PG 1T (14) to 1G (5)

1950 Twickenham
**England** 1T (3) to 0

1951 Dublin
**Ireland** 1PG (3) to 0

1952 Twickenham
**England** 1T (3) to 0

1953 Dublin
**Drawn** 2PG 1T (9) each

1954 Twickenham
**England** 1G 1PG 2T (14) to 1PG (3)

1955 Dublin
**Drawn** Ireland 1PG 1T (6)
England 2T (6)

1956 Twickenham
**England** 1G 3PG 2T (20) to 0

1957 Dublin
**England** 1PG 1T (6) to 0

1958 Twickenham
**England** 1PG 1T (6) to 0

1959 Dublin
**England** 1PG (3) to 0

1960 Twickenham
**England** 1G 1DG (8) to 1G (5)

1961 Dublin
**Ireland** 1G 2PG (11) to 1G 1T (8)

1962 Twickenham
**England** 2G 1PG 1T (16) to 0

1963 Dublin
**Drawn** no score

1964 Twickenham
**Ireland** 3G 1T (18) to 1G (5)

1965 Dublin
**Ireland** 1G (5) to 0

1966 Twickenham
**Drawn** 1PG 1T (6) each

1967 Dublin
**England** 1G 1PG (8) to 1PG (3)

1968 Twickenham
**Drawn** England 2PG 1DG (9)
Ireland 3PG (9)

1969 Dublin
**Ireland** 1G 2PG 1DG 1T (17)
to 4PG 1T (15)

1970 Twickenham
**England** 2DG 1T (9) to 1PG (3)

1971 Dublin
**England** 3PG (9) to 2T (6)

1972 Twickenham
**Ireland** 1G 1DG 1PG 1T (16)
to 1G 2PG (12)

1973 Dublin
**Ireland** 2G 1PG 1DG (18)
to 1G 1PG (9)

1974 Twickenham
**Ireland** 2G 1PG 1DG 2T (26) to 1G 5PG (21)

1975 Dublin
**Ireland** 2G (12) to 1G 1DG (9)

1976 Twickenham
**Ireland** 2PG 1DG 1T (13) to 4PG (12)

1977 Dublin
**England** 1T (4) to 0

1978 Twickenham
**England** 2G 1PG (15) to 2PG 1DG (9)

# ENGLAND v WALES

**Played 83   England won 33, Wales won 39, Drawn 11**

1881 Blackheath (London)
**England** 7G 1DG 6T to 0

1882 No Match

1883 Swansea
**England** 2G 4T to 0

1884 Leeds
**England** 1G 2T to 1G

1885 Swansea
**England** 1G 4T to 1G 1T

1886 Blackheath
**England** 1GM 2T to 1G

1887 Llanelli
**Drawn** no score

1888 No Match

1889 No Match

1890 Dewsbury
**Wales** 1T to 0

1891 Newport
**England** 2G 1T (7) to 1G (3)

1892 Blackheath
**England** 3G 1T (17) to 0

1893 Cardiff
**Wales** 1G 1PG 2T (14) to 1G 3T (11)

1894 Birkenhead
**England** 4G 1GM (24) to 1T (3)

1895 Swansea
**England** 1G 3T (14) to 2T (6)

1896 Blackheath
**England** 2G 5T (25) to 0

1897 Newport
**Wales** 1G 2T (11) to 0

1898 Blackheath
**England** 1G 3T (14) to 1DG 1T (7)

1899 Swansea
**Wales** 4G 2T (26) to 1T (3)

1900 Gloucester
**Wales** 2G 1PG (13) to 1T (3)

1901 Cardiff
**Wales** 2G 1T (13) to 0

1902 Blackheath
**Wales** 1PG 2T (9) to 1G 1T (8)

1903 Swansea
**Wales** 3G 2T (21) to 1G (5)

1904 Leicester
**Drawn** England 1G 1PG 2T (14) Wales 2G 1GM (14)

1905 Cardiff
**Wales** 2G 5T (25) to 0

1906 Richmond (London)
**Wales** 2G 2T (16) to 1T (3)

1907 Swansea
**Wales** 2G 4T (22) to 0

1908 Bristol
**Wales** 3G 1DG 1PG 2T (28) to 3G 1T (18)

1909 Cardiff
**Wales** 1G 1T (8) to 0

1910 Twickenham
**England** 1G 1PG 1T (11) to 2T (6)

1911 Swansea
**Wales** 1PG 4T (15) to 1G 2T (11)

1912 Twickenham
**England** 1G 1T (8) to 0

1913 Cardiff
**England** 1G 1DG 1T (12) to 0

1914 Twickenham
**England** 2G (10) to 1G 1DG (9)

1920 Swansea
**Wales** 1G 2DG 1PG 1T (19) to 1G (5)

1921 Twickenham
**England** 1G 1DG 3T (18) to 1T (3)

1922 Cardiff
**Wales** 2G 6T (28) to 2T (6)

1923 Twickenham
**England** 1DG 1T (7) to 1T (3)

1924 Swansea
**England** 1G 4T (17) to 3T (9)

1925 Twickenham
**England** 1PG 3T (12) to 2T (6)

1926 Cardiff
**Drawn** 1T (3) each

1927 Twickenham
**England** 1G 1PG 1GM (11) to 1PG 2T (9)

1928 Swansea
**England** 2G (10) to 1G 1T (8)

1929 Twickenham
**England** 1G 1T (8) to 1T (3)

1930 Cardiff
**England** 1G 1PG 1T (11) to 1T (3)

1931 Twickenham
**Drawn** England 1G 2PG (11) Wales 1G 1GM 1T (11)

74

1932 Swansea
**Wales** 1G 1DG 1PG (12) to 1G (5)

1933 Twickenham
**Wales** 1DG 1T (7) to 1T (3)

1934 Cardiff
**England** 3T (9) to 0

1935 Twickenham
**Drawn** England 1PG (3) Wales 1T (3)

1936 Swansea
**Drawn** no score

1937 Twickenham
**England** 1DG (4) to 1T (3)

1938 Cardiff
**Wales** 1G 2PG 1T (14) to 1G 1T (8)

1939 Twickenham
**England** 1T (3) to 0

1947 Cardiff
**England** 1G 1DG (9) to 2T (6)

1948 Twickenham
**Drawn** England 1PG (3) Wales 1T (3)

1949 Cardiff
**Wales** 3T (9) to 1DG (3)

1950 Twickenham
**Wales** 1G 1PG 1T (11) to 1G (5)

1951 Swansea
**Wales** 4G 1T (23) to 1G (5)

1952 Twickenham
**Wales** 1G 1T (8) to 2T (6)

1953 Cardiff
**England** 1G 1PG (8) to 1PG (3)

1954 Twickenham
**England** 3T (9) to 1PG 1T (6)

1955 Cardiff
**Wales** 1PG (3) to 0

1956 Twickenham
**Wales** 1G 1T (8) to 1PG (3)

1957 Cardiff
**England** 1PG (3) to 0

1958 Twickenham
**Drawn** England 1T (3) Wales 1PG (3)

1959 Cardiff
**Wales** 1G (5) to 0

1960 Twickenham
**England** 1G 2PG 1T (14) to 2PG (6)

1961 Cardiff
**Wales** 2T (6) to 1T (3)

1962 Twickenham
**Drawn** no score

1963 Cardiff
**England** 2G 1DG (13) to 1PG 1T (6)

1964 Twickenham
**Drawn** 2T (6) each

1965 Cardiff
**Wales** 1G 1DG 2T (14) to 1PG (3)

1966 Twickenham
**Wales** 1G 2PG (11) to 1PG 1T (6)

1967 Cardiff
**Wales** 5G 2PG 1DG (34) to 4PG 3T (21)

1968 Twickenham
**Drawn** England 1G 1PG 1T (11)
Wales 1G 1DG 1T (11)

1969 Cardiff
**Wales** 3G 2PG 1DG 2T (30) to 3PG (9)

1970 Twickenham
**Wales** 1G 1DG 3T (17) to 2G 1PG (13)

1971 Cardiff
**Wales** 2G 2DG 1PG 1T (22)
to 1PG 1T (6)

1972 Twickenham
**Wales** 1G 2PG (12) to 1PG (3)

1973 Cardiff
**Wales** 1G 1PG 4T (25) to 2PG 1DG (9)

1974 Twickenham
**England** 1G 2PG 1T (16)
to 1G 2PG (12)

1975 Cardiff
**Wales** 1G 2PG 2T (20) to 1T (4)

1976 Twickenham
**Wales** 3G 1PG (21) to 3PG (9)

1977 Cardiff
**Wales** 2PG 2T (14) to 3PG (9)

1978 Twickenham
**Wales** 3PG (9) to 2PG (6)

## ENGLAND v FRANCE
**Played 53   England won 29, France won 18, Drawn 6**

1906 Paris
**England** 4G 5T (35) to 1G 1T (8)

1907 Richmond (London)
**England** 5G 1DG 4T (41)
to 2G 1PG (13)

1908 Paris
**England** 2G 3T (19) to 0

1909 Leicester
**England** 2G 4T (22) to 0

1910 Paris
**England** 1G 2T (11) to 1T (3)

1911 Twickenham
**England** 5G 2PG 2T (37) to 0

1912 Paris
**England** 1G 1DG 3T (18) to 1G 1T (8)

1913 Twickenham
**England** 1G 5T (20) to 0

1914 Paris
**England** 6G 3T (39) to 2G 1T (13)

1920 Twickenham
**England** 1G 1PG (8) to 1T (3)

1921 Paris
**England** 2G (10) to 2PG (6)

1922 Twickenham
**Drawn** England 1G 2PG (11)
France 1G 2T (11)

1923 Paris
**England** 1G 1DG 1T (12) to 1PG (3)

1924 Twickenham
**England** 2G 3T (19) to 1DG 1T (7)

1925 Paris
**England** 2G 1GM (13) to 1G 2T (11)

1926 Twickenham
**England** 1G 2T (11) to 0

1927 Paris
**France** 1T (3) to 0

1928 Twickenham
**England** 3G 1T (18) to 1G 1T (8)

1929 Paris
**England** 2G 2T (16) to 2T (6)

1930 Twickenham
**England** 1G 2T (11) to 1G (5)

1931 Paris
**France** 2DG 2T (14) to 2G 1T (13)

1947 Twickenham
**England** 2T (6) to 1PG (3)

1948 Paris
**France** 1G 1DG 2T (15) to 0

1949 Twickenham
**England** 1G 1DG (8) to 1DG (3)

1950 Paris
**France** 2T (6) to 1T (3)

1951 Twickenham
**France** 1G 1PG 1T (11) to 1T (3)

1952 Paris
**England** 2PG (6) to 1T (3)

1953 Twickenham
**England** 1G 2T (11) to 0

1954 Paris
**France** 1G 1DG 1T (11) to 1T (3)

1955 Twickenham
**France** 2G 2DG (16) to 2PG 1T (9)

1956 Paris
**France** 1G 2PG 1T (14) to 2PG 1T (9)

1957 Twickenham
**England** 3T (9) to 1G (5)

1958 Paris
**England** 1G 1PG 2T (14) to 0

1959 Twickenham
**Drawn** 1PG (3) each

1960 Paris
**Drawn** France 1PG (3) England 1T (3)

1961 Twickenham
**Drawn** 1G (5) each

1962 Paris
**France** 2G 1T (13) to 0

1963 Twickenham
**England** 2PG (6) to 1G (5)

1964 Paris
**England** 1PG 1T (6) to 1T (3)

1965 Twickenham
**England** 2PG 1T (9) to 1PG 1T (6)

1966 Paris
**France** 2G 1T (13) to 0

1967 Twickenham
**France** 2G 1DG 1PG (16)
to 3PG 1DG (12)

1968 Paris
**France** 1G 2DG 1PG (14) to 1DG
2PG (9)

1969 Twickenham
**England** 2G 3PG 1T (22) to 1G 1DG (8)

1970 Paris
**France** 4G 2DG 1PG 2T (35)
to 2G 1PG (13)

1971 Twickenham
**Drawn** England 1G 3PG (14)
France 1G 1PG 1DG 1T (14)

1972 Paris
**France** 5G 1PG 1T (37) to 1G 2PG (12)

1973 Twickenham
**England** 2PG 2T (14) to 1G (6)

1974 Paris
**Drawn** 1G 1PG 1DG (12) each

1975 Twickenham
**France** 4G 1PG (27) to 4PG 2T (20)

1976 Paris
**France** 3G 3T (30) to 1G 1PG (9)

1977 Twickenham
**France** 1T (4) to 1PG (3)

1978 Paris
**France** 2G 1PG (15) to 2DG (6)

75

# ENGLAND v NEW ZEALAND
**Played 10   England won 2, New Zealand won 8, Drawn 0**

1905 Crystal Palace (London)
**New Zealand** 5T (15) to 0

1925 Twickenham
**New Zealand** 1G 1PG 3T (17)
to 1G 1PG 1T (11)

1936 Twickenham
**England** 1DG 3T (13) to 0

1954 Twickenham
**New Zealand** 1G (5) to 0

1963 *1* Auckland
**New Zealand** 3G 1DG 1PG (21)
to 1G 2PG (11)

    *2* Christchurch
**New Zealand** 1GM 2T (9)
to 1PG 1T (6)
*New Zealand won series 2–0*

1964 Twickenham
**New Zealand** 1G 2PG 1T (14) to 0

1967 Twickenham
**New Zealand** 4G 1T (23)
to 1G 1PG 1T (11)

1973 Twickenham
**New Zealand** 1G 1DG (9) to 0

1973 Auckland
**England** 2G 1T (16) to 1G 1T (10)

## ENGLAND v SOUTH AFRICA
**Played 7   England won 2, South Africa won 4, Drawn 1**

1906 Crystal Palace (London)
**Drawn** 1T (3) each

1913 Twickenham
**South Africa** 2PG 1T (9) to 1T (3)

1932 Twickenham
**South Africa** 1DG 1T (7) to 0

1952 Twickenham
**South Africa** 1G 1PG (8) to 1T (3)

1961 Twickenham
**South Africa** 1G (5) to 0

1969 Twickenham
**England** 1G 1PG 1T (11) to 1G 1PG (8)

1972 Johannesburg
**England** 1G 4PG (18) to 3PG (9)

## ENGLAND v AUSTRALIA
**Played 9   England won 3, Australia won 6, Drawn 0**

1909 Blackheath (London)
**Australia** 3T (9) to 1T (3)

1948 Twickenham
**Australia** 1G 2T (11) to 0

1958 Twickenham
**England** 1PG 2T (9) to 1DG 1PG (6)

1963 Sydney
**Australia** 3G 1T (18) to 3T (9)

1967 Twickenham
**Australia** 1G 3DG 2PG 1T (23)
to 1G 2PG (11)

1973 Twickenham
**England** 1G 2PG 2T (20) to 1PG (3)

1975 *1* Sydney
**Australia** 2PG 2DG 1T (16)
to 1G 1PG (9)

    *2* Brisbane
**Australia** 2G 2PG 3T (30)
to 2G 3PG (21)
*Australia won series 2–0*

1976 Twickenham
**England** 1G 3PG 2T (23) to 2PG (6)

## SCOTLAND v IRELAND
**Played 88   Scotland won 45, Ireland won 40, Drawn 3**

1877 Belfast
**Scotland** 6G 2T to 0

1878 No Match

1879 Belfast
**Scotland** 2G 1T to 0

1880 Glasgow
**Scotland** 3G 2T to 0

1881 Belfast
**Ireland** 1G to 1T

1882 Glasgow
**Scotland** 2T to 0

1883 Belfast
**Scotland** 1G 1T to 0

1884 Raeburn Place (Edinburgh)
**Scotland** 2G 2T to 1T

1885 Raeburn Place
**Scotland** 1G 2T to 0

1886 Raeburn Place
**Scotland** 4G 2T to 0

1887 Belfast
**Scotland** 2G 2T to 0

1888 Raeburn Place
**Scotland** 1G to 0

1889 Belfast
**Scotland** 1DG to 0

1890 Raeburn Place
**Scotland** 1DG 1T to 0

1891 Belfast
**Scotland** 4G 2T (14) to 0

1892 Raeburn Place
**Scotland** 1T (2) to 0

1893 Belfast
**Drawn** no score

1894 Dublin
**Ireland** 1G (5) to 0

1895 Raeburn Place
**Scotland** 2T (6) to 0

1896 Dublin
**Drawn** no score

1897 Powderhall (Edinburgh)
**Scotland** 1G 1PG (8) to 1T (3)

1898 Belfast
**Scotland** 1G 1T (8) to 0

1899 Inverleith (Edinburgh)
**Ireland** 3T (9) to 1PG (3)

1900 Dublin
**Drawn** no score

1901 Inverleith (Edinburgh)
**Scotland** 3T (9) to 1G (5)

1902 Belfast
**Ireland** 1G (5) to 0

1903 Inverleith
**Scotland** 1T (3) to 0

1904 Dublin
**Scotland** 2G 3T (19) to 1T (3)

1905 Inverleith
**Ireland** 1G 2T (11) to 1G (5)

1906 Dublin
**Scotland** 2G 1GM (13) to 2T (6)

1907 Inverleith
**Scotland** 3G (15) to 1PG (3)

1908 Dublin
**Ireland** 2G 2T (16) to 1G 1PG 1T (11)

1909 Inverleith
**Scotland** 3T (9) to 1PG (3)

1910 Belfast
**Scotland** 1G 3T (14) to 0

1911 Inverleith
**Ireland** 2G 2T (16) to 1DG 2T (10)

1912 Dublin
**Ireland** 1DG 1PG 1T (10) to 1G 1T (8)

1913 Inverleith
**Scotland** 4G 3T (29) to 2G 1DG (14)

1914 Dublin
**Ireland** 2T (6) to 0

1920 Inverleith
**Scotland** 2G 1PG 2T (19) to 0

1921 Dublin
**Ireland** 3T (9) to 1G 1T (8)

1922 Inverleith
**Scotland** 2T (6) to 1T (3)

1923 Dublin
**Scotland** 2G 1T (13) to 1T (3)

1924 Inverleith
**Scotland** 2G 1T (13) to 1G 1T (8)

1925 Dublin
**Scotland** 2G 1DG (14)
to 1G 1PG (8)

1926 Murrayfield
**Ireland** 1T (3) to 0

1927 Dublin
**Ireland** 2T (6) to 0

1928 Murrayfield
**Ireland** 2G 1T (13) to 1G (5)

1929 Dublin
**Scotland** 2G 2T (16) to 1DG 1T (7)

1930 Murrayfield
**Ireland** 1G 3T (14) to 1G 2T (11)

1931 Dublin
**Ireland** 1G 1T (8) to 1G (5)

1932 Murrayfield
**Ireland** 4G (20) to 1G 1T (8)

1933 Dublin
**Scotland** 2DG (8) to 2T (6)

1934 Murrayfield
**Scotland** 2G 1PG 1T (16) to 3T (9)

1935 Dublin
**Ireland** 4T (12) to 1G (5)

1936 Murrayfield
**Ireland** 1DG 2T (10) to 1DG (4)

1937 Dublin
**Ireland** 1G 2T (11) to 1DG (4)

1938 Murrayfield
**Scotland** 2G 1DG 1PG 2T (23)
to 1G 3T (14)

1939 Dublin
**Ireland** 1PG 1GM 2T (12) to 1T (3)

1947 Murrayfield
**Ireland** 1T (3) to 0

1948 Dublin
**Ireland** 2T (6) to 0

1949 Murrayfield
**Ireland** 2G 1PG (13) to 1PG (3)

1950 Dublin
**Ireland** 3G 2PG (21) to 0

1951 Murrayfield
**Ireland** 1DG 1T (6) to 1G (5)

1952 Dublin
**Ireland** 1PG 3T (12) to 1G 1PG (8)

1953 Murrayfield
**Ireland** 4G 2T (26) to 1G 1PG (8)

1954 Belfast
**Ireland** 2T (6) to 0

1955 Murrayfield
**Scotland** 2PG 1DG 1T (12) to 1PG (3)

1956 Dublin
**Ireland** 1G 3T (14) to 2G (10)

1957 Murrayfield
**Ireland** 1G (5) to 1PG (3)

1958 Dublin
**Ireland** 2PG 2T (12) to 2T (6)

1959 Murrayfield
**Ireland** 1G 1PG (8) to 1PG (3)

1960 Dublin
**Scotland** 1DG 1T (6) to 1G (5)

1961 Murrayfield
**Scotland** 2G 1PG 1T (16) to 1G 1T (8)

1962 Dublin
**Scotland** 1G 1DG 2PG 2T (20) to 1PG 1T (6)

1963 Murrayfield
**Scotland** 1PG (3) to 0

1964 Dublin
**Scotland** 2PG (6) to 1PG (3)

1965 Murrayfield
**Ireland** 2G 1DG 1T (16) to 1DG 1PG (6)

1966 Dublin
**Scotland** 1G 2T (11) to 1PG (3)

1967 Murrayfield
**Ireland** 1G (5) to 1PG (3)

1968 Dublin
**Ireland** 1G 1PG 2T (14) to 2PG (6)

1969 Murrayfield
**Ireland** 2G 2T (16) to 0

1970 Dublin
**Ireland** 2G 2T (16) to 1G 1DG 1T (11)

1971 Murrayfield
**Ireland** 1G 2PG 2T (17) to 1G (5)

1972 No Match

1973 Murrayfield
**Scotland** 2PG 3DG 1T (19) to 2PG 2T (14)

1974 Dublin
**Ireland** 1G 1PG (9) to 2PG (6)

1975 Murrayfield
**Scotland** 2PG 2DG 2T (20) to 1G 1PG 1T (13)

1976 Dublin
**Scotland** 4PG 1DG (15) to 2PG (6)

1977 Murrayfield
**Scotland** 2PG 1DG 3T (21) to 1G 3PG 1DG (18)

1978 Dublin
**Ireland** 1G 2PG (12) to 3PG (9)

# SCOTLAND v WALES
**Played 82   Scotland won 34, Wales won 46, Drawn 2**

1883 Raeburn Place (Edinburgh)
**Scotland** 3G to 1G

1884 Newport
**Scotland** 1DG 1T to 0

1885 Glasgow
**Drawn** no score

1886 Cardiff
**Scotland** 2G 1T to 0

1887 Raeburn Place
**Scotland** 4G 8T to 0

1888 Newport
**Wales** 1T to 0

1889 Raeburn Place
**Scotland** 2T to 0

1890 Cardiff
**Scotland** 1G 2T to 1T

1891 Raeburn Place
**Scotland** 1G 2DG 5T (14) to 0

1892 Swansea
**Scotland** 1G 1T (7) to 1T (2)

1893 Raeburn Place
**Wales** 1PG 3T (9) to 0

1894 Newport
**Wales** 1DG 1T (7) to 0

1895 Raeburn Place
**Scotland** 1G (5) to 1DG (4)

1896 Cardiff
**Wales** 2T (6) to 0

1897 No Match

1898 No Match

1899 Inverleith (Edinburgh)
**Scotland** 1GM 2DG 3T (21) to 2G (10)

1900 Swansea
**Wales** 4T (12) to 1T (3)

1901 Inverleith
**Scotland** 3G 1T (18) to 1G 1T (8)

1902 Cardiff
**Wales** 1G 3T (14) to 1G (5)

1903 Inverleith
**Scotland** 1PG 1T (6) to 0

1904 Swansea
**Wales** 3G 1PG 1T (21) to 1T (3)

1905 Inverleith
**Wales** 2T (6) to 1T (3)

1906 Cardiff
**Wales** 3T (9) to 1PG (3)

1907 Inverleith
**Scotland** 2T (6) to 1PG (3)

1908 Swansea
**Wales** 2T (6) to 1G (5)

1909 Inverleith
**Wales** 1G (5) to 1PG (3)

1910 Cardiff
**Wales** 1G 3T (14) to 0

1911 Inverleith
**Wales** 2G 1DG 6T (32)
to 1DG 2T (10)

1912 Swansea
**Wales** 2G 2DG 1T (21) to 2T (6)

1913 Inverleith
**Wales** 1G 1T (8) to 0

1914 Cardiff
**Wales** 2G 2DG 1PG 1T (24) to 1G (5)

1920 Inverleith
**Scotland** 2PG 1T (9) to 1G (5)

1921 Swansea
**Scotland** 1G 1PG 2T (14) to 2DG (8)

1922 Inverleith
**Drawn** Scotland 1PG 2T (9)
Wales 1G 1DG (9)

1923 Cardiff
**Scotland** 1G 2T (11) to 1G 1PG (8)

1924 Inverleith
**Scotland** 4G 1PG 4T (35) to 2G (10)

1925 Swansea
**Scotland** 1G 1DG 5T (24)
to 1G 1PG 2T (14)

1926 Murrayfield
**Scotland** 1G 1PG (8) to 1G (5)

1927 Cardiff
**Scotland** 1G (5) to 0

1928 Murrayfield
**Wales** 2G 1T (13) to 0

1929 Swansea
**Wales** 1G 3T (14) to 1DG 1PG (7)

1930 Murrayfield
**Scotland** 1G 1DG 1T (12)
to 1G 1DG (9)

1931 Cardiff
**Wales** 2G 1T (13) to 1G 1T (8)

1932 Murrayfield
**Wales** 1PG 1T (6) to 0

1933 Swansea
**Scotland** 1G 1PG 1T (11) to 1T (3)

1934 Murrayfield
**Wales** 2G 1T (13) to 1PG 1T (6)

1935 Cardiff
**Wales** 1DG 2T (10) to 2T (6)

1936 Murrayfield
**Wales** 2G 1T (13) to 1T (3)

1937 Swansea
**Scotland** 2G 1T (13) to 2T (6)

1938 Murrayfield
**Scotland** 1G 1PG (8) to 2T (6)

1939 Cardiff
**Wales** 1G 1PG 1T (11) to 1PG (3)

1947 Murrayfield
**Wales** 2G 1PG 3T (22) to 1G 1PG (8)

1948 Cardiff
**Wales** 1G 1PG 2T (14) to 0

1949 Murrayfield
**Scotland** 2T (6) to 1G (5)

1950 Swansea
**Wales** 1DG 1PG 2T (12) to 0

1951 Murrayfield
**Scotland** 2G 1DG 1PG 1T (19) to 0

1952 Cardiff
**Wales** 1G 2PG (11) to 0

1953 Murrayfield
**Wales** 1PG 3T (12) to 0

1954 Swansea
**Wales** 1PG 4T (15) to 1T (3)

1955 Murrayfield
**Scotland** 1G 1DG 1PG 1T (14)
to 1G 1T (8)

1956 Cardiff
**Wales** 3T (9) to 1PG (3)

1957 Murrayfield
**Scotland** 1DG 1PG 1T (9)
to 1PG 1T (6)

1958 Cardiff
**Wales** 1G 1T (8) to 1PG (3)

1959 Murrayfield
**Scotland** 1PG 1T (6) to 1G (5)

1960 Cardiff
**Wales** 1G 1PG (8) to 0

1961 Murrayfield
**Scotland** 1T (3) to 0

1962 Cardiff
**Scotland** 1G 1T (8) to 1DG (3)

1963 Murrayfield
**Wales** 1DG 1PG (6) to 0

1964 Cardiff
**Wales** 1G 1PG 1T (11) to 1T (3)

1965 Murrayfield
**Wales** 1G 2PG 1T (14) to 2DG 2PG (12)

1966 Cardiff
**Wales** 1G 1T (8) to 1PG (3)

1967 Murrayfield
**Scotland** 1G 1DG 1T (11) to 1G (5)

1968 Cardiff
**Wales** 1G (5) to 0

1969 Murrayfield
**Wales** 1G 2PG 2T (17) to 1PG (3)

1970 Cardiff
**Wales** 3G 1T (18) to 1DG 1PG 1T (9)

1971 Murrayfield
**Wales** 2G 1PG 2T (19) to 4PG 2T (18)

1972 Cardiff
**Wales** 3G 3PG 2T (35) to 1G 2PG (12)

| | |
|---|---|
| 1973 Murrayfield<br>**Scotland** 1G 1T (10) to 3PG (9) | 1976 Cardiff<br>**Wales** 2G 3PG 1DG 1T (28) to 1G (6) |
| 1974 Cardiff<br>**Wales** 1G (6) to 0 | 1977 Murrayfield<br>**Wales** 2G 2PG (18) to 1G 1DG (9) |
| 1975 Murrayfield<br>**Scotland** 3PG 1DG (12) to 2PG 1T (10) | 1978 Cardiff<br>**Wales** 1PG 1DG 4T (22) to 2PG 2T (14) |

# SCOTLAND v FRANCE

**Played 48    Scotland won 23, France won 23, Drawn 2**

| | |
|---|---|
| 1910 Inverleith (Edinburgh)<br>**Scotland** 3G 4T (27) to 0 | 1953 Paris<br>**France** 1G 1DG 1PG (11) to 1G (5) |
| 1911 Paris<br>**France** 2G 2T (16) to 1G 1DG 2T (15) | 1954 Murrayfield<br>**France** 1T (3) to 0 |
| 1912 Inverleith<br>**Scotland** 5G 1PG 1T (31) to 1T (3) | 1955 Paris<br>**France** 1PG 4T (15) to 0 |
| 1913 Paris<br>**Scotland** 3G 2T (21) to 1T (3) | 1956 Murrayfield<br>**Scotland** 2PG 2T (12) to 0 |
| 1914 No Match | 1957 Paris<br>**Scotland** 1DG 1PG (6) to 0 |
| 1920 Paris<br>**Scotland** 1G (5) to 0 | 1958 Murrayfield<br>**Scotland** 1G 1PG 1T (11) to 2PG 1T (9) |
| 1921 Inverleith<br>**France** 1T (3) to 0 | 1959 Paris<br>**France** 2DG 1T (9) to 0 |
| 1922 Paris<br>**Drawn** 1T (3) each | 1960 Murrayfield<br>**France** 2G 1T (13) to 1G 1PG 1T (11) |
| 1923 Inverleith<br>**Scotland** 2G 2T (16) to 1GM (3) | 1961 Paris<br>**France** 1G 1DG 1PG (11) to 0 |
| 1924 Paris<br>**France** 4T (12) to 1DG 1PG 1T (10) | 1962 Murrayfield<br>**France** 1G 2PG (11) to 1PG (3) |
| 1925 Inverleith<br>**Scotland** 2G 5T (25) to 1DG (4) | 1963 Paris<br>**Scotland** 1G 1DG 1PG (11)<br>to 1DG 1PG (6) |
| 1926 Paris<br>**Scotland** 1G 1PG 4T (20) to 1PG 1T (6) | 1964 Murrayfield<br>**Scotland** 2G (10) to 0 |
| 1927 Murrayfield<br>**Scotland** 4G 1PG (23) to 2T (6) | 1965 Paris<br>**France** 2G 2T (16) to 1G 1T (8) |
| 1928 Paris<br>**Scotland** 5T (15) to 2T (6) | 1966 Murrayfield<br>**Drawn** Scotland 1T (3) France 1PG (3) |
| 1929 Murrayfield<br>**Scotland** 1PG 1T (6) to 1T (3) | 1967 Paris<br>**Scotland** 2PG 1DG (9) to 1G 1T (8) |
| 1930 Paris<br>**France** 1DG 1T (7) to 1T (3) | 1968 Murrayfield<br>**France** 1G 1T (8) to 1PG 1T (6) |
| 1931 Murrayfield<br>**Scotland** 2PG (6) to 1DG (4) | 1969 Paris<br>**Scotland** 1PG 1T (6) to 1PG (3) |
| 1947 Paris<br>**France** 1G 1T (8) to 1PG (3) | 1970 Murrayfield<br>**France** 1G 1DG 1T (11) to 2PG 1T (9) |
| 1948 Murrayfield<br>**Scotland** 2PG 1T (9) to 1G 1PG (8) | 1971 Paris<br>**France** 2G 1PG (13) to 1G 1PG (8) |
| 1949 Paris<br>**Scotland** 1G 1T (8) to 0 | 1972 Murrayfield<br>**Scotland** 1G 1PG 1DG 2T (20)<br>to 1G 1PG (9) |
| 1950 Murrayfield<br>**Scotland** 1G 1T (8) to 1G (5) | 1973 Paris<br>**France** 3PG 1DG 1T (16)<br>to 2PG 1DG 1T (13) |
| 1951 Paris<br>**France** 1G 2PG 1T (14) to 2PG 2T (12) | |
| 1952 Murrayfield<br>**France** 2G 1PG (13) to 1G 2PG (11) | |

1974 Murrayfield
**Scotland** 1G 3PG 1T (19)
to 1PG 1DG (6)

1975 Paris
**France** 1PG 1DG 1T (10) to 3PG (9)

1976 Murrayfield
**France** 3PG 1T (13) to 1PG 1DG (6)

1977 Paris
**France** 2G 1PG 2T (23) to 1PG (3)

1978 Murrayfield
**France** 1G 3PG 1T (19) to 1G 1PG 1DG 1T (16)

## SCOTLAND v NEW ZEALAND
**Played 7   Scotland won 0, New Zealand won 6, Drawn 1**

1905 Inverleith (Edinburgh)
**New Zealand** 4T (12) to 1DG 1T (7)

1935 Murrayfield
**New Zealand** 3G 1T (18) to 1G 1T (8)

1954 Murrayfield
**New Zealand** 1PG (3) to 0

1964 Murrayfield
**Drawn** no score

1967 Murrayfield
**New Zealand** 1G 2PG 1T (14) to 1DG (3)

1972 Murrayfield
**New Zealand** 1G 2T (14) to 1DG 2PG (9)

1975 Auckland
**New Zealand** 4G (24) to 0

## SCOTLAND v SOUTH AFRICA
**Played 8   Scotland won 3, South Africa won 5, Drawn 0**

1906 Glasgow
**Scotland** 2T (6) to 0

1912 Inverleith
**South Africa** 2G 2T (16) to 0

1932 Murrayfield
**South Africa** 2T (6) to 1T (3)

1951 Murrayfield
**South Africa** 7G 1DG 2T (44) to 0

1960 Port Elizabeth
**South Africa** 3G 1T (18) to 2G (10)

1961 Murrayfield
**South Africa** 2PG 2T (12) to 1G (5)

1965 Murrayfield
**Scotland** 1G 1DG (8) to 1G (5)

1969 Murrayfield
**Scotland** 1PG 1T (6) to 1PG (3)

## SCOTLAND v AUSTRALIA
**Played 6   Scotland won 4, Australia won 2, Drawn 0**

1947 Murrayfield
**Australia** 2G 2T (16) to 1DG 1PG (7)

1958 Murrayfield
**Scotland** 2PG 2T (12) to 1G 1T (8)

1966 Murrayfield
**Scotland** 1G 1PG 1T (11) to 1G (5)

1968 Murrayfield
**Scotland** 2PG 1T (9) to 1PG (3)

1970 Sydney
**Australia** 1G 1PG 5T (23) to 1PG (3)

1975 Murrayfield
**Scotland** 1G 1T (10) to 1PG (3)

## IRELAND v WALES
**Played 80   Ireland won 26, Wales won 49, Drawn 5**

1882 Dublin
**Wales** 2G 2T to 0

1883 No Match

1884 Cardiff
**Wales** 1DG 2T to 0

1885 No Match

1886 No Match

1887 Birkenhead
**Wales** 1DG 1T to 3T

1888 Dublin
**Ireland** 1G 1DG 1T to 0

1889 Swansea
**Ireland** 2T to 0

1890 Dublin
**Drawn** 1G each

1891 Llanelli
**Wales** 1G 1DG (6) to 1DG 1T (4)

1892 Dublin
**Ireland** 1G 2T (9) to 0

1893 Llanelli
**Wales** 1T (2) to 0

1894 Belfast
**Ireland** 1PG (3) to 0

1895 Cardiff
**Wales** 1G (5) to 1T (3)

1896 Dublin
**Ireland** 1G 1T (8) to 1DG (4)

1897 No Match

1898 Limerick
**Wales** 1G 1PG 1T (11) to 1PG (3)

1899 Cardiff
**Ireland** 1T (3) to 0

1900 Belfast
**Wales** 1T (3) to 0

1901 Swansea
**Wales** 2G (10) to 3T (9)

1902 Dublin
**Wales** 1G 1DG 2T (15) to 0

1903 Cardiff
**Wales** 6T (18) to 0

1904 Belfast
**Ireland** 1G 3T (14) to 4T (12)

1905 Swansea
**Wales** 2G (10) to 1T (3)

1906 Belfast
**Ireland** 1G 2T (11) to 2T (6)

1907 Cardiff
**Wales** 2G 1DG 1PG 4T (29) to 0

1908 Belfast
**Wales** 1G 2T (11) to 1G (5)

1909 Swansea
**Wales** 3G 1T (18) to 1G (5)

1910 Dublin
**Wales** 1DG 5T (19) to 1T (3)

1911 Cardiff
**Wales** 2G 1PG 1T (16) to 0

1912 Belfast
**Ireland** 1G 1DG 1T (12) to 1G (5)

1913 Swansea
**Wales** 2G 1PG 1T (16) to 2G 1PG (13)

1914 Belfast
**Wales** 1G 2T (11) to 1T (3)

1920 Cardiff
**Wales** 3G 1DG 3T (28) to 1DG (4)

1921 Belfast
**Wales** 1PG 1T (6) to 0

1922 Swansea
**Wales** 1G 2T (11) to 1G (5)

1923 Dublin
**Ireland** 1G (5) to 1DG (4)

1924 Cardiff
**Ireland** 2G 1T (13) to 1DG 2T (10)

1925 Belfast
**Ireland** 2G 1PG 2T (19) to 1T (3)

1926 Swansea
**Wales** 1G 2T (11) to 1G 1PG (8)

1927 Dublin
**Ireland** 2G 1PG 2T (19) to 1G 1DG (9)

1928 Cardiff
**Ireland** 2G 1T (13) to 2G (10)

1929 Belfast
**Drawn** 1G (5) each

1930 Swansea
**Wales** 1PG 3T (12) to 1DG 1PG (7)

1931 Belfast
**Wales** 1G 1DG 2T (15) to 1T (3)

1932 Cardiff
**Ireland** 4T (12) to 1DG 2T (10)

1933 Belfast
**Ireland** 1DG 1PG 1T (10) to 1G (5)

1934 Swansea
**Wales** 2G 1T (13) to 0

1935 Belfast
**Ireland** 2PG 1T (9) to 1PG (3)

1936 Cardiff
**Wales** 1PG (3) to 0

1937 Belfast
**Ireland** 1G (5) to 1PG (3)

1938 Swansea
**Wales** 1G 1PG 1T (11) to 1G (5)

1939 Belfast
**Wales** 1DG 1T (7) to 0

1947 Swansea
**Wales** 1PG 1T (6) to 0

1948 Belfast
**Ireland** 2T (6) to 1T (3)

1949 Swansea
**Ireland** 1G (5) to 0

1950 Belfast
**Wales** 2T (6) to 1PG (3)

1951 Cardiff
**Drawn** Wales 1PG (3) Ireland 1T (3)

1952 Dublin
**Wales** 1G 1PG 2T (14) to 1PG (3)

1953 Swansea
**Wales** 1G (5) to 1T (3)

1954 Dublin
**Wales** 1DG 3PG (12) to 2PG 1T (9)

1955 Cardiff
**Wales** 3G 1PG 1T (21) to 1PG (3)

1956 Dublin
**Ireland** 1G 1DG 1PG (11) to 1PG (3)

1957 Cardiff
**Wales** 2PG (6) to 1G (5)

1958 Dublin
**Wales** 3T (9) to 1PG 1T (6)

1959 Cardiff
**Wales** 1G 1T (8) to 1PG 1T (6)

1960 Dublin
**Wales** 2G (10) to 2PG 1T (9)

1961 Cardiff
**Wales** 2PG 1T (9) to 0

1962 Dublin
**Drawn** Ireland 1DG (3) Wales 1PG (3)

1963 Cardiff
**Ireland** 1G 1DG 2PG (14)
to 1DG 1T (6)

1964 Dublin
**Wales** 3G (15) to 2PG (6)

1965 Cardiff
**Wales** 1G 1DG 1PG 1T (14)
to 1G 1PG (8)

1966 Dublin
**Ireland** 1DG 1PG 1T (9) to 1PG 1T (6)

1967 Cardiff
**Ireland** 1T (3) to 0

1968 Dublin
**Ireland** 1PG 1DG 1T (9)
to 1PG 1DG (6)

1969 Cardiff
**Wales** 3G 1DG 1PG 1T (24)
to 1G 2PG (11)

1970 Dublin
**Ireland** 1G 1DG 1PG 1T (14) to 0

1971 Cardiff
**Wales** 1G 2PG 1DG 3T (23) to 3PG (9)

1972 No Match

1973 Cardiff
**Wales** 1G 2PG 1T (16) to 1G 2PG (12)

1974 Dublin
**Drawn** Ireland 3PG (9)
Wales 1G 1PG (9)

1975 Cardiff
**Wales** 3G 2PG 2T (32) to 1T (4)

1976 Dublin
**Wales** 3G 4PG 1T (34) to 3PG (9)

1977 Cardiff
**Wales** 2G 2PG 1DG 1T (25) to 3PG (9)

1978 Dublin
**Wales** 4PG 2T (20) to 3PG 1DG 1T (16)

# IRELAND v FRANCE

**Played 51   Ireland won 24, France won 24, Drawn 3**

1909 Dublin
**Ireland** 2G 1PG 2T (19) to 1G 1T (8)

1910 Paris
**Ireland** 1G 1T (8) to 1T (3)

1911 Cork
**Ireland** 3G 1DG 2T (25) to 1G (5)

1912 Paris
**Ireland** 1G 2T (11) to 2T (6)

1913 Cork
**Ireland** 3G 3T (24) to 0

1914 Paris
**Ireland** 1G 1T (8) to 2T (6)

1920 Dublin
**France** 5T (15) to 1DG 1T (7)

1921 Paris
**France** 4G (20) to 2G (10)

1922 Dublin
**Ireland** 1G 1PG (8) to 1T (3)

1923 Paris
**France** 1G 3T (14) to 1G 1T (8)

1924 Dublin
**Ireland** 2T (6) to 0

1925 Paris
**Ireland** 1PG 2T (9) to 1T (3)

1926 Belfast
**Ireland** 1G 1PG 1T (11) to 0

1927 Paris
**Ireland** 1G 1PG (8) to 1T (3)

1928 Belfast
**Ireland** 4T (12) to 1G 1T (8)

1929 Paris
**Ireland** 2T (6) to 0

1930 Belfast
**France** 1G (5) to 0

1931 Paris
**France** 1T (3) to 0

1947 Dublin
**France** 4T (12) to 1G 1PG (8)

1948 Paris
**Ireland** 2G 1T (13) to 2T (6)

1949 Dublin
**France** 2G 2PG (16) to 3PG (9)

1950 Paris
**Drawn** France 1DG (3) Ireland 1PG (3)

1951 Dublin
**Ireland** 1PG 2T (9) to 1G 1T (8)

1952 Paris
**Ireland** 1G 1PG 1T (11) to 1G 1PG (8)

1953 Belfast
**Ireland** 2G 2T (16) to 1DG (3)

1954 Paris
**France** 1G 1T (8) to 0

1955 Dublin
**France** 1G (5) to 1PG (3)

1956 Paris
**France** 1G 2DG 1T (14) to 1G 1PG (8)

1957 Dublin
**Ireland** 1G 1PG 1T (11) to 2PG (6)

1958 Paris
**France** 1G 1DG 1PG (11) to 2PG (6)

1959 Dublin
**Ireland** 1DG 1PG 1T (9) to 1G (5)

1960 Paris
**France** 1G 3DG 3T (23) to 2T (6)

1961 Dublin
**France** 2DG 2PG 1T (15) to 1PG (3)

1962 Paris
**France** 1G 2T (11) to 0

1963 Dublin
**France** 3G 2DG 1T (24) to 1G (5)

1964 Paris
**France** 3G 1DG 3T (27) to 1DG 1T (6)

1965 Dublin
**Drawn** 1T (3) each

1966 Paris
**France** 1G 1PG 1T (11) to 1DG 1PG (6)

1967 Dublin
**France** 1G 2DG (11) to 1PG 1T (6)

1968 Paris
**France** 2G 1PG 1DG (16) to 2PG (6)

1969 Dublin
**Ireland** 1G 1DG 3PG (17) to 2PG 1T (9)

1970 Paris
**France** 1G 1DG (8) to 0

1971 Dublin
**Drawn** Ireland 2PG 1T (9)
France 2PG 1DG (9)

1972 Paris
**Ireland** 2PG 2T (14) to 1G 1PG (9)

*1972 Dublin
**Ireland** 3G 2PG (24) to 1G 2T (14)

1973 Dublin
**Ireland** 2PG (6) to 1T (4)

1974 Paris
**France** 1G 1PG (9) to 2PG (6)

1975 Dublin
**Ireland** 2G 1PG 2DG 1T (25)
to 1PG 1DG (6)

1976 Paris
**France** 2G 2PG 2T (26) to 1PG (3)

1977 Dublin
**France** 1G 3PG (15) to 2PG (6)

1978 Paris
**France** 2PG 1T (10) to 3PG (9)

*Non-championship match*

# IRELAND v NEW ZEALAND
**Played 8   Ireland won 0, New Zealand won 7, Drawn 1**

1905 Dublin
**New Zealand** 3G (15) to 0

1924 Dublin
**New Zealand** 1PG 1T (6) to 0

1935 Dublin
**New Zealand** 1G 2PG 2T (17)
to 2PG 1T (9)

1954 Dublin
**New Zealand** 1G 1DG 1PG 1T (14)
to 1PG (3)

1963 Dublin
**New Zealand** 1PG 1T (6) to 1G (5)

1973 Dublin
**Drawn** Ireland 2PG 1T (10)
New Zealand 1G 1T (10)

1974 Dublin
**New Zealand** 1G 3PG (15) to 2PG (6)

1976 Wellington
**New Zealand** 1PG 2T (11) to 1PG (3)

# IRELAND v SOUTH AFRICA
**Played 8   Ireland won 1, South Africa won 6, Drawn 1**

1906 Belfast
**South Africa** 1PG 4T (15)
to 1PG 3T (12)

1912 Dublin
**South Africa** 4G 6T (38) to 0

1931 Dublin
**South Africa** 1G 1T (8) to 1PG (3)

1951 Dublin
**South Africa** 1G 1DG 3T (17) to 1G (5)

1960 Dublin
**South Africa** 1G 1T (8) to 1PG (3)

1961 Cape Town
**South Africa** 3G 1PG 2T (24)
to 1G 1PG (8)

1965 Dublin
**Ireland** 2PG 1T (9) to 1PG 1T (6)

1970 Dublin
**Drawn** 1G 1PG (8) each

## IRELAND v AUSTRALIA
**Played 6   Ireland won 4, Australia won 2, Drawn 0**

1947 Dublin
**Australia** 2G 2T (16) to 1PG (3)

1958 Dublin
**Ireland** 1PG 2T (9) to 2T (6)

1967 Dublin
**Ireland** 2DG 1PG 2T (15) to 1G 1DG (8)

1967 Sydney
**Ireland** 1G 1DG 1T (11) to 1G (5)

1968 Dublin
**Ireland** 2G (10) to 1T (3)

1976 Dublin
**Australia** 1G 2PG 2T (20) to 2PG 1T (10)   85

## WALES v FRANCE
**Played 51   Wales won 34, France won 14, Drawn 3**

1908 Cardiff
**Wales** 3G 1PG 6T (36) to 1DG (4)

1909 Paris
**Wales** 7G 4T (47) to 1G (5)

1910 Swansea
**Wales** 8G 1PG 2T (49)
to 1G 2PG 1T (14)

1911 Paris
**Wales** 3G (15) to 0

1912 Newport
**Wales** 1G 3T (14) to 1G 1T (8)

1913 Paris
**Wales** 1G 2T (11) to 1G 1T (8)

1914 Swansea
**Wales** 5G 2T (31) to 0

1920 Paris
**Wales** 2T (6) to 1G (5)

1921 Cardiff
**Wales** 2PG 2T (12) to 1DG (4)

1922 Paris
**Wales** 1G 2T (11) to 1T (3)

1923 Swansea
**Wales** 2G 1PG 1T (16) to 1G 1T (8)

1924 Paris
**Wales** 1DG 2T (10) to 2T (6)

1925 Cardiff
**Wales** 1G 2T (11) to 1G (5)

1926 Paris
**Wales** 1DG 1T (7) to 1G (5)

1927 Swansea
**Wales** 2G 5T (25) to 1DG 1T (7)

1928 Paris
**France** 1G 1T (8) to 1T (3)

1929 Cardiff
**Wales** 1G 1T (8) to 1T (3)

1930 Paris
**Wales** 2DG 1T (11) to 0

1931 Swansea
**Wales** 5G 1DG 2T (35) to 1T (3)

1947 Paris
**Wales** 1PG (3) to 0

1948 Swansea
**France** 1G 2T (11) to 1PG (3)

1949 Paris
**France** 1G (5) to 1T (3)

1950 Cardiff
**Wales** 3G 1PG 1T (21) to 0

1951 Paris
**France** 1G 1PG (8) to 1T (3)

1952 Swansea
**Wales** 1DG 2PG (9) to 1G (5)

1953 Paris
**Wales** 2T (6) to 1PG (3)

1954 Cardiff
**Wales** 2G 3PG (19) to 2G 1PG (13)

1955 Paris
**Wales** 2G 2PG (16)
to 1G 1DG 1PG (11)

1956 Cardiff
**Wales** 1G (5) to 1T (3)

1957 Paris
**Wales** 2G 1PG 2T (19)
to 2G 1T (13)

1958 Cardiff
**France** 2G 2DG (16) to 1PG 1T (6)

1959 Paris
**France** 1G 1PG 1T (11) to 1PG (3)

1960 Cardiff
**France** 2G 2T (16) to 1G 1PG (8)

1961 Paris
**France** 1G 1T (8) to 2T (6)

1962 Cardiff
**Wales** 1PG (3) to 0

1963 Paris
**France** 1G (5) to 1PG (3)

1964 Cardiff
**Drawn** 1G 2PG (11) each

1965 Paris
**France** 2G 1PG 1DG 2T (22)
to 2G 1T (13)

1966 Cardiff
**Wales** 2PG 1T (9) to 1G 1T (8)

1967 Paris
**France** 1G 2DG 1PG 2T (20)
to 1G 2PG 1DG (14)

1968 Cardiff
**France** 1G 1PG 1DG 1T (14)
to 2PG 1T (9)

1969 Paris
**Drawn** France 1G 1PG (8)
Wales 1G 1T (8)

1970 Cardiff
**Wales** 1G 2PG (11) to 2T (6)

1971 Paris
**Wales** 1PG 2T (9) to 1G (5)

1972 Cardiff
**Wales** 4PG 2T (20) to 2PG (6)

1973 Paris
**France** 3PG 1DG (12) to 1DG (3)

1974 Cardiff
**Drawn** 3PG 1DG 1T (16) each

1975 Paris
**Wales** 1G 1PG 4T (25) to 2PG 1T (10)

1976 Cardiff
**Wales** 5PG 1T (19) to 1G 1PG 1T (13)

1977 Paris
**France** 1G 2PG 1T (16) to 3PG (9)

1978 Cardiff
**Wales** 1G 2DG 1T (16) to 1DG 1T (7)

## WALES v NEW ZEALAND
**Played 9   Wales won 3, New Zealand won 6, Drawn 0**

1905 Cardiff
**Wales** 1T (3) to 0

1924 Swansea
**New Zealand** 2G 1PG 2T (19) to 0

1935 Cardiff
**Wales** 2G 1T (13) to 1G 1DG 1T (12)

1953 Cardiff
**Wales** 2G 1PG (13) to 1G 1PG (8)

1963 Cardiff
**New Zealand** 1DG 1PG (6) to 0

1967 Cardiff
**New Zealand** 2G 1PG (13)
to 1DG 1PG (6)

1969 *1* Christchurch
**New Zealand** 2G 1PG 2T (19) to 0

*2* Auckland
**New Zealand** 3G 1DG 5PG (33)
to 2PG 2T (12)

*New Zealand won series 2–0*

1972 Cardiff
**New Zealand** 5PG 1T (19)
to 4PG 1T (16)

## WALES v SOUTH AFRICA
**Played 7   Wales won 0, South Africa won 6, Drawn 1**

1906 Swansea
**South Africa** 1G 2T (11) to 0

1912 Cardiff
**South Africa** 1PG (3) to 0

1931 Swansea
**South Africa** 1G 1T (8) to 1T (3)

1951 Cardiff
**South Africa** 1DG 1T (6) to 1T (3)

1960 Cardiff
**South Africa** 1PG (3) to 0

1964 Durban
**South Africa** 3G 1DG 2PG (24) to
1PG (3)

1970 Cardiff
**Drawn** 1PG 1T (6) each

## WALES v AUSTRALIA
**Played 7   Wales won 6, Australia won 1, Drawn 0**

1908 Cardiff
**Wales** 1PG 2T (9) to 2T (6)

1947 Cardiff
**Wales** 2PG (6) to 0

1958 Cardiff
**Wales** 1DG 1PG 1T (9) to 1T (3)

1966 Cardiff
**Australia** 1G 1DG 1PG 1T (14)
to 1G 1PG 1T (11)

1969 Sydney
**Wales** 2G 2PG 1T (19) to 2G 2PG (16)

1973 Cardiff
**Wales** 4PG 3T (24) to 0

1975 Cardiff
**Wales** 3G 1PG 1DG 1T (28) to 1PG (3)

# FRANCE v NEW ZEALAND
**Played 14   France won 3, New Zealand won 11, Drawn 0**

1906 Paris
**New Zealand** 4G 6T (38) to 1G 1T (8)

1925 Toulouse
**New Zealand** 3G 5T (30) to 2T (6)

1954 Paris
**France** 1T (3) to 0

1961 *1* Auckland
**New Zealand** 2G 1DG (13) to 2DG (6)

*2* Wellington
**New Zealand** 1G (5) to 1T (3)

*3* Christchurch
**New Zealand** 4G 3PG 1T (32) to 1T (3)

*New Zealand won series 3–0*

1964 Paris
**New Zealand** 1DG 1PG 2T (12) to 1PG (3)

1967 Paris
**New Zealand** 3G 1PG 1T (21) to 3PG 1DG 1T (15)

1968 *1* Christchurch
**New Zealand** 3PG 1T (12) to 1DG 2PG (9)

*2* Wellington
**New Zealand** 3PG (9) to 1PG (3)

*3* Auckland
**New Zealand** 2G 1DG 2PG (19) to 1DG 3T (12)

*New Zealand won series 3–0*

1973 Paris
**France** 1G 1PG 1T (13) to 2PG (6)

1977 *1* Toulouse
**France** 1G 1DG 3PG (18) to 1DG 2PG 1T (13)

*2* Paris
**New Zealand** 1G 1DG 2PG (15) to 1PG (3)

# FRANCE v SOUTH AFRICA
**Played 18   France won 3, South Africa won 11, Drawn 4**

1913 Bordeaux
**South Africa** 4G 1PG 5T (38) to 1G (5)

1952 Paris
**South Africa** 2G 1PG 4T (25) to 1DG (3)

1958 *1* Cape Town
**Drawn** South Africa 1T (3) France 1DG (3)

*2* Johannesburg
**France** 2DG 1PG (9) to 1G (5)

*France won series 1–0, with 1 draw*

1961 Paris
**Drawn** no score

1964 Springs (SA)
**France** 1G 1PG (8) to 1PG 1T (6)

1967 *1* Durban
**South Africa** 4G 1PG 1T (26) to 1T (3)

*2* Bloemfontein
**South Africa** 2G 1PG 1T (16) to 1PG (3)

*3* Johannesburg
**France** 2G 2DG 1PG (19) to 1G 2PG 1T (14)

*4* Cape Town
**Drawn** South Africa 1DG 1PG (6) France 1PG 1T (6)

*South Africa won series 2–1, with 1 draw*

1968 *1* Bordeaux
**South Africa** 4PG (12) to 3T (9)

*2* Paris
**South Africa** 2G 1PG 1T (16) to 1G 2DG (11)

*South Africa won series 2–0*

1971 *1* Bloemfontein
**South Africa** 2G 1DG 3PG (22) to 2PG 1T (9)

*2* Durban
**Drawn** 1G 1DG (8) each

*South Africa won series 1–0, with 1 draw*

1974 *1* Toulouse
**South Africa** 3PG 1T (13) to 1T (4)

*2* Paris
**South Africa** 2PG 1T (10) to 2T (8)

*South Africa won series 2–0*

1975 *1* Bloemfontein
**South Africa** 3G 4PG 2T (38) to 3G 1PG 1T (25)

*2* Pretoria
**South Africa** 2G 7PG (33) to 1G 3PG 1DG (18)

*South Africa won series 2–0*

# FRANCE v AUSTRALIA
**Played 11   France won 8, Australia won 2, Drawn 1**

1948 Paris
**France** 2G 1T (13) to 2PG (6)

1958 Paris
**France** 2G 2DG 1T (19) to 0

88

1961 Sydney
**France** 2DG 3T (15) to 1G 1PG (8)

1967 Paris
**France** 1G 1DG 4PG (20)
to 1G 1DG 1PG 1T (14)

1968 Sydney
**Australia** 1G 1DG 1PG (11) to 2G (10)

1971 *1* Toulouse
**Australia** 1G 1PG 1T (13) to 1PG 2T (11)

*2* Paris
**France** 1G 4PG (18) to 3PG (9)

*Series drawn 1–1*

1972 *1* Sydney
**Drawn** Australia 2PG 2T (14)
France 1G 2T (14)

*2* Brisbane
**France** 2G 1T (16) to 5PG (15)

*France won series 1–0, with 1 draw*

1976 *1* Bordeaux
**France** 3G (18) to 4PG 1DG (15)

*2* Paris
**France** 2G 1PG 1DG 4T (34) to 2PG (6)

*France won series 2–0*

# NEW ZEALAND v SOUTH AFRICA
**Played 34   New Zealand won 13, South Africa won 19, Drawn 2**

1921 *1* Dunedin
**New Zealand** 2G 1T (13) to 1G (5)

*2* Auckland
**South Africa** 1G 1DG (9) to 1G (5)

*3* Wellington
**Drawn** no score

*Series drawn 1–1, with 1 draw*

1928 *1* Durban
**South Africa** 2DG 2PG 1T (17) to 0

*2* Johannesburg
**New Zealand** 1DG 1PG (7)
to 1PG 1GM (6)

*3* Port Elizabeth
**South Africa** 1G 2T (11) to 2T (6)

*4* Cape Town
**New Zealand** 1DG 2PG 1T (13)
to 1G (5)

*Series drawn 2–2*

1937 *1* Wellington
**New Zealand** 1DG 2PG 1T (13)
to 1DG 1T (7)

*2* Christchurch
**South Africa** 2G 1PG (13) to 2T (6)

*3* Auckland
**South Africa** 1G 4T (17) to 2PG (6)

*South Africa won series 2–1*

1949 *1* Cape Town
**South Africa** 5PG (15)
to 1G 1DG 1PG (11)

*2* Johannesburg
**South Africa** 1DG 1PG 2T (12)
to 1DG 1PG (6)

*3* Durban
**South Africa** 3PG (9) to 1T (3)

*4* Port Elizabeth
**South Africa** 1G 1DG 1PG (11)
to 1G 1T (8)

*South Africa won series 4–0*

1956 *1* Dunedin
**New Zealand** 2G (10) to 1PG 1T (6)

*2* Wellington
**South Africa** 1G 1T (8) to 1T (3)

*3* Christchurch
**New Zealand** 1G 2PG 2T (17)
to 2G (10)

*4* Auckland
**New Zealand** 1G 2PG (11) to 1G (5)

*New Zealand won series 3–1*

1960 *1* Johannesburg
**South Africa** 2G 1PG (13) to 0

*2* Cape Town
**New Zealand** 1G 1DG 1PG (11)
to 1T (3)

*3* Bloemfontein
**Drawn** 1G 2PG (11) each

*4* Port Elizabeth
**South Africa** 1G 1PG (8) to 1PG (3)

*South Africa won series 2–1, with 1 draw*

1965 *1* Wellington
**New Zealand** 2T (6) to 1DG (3)

*2* Dunedin
**New Zealand** 2G 1T (13) to 0

*3* Christchurch
**South Africa** 2G 1PG 2T (19)
to 2G 1PG 1T (16)

*4* Auckland
**New Zealand** 1G 1DG 4T (20)
to 1PG (3)

*New Zealand won series 3–1*

1970 *1* Pretoria
**South Africa** 1G 2PG 1DG 1T (17)
to 1PG 1T (6)

*2* Cape Town
**New Zealand** 1PG 2T (9) to 1G 1PG (8)

*3* Port Elizabeth
**South Africa** 1G 2PG 1T (14) to 1PG (3)

*4* Johannesburg
**South Africa** 1G 4PG 1T (20)
to 1G 4PG (17)

*South Africa won series 3–1*

1976 *1* Durban
**South Africa** 1G 1PG 1DG 1T (16)
to 1PG 1T (7)

*2* Bloemfontein
**New Zealand** 1G 2PG 1DG (15)
to 3PG (9)

*3* Cape Town
**South Africa** 1G 2PG 1DG (15)
to 2PG 1T (10)

*4* Johannesburg
**South Africa** 1G 2PG 1DG (15)
to 1PG 1DG 2T (14)

*South Africa won series 3–1*

# NEW ZEALAND v AUSTRALIA
**Played 64   New Zealand won 47, Australia won 13, Drawn 4**

1903 Sydney
**New Zealand** 1G 1PG 2GM 2T (22)
to 1PG (3)

1905 Dunedin
**New Zealand** 1G 3T (14) to 1T (3)

1907 *1* Sydney
**New Zealand** 4G 2T (26)
to 1PG 1GM (6)

*2* Brisbane
**New Zealand** 1G 3T (14) to 1G (5)

*3* Sydney
**Drawn** 1G (5) each

*New Zealand won series 2–0, with 1 draw*

1910 *1* Sydney
**New Zealand** 2T (6) to 0

*2* Sydney
**Australia** 1G 2T (11) to 0

*3* Sydney
**New Zealand** 2G 6T (28) to 2G 1PG (13)

*New Zealand won series 2–1*

1913 *1* Wellington
**New Zealand** 3G 5T (30) to 1G (5)

*2* Dunedin
**New Zealand** 3G 1DG 2T (25)
to 2G 1T (13)

*3* Christchurch
**Australia** 2G 2T (16) to 1G (5)

*New Zealand won series 2–1*

1914 *1* Sydney
**New Zealand** 1G (5) to 0

*2* Brisbane
**New Zealand** 1G 4T (17) to 0

*3* Sydney
**New Zealand** 2G 4T (22) to 1DG 1T (7)

*New Zealand won series 3–0*

1929 *1* Sydney
**Australia** 2PG 1T (9) to 1G 1PG (8)

*2* Brisbane
**Australia** 1G 2PG 2T (17) to 1PG 2T (9)

*3* Sydney
**Australia** 3PG 2T (15) to 2G 1T (13)

*Australia won series 3–0*

1931 Auckland
**New Zealand** 1G 4PG 1T (20)
to 2G 1T (13)

1932 *1* Sydney
**Australia** 2G 2PG 2T (22)
to 2G 1DG 1T (17)

*2* Brisbane
**New Zealand** 1G 1DG 1PG 3T (21)
to 1T (3)

*3* Sydney
**New Zealand** 3G 2T (21) to 2G 1T (13)

*New Zealand won series 2–1*

1934 *1* Sydney
**Australia** 2G 3PG 2T (25)
to 1G 2T (11)

*2* Sydney
**Drawn** 1T (3) each

*Australia won series 1–0, with 1 draw*

1936 *1* Wellington
**New Zealand** 1G 2T (11)
to 1PG 1T (6)

*2* Dunedin
**New Zealand** 4G 1PG 5T (38)
to 2G 1PG (13)

*New Zealand won series 2–0*

1938 *1* Sydney
**New Zealand** 3G 2PG 1T (24)
to 3PG (9)

*2* Brisbane
**New Zealand** 2G 1DG 2T (20)
to 1G 1PG 2T (14)

*3* Sydney
**New Zealand** 1G 2PG 1T (14)
to 1PG 1T (6)

*New Zealand won series 3–0*

1946 *1* Dunedin
**New Zealand** 5G 2T (31) to 1G 1T (8)

*2* Auckland
**New Zealand** 1G 3PG (14) to 2G (10)

*New Zealand won series 2–0*

1947 *1* Brisbane
**New Zealand** 2G 1T (13) to 1G (5)

*2* Sydney
**New Zealand** 3G 4PG (27)
to 1G 3PG (14)

*New Zealand won series 2–0*

1949 *1* Wellington
**Australia** 1G 2T (11) to 1PG 1T (6)

90

*2* Auckland
**Australia** 2G 1PG 1T (16)
to 1DG 1PG 1T (9)

*Australia won series 2–0*

1951 *1* Sydney
**New Zealand** 1G 1PG (8) to 0

*2* Sydney
**New Zealand** 1G 1DG 3T (17)
to 1G 1PG 1T (11)

*3* Brisbane
**New Zealand** 2G 2T (16) to 2PG (6)

*New Zealand won series 3–0*

1952 *1* Christchurch
**Australia** 1G 1DG 2T (14) to 1PG 2T (9)

*2* Wellington
**New Zealand** 1DG 2PG 2T (15)
to 1G 1PG (8)

*Series drawn 1–1*

1955 *1* Wellington
**New Zealand** 2G 1PG 1T (16)
to 1G 1PG (8)

*2* Dunedin
**New Zealand** 1G 1DG (8) to 0

*3* Auckland
**Australia** 1T (8) to 1T (3)

*New Zealand won series 2–1*

1957 *1* Sydney
**New Zealand** 2G 3PG 2T (25)
to 1G 2PG (11)

*2* Brisbane
**New Zealand** 2G 1DG 1GM 2T (22)
to 2PG 1T (9)

*New Zealand won series 2–0*

1958 *1* Wellington
**New Zealand** 2G 5T (25) to 1T (3)

*2* Christchurch
**Australia** 1PG 1T (6) to 1T (3)

*3* Auckland
**New Zealand** 1G 4PG (17)
to 1G 1PG (8)

*New Zealand won series 2–1*

1962 *1* Brisbane
**New Zealand** 1G 1DG 1PG 3T (20)
to 2PG (6)

*2* Sydney
**New Zealand** 1G 2PG 1T (14) to 1G (5)

*New Zealand won series 2–0*

1962 *1* Wellington
**Drawn** New Zealand 2PG 1T (9)
Australia 3PG (9)

*2* Dunedin
**New Zealand** 1PG (3) to 0

*3* Auckland
**New Zealand** 2G 1DG 1T (16)
to 1G 1PG (8)

*New Zealand won series 2–0, with 1 draw*

1964 *1* Dunedin
**New Zealand** 1G 1DG 2PG (14)
to 2PG 1T (9)

*2* Christchurch
**New Zealand** 3G 1T (18) to 1T (3)

*3* Wellington
**Australia** 1G 1DG 3PG 1T (20) to 1G (5)

*New Zealand won series 2–1*

1967 Wellington
**New Zealand** 4G 1DG 2PG (29)
to 1PG 2T (9)

1968 *1* Sydney
**New Zealand** 3G 1PG 3T (27)
to 1G 2PG (11)

*2* Brisbane
**New Zealand** 2G 2PG 1T (19)
to 5PG 1T (18)

*New Zealand won series 2–0*

1972 *1* Wellington
**New Zealand** 3G 1DG 2T (29)
to 2PG (6)

*2* Christchurch
**New Zealand** 2G 2PG 3T (30)
to 1G 1DG 2T (17)

*3* Auckland
**New Zealand** 4G 2PG 2T (38)
to 1PG (3)

*New Zealand won series 3–0*

1974 *1* Sydney
**New Zealand** 1PG 2T (11) to 1G (6)

*2* Brisbane
**Drawn** 1G 2PG 1T (16) each

*3* Sydney
**New Zealand** 2G 1T (16) to 2PG (6)

*New Zealand won series 2–0, with 1 draw*

# SOUTH AFRICA v AUSTRALIA
**Played 28   South Africa won 21, Australia won 7, Drawn 0**

1933 *1* Cape Town
**South Africa** 1G 1PG 3T (17) to 1PG (3)

*2* Durban
**Australia** 3G 1PG 1T (21) to 1PG 1T (6)

*3* Johannesburg
**South Africa** 1G 1DG 1T (12) to 1T (3)

*4* Port Elizabeth
**South Africa** 1G 1PG 1T (11) to 0

*5* Bloemfontein
**Australia** 1G 1DG 2T (15) to 1DG (4)

*South Africa won series 3–2*

1937 *1* Sydney
**South Africa** 1PG 2T (9) to 1G (5)

*2* Sydney
**South Africa** 4G 2T (26)
to 1G 2PG 2T (17)

*South Africa won series 2–0*

1953 *1* Johannesburg
**South Africa** 2G 2PG 3T (25) to 1PG (3)

*2* Cape Town
**Australia** 3G 1T (18) to 1G 3T (14)

*3* Durban
**South Africa** 3G 1T (18) to 1G 1PG (8)

*4* Port Elizabeth
**South Africa** 2G 2DG 2PG (22)
to 2PG 1T (9)

*South Africa won series 3–1*

1956 *1* Sydney
**South Africa** 1PG 2T (9) to 0

*2* Brisbane
**South Africa** 1DG 2T (9) to 0

*South Africa won series 2–0*

1961 *1* Johannesburg
**South Africa** 2G 6T (28) to 1PG (3)

*2* Port Elizabeth
**South Africa** 1G 1DG 3PG 2T (23)
to 1G 2PG (11)

*South Africa won series 2–0*

1963 *1* Pretoria
**South Africa** 1G 2PG 1T (14) to 1T (3)

*2* Cape Town
**Australia** 1DG 1PG 1T (9) to 1G (5)

*3* Johannesburg
**Australia** 1G 1DG 1PG (11) to 3PG
(9)

*4* Port Elizabeth
**South Africa** 2G 3PG 1T (22)
to 1DG 1PG (6)

*Series drawn 2–2*

1965 *1* Sydney
**Australia** 4PG 2T (18) to 1G 1PG 1T (11)

*2* Brisbane
**Australia** 4PG (12) to 1G 1T (8)

*Australia won series 2–0*

1969 *1* Johannesburg
**South Africa** 3G 3PG 2T (30)
to 1G 2PG (11)

*2* Durban
**South Africa** 2G 1PG 1T (16) to 3PG (9)

*3* Cape Town
**South Africa** 1G 1PG 1T (11) to 1PG (3)

*4* Bloemfontein
**South Africa** 2G 2PG 1T (19)
to 1G 1PG (8)

*South Africa won series 4–0*

1971 *1* Sydney
**South Africa** 2G 1DG 1PG 1T (19)
to 1G 2PG (11)

*2* Brisbane
**South Africa** 1G 1PG 2T (14)
to 1DG 1PG (6)

*3* Sydney
**South Africa** 3G 1PG (18) to 1PG 1T (6)

*South Africa won series 3–0*

91

## GRAND SLAM WINNERS

**Wales** 8 times: 1908, 1909, 1911, 1950, 1952, 1971, 1976, 1978.
**England** 7 times: 1913, 1914, 1921, 1923, 1924, 1928, 1957.
**France** twice: 1968, 1977.
**Scotland** once: 1925.
**Ireland** once: 1948.

92

## TRIPLE CROWN WINNERS

**Wales** 15 times: 1893, 1900, 1902, 1905, 1908, 1909, 1911, 1950, 1952, 1965, 1969, 1971, 1976, 1977, 1978.
**England** 14 times: 1883, 1884, 1892, 1913, 1914, 1921, 1923, 1924, 1928, 1934, 1937, 1954, 1957, 1960.
**Scotland** 8 times: 1891, 1895, 1901, 1903, 1907, 1925, 1933, 1938.
**Ireland** 4 times: 1894, 1899, 1948, 1949.

## INTERNATIONAL CHAMPIONSHIP WINNERS

| Year | Winner | Year | Winner | Year | Winner | Year | Winner |
|---|---|---|---|---|---|---|---|
| 1883 | England | 1906 | { Ireland / Wales | 1931 | Wales | 1956 | Wales |
| 1884 | England | 1907 | Scotland | 1932 | { England / Wales / Ireland | 1957 | England |
| 1885* | — | 1908 | Wales | | | 1958 | England |
| 1886 | { England / Scotland | 1909 | Wales | 1933 | Scotland | 1959 | France |
| 1887 | Scotland | 1910 | England | 1934 | England | 1960 | { France / England |
| 1888* | — | 1911 | Wales | 1935 | Ireland | | |
| 1889* | — | 1912 | { England / Ireland | 1936 | Wales | 1961 | France |
| 1890 | { England / Scotland | 1913 | England | 1937 | England | 1962 | France |
| 1891 | Scotland | 1914 | England | 1938 | Scotland | 1963 | England |
| 1892 | England | 1920 | { England / Scotland / Wales | 1939 | { England / Wales / Ireland | 1964 | { Scotland / Wales |
| 1893 | Wales | | | | | 1965 | Wales |
| 1894 | Ireland | 1921 | England | 1947 | { Wales / England | 1966 | Wales |
| 1895 | Scotland | 1922 | Wales | | | 1967 | France |
| 1896 | Ireland | 1923 | England | 1948 | Ireland | 1968 | France |
| 1897* | — | 1924 | England | 1949 | Ireland | 1969 | Wales |
| 1898* | — | 1925 | Scotland | 1950 | Wales | 1970 | { France / Wales |
| 1899 | Ireland | 1926 | { Scotland / Ireland | 1951 | Ireland | | |
| 1900 | Wales | | | 1952 | Wales | 1971 | Wales |
| 1901 | Scotland | 1927 | { Scotland / Ireland | 1953 | England | 1972* | — |
| 1902 | Wales | | | 1954 | { England / France / Wales | 1973 | Quintuple tie |
| 1903 | Scotland | 1928 | England | | | 1974 | Ireland |
| 1904 | Scotland | 1929 | Scotland | 1955 | { France / Wales | 1975 | Wales |
| 1905 | Wales | 1930 | England | | | 1976 | Wales |
| | | | | | | 1977 | France |
| | | | | | | 1978 | Wales |

*Matches not completed, for various reasons*

Wales have won the title outright most times, 20; England have won it 17 times, Scotland 11, Ireland 8, and France 6.

*A dramatic start to an international career: new England full-back David Caplan comes close to scoring in the opening minutes of the 1978 Calcutta Cup match at Murrayfield. However, he had grounded the ball outside the line first.*

# BEWARE THE ICONOCLASTS

**Cliff Morgan** *Cardiff, Bective Rangers, Wales, British Isles; Head of Outside Broadcasts, BBC Television*

For me the most arresting and attractive aspect of the game of Rugby Union football – a game which demands courage and judgment and style, sharp and specific talent and a sense of values – has always been its unique devotion to amateur principles. This in a world of sport where financial reward is quite often more important than fair play and straight dealing.

Lamentably we live in an age of iconoclasm, where the ideas and ideals of our forefathers are often a source of ridicule and sneered at. It is at its peril that the game of rugby football ever jumps on this particular bandwagon.

It was in 1955 in South Africa that I first stumbled across a book written by Robert Ruark called *Something of Value*. He took the title from an old Basuto proverb – 'If a man does away with his traditional way of living and throws away his good customs, he had better first make certain he has something of value to replace them'. It struck me then as a sound philosophy and nothing that has happened since has induced me to change my mind.

I mention all this because quite a few people, including the odd journalist, have been urging that rugby union players should become paid gladiators. It has become a popular topic to nibble at – perhaps because last season was quite the best that most of us can remember. Unquestionably rugby union, as a spectacle, has improved out of all recognition over the past ten years or so. It has become a top box-office attraction, and there is nothing wrong with that. The game, at all levels, needs money. But the inherent danger is the all-too-easy assumption that paying the top players ties in with the interests and needs of the millions who run and tackle and scrummage and side-step on the rugby fields of the world.

If rugby were to be simply a show-case for selected stars, it would be another matter. But those who care know it to be much, much more than that. It is a game which provides a unique opportunity for men – big and small, fast and not so fast, talented and not so talented – to take part in a recreation which, if not better than any other game, is certainly very different. It has its own character and one of the fundamentals is that it should be amateur.

You have only to visit Gala YMCA, Wigan, Ipswich, Haverfordwest and Greystones and many hundreds of the small clubs

Two of the top players who have had to give so much in time and effort in the cause of rugby. Above: Phil Bennett, captain of the 1977 Lions in New Zealand, lays down the law to his team during a break. Below: Sid Going, the All Blacks' scrum-half, manages to avoid the attentions of Terry Cobner while sending out a typical pass in one of the international matches on the same tour.

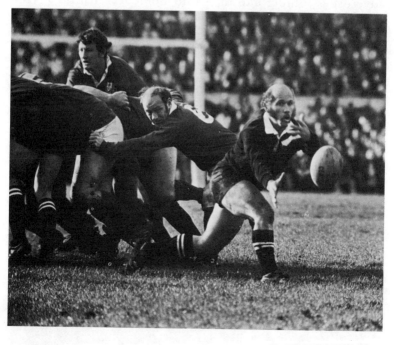

in these islands to know what the game is all about. Men and women giving their time and expertise; club nights and raffle tickets; taking turns at running the bar; washing the kit, etc. This is where you find the unsung guardians of the game who never plead poverty but practise invention. Without them the game at international level would be impossible. Without them the game would be less rich. It is all very well for the big clubs to get free jerseys, but it means that the schoolboys and the smaller clubs pay more on the manufacturer's price. Running small clubs is not easy, but it is so worthwhile. The rewards may not be tangible, but the quality of life and friendship is something money will never buy.

96

If all this changed – and money could bring it about – we could easily see the game being overtaken by all the things that threaten modern sport: 'phoney' build-ups; crowd eruptions; 'conning' of referees; violence on the terraces; and so on. Because of its very nature rugby, a game of bodily contact, could become far too dangerous to play. Our administrators must ensure that the almighty dollar does not rule. Commercial exploitation is as evil as political exploitation.

Yet one can understand, looking around the game these days, why the paying of players is often discussed. Rugby has become big business and there is a flood of money from sponsors and advertising coming into the game. Some feel that the players should have their slice of the cake. Without the star attractions, it is argued, there would be no crowds; and without the same players' appearance on television there would be no revenue from sponsors or advertisers.

My own feeling is that there is room for compromise in this. Administrators should certainly treat the top players well. They should give them the very best travelling arrangements and accommodation when they have to make long journeys and stay away from home for many months, as on a Lions tour. Everything should be done for their comfort. Otherwise how can they be expected to produce their best performance on the field? At home internationals, too, players, and their wives, should be given the best possible treatment. A few nights at a comfortable hotel, special dinner parties, the odd treat to the theatre and so on. I see no harm in that. I believe that if players at international level – who, let us face it, have to sacrifice so much – felt that they were getting the odd privilege, and were being treated well, most of them would not be interested in playing the game for money.

It so happens that I am a great fan of Rugby League and some of the most decent people I have met in sport are in the professional game. If a player wants to make rugby his life and earn the best part of his living that way there is nothing dis-honourable about it. But it is a simple fact that if a man takes this decision he cannot expect to have the same sort of existence in sport as the man who plays for enjoyment only. Rugby League exists to provide opportunity for those who want the game to be the most important part of their lives. I believe Rugby Union should be available in its present form as an outlet for millions who want to play a game as a relaxation from their daily work, and something for which they will make sacrifices at junior and club and international level.

There must be a cold shiver in rugby's corridors of power at the moment with the efforts being made to create a sort of Packer rugby circus. There is so much money available for this sort of thing these days. Here again it is a case of big money catering for the élite, and to hell with the future of the game and its players. I do not believe the rugby fans will flock to see exhibition games between the same players time and again. The pulse only quickens when Scotland play England or Wales meet Ireland, in the quest for the Triple Crown.

I should hate the game to lose its spirit . . . a spirit created over the past century by people who cared. Fifty years ago that immortal rugby man Lord Wakefield wrote 'The spirit of a game is an elusive quality, for we play without analysing our motives'. He went on to say that the spirit of rugby stood apart . . .

> 'Our game is meant to be played swept clean of all those mean and petty infringements of the rules which could so easily creep in . . . As to the rigour of the game, that we must have – a wholehearted joy in the hardness of it, a desire to do our best, to play fair and ask no favour. And, above all, there is no fear of defeat but simply an effort to win because that is the object of the game. If defeat comes our way, it is a lesson rather than a loss; while if we win we are satisfied that our best should have been good enough.'

I am an apostle of those words and was distressed to hear, for the first time, the phrase 'professional foul' being bandied about after the Ireland v Wales game last season. Payments of money to players would make the professional foul the norm. May we be preserved from such sacrilege.

Rugby union has a soul. It could be lost unless we hold on to what has been handed down from the past. 'If a man gives up his traditional way of living . . .' Robert Ruark's words and that Basuto proverb are worth a close look by everyone with the future of the game at heart.

# THE 1977-78 SEASON IN ENGLAND

**Peter Robbins** *The Financial Times*

Bearing in mind that England are still in the process of rehabilitation, the team had a good season and looked a better side than the previous year. They had the misfortune to open against France in Paris and lost 6–15 after twice leading. Injuries to Maxwell (who subsequently retired entirely from rugby), Dixon, and Cowling were an enormous blow. As if that were not enough, the next match was against Wales at Twickenham where, in dreadful conditions, England lost 6–9 with Bennett kicking three penalty goals to two from Hignell. Yet again the losers had the galling experience of having a good share of the game, only to be denied a share of the spoils at the last gasp. The cynics then put it about that the two remaining games, against Scotland and Ireland, were for the second division championship. This was as untrue as it was harsh.

For all that, the match against Scotland was vital to England's players, and to the national morale. In the event, a fine pack once again laid the foundation for a 15–0 victory over a poorish Scottish side. Hignell dropped out at full-back, which gave Caplan, of Headingley, the first cap he should have been given against France. It was a piece of misfortune for Hignell, but paradoxically it gave England a much needed boost behind the scrum and an extra dimension in attack. Caplan, indeed, was nearly over for a try in the first minute, following a daring intervention in the line. Ireland were beaten 15–9 at Twickenham after a fierce game, and so, in retrospect, the Welsh match had cost England the rare prize of the Triple Crown.

England were blessed in Beaumont with a captain of total commitment. He was an outstanding example to his team and had clearly benefited enormously from his call to New Zealand with the Lions in the summer. He was surrounded by some extremely experienced players in Wheeler, Cotton, Burton (for France and Wales), Dixon, and Rafter. Nigel Horton was dropped after the Welsh game, which raised a few eyebrows, but his replacement, Colclough, played energetically against Scotland and Ireland, which seemed to support the selectors.

The team's chief problem, as ever, was at half-back. Old was dropped after Paris and a cap given to John Horton, of Bath, who occasionally showed the range of talents at his disposal. Malcolm Young, of Gosforth, has served England well at scrum-half and there is no grittier player in the position;

nonetheless England desperately needed a touch of class here to capitalise on the marvellous ruck and maul possession won by such a splendid pack. Dodge made a very good impression in the centre, but the two backs who stood out were Slemen, on the wing, and Caplan. Slemen's defence in every game was quite outstanding.

Earlier in the season an England XV beat the American Eagles conclusively 37–11, and England Under 23 beat their French counterparts 10–3 at Orrell, a game in which John Scott, the Under 23 captain, did his cause no harm and he was subsequently capped for the national side at No. 8. Later England Under 23 beat both English Students and Holland, at Hilversum, and England 'B', appearing for the first time, had a successful tour to Rumania.

The system of regional and divisional games did not please everybody. This was partly because it took so many players away so frequently, and partly because there were those who alleged that the national team had been picked despite, rather than because of, the evidence of these games. In the divisional competition the North beat the Midlands 22–7 in the final, with London unexpectedly beating the South and South-West 22–15 in the play-off between the semi-final losers. I myself felt the system to be of value, but this season's visits by Argentina and New Zealand have forced a return to the former trial system.

In the County Championship, North Midlands won the title for the first time, after first beating Yorkshire in the semi-final at Moseley. There they won a most entertaining game 14-10, and owed much to the brilliance of Cusworth at fly-half. Gloucestershire, having disposed of Kent fairly comfortably 19–9 in the semi-final at Blackheath, were hot favourites to carry off the title yet again. Once more, however, Cusworth was in great form and took full advantage of some wayward kicking by Wilkins, the Gloucestershire fly-half. North Midlands' 10–7 victory was even more remarkable as Fidler, for the losers, won a massive amount of possession from the line-out. It helped the winners that his scrum-half Howells, a replacement for Kingston, misread so many promising situations and kicked so inaccurately that North Midlands were able to counter-attack time and again. Their victory was good for rugby in general but most of all in their own area.

Prior to Christmas the 'Varsity Match had taken place, and rarely can one side, in this case Cambridge, have won so much possession and lost the match. Oxford ultimately won 16–10 and owed it most of all to their magnificent defence, with Hopkins, at full-back, pre-eminent. Gareth Davies, at fly-half for Oxford, dropped only one pass through the afternoon and his tactical assessment was always shrewd and correct, as one might expect from an established Cardiff player. Hignell, the Light Blues' captain, at full-back, was not fully match-fit, and was given a bad time by Davies's kicking. Moreover, White, Mitchell, and Moir, the Oxford loose forwards, successfully constricted the Irish international Robbie, at scrum-half for Cambridge. Robbie's partner, Breakey, dropped innumerable passes, as did his centres, Fosh and Davies, in the face of some fierce tackling by Bryan and Watkinson.

The surprise of the John Player Cup competition was the progress of the Harlequins to the semi-final. There they met and lost to Gloucester, who had previously made heavy weather of beating a gallant Wasps side 13–3 at Sudbury. Richards was outstanding for Wasps. Moseley, the hot favourites, had lost 14–0 to Bristol, who in turn were knocked out, but only just, by Coventry. This gave Coventry a semi-final against Leicester at Leicester, where the home team, after leading 12–6 at half-time, were suddenly jolted by a superb try from Cowman, converted by Rossborough. At that point, Coventry could have won on the try-count, but gross defensive lapses finally gave Leicester victory 25–16.

The final at Twickenham was not the greatest of games. Leicester gave Gloucester a fright in the last minute, but the West Country side clung on to win 6–3. Once again the power of their pack, which one has to admire, won the day. Leicester planned to run the ball whenever possible, but Kenney, their usually alert scrum-half, had a difficult day. Much credit goes to the Leicester loose forwards, Adey, Forfar, and Johnson, but not even they could stop the Gloucester juggernaut.

On the club scene, Coventry again had a mixed season and Moseley, after a dazzling start, fell away badly. London Irish delighted their supporters with their John Player run, but it ought to have been extended. They lost, when they should have won, to Harlequins. Waterloo rather fell from grace, but at least won 26 matches. It was good to see Cheltenham, so long the whipping boys of their opponents, make some sort of a comeback, with 12 wins. No one likes to see a club of such traditions in a perpetual trough, and it says much for their administrators that they re-emerged to something like their proper status. Bristol and Bedford were two of the most entertaining sides I saw, and were also among the better organised.

Among individuals I saw, far and away the most impressive scrum-half was Howells of Gloucestershire, despite his display in the county final. He was close run by Kenney of Leicester, Peck of Bedford, and Carfoot of Waterloo. Fidler was still the best non-capped lock, and Brain, the Moseley hooker, took over from his club colleague Cox as an England prospect.

*The England team v Wales at Twickenham.*
*Back row: A J Hignell, M A C Slemen, J P Scott, N E Horton, B G Nelmes, R J Mordell,*
*P W Dodge, M Rafter, P J Wheeler. Front row: J P Horton, M Young, W B Beaumont*
*(capt), P J Squires, B J Corless, M A Burton.*

*Action from the 1978 John Player Cup final: Bob Clewes of Gloucester is bundled into touch by*
*Leicester's Steve Kenny and 'Dusty' Hare.*

There were three notable retirements. Firstly, a collective one – St Luke's College merged with Exeter University, and the RFU, in theory, lost one of its most prolific producers of rugby talent. However, the University could well take over the same role. Bob Taylor of Northampton, England, and the Lions decided to call it a day after a long and distinguished career, while Mike Burton surprised everyone by opting out of the game at the comparatively early age of 32.

The England Colts beat Welsh Youth 12–7 at Cardiff, where fly-half Colin Price, of Lydney, and the two wings, Mark Gregory, of Old Askeans, and Mark Tyrell, of Hampshire, were outstanding on the day. The Colts, however, lost to a good French side at Camborne, 3–11. Unfortunately England Schools, after their prodigious efforts the previous season, fared less well this time. Perhaps we are beginning to see the effects of the liberalising of PE programmes in schools. There are those who are decidedly worried about the fall-off in rugby at this level. All the more important, then, to foster the England Colts.

## RFU CLUB MERIT TABLES 1977–78

### North

| | P | W | D | F | A | Pts | % |
|---|---|---|---|---|---|---|---|
| Liverpool | 12 | 10 | 0 | 147 | 92 | 20 | 83·33 |
| Gosforth | 11 | 9 | 0 | 283 | 84 | 18 | 81·82 |
| Sale | 12 | 9 | 1 | 159 | 123 | 19 | 79·17 |
| Broughton Pk | 14 | 9 | 2 | 255 | 123 | 20 | 71·43 |
| Orrell | 14 | 10 | 0 | 229 | 161 | 20 | 71·43 |
| Wakefield | 12 | 8 | 1 | 215 | 125 | 17 | 70·83 |
| Waterloo | 10 | 6 | 1 | 144 | 72 | 13 | 65·00 |
| Fylde | 11 | 7 | 0 | 186 | 143 | 14 | 63·44 |
| Roundhay | 12 | 7 | 0 | 106 | 136 | 14 | 58·33 |
| Wilmslow | 15 | 8 | 0 | 202 | 179 | 16 | 53·33 |
| Halifax | 17 | 9 | 0 | 178 | 183 | 18 | 52·94 |
| Morley | 10 | 4 | 0 | 102 | 138 | 8 | 40·00 |
| Headingley | 15 | 3 | 3 | 111 | 190 | 9 | 30·00 |
| Northern | 13 | 3 | 1 | 123 | 172 | 7 | 26·92 |
| Harrogate | 15 | 3 | 0 | 130 | 253 | 6 | 20·00 |
| Manchester | 13 | 2 | 1 | 96 | 188 | 5 | 19·23 |
| Hull | 13 | 2 | 0 | 108 | 252 | 4 | 15·38 |
| West Hartlepool | 13 | 2 | 0 | 120 | 280 | 4 | 15·38 |

*Top four qualify for 1978–79 John Player Cup.*

### Midlands

| | P | W | D | F | A | Pts | % |
|---|---|---|---|---|---|---|---|
| Bedford | 8 | 7 | 0 | 209 | 94 | 14 | 87·05 |
| Moseley | 8 | 5 | 1 | 206 | 81 | 11 | 68·75 |
| Coventry | 8 | 5 | 1 | 142 | 93 | 11 | 68·75 |
| Northampton | 6 | 4 | 0 | 91 | 74 | 8 | 66·67 |
| Leicester | 8 | 5 | 0 | 219 | 127 | 10 | 62·05 |
| Birmingham | 7 | 3 | 0 | 92 | 105 | 6 | 42·86 |
| Rugby | 8 | 3 | 0 | 76 | 172 | 6 | 37·05 |
| Nuneaton | 7 | 1 | 0 | 57 | 226 | 2 | 14·29 |
| Nottingham | 8 | 0 | 0 | 74 | 194 | 0 | — |

*Top five qualify for John Player Cup.*

### London

| | P | W | D | F | A | Pts | % |
|---|---|---|---|---|---|---|---|
| London Scottish | 9 | 7 | 2 | 158 | 84 | 16 | 88·89 |
| London Welsh | 9 | 7 | 1 | 143 | 68 | 15 | 83·33 |
| London Irish | 7 | 5 | 1 | 67 | 41 | 11 | 78·57 |
| Rosslyn Pk | 8 | 3 | 3 | 116 | 84 | 9 | 56·25 |
| Harlequins | 6 | 2 | 2 | 64 | 82 | 6 | 50·00 |
| Richmond | 7 | 3 | 1 | 45 | 50 | 7 | 50·00 |
| Blackheath | 8 | 2 | 1 | 100 | 117 | 5 | 31·25 |
| Saracens | 8 | 2 | 0 | 86 | 123 | 4 | 25·00 |
| Wasps | 9 | 1 | 1 | 98 | 123 | 3 | 16·67 |
| Met Police | 7 | 1 | 0 | 42 | 167 | 2 | 14·29 |

*Top six qualify for John Player Cup.*

### South and South-West

| | P | W | D | F | A | Pts | % |
|---|---|---|---|---|---|---|---|
| Gloucester | 7 | 6 | 0 | 109 | 69 | 12 | 85·71 |
| Exeter | 7 | 4 | 0 | 135 | 77 | 8 | 57·14 |
| Bath | 7 | 4 | 0 | 125 | 85 | 8 | 57·14 |
| Plymouth Albion | 8 | 4 | 0 | 121 | 112 | 8 | 50·00 |
| Bristol | 7 | 3 | 0 | 103 | 75 | 6 | 42·86 |
| Falmouth | 6 | 0 | 0 | 15 | 190 | 0 | — |

*Top four qualify for John Player Cup.*

# ENGLISH INTERNATIONAL PLAYERS
*(up to 30 April 1978)*

## ABBREVIATIONS

| | |
|---|---|
| *A* Australia | *W* Wales |
| *F* France | (C) Centenary match v Scotland at Murrayfield, 1971 (non-championship) |
| *I* Ireland | |
| *M* Maoris | P England v President's Overseas XV, at Twickenham, in RFU's Centenary season, 1970–71 |
| *NSW* New South Wales | |
| *NZ* New Zealand | (R) Replacement |
| *S* Scotland | Note: Years given for Five Nations' matches are for second half of season; e.g. 1972 means season 1971–72 |
| *SA* South Africa | |

**Aarvold, C D** (Durham) 1928 *S, I, W, F, NSW*, 1929 *I, W, F*, 1931 *S, W, F*, 1932 *S, I, W, SA*, 1933 *W*
**Adams, A A** (London Hospital) 1910 *F*
**Adams, F R** (Richmond) 1875 *S, I*, 1876 *S*, 1877 *I*, 1878 *S*, 1879 *S, I*
**Adey, G J** (Leicester) 1976 *I, F*
**Adkins, S J** (Coventry) 1950 *I, F, S*, 1953 *I, F, S, W*
**Agar, A E** (Harlequins) 1952 *SA, W, S, I, F*, 1953 *W, I*
**Alcock, A** (Guy's Hospital) 1907 *SA*
**Alderson, F H R** (Hartlepool R) 1891 *S, I, W*, 1892 *S, W*, 1893 *W*
**Alexander, H** (Richmond) 1900 *S, I*, 1901 *S, I, W*, 1902 *I, W*
**Alexander, W** (Northern) 1927 *F*
**Allison, D F** (Coventry) 1956 *W, I, S, F*, 1957 *W*, 1958 *W, S*
**Allport, A** (Blackheath) 1892 *W*, 1893 *I*, 1894 *S, I, W*
**Anderson, S** (Rockcliff) 1899 *I*
**Anderson, W F** (Orrell) 1973 *NZ*
**Anderson, C** (Manchester FW) 1889 *M*
**Archer, H** (Bridgwater A) 1909 *W, I, F*
**Armstrong, R** (Northern) 1925 *W*
**Arthur, T G** (Wasps) 1966 *W, I*
**Ashby, R C** (Wasps) 1966 *I, F*, 1967 *A*
**Ashcroft, A** (Waterloo) 1956 *W, I, S, F*, 1957 *W, I, S, F*, 1958 *W, I, S, F, A*, 1959 *I, S, F*
**Ashcroft, A H** (Birkenhead Park) 1909 *A*
**Ashford, W** (Richmond) 1897 *I, W*, 1898 *S, W*
**Ashworth, A** (Oldham) 1892 *I*
**Askew, J G** (Cambridge U) 1930 *I, W, F*
**Aslett, A R** (Richmond) 1926 *S, I, W, F*, 1929 *S, F*
**Assinder, E W** (O Edwardians) 1909 *W, A*
**Aston, R L** (Blackheath) 1890 *S, I*
**Auty, J R** (Headingley) 1935 *S*

**Baker, D G S** (OMTs) 1955 *W, I, F, S*
**Baker, E M** (Moseley) 1895 *S, I, W*, 1896 *S, I, W*, 1897 *W*
**Baker, H C** (Clifton) 1887 *W*
**Bance, J F** (Bedford) 1954 *S*
**Barr, R J** (Leicester) 1932 *SA, W, I*
**Barrett, E I M** (Lennox) 1903 *S*
**Barrington, T J M** (Bristol) 1931 *W, I*
**Barrington-Ward, L E** (Edinburgh U) 1910 *S, I, W, F*
**Barron, J H** (Bingley) 1896 *S*, 1897 *I, W*
**Bartlett, J T** (Waterloo) 1951 *W*
**Bartlett, R M** (Harlequins) 1957 *W, I, F, S*, 1958 *I, F, S*
**Barton, J** (Coventry) 1967 *I, F, W*, 1972 *F*
**Batchelor, T B** (Oxford U) 1907 *F*
**Bateson, A H** (Otley) 1930 *S, I, W, F*
**Bateson, H D** (Liverpool) 1879 *I*
**Batson, T** (Blackheath) 1872 *S*, 1874 *S*, 1875 *I*

**Batten, J M** (Cambridge U) 1874 *S*
**Baume, J L** (Northern) 1950 *S*
**Baxter, J** (Birkenhead Park) 1900 *S, I, W*
**Bazley, R C** (Waterloo) 1952 *I, F*, 1953 *I, F, W, S*, 1955 *I, F, W, S*
**Beaumont, W B** (Fylde) 1975 *I, A* (2[1R]), 1976 *A, W, S, I, F*, 1977 *S, I, F, W*, 1978 *F, W, S, I*
**Bedford, H** (Morley) 1889 *M*, 1890 *S, I*
**Bedford, L L** (Headingley) 1931 *W, I*
**Beer, I D S** (Harlequins) 1955 *F, S*
**Beese, M C** (Liverpool) 1972 *I, F, W*
**Bell, F J** (Northern) 1900 *W*
**Bell, H** (Brighton) 1884 *I*
**Bell, J L** (Darlington) 1878 *I*
**Bell, P J** (Blackheath) 1968 *W, I, F, S*
**Bell, R W** (Northern) 1900 *S, I, W*
**Bendon, G J** (Wasps) 1959 *W, I, F, S*
**Bennett, N O** (St Mary's Hospital) 1947 *S, W, F*, 1948 *S, I, W, A*
**Bennett, W N** (Bedford) 1975 *S, A*, 1976 *S* (R)
**Bennetts, B B** (Penzance) 1909 *W, A*
**Bentley, J E** (Gipsies) 1871 *S*, 1872 *S*
**Berridge, M J** (Northampton) 1949 *I, W*
**Berry, H** (Gloucester) 1910 *S, I, W, F*
**Berry, J** (Tyldesley) 1891 *S, I, W*
**Berry, J T W** (Leicester) 1939 *W, I, S*
**Beswick, E** (Swinton) 1882 *S, I*
**Biggs, J M** (UCH) 1878 *S*, 1879 *I*
**Birkett, J G G** (Harlequins) 1906 *S, F*, 1907 *S, W, F, SA*, 1908 *S, I, W, F*, 1910 *S, I, W*, 1911 *S, I, W, F*, 1912 *S, I, W, F*
**Birkett, L** (Clapham R) 1875 *S*, 1877 *S, I*
**Birkett, R H** (Clapham R) 1871 *S*, 1875 *S*, 1876 *S*, 1877 *I*
**Bishop, C C** (Blackheath) 1927 *F*
**Black, B H** (Blackheath) 1930 *S, I, W, F*, 1931 *S, I, W, F*, 1932 *S*, 1933 *W*
**Blacklock, J H** (Aspatria) 1898 *I*, 1899 *I*
**Blakiston, A F** (Northampton) 1920 *S, I, W, F*, 1921 *S, I, W, F*, 1922 *W*, 1923 *S, F*, 1924 *S, I, W, F*, 1925 *S, I, W, F, NZ*
**Blatherwick, T** (Manchester) 1878 *I*
**Body, J A** (Gipsies) 1872 *S*, 1873 *S*
**Bolton, C A** (United Services) 1909 *F*
**Bolton, R** (Harlequins) 1933 *W*, 1936 *S*, 1937 *S*, 1938 *W, I*
**Bolton, W N** (Blackheath) 1882 *S, I*, 1883 *S, I, W*, 1884 *S, I, W*, 1885 *I*, 1887 *S, I*
**Bonaventura, M S** (Blackheath) 1931 *W*
**Bonham-Carter, E** (Oxford U) 1891 *S*
**Bonsor, F** (Bradford) 1886 *S, I, W*, 1887 *S, W*, 1889 *M*
**Boobbyer, B** (Rosslyn Park) 1950 *W, I, F, S*, 1951 *W, F*, 1952 *I, F, S*

104

*The USA found the combined skills of the England XV too much for them at Twickenham. Here Mike Rafter, of Bristol, draws full-back Robbie Bordley while giving a well-timed pass to his fellow-flanker Peter Dixon.*

**Daniell, J** (Richmond) 1899 *W*, 1900 *S, I*, 1902 *S, I*, 1904 *S, I*

**Darby, A J L** (Birkenhead Park) 1899 *I*

**Davenport, A** (Ravenscourt Park) 1871 *S*

**Davey, J** (Redruth) 1908 *S*, 1909 *W*

**Davey, R F** (Teignmouth) 1931 *W*

**Davidson, Jas** (Aspatria) 1897 *S*, 1898 *S, W*, 1899 *S, I*

**Davidson, Jos** (Aspatria) 1899 *S, W*

**Davies, P H** (Sale) 1927 *I*

**Davies, V G** (Harlequins) 1922 *W*, 1925 *NZ*

**Davies, W J A** (United Services, RN) 1913 *S, I, W, F, SA*, 1914 *S, I, F*, 1920 *S, I, F*, 1921 *S, I, W, F*, 1922 *S, I, F*, 1923 *S, I, W, F*

**Davies, W P C** (Harlequins) 1953 *S*, 1954 *NZ, I*, 1955 *S, I, W, F*, 1956 *W*, 1957 *S, F*, 1958 *W*

**Davis, A M** (Harlequins) 1963 *W, I, S, NZ* (2), 1964 *W, I, S, NZ, F*, 1966 *W*, 1967 *A*, 1969 *SA*, 1970 *W, I, S*

**Dawson, E F** (RIEC) 1878 *I*

**Day, H L V** (Leicester) 1920 *W*, 1922 *W, F*, 1926 *S*

**Dean, G J** (Harlequins) 1931 *I*

**Dee, J M** (Hartlepool R) 1962 *S*, 1963 *NZ*

**Devitt, Sir T G** (Blackheath) 1926 *I, F*, 1928 *W, NSW*

**Dewhurst, J H** (Richmond) 1887 *S, I, W*, 1890 *W*

**De Winton, R F C** (Marlborough N) 1893 *W*

**Dibble, R** (Bridgwater A) 1906 *S, F*, 1907 *SA*, 1908 *S, I, W, F*, 1909 *S, I, W, F, A*, 1910 *S*, 1911 *S, W, F*, 1912 *S, I, W*

**Dicks, J** (Northampton) 1934 *W, I, S*, 1935 *W, I, S*, 1936 *S*, 1937 *I*

**Dillon, E W** (Blackheath) 1904 *S, I, W*, 1905 *W*

**Dingle, A J** (Hartlepool R) 1913 *I*, 1914 *S, F*

**Dixon, P J** (Harlequins, Gosforth) 1971 *P*, 1972 *S, I, W, F*, 1973 *I, F, S*, 1974 *S, I, F, W*, 1975 *I*, 1976 *F*, 1977 *S, I, F, W*, 1978 *F, S, I*

**Dobbs, G E B** (Devonport A) 1906 *I, W*

**Doble, S A** (Moseley) 1972 *SA*, 1973 *NZ, W*

**Dobson, D D** (Newton Abbot) 1902 *S, I, W*, 1903 *S, I, W*

**Dobson, T H** (Bradford) 1895 *S*

**Dodge, P W** (Leicester) 1978 *W, S, I*

**Donnelly, M P** (Oxford U) 1947 *I*

**Dovey, B A** (Rosslyn Park) 1963 *W, I*

**Down, P J** (Bristol) 1909 *A*

**Dowson, A O** (Moseley) 1899 *S*

**Drake-Lee, N J** (Cambridge U and Leicester) 1963 *W, I, F, S*, 1964 *W, I, NZ*, 1965 *W*

**Duckett, H** (Bradford) 1893 *S, I*

**Duckham, D J** (Coventry) 1969 *I, F, S, W, SA*, 1970 *I, F, S, W*, 1971 *I, F, S* (2[1C]), *W, P*, 1972 *I, F, S, W*, 1973 *NZ, W, I, F, S, NZ, A*, 1974 *S, I, F, W*, 1975 *I, F, W*, 1976 *A, W, S*

**Dudgeon, H W** (Richmond) 1897 *S*, 1898 *S, I, W*, 1899 *S, I, W*

**Dugdale, J M** (Ravenscourt Park) 1871 *S*

**Duncan, R F H** (Guy's Hospital) 1922 *S, I, F*

**Dunkley, P E** (Harlequins) 1931 *I, S*, 1936 *I, S, W, NZ*

**Duthie, J** (W Hartlepool) 1903 *W*

**Dyson, J W** (Huddersfield) 1890 *S*, 1892 *S*, 1893 *S, I*

**Ebdon, P J** (Wellington) 1897 *I, W*

**Eddison, J H** (Headingley) 1912 *S, I, F, W*

**Edgar, C S** (Birkenhead Park) 1901 *S*

**Edwards, R** (Newport) 1921 *S, I, W, F*, 1922 *W, F*, 1923 *W*, 1924 *S, W, F*, 1925 *NZ*

**Elliot, C H** (Sunderland) 1886 *W*

**Elliot, E W** (Sunderland) 1901 *S, I, W*, 1904 *W*

**Elliot, W** (United Services, RN) 1932 *I, S*, 1933 *I, S, W*, 1934 *I, W*

**Elliott, A E** (St Thomas's Hospital) 1894 *S*

**Ellis, J** (Wakefield) 1939 *S*

**Ellis, S S** (Queen's House) 1880 *I*

**Emmott, C** (Bradford) 1892 *W*

**Enthoven, H J** (Richmond) 1878 *I*

**Estcourt, N S D** (Blackheath) 1955 *S*

**Evans, E** (Sale) 1948 *A*, 1950 *W*, 1951 *I, F, S*, 1952 *W, I, F, S, SA*, 1953 *I, F, S*, 1954 *W, I, F, NZ*, 1956 *W, I, F, S*, 1957 *W, I, F, S*, 1958 *A, W, I, F, S*

**Evans, G W** (Coventry) 1972 *S*, 1973 *W* (R), *F, S, NZ,* 1974 *S, I, F, W*
**Evans, N L** (RNEC) 1932 *W, I, S,* 1933 *W, I*
**Evanson, A M** (Richmond) 1883 *S, I, W,* 1884 *S*
**Evanson, W A D** (Richmond) 1875 *S,* 1877 *S,* 1878 *S,* 1879 *S, I*
**Evershed, F** (Blackheath) 1889 *M,* 1890 *S, I, W,* 1892 *S, I, W,* 1893 *S, I, W*
**Eyres, W C T** (Richmond) 1927 *I*

**Fagan, A St L** (Richmond) 1887 *I*
**Fairbrother, K E** (Coventry) 1969 *I, F, S, W, SA,* 1970 *I, F, S, W,* 1971 *I, F, W*
**Faithfull, C K T** (Harlequins) 1924 *I,* 1926 *S, F*
**Fallas, H** (Wakefield T) 1884 *I*
**Fegan, J H C** (Blackheath) 1895 *S, I, W*
**Fernandes, C W L** (Leeds) 1881 *S, I, W*
**Field, E** (Middlesex W) 1893 *I, W*
**Fielding, K J** (Moseley, Loughborough Colls) 1969 *I, F, S, SA,* 1970 *I, F,* 1972 *I, F, S, W*
**Finch, R T** (Cambridge U) 1880 *S*
**Finlan, J F** (Moseley) 1967 *I, F, S, W, NZ,* 1968 *I, W,* 1969 *I, F, S, W,* 1970 *F,* 1973 *NZ*
**Finlinson, H W** (Blackheath) 1895 *S, I, W*
**Finney, S** (RIE Coll) 1872 *S,* 1873 *S*
**Firth, F** (Halifax) 1894 *S, I, W*
**Fletcher, N C** (OMTs) 1901 *S, I, W,* 1903 *S*
**Fletcher, T** (Seaton) 1897 *W*
**Fletcher, W R B** (Marlborough N) 1873 *S,* 1875 *S*
**Fookes, E F** (Sowerby Bridge) 1896 *S, I, W,* 1897 *S, I, W,* 1898 *I, W,* 1899 *S, I*
**Ford, P J** (Gloucester) 1964 *W, I, F, S*
**Forrest, J W** (United Services, RN) 1930 *S, I, W, F,* 1931 *S, I, W, F,* 1934 *S, I*
**Forrest, R** (Wellington) 1899 *W,* 1900 *S,* 1902 *S, I,* 1903 *S, I*
**Foulds, R T** (Waterloo) 1929 *I, W*
**Fowler, F D** (Manchester) 1878 *S,* 1879 *S*
**Fowler, H** (Oxford U) 1878 *S,* 1881 *S, W*
**Fowler, R H** (Leeds) 1877 *I*
**Fox, F H** (Wellington) 1890 *S, W*
**Francis, T E S** (Cambridge U) 1926 *S, I, W, F*
**Frankcom, G P** (Cambridge U and Bedford) 1965 *W, I, F, S*
**Fraser, E C** (Blackheath) 1875 *I*
**Fraser, G** (Richmond) 1902 *S, I, W,* 1903 *I, W*
**Freakes, H D** (Oxford U) 1938 *W,* 1939 *W, I*
**Freeman, H** (Marlborough N) 1872 *S,* 1873 *S,* 1874 *S*
**French, R J** (St Helens) 1961 *W, I, F, S*
**Fry, H A** (Liverpool) 1934 *W, I, S*
**Fry, T W** (Queen's House) 1880 *S, I,* 1881 *W*
**Fuller, H G** (Bath) 1882 *S, I,* 1883 *S, I, W,* 1884 *W*

**Gadney, B C** (Headingley) 1932 *I, S,* 1933 *I, S,* 1934 *I, S, W,* 1935 *I,* 1936 *I, S, W, NZ,* 1937 *S,* 1938 *W*
**Gamlin, H T** (Blackheath) 1899 *S, W,* 1900 *S, I, W,* 1901 *S,* 1902 *S, I, W,* 1903 *S, I, W,* 1904 *S, I, W*
**Gardner, E R** (Devonport Services) 1921 *S, I, W,* 1922 *I, W, F,* 1923 *S, I, W, F*
**Gardner, H P** (Richmond) 1878 *I*
**Garnett, H W T** (Bradford) 1877 *S*
**Gavins, M N** (Leicester) 1961 *W*
**Gay, D J** (Bath) 1968 *W, I, F, S*
**Gent, D R** (Gloucester) 1906 *I, W, NZ,* 1910 *I, W*
**Genth, J S M** (Manchester) 1874 *S,* 1875 *S*
**George, J T** (Falmouth) 1947 *S, F,* 1949 *I*
**Gerrard, R A** (Bath) 1932 *SA, W, I, S* 1933 *W, I, S,* 1934 *W, I, S,* 1936 *W, I, S, NZ*
**Gibbs, G A** (Bristol) 1947 *F,* 1948 *I*
**Gibbs, J C** (Harlequins) 1925 *W, NZ,* 1926 *F,* 1927 *S, I, W, F*
**Gibbs, N** (Harlequins) 1954 *S, F*
**Giblin, L F** (Blackheath) 1896 *I, W,* 1897 *S*
**Gibson, A S** (Manchester) 1871 *S*
**Gibson, C O P** (Northern) 1901 *W*
**Gibson, G R** (Northern) 1899 *W,* 1901 *S*
**Gibson, T A** (Northern) 1905 *S, W*
**Gilbert, F G** (Devonport Services) 1923 *I, W*
**Gilbert, R** (Devonport A) 1908 *S, I, W*
**Giles, J L** (Coventry) 1935 *W, I,* 1937 *W, I,* 1938 *I, S*
**Gittings, W J** (Coventry) 1967 *NZ*
**Glover, P B** (Bath) 1967 *A,* 1971 *F, P*
**Godfray, R E** (Richmond) 1906 *NZ*

**Godwin, H O** (Coventry) 1959 *F, S,* 1963 *S, NZ* (2), *A,* 1964 *F, S, NZ, I,* 1967 *NZ*
**Gordon-Smith, G W** (Blackheath) 1900 *S, I, W*
**Gotley, A L H** (Oxford U) 1910 *S, F,* 1911 *S, I, W, F*
**Graham, D** (Aspatria) 1901 *W*
**Graham, H J** (Wimbledon H) 1875 *S, I,* 1876 *S, I*
**Graham, J D G** (Wimbledon H) 1876 *I*
**Gray, A** (Otley) 1947 *S, I, W*
**Green, J** (Skipton) 1905 *I,* 1906 *S, F,* 1907 *S, I, W, F, SA*
**Green, J F** (West Kent) 1871 *S*
**Greenwell, J H** (Rockcliff) 1893 *I, W*
**Greenwood, J E** (Cambridge U) 1912 *F,* 1913 *S, I, W, F, SA,* 1914 *S, W, F,* 1920 *S, I, W, F*
**Greenwood, J R H** (Waterloo) 1966 *I, F, S,* 1967 *A,* 1969 *I*
**Greg, W** (Manchester) 1876 *S, I*
**Gregory, G G** (Bristol) 1931 *I, S, F,* 1932 *I, S, SA, W,* 1933 *I, S, W,* 1934 *I, S, W*
**Gregory, J A** (Blackheath) 1949 *W*
**Grylls, W M** (Redruth) 1905 *I*
**Guest, R H** (Waterloo) 1939 *S, I, W,* 1947 *S, I, W, F,* 1948 *S, I, W, A,* 1949 *S, F*
**Guillemard, A G** (West Kent) 1871 *S,* 1872 *S*
**Gummer, C H A** (Plymouth A) 1929 *F*
**Gunner, C R** (Marlborough N) 1876 *I*
**Gurdon, C** (Richmond) 1880 *S, I,* 1881 *S, I, W,* 1882 *S, I,* 1883 *S,* 1884 *S, W,* 1885 *I,* 1886 *S, I, W*
**Gurdon, E T** (Richmond) 1878 *S,* 1879 *I,* 1880 *S,* 1881 *S, I, W,* 1882 *S,* 1883 *S, I, W,* 1884 *S, I, W,* 1885 *I, W,* 1886 *S*

**Haigh, L** (Manchester) 1910 *S, I, W,* 1911 *S, I, W, F*
**Hale, P M** (Moseley) 1969 *SA,* 1970 *I, W*
**Hall, C** (Gloucester) 1901 *S, I*
**Hall, J** (N Durham) 1894 *S, I, W*
**Hall, N M** (Richmond) 1947 *S, I, W, F,* 1949 *I, W,* 1952 *S, I, W, F, SA,* 1953 *S, I, W, F,* 1955 *I, W*
**Hamersley, A St G** (Marlborough N) 1871 *S,* 1872 *S,* 1873 *S,* 1874 *S*
**Hamilton-Hill, E A** (Harlequins) 1936 *NZ, W, I*
**Hamilton-Wickes, R H** (Cambridge U) 1924 *I,* 1925 *S, I, W, F, NZ,* 1926 *S, I, W,* 1927 *W*
**Hammett, E D G** (Newport) 1920 *S, W, F,* 1921 *S, I, W, F,* 1922 *W*
**Hammond, C E L** (Harlequins) 1905 *S,* 1906 *S, I, W, F, NZ,* 1908 *I, W*
**Hancock, A W** (Northampton) 1965 *F, S,* 1966 *F*
**Hancock, G E** (Birkenhead Park) 1939 *W, I, S*
**Hancock, J H** (Newport) 1955 *W, I*
**Hancock, P F** (Blackheath) 1886 *I, W,* 1890 *W*
**Hancock, P S** (Richmond) 1904 *S, I, W*
**Handford, F G** (Manchester) 1909 *S, I, W, F*
**Hands, R H M** (Blackheath) 1910 *S, F*
**Hanley, J** (Plymouth A) 1927 *S, W, F,* 1928 *S, I, W, F*
**Hannaford, R C** (Bristol) 1971 *W, I, F*
**Hanvey, R J** (Aspatria) 1926 *S, I, W, F*
**Harding, E H** (Devonport Services) 1931 *I*
**Harding, V S J** (Saracens) 1961 *F, S,* 1962 *F, S, W, I*
**Hardwick, P F** (Percy Park) 1902 *S, I,* 1903 *S, I, W,* 1904 *S, I, W*
**Hardy, E M P** (Blackheath) 1951 *I, F, S*
**Hare, W H** (Nottingham, Leicester) 1974 *W,* 1978 *F*
**Harper, C H** (Exeter) 1899 *W*
**Harris, S W** (Blackheath) 1920 *S, I*
**Harris, T W** (Northampton) 1929 *S,* 1932 *I*
**Harrison, A C** (Hartlepool R) 1931 *I, S*
**Harrison, A L** (United Services, RN) 1914 *I, F*
**Harrison, G** (Hull) 1877 *S, I,* 1879 *S, I,* 1880 *S,* 1885 *I, W*
**Harrison, H C** (United Services, RN) 1909 *S,* 1914 *S, I, F*
**Hartley, B C** (Blackheath) 1901 *S,* 1902 *S*
**Haslett, L W** (Birkenhead Park) 1926 *I, F*
**Hastings, G W D** (Gloucester) 1955 *W, I, F, S,* 1957 *W, I, F, S,* 1958 *W, I, F, S, A*
**Havelock, H** (Hartlepool R) 1908 *I, W, F*
**Hawcridge, J J** (Bradford) 1885 *I, W*
**Hayward, L W** (Cheltenham) 1910 *I*
**Hazell, D St G** (Leicester) 1955 *W, I, F, S*
**Hearn, R D** (Bedford) 1966 *F, S,* 1967 *F, S, I, W*
**Heath, A H** (Oxford U) 1876 *S*
**Heaton, J** (Waterloo) 1935 *S, I, W,* 1939 *S, I, W,* 1947 *S, I, F*

106

107

Nicholson, T (Rockcliff) 1893 *I*
Ninnes, B F (Coventry) 1971 *W*
Norman, D J (Leicester) 1932 *W, SA*
North, E H G (Blackheath) 1891 *S, I, W*
Northmore, S (Millom) 1897 *I*
Novak, M J (Harlequins) 1970 *W, S, F*
Novis, A L (Blackheath) 1929 *S, F*, 1930 *I, W, F*, 1933 *S, I*

Oakeley, F E (United Services, RN) 1913 *S*, 1914 *S, I, F*
Oakes, R F (Hartlepool R) 1897 *S, I, W*, 1898 *S, I, W*, 1899 *S, W*
Oakley, L F L (Bedford) 1951 *W*
Obolensky, A (Oxford U) 1936 *S, I, W, NZ*
Old, A G B (Middlesbrough, Leicester, Sheffield) 1972 *S, I, W, F, SA*, 1973 *NZ, A*, 1974 *S, I, F, W*, 1975 *I, A*, 1976 *S, I*, 1978 *F*
Oldham, W L (Coventry) 1908 *S*, 1909 *A*
O'Neill, A (Teignmouth and Torquay A) 1901 *S, I, W*
Openshaw, W E (Manchester) 1879 *I*
Osborne, R R (Manchester) 1871 *S*
Osborne, S H (Oxford U) 1905 *S*
Oughtred, B (Hull and E Riding) 1901 *S*, 1902 *S, I, W*, 1903 *I, W*
Owen, J E (Coventry) 1963 *W, I, F, S, A*, 1964 *NZ*, 1965 *W, I, F, S*, 1966 *I, F, S*, 1967 *NZ*
Owen-Smith, H G O (St Mary's Hospital) 1934 *W, I, S*, 1936 *W, I, S, NZ*, 1937 *W, I, S*

Page, J J (Bedford, Northampton) 1971 *W, I, F, S*, 1975 *S*
Pallant, J N (Notts) 1967 *I, F, S*
Palmer, A C (London Hospital) 1909 *S, I*
Palmer, F H (Richmond) 1905 *W*
Palmer, G V (Richmond) 1928 *S, I, F*
Pargetter, T A (Coventry) 1962 *S*, 1963 *F, NZ*
Parker, G W (Gloucester) 1938 *I, S*
Parker, Hon S (Liverpool) 1874 *S*, 1875 *S*
Parsons, E J (RAF) 1939 *S*
Parsons, M J (Northampton) 1968 *W, I, F, S*
Patterson, W M (Sale) 1961 *S, SA*
Pattisson, R M (Blackheath) 1883 *S, I*
Paul, J E (RIE Coll) 1875 *S*
Payne, A T (Bristol) 1935 *I, S*
Payne, C M (Harlequins) 1964 *I, F, S*, 1965 *I, F, S*, 1966 *I, F, S, W*
Payne, J H (Broughton) 1882 *S*, 1883 *S, I, W*, 1884 *I*, 1885 *I, W*
Pearson, A W (Blackheath) 1875 *S, I*, 1876 *I, S*, 1877 *S*, 1878 *S, I*
Peart, T G A H (Hartlepool R) 1964 *F, S*
Pease, F E (Hartlepool R) 1887 *I*
Penny, S H (Leicester) 1909 *A*
Penny, W J (United Hospitals) 1878 *I*, 1879 *I, S*
Percival, L J (Rugby) 1891 *I*, 1892 *I*, 1893 *S*
Periton, H G (Waterloo) 1925 *W*, 1926 *W, S, I, F*, 1927 *W, S, I, F*, 1928 *S, I, F, NSW*, 1929 *S, I, F, W*, 1930 *S, I, F, W*
Perrott, E S (O Cheltonians) 1875 *I*
Perry, D G (Bedford) 1963 *F, S, NZ* (2), *A*, 1964 *I, W, NZ*, 1965 *I, W, F, S*, 1966 *I, W, F*
Perry, S V (Cambridge U) 1947 *I, W*, 1948 *I, W, S, F, A*
Peters, J (Plymouth) 1906 *S, F*, 1907 *S, I*, 1908 *W*
Phillips, C (Birkenhead Park) 1880 *S*, 1881 *I, S*
Phillips, M S (Fylde) 1958 *S, I, F, A*, 1959 *S, I, F, W*, 1960 *S, I, F, W*, 1961 *W, I*, 1963 *S, I, F, W, A, NZ* (2), 1964 *S, I, F, W, NZ*
Pickering, A S (Harrogate) 1907 *I*
Pickering, R D A (Bradford) 1967 *I, F, S, W*, 1968 *F, S*
Pickles, R C W (Bristol) 1922 *I, F*
Pierce, R (Liverpool) 1898 *I*, 1903 *S*
Pilkington, W N (Cambridge U) 1898 *S*
Pillman, C H (Blackheath) 1910 *S, I, W, F*, 1911 *S, I, W, F*, 1912 *W, F*, 1913 *S, I, W, F, SA*, 1914 *S, I, W*
Pillman, R L (Blackheath) 1914 *F*
Pinch, J (Lancaster) 1896 *I, W*, 1897 *S*
Pinching, W W (Guy's Hospital) 1872 *S*
Pitman, I J (Oxford U) 1922 *S*
Plummer, K C (Bristol) 1969 *W*, 1976 *S, I, F*
Poole, F O (Oxford U) 1895 *S, I, W*
Poole, R W (Hartlepool R) 1896 *S*

Pope, E B (Blackheath) 1931 *W, S, F*
Portus, G V (Blackheath) 1908 *I, F*
Poulton, R W (later **Poulton Palmer**), (Oxford U, Harlequins and Liverpool) 1909 *S, I, F*, 1910 *W*, 1911 *S*, 1912 *S, I, W*, 1913 *S, I, W, F, SA*, 1914 *S, I, W, F*
Powell, D L (Northampton) 1966 *W, I*, 1969 *W, I, F, S*, 1971 *W, I, F, S* (2[1C])
Pratten, W E (Blackheath) 1927 *S, F*
Preece, I (Coventry) 1948 *I, S, F*, 1949 *S, F*, 1950 *I, S, F, W*, 1951 *I, F, W*
Preece, P S (Coventry) 1972 *SA*, 1973 *NZ, W, I, F, S, NZ*, 1975 *I, F, W, A*, 1976 *W* (R)
Prentice, F D (Leicester) 1928 *S, I, F*
Prescott, R E (Harlequins) 1937 *W, I*, 1938 *I*, 1939 *W, I, S*
Price, H L (Harlequins) 1922 *S, I*, 1923 *I, W*
Price, J (Coventry) 1961 *I*
Price, P L A (RIE Coll) 1877 *S, I*, 1878 *S*
Price, T W (Cheltenham) 1948 *S, F*, 1949 *S, F, W, I*
Prout, D H (Northampton) 1968 *W, I*
Pullin, J V (Bristol) 1966 *W*, 1968 *W, I, F, S*, 1969 *W, I, F, S, SA*, 1970 *W, I, F, S*, 1971 *W, I, F, S* (2[1C]), *P*, 1972 *W, I, F, S, SA*, 1973 *NZ, W, I, F, S, NZ, A*, 1974 *S, I, F, W*, 1975 *I, W* (R), *S, A* (2), 1976 *F*
Purdy, S J (Rugby) 1962 *S*
Pyke, J (St Helens Recreation) 1892 *W*
Pym, J A (Blackheath) 1912 *S, I, W, F*

Quinn, J P (New Brighton) 1954 *W, I, S, F, NZ*

Rafter, M (Bristol) 1977 *S, F, W*, 1978 *F, W, S, I*
Ralston, C W (Richmond) 1971 *S* (C), *P*, 1972 *S, I, W, F, SA*, 1973 *NZ, W, I, F, S, NZ, A*, 1974 *S, I, F, W*, 1975 *I, F, W, S*
Ramsden, H E (Bingley) 1898 *S, W*
Ranson, J M (Rosslyn Park) 1963 *NZ* (2), *A*, 1964 *W, I, F, S*
Raphael, J E (OMTs) 1902 *S, I, W*, 1905 *S, W*, 1906 *S, W, F, NZ*
Ravenscroft, J (Birkenhead Park) 1881 *I*
Rawlinson, W C W (Blackheath) 1876 *S*
Redmond, G F (Cambridge U) 1970 *F*
Redwood, B W (Bristol) 1968 *W, I*
Reeve, J S R (Harlequins) 1929 *F*, 1930 *F, S, I, W*, 1931 *S, I, W*
Regan, M (Liverpool) 1953 *W, I, F, S*, 1954 *W, I, F, S, NZ*, 1956 *I, F, S*
Rew, H (Blackheath) 1929 *S, F*, 1930 *S, F*, 1931 *S, F, W*, 1934 *S, W, I*
Reynolds, F J (O Cranleighans) 1937 *S*, 1938 *S, I*
Reynolds, S (Richmond) 1900 *S, I, W*, 1901 *I*
Rhodes, J (Castleford) 1896 *S, I, W*
Richards, E E (Plymouth A) 1929 *S, F*
Richards, J (Bradford) 1891 *S, I, W*
Richards, S B (Richmond) 1965 *W, I, F, S*, 1967 *W, I, F, S, A*
Richardson, J V (Birkenhead Park) 1928 *S, I, W, F, NSW*
Richardson, W R (Manchester) 1881 *I*
Rickards, C H (Gipsies) 1873 *S*
Rimmer, G (Waterloo) 1949 *W, I*, 1950 *W*, 1951 *W, I, F*, 1952 *W, SA*, 1954 *W, I, S, NZ*
Rimmer, L I (Bath) 1961 *S, I, W, F, SA*
Ripley, A G (Rosslyn Park) 1972 *S, I, W, F, S, A*, 1973 *NZ, W, I, F, S, NZ, A*, 1974 *S, I, F, W*, 1975 *I, F, S, A* (2), 1976 *A, W, S*
Risman, A B W (Loughborough Colls) 1959 *W, I, F, S*, 1961 *W, I, F, SA*
Ritson, J A S (Northern) 1910 *S, F*, 1912 *F*, 1913 *S, I, W, F, SA*
Rittson–Thomas, G C (Oxford U) 1951 *W, I, F*
Robbins, P G D (Moseley) 1956 *W, I, S, F*, 1957 *W, I, S, F*, 1958 *W, I, S, A*, 1960 *W, I, S, F*, 1961 *W, SA*, 1962 *S*
Roberts, A D (Northern) 1911 *S, I, W, F*, 1912 *S, I, F*, 1914 *I*
Roberts, E W (RNE Coll) 1901 *I, W*, 1906 *I, W, NZ*, 1907 *S*
Roberts, G D (Harlequins) 1907 *S*, 1908 *W, F*
Roberts, J (Sale) 1960 *W, I, F, S*, 1961 *W, I, F, S, SA*, 1962 *W, I, F, S*, 1963 *W, I, F, S*, 1964 *NZ*
Roberts, R S (Coventry) 1932 *I*
Roberts, S (Swinton) 1887 *I, W*
Roberts, V G (Harlequins) 1947 *F*, 1949 *F, W, I, S*, 1950 *F, I, S*, 1951 *F, W, I, S*, 1956 *F, W, I, S*

**Robertshaw, R** (Bradford) 1886 *S, I, W,* 1887 *S, W*
**Robinson, A** (Blackheath) 1889 *M,* 1890 *S, I, W*
**Robinson, E F** (Coventry) 1954 *S,* 1961 *S, I, F*
**Robinson, G C** (Percy Park) 1897 *S, I,* 1898 *I,* 1899 *W,* 1900 *S, I,* 1901 *S, I*
**Robinson, J J** (Headingley) 1893 *S,* 1902 *S, I, W*
**Robson, A** (Northern) 1924 *S, I, W, F,* 1926 *W*
**Robson, M** (Oxford U) 1930 *S, I, W, F*
**Rogers, D P** (Bedford) 1961 *I, F, S,* 1962 *I, F, W,* 1963 *I, F, S, W, NZ* (2), *A,* 1964 *I, F, S, W, NZ,* 1965 *I, F, S, W,* 1966 *I, F, S, W,* 1967 *S, W, A, NZ,* 1969 *I, F, S*
**Rogers, J H** (Moseley) 1890 *S, I, W,* 1891 *S*
**Rogers, W L Y** (Blackheath) 1905 *I, W*
**Rollitt, D M** (Bristol) 1967 *I, F, S, W,* 1969 *I, F, S, W,* 1975 *S, A* (2)
**Roncoroni, A D S** (West Herts and Richmond) 1933 *W, I, S*
**Rossborough, P A** (Coventry) 1971 *W,* 1973 *NZ, A,* 1974 *S, I,* 1975 *I, F*
**Rosser, D W A** (Wasps) 1965 *S, I, W, F,* 1966 *W*
**Rotherham, Alan** (Richmond) 1883 *S, W,* 1884 *S, W,* 1885 *I, W,* 1886 *S, I, W,* 1887 *S, I, W*
**Rotherham, Arthur** (Richmond) 1898 *S, W,* 1899 *S, W, I*
**Roughley, D F K** (Liverpool) 1973 *A,* 1974 *S, I*
**Rowell, R E** (Leicester) 1964 *W,* 1965 *W*
**Rowley, A J** (Coventry) 1932 *SA*
**Rowley, H C** (Manchester) 1879 *S, I,* 1880 *S, I,* 1881 *S, I, W,* 1882 *S, I*
**Royds, P M R** (Blackheath) 1898 *S, W,* 1899 *W*
**Royle, A V** (Broughton R) 1889 *M*
**Rudd, E L** (Liverpool) 1965 *W, I, S,* 1966 *W, I, S*
**Russell, R F** (Leicester) 1906 *NZ*
**Rutherford, D** (Gloucester) 1960 *W, I, F, S,* 1961 *SA,* 1965 *W, I, F, S,* 1966 *W, I, F, S,* 1967 *NZ*
**Ryalls, H J** (N Brighton) 1885 *I, W*
**Ryan, P H** (Richmond) 1955 *W, I*

**Sadler, E H** (Army) 1933 *S, I*
**Sagar, J W** (Cambridge U) 1901 *I, W*
**Sample, C H** (Cambridge U) 1884 *I,* 1885 *I,* 1886 *S*
**Sanders, D L** (Harlequins) 1954 *W, I, S, F, NZ,* 1956 *W, I, S, F*
**Sanders, F W** (Plymouth A) 1923 *S, I, F*
**Sandford, J R P** (Marlborough N) 1906 *I*
**Sangwin, R D** (Hull and E Riding) 1964 *W, NZ*
**Savage, K F** (Northampton) 1966 *W, I, F, S,* 1967 *W, I, F, S, A, NZ,* 1968 *W, F, S*
**Sawyer, C M** (Broughton) 1880 *S,* 1881 *I*
**Saxby, L E** (Gloucester) 1932 *W, SA*
**Schofield, J W** (Manchester) 1880 *I*
**Scholfield, J A** (Preston Grasshoppers) 1911 *W*
**Schwarz, R O** (Richmond) 1899 *S,* 1901 *I, W*
**Scorfield, E S** (Percy Park) 1910 *F*
**Scott, C T** (Blackheath) 1900 *I, W,* 1901 *I, W*
**Scott, E K** (St Mary's Hospital and Redruth) 1947 *W,* 1948 *W, S, I, A*
**Scott, F S** (Bristol) 1907 *W*
**Scott, H** (Manchester) 1955 *F*
**Scott, J P** (Rosslyn Park) 1978 *F, W, S, I*
**Scott, J S M** (Oxford U) 1958 *F*
**Scott, M T** (Cambridge U) 1887 *I,* 1890 *I, S*
**Scott, W M** (Cambridge U) 1889 *M*
**Seddon, R L** (Broughton R) 1887 *S, I, W*
**Sellar, K A** (United Services, RN) 1927 *S, I, W,* 1928 *W, I, F, NSW*
**Sever, H S** (Sale) 1936 *S, I, W, NZ,* 1937 *S, I, W,* 1938 *S, I, W*
**Shackleton, I R** (Cambridge U) 1969 *SA,* 1970 *S, I, W*
**Sharp, R A W** (Oxford U. Wasps and Redruth) 1960 *W, I, F, S,* 1961 *I, F,* 1962 *W, I, F,* 1963 *W, I, F, S,* 1967 *A*
**Shaw, C H** (Moseley) 1906 *S,* 1907 *S, I, W, F, SA*
**Shaw, F** (Cleckheaton) 1898 *I*
**Shaw, J F** (RNE Coll) 1898 *S, W*
**Sherrard, C W** (Blackheath) 1871 *S,* 1872 *S*
**Sherriff, G A** (Saracens) 1966 *S,* 1967 *A, NZ*
**Shewring, H E** (Bristol) 1905 *I,* 1906 *S, W, F, NZ,* 1907 *S, I, W, F, SA*
**Shooter, J P** (Morley) 1899 *S, I,* 1900 *S, I*
**Shuttleworth, D W** (Headingley) 1951 *S,* 1953 *S*
**Sibree, H J H** (Harlequins) 1908 *F,* 1909 *S, I*
**Silk, N** (Harlequins) 1965 *W, I, F, S*
**Simpson, C P** (Harlequins) 1965 *W*

**Simpson, T** (Rockcliff) 1902 *S,* 1903 *S, I, W,* 1904 *S, I,* 1905 *S, I,* 1906 *S,* 1907 *SA,* 1909 *F*
**Sladen, G M** (United Services, RN) 1929 *S, I, W*
**Slemen, M A C** (Liverpool) 1976 *I, F,* 1977 *S, I, F, W,* 1978 *F, W, S, I*
**Slocock, L A N** (Liverpool) 1907 *S, I, W, F,* 1908 *S, I, W, F*
**Slow, C F** (Leicester) 1934 *S*
**Small, H D** (Oxford U) 1950 *W, I, F, S*
**Smallwood, A M** (Leicester) 1920 *I, F,* 1921 *S, I, W, F,* 1922 *S, I,* 1923 *S, I, W, F,* 1925 *S, I*
**Smart, S** (Gloucester) 1913 *S, I, W, F, SA,* 1914 *S, I, W, F,* 1920 *S, I, W*
**Smeddle, R W** (Cambridge U) 1929 *S, I, W,* 1931 *F*
**Smith, C C** (Gloucester) 1901 *W*
**Smith, D F** (Richmond) 1910 *I, W*
**Smith, J V** (Cambridge U and Rosslyn Park) 1950 *W, I, F, S*
**Smith, K** (Roundhay) 1974 *F, W,* 1975 *W, S*
**Smith, M J K** (Oxford U) 1956 *W*
**Smith, S J** (Sale) 1973 *I, F, S, A,* 1974 *I, F,* 1975 *W* (R), 1976 *F,* 1977 *F* (R)
**Smith, S R** (Richmond) 1959 *W, F, S,* 1964 *F, S*
**Smith, T A** (Northampton) 1951 *W*
**Soane, F** (Bath) 1893 *S,* 1894 *S, I, W*
**Sobey, W H** (O Millhillians) 1930 *S, W, F,* 1932 *W, SA*
**Solomon, B** (Redruth) 1910 *W*
**Sparks, R H W** (Plymouth A) 1928 *S, I, F,* 1929 *S, I, W,* 1931 *S, I, F*
**Speed, H** (Castleford) 1894 *S, I, W,* 1896 *S*
**Spence, F W** (Birkenhead Park) 1890 *I*
**Spencer, J** (Harlequins) 1966 *W*
**Spencer, J S** (Cambridge U and Headingley) 1969 *I, F, S, W, SA,* 1970 *I, F, S, W,* 1971 *I, S* (2[1C]), *W, P*
**Spong, R S** (O Millhillians) 1929 *F,* 1930 *F, S, I, W,* 1931 *F.* 1932 *W, SA*
**Spooner, R H** (Liverpool) 1903 *W*
**Springman, H H** (Liverpool) 1879 *S,* 1887 *S*
**Spurling, A** (Blackheath) 1882 *I*
**Spurling, N** (Blackheath) 1886 *S, I,* 1887 *W*
**Squires, P J** (Harrogate) 1973 *F, S, NZ, A,* 1974 *S, I, F, W,* 1975 *I, F, W, S, A* (2), 1976 *A, W,* 1977 *S, I, F, W,* 1978 *F, W, S, I*
**Stafford, R C** (Bedford) 1912 *S, I, W, F*
**Stafford, W F H** (RE) 1874 *S*
**Stanbury, E** (Plymouth A) 1926 *S, I, W,* 1927 *S, I, W, F,* 1928 *S, I, W, F, NSW,* 1929 *S, I, W, F*
**Standing, G** (Blackheath) 1883 *I, W*
**Stanger-Leathes, C F** (Northern) 1905 *I*
**Stark, K J** (O Alleynians) 1927 *S, I, W, F,* 1928 *S, I, W, F, NSW*
**Starks, A** (Castleford) 1896 *I, W*
**Starmer-Smith, N C** (Harlequins) 1969 *SA,* 1970 *I, W, S, F,* 1971 *S* (C), *P*
**Start, S P** (United Services, RN) 1907 *S*
**Steeds, J H** (Saracens) 1949 *S, F,* 1950 *S, F, I*
**Steele-Bodger, M R** (Cambridge U) 1947 *S, I, W, F,* 1948 *S, I, W, F, A*
**Steinthal, F E** (Ilkley) 1913 *F, W*
**Stevens, C B** (Penzance-Newlyn, Harlequins) 1969 *SA,* 1970 *I, W, S,* 1971 *P,* 1972 *I, W, S, F, SA,* 1973 *NZ, W, I, F, S, NZ, A,* 1974 *S, I, F, W,* 1975 *I, F, W, S*
**Still, E R** (Oxford U and Ravenscourt P) 1873 *S*
**Stirling, R V** (Wasps) 1951 *W, I, F, S,* 1952 *W, I, F, S, SA,* 1953 *W, I, F, S,* 1954 *W, I, F, S, NZ*
**Stoddart, A E** (Blackheath) 1885 *I, W,* 1886 *I, W, S,* 1889 *M,* 1890 *I, W,* 1893 *S, W*
**Stoddart, W B** (Liverpool) 1897 *S, I, W*
**Stokes, F** (Blackheath) 1871 *S,* 1872 *S,* 1873 *S*
**Stokes, L** (Blackheath) 1875 *I,* 1876 *S,* 1877 *S, I,* 1878 *S,* 1879 *S, I,* 1880 *S, I,* 1881 *S, I, W*
**Stone, F le S** (Blackheath) 1914 *F*
**Stoop, A D** (Harlequins) 1905 *S,* 1906 *S, F,* 1907 *W, F, SA,* 1910 *S, I, W,* 1911 *S, I, W, F,* 1912 *S, W*
**Stoop, F M** (Harlequins) 1910 *S,* 1911 *I, F,* 1913 *SA*
**Stout, F M** (Richmond) 1897 *I, W,* 1898 *I, W, S,* 1899 *I, S,* 1903 *S,* 1904 *S, I, W,* 1905 *S, I, W*
**Stout, P W** (Richmond) 1898 *S, W,* 1899 *S, W, I*
**Strong, E L** (Oxford U) 1884 *S, I, W*
**Summerscales, G E** (Durham City) 1906 *NZ*
**Sutcliffe, J W** (Heckmondwike) 1889 *M*
**Swarbrick, D W** (Oxford U) 1947 *W, I, F,* 1948 *W, A,* 1949 *I*
**Swayne, D H** (Oxford U) 1931 *W*

**Swayne, J W R** (Bridgwater) 1929 *W*
**Sykes, A R V** (Blackheath) 1914 *F*
**Sykes, F D** (Northampton) 1955 *F, S,* 1963 *NZ, A*
**Sykes, P W** (Wasps) 1948 *F,* 1952 *F, S, I,* 1953 *F, I, W*
**Syrett, R E** (Wasps) 1958 *W, I, F, A,* 1960 *W, I, F, S,* 1962 *W, I, F*

**Tallent, J A** (Cambridge U and Blackheath) 1931 *S, F,* 1932 *W, SA,* 1935 *I*
**Tanner, C C** (Cambridge U and Gloucester) 1930 *S,* 1932 *S, I, W, SA*
**Tarr, F N** (Leicester) 1909 *W, F, A,* 1913 *S*
**Tatham, W M** (Oxford U) 1882 *S,* 1883 *S, I, W,* 1884 *S, I, W*
**Taylor, A S** (Blackheath) 1883 *I, W,* 1886 *I, W*
**Taylor, E W** (Rockcliff) 1892 *I,* 1893 *I,* 1894 *I, S, W,* 1895 *I, S, W,* 1896 *I, W,* 1897 *I, S, W,* 1899 *I*
**Taylor, F** (Leicester) 1920 *I, F*
**Taylor, F M** (Leicester) 1914 *W*
**Taylor, H H** (Blackheath) 1879 *S,* 1880 *S,* 1881 *I, W,* 1882 *S*
**Taylor, J T** (W Hartlepool) 1897 *I,* 1899 *I,* 1900 *I,* 1901 *I, W,* 1902 *I, W, S,* 1903 *I, W,* 1905 *S*
**Taylor, P J** (Northampton) 1955 *W, I,* 1962 *W, I, F, S*
**Taylor, R B** (Northampton) 1966 *W,* 1967 *W, I, F, S, NZ,* 1969 *W, F, S, SA,* 1970 *W, I, F, S,* 1971 *S* (2[1C])
**Taylor, W J** (Blackheath) 1928 *S, I, W, F, NSW*
**Teden, D E** (Richmond) 1939 *W, I, S*
**Teggin, A** (Broughton R) 1884 *I,* 1885 *W,* 1886 *S, I,* 1887 *S, I*
**Tetley, T S** (Bradford) 1876 *S*
**Thomas, C** (Barnstaple) 1895 *S, I, W,* 1899 *I*
**Thompson, P H** (Waterloo) 1956 *W, I, S, F,* 1957 *W, I, S, F,* 1958 *W, I, S, F, A,* 1959 *W, I, S, F*
**Thomson, G T** (Halifax) 1878 *S,* 1882 *S, I,* 1883 *S, I, W,* 1884 *S, I,* 1885 *I*
**Thomson, W B** (Blackheath) 1892 *W,* 1895 *W, S, I*
**Thorne, J D** (Bristol) 1963 *W, I, F*
**Tindall, V R** (Liverpool U) 1951 *W, I, F, S*
**Tobin, F** (Liverpool) 1871 *S*
**Todd, A F** (Blackheath) 1900 *S, I*
**Todd, R** (Manchester) 1877 *S*
**Toft, H B** (Waterloo) 1936 *S,* 1937 *S, W, I,* 1938 *S, W, I,* 1939 *S, W, I*
**Toothill, J T** (Bradford) 1890 *S, I,* 1891 *I, W,* 1892 *S, I. W.* 1893 *S, I, W.* 1894 *I, W*
**Tosswill, L R** (Exeter) 1902 *S, I, W*
**Touzel, C J C** (Liverpool) 1877 *S, I*
**Towell, A C** (Bedford) 1948 *F,* 1951 *S*
**Travers, B H** (Harlequins) 1947 *I, W,* 1948 *W, A,* 1949 *S, F*
**Treadwell, W T** (Wasps) 1966 *S, I, F*
**Tristram, H B** (Oxford U) 1883 *S,* 1884 *S, W,* 1885 *W,* 1887 *S*
**Troop, C L** (Aldershot S) 1933 *S, I*
**Tucker, J S** (Bristol) 1922 *W,* 1925 *S, I, W, F, NZ,* 1926 *S, I, W, F,* 1927 *S, I, W, F,* 1928 *S, I, W, F, NSW,* 1929 *I, W, F,* 1930 *S, I, W, F,* 1931 *W*
**Tucker, W E** (Blackheath) 1894 *I, W,* 1895 *I, W, S*
**Tucker, W E** (Blackheath) 1926 *I,* 1930 *I, W*
**Turner, D P** (Richmond) 1871 *S,* 1872 *S,* 1873 *S,* 1874 *S,* 1875 *S, I*
**Turner, E B** (St George's Hospital) 1876 *I,* 1877 *I,* 1878 *I*
**Turner, G R** (St George's Hospital) 1876 *S*
**Turner, H J C** (Manchester) 1871 *S*
**Turner, M F** (Blackheath) 1948 *S, F*
**Turquand-Young, D** (Richmond) 1928 *W, NSW,* 1929 *S, I, F*
**Twynam, H T** (Richmond) 1879 *I,* 1880 *I,* 1881 *W,* 1882 *I,* 1883 *I,* 1884 *I, S, W*

**Underwood, A M** (Exeter) 1962 *W, I, F, S,* 1964 *S*
**Unwin, E J** (Rosslyn Park and Army) 1937 *S,* 1938 *S, W, I*
**Unwin, G T** (Blackheath) 1898 *S*
**Uren, R** (Waterloo) 1948 *S, I, F,* 1950 *I*
**Uttley, R M** (Gosforth) 1973 *I, F, S, NZ, A,* 1974 *I, F, W,* 1975 *F, W, S, A* (2), 1977 *S, I, F, W*

**Valentine, J** (Swinton) 1890 *W,* 1896 *W, S, I*
**Vanderspar, C H R** (Richmond) 1873 *S*
**Van Ryneveld, C B** (Oxford U) 1949 *S, I, W, F*
**Varley, H** (Liversedge) 1892 *S*

**Vassall, H** (Blackheath) 1881 *S, W,* 1882 *S, I,* 1883 *W*
**Vassall, H H** (Blackheath) 1908 *I*
**Vaughan, D B** (Headingley) 1948 *S, I, W, A,* 1949 *S, I, F,* 1950 *W*
**Vaughan-Jones, A** (Army) 1932 *S, I,* 1933 *W*
**Verelst, C L** (Liverpool) 1876 *I,* 1878 *I*
**Vernon, G F** (Blackheath) 1878 *S, I,* 1880 *S, I,* 1881 *I*
**Vickery, G** (Aberavon) 1905 *I*
**Vivyan, E J** (Devonport A) 1901 *W,* 1904 *W, S, I*
**Voyce, A T** (Gloucester) 1920 *S, I,* 1921 *S, I, W, F,* 1922 *S, I, W, F,* 1923 *S, I, W, F,* 1924 *S, I, W, F,* 1925 *S, I, W, F, NZ,* 1926 *S, I, W, F*

111

**Wackett, J A S** (Rosslyn Park) 1959 *W, I*
**Wade, C G** (Richmond) 1883 *S, I, W,* 1884 *S, W,* 1885 *W,* 1886 *I, W*
**Wade, M R** (Cambridge U) 1962 *W, I, F*
**Wakefield, W W** (Harlequins) 1920 *S, I, W, F,* 1921 *S, I, W, F,* 1922 *S, I, W, F,* 1923 *S, I, W, F,* 1924 *S, I, W, F,* 1925 *S, I, W, F, NZ,* 1926 *S, I, W, F,* 1927 *S, F*
**Walker, G A** (Blackheath) 1939 *W, I*
**Walker, H W** (Coventry) 1947 *S, I, W, F,* 1948 *A, S, I, W, F*
**Walker, R** (Manchester) 1874 *S,* 1875 *I,* 1876 *S,* 1879 *S,* 1880 *S*
**Wallens, J N S** (Waterloo) 1927 *F*
**Walton, E J** (Castleford) 1901 *I, W,* 1902 *I, S*
**Walton, W** (Castleford) 1894 *S*
**Ward, G** (Leicester) 1913 *S, W, F,* 1914 *S, W, I*
**Ward, H** (Bradford) 1895 *W*
**Ward, J I** (Richmond) 1881 *I,* 1882 *I*
**Ward, J W** (Castleford) 1896 *S, I, W*
**Wardlow, C S** (Northampton) 1969 *SA* (R), 1971 *W, I, F, S,* (2[1C])
**Warfield, P J** (Rosslyn Park and Durham U) 1973 *NZ, W, I,* 1975 *I, F, S*
**Warr, A L** (Oxford U) 1934 *W, I*
**Watkins, J A** (Gloucester) 1972 *SA,* 1973 *NZ, W, NZ, A,* 1975 *F, W*
**Watkins, J K** (United Services, RN) 1939 *W, I, S*
**Watson, F B** (United Services, RN) 1908 *S,* 1909 *S*
**Watson, J H D** (Blackheath) 1914 *S, W, F*
**Watt, D E J** (Bristol) 1967 *I, F, S, W*
**Webb, C S H** (Devonport Services, RN) 1932 *SA, W, I, S,* 1933 *W, I, S,* 1935 *S,* 1936 *W, I, S, NZ*
**Webb, J W G** (Northampton) 1926 *S, F,* 1929 *S*
**Webb, R E** (Coventry) 1967 *S, W, NZ,* 1968 *S, I, F,* 1969 *S, W, I, F,* 1972 *I, F*
**Webb, St L H** (Bedford) 1959 *W, I, F, S*
**Webster, J G** (Moseley) 1972 *W, I, SA,* 1973 *NZ, W, NZ,* 1974 *S, W,* 1975 *I, F, W*
**Wedge, T G** (St Ives) 1907 *F,* 1909 *W*
**Weighill, R H G** (RAF, Harlequins) 1947 *S, F,* 1948 *S, F*
**Wells, C M** (Cambridge U, Harlequins) 1893 *S,* 1894 *S, W,* 1896 *S,* 1897 *S, W*
**West, B R** (Loughborough Colls, Northampton) 1968 *W, I, F, S,* 1969 *SA,* 1970 *W, I, S*
**Weston, H T F** (Northampton) 1901 *S*
**Weston, L E** (W of Scotland) 1972 *S, F*
**Weston, M P** (Richmond, Durham City) 1960 *W, I, F, S,* 1961 *W, I, F, S, SA,* 1962 *W, I, F,* 1963 *W, I, F, S, NZ* (2), *A,* 1964 *W, I, F, S, NZ,* 1965 *F, S,* 1966 *S,* 1968 *F, S*
**Weston, W H** (Northampton) 1933 *I, S,* 1934 *I, S,* 1935 *I, S, W,* 1936 *S, W, NZ,* 1937 *I, S, W,* 1938 *I, S, W*
**Wheatley, A A** (Coventry) 1937 *W, I, S,* 1938 *W, S*
**Wheatley, H F** (Coventry) 1936 *I,* 1937 *S,* 1938 *S, W,* 1939 *I, S, W*
**Wheeler, P J** (Leicester) 1975 *F, W,* 1976 *A, W, S, I,* 1977 *S, I, F, W,* 1978 *F, W, S, I*
**White, D F** (Northampton) 1947 *S, I, W,* 1948 *I, F,* 1951 *S,* 1952 *S, W, F, SA, I,* 1953 *S, I, W*
**Whiteley, E C P** (O Alleynians) 1931 *S, F*
**Whiteley, W** (Bramley) 1896 *W*
**Whitley, H** (Northern) 1929 *W*
**Wightman, B J** (Moseley, Coventry) 1959 *W,* 1963 *W, I, NZ, A*
**Wigglesworth, H** (Thornes) 1884 *I*
**Wilkins, D T** (United Services, RN, Roundhay) 1951 *W, I, F, S,* 1952 *W, I, F, S, SA,* 1953 *W, I, F, S*
**Wilkinson, E** (Bradford) 1886 *S, I, W,* 1887 *S, W*
**Wilkinson, H** (Halifax) 1889 *M*
**Wilkinson, H** (Halifax) 1929 *S, I, W,* 1930 *F*
**Wilkinson, P** (Law Club) 1872 *S*

**Wilkinson, R M** (Bedford) 1975 *A*, 1976 *A, W, S, I, F*
**Willcocks, T J** (Plymouth) 1902 *W*
**Willcox, J G** (Oxford U, Harlequins) 1961 *I, F, S,* 1962 *I, F, S, W,* 1963 *I, F, S, W,* 1964 *I, F, S, W, NZ*
**William-Powlett, P B R W** (United Services, RN) 1922 *S*
**Williams, C G** (Gloucester and RAF) 1976 *F*
**Williams, C S** (Manchester) 1910 *F*
**Williams, J E** (O Millhillians and Sale) 1954 *F,* 1955 *F, W, I, S,* 1956 *F, I, S,* 1965 *W*
**Williams, J M** (Penzance-Newlyn) 1951 *I, S*
**Williams, S G** (Devonport A) 1902 *S, I, W,* 1903 *S, I,* 1907 *S, I*
**Williams, S H** (Newport) 1911 *S, I, W, F*
**Williamson, R H** (Oxford U) 1908 *S, I, W,* 1909 *F, A*
**Wilson, A J** (Camborne S of M) 1909 *I*
**Wilson, C E** (Blackheath) 1898 *I*
**Wilson, C P** (Cambridge U, Marlborough N) 1881 *W*
**Wilson, D S** (Met Police, Harlequins) 1953 *F,* 1954 *F, W, NZ, I, S,* 1955 *F, S*
**Wilson, G S** (Tyldesley) 1929 *I, W*
**Wilson, K J** (Gloucester) 1963 *F*
**Wilson, R P** (Liverpool OB) 1891 *S, I, W*
**Wilson, W C** (Richmond) 1907 *S, I*
**Winn, C E** (Rosslyn Park) 1952 *SA, W, S, I, F,* 1954 *W, S, F*
**Wintle, T C** (Northampton) 1966 *S,* 1969 *S, I, F, W*
**Wodehouse, N A** (United Services, RN) 1910 *F,* 1911 *S, I, W, F,* 1912 *S, I, W, F,* 1913 *S, I, W, F, SA*
**Wood, A** (Halifax) 1884 *I*
**Wood, A E** (Gloucester, Cheltenham) 1908 *I, W, F*
**Wood, G W** (Leicester) 1914 *W*
**Wood, R** (Liversedge) 1894 *I*
**Wood, R D** (Liverpool OB) 1901 *I,* 1903 *I, W*
**Woodgate, E E** (Paignton) 1952 *W*
**Woodhead, E** (Huddersfield) 1880 *I*

**Woodruff, C G** (Harlequins) 1951 *W, I, F, S*
**Woods, S M J** (Cambridge U, Wellington) 1890 *S, I, W,* 1891 *S, I, W,* 1892 *S, I,* 1893 *I, W,* 1895 *S, I, W*
**Woods, T** (Bridgwater) 1908 *S*
**Woods, T** (United Services, RN) 1920 *S,* 1921 *S, I, W, F*
**Woodward, J E** (Wasps) 1952 *W, SA, S,* 1953 *W, S, I, F,* 1954 *W, S, I, F, NZ,* 1955 *W, I,* 1956 *S*
**Wooldridge, C S** (Oxford U, Blackheath) 1883 *S, I, W,* 1884 *S, I, W,* 1885 *I*
**Wordsworth, A J** (Cambridge U) 1975 *A* (R)
**Worton, J R B** (Harlequins, Army) 1926 *W,* 1927 *W*
**Wrench, D F B** (Harlequins) 1964 *F, S*
**Wright, C C G** (Cambridge U, Blackheath) 1909 *S, I*
**Wright, F T** (Edinburgh Acads, Manchester) 1881 *S*
**Wright, I D** (Northampton) 1971 *W, I, F, S* (R)
**Wright, J C** (Met Police) 1934 *W*
**Wright, J F** (Bradford) 1890 *W*
**Wright, T P** (Blackheath) 1960 *W, I, F, S,* 1961 *W, I, F, S, SA,* 1962 *W, I, F, S*
**Wright, W H G** (Plymouth) 1920 *W, F*
**Wyatt, D M** (Bedford) 1976 *S* (R)

**Yarranton, P G** (RAF, Wasps) 1954 *W, NZ, I,* 1955 *F, S*
**Yiend, W** (Hartlepool R, Gloucester) 1892 *S, I, W,* 1893 *S, I* 1889 *M*
**Young, A T** (Cambridge U, Blackheath, Army) 1924 *S, I, W, F,* 1925 *F, NZ,* 1926 *S, I, F,* 1927 *S, I, F,* 1928 *S, I, W, F, NSW,* 1929 *I*
**Young, J R C** (Oxford U, Harlequins) 1958 *I,* 1960 *I, W, F, S,* 1961 *I, W, F, SA*
**Young, M** (Gosforth) 1977 *S, I, F, W,* 1978 *F, W, S, I*
**Young, P D** (Dublin Wands) 1954 *W, NZ, I, S, F,* 1955 *W, I, S, F*

112

*Two new caps who served England with distinction in 1977–78: Dave Caplan, of Headingley, shapes to kick with Paul Dodge, of Leicester, in attendance.*

# ENGLISH INTERNATIONAL RECORDS

*From 1890–91, when uniform points-scoring was first adopted by International Board countries, to 30 April 1978. Both team and individual records are against International Board countries only, except for the match against the RFU President's XV in the 1970–71 centenary season.*

## TEAM RECORDS

### Highest score
41 v France (41–13) 1907 Richmond
*v individual countries*
27 v Scotland (27–14) 1967 Twickenham
36 v Ireland (36–14) 1938 Dublin
25 v Wales (25–0) 1896 Blackheath
  (London)
41 v France (41–13) 1907 Richmond
16 v N Zealand (16–10) 1973 Auckland
18 v S Africa (18–9) 1972 Johannesburg
23 v Australia (23–6) 1976 Twickenham

---

### Biggest winning points margin
37 v France (37–0) 1911 Twickenham
*v individual countries*
20 v Scotland (26–6) 1977 Twickenham
22 v Ireland (36–14) 1938 Dublin
25 v Wales (25–0) 1896 Blackheath
37 v France (37–0) 1911 Twickenham
13 v N Zealand (13–0) 1936 Twickenham
 9 v S Africa (18–9) 1972 Johannesburg
17 v Australia $\begin{cases} (20–3) \ 1973 \ \text{Twickenham} \\ (23–6) \ 1976 \ \text{Twickenham} \end{cases}$

---

### Highest score by opposing team
37 France (12–37) 1972 Colombes (Paris)
*by individual countries*
28 Scotland (19–28) 1931 Murrayfield
26 Ireland (21–26) 1974 Twickenham
34 Wales (21–34) 1967 Cardiff
37 France (12–37) 1972 Colombes
23 N Zealand (11–23) 1967 Twickenham
 9 S Africa $\begin{cases} (3–9) \ 1913 \ \text{Twickenham} \\ (18–9) \ 1972 \ \text{Johannesburg} \end{cases}$
30 Australia (21–30) 1975 Brisbane

---

### Biggest losing points margin
25 $\begin{cases} \text{v Wales (0–25) 1905 Cardiff} \\ \text{v France (12–37) 1972 Colombes} \end{cases}$
*v individual countries*
20 v Scotland (6–26) 1971 Murrayfield
22 v Ireland (0–22) 1947 Dublin
25 v Wales (0–25) 1905 Cardiff

25 v France (12–37) 1972 Colombes
15 v N Zealand (0–15) 1905 Crystal
  Palace (London)
 7 v S Africa (0–7) 1932 Twickenham
12 v Australia (11–23) 1967 Twickenham

---

### Most points by England in International Championship in a season—82
(in season 1913–14)

---

### Most tries by England in International Championship in a season—20
(in season 1913–14)

---

### Most tries by England in an international
9 $\begin{cases} \text{v France (35–8) 1906 Parc des} \\ \text{Princes (Paris)} \\ \text{v France (41–13) 1907 Richmond} \\ \text{v France (39–13) 1914 Colombes} \end{cases}$

*England scored 13 tries v Wales at Blackheath in 1881, before uniform scoring was adopted.*

---

### Most tries against England in an international
8 by Wales (6–28) 1922 Cardiff

---

## INDIVIDUAL RECORDS

### Most capped player
J V Pullin  42  1966–76
*in individual positions*
*Full-back*
R Hiller  19  1968–72
*Wing*
C N Lowe  25*  1913–23
*Centre*
J Butterfield  28*  1953–59
*Fly-half*
W J A Davies  22  1913–23
*Scrum-half*
R E G Jeeps  24  1956–62

114

*Prop*
C R Jacobs   29   1956–64
*Hooker*
J V Pullin   42   1966–76
*Lock*
J D Currie   25†   1956–62
*Flanker*
D P Rogers } 34 { 1961–69
A Neary   }      { 1971–78
*No 8*
A G Ripley   24   1972–76

*David Duckham, England's most capped back, has
played 14 times at centre, and 22 times on the wing,
making a total of 36 caps*
*M P Weston won 5 of his 29 caps as a fly-half, and 24 in the
centre*
*†W W Wakefield won his 31 caps variously at prop,
lock, and No 8*
*R Cove-Smith, 29 caps, played 22 times at lock and
7 times at No 8*

**Most points in internationals – 138**
R Hiller (19 appearances) 1968–72

**Most points in an international – 22**
D Lambert v France 1911 Twickenham

**Most tries in an international – 5**
D Lambert v France 1907 Richmond
(on first appearance)

**Most tries in an international – 5**
D Lambert v France 1907 Richmond

**Most points in International
Championship in a season – 38**
R W Hosen (4 appearances) 1966–67

**Most tries in International
Championship in a season – 8**
C N Lowe (4 appearances) 1913–14

**Most points on overseas tour – 48**
W N Bennett (4 appearances) Australia
1975

**Most points in any tour match – 36**
W N Bennett v Western Australia 1975
Perth

**Most tries in any tour match – 4**
A J Morley v Western Australia 1975
Perth
P S Preece v New South Wales 1975
Sydney

*Fran Cotton on the burst
against Scotland at
Murrayfield, with Mike
Rafter (left) and Peter
Dixon in support. Cotton,
25 caps, needs only four
more to equal Ron Jacobs's
record for an England
prop.*

# ENGLISH INTER-DIVISIONAL TOURNAMENT 1977-78

## 17 December, Twickenham
**North 22** (2G 1DG 1PG 1T)   **Midlands 7** (1PG 1T)

A new event in England's rugby calendar, the Inter-Divisional Tournament stemmed largely from a series of meetings with county and club administrators which were organised by R E G Jeeps, the 1976–77 RFU President, during his year of office. He was able to persuade them that such a tournament would provide a better basis for selecting a successful England team. In the event, the country was divided, for the purposes of the tournament, into four 'divisions' (sub-divided into eight regions), with a national selector acting as chairman of the divisional selection committees in each case. Each division was divided into roughly the two regions from which teams are selected to play overseas touring teams on their visits to England, an exception being that Gloucestershire, in the South and South-West, were seconded to the southern counties for the inter-regional trial.

Four inter-regional matches, or divisional trials, were held on 3 December, followed by two inter-divisional matches a week later. The winners of these, in turn, met in the Divisional final at Twickenham on 17 December, with the two losers playing off for third and fourth places at the same venue in the morning. The outcome was that the North emerged as the first Divisional champions. After demolishing London 52–6 on the Wasps ground at Sudbury, they went on to beat the Midlands 22–7 in the final at Twickenham without being unduly stretched. The Midlands had previously accounted for the South and South-West at Bath, 19–3. There was a surprise, nevertheless, in the losers' play-off at Twickenham, with London, after their thrashing by the North, salvaging some of their pride by beating South and South-West 22–15 to take third place. The final order read: 1, The North; 2, The Midlands; 3, London; 4, South and South-West.

In the final itself, the four Lions in the North's pack – Beaumont, Cotton, Dixon, and Neary – played a large part in their side's success. Additionally Malcolm Young upheld his England status with a lively display at scrum-half and Caplan, who was later to win his first cap, showed his capabilities as an attacking full-back by scoring two tries. The best moment of the match came in the second half when Maxwell, the North centre, burst clean through past Corless from just inside half-way for a superb individual try. Altogether seven of the North team were picked for the first international, against France.

Horton, the Lancashire fly-half, opened the scoring in the ninth minute with a well-taken dropped goal for the North, to which Hare replied with a mammoth penalty goal from a metre inside his own half for the Midlands. An unconverted try by Caplan, taking an inside pass from Carleton, gave the North a lead of 7–3 at half-time. From then on they forged further ahead with a penalty goal by Young, a second try by Caplan, converted by Young, and Maxwell's splendid try, which Caplan converted from wide out. At 22–3 the match was virtually over, but the Midlands had the last word. From a short penalty, Cooper, Corless, and Dodge moved the ball rapidly to Knee, who ran in for an unconverted try near the corner.

In the play-off for third place, London surprised everyone by beating the South and South-West with something to spare. Perhaps the early kick-off time of 11.15 a.m. had something to do with it, for the losers took an uncommonly long time to warm up. They were 13–6 down at half-time, after Demming and Ball had scored tries in reply to one by Kent (converted by Sorrell) and Ball had kicked a penalty goal and conversion. Injuries to full-back Bushell and centre threequarter Cooke in the first 25 minutes had brought on Ralston, of Rosslyn Park, and Bryan, of the Harlequins, as replacements for London, and it did no harm to their cause. Ralston came up into the line to feed Demming for the latter's try, and Bryan looked sounder in defence than Cooke.

In the second half, the South and South-West fared much better. Their forwards began to look much more like a West Country pack, and Nelmes, always prominent in the loose, drove over for a try after a surging run by Pomphrey. Sorrell converted, and also kicked a penalty goal; but three more penalty goals by Ball for injudicious offences by the South and South-West enabled London to keep their seven-points winning margin.

In the previous round, on the Wasps ground at Sudbury, an apathetic London side were never in the hunt against the North, who ran up nine tries and by the end were scoring almost as they pleased. At Bath, the Midlands scored 13 of their 19 points in the last 10 minutes, so the South and South-West did rather better than the score of 19–3 might indicate. The pitch was so heavy after rain that the match was mainly a slugging affair between the forwards, with the bulk of the scores coming from defensive mistakes. An exception was Knee's try for the Midlands after clever approach-work by Cooper and Corless.

## TEAMS IN THE FINAL

**North:** D W N Caplan (Headingley); P J Squires (Harrogate), A M Bond (Broughton Park), A W Maxwell (Headingley), J Carleton (Orrell); J P Horton (Bath), M Young (Gosforth); *No 8* P Moss (Orrell); *Second Row* P J Dixon (Gosforth), W B Beaumont (Fylde) (*capt*), J Butler (Egremont), A Neary (Broughton Park); *Front Row* F E Cotton (Sale), K Pacey (Broughton Park), C White (Gosforth)  *Replacements* T Roberts (Gosforth) for Butler (33 mins), J Bell (Middlesbrough) for Cotton (70 mins)

**Scorers** *Tries:* Caplan (2), Maxwell  *Conversions:* Caplan, Young  *Dropped Goal:* Horton  *Penalty Goal:* Young

**Midlands:** W H Hare (Leicester); P Knee (Coventry), B J Corless (Moseley) (*capt*), P W Dodge (Leicester), R Barnwell (Leicester); M J Cooper (Moseley), I Peck (Bedford); *No 8* N Jeavons (Moseley); *Second Row* J Shipsides (Coventry), R Field (Moseley), I Darnell (Coventry), D Warren (Moseley); *Front Row* W H Greaves (Moseley), G N Cox (Moseley), R J Cowling (Leicester)  *Replacement* D Nutt (Moseley) for Darnell (69 mins)

**Scorers** *Try:* Knee  *Penalty Goal:* Hare

**Referee** A Welsby (Lancashire)

## PLAY-OFF FOR 3rd AND 4th PLACES

### 17 December, Twickenham
### London 22 (1G 4PG 1T)  South & South-West 15 (2G 1PG)

**London:** K M Bushell (Harlequins); R Demming (Bedford), D Croydon (Saracens), D A Cooke (Harlequins), S Tiddy (Rosslyn Park); I Ball (Wasps), M Conner (Wasps); *No 8* E Bignell (Blackheath); *Second Row* A Alexander (Harlequins), N D Mantell (Rosslyn Park), M Colclough (Angoulême), R J Mordell (Rosslyn Park); *Front Row* K Cairns (Bedford), P d'A Keith-Roach (Rosslyn Park) (*capt*), T C Claxton (Harlequins)  *Replacements* C Ralston (Rosslyn Park) for Bushell (16 mins), T A Bryan (Harlequins) for Cooke (25 mins)

**Scorers** *Tries:* Demming, Ball  *Conversion:* Ball  *Penalty Goals:* Ball (4)

**South & South-West:** D Sorrell (Bristol); D Newman (Bristol), C P Kent (Rosslyn Park), M C Beese (Bath), R J Clewes (Gloucester); C G Williams (Gloucester), S M Lewis (Ebbw Vale); *No 8* J Scott (Rosslyn Park); *Second Row* G Parsons (Bath), S Boyle (Gloucester), N Pomphrey (Bristol), M Rafter (Bristol); *Front Row* M A Burton (Gloucester), J Lockyer (Exeter) (*capt*), B G Nelmes (Cardiff)  *Replacement* J Leigh (Bristol) for Williams (35 mins)

**Scorers** *Tries:* Kent, Nelmes  *Conversions:* Sorrell (2)  *Penalty Goal:* Sorrell

**Referee** P E Hughes (Lancashire)

## SEMI-FINALS

### 10 December, Sudbury (Wasps)
### London 6 (2PG)  North 52 (5G 2PG 4T)

**London:** C S Ralston (Rosslyn Park); R Demming (Bedford), N R French (Wasps), D A Cooke (Harlequins), G Wood (Harlequins); I Ball (Wasps), I George (Rosslyn Park); *No 8* N D Mantell (Rosslyn Park); *Second Row* A Alexander (Harlequins), A K Rodgers (Bedford), M Colclough (Angoulême), D H Cooke (Harlequins); *Front Row* K Cairns (Bedford), P d'A Keith-Roach (Rosslyn Park) (*capt*), T C Claxton (Harlequins)  *Replacements* J Palmer (Bath) for French (5 mins), K M Bushell (Harlequins) for Ball (51 mins)

**Scorer** *Penalty Goals:* Ball (2)

117

**North:** D W N Caplan (Headingley); P J Squires (Harrogate), A M Bond (Broughton Park), A W Maxwell (Headingley), J Carleton (Orrell); A G B Old (Sheffield), M Young (Gosforth); *No 8* P Moss (Orrell); *Second Row* P J Dixon (Gosforth), W B Beaumont (Fylde) (*capt*), J Hedley (Gosforth), R Anderson (Gosforth); *Front Row* F E Cotton (Sale), P Hryschko (Wakefield), C White (Gosforth) *Replacements* S J Smith (Sale) for Young (53 mins), T Roberts (Gosforth) for Hedley (79 mins)
**Scorers** *Tries:* Squires (3), Carleton (2), Moss (2), Beaumont, Hedley *Conversions:* Old (5) *Penalty Goals:* Old (2)
**Referee** L Prideaux (North Midlands)

## 10 December, Bath
## South & South-West 3 (1PG)   Midlands 19 (2G 1PG 1T)

**South & South-West:** D P Sorrell (Bristol); A J Morley (Bristol), P Johnson (Clifton), N Hunt (Bristol), R Mogg (Gloucester); J Leigh (Bristol), S M Lewis (Ebbw Vale); *No 8* J P Scott (Rosslyn Park); *Second Row* M Rafter (Bristol), S Boyle (Gloucester), N Pomphrey (Bristol), G Parsons (Bath); *Front Row* M A Burton (Gloucester), J Lockyer (Exeter) (*capt*), B G Nelmes (Cardiff)
**Scorer** *Penalty Goal:* Sorrell
**Midlands:** W H Hare (Leicester); P Knee (Coventry), B J Corless (Moseley) (*capt*), P W Dodge (Leicester), R C Barnwell (Leicester); M J Cooper (Moseley), C J Gifford (Moseley); *No 8* G J Adey (Leicester); *Second Row* J Shipsides (Coventry), R Field (Moseley), N E Horton (Toulouse), D Warren (Moseley); *Front Row* W H Greaves (Moseley), G N Cox (Moseley), R J Cowling (Leicester) *Replacement* N Jeavons (Moseley) for Adey (70 mins)
**Scorers** *Tries:* Knee, Adey, Barnwell *Conversions:* Hare (2) *Penalty Goal:* Hare
**Referee** B Head-Rapson (Notts, Lincs, & Derby)

## INTER-REGIONAL MATCHES

## 3 December, Headingley
## North-East 9 (3PG)   North-West 16 (1G 2PG 1T)

**North-East:** D W N Caplan (Headingley); P J Squires (Harrogate), A W Maxwell (Headingley), A Tindle (Northern), N Bennett (Wakefield); A G B Old (Sheffield), M Young (Gosforth); *No 8* J Dowson (Wakefield) (*capt*); *Second Row* K Higgins (Wakefield), T C Roberts (Gosforth), J Hedley (Gosforth), R Anderson (Gosforth); *Front Row* J Bell (Middlesbrough), P Hryschka (Wakefield), C White (Gosforth) *Replacement* S Rule (Sale) for Maxwell (59 mins)
**Scorer** *Penalty Goals:* Old (3)
**North-West:** D G Gullick (Orrell); J Carleton (Orrell), A M Bond (Broughton Park), M Burke (Waterloo), M A C Slemen (Liverpool); J P Horton (Bath), S J Smith (Sale); *No 8* P Moss (Orrell); *Second Row* P J Dixon (Gosforth), W B Beaumont (Fylde) (*capt*), J Butler (Egremont), A Neary (Broughton Park); *Front Row* F E Cotton (Sale), K Pacey (Broughton Park), S Miles (New Brighton)
**Scorers** *Tries:* Slemen (2) *Conversion:* Gullick *Penalty Goals:* Gullick (2)
**Referee** B Head-Rapson (Notts, Lincs, and Derby)

## 3 December, Coventry
## Midlands West 12 (4PG)   Midlands East 6 (1G)

**Midlands West:** P A Rossborough (Coventry); P F Knee (Coventry), B J Corless (Moseley) (*capt*), G W Evans (Coventry), R C Barnwell (Coventry); M J Cooper (Moseley), C J Gifford (Moseley); *No 8* N Jeavons (Moseley); *Second Row* J Shipsides (Coventry), R Field (Moseley), I R Darnell (Coventry), D G Warren

(Moseley); *Front Row* W H Greaves (Moseley), G N Cox (Moseley), T F Corless
(Moseley) *Replacement* J J Pearce (Nottingham) for T F Corless (65 mins)
**Scorer** *Penalty Goals:* Rossborough (4)
**Midlands East:** W H Hare (Leicester); R Barker (Leicester), P W Dodge
(Leicester), B Hall (Leicester) *(capt)*, P McGuckian (Northampton); L Cusworth
(Moseley), I Peck (Bedford); *No 8* G J Adey (Leicester); *Second Row* J Kempin
(Leicester), V Cannon (Northampton), R M Wilkinson (Bedford), I Smith
(Leicester); *Front Row* W Dickenson (Richmond), M Howe (Bedford), R J Cowling
(Leicester) *Replacement* I K George (Rosslyn Park) for Peck (45 mins)
**Scorers** *Try:* Dodge *Conversion:* Hare
**Referee** M J Fisk (Yorkshire)

## 3 December, Exeter
## South-West 18 (2G 1DG 1PG)  South 13 (1G 1PG 1T)

**South-West:** P Winnan (Penryn); B Trevaskis (Falmouth), N Hunt (Bristol),
D Course (Maidenhead), D Newman (Bristol); J Leigh (Bristol), S M Lewis (Ebbw
Vale); *No 8* J P Scott (Rosslyn Park); *Second Row* G Parsons (Avon & Somerset
Police), R G Corin (St Ives), N Williams (Bristol), M Baker (Bristol); *Front Row*
T Pryor (Redruth), J Lockyer (Exeter) *(capt)*, C Mills (Exeter)
**Scorers** *Tries:* Newman, Parsons *Conversions:* Winnan (2) *Dropped Goal:*
Winnan *Penalty Goal:* Winnan
**South:** D P Sorrell (Bristol); R J Clewes (Gloucester), A J Morley (Bristol),
P Johnson (Clifton), R R Mogg (Gloucester); C G Williams (Gloucester),
D Kingston (Gloucester); *No 8* D M Rollitt (Richmond); *Second Row* M Rafter
(Bristol) *(capt)*, S B Boyle (Gloucester), N Pomphrey (Bristol), C Sharpe
(Richmond); *Front Row* M A Burton (Gloucester), S Mills (Gloucester),
B G Nelmes (Cardiff)
**Scorers** *Tries:* Kingston, Clewes *Conversion:* Sorrell *Penalty Goal:* Sorrell
**Referee** O E Doyle (Ireland)

## 3 December, Esher
## London South 12 (4PG)  London North 25 (3G 1PG 1T)

**London South:** I Williamson (Blackheath) *(capt)*; C Lambert (Harlequins),
D A Cooke (Harlequins), S G Jackson (Blackheath), G E Wood (Harlequins);
W N Bennett (London Welsh), J Hartley (Blackheath); *No 8* N D Mantell (Rosslyn
Park); *Second Row* D H Cooke (Harlequins), M A Hess (Richmond), M Colclough
(Angoulême), E Bignell (Blackheath); *Front Row* C McGregor (Saracens), N Vinter
(Richmond), R Fairclough (Saracens)
**Scorer** *Penalty Goals:* Williamson (4)
**London North:** C S Ralston (Rosslyn Park); R O Demming (Bedford),
N R French (Wasps), D J Croydon (Saracens), D M Wyatt (Bedford); I Ball
(Wasps), M Conner (Wasps); *No 8* A G Ripley (Rosslyn Park); *Second Row*
A Alexander (Harlequins), A K Rodgers (Bedford), A Jaszcak (Saracens),
R J Mordell (Rosslyn Park); *Front Row* K Cairns (Bedford), P d'A Keith-Roach
(Rosslyn Park) *(capt)*, T C Claxton (Harlequins)
**Scorers** *Tries:* Demming (2), Conner, Ball *Conversions:* Ball (3) *Penalty Goal:*
Ball
**Referee** M D M Rea (Ireland)

# ENGLISH COUNTY CHAMPIONSHIP 1977-78

**31 December, Moseley**
**North Midlands 10** (2PG 1T)    **Gloucestershire 7** (1PG 1T)

North Midlands have existed as a constituent body since 1920, but this was the first time they had ever won the County Championship. Oddly enough their only previous appearance in the final, in 1922, was against the same opponents, Gloucestershire, when they lost by 19 points to nil. Thus they had to wait a long time to level matters, but their success, when it came, was thoroughly well earned. Gloucestershire were making their eighth appearance in the final in the last nine seasons, and had won the title four times in the process; in 1972, 1974, 1975, and 1976. Not unnaturally they began as favourites, but North Midlands, with no fewer than 11 of the successful Moseley side in their ranks, showed that they, too, were worthy finalists.

The Gloucestershire pack, based as so often on the strong Bristol and Gloucester clubs, began the game with such power and authority that everything seemed to point to them winning again. Fidler, their big lock, dominated the line-outs, and their hefty front-row men at first carried all before them. But Cusworth, the North Midlands fly-half, who ended up as the player of the day, saved his side repeatedly with shrewd defensive kicking, and gradually the home pack began to fight back. Eventually Gloucestershire's initial dominance was blunted, and with Butler, their ace goal-kicker, out of form – he missed with five attempts out of six – North Midlands were never out of challenging range.

The scores were level at half-time, 3–3 – an early penalty goal by Butler for Gloucestershire being replied to by one from Meanwell. Shortly after the break Meanwell kicked his second penalty goal, to make it 6–3, but Gloucestershire then went ahead with an unconverted try by Mills. This came following a break from a line-out by their forwards. At 7–6 there was much excitement, with the big Gloucestershire contingent in the crowd scenting victory, but then came Cusworth's big moment. From a clearing kick by Butler which missed touch, the fly-half collected the ball near halfway, sold two superlative dummies, and put Corless away on the right. He then took the return pass and handed on to Nutt, who dived over halfway out for the winning try. It was beautifully done, and for this effort alone, plus their refusal to give in to Gloucestershire's pack, the winners could claim to be worthy champions.

In their semi-final, North Midlands owed much to Malcolm Swain, their Wales 'B' centre, for their 14-10 win over Yorkshire at Moseley. Swain scored all three of their tries with some forceful running, and again it was Cusworth who sparked off the second of the tries with a cheeky dummy-scissors from behind his own line. Yorkshire were still 10-4 ahead with barely 10 minutes to go, but they cracked at the end against the better North Midlands forwards. In the second semi-final, at Blackheath, Kent gave Gloucestershire an unexpectedly hard game before going down 19-9. Six minutes from the end there were only four points in it, the score standing at 13-9. Then a try by Haines, following a great run by Morley, and Butler's conversion finally bolted the door.

Kent had done well to reach the semi-finals for the first time in 28 years. They beat Middlesex 12-0 at Blackheath in the London divisional play-off. Yorkshire, likewise, had taken the honours in the Northern division, their most satisfying win surely being that against their arch-rivals Lancashire, the reigning champions, whom they beat 12-7 at Bradford. None the less, they still had to account for both Northumberland and Cheshire away from home to top the division.

Gloucestershire carried all before them in the South and South-West, and in the Midlands Notts, Lincs, and Derby were far from disgraced in holding North Midlands to 13-6 in the divisional play-off at Moseley.

## TEAMS IN THE FINAL

**North Midlands:** C Meanwell (Moseley); M A Hall (Dixonians), B J Corless (Moseley), M K Swain (Moseley), P J Mumford (Birmingham); L Cusworth (Moseley), P C Bullock (Birmingham); *No 8* D Nutt (Moseley); *Second Row* J C White (Moseley), B Ayre (Moseley), N J Bakewell (Coventry), D G Warren (Moseley) *(capt)*; *Front Row* W H Greaves (Moseley), G N J Cox (Moseley), T F Corless (Moseley)

**Scorers** *Try:* Nutt  *Penalty Goals:* Meanwell (2)

**Gloucestershire:** P E Butler (Gloucester); R J Clewes (Gloucester), C G Williams (Gloucester), P C Johnson (Clifton), M Ward (Bristol); I N Wilkins (St Paul's College, Cheltenham), P Howell (Gloucester); *No 8* N Pomphrey (Bristol); *Second Row* M Rafter (Bristol) *(capt)*, J H Fidler (Gloucester), S B Boyle (Gloucester), J H Haines (Gloucester); *Front Row* M A Burton (Gloucester), S G F Mills (Gloucester), A Sheppard (Bristol)

**Scorers** *Try:* Mills  *Penalty Goal:* Butler

**Referee** R C Quittenton (Sussex)

*Barry Ayre (centre), the North Midlands' lock, manages to deflect the ball back from a line-out in the County Championship semi-final against Yorkshire at Moseley.*

## SEMI-FINALS

### 26 November, Blackheath
### Kent 9 (1G 1PG)   Gloucestershire 19 (1G 1DG 2PG 1T)

**Kent:** I Williamson (Blackheath) (*capt*); D Sibley (Blackheath), A Crust (Blackheath), D A Cooke (Harlequins), A Mort (Richmond); D Slater (Blackheath), J Hartley (Blackheath); *No 8* E Bignell (Blackheath); *Second Row* J Baxter (Blackheath), A Patrick (Metropolitan Police), W Mainprize (Metropolitan Police), K Short (London Irish); *Front Row* A Trotter (Blackheath), A Wolstenholme (St Luke's College, Exeter), N Gray (Rosslyn Park)
**Scorers** *Try:* Cooke   *Conversion:* Williamson   *Penalty Goal:* Williamson
**Gloucestershire:** P E Butler (Gloucester); R J Clewes (Gloucester), A J Morley (Bristol), P C Johnson (Clifton), R R Mogg (Gloucester); C G Williams (Gloucester), P Kingston (Gloucester); *No 8* D M Rollitt (Richmond); *Second Row* M Rafter (Bristol) (*capt*), N Pomphrey (Bristol), A Turton (Stroud), J H Haines (Gloucester); *Front Row* M A Burton (Gloucester), S Mills (Gloucester), A Sheppard (Bristol)
**Scorers** *Tries:* Clewes, Haines   *Conversion:* Butler   *Dropped Goal:* Butler   *Penalty Goals:* Butler (2)
**Referee** P E Hughes (Lancashire)

### 26 November, Moseley
### North Midlands 14 (1G 2T)   Yorkshire 10 (1DG 1PG 1T)

**North Midlands:** C Meanwell (Moseley); A C Thomas (Moseley), B J Corless (Moseley), M K Swain (Moseley), P J Mumford (Birmingham); L Cusworth (Moseley), P C Bullock (Birmingham); *No 8* D Nutt (Moseley); *Second Row* D G Warren (Moseley) (*capt*), B Ayre (Moseley), N J Bakewell (Coventry), J C White (Moseley); *Front Row* W H Greaves (Moseley), G N J Cox (Moseley), T F Corless (Moseley) *Replacement* T C Clarke (Birmingham) for Nutt (65 mins)
**Scorers** *Tries:* Swain (3)   *Conversion:* Meanwell
**Yorkshire:** D W N Caplan (Headingley); P J Squires (Harrogate), A W Maxwell (Headingley), I R McGeechan (Headingley), N Bennett (Wakefield); A G B Old (Sheffield), I Orum (Roundhay); *No 8* J Dowson (Wakefield) (*capt*); *Second Row* R Davenport (Bradford), T Jones (Middlesbrough), D White (Middlesbrough), K Higgins (Wakefield); *Front Row* J Bell (Middlesbrough), J Billington (Huddersfield), D Ashton (Morley)   *Replacement* R Cardus (Roundhay) for McGeechan (79 mins)
**Scorers** *Try:* Bennett   *Dropped Goal:* McGeechan   *Penalty Goal:* Old
**Referee** P J Kingham (Surrey)

## DIVISIONAL MATCHES

### Northern Division

**Yorkshire** beat Cumbria 25–6, Lancashire 12–7, Northumberland 22–12, and Cheshire 12–0; drew with Durham 15–15
**Lancashire** beat Cumbria 21–3, Northumberland 15–6, Cheshire 13–3, and Durham 33–12; lost to Yorkshire 7–12
**Northumberland** beat Cheshire 29–6, Durham 20–7, and Cumbria 10–0; lost to Lancashire 6–15 and Yorkshire 12–22
**Cheshire** beat Durham 18–3 and Cumbria 33–12; lost to Northumberland 6–29, Lancashire 3–13, and Yorkshire 0–12

**Durham** drew with Yorkshire 15–15 and Cumbria 0–0; lost to Cheshire 3–18, Northumberland 7–20, and Lancashire 12–33
**Cumbria** drew with Durham 0–0; lost to Lancashire 3–21, Yorkshire 6–25, Cheshire 12–33, and Northumberland 0–10

|                    | P | W | D | L | F  | A  | Pts |
|--------------------|---|---|---|---|----|----|-----|
| Yorkshire          | 5 | 4 | 1 | 0 | 86 | 40 | 9   |
| Lancashire         | 5 | 4 | 0 | 1 | 89 | 36 | 8   |
| Northumberland     | 5 | 3 | 0 | 2 | 77 | 50 | 6   |
| Cheshire           | 5 | 2 | 0 | 3 | 60 | 69 | 4   |
| Durham             | 5 | 0 | 2 | 3 | 37 | 86 | 2   |
| Cumbria            | 5 | 0 | 1 | 4 | 21 | 89 | 1   |

## Midland Division

*East Region*
**Notts, Lincs, and Derby** beat Leicestershire 18–13 and East Midlands 18–9
**East Midlands** beat Leicestershire 13–0; lost to Notts, Lincs, and Derby 9–18
**Leicestershire** lost to East Midlands 0–13 and Notts, Lincs, and Derby 13–18

|                       | P | W | D | L | F  | A  | Pts |
|-----------------------|---|---|---|---|----|----|-----|
| Notts, Lincs, & Derbys| 2 | 2 | 0 | 0 | 36 | 22 | 4   |
| East Midlands         | 2 | 1 | 0 | 1 | 22 | 18 | 2   |
| Leicestershire        | 2 | 0 | 0 | 2 | 13 | 31 | 0   |

*West Region*
**North Midlands** beat Staffordshire 13–3 and Warwickshire 23–6
**Warwickshire** beat Staffordshire 22–15; lost to North Midlands 6–23
**Staffordshire** lost to North Midlands 3–13 and Warwickshire 15–22

|                | P | W | D | L | F  | A  | Pts |
|----------------|---|---|---|---|----|----|-----|
| North Midlands | 2 | 2 | 0 | 0 | 36 | 9  | 4   |
| Warwickshire   | 2 | 1 | 0 | 1 | 28 | 38 | 2   |
| Staffordshire  | 2 | 0 | 0 | 2 | 18 | 35 | 0   |

*In the inter-region play-off North Midlands beat Notts, Lincs, & Derby 13–6 at Moseley to qualify for the semi-finals*

## South-Western and Southern Division

*South-West Region*
**Gloucestershire** beat Devon 20–6, Somerset 20–8, and Cornwall 35–13
**Devon** beat Cornwall 18–12 and Somerset 19–13; lost to Gloucestershire 6–20
**Cornwall** beat Somerset 15–12; lost to Devon 12–18 and Gloucestershire 13–35
**Somerset** lost to Cornwall 12–15, Gloucestershire 8–20, and Devon 13–19

|                 | P | W | D | L | F  | A  | Pts |
|-----------------|---|---|---|---|----|----|-----|
| Gloucestershire | 3 | 3 | 0 | 0 | 75 | 27 | 6   |
| Devon           | 3 | 2 | 0 | 1 | 43 | 45 | 4   |
| Cornwall        | 3 | 1 | 0 | 2 | 40 | 65 | 2   |
| Somerset        | 3 | 0 | 0 | 3 | 33 | 54 | 0   |

*Southern Region*
**Oxfordshire** beat Buckinghamshire 18–12, Dorset–Wilts 19–15, and Berkshire 22–9

**Buckinghamshire** beat Berkshire 7–6 and Dorset–Wilts 22–9; lost to Oxfordshire 12–18
**Berkshire** drew with Dorset–Wilts 12–12; lost to Buckinghamshire 6–7 and Oxfordshire 9–22
**Dorset–Wilts** drew with Berkshire 12–12; lost to Oxfordshire 15–19 and Buckinghamshire 9–22

|                     | P | W | D | L | F  | A  | Pts |
|---------------------|---|---|---|---|----|----|-----|
| **Oxfordshire**     | 3 | 3 | 0 | 0 | 59 | 36 | 6   |
| **Buckinghamshire** | 3 | 2 | 0 | 1 | 41 | 33 | 4   |
| **Berkshire**       | 3 | 0 | 1 | 2 | 27 | 41 | 1   |
| **Dorset–Wilts**    | 3 | 0 | 1 | 2 | 36 | 53 | 1   |

*In the inter-region play-off Gloucestershire beat Oxfordshire 29–15 at Oxford (Iffley Road) to qualify for the semi-finals*

# London Division

*A Group*
**Middlesex** beat Surrey 28–4 and Eastern Counties 31–13
**Eastern Counties** beat Surrey 31–0; lost to Middlesex 13–31
**Surrey** lost to Eastern Counties 0–31 and Middlesex 4–28

|                      | P | W | D | L | F  | A  | Pts |
|----------------------|---|---|---|---|----|----|-----|
| **Middlesex**        | 2 | 2 | 0 | 0 | 59 | 17 | 4   |
| **Eastern Counties** | 2 | 1 | 0 | 1 | 44 | 31 | 2   |
| **Surrey**           | 2 | 0 | 0 | 2 | 4  | 59 | 0   |

*B Group*
**Kent** beat Hampshire 28–13, Sussex 21–6, and Hertfordshire 15–13
**Hampshire** beat Hertfordshire 13–6 and Sussex 16–0; lost to Kent 13–28
**Hertfordshire** beat Sussex 16–6; lost to Hampshire 6–13 and Kent 13–15
**Sussex** lost to Hertfordshire 6–16, Kent 6–21, and Hampshire 0–16

|                   | P | W | D | L | F  | A  | Pts |
|-------------------|---|---|---|---|----|----|-----|
| **Kent**          | 3 | 3 | 0 | 0 | 64 | 32 | 6   |
| **Hampshire**     | 3 | 2 | 0 | 1 | 42 | 34 | 4   |
| **Hertfordshire** | 3 | 1 | 0 | 2 | 35 | 34 | 2   |
| **Sussex**        | 3 | 0 | 0 | 3 | 12 | 53 | 0   |

*In the inter-group play-off, Kent beat Middlesex 14–0 at Blackheath to qualify for the semi-finals*

NOTE: *For past County Champions and runners-up, please see page 312.*

# RFU CLUB COMPETITION 1977–78

(*for the John Player Cup*)

**Michael Austin** *Coventry Evening Telegraph*

**15 April, Twickenham**
**Gloucester 6** (1G)   **Leicester 3** (1PG)

A wealth of possession paved the way for Gloucester's victory over Leicester in the 1978 final, but the match, as a spectacle, was disappointing. This was unfortunate because the attendance – 24,000 – more than doubled the previous highest for this event.

Gloucester alone brought 12,000 supporters with them, but they had only one try to cheer – by Mogg, on the left wing, just before half-time. Kenney and Bleddyn Jones, the Leicester half-backs, lost control of the ball in defence and Duggan was tackled when trying to tidy up possession. Gloucester's forwards moved in and the ball went via Burton, Howells, and Williams to lock forward Boyle, who made the decisive thrust before sending Mogg over, under a pile of defenders, at the corner. Peter Butler, who scored 40 of his side's 88 points in the competition, kicked a fine goal from the edge of touch, to underline a series of goal-kicking failures by Leicester.

The winners were penalised 17 times to Leicester's seven, but Hare, at full-back for the losers, succeeded with only one of his six penalty attempts. Three of his misses were from comfortable range – in marked contrast to his remarkable accuracy in the semi-final win over Coventry.

Leicester, who had been plagued by injuries, knew that to win the competition, on their first appearance beyond the quarter-final stage, they needed to run the ball at their opponents from almost everywhere; but Gloucester, with one of the most formidable tight-forward platforms in British rugby, deprived them of the necessary possession. Gloucester hooker Steve Mills heeled three times against the head and Fidler dominated the line-out, which was Leicester's weakest department.

Gloucester, thanks to Mogg and Butler, led 6–0 at half-time, after which Leicester, with the wind in their favour, fared rather better. Hare at last kicked a penalty goal, from 35 metres, to reduce the leeway and shone in general play, despite his goal-kicking lapses. Near the end Gloucester had a fright when Barker ran clear on the left for Leicester, but a great tackle by Mogg, coming across from the far wing, saved the situation. Gloucester, with so much possession, should have won much more easily, but their backs failed to exploit their advantage.

As it is, they join Coventry and Gosforth as twice winners of a competition which was boosted this time by an extra £10,000 revenue from the sponsors. It brought the season's total to £50,000 and completed John Player's contract with the RFU to provide £120,000 over a period of three years.

In the run-up to the final, Leicester, like Gosforth the previous season, were helped by continually being drawn at home. 127 They did not leave Welford Road until they played at Twickenham. Additionally, they had a happy knack of rallying to bring off late wins. Rosslyn Park, Northampton, and Coventry all held second-half leads against them before being overtaken. Hare scored 42 of his side's 82 points in the competition, but there were only seven tries in Leicester's total. This underlines what a blow it was when Hare was off-form with his goal-kicking at Twickenham.

Gloucester, led by former England flanker John Watkins, had their most important win when they eliminated Gosforth 19–10 in the second round at Gloucester. Gosforth, winners of the competition in the two previous years, had again been strongly fancied, but missed Roger Uttley, who was out with injury throughout the season. Gloucester, in contrast, had the distinction of fielding an unchanged side throughout.

In general the competition produced few surprise results, though away teams did slightly better than in the previous season. In the 30 games leading to the final there were 11 away-winners – two more than in 1976–77. There were also some good performances by non-favoured clubs. Walsall, at home, held Northampton to 16–8 and Wilmslow lost by a mere point to Coventry at Coventry in another first-round tie. Liverpool sprang a major shock with a 13–9 victory over London Welsh at Old Deer Park to reach the quarter-finals.

Disruption of the competition through frost meant that several clubs were called on to play tough cup-ties on successive Saturdays. It was asking too much of Liverpool and Wakefield. A week after beating London Welsh, Liverpool returned to the Metropolis for a gruelling match against Harlequins, who won 18–6. Wakefield, having won at Nottingham, failed to reproduce their best form and lost 21–4 at Northampton. As in 1976–77, only one match needed to be decided on the 'away team' rule. Wasps went through in this way after drawing 9–9 at Richmond, but were then knocked out by Gloucester.

The 1978–79 competition will again bring in clubs for whom knockout matches at the highest level are a new experience. That, probably, is the tournament's biggest justification; but it is a bonus that the final rounds, too, are now beginning to make a real impact with the public.

## TEAMS IN THE FINAL

**Gloucester:** P E Butler; R J Clewes, B J Vine, R Jardine, R R Mogg;
C G Williams, P R Howell; *No 8* J F Simonett; *Second Row* J A Watkins *(capt)*,
S B Boyle, J H Fidler, V J Wooley; *Front Row* M A Burton, S G F Mills,
G A F Sargent
**Scorers** *Try:* Mogg *Conversion:* Butler
**Leicester:** W H Hare; M J Duggan, P W Dodge, B P Hall *(capt)*, R G Barker;
B Jones, S Kenney; *No 8* G J Adey; *Second Row* S R Johnson, N J Joyce,
A G Hazlerigg, D J Forfar; *Front Row* S P Redfern, P J Wheeler, R E Needham
**Scorer** *Penalty Goal:* Hare
**Referee** R C Quittenton (London)

## RESULTS
### First round

| | |
|---|---|
| Morley 3 Gosforth 12 | |
| Waterloo 10 Bedford 4 | |
| Liverpool 18 Sale 4 | |
| Walsall 8 Northampton 16 | |
| Nottingham 12 Wakefield 17 | |
| Coventry 7 Wilmslow 6 | |
| Moseley 38 Blackheath 12 | |
| Leicester 9 Hartlepool Rovers 3 | |
| Exeter 20 Bath 6 | |
| Bristol 19 Falmouth 6 | |
| Gloucester 38 Lydney 6 | |
| Saracens 3 London Welsh 14 | |
| US Portsmouth 6 Harlequins 19 | |
| Esher 10 London Irish 32 | |
| Richmond 9 Wasps 9* | |
| Rosslyn Park 58 High Wycombe 0 | |

*\*Wasps won on 'away team' rule*

### Second round

| | |
|---|---|
| Bristol 14 Moseley 0 | |
| Exeter 0 Coventry 34 | |
| Gloucester 19 Gosforth 10 | |
| Harlequins 17 London Irish 15 | |
| Leicester 25 Rosslyn Park 16 | |
| Wasps 10 Waterloo 9 | |
| London Welsh 9 Liverpool 13 | |
| Northampton 21 Wakefield 4 | |

### Third round

| | |
|---|---|
| Harlequins 18 Liverpool 6 | |
| Leicester 20 Northampton 11 | |
| Coventry 16 Bristol 13 | |
| Wasps 3 Gloucester 13 | |

### Semi-finals

| | |
|---|---|
| Leicester 25 Coventry 16 | |
| Harlequins 6 Gloucester 12 | |

## Final

Gloucester 6 Leicester 3

## Previous finals

| | |
|---|---|
| 1972 | Gloucester 17 Moseley 6 |
| 1973 | Coventry 27 Bristol 15 |
| 1974 | Coventry 26 London Scottish 6 |
| 1975 | Bedford 28 Rosslyn Park 12 |
| 1976 | Gosforth 23 Rosslyn Park 14 |
| 1977 | Gosforth 27 Waterloo 11 |

## County Cup Winners 1977–78

| | |
|---|---|
| Berkshire | **Abbey** |
| Buckinghamshire | **High Wycombe** |
| Cheshire | **Sale** |
| Cornwall | **Camborne** |
| Cumbria | **Aspatria** |
| Devon | **Exeter** |
| Dorset-Wilts | **Salisbury** |
| Durham | **Hartlepool Rovers** |
| Eastern Counties | **Ipswich** |
| East Midlands | **Peterborough** |
| Gloucestershire | **Matson** |
| Hampshire | **Havant** |
| Hertfordshire | **Letchworth** |
| Kent | **Blackheath** |
| Lancashire | **Orrell** |
| Leicestershire | **Loughborough Students** |
| Middlesex | **Wasps** |
| North Midlands | **Worcester** |
| Northumberland | **Gosforth** |
| Notts, Lincs, Derbys | **Chesterfield** |
| Oxfordshire | **Oxford** |
| Somerset | **Avon and Somerset Constabulary** |
| Staffordshire | **Walsall** |
| Surrey | **Esher** |
| Sussex | **Lewes** |
| Warwickshire | **Newbold-on-Avon** |
| Yorkshire | **Wakefield** |

# THE UNIVERSITY MATCH 1977

**6 December, Twickenham**
**Oxford University 16** (4PG 1T)
**Cambridge University 10** (2PG 1T)

Oxford, to the joy of their long-suffering supporters in the crowd of 32,000, put an end to Cambridge's record-breaking sequence of five wins, and ensured in the process that two other records should remain unbroken. Had Cambridge won, they would have taken the lead in the series for the first time since it began in 1872. Instead, Oxford still lead by 42 wins to 41, with 13 matches drawn. Likewise C D (now Sir Carl) Aarvold remains the only Light Blue to have taken part in four winning University matches (in his case from 1926 to 1929). Two of the Cambridge team, the captain Alastair Hignell and their right wing O'Callaghan, the former All Black international, were well placed to equal Aarvold's feat. They had taken part in the previous three wins; but this time Oxford managed to thwart them.

This is by way of postscript to a thoroughly entertaining match. Both sides gave themselves to their task with the usual do-or-die commitment, and if the higher skills were sometimes lacking, the pace and fury of the exchanges were well in tune with tradition. There was suspense, too, right up to the end. Cambridge launched several attacks in the closing stages, and still needed only a try and conversion to draw.

What really determined the match, on a grey and drizzly day, was Oxford's excellent goal-kicking. Tony Watkinson, their 22-year-old centre, a freshman post-graduate from Sheffield University, kicked four penalty goals in four attempts, and narrowly missed converting Oxford's only try. It was quality goal-kicking, in such unpromising conditions. Hignell, in contrast, missed two kicks at goal for Cambridge in the second half, when his side badly needed the points, and was well off target with a drop-kick in the crucial closing stages. These gifts of fortune apart, it was great work by the Oxford pack, superbly supported by the kicking of fly-half Gareth Davies, the Cardiff freshman, that set up the positions from which Watkinson, in the event, was able to kick his penalty goals. The Oxford outsides tackled superbly, and Hopkins, at full-back, hardly put hand or foot wrong throughout.

Cambridge started the game with a rush and threatened two or three scores in the first quarter of an hour. They did, in fact, get one, a straight-on penalty goal by Hignell, but thereafter the game began to go more Oxford's way. Watkinson kicked the first of his penalty goals and shortly afterwards Moir, one of a highly efficient Dark Blue loose-forward trio, powered his way over for an unconverted try after taking a short pass from his scrum-half Faktor. Two more penalty goals by Watkinson made it 13–3 to Oxford at half-time.

131

Any complacency they may have felt was dispelled soon after the interval when Greig crossed for Cambridge on the left after chasing a diagonal kick by Breakey. Hignell failed to convert. Watkinson then kicked his fourth penalty goal for the winners, and all Cambridge could then muster before the end was a penalty goal by Robbie.

Butler, at No 8, was the losers' most prominent player, but their half-backs Robbie, the Irish international freshman, and Breakey had a disappointing afternoon against the quick-breaking Oxford flankers. Breakey, especially, tried to do too much on his own. Hignell, who had been injured for most of the term, should probably never have played. His lack of match-play led to some uncharacteristic errors.

**Oxford University:** K M Hopkins (Maesteg GS & St Edmund Hall); R M C Hoolahan (Reigate GS & St Edmund Hall), A Watkinson (Belmont Abbey & St Edmund Hall), T A Bryan (Hampton GS & St Edmund Hall) (*capt*), D C Willis (Haberdashers' Aske's & Worcester); W G Davies (Gwendraeth GS & St Catherine's), S J Faktor (Latymer Upper & University); *No 8* M J P Moir (Ampleforth & Lincoln); *Second Row* M D Mitchell (Westerford HS, Cape Town, & St Catherine's), R G Robinson (Oundle & Lincoln), K J Budge (Rossall & University), G L White (Diocesan College, Cape Town, & University); *Front Row* T P Enevoldson (Royal GS, Newcastle, & Brasenose), B Light (Lewis School, Pengam, & St Edmund Hall), E C Horne (Emanuel & Jesus)
**Scorers** *Try:* Moir *Penalty Goals:* Watkinson (4)

**Cambridge University:** A J Hignell (Denstone & Fitzwilliam) (*capt*); M W O'Callaghan (Christchurch Boys HS, NZ, & Emmanuel), M K Fosh (Harrow & Magdalene), J S Davies (Christ Coll, Brecon, & St John's), I A Greig (Queen's Coll, Queenstown, SA, & Downing); J N F Breakey (Fettes & Christ's), J C Robbie (Dublin HS & Christ's); *No 8* E T Butler (Monmouth & Fitzwilliam); *Second Row* R J Stead (Radley & Selwyn), N R M Heath (Solihull & Downing), J N Ford (Millfield & Emmanuel), S F Glanvill (Exeter & Pembroke); *Front Row* P A V Shaw (Queen Elizabeth GS, Wakefield, & Downing), K F Geoghegan (Gonzaga Coll, Dublin, & King's), R J Brooman (Merchant Taylor's, Northwood, & Trinity) *Replacements* H Stevenson (Haberdashers' Aske's & St Catharine's) for Shaw (15 mins), G Crothers (Belfast RA & Hughes Hall) for O'Callaghan (75 mins)
**Scorers** *Try:* Greig *Penalty Goals:* Hignell, Robbie
**Referee** C Norling (Wales)

*Opposite page, top: Alastair Hignell, the Cambridge captain and full-back, is caught in possession by Steve Faktor, Oxford's scrum-half. Hignell had been injured for most of the season and there were doubts about him playing: in the event his lack of match fitness showed up. Bottom: Faktor in action again with a well-timed pass to his fly-half.*

# UNIVERSITY MATCH RESULTS

### 96 Matches played   Oxford 42 wins   Cambridge 41 wins   13 Draws

*Match played at Oxford 1871–72; Cambridge 1872–73; The Oval 1873–74 to 1879–80; Blackheath 1880–81 to 1886–87; Queen's Club 1887–88 to 1920–21; then Twickenham.*

| Season | | |
|---|---|---|
| 1871–72 | **Oxford** | 1G 1T to 0 |
| 1872–73 | **Cambridge** | 1G 1T to 0 |
| 1873–74 | Drawn | 1T each |
| 1874–75* | Drawn | Oxford 2T to 0 |
| 1875–76 | **Oxford** | 1T to 0 |
| 1876–77 | **Cambridge** | 1G 2T to 0 |
| 1877–78 | **Oxford** | 2T to 0 |
| 1878–79 | Drawn | No score |
| 1879–80 | **Cambridge** | 1G 1DG to 1DG |
| 1880–81 | Drawn | 1T each |
| 1881–82 | **Oxford** | 2G 1T to 1G |
| 1882–83 | **Oxford** | 1T to 0 |
| 1883–84 | **Oxford** | 3G 4T to 1G |
| 1884–85 | **Oxford** | 3G 1T to 1T |
| 1885–86 | **Cambridge** | 2T to 0 |
| 1886–87 | **Cambridge** | 3T to 0 |
| 1887–88 | **Cambridge** | 1DG 2T to 0 |
| 1888–89 | **Cambridge** | 1G 2T to 0 |
| 1889–90 | **Oxford** | 1G 1T to 0 |
| 1890–91 | Drawn | 1G each |
| 1891–92 | **Cambridge** | 2T to 0 |
| 1892–93 | Drawn | No score |
| 1893–94 | **Oxford** | 1T to 0 |
| 1894–95 | Drawn | 1G each |
| 1895–96 | **Cambridge** | 1G to 0 |
| 1896–97 | **Oxford** | 1G 1DG to 1G 1T |
| 1897–98 | **Oxford** | 2T to 0 |
| 1898–99 | **Cambridge** | 1G 2T to 0 |
| 1899–1900 | **Cambridge** | 2G 4T to 0 |
| 1900–01 | **Oxford** | 2G to 1G 1T |
| 1901–02 | **Oxford** | 1G 1T to 0 |
| 1902–03 | Drawn | 1G 1T each |
| 1903–04 | **Oxford** | 3G 1T to 2G 1T |
| 1904–05 | **Cambridge** | 3G to 2G |
| 1905–06 | **Cambridge** | 3G (15) to 2G 1T (13) |
| 1906–07 | **Oxford** | 4T (12) to 1G 1T (8) |
| 1907–08 | **Oxford** | 1G 4T (17) to 0 |
| 1908–09 | Drawn | 1G (5) each |
| 1909–10 | **Oxford** | 4G 5T (35) to 1T (3) |
| 1910–11 | **Oxford** | 4G 1T (23) to 3G 1T (18) |
| 1911–12 | **Oxford** | 2G 3T (19) to 0 |
| 1912–13 | **Cambridge** | 2G (10) to 1T (3) |
| 1913–14 | **Cambridge** | 1DG 3T (13) to 1T (3) |
| 1914–18 | *No matches* | |
| 1919–20 | **Oxford** | 1DG 1PG (7) to 1G (5) |
| 1920–21 | **Oxford** | 1G 4T (17) to 1G 3T (14) |
| 1921–22 | **Oxford** | 1G 2T (11) to 1G (5) |
| 1922–23 | **Cambridge** | 3G 2T (21) to 1G 1T (8) |
| 1923–24 | **Oxford** | 3G 2T (21) to 1G 1PG 2T (14) |
| 1924–25 | **Oxford** | 1G 2T (11) to 2T (6) |
| 1925–26 | **Cambridge** | 3G 6T (33) to 1T (3) |
| 1926–27 | **Cambridge** | 3G 5T (30) to 1G (5) |
| 1927–28 | **Cambridge** | 2G 2PG 2T (22) to 1G 3T (14) |
| 1928–29 | **Cambridge** | 1G 3T (14) to 1DG 1PG 1T (10) |
| 1929–30 | **Oxford** | 1G 1DG (9) to 0 |

| Season | | |
|---|---|---|
| 1930–31 | Drawn | Oxford 1PG (3) |
| | | Cambridge 1T (3) |
| 1931–32 | **Oxford** | 1DG 2T (10) to 1T (3) |
| 1932–33 | **Oxford** | 1G 1T (8) to 1T (3) |
| 1933–34 | **Oxford** | 1G (5) to 1T (3) |
| 1934–35 | **Cambridge** | 2G 1DG 1PG 4T (29) to 1DG (4) |
| 1935–36 | Drawn | No score |
| 1936–37 | **Cambridge** | 2T (6) to 1G (5) |
| 1937–38 | **Oxford** | 1G 4T (17) to 1DG (4) |
| 1938–39 | **Cambridge** | 1G 1PG (8) to 2PG (6) |
| 1939–45 | *War-time series* | |
| 1945–46 | **Cambridge** | 1G 2T (11) to 1G 1PG (8) |
| 1946–47 | **Oxford** | 1G 1DG 2T (15) to 1G (5) |
| 1947–48 | **Cambridge** | 2PG (6) to 0 |
| 1948–49 | **Oxford** | 1G 1DG 2T (14) to 1DG 1PG (8) |
| 1949–50 | **Oxford** | 1T (3) to 0 |
| 1950–51 | **Oxford** | 1G 1PG (8) to 0 |
| 1951–52 | **Oxford** | 2G 1T (13) to 0 |
| 1952–53 | **Cambridge** | 1PG 1T (6) to 1G (5) |
| 1953–54 | Drawn | Oxford 1PG 1T (6) |
| | | Cambridge 2PG (6) |
| 1954–55 | **Cambridge** | 1PG (3) to 0 |
| 1955–56 | **Oxford** | 1PG 2T (9) to 1G (5) |
| 1956–57 | **Cambridge** | 1G 1DG 1PG 1T (14) to 2PG 1T (9) |
| 1957–58 | **Oxford** | 1T (3) to 0 |
| 1958–59 | **Cambridge** | 1G 1PG 3T (17) to 1PG 1T (6) |
| 1959–60 | **Oxford** | 3PG (9) to 1PG (3) |
| 1960–61 | **Cambridge** | 2G 1T (13) to 0 |
| 1961–62 | **Cambridge** | 1DG 2T (9) to 1DG (3) |
| 1962–63 | **Cambridge** | 2G 1PG (17) to 0 |
| 1963–64 | **Cambridge** | 1G 1DG 1PG (11) |
| 1964–65 | **Oxford** | 2G 1PG 2T (19) to 1PG 1GM (6) |
| 1965–66 | Drawn | 1G each |
| 1966–67 | **Oxford** | 1G 1T (8) to 1DG 1T (6) |
| 1967–68 | **Cambridge** | 1T 1PG (6) to 0 |
| 1968–69 | **Cambridge** | 1T 1PG 1DG (9) to 2T (6) |
| 1969–70 | **Oxford** | 3PG (9) to 2PG (6) |
| 1970–71 | **Oxford** | 1G 1DG 2T (14) to 1PG (3) |
| 1971–72 | **Oxford** | 3PG 3T (21) to 1PG (3) |
| 1972–73 | **Cambridge** | 1G 1PG 1DG 1T (16) to 2PG (6) |
| 1973–74 | **Cambridge** | 1DG 1PG 2T (14) to 1G 2PG (12) |
| 1974–75 | **Cambridge** | 1G 2PG 1T (16) to 5PG (15) |
| 1975–76 | **Cambridge** | 2G 5PG 1DG 1T (34) to 3PG 1DG (12) |
| 1976–77 | **Cambridge** | 1G 3PG (15) to 0 |
| 1977–78 | **Oxford** | 4PG 1T (16) to 2PG 1T (10) |

*At this date no match could be won unless a goal was scored.*

### THE WAR-TIME MATCHES

| Season | | | | | |
|---|---|---|---|---|---|
| 1939–40 | **Oxford** | 1G 1DG 2T (15) to 1T (3) (at Cambridge) | | **Cambridge** | 1G 3T (14) to 2G 1T (13) (at Oxford) |
| 1940–41 | **Cambridge** | 1G 2T (11) to 1G 1DG (9) (at Oxford) | | **Cambridge** | 2G 2T (16) to 1T (3) (at Cambridge) |
| | **Cambridge** | 2G 1T (13) to 0 (at Cambridge) | 1943–44 | **Cambridge** | 2G 1T (13) to 1DG (4) (at Cambridge) |
| 1941–42 | **Cambridge** | 1PG 2T (9) to 1PG 1T (6) (at Cambridge) | | **Oxford** | 2T (6) to 1G (5) (at Oxford) |
| | **Cambridge** | 1G 2PG 2T (17) to 1G 1T (8) (at Oxford) | 1944–45 | Drawn | 1T (3) each (at Oxford) |
| 1942–43 | **Cambridge** | 1G 1DG (9) to 0 (at Oxford) | | **Cambridge** | 2G 2T (16) to 1DG (4) (at Cambridge) |

# UNIVERSITY BLUES 1872–1977
*(Each year indicates a separate appearance)*

## OXFORD

|  |  |
|---|---|
| Abbott, J S | 1954–55 |
| Abell, G E B | 1923–24–25–26 |
| Adamson, J A | 1928–29–31 |
| Adcock, J R L | 1961 |
| Aitken, G G | 1922–24 |
| Aldridge, J E | 1888 |
| Alexander, H | 1897–98 |
| Alexander, P C | 1930 |
| Allaway, R C P | 1953–54–55 |
| Allen, C P | 1881–82–83 |
| Allen, T | 1909 |
| Allen, W C | 1910 |
| Allison, M G | 1955 |
| Almond, R G P | 1937 |
| Ashby, C J | 1973 |
| Asher, A G G | 1881–82–83–84 |
| Asquith, P R | 1974 |
| Atkinson, C C | 1876 |
| Back, A | 1878 |
| Badenoch, D F | 1971 |
| Baden-Powell, F S | 1873 |
| Baggaley, J C | 1953–54 |
| Bain, D McL | 1910–11–12–13 |
| Bainbrigge, J H | 1874–76–77 |
| Baird, J S | 1966–67 |
| Baiss, R S H | 1894–95 |
| Baker, C D | 1891–93 |
| Baker, D G S | 1951–52 |
| Baker, E M | 1893–94–95–96 |
| Baker, R T | 1968 |
| Balfour, E R | 1893–94–95 |
| Bannerman, J MacD | 1927–28 |
| Barker, A C | 1966–67 |
| Barry, C E | 1897–98–99 |
| Barry, D M | 1968–69–70 |
| Barwick, W M | 1880–81 |
| Bass, R G | 1961 |
| Batchelor, T B | 1906 |
| Bateson, H D | 1874–75–77 |
| Baxter, T J | 1958–59 |
| Beamish, S H | 1971 |
| Bedford, T P | 1965–66–67 |
| Behn, A R | 1968–69 |
| Bell, D L | 1970 |
| Benson, E T | 1928 |
| Bentley, P J | 1960 |
| Berkeley, W V | 1924–25–26 |
| Berry, C W | 1883–84 |
| Bettington, R H B | 1920–22 |
| Bevan, J H | 1946 |
| Binham, P A | 1971 |
| Birrell, R H B | 1953 |
| Black, B H | 1929 |
| Blair, A S | 1884 |
| Blencowe, L C | 1907–08 |
| Bloxham, C T | 1934–35–36–37 |
| Blyth, P H | 1885–86 |
| Bolton, W H | 1873–74–75 |
| Bonham-Carter, E | 1890–91 |
| Boobbyer, B | 1949–50–51 |
| Booker, J L | 1880 |
| Booth, J L | 1956 |
| Bos, F H ten | 1958–59–60 |
| Boswell, J D | 1885–86–87 |
| Botfield, A S G | 1871 |
| Botting, I J | 1949–50 |
| Bourdillon, H | 1873–74–75 |
| Bourns, C | 1903 |
| Bowers, J B | 1932–34 |
| Boyce, A W | 1952–53 |
| Boyd, A de H | 1924 |
| Boyd, E F | 1912 |
| Boyle, D S | 1967–68–69 |
| Brace, D O | 1955–56 |
| Bradby, G F | 1882–85 |
| Bradford, C C | 1887 |
| Branfoot, E P | 1878–79 |
| Bremridge, H | 1876–77 |
| Brett, J A | 1935–36–37 |
| Brewer, R J | 1965 |
| Brewer, T J | 1951 |
| Bridge, D J W | 1946–47–48 |
| Brierley, H | 1871 |
| Britton, R B | 1963–64 |
| Bromet, W E | 1889 |
| Brooks, M J | 1873 |
| Brooks, W | 1872 |
| Broster, L R | 1912 |
| Broughton, R C | 1965 |
| Brown, L G | 1910–11–12 |
| Brunskill, R F | 1873–74 |
| Bryan, T A | 1975–76–77 |
| Bryer, L W | 1953 |
| Buchanan, F G | 1909–10 |
| Bucknall, A L | 1965–66 |
| Budge, K J | 1977 |
| Budworth, R T D | 1887–88–89 |
| Bullard, G L | 1950–51 |
| Bullock, H | 1910–11 |
| Bulpett, C W L | 1871 |
| Burnet, P J | 1960 |
| Burrow, K C | 1933 |
| Burse, R M | 1974 |
| Bush, A | 1934 |
| Bussell, J G | 1903–04 |
| Butcher, W M | 1954 |
| Butler, F E R | 1959–60 |
| Button, E L | 1936 |
| Byers, R M | 1926 |
| Caccia, H A | 1926 |
| Cadell, P R | 1890 |
| Cairns, A G | 1899–1900–01 |
| Campbell, E | 1919–20–21 |
| Cannell, L B | 1948–49–50 |
| Cardale, C F | 1929–30 |
| Carey, G M | 1891–92–94 |
| Carey, W J | 1894–95–96–97 |
| Carlyon, H B | 1871 |
| Carroll, B M | 1970–71 |
| Carroll, P R | 1968–69–70 |
| Carter, C R | 1885 |
| Cartwright, V H | 1901–02–03–04 |
| Cass, T | 1961 |
| Castens, H H | 1886–87 |
| Cattell, R H B | 1893 |
| Cave, H W | 1881 |
| Cawkwell, G L | 1946–47 |
| Chadwick, A J | 1898–99 |
| Chambers, J C | 1921 |
| Champain, F H B | 1897–98–99 |
| Champneys, F W | 1874–75–76 |
| Charles, A E S | 1932 |
| Cheesman, W I | 1910–11 |
| Cheyne, H | 1903–04 |
| Cholmondeley, F G | 1871–73 |
| Christopherson, P | 1886–87–88 |
| Clarke, E J D | 1973 |
| Clarke, I A | 1913 |
| Clauss, P R | 1889–90–91 |
| Clements, B S | 1975 |
| Cleveland, C R | 1885–86 |
| Cochran, P C | 1889–91 |
| Cohen, B A | 1884 |
| Coker, J B H | 1965 |
| Cole, B W | 1945 |
| Coles, D G G | 1937–38 |
| Coles, P | 1884–85–86 |
| Coles, S C | 1954–56–57 |
| Collingwood, J A | 1961–62 |
| Colvile, A H | 1892–93 |
| Conway-Rees, J | 1891–92–93 |
| Cooke, J L | 1968–69 |
| Cooke, P | 1936–37 |
| Cooke, W R | 1976 |
| Cookson, G H F | 1891–92 |
| Cooper, A H | 1951 |
| Cooper, M McG | 1934–35–36 |
| Cooper, R A | 1937 |
| Cooper, R M | 1946 |
| Cornish, W H | 1876 |
| Couper, T | 1899–1900 |
| Court, E D | 1882–83 |
| Cousins, F C | 1885–86 |
| Coutts, I D F | 1951 |
| Coventry, R G T | 1889–90–91 |
| Cowen, T J | 1938 |
| Cowlishaw, F I | 1890–91 |
| Cox, G V | 1878 |
| Cozens-Hardy, B | 1904–05–06 |
| Crabbie, J E | 1898–99–1900–01 |
| Craig, F J R | 1963–64–65 |
| Cranmer, P | 1933–34 |
| Crawfurd, J W F A | 1900 |
| Creese, N A H | 1951 |
| Cridlan, A G | 1928–29–30 |
| Croker, J R | 1966–67 |
| Crole, G B | 1913–19 |
| Cronje, S N | 1907–08 |
| Crosse, C W | 1874 |
| Crump, L M | 1896 |
| Cuff, T W | 1945 |
| Cunningham, G | 1907–08–09 |
| Currie, J D | 1954–55–56–57 |
| Curry, J A H | 1961 |
| Curtis, A B | 1949 |
| Dalby, C | 1923 |
| Davey, P | 1967 |
| Davey, R A E | 1972 |
| David, A M | 1921–22 |
| Davies, D B | 1905–06–07 |
| Davies, D E | 1951 |
| Davies, D M | 1958–59–60 |
| Davies, J A B | 1920 |
| Davies, L L J | 1927 |
| Davies, R | 1969 |
| Davies, R H | 1955–56–57 |
| Davies, S J T | 1972–73 |
| Davies, W G | 1977 |
| Davis, R A | 1974–75 |
| Dawkins, P M | 1959–60–61 |
| Deacon, E A | 1871–72 |
| De Winton, R F C | 1888–89–90 |
| Diamond, A J | 1957 |
| Dickson, M R | 1903 |
| Dickson, W M | 1912 |
| Diggle, P R | 1908–09 |
| Dingle, A J | 1911 |
| Disney, P C W | 1935 |
| Dixon, P J | 1967–68–69–70 |
| Dobson, D D | 1899–1900–01 |
| Donald, D G | 1911–12–13 |
| Donaldson, C L | 1895 |
| Donaldson, D W | 1893 |
| Donaldson, W P | 1892–93–94 |
| Donnelly, M P | 1946 |
| Donovan, T J | 1971 |
| Douglas, A I | 1970–71 |
| Dorman, J M A | 1964 |
| Dowson, A O | 1896 |

134

| | | | | | |
|---|---|---|---|---|---|
| Swanzy, A J | 1901–02 | Vassall, H | 1879–80–81–82 | Whyte, A G D | 1963 |
| Swarbrick, D W | 1946–47–48 | Vassall, H H | 1906–07–08 | Whyte, D J | 1963 |
| Swayne, D H | 1930–31 | Vecqueray, A H | 1877–78 | Wilcock, R M | 1962 |
| Sweatman, E A | 1927 | Vecqueray, G C | 1873 | Wilcock, S H | 1957–58–59 |
| | | Vidal, R W S | 1872 | Willcox, J G | 1959–60–61–62 |
| Taberer, H M | 1892 | Vincent, A N | 1948–49 | Wilkinson, J V S | 1904 |
| Tahany, M P | 1945 | | | Wilkinson, W E | 1891 |
| Tanner, T L | 1931 | | | Williams, C D | 1945 |
| Tarr, F N | 1907–08–09 | Wade, C G | 1882–83–84 | Williams, J R | 1969 |
| Tatham, W M | 1881–82–83 | Waide, S L | 1932 | Williamson, A C | 1913 |
| Taylor, E G | 1926–27–28 | Wake, H B L | 1922 | Williamson, R H | 1906–07–08 |
| Taylor, J A | 1974 | Wakefield, W H | 1891–92 | Willis, D C | 1975–76–77 |
| Terry, H F | 1900–01 | Wakelin, W S | 1964 | Wilson, C T M | 1948 |
| Theron, T P | 1923 | Waldock, F A | 1919 | Wilson, D B | 1874 |
| Thomas, T R | 1938 | Waldock, H F | 1919–20 | Wilson, G A | 1946–48 |
| Thomas, W E | 1911–12 | Waldron, O C | 1965–67 | Wilson, J | 1967–68 |
| Thomas, W L | 1893–94 | Walford, M M | 1935–36–37 | Wilson, J H G | 1888–89–90 |
| Thomson, B E | 1951–52 | Walker, A | 1880 | Wilson, N G C | 1967 |
| Thomson, C | 1896 | Walker, J C | 1955 | Wilson, R W | 1956 |
| Thomson, F W | 1912–13 | Walker, J G | 1879–80–81 | Wilson, S | 1963–64 |
| Thomson, W J | 1895–96 | Walker, M | 1950–51 | Wilson, S E | 1890 |
| Thorburn, C W | 1964 | Wall, T W | 1875–76–77 | Wilson, T W | 1887 |
| Thorniley-Walker, M J | 1967 | Wallace, A C | 1922–23–24–25 | Wimperis, E J | 1951 |
| Tongue, P K | 1975 | Walton, E J | 1900–01 | Winn, C E | 1950 |
| Torry, P J | 1968–69 | Ward, J M | 1972 | Winn, R R | 1953 |
| Travers, B H | 1946–47 | Ware, M A | 1961–62 | Witney, N K-J | 1970–71 |
| Tristram, H B | 1882–83–84 | Warr, A L | 1933–34 | Wix, R S | 1904–05–06–07 |
| Troup, D S | 1928 | Waterman, J S | 1974 | Wood, A E | 1904 |
| Tudor, H A | 1878–79–80–81 | Wates, C S | 1961 | Wood, D E | 1952–53 |
| Turcan, H H | 1928 | Watkins, L | 1879 | Wood, G F | 1919 |
| Turner, A B | 1884 | Watkinson, A F | 1977 | Woodhead, P G | 1974 |
| Turner, F H | 1908–09–10 | Watson, P W | 1954–55 | Wooldridge, C S | 1882 |
| | | Watt, K A | 1976 | Wordsworth, C R | 1922–23–24 |
| Unwin, G T | 1894–95–96 | Watts, I H | 1937–38 | Wordsworth, C W | 1902 |
| | | Watts, L D | 1957–58 | Wordsworth, J R | 1885 |
| Valentine, A C | 1923–24–25 | Wesche, V V G | 1924 | Wray, M O | 1933–34 |
| Van Der Riet, E F | 1920–21 | Weston, B A G | 1957 | Wydell, H A | 1951 |
| Van Ryneveld, A J | 1946–47–48 | Weston, J W | 1871 | Wynter, E C C | 1947 |
| Van Ryneveld, C B | 1947–48–49 | White, G L | 1976–77 | | |
| | | White, N T | 1905–06 | Young, J R C | 1957–58 |

136

## CAMBRIDGE

| | | | | | |
|---|---|---|---|---|---|
| Aarvold, C D | 1925–26–27–28 | Bartlett, R M | 1951 | Boughton-Leigh, C E W | 1878 |
| Adams, G C A | 1929 | Bateman–Champain, P J C | 1937 | Boulding, P V | 1975–76 |
| Adams, H F S | 1884–85 | Batten, J M | 1871–72–73–74 | Bowcott, H M | 1927–28 |
| Agnew, C M | 1875–76 | Batty, P A | 1919–20 | Bowcott, J E | 1933 |
| Agnew, G W | 1871–72–73 | Baxter, R | 1871–72–73 | Bowen, R W | 1968 |
| Agnew, W L | 1876–77–78 | Baxter, W H B | 1912–13 | Bowhill, J W | 1888–89 |
| Albright, G S | 1877 | Bealey, R J | 1874 | Bowman, J H | 1933–34 |
| Alderson, F H R | 1887–88 | Bearne, K R F | 1957–58–59 | Boyd, C W | 1909 |
| Alexander, E P | 1884–85–86 | Beazley, T A G | 1971 | Brandram, R A | 1896 |
| Alexander, J W | 1905–06 | Bedell-Sivright, D R | | Brash, J C | 1959–60–61 |
| Allan, C J | 1962 | | 1899–1900–01–02 | Brathwaite, G A | 1934 |
| Allan, J L F | 1956 | Bedell-Sivright, J V | | Breakey, J N F | 1974–75(R)–77 |
| Allen, A D | 1925–26–27 | | 1900–01–02–03 | Bree-Frink, F C | 1888–89–90 |
| Allen, D B | 1975 | Beer, I D S | 1952–53–54 | Briggs, P D | 1962 |
| Allen, J | 1875–76 | Bell, R W | 1897–98–99 | Bromet, E | 1887–88 |
| Anderson, W T | 1931–32 | Bell, S P | 1894–95–96 | Brook, P W P | 1928–29–30–31 |
| Anthony, A J | 1967 | Bennett, G M | 1897–98 | Brookstein, R | 1969 |
| Archer, G M D | 1950–51 | Benthall, E C | 1912 | Brooman, R J | 1977 |
| Arthur, T G | 1962 | Beringer, F R | 1951–52 | Browell, H H | 1877–78 |
| Ashcroft, A H | 1908–09 | Beringer, G G | 1975–76 | Brown, A C | 1920–21 |
| Ashford, C L | 1929 | Berman, J V | 1966 | Brown, S L | 1975–76 |
| Askew, J G | 1929–30–31 | Berry, S P | 1971 | Browning, O C | 1934 |
| Asquith, J P K | 1953 | Bevan, G A J | 1951 | Bruce Lockhart, J H | 1910 |
| Aston, R L | 1889–90 | Bevan, J A | 1877–80 | Bruce Lockhart, L | 1945–46 |
| Atkinson, M L | 1908–09 | Bevan, W | 1887 | Bruce Lockhart, R B | 1937–38 |
| | | Biggar, M A | 1971 | Brutton, E B | 1883–85–86 |
| Back, F F | 1871–72 | Bird, D R J | 1958–59 | Bryce, R D H | 1965 |
| Bailey, G H | 1931 | Birdwood, C R B | 1932 | Bull, H A | 1874–75 |
| Balding, I A | 1961 | Bishop, C C | 1925 | Bunting, W L | 1894–95 |
| Balfour, A | 1896–97 | Black, M A | 1897–98 | Burt-Marshall, J | 1905 |
| Bance, J F | 1945 | Blair, P C B | 1910–11–12–13 | Burton, B C | 1882–83 |
| Barker, R E | 1966 | Blake, W H | 1875 | Bussey, W M | 1960–61–62 |
| Barlow, C S | 1923–24–25–26 | Boggon, R P | 1956 | Butler, E T | 1976–77 |
| Barlow, R M M | 1925 | Bole, E | 1945–46–47 | | |
| Barrow, C | 1950 | Bonham–Carter, J | 1873 | Campbell, D A | 1936 |
| Barter, A F | 1954–55–56 | Bordass, J H | 1923–24 | Campbell, H H | 1946 |

137

| | |
|---|---|
| Rendall, H D | 1892–93 |
| Reynolds, E P | 1909 |
| Rice, E | 1880–81 |
| Richards, T B | 1955 |
| Richardson, W P | 1883 |
| Rigby, J C A | 1892 |
| Riley, H | 1871–72–73 |
| Ritchie, W T | 1903–04 |
| Robbie, J C | 1977 |
| Roberts, A F | 1901–02 |
| Roberts, A J R | 1901–02 |
| Roberts, J | 1952–53–54 |
| Roberts, J | 1927–28 |
| Robertson, D D | 1892 |
| Robertson, I | 1967 |
| Robinson, A | 1886–87 |
| Robinson, B F | 1891–92–93 |
| Robinson, J J | 1892 |
| Robinson, P J | 1962 |
| Rocyn-Jones, D N | 1923 |
| Roden, W H | 1936–37 |
| Rodgers, A K | 1968–69–70 |
| Roffey, D B | 1874–75 |
| Rose, H | 1872 |
| Rosser, D W A | 1962–63–64 |
| Rosser, M F | 1972–73 |
| Ross-Skinner, W M | 1924 |
| Rotherham, A | 1890–91 |
| Rottenburg, H | 1898 |
| Rowell, W I | 1890 |
| Ryan, C J | 1966 |
| Ryan, P H | 1952–53 |
| Ryder, D C D | 1921–23 |
| | |
| Salmon, W B | 1883 |
| Sagar, J W | 1899–1900 |
| Sample, C H | 1882–83–84 |
| Sample, H W | 1884 |
| Sanderson, A B | 1901 |
| Saunders-Jacobs, S M | 1929 |
| Saville, C D | 1967–68–69–70 |
| Sawyer, B T C | 1910 |
| Saxon, K R J | 1919–21 |
| Scholfield, J A | 1909–10 |
| Schwarz, R O | 1893 |
| Scotland, K J F | 1958–59–60 |
| Scott, A W | 1945–48 |
| Scott, C T | 1899 |
| Scott, J M | 1927 |
| Scott, M T | 1885–86–87 |
| Scott, R R F | 1957 |
| Scott, W B | 1923–24 |
| Scott, W M | 1888 |
| Scoular, J G | 1905–06 |
| Seddon, E R H | 1921 |
| Shackleton, I R | 1968–69–70 |
| Shaw, P A V | 1977 |
| Shepherd, J K | 1950 |
| Sherrard, P | 1938 |
| Shipsides, J | 1970 |
| Shirer, J A | 1885 |
| Silk, D R W | 1953–54 |
| Sim, R G | 1966–67 |
| Simpson, C P | 1890 |
| Simpson, F W | 1930–31 |
| Sisson, J P | 1871 |
| Skinner, R C O | 1970–71 |
| Slater, K J P | 1964 |
| Smallwood, A M | 1919 |
| Smeddle, R W | 1928–29–30–31 |
| Smith, A F | 1873–74 |
| Smith, A R | 1954–55–56–57 |
| Smith, H K P | 1920 |
| Smith, H Y L | 1878–79–80–81 |
| Smith, J | 1889 |
| Smith, J J E | 1926 |
| Smith, J M | 1972 |

| | |
|---|---|
| Smith, J V | 1948–49–50 |
| Smith, K P | 1919 |
| Smith, M A | 1966–67 |
| Smith, P K | 1970 |
| Smith, S R | 1958–59 |
| Sobey, W H | 1925–26 |
| Spencer, J S | 1967–68–69 |
| Spicer, N | 1901–02 |
| Spray, K A N | 1946–47 |
| Sprot, A | 1871 |
| Staunton, H | 1891 |
| Stead, R J | 1977 |
| Steeds, J H | 1938 |
| Steel, D Q | 1877 |
| Steele, H K | 1970 |
| Steele, J T | 1879–80 |
| Steele-Bodger, M R | 1945–46 |
| Stevenson, H | 1977(R) |
| Stevenson, L E | 1884–85 |
| Steward, R | 1875–76 |
| Stewart, A A | 1975–76 |
| Stewart, J R | 1935 |
| Stokes, R R | 1921 |
| Stone, R J | 1901 |
| Storey, E | 1878–79–80 |
| Storey, L H T | 1909 |
| Storey, T W P | 1889–90–91–92 |
| Style, H B | 1921 |
| Surtees, A A | 1886 |
| Sutherland, J F | 1908 |
| Swanson, J C | 1938 |
| Swayne, F G | 1884–85–86 |
| Symington, A W | 1911–12–13 |
| Synge, J S | 1927 |
| | |
| Tait, J G | 1880–82 |
| Talbot, S C | 1900 |
| Tallent, J A | 1929–30–31 |
| Tanner, C C | 1930 |
| Tarsh, D N | 1955 |
| Taylor, A S | 1879–80–81 |
| Taylor, H B J | 1894–96 |
| Taylor, W J | 1926 |
| Templer, J L | 1881–82 |
| Thomas, B | 1960–61–62 |
| Thomas, D R | 1972–73–74 |
| Thomas, H W | 1912 |
| Thomas, J | 1945 |
| Thomas, N B | 1966 |
| Thomas, R C C | 1949 |
| Thomas, T J | 1895–96 |
| Thomas, W H | 1886–87 |
| Thompson, M J M | 1950 |
| Thompson, R | 1890 |
| Thompson, R V | 1948–49 |
| Thorman, W H | 1890 |
| Thorne, C | 1911 |
| Thornton, J F | 1976 |
| Threlfall, R | 1881–83 |
| Todd, A F | 1893–94–95 |
| Todd, T | 1888 |
| Touzel, C J C | 1874–75–76 |
| Tredwell, J R | 1968 |
| Trethewy, A | 1888 |
| Trubshaw, A R | 1919 |
| Tucker, W E | 1892–93–94 |
| Tucker, W E | 1922–23–24–25 |
| Tudsbery, F C T | 1907–08 |
| Turnbull, B R | 1924–25 |
| Turner, J A | 1956 |
| Turner, M F | 1946 |
| | |
| Umbers, R H | 1954 |
| Ure, C McG | 1911 |
| | |
| Valentine, G E | 1930 |
| Van Schalkwijk, J | 1906 |
| Vaughan, G P | 1949 |

| | |
|---|---|
| Vaux, J G | 1957 |
| Vincent, C A | 1913 |
| Vivian, J M | 1976 |
| | |
| Wace, H | 1873–74 |
| Wade, M R | 1958–59–60–61 |
| Waddell, G H | 1958–60–61 |
| Wainwright, J F | 1956 |
| Wakefield, W W | 1921–22 |
| Walker, A W | 1929–30 |
| Walker, E E | 1899–1900 |
| Walker, R M | 1963 |
| Walkey, J R | 1902 |
| Wallace, W M | 1912–13 |
| Waller, G S | 1932 |
| Wallis, H T | 1895–96 |
| Ward, R O C | 1903 |
| Ware, C H | 1882 |
| Warfield, P J | 1974 |
| Warlow, S | 1972–74 |
| Waters, F H | 1927–28–29 |
| Waters, J B | 1902–03–04 |
| Watherston, J G | 1931 |
| Watson, C F K | 1919–20 |
| Watt, J R | 1970 |
| Webb, G K M | 1964–65 |
| Webster, A P | 1971 |
| Wells, C M | 1891–92 |
| Wells, T U | 1951 |
| Wetson, M T | 1958–59–60 |
| Wheeler, P J F | 1951–52–53 |
| White, J B | 1922 |
| White, W N | 1947 |
| Whiteway, S E A | 1893 |
| Wiggins, C E M | 1928 |
| Wiggins, C M | 1964 |
| Wilkinson, R M | 1971–72–73 |
| Will, J G | 1911–12–13 |
| Williams, A G | 1926–27 |
| Williams, C C U | 1950 |
| Williams, C H | 1930 |
| Williams, C R | 1971–72–73 |
| Williams, D B | 1973 |
| Williams, E J H | 1946 |
| Williams, H A | 1876 |
| Williams, J M | 1949 |
| Williams, L T | 1874–75 |
| Williams, N E | 1950 |
| Williams, P T | 1888–89 |
| Williamson, I S | 1972 |
| Willis, H | 1949–50–51 |
| Wilson, A H | 1911–12–13 |
| Wilson, C P | 1877–78–79–80 |
| Wilton, C W | 1936 |
| Winthrop, W Y | 1871 |
| Wintle, T C | 1960–61 |
| Wood, G E | 1974–75–76 |
| Wood, G E C | 1919 |
| Woodall, B J C | 1951 |
| Woodroffe, O P | 1952 |
| Woods, S M J | 1888–89–90 |
| Wooller, W | 1933–34–35 |
| Wordsworth, A J | 1973–75 |
| Wotherspoon, W | 1888–89 |
| Wrench, D F B | 1960 |
| Wright, C C G | 1907–08 |
| Wrigley, P T | 1877–78–79–80 |
| Wynne, E H | 1887 |
| | |
| Yetts, R M | 1879–80–81 |
| Young, A B S | 1919–20 |
| Young, A T | 1922–23–24 |
| Young, J S | 1935 |
| Young, J V | 1906 |
| Young, P D | 1949 |
| Young, S K | 1974 |
| Young, W B | 1935–36–37 |

# THE BARBARIANS 1977–78

It was felt to be a great honour by the Barbarians when they were invited to play the British Lions, on their return from New Zealand, in a special match which represented rugby's major celebration of the Queen's Silver Jubilee. It also produced a cheque for £100,000 for the Jubilee Trust Fund Appeal, as well as contributions to other charities.

The Lions won the game itself, on 10 September, before a capacity crowd at Twickenham and in the presence of the Prince of Wales, by a goal, three penalty goals, and two tries (23 points) to a goal and two tries (14 points), and the fare provided was well up to the expected standard. The Barbarians faced a side made up entirely of Lions international match players, while their own team included six Welsh internationals, three from England, one from Scotland, and all three French Grand Slam flankers of 1977 in Rives, Skréla, and Bastiat. There were two uncapped players – David McKay, of Rosslyn Park, and David Richards, of Swansea.

In a thoroughly competitive match the Lions won deservedly – largely because of their magnificent forward play and, to a lesser extent, the shortcomings of the Baa–Baas as goal-kickers. The hectic exchanges of the opening minutes soon died down, but the abrasiveness of the battle up front and the competitiveness of the game as a whole certainly did not. Bennett kicked two early penalty goals for the Lions before Irvine produced one of his characteristic long runs, on a wide arc, to breach the Barbarian defence. It led to a fine try, by Fenwick, which Bennett converted, and Irvine himself kicked a superbly-struck penalty goal from 50 metres to put the Barbarians 0–15 down at half-time.

In the second half, the Barbarians raised their effort to come more into the game. A clear overlap on the left wing was not used to advantage, but further pressure brought results. Gravell ran on following a 'crash ball' through the Lions midfield to give J P R Williams a scoring pass and the Barbarians' first try. Gerald Davies, hardly the most likely of goal-kickers, converted.

This was the signal for the Lions to mount a further onslaught. Fenwick outsmarted the Barbarian defence and placed a neat chip-kick to the wing for Evans to gather and score. Then Irvine broke away to add a third try – unconverted, as was that of Evans. In a final rally the Barbarians produced some of the best rugby of the game, with Rives very much the inspiration in two final tries. First he gave the pass that enabled Gravell to run through and score. Then, a few minutes later, he made the running for a try by McKay.

This was no exhibition match, as far as the players were concerned, but it produced an enthralling contest, and a display befitting a Royal occasion. The dinner in the evening, with an unprecedented gathering of Lions and Barbarians, past and present, provided a fitting climax to a memorable day.

**British Isles:** A R Irvine (Heriot's FP and Scotland); P J Squires (Harrogate and England), S P Fenwick (Bridgend and Wales), I R McGeechan (Headingley and Scotland), G L Evans (Newport and Wales); P Bennett (Llanelli and Wales) *(capt)*, D W Morgan (Stewart's Melville and Scotland); *No 8* W P Duggan (Blackrock Coll and Ireland); *Second Row* D L Quinnell (Llanelli and Wales), W B Beaumont (Fylde and England), G L Brown (West of Scotland and Scotland), A Neary (Broughton Park and England); *Front Row* F E Cotton (Sale and England), P J Wheeler (Leicester and England), G Price (Pontypool and Wales) *Replacement* H E Rees (Neath) for Squires (60 mins)
**Scorers** *Tries:* Fenwick, Evans, Irvine *Conversion:* Bennett *Penalty Goals:* Bennett (2), Irvine
**Barbarians:** J P R Williams (Bridgend and Wales); T G R Davies (Cardiff and Wales) *(capt)*, R W R Gravell (Llanelli and Wales), C P Kent (Rosslyn Park and England), D J McKay (Rosslyn Park); D S Richards (Swansea), G O Edwards (Cardiff and Wales); *No 8* J-P Bastiat (Dax and France); *Second Row* J-C Skréla (Stade Toulousain and France), R M Wilkinson (Bedford and England), G A D Wheel (Swansea and Wales), J-P Rives (Stade Toulousain and France); *Front Row* F M D Knill (Cardiff and Wales), D F Madsen (Gosforth and Scotland), B G Nelmes (Cardiff and England)
**Scorers** *Tries:* Williams, Gravell, McKay *Conversion:* Davies
**Referee** N R Sanson (Scotland)

Understandably, the game against the Lions was the high-spot of the Barbarians' season, but their subsequent matches produced much entertaining rugby, with only one more defeat.

At Leicester, in front of one of the biggest crowds seen for a club match at Welford Road, the Baa-Baas prevented the home team adding to their wins of the previous two years. It was a most exciting contest, and a credit to both teams, for in spite of the muddy conditions the players went in for all-out attack. Although Leicester's forwards posed a problem, the Barbarians won by two goals to one, all the scores coming in the second half. The winning try was unusual in that its scorer, Alun Lewis, the British Lions' scrum-half, was on the field as a replacement left-wing for the injured Elgan Rees.

After this close contest, the Mobbs Memorial Match, at Northampton, proved a comparative romp for the Barbarians in perfect conditions. However, the match was not as one-sided as the scoreline, 40–12, might suggest. East Midlands, in fact, were leading at half-time, but after the interval, with the wind at their backs, the Barbarians took command in style. Altogether they scored eight tries, including a hat-trick by the new England full-back, David Caplan. It was a record ninth successive victory for the Barbarians in this match.

The Easter tour of South Wales had its ups and downs, the opening game, at Penarth, producing the highest score in Barbarian history – 84 points, including 15 tries. By an odd coincidence the Barbarians again produced a scrum-half, on this occasion Alan Lawson, as a replacement try-scorer on the left wing.

Perhaps inspired by the previous day's frolics, the touring team did well to beat Cardiff by 12 clear points, 20–8, in front of 16,000 spectators at the Arms Park – the most the new club ground has held. Superb defence, good forward play – under the leadership of Terry Cobner – a lively scrum-half performance by Alan Lawson, and a fine try by John Scott had much to do with the Baa–Baas' success.

Injuries took their toll in the last two matches of the tour. Against Swansea, shortly afterwards to become Welsh Cup champions, the touring team were leading by nine points at half-time, but then the home side took full advantage of the Barbarians' state of disarray, arising from all their injuries. These had reached the point where Malcolm Young, the England scrum-half, had to operate as a replacement wing-forward for more than half the game. Eventually, with the help of six second-half tries, Swansea recorded their biggest win in this match since 1904. In the final game at Newport only the relentless rain deprived the home team of victory. For the first time in Barbarian history the match was abandoned – after 68 minutes by referee Jeff Kelleher. Newport, at that stage, were 13 points up and in a commanding position; but with the players on both sides floundering in pools of water, the end was a merciful release.

## PLAYERS 1977–78

**Abbreviations** BI–British Isles, L–Leicester, EM–East Midlands, SW1–Penarth, SW2–Cardiff, SW3–Swansea, SW4–Newport, R–Replacement *New Barbarian*

**Full-backs** J P R Williams (Bridgend) [BI]; D W N Caplan* (Headingley) [EM, SW1, SW4]; A J Hignell* (Cambridge U) [L]; B H Hay (Boroughmuir) [SW2, SW3]

**Threequarters** T G R Davies (Cardiff) [BI]; D J McKay (Rosslyn Park) [BI]; W B B Gammell* (Edinburgh Wanderers) [EM, SW2, SW3]; G L Evans* (Newport) [EM]; M W O'Callaghan* (Cambridge U) [L]; H E Rees (Neath) [L, SW1, SW3]; V L Jenkins* (Bridgend) [SW1, SW4]; M A C Slemen (Liverpool) [SW2, SW4]; R W R Gravell (Llanelli) [BI]; C P Kent (Rosslyn Park) [BI]; J M Renwick (Hawick) [EM, L]; M K Swain* (Moseley) [EM, SW1, SW3, SW4];

I R McGeechan (Headingley) [L]; A R McKibbin* (London Irish) [SW1];
A G Cranston* (Hawick) [SW2, SW3]; P W Dodge* (Leicester) [SW2, SW4];
A D Lewis (London Welsh) [L (R)]
**Half-backs** P Bennett (Llanelli) [SW1]; D S Richards (Swansea) [BI, L];
M J Cooper (Moseley) [EM, SW2, SW4]; A J P Ward* (Garryowen) [SW3];
G O Edwards (Cardiff) [BI]; D B Williams (Newport) [EM]; M Young (Gosforth)
[SW1, SW3 (R), SW4]; A J M Lawson (London Scottish) [L, SW1 (R), SW2, SW3]
**Forwards** B G Nelmes (Cardiff) [BI, L]; F M D Knill (Cardiff) [BI, SW4];        143
G Howls* (Ebbw Vale) [L]; J McLauchlan (Jordanhill) [EM]; T Pryor* (Redruth)
[EM, SW1, SW3]; C White* (Gosforth) [SW1, SW3 (R)]; S J Richardson*
(Aberavon) [SW2, SW3]; W H Graves (Moseley) [SW2, SW4]; D F Madsen
(Gosforth) [BI, EM, SW1, SW3]; P C Whelan* (Garryowen) [L]; P J Wheeler
(Leicester) [SW2, SW4]; R M Wilkinson (Bedford) [BI, L (R), SW3, SW4];
G A D Wheel (Swansea) [BI]; A J Tomes (Hawick) [L]; W B Beaumont (Fylde) [L,
SW2, SW3]; C Davis* (Newbridge) [EM, SW1, SW4]; J Murray* (Cork
Constitution) [EM]; A J Martin (Aberavon) [SW1]; M J Colclough* (Angoulême)
[SW2, SW3]; J-P Rives (Stade Toulousain) [BI]; J-C Skréla (Stade Toulousain) [BI];
J-P Bastiat* (Dax) [BI]; M A Biggar (London Scottish) [L]; T P David
(Pontypridd) [L, EM, SW1, SW4]; N D Mantell (Rosslyn Park) [L]; D G Leslie
(West of Scotland) [EM]; J Dowson* (Wakefield) [EM]; A G Ripley (Rosslyn Park)
[SW1, SW4]; D S M MacDonald (West of Scotland) [SW1, SW4]; M J Rafter*
(Bristol) [SW2, SW3]; T J Cobner (Pontypool) [SW2]; J P Scott* (Rosslyn Park)
[SW2, SW3]

## RESULTS 1977–78

**Played 6   Won 4   Lost 2   Pts for 185   Against 97**

**1977**
10 September   **Lost to BRITISH ISLES** at Twickenham
1G 2T (14) to 1G 3PG 2T (23)

27 December   **Beat Leicester** at Leicester
2G (12) to 1G (6)

**1978**
8 March   **Beat East Midlands** at Northampton
4G 4T (40) to 1G 1DG 1PG (12)

24 March   **Beat Penarth** at Penarth
12G 3T (84) to 2G (12)

25 March   **Beat Cardiff** at Cardiff
2G 2T (20) to 2T (8)

27 March   **Lost to Swansea** at Swansea
2G 1PG (15) to 3G 1DG 1PG 3T (36)

28 March   Match v **Newport** abandoned after 68 minutes, with
Newport leading by 1G 1PG 1T (13) to 0

# THE INTER-SERVICES TOURNAMENT 1977–78

**Rupert Cherry**

For only the seventh time since the triangular Inter-Services Tournament began 58 years ago the series ended in a triple tie. It was probably a just result because no team really measured up to the description of champions. The Navy, defending the title, began by beating the Army by a single point in a thrilling match. Even if the skill was not out of the very top drawer, both sides played well, running the ball as much as they could.

The standard, alas, was not maintained. In their next game the Navy, facing a combination of strong wind and driving rain as well as the RAF, were no match for either. Pugh, the RAF captain, scored a try and Green, his partner at half-back, did the rest with his goal-kicking. This gave the RAF an excellent chance of winning the tournament, but they failed to take it. Frost had forced the postponement of their match with the Army until near the end of the season, when although not quite at full strength, the Army proved to be the steadier of two rather mediocre sides.

## 4 March, Twickenham
### Royal Navy 17 (1G 1PG 2T)   Army 16 (1G 2PG 1T)

**Royal Navy:** Lt P R Lea (HMS Seahawk); Lt C R English (HMS Thunderer), PO J Hopkins (HMS Osprey), Lt Cdr A G Jones (HMS Sultan), PO A Hamlett (HMS Collingwood); Sub Lt J Leigh (BRNC, Dartmouth), Lt K H Martin (HMS Royal Arthur); *No 8* Lt  L C P Merrick (HMS Pembroke); *Second Row* CPO P Dunn (HMS Heron) (*capt*), CPO M J Lane (HMS Defiance), Lt C A Richards (HMS Centurion), L/Cpl R Tinson (RM Depot, Deal); *Front Row* LPT T H W Davies (HMS Drake), Lt P H Plumb (HMS Dryad), Lt J C Ackerman (HMS Daedalus)
**Scorers** *Tries:* English, Hamlett, Richards  *Conversion:* Leigh *Penalty Goal:* Leigh
**Army:** Lt P J Wright (King's Own Borderers); Cpl K A'Hearne (Royal Regt of Wales), Cpl S G Jackson (RAMC), Lt D E Stevens (RE), Cpl D B Reynolds (REME); Lt W A N Atkinson (Duke of Wellington's Regt), Cpl G Davies (Queen's Dragoon Guards); *No 8* Capt A J Hoon (RE) (*capt*); *Second Row* Cpl G O W Williams (Duke of Wellington's Regt), Cpl D P McCracken (RMP), Capt J M Bowles (RCT), Lt J Baxter (RA); *Front Row* Cpl N J Gray (RE), Cpl R J Matthews (RE), Cpl M Jenkins (Royal Regt of Wales)
**Scorers** *Tries:* Davies, A'Hearne  *Conversion:* Atkinson  *Penalty Goals:* McCracken, Atkinson
**Referee** C Norling (Wales)

## 25 March, Twickenham
### RAF 15 (1G 2PG 1DG)   Royal Navy 8 (2T)

**RAF:** AC P Bate (Swinderby); Cpl M Smith (Sealand), Cpl R Seward (Brize Norton), Cpl S Grey (Uxbridge), J/Tech S Rogers (Scampton); Cpl A Green

(Northolt), J/Tech K Pugh (Scampton) (*capt*); *No 8* F/O N Gillingham
(Waddington); *Second Row* Cpl W Jenkins (Stanmore Park), SAC J Orwin (Brize
Norton), Cpl C Rayner (Brize Norton), SAC G Still (Hereford); *Front Row*
SAC B Dix (Stafford), Sgt A McCrindle (HQ 18 Group), Cpl M Jones (Marham)
**Scorers** *Try:* Pugh  *Conversion:* Green  *Penalty Goals:* Green (2)  *Dropped Goal:*
Green
**Royal Navy:** Lt G H Fabian (HMS Seahawk); Lt C R English (HMS Thunderer),
PO J Hopkins (HMS Osprey), Lt Cmdr A G Jones (HMS Sultan), PO A Hamlett
(HMS Collingwood); Sub Lt J Leigh (BRNC, Dartmouth), Lt K H Martin
(HMS Royal Arthur); *No 8* PO M H Connolly (HMS Hermes); *Second Row*
CPO P Dunn (HMS Heron) (*capt*), CPO M J Lane (HMS Defiance),
Lt C A Richards (HMS Centurion, DNR), Cpl R Tinson (RM Depot, Deal); *Front
Row* LPT T H W Davies (HMS Drake), Lt P Norrington-Davies (HMS
Greenwich), Lt J C Ackerman (HMS Daedalus)
**Scorers** *Tries:* Tinson, Martin
**Referee** Corris Thomas (Wales)

## 22 April, Twickenham
## Army 16 (1G 2PG 1T)   RAF 6 (2PG)

**Army:** L/Cpl B J Abbott (REME); L/Cpl K A'Hearne (Royal Regt of Wales),
Sgt D Prowse (REME), Cpl S G Jackson (RAMC), Cpl D B Reynolds (REME);
Lt W A N Atkinson (Duke of Wellington's Regt), Cpl G Davies (Queen's
Dragoon Guards); *No 8* Capt A J Hoon (RE) (*capt*); *Second Row*
Cpl G O W Williams (Duke of Wellington's Regt), S/Sgt P Smith (RAOC),
Capt J M Bowles (RCT), Lt J Baxter (RA); *Front Row* Cpl N J Gray (RE),
Cpl R J Matthews (RE), Cpl M Jenkins (Royal Regt of Wales)
**Scorers** *Tries:* A'Hearne, Bowles  *Conversion:* Abbott  *Penalty Goals:* Abbott (2)
**RAF:** A/C P Bate (Brize Norton); Cpl M Smith (Sealand), Cpl S Grey (Uxbridge),
Cpl R Seward (Brize Norton), J/Tech S Rogers (Scampton); Cpl A Green
(Northolt), Cpl K Pugh (Scampton) (*capt*); *No 8* F/O N Gillingham (Waddington);
*Second Row* SAC G Still (Hereford), SAC J Orwin (Brize Norton), Cpl C Rayner
(Brize Norton), Cpl W Jenkins (Stanmore Park); *Front Row* SAC B Dix (Stafford),
Sgt A McCrindle (Northwood), Cpl M Jones (Raynham)
**Scorer** *Penalty Goals:* Green (2)
**Referee** R C Quittenton (England)

### Inter-Services Tournament Champions

*The Army have won the Tournament outright 23 times, the Royal Navy 14 times, and the RAF 7
times.*

| | | | | |
|---|---|---|---|---|
| 1920 **Navy** | 1930 **Army** | 1947 **RAF** | 1957 **Army** | 1968 **Army** |
| 1921 **Navy** | 1931 **Navy** | 1948 Triple Tie | 1958 **RAF** | 1969 **Army** |
| 1922 **Navy** | 1932 **Army** | 1949 {**Army** **RAF** | 1959 **RAF** | 1970 **Navy** |
| 1923 **RAF** | 1933 **Army** | | 1960 **Army** | 1971 **RAF** |
| 1924 Triple Tie | 1934 **Army** | 1950 **Army** | 1961 **Navy** | 1972 **Army** |
| 1925 {**Army** **RAF** | 1935 Triple Tie | 1951 **Navy** | 1962 **RAF** | 1973 **Navy** |
| | 1936 **Army** | 1952 **Army** | 1963 **Army** | 1974 **Navy** |
| 1926 **Army** | 1937 **Army** | 1953 **Army** | 1964 **Army** | 1975 Triple Tie |
| 1927 **Navy** | 1938 **Navy** | 1954 Triple Tie | 1965 **Army** | 1976 **Army** |
| 1928 **Army** | 1939 **Navy** | 1955 **RAF** | 1966 **Navy** | 1977 **Navy** |
| 1929 **Army** | 1946 **Army** | 1956 Triple Tie | 1967 **Army** | 1978 Triple Tie |

**Royal Navy v Army** Royal Navy have won 28, Army 31, and 2 matches have been drawn
**Royal Navy v RAF** Royal Navy have won 33, RAF 16, and 4 matches have been drawn
**Army v RAF** Army have won 32, RAF 14, and 7 matches have been drawn

# UAU CHAMPIONSHIP 1977–78

**8 March, Twickenham**
**Loughborough Students 17** (1G 1PG 2T)
**Bristol University 0**

The 1978 final failed almost completely to live up to expectations. Instead of a flowing game between two sides committed to attacking rugby, the match stuttered badly. Bristol played substantially below their best and, hampered by the early loss of fly-half Masters, became almost willing victims of the formidable Loughborough loose forwards.

In the first half Bristol had the wind at their backs, but failed to seize an early advantage, squandering five attempts at goal. Their best opportunities lay with the running game and they gained ample possession from the set pieces, notably through the work of Troughton at the line-out; but keen tackling by the opposition and poor passing contributed to a general lack of penetration. Loughborough, after a hesitant start, played a more disciplined type of game and took the lead with a try by Whiteley after Woodward and Morgan had created the opening.

After 25 minutes Masters left the field and Barclay became the first replacement to appear in a UAU final. This disrupted Bristol's back play even more, and although they continued to run the ball from all parts of the field, there was a general looseness in their play which was eagerly fed on by the marauding Morgan. Loughborough's support play was of a much higher quality and when Whiteley increased their lead with a penalty goal early in the second half, the writing was on the wall. Woodward then scored a try and Howard Thomas added another, converted by Whiteley, which put the result beyond doubt.

**Loughborough Students:** A J Whiteley (Bingley GS); P Iddon (Merchant Taylors', Crosby), R Bodenham (Brockley CS), C Woodward (HMS Conway), A K Williams (St Julian's, Newport); R Owen (Pen-y-dre CS, Merthyr), I G Wright (Hutton GS); *No 8* C J O'Callaghan (St Joseph's, Port Talbot) (*capt*); *Second Row* H Thomas (Glyn GS), J Watts (Bransgrove CS, Harlow), P J de Lacy (Hull GS), B D Morgan (Maesydderwen CS); *Front Row* M G Thomas (Duffryn CS, Port Talbot), S Hardy (Great Baddow CS), I Lindley (Bingley GS)
**Scorers** *Tries:* Whiteley, Woodward, H Thomas  *Conversion:* Whiteley  *Penalty Goal:* Whiteley
**Bristol University:** R W Wright (Woodlands, Coventry); I Horsfall (Worth),

J Watson (Broxbourne) (*capt*), D Bowrey (Queen Elizabeth Hosp, Bristol),
M Chapman (Hurstpierpoint); J P Masters (Sandbach), J Chandler (Whitgift); *No 8*
P G H Horton (Solihull); *Second Row* P Cumber (Hampton GS), K Francis
(Skinner's, Tunbridge Wells), A Troughton (Warwick), A Evans (Clifton); *Front
Row* W A Hobhouse (Eton), I Paterson (Bangor GS), D J Doole (Harrow CGS)
*Replacement* I Barclay (Queen Elizabeth GS, Barnet) for Masters (25 mins)
**Referee** R C Quittenton (London)
(Loughborough have now won the Championship 16 times, Swansea 7,
Liverpool 6, Bristol 5, Durham and Manchester 4 each, Cardiff 3, Bangor twice,
Birmingham, Leeds, Newcastle and UWIST once each.)

147

The earlier rounds of the Championship were closely con-
tested, not least at the semi-final stage, when both matches were
settled only in the closing minutes. In each case the standard of
play was of high quality and the match between Durham and
Loughborough at Sheffield was much enjoyed by a large
crowd. Durham had hoped to win through their forwards, but
could not penetrate a stout defence. Loughborough's back
division brought off some sparkling movements and they were
worthy winners on a day when there was not much between the
two teams. In the second semi-final at Warwick, Bristol just
managed to beat Leeds with a dropped goal in the dying seconds. They had shown more attacking skill than their opponents, but the latter were able to stay in the game through the
goalkicking of their scrum-half Merriman.

One of the surprises of the season was the apparent decline in
Welsh rugby supremacy. Swansea were comfortably beaten by
Bristol in the quarter-final, and though UWIST had more
excuse for being knocked out at the same ᵛ stage at
Loughborough, it seemed obvious that back play in the Prin-
cipality had deteriorated. Once more East Anglia gave notice
that the newer institutions were becoming a force, although
they were heavily beaten by Durham.

The changing pattern of student rugby will be given an extra
tinge this season with the amalgamation of Exeter University
and St Luke's. It creates a further power in the south west,
with the possibility of a meeting with Loughborough at
Twickenham in the Championship final. On the national scene,
the decision to award the English Students XV a fixture with
the touring Argentinians was a further encouragement, and the
match at Gloucester in October will be eagerly awaited.

**Results of representative matches:** Welsh Universities 12, Scottish Universities
12 (Swansea); Scottish Universities 10, English Universities 4 (Dundee); English
Universities 7, Welsh Universities 3 (Birmingham); UAU 12, British Colleges 17
(Fylde); British Polytechnics 12, UAU 8 (Coventry); French Universities 25,
British Universities 3 (Béthune)

# DIVISIONAL RESULTS
## Eastern Division
### NORTH-EAST GROUP

| | P | W | D | L | F | A | Pts |
|---|---|---|---|---|---|---|---|
| **Durham** | 2 | 2 | 0 | 0 | 44 | 3 | 4 |
| **Newcastle** | 2 | 1 | 0 | 1 | 23 | 26 | 2 |
| **Hull** | 2 | 0 | 0 | 2 | 3 | 41 | 0 |

### EAST-MIDLANDS GROUP

| | P | W | D | L | F | A | Pts |
|---|---|---|---|---|---|---|---|
| **Leeds** | 3 | 3 | 0 | 0 | 109 | 25 | 6 |
| **Sheffield** | 3 | 2 | 0 | 1 | 23 | 44 | 4 |
| **Nottingham** | 3 | 1 | 0 | 2 | 25 | 33 | 2 |
| **Bradford** | 3 | 0 | 0 | 3 | 18 | 73 | 0 |

*Winners of each group play runners-up in other group in Round 1 of the National Draw*

## Western Division
### NORTH-WEST GROUP

| | P | W | D | L | F | A | Pts |
|---|---|---|---|---|---|---|---|
| **Manchester** | 4 | 4 | 0 | 0 | 71 | 25 | 8 |
| **Lancaster** | 4 | 3 | 0 | 1 | 53 | 35 | 6 |
| **Liverpool** | 4 | 2 | 0 | 2 | 31 | 28 | 4 |
| **Keele** | 4 | 1 | 0 | 3 | 26 | 45 | 2 |
| **Salford** | 4 | 0 | 0 | 4 | 21 | 69 | 0 |

### WEST-MIDLANDS GROUP

| | P | W | D | L | F | A | Pts |
|---|---|---|---|---|---|---|---|
| **Loughborough** | 4 | 4 | 0 | 0 | 126 | 28 | 8 |
| **Warwick** | 4 | 3 | 0 | 1 | 60 | 34 | 6 |
| **Aston** | 4 | 2 | 0 | 2 | 44 | 63 | 4 |
| **Birmingham** | 4 | 1 | 0 | 3 | 49 | 71 | 2 |
| **Leicester** | 4 | 0 | 0 | 4 | 32 | 115 | 0 |

*Winners of each group play runners-up in other group in Round 1 of the National Draw*
*Third-placed teams in each group play off for place in National Draw*

**PLAY-OFF**
**Liverpool beat Aston 26–6** at Liverpool

## Southern Division
### SOUTH-EAST GROUP
**(a) North Thames**

| | P | W | D | L | F | A | Pts |
|---|---|---|---|---|---|---|---|
| **East Anglia** | 4 | 4 | 0 | 0 | 160 | 21 | 8 |
| **Brunel** | 4 | 3 | 0 | 1 | 209 | 39 | 6 |
| **The City** | 4 | 2 | 0 | 2 | 39 | 92 | 4 |
| **UCL** | 4 | 1 | 0 | 3 | 57 | 108 | 2 |
| **Essex** | 4 | 0 | 0 | 4 | 22 | 227 | 0 |

**(b) South Thames**

| | P | W | D | L | F | A | Pts |
|---|---|---|---|---|---|---|---|
| **Surrey** | 3 | 3 | 0 | 0 | 46 | 24 | 6 |
| **Kent** | 3 | 2 | 0 | 1 | 71 | 20 | 4 |
| **LSE** | 3 | 1 | 0 | 2 | 27 | 44 | 2 |
| **Sussex** | 3 | 0 | 0 | 3 | 15 | 71 | 0 |

*Winners of North Thames and South Thames play off for South-East Group title (both go into National Draw)*

**Result: East Anglia beat Surrey 14–6** at Guildford

*Runners-up in North Thames and South Thames play off for place in Divisional 'decider' against third-placed team in South-West group, for place in National Draw*

**PLAY-OFF**
**Brunel beat Kent 32–4** at Canterbury

## SOUTH-WEST GROUP

|  | P | W | D | L | F | A | Pts |
|---|---|---|---|---|---|---|---|
| **Bristol** | 4 | 4 | 0 | 0 | 149 | 34 | 8 |
| **Exeter** | 4 | 3 | 0 | 1 | 58 | 46 | 6 |
| **Southampton** | 4 | 2 | 0 | 2 | 54 | 39 | 4 |
| **Reading** | 4 | 1 | 0 | 3 | 41 | 91 | 2 |
| **Bath** | 4 | 0 | 0 | 4 | 27 | 119 | 0 |

*Winners of each group play runners-up in other group in Round 1 of National Draw*
*Third-placed team plays winner of play off in South-East group for a place in the National Draw*

**PLAY-OFF**
**Brunel beat Southampton 40–3** at Uxbridge

---

# Welsh Division

|  | P | W | D | L | F | A | Pts |
|---|---|---|---|---|---|---|---|
| **Swansea** | 5 | 5 | 0 | 0 | 92 | 32 | 10 |
| **UWIST** | 5 | 4 | 0 | 1 | 73 | 34 | 8 |
| **Bangor** | 5 | 2 | 0 | 3 | 54 | 54 | 4 |
| **Aberystwyth** | 5 | 2 | 0 | 3 | 27 | 38 | 4 |
| **Cardiff** | 5 | 2 | 0 | 3 | 55 | 85 | 4 |
| **Cardiff Medicals** | 5 | 0 | 0 | 5 | 38 | 96 | 0 |

*Winners and runners-up go direct into the National Draw*

---

**ROUND 1 (National Draw)**
**Durham beat Sheffield 15–0** at Durham
**Leeds beat Newcastle 19–0** at Leeds
**Manchester beat Warwick 8–3** at Manchester
**Loughborough beat Lancaster 24–0** at Loughborough
**East Anglia beat Exeter 12–10** at Norwich
**Bristol beat Surrey 55–0** at Bristol
**Swansea beat Brunel 34–16** at Swansea
**UWIST beat Liverpool 12–0** at Cardiff

**QUARTER-FINALS**
**Bristol beat Swansea 31–7** at Swansea
**Leeds beat Manchester 34–8** at Leeds
**Durham beat East Anglia 34–7** at Norwich
**Loughborough beat UWIST 12–3** at Loughborough

**SEMI-FINALS**
**Bristol beat Leeds 15–12** at Coventry
**Loughborough beat Durham 14–12** at Sheffield

**FINAL**
**Loughborough beat Bristol 17–0** at Twickenham

**UAU SEVENS TOURNAMENT** (at The City University, London)
**Quarter-Finals:** Manchester 12, Bradford 6; Loughborough I 40, Nottingham 0;
Loughborough II 19, Bristol 16; Reading I 13, Durham I 6
**Semi-Finals:** Loughborough I 24, Manchester 0; Reading I 10, Loughborough II 4
**Final:** Loughborough I 38, Reading I 4

# HOSPITALS' CHALLENGE CUP 1977–78

**8 March, Richmond Athletic Ground**
**St Mary's Hospital 30** (2G 1DG 1PG 3T)
**The London Hospital 12** (1G 1DG 1PG)

St Mary's won the Hospitals' Cup for the 19th time, and thoroughly deserved to do so. It was one of the best finals for many years, with the winners' score being the highest recorded since Guy's beat The London 42–3 in 1922.

St Mary's came into the Cup picture again because, as so often in the past, they had an excellent back division, including Alun Lewis, the British Lion, at scrum-half, and Alistair McKibbin, the Ireland centre. But The London pack and Condon, their Ireland 'B' scrum-half, also acquitted themselves well.

Young and McKibbin scored unconverted tries for Mary's early on, but Condon then kicked a penalty goal, converted a try by Holman and dropped a goal from 40 metres to put The London 12–8 ahead. St Mary's came back with a splendid try by Alun Lewis, after seven players had handled, and after that there was no stopping them.

The Hospitals' Cup had been stolen from St Bartholomew's library in the close season, so St Mary's were presented with the original cup, first played for in 1875, which St Thomas's won outright in the 1890s. A new cup is being made.

**St Mary's:** M J Meredith (*capt*); C Elias, A R McKibbin, M Greenhalgh, R Young; C Ralston, A D Lewis; *No 8* I Lloyd; *Second Row* A Wakefield, P Sampson, J Mountjoy, M Hickey; *Front Row* A Moir, M Dunkerton, N Enevoldson
*Replacement* M Williams for Young (70 mins)
**Scorers** *Tries:* Young, McKibbin, Lewis, Ralston, Elias *Conversions:* Greenhalgh (2) *Penalty Goal:* Greenhalgh *Dropped Goal:* Ralston
**The London:** S Hignell; A Williams, R Holman, C Lammiman, B Whitmill; H Condon, M Williams; *No 8* J O'Brien; *Second Row* T Lewis, P Szypryt, R Kerr, S Daniels; *Front Row* S Young, D Cousins, D Chidwick (*capt*)
**Scorers** *Try:* Holman *Conversion:* Condon *Penalty Goal:* Condon *Dropped Goal:* Condon
**Referee** R F Johnson (London Society)

**Full results**
**1st round:** UCH 12, Middlesex 18; Guy's 16, Charing Cross 0 (after 7–7 draw); St George's 9 Royal Free 52; KCH 12, St Thomas's 3
**2nd round:** St Bartholomew's 25, Middlesex 0; The London 9, Guy's 3; St Mary's 44, Royal Free 6; Westminster 16, KCH 0
**Semi-finals:** St Bartholomew's 6, The London 10 (after 3–3 draw); St Mary's 3, Westminster 0
**Final:** The London 12, St Mary's 30

*Guy's have won the Cup 30 times, St Mary's 19, St Thomas's 17, The London 10, St Bartholomew's 9, St George's 3, Westminster twice, and Middlesex once.*

# THE MIDDLESEX SEVENS 1978

**Rupert Cherry**

Most people expected Richmond to win the 1978 Middlesex Sevens as they had done in three of the four previous years; London Scottish dearly would have liked to do so in their centenary year; but as it turned out the Harlequins stole the show before the usual crowd of nearly 60,000, and set three new records in beating Rosslyn Park 40–12 in the final. It was the eighth time the 'Quins had won the tournament since it began in 1926 – one more than the seven times of London Welsh; and the score in the final set new high-watermarks for the winners' total and winning margin.

Richmond were knocked out in the first round of the day, by Blackheath, but the Harlequins, who put their trust in sheer speed to carry them through – they played their wing-threequarter Lambert as a prop – looked wellnigh unstoppable right from the start. Their running was swift and sure, and they covered and tackled like fiends. In addition, the speed of Wood, the cleverness and enterprise of Gilbert, and splendid goal-kicking by Lamden contributed much to their success. They played a magnificent semi-final to beat London Welsh 12–10, with Gilbert excelling himself. Both he and Alexander made superb tackles on the swift British Lion Clive Rees to prevent certain tries, and Gilbert's 55 metres dash for a try of his own was one of the best things of the day.

Rosslyn Park defeated Loughborough Students in another fine semi-final by the same score and, being in the top half of the draw, came to the final fresher than the Harlequins. But they had lost two forwards, Scott and Bazelle, in the semi-final and were hardly in the game. Wood, Gilbert, and Lamden were too fast and clever for them, and at half-time the 'Quins led 24–0. Ian George revived some slight hope for the Park with a try and Lloyd ran beautifully for a second one, with George converting both. However, the Harlequins came back strongly, and at the end they were running the Park off their feet.

The two 'guest' sides, Gosforth and Hawick, were both eliminated early on – Gosforth in the first round of the day and Hawick in the second. No fewer than 240 teams had taken part in the preliminary rounds on the previous Saturday. Hemel Hempstead, Maidstone, and Old Reigatians II were among those who came through, but all fell by the wayside at their first attempt.

## RESULTS

**Sixth round:** Gosforth 4, St Luke's College, Exeter 12; Loughborough Students 16, Wasps 12; Rosslyn Park 32, Hemel Hempstead 0; London Scottish 12, Bath 18; Hawick 12, Old Reigatians II 6; Maidstone 6, Harlequins 26; London Irish 0, London Welsh 32; Blackheath 18, Richmond 12

**Seventh round:** St Luke's 6, Loughborough 18; Rosslyn Park 14, Bath 6; Hawick 6, Harlequins 14; London Welsh 24, Blackheath 4

**Semi-finals:** Loughborough 10, Rosslyn Park 12; Harlequins 12, London Welsh 10

**Final:** Harlequins 40, Rosslyn Park 12

152

### TEAMS IN THE FINAL

**Harlequins:** G E Wood; D A Cooke (*capt*); G Gilbert, C St. J Lamden; A C Alexander, K J Douglas, C W Lambert

**Scorers** *Tries:* Lambert, Douglas (2), Wood (2), Cooke, Lamden, Gilbert *Conversions:* Lamden (3), Lambert

**Rosslyn Park:** G Lloyd; R Fisher; N Anderson, I George; D Starling, P J Warfield, A G Ripley (*capt*)

**Scorers** *Tries:* George, Lloyd *Conversions:* George (2)

**Referee** R C Quittenton

## WINNERS

| | | | | |
|---|---|---|---|---|
| 1926 | **Harlequins** | | 1953 | **Richmond** |
| 1927 | **Harlequins** | | 1954 | **Rosslyn Park** |
| 1928 | **Harlequins** | | 1955 | **Richmond** |
| 1929 | **Harlequins** | | 1956 | **London Welsh** |
| 1930 | **London Welsh** | | 1957 | **St Luke's College** |
| 1931 | **London Welsh** | | 1958 | **Blackheath** |
| 1932 | **Blackheath** | | 1959 | **Loughborough Colleges** |
| 1933 | **Harlequins** | | 1960 | **London Scottish** |
| 1934 | **Barbarians** | | 1961 | **London Scottish** |
| 1935 | **Harlequins** | | 1962 | **London Scottish** |
| 1936 | **Sale** | | 1963 | **London Scottish** |
| 1937 | **London Scottish** | | 1964 | **Loughborough Colleges** |
| 1938 | **Metropolitan Police** | | 1965 | **London Scottish** |
| 1939 | **Cardiff** | | 1966 | **Loughborough Colleges** |
| 1940 | **St Mary's Hospital** | | 1967 | **Harlequins** |
| 1941 | **Cambridge University** | | 1968 | **London Welsh** |
| 1942 | **St Mary's Hospital** | | 1969 | **St Luke's College** |
| 1943 | **St Mary's Hospital** | | 1970 | **Loughborough Colleges** |
| 1944 | **St Mary's Hospital** | | 1971 | **London Welsh** |
| 1945 | **Notts** | | 1972 | **London Welsh** |
| 1946 | **St Mary's Hospital** | | 1973 | **London Welsh** |
| 1947 | **Rosslyn Park** | | 1974 | **Richmond** |
| 1948 | **Wasps** | | 1975 | **Richmond** |
| 1949 | **Heriot's FP** | | 1976 | **Loughborough Colleges** |
| 1950 | **Rosslyn Park** | | 1977 | **Richmond** |
| 1951 | **Richmond II** | | 1978 | **Harlequins** |
| 1952 | **Wasps** | | | |

*Harlequins have won the title 8 times, London Welsh 7, London Scottish 6 times, Richmond 6 times (including once by Richmond II), St Mary's Hospital and Loughborough Colleges 5 times, Rosslyn Park 3 times, Blackheath, Wasps, and St Luke's College twice and Barbarians, Sale, Metropolitan Police, Cardiff, Cambridge University, Notts, and Heriot's FP once each.*

# SCHOOLS RUGBY 1977–78

**George Abbott** *The Daily Telegraph*

After the salutary lessons of the Australian Schools' tour had been absorbed (see p 160), the 'home' countries settled down to a programme of international matches which lacked only two to make it a complete Five Nations Tournament. In the 19 Group England and Scotland played all four of the other countries, while Wales and France met all except Ireland.

It soon became clear that England's leading position, undisputed since 1975, was at considerable risk. Their first game was against France at Châteauroux, where they put up a stout fight against bigger and stronger opponents, but went down 10–12. An unchanged team suffered a second narrow defeat at the hands of a lively Ireland team at Lansdowne Road, but then came two victories, over Scotland and Wales. It was recognised from an early stage that this England 'squad' was not a particularly talented one, but the players were very competitive and showed great spirit. In the five seasons, plus a tour of Australia, during which the former England lock Mike Davis has been in charge of their coaching, England's 19 Group players have won 17 matches, drawn 2 and lost only 4. The decisive 21–10 victory over Wales at Gosforth made a fitting finale to Davis's inspired period of guidance.

Ireland confirmed the good impression they made against Australia in December by gaining two competent victories over England and Scotland. With a hard-working, enthusiastic pack and speedy backs they were probably the best of the home countries, but this must remain a matter for conjecture, since they did not play Wales or France.

Wales, for all their natural talent, were again a little disappointing. They proved too strong for Scotland (who were consistently outweighed and lost all four matches) and their forwards rose to the occasion in a punishing and ill-tempered match at Neath against France; but the English pack mastered them at Gosforth.

At the lower age level it was again impossible to play the traditional game between England and Wales because of the different age limits fixed by the two countries. England, playing as Under-16s, entertained Portugal at Twickenham and had an easy 42–0 victory over a keen but inexperienced side. Later they visited France, where they won the official international match 13–8 at Poitiers in a rousing finish. The English boys came from behind to score the winning try with only three minutes left for play. France's organisation at this level has improved greatly in the last year or so and they are now formidable opponents.

Wales took their Under-15 team on tour to Scotland. In their first game they played opponents of long standing, the South of Scotland, at Hawick. The Scottish side, in winning 10–4, recorded their third victory out of 28 matches, of which Wales have won 23 and two have been drawn. A second game was played against Edinburgh Schools at Inverleith and resulted in a 22–4 win for Wales. The Welsh selectors made several changes for their final fixture, against Italy at Cardiff. This was the third meeting of the two countries in the last three years and the result, like those of the other two, was a victory for Wales – by 64 points to nil.

154

Comparisons between school XVs, however tempting, are nearly always inconclusive, but it is fair to say that among the best in their groups and areas were *Bryanston*, *Campion* (Hornchurch), *Emanuel*, *Felsted*, *Gresham's*, *Haberdashers' Aske's* (Elstree), *Plymouth*, *St Brendan's*, *Sedbergh*, *Sherborne*, *West Park GS* (St Helens) and *Woolverstone Hall* (Ipswich).

Four of these schools are situated in East Anglia, where *Felsted*, with the most testing fixture list of the four, won 12 matches, including three on a tour in the West. They lost only to *Gresham's*, whose young and talented side won all eight school games. *Woolverstone Hall*, playing open and attractive rugby, had an unbroken run of 16 successes. One of these was against *Campion*, another enterprising team dedicated to attack, who recorded 20 victories and only two defeats.

*Emanuel*, with a powerful pack and strong-running backs, had few, if any, superiors in the South-East. Unbeaten with 15 wins and two draws, they became the first school to overcome *Haberdashers' Aske's* (Elstree) since 1973. The margin, in a tense encounter, was a single penalty goal. Haberdashers' suffered no other setback and their efficient team gained 13 victories; the hardest-earned was against *Queen Elizabeth's* (Barnet), whose pack was exceptionally strong.

Other useful sides in the south-east included *Epsom*, whose direct, thrustful running brought them 11 successes in their 13 school matches; *KCS, Wimbledon*, who thanks mainly to their strength at scrum-half and loose forward won 12 games and lost only to Reigate GS and Woolverstone Hall; and *Reigate GS*, who worthily upheld their high reputation, in spite of losing six of their 18 games. *Dulwich* recovered from an uncertain injury-hit start to win their last seven matches. They beat *St Paul's*, who, with nine wins and three losses, had a fine season.

A well balanced *Bryanston* team, with power in the pack and plenty of scoring ability behind the scrum, won all 15 engagements, including 13 against schools. *Sherborne* did equally well, in a shorter fixture list. Their pack was big and talented and of their nine school opponents only Christ College, Brecon gave them serious trouble. *Downside*, who joined forces with Sherborne in touring British Columbia at the end of the season, possessed some very capable backs. They had nine victories and lost only to Sherborne and Blackrock College, from Dublin. *Canford* lost to Sherborne, Downside and Bryanston, but their other nine fixtures brought eight wins and a draw – a very satisfactory performance from a team which made steady improvement.

*Bishop Wordsworth's* (Salisbury) have strengthened their fixture list in recent years and are trying to improve it still further. Their XV of 1977–78 won 21 out of 22 games, scoring 629 points to 144, and would have been a match for most schools with their effective ball-winning and support play. Millfield, Plymouth and St Brendan's are highly regarded, not only in the West of England, and all three were well represented. *Millfield* lost narrowly to the other two, but the pace and skill of their backs were normally too much for most opposition. With strength, talent and experience both in and outside the scrum, *Plymouth* scored freely, totalling more than 450 points in winning 12 games and drawing one. *St Brendan's*, with a solid pack and a sound pair of half-backs, had 11 victories to set against defeats by Emanuel and Christ, Brecon.

*Rugby*, following their unbeaten 1976 season, gave some sound performances in winning nine out of 12 inter-school matches. Their major strength lay in the pack and particularly in an experienced back row. They drew with *Uppingham*, who did well with a young team containing only one old colour and ended up with six wins and three defeats. Rugby also inflicted one of only two defeats suffered by a competent *Oundle* side, who scored 39 tries in their ten games against schools. *Oakham* had a pleasing success against Uppingham, but the outstanding feature of their season was their tour of Japan, the first ever by a British school, in December. *Bablake* (Coventry) played 21 matches, winning 17, drawing one and losing three. The team's main asset was the strength of their pack, which seldom failed to dominate the opposition.

*Wellington* (Berkshire) had some notable successes, with Haileybury, Radley, Monmouth and Marlborough among their nine victims; they lost twice, to St Paul's and Epsom. *Lord Wandsworth* (Basingstoke), inspired by an accomplished pair of half-backs, won 10 games in a row before losing the last. *Wrekin* had an outstanding fly-half in M H Perry, who scored 254 points. They won 12 games and drew one, and although they lost five times it was often in close contests which could easily have gone either way. *Ernest Bailey GS* (Matlock), with a strengthened fixture list, completed another successful season, winning 17 out of 20 matches. As 13 of the side will be available this season, hopes are high for 1978-79. They had home-and-away fixtures with *Mount St Mary's*, winning one and losing one. The latter had fast and clever backs, who helped to produce a record of 17 victories and five defeats.

Unbeaten in 1975 and 1976, *Ampleforth* again had a strong XV, who defeated eight of their 11 rivals and drew with Coleraine Academical Institution, from Northern Ireland. They lost narrowly to Sedbergh and also to *Leeds GS*, who had a good season (won 17, lost 5), and lacked authority only in midfield. The strength of the *Bradford GS* pack contributed substantially to many successes, notably a 25–0 win over Sedbergh. *Queen Elizabeth GS, Wakefield* had fast and clever backs and their light forwards made considerable improvement. Their final record was 17 wins and five losses.

*Giggleswick* enjoyed a happy season with eight victories out of 11 school matches. They had a very competent pack and the XV included two talented players in M J Dixon (hooker) and S M Hartley (scrum-half). In March they toured Bermuda for two weeks and won all five matches there, scoring 300 points to 25.

*Sedbergh's* heavy defeat at Bradford was by no means typical. They won all of their other 10 school matches, with Ampleforth, Rossall, Stonyhurst and Fettes among their victims.

A lively, fast-moving *King's, Macclesfield* XV scored freely in winning 15 games out of 18. P Hughes (right wing) equalled the school's try-scoring record, with 28. *Rossall*, the only English school to overcome King's, Macclesfield, had several gifted players. The team had to be rebuilt to a large extent, but finished with the highly creditable figures of 13 wins, three defeats and a draw. *West Park GS* had their strength well distributed throughout the XV. They played 28 matches against schools, winning 26 and losing two. Their close neighbours and rivals, *Cowley*, suffered at times through a shortage of weight and size in the pack, but won 16 and drew one of their 21 games. *De La Salle* (Salford) were again a force, with mobile loose forwards and two high-scoring wings. Their final record was 21 victories, three defeats and a draw. *Whitehaven GS* in Cumbria had an inspiring performer at fly-half in their captain S Lowdon, who was unlucky with injury after playing for the England

Schools (19 Gp) against Australia. They won 12 and drew one of their 16 matches and their three defeats were largely due to lack of physique in the pack.

Two of the Welsh comprehensive schools had particularly impressive results. *Dwr-y-Felin* (Neath), whose main strength lay in their powerful forwards, won 20 out of 22 games. One of their defeats was against a very talented touring side of Maoris from New Zealand – St Stephen's College, near Auckland. *Dyffryn* (Port Talbot), not as well known outside Wales as Dwr-y-Felin, had an excellent set of backs and lively loose forwards. They won all of their 26 matches. Injury problems hit a potentially strong *Monmouth* team and they did not fulfil the highest hopes; but their eight victims included *Llandovery*, who were young and light, and *Christ, Brecon*. The last-named had a very useful XV, with a particularly strong threequarter line, and did well to go through a varied and testing fixture list with 13 wins and 4 defeats.

157

The outstanding record among the Scottish schools belonged to *Stewart's Melville*, who won all 22 games. They had notable team-spirit under a fine captain, C Spence – a full-back with a ready eye for an opening. *Trinity College, Glenalmond* were well equipped all round; they had 11 victories and lost only to *Fettes*. The latter, in turn, went down narrowly on two visits to England – to Rossall and Sedbergh – but accounted for all their Scottish rivals except *George Heriot's*.

*Bangor GS* had the coveted distinction of winning the Ulster Schools Cup, but should not necessarily be ranked above *Royal Belfast Academical Institution* (W 26, D 1, L 3), *Coleraine Academical Institution* (W 22, D 1, L 2) or *Regent House*, whose XV suffered a few set-backs, but whose VII had a great double success in the Ulster Schools and Rosslyn Park Open tournaments. The Senior Schools Cups in the other Irish provinces were won by *Clongowes Wood College* (Leinster), *Presentation Brothers' College, Cork* (Munster) and *St Joseph's College, Garbally* (Connacht).

No outstanding team emerged in the major seven-a-side competitions, but *Bedford* gave some fine displays in winning the Rosslyn Park Festival event and *Rydal* were worthy winners in a strong field at Oxford.

The following players took part in the 19 Group international matches. (Countries played against are shown in square brackets.)

Abbreviations: *A*–Australia, *E*–England, *F*–France, *I*–Ireland, *S*–Scotland, *W*–Wales, *(R)*–Replacement.

# ENGLAND

**Full-backs** M D Schiefler (St Brendan's) [*A, F, I*], R Bowers (QEGS, Wakefield) [*A(R)*], M E Drane (Loughborough GS) [*S, W*]
**Threequarters** D M Trick (Bryanston) [*A, F, I, S, W*], M R D Jellings (Haywards Heath) [*A*], S I D Lowdon (Whitehaven GS) [*A*], J E Williams (Campion, Hornchurch) [*F, I*], J Pedley(Rossall) [*S, W*], B Barley (Normanton HS) [*F, I, S, W*], M J Nelson (Nelson & Colne C of E) [*A*], P M B Stapleton (London Oratory) [*F, I*], C R Pitts (K E VI, Retford) [*S, W*]
**Half-backs** A J Kift (Exeter Coll) [*A*], M E Drane (Loughborough GS) [*F, I*], M D Schiefler (St Brendan's) [*S, W*], N G Youngs (Gresham's) [*A, F, I, S, W*]
**Forwards** D J Rose (Pocklington) [*A, F, I*], I Taylor (Cowley) [*S*], T Rhodes (West Park GS, St Helens) [*S(R), W*], D A Vickery (Exeter Coll) [*I(R)*], S Adkins (Bablake, Coventry) [*W*], R J Pearson (Oundle) [*A, F, I, S*],C M P Mather (Rugby) [*A*], J G Merison (Radley) [*F, I, S, W*], A Papaloizou (Queen Elizabeth's, Barnet) [*A*], C Butcher (St Peter's, Bournemouth) [*A*], R W B Smart (RGS, Newcastle) [*F, I, S, W*], P M Gale (Millfield) [*F, I*], J A Taylor (Henry Mellish, Nottingham) [*I(R), S, W*], P Faulkner (Blackpool Collegiate) [*A, F, I, S, W*], P Wallace (Hartland, Worksop) [*W(R)*], B J Kenny (Sherborne) [*A, F, I, S, W*], M H Piccirillo (Plymouth) [*A*], G B Marsh (Queen Elizabeth's, Barnet) [*A(R), F, I, S, W*]
N G Youngs was captain against Australia, France, Ireland and Scotland, and R W B Smart against Wales.

# SCOTLAND

**Full-backs** R B Nelson (Hutchesons' GS) [*F, W, E*], C St J Spence (Stewart's Melville) [*I*], D A M Clarke (George Heriot's) [*I(R)*]
**Threequarters** T Paterson-Brown (Trinity College, Glenalmond) [*F, W*], G W A McCutcheon (Hutchesons' GS) [*E, I*], G C S Gordon (Trinity College, Glenalmond) [*F, W, E, I*], J F Paton (Loretto) [*F, W*], G M Hastings (George Watson's) [*W(R), E, I*], D A Smellie (Strathallan) [*F, W, E*], R B Nelson (Hutchesons' GS) [*I*]
**Half-backs** N J Marshall (Morrison's Academy) [*F, W, E, I*], R Stevenson (George Heriot's) [*F, W*], G R T Baird (Merchiston Castle) [*E, I*]
**Forwards** A J Kendall (Fettes) [*F, W*], N T Roberts (Trinity College, Glenalmond) [*E, I*], M R Ferguson (Stewart's Melville) [*F, W, E, I*], A J S Morton (Ayr Academy) [*F, W, E, I*], P M Lillington (Fettes) [*F, W*], K Goudie (Stewart's Melville) [*F, W, E, I*], G R Marshall (Currie HS) [*E, I*], L T Purves (Galashiels Academy) [*F, W*], J A Turnbull (Merchiston Castle) [*E*], D R W Denham (Royal High School) [*E(R), I*], J K Murdoch (Belmont Academy) [*F, W, E*], R D Graham (North Berwick HS) [*I*], W M Anderson (Fettes) [*F, W, E, I*]
P M Lillington was captain against France and Wales, and G C S Gordon against England and Ireland.

# IRELAND

**Full-back** R W Hopkins (Terenure) [*A, E, S*]
**Threequarters** P S A Nowlan (Wesley) [*A, E, S*], B M Keogh (Christian Brothers', Monkstown) [*A, E, S*], P Bauress (Blackrock) [*A, E, S*], K Forkin (St Michael's) [*A(R)*], K J Hooks (Bangor GS) [*A, E, S*]
**Half-backs** P M Dean (St Mary's, Rathmines) [*A, E, S*], P R McDonnell (St Mary's, Rathmines) [*A, E, S*]

**Forwards** A C Blair (Dublin HS) [*A, E, S*], C Jennings (St Gerard's, Bray) [*A, E*], T Crotty (Christian Brothers', Cork) [*S*], P M Matthews (Regent House) [*A, E, S*], P C Collins (Christian Brothers', Cork) [*A, E, S*], M F Moylett (Castleknock) [*A, E, S*], R J Blair (Methodist, Belfast) [*A, E, S*], J O Douglas (Methodist, Belfast) [*A, E, S*], W B Iveston (Regent House [*A, E, S*]
P M Matthews was captain in all three matches.

# WALES

**Full-back** D G Thomas (Ystalyfera) [*A, S, F, E*]
**Threequarters** C T Edwards (Cross Keys) [*A, S, F, E*], I P Goslin (Cross Keys) [*A, S, F, E*], A G Davies (Preseli, Crymych) [*A*], H J Jenkins (Cynffig Hill) [*S, F*], P Jones (Glanafon, Port Talbot) [*E*], P M Hamer (Cwmtawe) [*A*], S C Evans (Heol Ddu, Bargoed) [*S, F, E*]
**Half-backs** J J Robinson (Heol Ddu, Bargoed) [*A, S, F, E*], J Greenway (Dyffryn, Port Talbot) [*A*], H O Wooldridge (Gowerton) [*S, F, E*]
**Forwards** K R Moose (John Bright, Llandudno) [*A, S, F(R), E*], O M Golding (St Cyres, Penarth) [*A, S, F, E*], N Robinson (Dwr-y-Felin, Neath) [*A, S, F*], J Lye (Rhydfelin, Pontypridd) [*E(R)*], M Hall (Bryntirion, Bridgend) [*A, S, F, E*], A L Vaughan (Dwr-y-Felin, Neath) [*A, F, E*], S L Cooper (Howardian, Cardiff) [*S, F, E*], T D Jones (Ynysawdre, Bridgend) [*A*], R Hawkins (St Martin's, Caerffili) [*S, F, E*], L S Jones (Coed-y-Lan, Pontypridd) [*A, S, F, E*], M A Gorecki (Emmanuel, Swansea) [*A, S, F, E*], P Souto (St Illtyd's, Cardiff) [*F(R)*]
O M Golding was captain in all four matches.

## MATCH DETAILS (19 Group)

**29 December, Edinburgh**

---

**SCOTLAND 3** (1PG)   **FRANCE 8** (2T)
**Scotland** *Penalty Goal:* Nelson
**France** *Tries:* Bonal, Bruned
**Referee** Corris Thomas (Wales)

**7 January, Glasgow**

---

**SCOTLAND 3** (1PG)   **WALES 26** (2G 2PG 2T)
**Scotland** *Penalty Goal:* Nelson
**Wales** *Tries:* Edwards, Jenkins, Wooldridge, Moose   *Conversions:* Thomas (2)
*Penalty Goals:* J Robinson, Wooldridge
**Referee** P E Hughes (England)

**25 March, Châteauroux**

---

**FRANCE 12** (3T)   **ENGLAND 10** (1G 1T)
**France** *Tries:* Moreti, Plantat, Sallefranque
**England** *Tries:* Trick (2)   *Conversion:* Drane
**Referee** A Bryce (Scotland)

**29 March, Neath**

---

**WALES 7** (1PG 1T)   **FRANCE 3** (1PG)
**Wales** *Try:* Wooldridge   *Penalty Goal:* Thomas
**France** *Penalty Goal:* Morrison
**Referee** L Prideaux (England)

**1 April, Dublin**

**IRELAND 22** (1G 1DG 3PG 1T)   **ENGLAND 16** (1G 2PG 1T)
**Ireland** *Tries:* Nowlan, Keogh   *Conversion:* McDonnell   *Dropped Goal:* Dean
*Penalty Goals:* Keogh, McDonnell (2)
**England** *Tries:* Youngs (2)   *Conversion:* Youngs   *Penalty Goals:* Youngs, Drane
**Referee** C Norling (Wales)

**4 April, Gloucester**

**ENGLAND 16** (4T)   **SCOTLAND 3** (1PG)
**England** *Tries:* Marsh, Barley, J A Taylor, Drane
**Scotland** *Penalty Goal:* Hastings
**Referee** Corris Thomas (Wales)

**7 April, Edinburgh**

**SCOTLAND 7** (1PG 1T)   **IRELAND 21** (2G 3PG)
**Scotland** *Try:* Hastings   *Penalty Goal:* Hastings
**Ireland** *Tries:* Hooks, Collins   *Conversions:* Bauress (2)   *Penalty Goals:*   Bauress,
McDonnell (2)
**Referee** J B Williamson (England)

**8 April, Gosforth**

**ENGLAND 21** (1G 2DG 3PG)   **WALES 10** (1DG 1PG 1T)
**England** *Try:* Drane   *Conversion:* Youngs   *Dropped Goals:* Youngs (2)   *Penalty
Goals:* Drane (2), Youngs
**Wales** *Try:* L S Jones   *Dropped Goal:* J Robinson   *Penalty Goal:* Thomas
**Referee** J A Short (Scotland)

# AUSTRALIAN SCHOOLS TO BRITISH ISLES 1977–78

It must be many years since a touring party of any kind won such widespread acclaim throughout the British Isles as the young Australians of 1977–78. The facts of their unbeaten tour speak eloquently for themselves, but the figures, impressive though they are, are unimportant compared with the manner in which they were achieved.

Brimming with talent, the Australians had such confidence in their attacking powers that they were able to introduce into their play a spirit of adventure all too rarely seen here, even among the schools. Kicking to touch was reduced to a minimum and they attacked consistently from positions deep in their own territory. Indeed, they were never more dangerous than when given space to develop their attacks. Against the Midlands at Leicester they scored from three consecutive kick-offs against without an opponent being able to touch the ball.

Subsequent opponents took the hint and placed their kick-offs high and short, so that their own forwards could arrive under the ball.

Superb ball-handling, speedy and aggressive running and incessant backing-up were the qualities that marked this team as being really exceptional. Tactically they presented a new–old concept of back play in their short, quick passing along the line to give space for the wings or for players looping outside them. Not for the Australians the long pass from the base of the scrum. At times the fly-half stood off no more than two or three yards and transferred the ball with lightning rapidity to his inside centre. The result was that they scored 103 tries and – perhaps even more remarkable, considering their adventurous style of play – conceded only five.

The three Ella brothers, extraordinarily gifted players, provided some of the most exciting moments. With their instinctive sense of position and elusive running they formed the spearhead of the attack, with G J Ella at full-back making an especially notable contribution. Melrose, the captain, at fly-half or inside centre, was particularly adept at taking and giving a pass in one or two strides and McPherson, Hawker and O'Connor provided speed and finishing power in full measure.

Although the forwards played a secondary role, they were equally invaluable in ball-winning and backing-up, with Roche and Nightingale in particular often making ground with powerful bursts.

The touring team made a most impressive start in scoring 12 tries to overwhelm London Counties at Sudbury. This riot of scoring set the pattern for the tour and subsequently only Ireland came anywhere near to holding their full-strength team. The international at Limerick was certainly a close thing for the visitors. They persisted in their tactics of passing the ball to the wings as swiftly as possible, but were met by determined Irish tackling in a great contest. The Irish defence earned high marks for conceding no more than two tries against their opponents' high-speed attacks.

Against Wales the Australians had a more comfortable passage, proving too good for the Welsh boys in all departments, with the three Ella brothers in top form. It was the cruellest of misfortunes that the final match against England at Twickenham should have been completely ruined as a spectacle by thick fog, which made play very nearly impossible. This was the game to which the Australians had looked forward with the keenest anticipation and they rose to the occasion in fine style. They outplayed the English boys and scored seven tries in an emphatic victory.

Mr Douglas Harrison, President of the Rugby Football Schools' Union, said in a farewell speech that, if these young players were typical, Australia had the material to become the greatest Rugby Union country in the world. The question is, alas – how many of them will go to the Rugby League?

162    In addition to their matches in the British Isles the Australians played All-Japan Schools in Tokyo and Holland at The Hague. They beat the Japanese 42–0 and Holland 34–4.

## THE TOURING PARTY

**Captain** T C Melrose    **Manager** R J Wallace
**Assistant Managers** G Mould, J Lucey

Appearances in the international matches are shown in square brackets (Abbreviations: *E*–England, *I*–Ireland, *W*–Wales)

### FULL-BACK

**G J Ella** (Matraville HS, NSW)
[*I, W, E*]

### THREEQUARTERS

**P J McPherson** (Waratah HS, NSW)
[*I, E*]

**P J Tuck** (Knox GS, NSW)

**M A Williams** (Brisbane State HS, Qld)

**M J Hawker** (Sydney C of E GS, NSW)    [*I, W, E*]

**M D O'Connor** (Phillip Coll, ACT)   [*W*]

**G A Ella** (Matraville HS, NSW)
[*I, W, E*]

**W J Lewis** (Brisbane State HS, Qld)

### HALF-BACKS

**M G Ella** (Matraville HS, NSW)
[*I, W, E*]

**T C Melrose (**Northmead HS, NSW)    [*I, W, E*]

**M J Egan** (St Joseph's Coll, NSW)

**D V Vaughan** (Hamilton Marist Bros, NSW)    [*I, W, E*]

*****D Lester** (Matraville HS, NSW)

### FORWARDS

**G R Bailey** (Brisbane State HS, Qld)
[*I*]

**G E Reed** (Marist Bros, ACT)

**A I MacLean** (Brisbane GS, Qld)

**I R Miller** (Killarney Heights HS, NSW)    [*I, W, E*]

**C Roche** (Brisbane State HS, Qld)    [*I, W, E*]

**G Gavalas** (Homebush Boys' HS, NSW)

**M J Maxwell** (Cranbrook School, NSW)    [*W, E*]

**W G Melrose** (Matraville HS, NSW)    [*I, W, E*]

**S N Nightingale** (St Columba's, Qld)    [*I, W, E*]

**B J Allan** (Ku-ring-ga HS, NSW)
[*W*]

**A M D'Arcy** (Nudgee Coll, Qld)
[*I, W, E*]

**M J Ilett** (Brisbane GS, Qld) [*I, W, E*]

**R Leslie** (Brisbane Boys' Coll, Qld)    [*I, E*]

**A W Ryan** (St Ignatius, NSW)

**J Matheson** (Pennant Hills HS, NSW)

*Replacement during tour*

## TOUR RECORD

| | | | | |
|---|---|---|---|---|
| **All matches** | Played 16 | Won 16 | Pts for 555 | Against 97 |
| **In British Isles** | Played 14 | Won 14 | Pts for 479 | Against 93 |

# MATCH DETAILS in British Isles

| 1977 | OPPONENTS | VENUE | RESULT |
|------|-----------|-------|--------|
| 4 December | London Counties | Sudbury | W 54–6 |
| 7 December | South-West | Gloucester | W 28–12 |
| 10 December | North Wales | Llandudno | W 66–0 |
| 14 December | Ulster | Bangor | W 30–7 |
| 17 December | IRELAND | Limerick | W 12–10 |
| 21 December | Leinster | Dublin | W 34–6 |
| 23 December | East Wales | Penygraig | W 14–6 |
| 28 December | WALES | Cardiff | W 25–6 |
| 31 December | West Wales | Gowerton | W 38–0 |
| **1978** | | | |
| 4 January | Southern Counties | Oxford | W 37–4 |
| 6 January | Midlands | Leicester | W 63–12 |
| 11 January | North | Lancaster | W 33–9 |
| 14 January | Sevenoaks School (Past & Present) | Sevenoaks | W 14–6 |
| 18 January | ENGLAND | Twickenham | W 31–9 |

## The Internationals

**17 December, Limerick**

**IRELAND 10** (2PG 1T)   **AUSTRALIA 12** (2G)
**IRELAND:** *Try:* Nowlan   *Penalty Goals:* McDonnell (2)
**AUSTRALIA:** *Tries:* G J Ella, G A Ella   *Conversions:* Melrose (2)
**Referee** M Messan (France)

**28 December, Cardiff**

**WALES 6** (2PG)   **AUSTRALIA 25** (2G 3PG 1T)
**WALES:** *Penalty Goals:* J Robinson (2)
**AUSTRALIA:** *Tries:* G A Ella, G J Ella, M G Ella   *Conversions:* Melrose, Nightingale   *Penalty Goals:* Melrose (2), Nightingale
**Referee** N R Sanson (Scotland)

**18 January, Twickenham**

**ENGLAND 9** (3PG)   **AUSTRALIA 31** (1PG 7T)
**ENGLAND:** *Penalty Goals:* Kift, Youngs (2)
**AUSTRALIA:** *Tries:* G J Ella (2), Hawker (3), G A Ella, McPherson   *Penalty Goal:* Nightingale
**Referee** J-P Bonnet (France)

*British Lion Douglas Morgan, captain of Scotland and Stewart's Melville FP, in action against England. Fellow Scots Donald MacDonald (West of Scotland) and Alan Tomes (Hawick) hold a watching brief.*

# THE 1977–78 SEASON IN SCOTLAND

**Bill McMurtrie** *Glasgow Herald*

Scotland's international season began in Tokyo's National Stadium in September and finished on home ground in the Calcutta Cup match against England at Murrayfield in March ... and the results, too, were worlds apart. In Tokyo the Scots, fielding five players at that time uncapped, beat the Japanese national XV 74–9, but six months later the full Scottish team lost 0–15 to England – the last defeat of a first 'whitewash' in the championship for 10 years.

Yet the home international season had begun on a hopeful note. A new coach, Nairn MacEwan, the former international flanker, who had lifted Highland from the fourth division of the national club league to the first in successive seasons, had said he would bring a fresh look to Scotland's game. He promised the 15-man rugby that Scotland had played in the Far East. His first challenge, against Ireland in Dublin, was expected to be the least difficult, but Ireland won 12–9, having produced the only try of the match. In the final seconds Scotland's new captain, Douglas Morgan, foregoing three probable points and a draw, decided to run a penalty in the opposition 22 in a bid for a try and victory – to no avail.

A fortnight later Scotland actually led France 13–0 shortly before half-time, after Shedden and Irvine had both scored tries; but the new French star, Jérôme Gallion, torpedoed that lead in the last minutes of the first half. At Cardiff, again, the story was similar. Scotland had their moments in the first half, but crucial tackles were missed and Wales, like France, put paid to the Scots with a scoring burst early in the second half.

Despite the defeats by France and Wales, MacEwan remained optimistic. '... we are looking for the Calcutta Cup, not the wooden spoon.' But in a game lacking atmosphere and spirit, from the Scottish point of view, England came through to their first win of the season. In the course of their four defeats, Scotland scored 39 points and conceded 68, with four tries for and nine against. The 'against' column had been reduced compared with 1977, but without the consolation of a victory.

Luck, though, was not on Scotland's side. Andy Irvine, the Rugby Union Writers' Club personality of 1977, injured a shoulder against France and could not play against Wales. Alastair McHarg, who took his total of caps to 41, was absent from the Calcutta Cup match because of a hand injury at Cardiff, and three other top-class players had to watch the campaign from the sidelines. Alan Lawson, of London Scottish, described by many as the 'best scrum-half in England', was ruled out through adhering to his refusal to stand by as a replacement; Gordon Brown missed a second successive full season of international rugby, this time because of a shoulder injury incurred on the Lions' tour of New Zealand; and his West of Scotland colleague, David Leslie, that lively and energetic flanker, was out of action with ankle damage.

Sandy Carmichael, another West of Scotland leading light and, like Brown, a Lion, departed from the international scene after winning his fiftieth cap by playing against Ireland. It seemed he had to be one of the scapegoats for the poor Scottish scrummaging in the Dublin defeat, but later changes produced little, if any, improvement. It was an area which caused MacEwan concern throughout the campaign. When the international matches were over, Carmichael announced his retirement as a player. The announcement came on an appropriate occasion, when he was presented with a National Playing Fields Association trophy to mark his contribution to Scottish sport. He left behind him two international records: the most caps won by any Scot and the most by any prop in world rugby.

The International Championship results dampened the enthusiasm the Scots had brought back from the Far East, where all five games were won easily, the touring team scoring 307 points and conceding only five tries. Yet of the five new caps who played in Scotland's four Championship matches, only Deans, the Hawick hooker, had been on that tour. The course, it seemed, had been changed in midstream.

Perhaps the first sign of pending problems was seen in the new 'B' international fixture against Ireland at Murrayfield in December, when the visitors won a drab match 7–3. Only five of the Scottish side had been in the Far East; continuity was being lost. Three months later, in a second 'B' international, against France at Le Havre, Scotland held their own until the French produced two late tries to win 11–3. A distinctly forgettable international season, for Scotland, was thus complete.

In the District Championship, Glasgow, Edinburgh, and the South shared the honours with two wins apiece. The North and Midlands side finished without a victory. Edinburgh began the tournament by beating Glasgow through two Douglas Morgan penalty goals to a try by Dobbs. Glasgow's place-kickers could do nothing right, and Edinburgh were allowed to continue their domination of the long-established Inter-city series. It was their sixth win in seven such matches and extended their overall lead to 48–35.

Yet, on the same day as the South beat Edinburgh 26–15, Glasgow revived with a 33–3 win against North and Midlands. No fewer than 17 of their points were scored by Ayr's full-back John Brown, on his district début. A week later Glasgow, avenging their 43–0 defeat at Kelso the previous year, halted the South's bid for a second successive clean sweep in the Championship. The Glasgow men won 19–6, with Brown contributing another 11 points. It was a performance that earned him a trial place in opposition to Andy Irvine.

On the club scene, Hawick, as has been their habit, dominated matters, winning the national title for the fifth time in the competition's five years and the Border League for the seventh consecutive season. They were unbeaten in the national league for the second time, and the only real change was in the name of the trophy they won. It was the same cup, but with the advent of sponsorship it was renamed the Schweppes Trophy. Only a 6–6 draw with Boroughmuir in February denied Hawick a 100 per cent league record, and it was a result that also allowed the Edinburgh club a brief glimpse of the championship. But Hawick finished off with victories against West of Scotland and Kilmarnock, and Boroughmuir had to be content with the runners-up position.

By scoring 40 points or more in four of their 11 championship matches, Hawick had established a built-in insurance against any possible need for a points-difference decision. Indeed, they

*The Scotland team v Ireland at Lansdowne Road.*
*Back row: A Welsby (touch judge), O E Doyle (touch judge), D F Madsen, D S M Mac-*
*Donald, A J Tomes, A F McHarg, M A Biggar, R Wilson, P E Hughes (referee). Front*
*row: C B Hegarty, B H Hay, I R McGeechan, Brig F H Coutts (SRU president),*
*D W Morgan (capt), A B Carmichael, J McLauchlan, A R Irvine. On ground: J M Ren-*
*wick, D Shedden.*

finished as top scorers in the whole championship with 324 points, their international centre, Jim Renwick, being responsible for more than a third of these with 115 points – the most by any player in the top two divisions. Hawick's two regular wings also topped the try table, McCartney getting 15 and Polson 12. Boroughmuir's international full-back Bruce Hay came next, with nine.

Throughout the season Boroughmuir, captained by a former Hawick player, Graham Hogg, seemed the only club likely to catch the champions. But the Edinburgh men were saddled with a handicap in October when, despite scoring four tries to one, they lost 21–22 to Gala at Netherdale. Kilmarnock, captained by Scotland 'B' scrum-half Hugh McHardy, proved themselves the most successful of the previously unrecognised clubs who have used the championship as a ladder. Having begun in Division 3, they reached the top level in successive seasons, and once there have steadily improved their position ... eighth in 1976, fourth in 1977, and now third in 1978. They also confirmed their place as the Glasgow district's top club by winning the local cup competition for the first time, beating Clarkston in the final.

In a tense relegation struggle Jordanhill saved themselves by beating Highland, a result that sent the Inverness club back down after two seasons in Division 1. The other relegation place was also settled by a Jordanhill result. Watsonians, thanks to a 7–7 draw against them, just managed to escape. It was a close and tense match, with Kenny Ross scoring the equalising try in the final move and so helping to send Melrose down.

Melrose and Highland have been replaced by Kelso, Division 2 champions for the second time, and newcomers Haddington. The latter, like Highland, began the league five years ago in the fourth division. Kelso went up comfortably, winning 10 successive championship games after a surprise defeat by Edinburgh Academicals in their opening match; but Haddington only just pipped Ayr for second place, on points-difference. In the final game Haddington had to beat Glasgow High by at least nine points to gain promotion – and won 19–7.

Two clubs shared the honours on the Border sevens circuit. Kelso took the Melrose and Jedforest trophies, and Boroughmuir won at Hawick and Langholm. Hawick, winners of three trophies the previous year, picked up only one – in the Gala tournament – and were runners-up twice.

## DISTRICT CHAMPIONSHIP

| | P | W | D | L | F | A | Pts |
|---|---|---|---|---|---|---|---|
| Glasgow | 3 | 2 | 1 | 0 | 56 | 15 | 4 |
| South | 3 | 2 | 0 | 1 | 57 | 34 | 4 |
| Edinburgh | 3 | 2 | 0 | 1 | 49 | 34 | 4 |
| North and Midlands | 3 | 0 | 0 | 3 | 7 | 86 | 0 |

# SCHWEPPES CLUB CHAMPIONSHIP

## Division 1

|  | P | W | D | L | F | A | Pts |
|---|---|---|---|---|---|---|---|
| Hawick | 11 | 10 | 1 | 0 | 324 | 68 | 21 |
| Boroughmuir | 11 | 9 | 1 | 1 | 241 | 95 | 19 |
| Kilmarnock | 11 | 8 | 0 | 3 | 163 | 122 | 16 |
| Heriot's FP | 11 | 6 | 0 | 5 | 154 | 147 | 12 |
| Langholm | 10 | 5 | 0 | 5 | 118 | 181 | 10 |
| West of Scotland | 10 | 4 | 1 | 5 | 123 | 103 | 9 |
| Gala | 10 | 4 | 0 | 6 | 139 | 177 | 8 |
| Jordanhill | 11 | 3 | 2 | 6 | 104 | 140 | 8 |
| Stewart's Melville FP | 10 | 4 | 0 | 6 | 127 | 178 | 8 |
| Watsonians | 11 | 3 | 1 | 7 | 74 | 162 | 7 |
| Melrose | 11 | 3 | 0 | 8 | 123 | 180 | 6 |
| Highland | 11 | 2 | 0 | 9 | 86 | 223 | 4 |

**Champions:** Hawick
**Relegated:** Melrose and Highland

## Division 2

|  | P | W | D | L | F | A | Pts |
|---|---|---|---|---|---|---|---|
| Kelso | 11 | 10 | 0 | 1 | 182 | 75 | 20 |
| Haddington | 11 | 8 | 0 | 3 | 149 | 101 | 16 |
| Ayr | 11 | 8 | 0 | 3 | 167 | 123 | 16 |
| Jedforest | 11 | 7 | 0 | 4 | 207 | 113 | 14 |
| Gordonians | 11 | 6 | 1 | 4 | 134 | 112 | 13 |
| Selkirk | 11 | 6 | 0 | 5 | 151 | 108 | 12 |
| Edinburgh Acads | 11 | 4 | 1 | 6 | 122 | 132 | 9 |
| Glasgow High | 11 | 3 | 2 | 6 | 116 | 115 | 8 |
| Clarkston | 11 | 4 | 0 | 7 | 95 | 168 | 8 |
| Edinburgh Wands | 11 | 3 | 0 | 8 | 105 | 162 | 6 |
| Dunfermline | 11 | 3 | 0 | 8 | 108 | 254 | 6 |
| Preston Lodge FP | 11 | 2 | 0 | 9 | 121 | 194 | 4 |

**Promoted:** Kelso (champions) and Haddington
**Relegated:** Dunfermline and Preston Lodge FP

## Division 3

|  | P | W | D | L | F | A | Pts |
|---|---|---|---|---|---|---|---|
| Leith Acads | 11 | 11 | 0 | 0 | 223 | 61 | 22 |
| Madras Coll FP | 11 | 9 | 0 | 2 | 149 | 103 | 18 |
| Royal High | 11 | 8 | 0 | 3 | 212 | 78 | 16 |
| Glasgow Acads | 11 | 8 | 0 | 3 | 217 | 111 | 16 |
| Trinity Acads | 11 | 5 | 1 | 5 | 149 | 95 | 11 |
| Howe of Fife | 11 | 5 | 1 | 5 | 123 | 106 | 11 |
| Harris FP | 11 | 4 | 2 | 5 | 108 | 104 | 10 |
| Hillhead | 11 | 3 | 2 | 6 | 86 | 175 | 8 |
| Perthshire | 11 | 4 | 0 | 7 | 112 | 210 | 8 |
| Edinburgh Univ | 11 | 3 | 0 | 8 | 139 | 169 | 6 |
| Aberdeen GSFP | 11 | 3 | 0 | 8 | 89 | 165 | 6 |
| Marr | 11 | 0 | 0 | 11 | 54 | 284 | 0 |

**Promoted:** Leith Acads (champions) and Madras College FP
**Relegated:** Aberdeen GSFP and Marr

## Division 4

|  | P | W | D | L | F | A | Pts |
|---|---|---|---|---|---|---|---|
| Kelvinside Acads | 11 | 9 | 0 | 2 | 162 | 92 | 18 |
| Penicuik | 11 | 8 | 1 | 2 | 199 | 65 | 17 |
| Aberdeen Univ | 11 | 8 | 0 | 3 | 136 | 81 | 16 |
| Musselburgh | 11 | 5 | 2 | 4 | 110 | 94 | 12 |
| Broughton | 11 | 6 | 0 | 5 | 136 | 135 | 12 |
| Kirkcaldy | 11 | 6 | 0 | 5 | 108 | 157 | 12 |
| Hutchesons' | 11 | 5 | 0 | 6 | 87 | 117 | 10 |
| Dundee Univ | 11 | 4 | 1 | 6 | 89 | 144 | 9 |
| Dalziel HSFP | 11 | 4 | 0 | 7 | 120 | 107 | 8 |
| Allan Glen's FP | 11 | 3 | 1 | 7 | 92 | 109 | 7 |
| Greenock Wands | 11 | 3 | 1 | 7 | 70 | 113 | 7 |
| Ardrossan Acads | 11 | 2 | 0 | 9 | 77 | 172 | 4 |

**Promoted:** Kelvinside Acads (champions) and Penicuik
**Relegated:** Greenock Wands and Ardrossan Acads

## Division 5
**Promoted:** Old Aloysians (champions) and Corstorphine
**Relegated:** Cartha Queen's Park and Glasgow Univ

## Division 6
**Promoted:** Dalkeith (champions) and Stirling County
**Relegated:** Aberdeenshire and Panmure

## Division 7
**Promoted:** Glenrothes (champions) and East Kilbride
**Relegated to district leagues:** Helensburgh, Hillfoots, and Lenzie

# BORDER LEAGUE

|  | P | W | D | L | F | A | Pts |
|---|---|---|---|---|---|---|---|
| Hawick | 11 | 9 | 0 | 2 | 253 | 59 | 18 |
| Gala | 10 | 5 | 0 | 5 | 174 | 164 | 10 |
| Selkirk | 9 | 5 | 0 | 4 | 105 | 111 | 10 |
| Jedforest | 11 | 5 | 0 | 6 | 105 | 127 | 10 |
| Melrose | 10 | 4 | 0 | 6 | 129 | 133 | 8 |
| Langholm | 10 | 4 | 0 | 6 | 92 | 179 | 8 |
| Kelso | 9 | 3 | 0 | 6 | 79 | 164 | 6 |

# SCOTTISH INTERNATIONAL PLAYERS
## (up to 30 April 1978)

**ABBREVIATIONS**

*A* Australia

*E* England

*F* France

*I* Ireland

*NSW* New South Wales

*NZ* New Zealand

*SA* South Africa

*W* Wales

(C) Centenary match v England at Murrayfield, 1971 (non-championship)

P Scotland v President's Overseas XV, at Murrayfield, in SFU's Centenary season, 1972–73

(R) Replacement

Note: Years given for Five Nations' matches are for second half of season; e.g. 1972 means season 1971–72

**Abercrombie, C H** (United Services) 1910 *E, I*, 1911 *W, F*, 1913 *W, F*
**Abercrombie, J G** (Edinburgh U) 1949 *I, W, F*, 1950 *E, I, W, F*
**Agnew, W C C** (Stewart's Coll FP) 1930 *I, W*
**Ainslie, R** (Edinburgh Inst FP) 1879 *E, I*, 1880 *E, I*, 1881 *E*, 1882 *E, I*
**Ainslie, T** (Edinburgh Inst FP) 1881 *E*, 1882 *E, I*, 1883 *E, I, W*, 1884 *E, I, W*, 1885 *I, W*
**Aitchison, G R** (Edinburgh Wands) 1883 *I*
**Aitchison, T G** (Gala) 1929 *E, I, W*
**Aitken, A I** (Edinburgh Inst FP) 1889 *I*
**Aitken, G G** (Oxford U) 1924 *E, I, W*, 1925 *E, I, W, F*, 1929 *F*
**Aitken, J** (Gala) 1977 *E, I, F*
**Aitken, R** (London Scottish) 1947 *W*
**Allan, B** (Glasgow Acads) 1881 *I*
**Allan, J L** (Melrose) 1952 *I, W, F*, 1953 *W*
**Allan, J L F** (Cambridge U) 1957 *E, I*
**Allan, J W** (Melrose) 1927 *F*, 1928 *I*, 1929 *E, I, W, F*, 1930 *E, F*, 1931 *E, I, W, F*, 1932 *I, W, SA*, 1934 *E, I*
**Allan, R C** (Hutchesons' GSFP) 1969 *I*
**Allardice, W D** (Aberdeen GSFP) 1948 *I, W, F, A*, 1949 *E, I, W, F*
**Allen, H W** (Glasgow Acads) 1873 *E*
**Anderson, A H** (Glasgow Acads) 1894 *I*
**Anderson, D G** (London Scottish) 1889 *I*, 1890 *E, I, W*, 1891 *E, W*, 1892 *E, W*
**Anderson, E** (Stewart's Coll FP) 1947 *E, I*
**Anderson, J W** (W of Scotland) 1872 *E*
**Anderson, T** (Merchiston) 1882 *I*
**Angus, A W** (Watsonians) 1909 *W*, 1910 *E, W, F*, 1911 *I, W*, 1912 *E, I, W, F, SA*, 1913 *W, F*, 1914 *E, I, W, F*, 1920 *E, I, W, F*
**Anton, P A** (St Andrew's U) 1873 *E*
**Arneil, R J** (Edinburgh Acads, Leicester and Northampton) 1968 *E, I, A*, 1969 *E, I, W, F, SA*, 1970 *E, I, W, F, A*, 1971 *E* (2[1C]), *I, W, F*, 1972 *E, W, F*, 1973 *NZ*
**Arthur, A** (Glasgow Acads) 1875 *E*, 1876 *E*
**Arthur, J W** (Glasgow Acads) 1871 *E*, 1872 *E*
**Asher, A G G** (Oxford U) 1882 *I*, 1884 *E, I, W*, 1885 *W*, 1886 *E, I*
**Auld, W** (W of Scotland) 1889 *W*, 1890 *W*
**Auldjo, L J** (Abertay) 1878 *E*

**Bain, D McL** (Oxford U) 1911 *E*, 1912 *E, W, F, SA*, 1913 *E, I, W, F*, 1914 *I, W*
**Balfour, A** (Watsonians) 1896 *E, I, W*, 1897 *E*
**Balfour, L M** (Edinburgh Acads) 1872 *E*
**Bannerman, E M** (Edinburgh Acads) 1872 *E*, 1873 *E*
**Bannerman, J M** (Glasgow HSFP) 1921 *E, I, W, F*, 1922 *E, I, W, F*, 1923 *E, I, W, F*, 1924 *E, I, W, F*, 1925 *E, I, W, F*, 1926 *E, I, W, F*, 1927 *E, I, W, F, NSW*, 1928 *E, I, W, F*, 1929 *E, I, W, F*

**Barnes, I A** (Hawick) 1972 *W*, 1974 *F* (R), 1975 *E* (R), *NZ*, 1977 *I, F, W*
**Barrie, R W** (Hawick) 1936 *E*
**Bearne, K R F** (Cambridge U, London Scottish) 1960 *W, F*
**Beattie, J A** (Hawick) 1929 *W, F*, 1930 *W*, 1931 *E, I, W, F*, 1932 *E, I, W, SA*, 1933 *E, I, W*, 1934 *E, I*, 1935 *E, I, W, NZ*, 1936 *E, I, W*
**Bedell-Sivright, D R** (Cambridge U, Edinburgh U) 1900 *W*, 1901 *E, I, W*, 1902 *E, I, W*, 1903 *I, W*, 1904 *E, I, W*, 1905 *NZ*, 1906 *E, I, W, SA*, 1907 *E, I, W*, 1908 *I, W*
**Bedell-Sivright, J V** (Cambridge U) 1902 *W*
**Begbie, T A** (Edinburgh Wands) 1881 *E, I*
**Bell, D L** (Watsonians) 1975 *I, F, W, E*
**Bell, J A** (Clydesdale) 1901 *E, I, W*, 1902 *E, I, W*
**Bell, L H I** (Edinburgh Acads) 1900 *E*, 1904 *I, W*
**Berkeley, W V** (Oxford U) 1926 *F*, 1929 *F, W, I*
**Berry, C W** (Fettesian-Lorettonians) 1884 *E, I*, 1885 *W*, 1887 *E, I, W*, 1888 *I, W*
**Bertram, D M** (Watsonians) 1922 *E, I, W, F*, 1923 *E, I, W, F*, 1924 *E, I, W, F*
**Biggar, A G** (London Scottish) 1969 *SA*, 1970 *E, I, F, A*, 1971 *E* (2[1C]), *I, W, F*, 1972 *F, W*
**Biggar, M A** (London Scottish) 1975 *I, F, W, E*, 1976 *W, E, I*, 1977 *I, F, W*, 1978 *I, F, W, E*
**Birkett, G A** (Harlequins, London Scottish) 1975 *NZ*
**Bishop, J M** (Glasgow Acads) 1893 *I*
**Bisset, A A** (RIE Coll) 1904 *W*
**Black, A W** (Edinburgh U) 1947 *W, F*, 1948 *E*, 1950 *E, I, W*
**Black, W P** (Glasgow HSFP) 1948 *E, I, W, F*, 1951 *E*
**Blackadder, W F** (W of Scotland) 1938 *E*
**Blaikie, C F** (Heriot's FP) 1963 *E, I*, 1966 *E*, 1968 *A*, 1969 *E, I, W, F*
**Blair, P C B** (Cambridge U) 1912 *SA*, 1913 *E, I, W, F*
**Bolton, W H** (W of Scotland) 1876 *E*
**Borthwick, J B** (Stewart's Coll FP) 1938 *I, W*
**Bos, F H ten** (Oxford U, London Scottish) 1959 *E*, 1960 *W, F, SA*, 1961 *E, I, W, F, SA*, 1962 *E, I, W, F*, 1963 *E, I, W, F*
**Boswell, J D** (W of Scotland) 1889 *I, W*, 1890 *E, I, W*, 1891 *E, I, W*, 1892 *E, I, W*, 1893 *E, I*, 1894 *E, I*
**Bowie, T C** (Watsonians) 1913 *E, I*, 1914 *E, I*
**Boyd, G M** (Glasgow HSFP) 1926 *E*
**Boyd, J L** (United Services) 1912 *E, SA*
**Boyle, A C W** (London Scottish) 1963 *I, W, F*
**Boyle, A H W** (St Thomas's Hospital, London Scottish) 1966 *A*, 1967 *F, NZ*, 1968 *I, W, F*
**Brash, J C** (Cambridge U) 1961 *E*
**Breakey, R W** (Gosforth) 1978 *E*
**Brewis, N T** (Edinburgh Inst FP) 1876 *E*, 1878 *E*, 1879 *E, I*, 1880 *E, I*
**Brewster, A K** (Stewart's-Melville FP) 1977 *E*
**Brown, A H** (Heriot's FP) 1928 *E*, 1929 *F, W*

**Brown, A R** (Gala) 1971 *E* (2[1C]), 1972 *E, W, F*
**Brown, C H C** (Dunfermline) 1929 *E*
**Brown, D I** (Cambridge U) 1933 *E, I, W*
**Brown, G L** (W of Scotland) 1969 *SA*, 1970 *E, I, W* (R), *F, A*, 1971 *E* (2[1C]), *I, W, F*, 1972 *E, W, F*, 1973 *NZ, E* (R), *P*, 1974 *W, E, I, F*, 1975 *I, F, W, E, A*, 1976 *F, W, E, I*
**Brown, J A** (Glasgow Acads) 1908 *I, W*
**Brown, J B** (Glasgow Acads) 1879 *E, I*, 1880 *E, I*, 1881 *E, I*, 1882 *E, I*, 1883 *E, W*, 1884 *E, I, W*, 1885 *I*, 1886 *E, I, W*
**Brown, P C** (W of Scotland, Gala) 1964 *E, I, W, F, NZ*, 1965 *E, I, SA*, 1966 *A*, 1969 *E, I*, 1970 *E, W, F*, 1971 *F* (2[1C]), *I, W, F*, 1972 *E, W, F*, 1973 *NZ, F, W, I, E, P*
**Brown, T G** (Heriot's FP) 1929 *W*
**Brown, W D** (Glasgow Acads) 1871 *E*, 1872 *E*, 1873 *E*, 1874 *E*, 1875 *E*
**Brown, W S** (Edinburgh Inst FP) 1880 *E, I*, 1882 *E, I*, 1883 *E, I, W*
**Browning, A** (Glasgow HSFP) 1920 *I*, 1922 *I, W, F*, 1923 *E, I, W*
**Bruce, C R** (Glasgow Acads) 1947 *E, I, W, F*, 1949 *E, I, W, F*
**Bruce, N S** (Blackheath, Army and London Scottish) 1958 *E, I, F, A*, 1959 *E, I, W, F*, 1960 *E, I, W, F, SA*, 1961 *E, I, W, F, SA*, 1962 *E, I, W, F*, 1963 *E, I, W, F*, 1964 *E, I, W, F, NZ*
**Bruce, R M** (Gordonians) 1948 *I, W, F, A*
**Bruce-Lockhart, J H** (London Scottish) 1913 *W*, 1920 *E*
**Bruce-Lockhart, L** (London Scottish) 1948 *E*, 1950 *W, F*, 1953 *E, I*
**Bruce-Lockhart, R B** (Cambridge U and London Scottish) 1937 *I*, 1939 *I, E*
**Bryce, C C** (Glasgow Acads) 1873 *E*, 1874 *E*
**Bryce, R D H** (W of Scotland) 1973 *I* (R)
**Bryce, W E** (Selkirk) 1922 *E, I, W*, 1923 *E, I, W, F*, 1924 *E, I, W, F*
**Brydon, W R C** (Heriot's FP) 1939 *W*
**Buchanan, A** (Royal HSFP) 1871 *E*
**Buchanan, F G** (Kelvinside Acads and Oxford U) 1910 *F*, 1911 *W, F*
**Buchanan, J C R** (Stewart's Coll FP) 1921 *E, I, W*, 1922 *E, I, W*, 1923 *E, I, W, F*, 1924 *E, I, W, F*, 1925 *I, F*
**Bucher, A M** (Edinburgh Acads) 1897 *E*
**Budge, G M** (Edinburgh Wands) 1950 *E, I, W, F*
**Bullmore, H H** (Edinburgh U) 1902 *I*
**Burnet, P J** (London Scottish and Edinburgh Acads) 1960 *SA*
**Burnet, W** (Hawick) 1912 *E*
**Burnet, W A** (W of Scotland) 1934 *W*, 1935 *E, I, W, NZ*, 1936 *E, I, W*
**Burrell, G** (Gala) 1950 *I, W, F*, 1951 *SA*

**Cairns, A G** (Watsonians) 1903 *E, I, W*, 1904 *E, I, W*, 1905 *E, I, W*, 1906 *E, I, W*
**Cameron, A** (Glasgow HSFP) 1948 *W*, 1950 *E, I*, 1951 *E, I, W, F, SA*, 1953 *E, I*, 1955 *E, I, W, F*, 1956 *I, W, F*
**Cameron, A D** (Hillhead HSFP) 1951 *F*, 1954 *W, F*
**Cameron, A W** (Watsonians) 1887 *W*, 1893 *W*, 1894 *I*
**Cameron, D** (Glasgow HSFP) 1953 *E, I*, 1954 *E, I, F, NZ*
**Cameron, N W** (Glasgow U) 1952 *E*, 1953 *W, F*
**Campbell, G T** (London Scottish) 1892 *E, I, W*, 1893 *E, I*, 1894 *E, I, W*, 1895 *E, I, W*, 1896 *E, I, W*, 1897 *I*, 1899 *I*, 1900 *E*
**Campbell, H H** (Cambridge U and London Scottish) 1947 *E, I*, 1948 *E, I*
**Campbell, J A** (W of Scotland) 1878 *E*, 1879 *E, I*, 1881 *E, I*
**Campbell, J A** (Cambridge U) 1900 *I*
**Campbell, N M** (London Scottish) 1956 *W, F*
**Campbell-Lamerton, M J** (Halifax, Army and London Scottish) 1961 *I, W, F, SA*, 1962 *I, W, F*, 1963 *E, I, W, F*, 1964 *E, I*, 1965 *E, I, W, F, SA*, 1966 *E, I, W, F*
**Carmichael, A B** (W of Scotland) 1967 *I, NZ*, 1968 *E, I, W, F, A*, 1969 *E, I, W, F, SA*, 1970 *E, I, W, F, A*, 1971 *E* (2[1C]), *I, W, F*, 1972 *E, W, F*, 1973 *NZ, F, W, I, E, P*, 1974 *W, E, I, F*, 1975 *I, F, W, E, NZ, A*, 1976 *F, W, E, I*, 1977 *E, I* (R), *F, W*, 1978 *I*
**Carmichael, J H** (Watsonians) 1921 *I, W, F*
**Carrick, J S** (Glasgow Acads) 1876 *E*, 1877 *E*

**Cassels, D Y** (W of Scotland) 1880 *E*, 1881 *I*, 1882 *E, I*, 1883 *E, I, W*
**Cathcart, C W** (Edinburgh U) 1872 *E*, 1873 *E*, 1876 *E*
**Cawkwell, G L** (Oxford U) 1947 *F*
**Chalmers, T** (Glasgow Acads) 1871 *E*, 1872 *E*, 1873 *E*, 1874 *E*, 1875 *E*, 1876 *E*
**Chambers, H F T** (Edinburgh U) 1888, *I, W*, 1889 *I, W*
**Charters, R G** (Hawick) 1955 *E, I, W*
**Chisholm, D H** (Melrose) 1964 *E, I*, 1965 *E, SA*, 1966 *E, I, F, A*, 1967 *W, F, NZ*, 1968 *I, W, F*
**Chisholm, R W T** (Melrose) 1955 *E, I*, 1956 *E, I, W, F*, 1958 *I, W, F, A*, 1960 *SA*
**Church, W C** (Glasgow Acads) 1906 *W*
**Clark, R L** (Edinburgh Wands, Royal Navy) 1972 *E, W, F*, 1973 *NZ, F, W, I, E, P*
**Clauss, P R A** (Oxford U) 1891 *E, I, W*, 1892 *E, W*, 1895 *I*
**Clay, A T** (Edinburgh Acads) 1886 *E, I, W*, 1887 *E, I, W*, 1888 *W*
**Clunies-Ross, A** (St Andrews U) 1871 *E*
**Coltman, S** (Hawick) 1948 *I*, 1949 *E, I, W, F*
**Colvile, A G** (Merchistonians, Blackheath) 1871 *E*, 1872 *E*
**Connell, G C** (Trinity Acads and London Scottish) 1968 *E, A*, 1969 *E, F*, 1970 *F*
**Cooper, M McG** (Oxford U) 1936 *I, W*
**Cordial, I F** (Edinburgh Wands) 1952 *E, I, W, F*
**Cotter, J L** (Hillhead HSFP) 1934 *E, I*
**Cottington, G S** (Kelso) 1934 *E, I*, 1935 *I, W*, 1936 *E*
**Coughtrie, S** (Edinburgh Acads) 1959 *E, I, W, F*, 1962 *E, I, W*, 1963 *E, I, W, F*
**Couper, J H** (W of Scotland) 1896 *I, W*, 1899 *I*
**Coutts, F H** (Melrose and Army) 1947 *E, I, W*
**Coutts, I D F** (Old Alleynians) 1951 *F*, 1952 *E*
**Cowan, R C** (Selkirk) 1961 *F*, 1962 *E, I, W, F*
**Cowie, W L K** (Edinburgh Wands) 1953 *E*
**Cownie, W B** (Watsonians) 1893 *E, I, W*, 1894 *E, I, W*, 1895 *E, I, W*
**Crabbie, G E** (Edinburgh Acads) 1904 *W*
**Crabbie, J E** (Edinburgh Acads and Oxford U) 1900 *W*, 1902 *I*, 1903 *I, W*, 1904 *E*, 1905 *W*
**Craig, J B** (Heriot's FP) 1939 *W*
**Cranston, A G** (Hawick) 1976 *W, E, I*, 1977 *E, W*, 1978 *F* (R), *W, E*
**Crawford, J A** (Army and London Scottish) 1934 *I*
**Crawford, W H** (United Services and RN) 1938 *E, I, W*, 1939 *E, W*
**Crichton-Miller, D** (Gloucester) 1931 *E, I, W*
**Crole, G B** (Oxford U) 1920 *E, I, W, F*
**Cross, M** (Merchistonians) 1875 *E*, 1876 *E*, 1877 *E, I*, 1878 *E*, 1879 *E, I*, 1880 *E, I*
**Cross, W** (Merchistonians) 1871 *E*, 1872 *E*
**Cumming, R S** (Aberdeen U) 1921 *W, F*
**Cunningham, G** (Oxford U) 1908 *I, W*, 1909 *E, W*, 1910 *E, I, F*, 1911 *E*
**Currie, L R** (Dunfermline) 1948 *I, W, F, A*, 1949 *E, I, W, F*

**Dalgleish, A** (Gala) 1890 *E, W*, 1891 *I, W*, 1892 *W*, 1893 *W*, 1894 *I, W*
**Dalgleish, K J** (Edinburgh Wands and Cambridge U) 1951 *E, I*, 1953 *W, F*
**Dallas, J D** (Watsonians) 1903 *E*
**Davidson, J A** (London Scottish and Edinburgh Wands) 1959 *E*, 1960 *E, I*
**Davidson, J N G** (Edinburgh U) 1952 *E, I, W, F*, 1953 *W, F*, 1954 *F*
**Davidson, J P** (RIE Coll) 1873 *E*, 1874 *E*
**Davidson, R S** (Royal HSFP) 1893 *E*
**Davies, D S** (Hawick) 1922 *E, I, W, F*, 1923 *E, I, W, F*, 1924 *E, F*, 1925 *E, I, W*, 1926 *E, I, W, F*, 1927 *I, W, F*
**Dawson, J C** (Glasgow Acads) 1948 *W, F, A*, 1949 *I, W, F*, 1950 *E, I, W, F*, 1951 *E, I, W, F, SA*, 1952 *E, I, W, F*, 1953 *E*
**Deans, C T** (Hawick) 1978 *F, W, E*
**Deans, D T** (Hawick) 1968 *E*
**Deas, D W** (Heriot's FP) 1947 *W, F*
**Dick, L G** (Loughborough Colls, Jordanhill, Swansea) 1972 *W* (R), *E*, 1974 *W, E, I, F*, 1975 *I, F, W, E, NZ, A*, 1976 *F*, 1977 *E*
**Dick, R C S** (Cambridge U and Guy's Hospital) 1934 *E, I, W*, 1935 *E, I, W, NZ*, 1936 *E, I, W*, 1937 *W*, 1938 *E, I, W*

172

**Gowans, J J** (Cambridge U, London Scottish) 1893 *W*, 1894 *E, W*, 1895 *E, I, W*, 1896 *E, I*
**Gowlland, G C** (London Scottish) 1908 *W*, 1909 *E, W*, 1910 *E, I, W, F*
**Gracie, A L** (Harlequins) 1921 *E, I, W, F*, 1922 *E, I, W, F*, 1923 *E, I, W, F*, 1924 *F*
**Graham, I N** (Edinburgh Acads) 1939 *E, I*
**Graham, J** (Kelso) 1926 *E, I*, 1927 *E, I, W, F, NSW*, 1928 *E, I, W, F*, 1930 *E, I*, 1932 *W, SA*
**Graham, J H S** (Edinburgh Acads) 1876 *E*, 1877 *E, I*, 1878 *E*, 1879 *E, I*, 1880 *E, I*, 1881 *E, I*
**Grant, D** (Hawick) 1965 *E, SA*, 1966 *E, I, W, F, A*, 1967 *E, I, W, F, NZ*, 1968 *F*
**Grant, D M** (East Midlands) 1911 *I, W*
**Grant, M L** (Harlequins) 1955 *F*, 1956 *W, F*, 1957 *F*
**Grant, T O** (Hawick) 1960 *E, I, SA*, 1964 *W, F, NZ*
**Grant, W St C** (Craigmount) 1873 *E*, 1874 *E*
**Gray, D** (West of Scotland) 1978 *E*
**Gray, G L** (Gala) 1935 *NZ*, 1937 *E, I, W*
**Gray, T** (Northampton and Heriot's FP) 1950 *E*, 1951 *E, F*
**Greenlees, H D** (Leicester) 1927 *NSW*, 1928 *W, F*, 1929 *E, I*, 1930 *E*
**Greenlees, J R C** (Cambridge U and Kelvinside Acads) 1900 *I*, 1902 *E, I, W*, 1903 *E, I, W*
**Greenwood, J T** (Dunfermline and Perthshire Acads) 1952 *F*, 1955 *E, I, W, F*, 1956 *E, I, W, F*, 1957 *E, W, F*, 1958 *E, I, W, F, A*, 1959 *I, W, F*
**Greig, A** (Glasgow HSFP) 1911 *I*
**Greig, L L** (Glasgow Acads and United Services) 1905 *NZ*, 1906 *SA*, 1907 *W*, 1908 *I, W*
**Greig, R C** (Glasgow Acads) 1893 *W*, 1897 *I*
**Grieve, C F** (Oxford U) 1935 *W*, 1936 *E*
**Grieve, R M** (Kelso) 1935 *E, I, W, NZ*, 1936 *E, I, W*
**Gunn, A W** (Royal HSFP) 1912 *I, W, F, SA*, 1913 *F*

**Hamilton, A S** (Headingley) 1914 *W*, 1920 *F*
**Hamilton, H M** (W of Scotland) 1874 *E*, 1875 *E*
**Hannah, R S M** (W of Scotland) 1971 *I*
**Harrower, P R** (London Scottish) 1885 *W*
**Hart, J G M** (London Scottish) 1951 *SA*
**Hart, T M** (Glasgow U) 1930 *I, W*
**Hart, W** (Melrose) 1960 *SA*
**Harvey, L** (Greenock Wands) 1899 *I*
**Hastie, A J** (Melrose) 1961 *E, I, W*, 1964 *E, I*, 1965 *E, SA*, 1966 *E, I, W, F, A*, 1967 *I, W, F, NZ*, 1968 *W, F*
**Hastie, I R** (Kelso) 1955 *F*, 1958 *E, F*, 1959 *I, W, F*
**Hastie, J D H** (Melrose) 1938 *E, I, W*
**Hay, B H** (Boroughmuir) 1975 *NZ, A*, 1976 *F*, 1978 *I, F, W, E*
**Hay-Gordon, J R** (Edinburgh Acads) 1875 *E*, 1877 *E, I*
**Hegarty, C B** (Hawick) 1978 *I, F, W, E*
**Hegarty, J J** (Hawick) 1951 *F*, 1953 *E, I, W, F*, 1955 *F*
**Henderson, B C** (Edinburgh Wands) 1963 *E*, 1964 *E, I, F*, 1965 *E, I, W, F*, 1966 *E, I, W, F*
**Henderson, F W** (London Scottish) 1900 *I, W*
**Henderson, I C** (Edinburgh Acads) 1939 *E, I*, 1947 *E, W, F*, 1948 *E, I, A*
**Henderson, J H** (Oxford U and Richmond) 1953 *E, I, W, F*, 1954 *E, I, W, F, NZ*
**Henderson, J M** (Edinburgh Acads) 1933 *E, I, W*
**Henderson, J Y M** (Watsonians) 1911 *E*
**Henderson, M M** (Dunfermline) 1937 *E, I, W*
**Henderson, N F** (London Scottish) 1892 *I*
**Henderson, R G** (Newcastle Northern) 1924 *E, I*
**Hendrie, K G P** (Heriot's FP) 1924 *I, W, F*
**Hendry, T L** (Clydesdale) 1893 *E, I, W*, 1895 *I*
**Henriksen, E H** (Royal HSFP) 1953 *I*
**Hepburn, D P** (Woodford) 1948 *E, I, W, F, A*, 1949 *E, I, W, F*
**Heron, G** (Glasgow Acads) 1874 *E*, 1875 *E*
**Hill, C C P** (St Andrew's U) 1912 *I, F*
**Hinshelwood, A J W** (London Scottish) 1966 *E, I, W, F, A*, 1967 *E, I, W, F, NZ*, 1968 *E, I, W, F, A*, 1969 *I, W, F, SA*, 1970 *W, F*
**Hodgson, C G** (London Scottish) 1968 *E, I*
**Hogg, C G** (Boroughmuir) 1978 *F (R), W (R)*
**Holms, W F** (RIE Coll) 1886 *E, W*, 1887 *E, I*, 1889 *I, W*
**Horsburgh, G B** (London Scottish) 1937 *E, I, W*, 1938 *E, I, W*, 1939 *E, I, W*
**Howie, D D** (Kirkcaldy) 1912 *E, I, W, F, SA*, 1913 *W, F*
**Howie, R A** (Kirkcaldy) 1924 *E, I, W, F*, 1925 *E, I, W*
**Hoyer-Millar, G C** (Oxford U) 1953 *I*

**Huggan, J L** (London Scottish) 1914 *E*
**Hume, J** (Royal HSFP) 1912 *F*, 1920 *F*, 1921 *E, I, W, F*, 1922 *F*
**Hume, J W G** (Oxford U and Edinburgh Wands) 1928 *I*, 1930 *F*
**Hunter, F** (Edinburgh U) 1882 *I*
**Hunter, J M** (Cambridge U) 1947 *F*
**Hunter, M D** (Glasgow High) 1974 *F*
**Hunter, W J** (Hawick) 1964 *W, F, NZ*, 1967 *E, I, W, F*
**Hutchison, W R** (Glasgow HSFP) 1911 *E*
**Hutton, A H M** (Dunfermline) 1932 *I*
**Hutton, J E** (Harlequins) 1930 *E*, 1931 *F*

173

**Inglis, H M** (Edinburgh Acads) 1951 *E, I, W, F, SA*, 1952 *I, W*
**Inglis, J M** (Selkirk) 1952 *E*
**Inglis, W M** (Cambridge U and Royal Engineers) 1937 *E, I, W*, 1938 *E, I, W*
**Innes, J R S** (Aberdeen GSFP) 1939 *E, I, W*, 1948 *E, I, W, F, A*
**Ireland, J C H** (Glasgow HSFP) 1925 *E, I, W*, 1926 *E, I, W, F*, 1927 *E, I, W, F*
**Irvine, A R** (Heriot's FP) 1973 *NZ, F, W, I, E, P*, 1974 *W, E, I, F*, 1975 *I, F, W, E, NZ, A*, 1976 *F, W, E, I*, 1977 *E, I, F, W*, 1978 *I, F*
**Irvine, D R** (Edinburgh Acads) 1878 *E*, 1879 *E, I*
**Irvine, R W** (Edinburgh Acads) 1871 *E*, 1872 *E*, 1873 *E*, 1874 *E*, 1875 *E*, 1876 *E*, 1877 *E, I*, 1878 *E*, 1879 *E, I*, 1880 *E, I*
**Irvine, T W** (Edinburgh Acads) 1885 *I*, 1886 *E, I, W*, 1887 *E, I, W*, 1888 *I, W*, 1889 *I*

**Jackson, K L T** (Oxford U) 1933 *E, I, W*, 1934 *W*
**Jackson, T G H** (Army) 1947 *E, W, F*, 1948 *E, I, W, F, A*, 1949 *E, I, W, F*
**Jackson, W D** (Hawick) 1964 *I*, 1965 *E, SA*, 1968 *A*, 1969 *E, I, W, F*
**Jamieson, J** (W of Scotland) 1883 *E, I, W*, 1884 *E, I, W*, 1885 *I, W*
**Johnston, H H** (Edinburgh Collegian FP) 1877 *E, I*
**Johnston, J** (Melrose) 1951 *SA*, 1952 *E, I, W, F*
**Johnston, W G S** (Cambridge U) 1935 *I, W*, 1937 *E, I, W*
**Johnston, W C** (Glasgow HSFP) 1922 *F*
**Junor, J E** (Glasgow Acads) 1876 *E*, 1877 *E, I*, 1878 *E*, 1879 *E*, 1881 *I*

**Keddie, R R** (Watsonians) 1967 *NZ*
**Keith, G J** (Wasps) 1968 *W, F*
**Keller, D H** (London Scottish) 1949 *E, I, W, F*, 1950 *I, W, F*
**Kelly, R F** (Watsonians) 1927 *NSW*, 1928 *E, W, F*
**Kemp, J W Y** (Glasgow HSFP) 1954 *W*, 1955 *E, I, W, F*, 1956 *E, I, W, F*, 1957 *E, I, W, F*, 1958 *E, I, W, F, A*, 1959 *E, I, W, F*, 1960 *E, I, W, F, SA*
**Kennedy, F** (Stewart's Coll FP) 1920 *E, I, W, F*, 1921 *E*
**Kennedy, N** (W of Scotland) 1903 *E, I, W*
**Ker, H T** (Glasgow Acads) 1887 *E, I, W*, 1888 *I*, 1889 *W*, 1890 *E, I*
**Kerr, D S** (Heriot's FP) 1923 *W, F*, 1924 *F*, 1926 *E, I*, 1927 *E, I, W*, 1928 *E, I*
**Kerr, G C** (Old Dunelmians and Edinburgh Wands) 1898 *E, I*, 1899 *E, I, W*, 1900 *E, I, W*
**Kerr, J M** (Heriot's FP) 1935 *NZ*, 1936 *E, I*, 1937 *I, W*
**Kerr, W** (London Scottish) 1953 *E*
**Kidston, D W** (Glasgow Acads) 1883 *E, W*
**Kidston, W H** (W of Scotland) 1874 *E*
**Kilgour, I J** (RMC Sandhurst) 1921 *F*
**King, J H F** (Selkirk) 1953 *E, W, F*, 1954 *E*
**Kininmonth, P W** (Oxford U and Richmond) 1949 *E, I, W, F*, 1950 *E, I, W, F*, 1951 *E, I, W, F, SA*, 1952 *I, W, F*, 1954 *E, I, W, F, NZ*
**Kinnear, R M** (Heriot's FP) 1926 *I, W, F*
**Knox, J** (Kelvinside Acads) 1903 *E, I, W*
**Kyle, W E** (Hawick) 1902 *E, I, W*, 1903 *E, I, W*, 1904 *E, I, W*, 1905 *E, I, W, NZ*, 1906 *E, I, W*, 1908 *E*, 1909 *E, I, W*, 1910 *W*

**Laidlaw, A S** (Hawick) 1897 *I*
**Laidlaw, F A L** (Melrose) 1965 *E, I, W, F, SA*, 1966 *E, I, W, F, A*, 1967 *E, I, W, F, NZ*, 1968 *I, W, F, A*, 1969 *E, I, W, F, SA*, 1970 *E, I, W, F, A*, 1971 *I, W, F*

174

**Robertson, D** (Edinburgh Acads) 1875 *E*
**Robertson, D D** (Cambridge U) 1893 *W*
**Robertson, I** (London Scottish and Watsonians) 1968 *E*, 1969 *E, SA*, 1970 *E, I, W, F, A*
**Robertson, I P M** (Watsonians) 1910 *F*
**Robertson, J** (Clydesdale) 1908 *E*
**Robertson, L** (London Scottish and United Services) 1908 *E*, 1911 *W*, 1912 *E, I, W, SA*, 1913 *E, I, W*
**Robertson, M A** (Gala) 1958 *F*
**Robertson, R D** (London Scottish) 1912 *F*
**Robson, A** (Hawick) 1954 *F*, 1955 *E, W, F, I*, 1956 *E, I, W, F*, 1957 *E, I, W, F*, 1958 *E, I, W, A*, 1959 *E, I, W, F*, 1960 *F*
**Rodd, J A T** (United Services, RN and London Scottish) 1958 *E, I, W, F, A*, 1960 *W, F*, 1962 *F*, 1964 *W, F, NZ*, 1965 *I, W, F*
**Rogerson, J** (Kelvinside Acads) 1894 *W*
**Roland, E T** (Edinburgh Acads) 1884 *E, I*
**Rollo, D M D** (Howe of Fife) 1959 *E*, 1960 *E, I, W, F, SA*, 1961 *E, I, W, F, SA*, 1962 *E, I, W, F*, 1963 *E, I, W, F*, 1964 *E, I, W, F, NZ*, 1965 *E, I, W, F, SA*, 1966 *E, I, W, F, A*, 1967 *E, I, W, F, NZ*, 1968 *I, W, F*
**Rose, D M** (Jedforest) 1951 *E, I, W, F, SA*, 1953 *W, F*
**Ross, A** (Kilmarnock) 1924 *W, F*
**Ross, A** (Royal HSFP) 1905 *E, I, W*, 1909 *I, W*
**Ross, A R** (Edinburgh U) 1911 *W*, 1914 *E, I, W*
**Ross, E J** (London Scottish) 1904 *W*
**Ross, G T** (Watsonians) 1954 *E, I, W, NZ*
**Ross, I A** (Hillhead HSFP) 1951 *E, I, W, F*
**Ross, J** (London Scottish) 1901 *E, I, W*, 1902 *W*, 1903 *E*
**Ross, K I** (Boroughmuir FP) 1961 *E, I, W, SA*, 1962 *E, I, W, F*, 1963 *E, W, F*
**Ross, W A** (Hillhead HSFP) 1937 *E, W*
**Rottenburg, H** (Cambridge U, London Scottish) 1899 *E, W*, 1900 *E, I, W*
**Roughead, W N** (Edinburgh Acads and London Scottish) 1927 *NSW*, 1928 *E, I, W, F*, 1930 *E, I*, 1931 *E, I, W, F*, 1932 *W*
**Rowand, R** (Glasgow HSFP) 1930 *W, F*, 1932 *E*, 1933 *E, I, W*, 1934 *W*
**Roy, A** (Waterloo) 1938 *E, I, W*, 1939 *E, I, W*
**Russell, W L** (Glasgow Acads) 1905 *NZ*, 1906 *E, I, W*

**Sampson, R W F** (London Scottish) 1939 *W*, 1947 *W*
**Sanderson, G A** (Royal HSFP) 1907 *E, I, W*, 1908 *I*
**Sanderson, J L P** (Edinburgh Acads) 1873 *E*
**Schulze, D G** (London Scottish) 1905 *E*, 1907 *E, I*, 1908 *E, I, W*, 1909 *E, I, W*, 1910 *E, I, W*, 1911 *W*
**Scobie, R M** (Royal Military Coll) 1914 *E, I, W*
**Scotland, K J F** (Heriot's FP, Cambridge U and Leicester) 1957 *E, I, W, F*, 1958 *E*, 1959 *E, I, W, F*, 1960 *E, I, W, F*, 1961 *E, I, W, F, SA*, 1962 *E, I, W, F*, 1963 *E, I, W, F*, 1965 *F*
**Scott, D M** (Langholm and Watsonians) 1950 *E, I*, 1951 *E, I, W, SA*, 1952 *I, W, F*, 1953 *F*
**Scott, J M B** (Edinburgh Acads) 1907 *E*, 1908 *E, I, W*, 1909 *E, I, W*, 1910 *E, I, W, F*, 1911 *I, W, F*, 1912 *E, I, W, SA*, 1913 *E, I, W*
**Scott, J S** (St Andrews U) 1950 *E*
**Scott, J W** (Stewart's Coll FP) 1925 *E, I, W, F*, 1926 *E, I, W, F*, 1927 *E, I, W, F, NSW*, 1928 *E, W, F*, 1929 *E, I, W, F*, 1930 *F*
**Scott, R** (Hawick) 1898 *I*, 1900 *E, I*
**Scott, T** (Langholm, Hawick) 1896 *W*, 1897 *E, I*, 1898 *E, I*, 1899 *E, I, W*, 1900 *E, I, W*
**Scott, T M** (Hawick) 1893 *E*, 1895 *E, I, W*, 1896 *E, W*, 1897 *E, I*, 1898 *E, I*, 1900 *I, W*
**Scott, W P** (W of Scotland) 1900 *I, E*, 1902 *E, I*, 1903 *E, I, W*, 1904 *E, I, W*, 1905 *E, I, W, NZ*, 1906 *E, I, W, SA*, 1907 *E, I, W*
**Scoular, J G** (Cambridge U) 1905 *NZ*, 1906 *E, I, W, SA*
**Selby, J A R** (Watsonians) 1920 *I, W*
**Shackleton, J A P** (London Scottish) 1959 *E*, 1963 *W, F*, 1964 *W, NZ*, 1965 *I, SA*
**Sharp, G** (Stewart's FP and Army) 1960 *F*, 1964 *W, F, NZ*
**Shaw, G D** (Sale) 1935 *NZ*, 1936 *W*, 1937 *E, I, W*, 1939 *I*
**Shaw, I** (Glasgow HSFP) 1937 *I*
**Shaw, J N** (Edinburgh Acads) 1921 *I, W*
**Shaw, R W** (Glasgow HSFP) 1934 *E, I, W*, 1935 *E, I, W, NZ*, 1936 *E, I, W*, 1937 *E, I, W*, 1938 *E, I, W*, 1939 *E, I, W*

**Shedden, D** (W of Scotland) 1973 *NZ, F, W, I, E, P*, 1976 *W, E, I*, 1977 *I, F, W*, 1978 *I, F, W*
**Shillinglaw, R B** (Gala and Army) 1960 *E, I, SA*, 1961 *F, SA*
**Simmers, B M** (Glasgow Acads) 1965 *W, F*, 1966 *A*, 1967 *I, W, F*, 1971 *F* (R)
**Simmers, W M** (Glasgow Acads) 1926 *E, I, W*, 1927 *E, I, W, F, NSW*, 1928 *E, I, W, F*, 1929 *E, I, W, F*, 1930 *E, I, W, F*, 1931 *E, I, W, F*, 1932 *E, I, W, SA*
**Simpson, J W** (Royal HSFP) 1893 *E, I*, 1894 *E, I, W*, 1895 *E, I, W*, 1896 *I, W*, 1897 *E*, 1899 *E, W*
**Simpson, R S** (Glasgow Acads) 1923 *I*
**Simson, E D** (Edinburgh U and London Scottish) 1902 *E*, 1903 *E, I, W*, 1904 *E, I, W*, 1905 *E, I, W, NZ*, 1906 *E, I, W*, 1907 *E, I, W*
**Simson, J T** (Watsonians) 1905 *NZ*, 1909 *E, I, W*, 1910 *W, F*, 1911 *I*
**Simson, R F** (London Scottish) 1911 *E*
**Sloan, A T** (Edinburgh Acads) 1914 *W*, 1920 *E, I, W, F*, 1921 *E, I, W, F*
**Sloan, D A** (Edinburgh Acads and London Scottish) 1950 *E, W, F*, 1951 *E, I*, 1953 *F*
**Sloan, T** (Glasgow Acads and Oxford U) 1905 *NZ*, 1906 *W, SA*, 1907 *E, W*, 1908 *W*, 1909 *I*
**Smeaton, P W** (Edinburgh Acads) 1881 *I*, 1883 *E, I*
**Smith, A R** (Oxford U) 1895 *E, I, W*, 1896 *I, W*, 1897 *E, I*, 1898 *E, I*, 1900 *E, I*
**Smith, A R** (Cambridge U, Gosforth, Ebbw Vale and Edinburgh Wands) 1955 *E, I, W*, 1956 *E, I, W, F*, 1957 *E, I, W, F*, 1958 *I, W, F, A*, 1959 *E, I, W, F*, 1960 *E, I, W, F, SA*, 1961 *E, I, W, F, SA*, 1962 *E, I, W, F*
**Smith, D W C** (London Scottish) 1949 *E, I, W, F*, 1950 *I, W, F*, 1953 *I*
**Smith, E R** (Edinburgh Acads) 1879 *I*
**Smith, G K** (Kelso) 1957 *E, I*, 1958 *W, F, A*, 1959 *E, I, W, F*, 1960 *E, I, W, F*, 1961 *E, I, W, F, SA*
**Smith, H O** (Watsonians) 1895 *W*, 1896 *E, I, W*, 1898 *E, I*, 1899 *E, I, W*, 1900 *E*, 1902 *E*
**Smith, I S** (Oxford U and Edinburgh U) 1924 *E, I, W*, 1925 *E, I, W, F*, 1926 *E, I, W, F*, 1927 *E, I, F*, 1929 *E, I, W, F*, 1930 *I, W, F*, 1931 *E, I, W, F*, 1932 *E, I, W, SA*, 1933 *E, I, W*
**Smith, I S G** (London Scottish) 1969 *SA*, 1970 *E, I, W, F*, 1971 *I, W, F*
**Smith, M A** (London Scottish) 1970 *E, I, W, A*
**Smith, R T** (Kelso) 1929 *E, I, W, F*, 1930 *I, W, F*
**Smith, S H** (Glasgow Acads) 1877 *I*, 1878 *E*
**Somerville, D** (Edinburgh Inst FP) 1879 *I*, 1882 *I*, 1883 *E, I, W*, 1884 *W*
**Speirs, L M** (Watsonians) 1906 *SA*, 1907 *E, I, W*, 1908 *E, I, W*, 1910 *E, W, F*
**Spence, K M** (Oxford U) 1953 *I*
**Spencer, E** (Clydesdale) 1898 *I*
**Stagg, P K** (Sale) 1965 *E, W, F, SA*, 1966 *E, I, W, F, A*, 1967 *E, I, W, F, NZ*, 1968 *E, I, W, F, A*, 1969 *I* (R), *W, F, SA*, 1970 *E, I, W, F, A*
**Steele, W C C** (Langholm, Bedford, RAF, London Scottish) 1969 *E*, 1971 *E* (2[1C]), *I, W, F*, 1972 *E, W, F*, 1973 *NZ, F, W, I, E*, 1975 *I, F, W, E, NZ* (R), 1976 *W, E, I*, 1977 *E*
**Stephen, A E** (W of Scotland) 1885 *W*, 1886 *I*
**Steven, R** (Edinburgh Wands) 1962 *I*
**Stevenson, A K** (Glasgow Acads) 1922 *F*, 1923 *E, W, F*
**Stevenson, A M** (Glasgow U) 1911 *F*
**Stevenson, G D** (Hawick) 1956 *E*, 1957 *F*, 1958 *E, I, W, F, A*, 1959 *E, I, W*, 1960 *E, I, W, SA*, 1961 *E, I, W, F, SA*, 1963 *I, W, F*, 1964 *E, I, W*, 1965 *F*
**Stevenson, H J** (Edinburgh Acads) 1888 *I, W*, 1889 *I, W*, 1890 *E, I, W*, 1891 *E, I, W*, 1892 *E, I, W*, 1893 *E, I*
**Stevenson, L E** (Edinburgh U) 1888 *W*
**Stevenson, R C** (London Scottish) 1897 *E, I*, 1898 *E*, 1899 *E, I, W*
**Stevenson, R C** (St Andrews U) 1910 *E, I, F*, 1911 *I, W, F*
**Stevenson, W H** (Glasgow Acads) 1925 *F*
**Stewart, A K** (Edinburgh U) 1874 *E*, 1876 *E*
**Stewart, A M** (Edinburgh Acads) 1914 *W*
**Stewart, C A R** (W of Scotland) 1880 *E, I*
**Stewart, C E B** (Kelso) 1960 *W*, 1961 *F*
**Stewart, J** (Glasgow HSFP) 1930 *F*
**Stewart, J L** (Edinburgh Acads) 1921 *I*
**Stewart, M S** (Stewart's Coll FP) 1932 *I, W, SA*, 1933 *E, I, W*, 1934 *E, I, W*

*Alastair McHarg, Scotland's most-capped lock, just fails, from the wrong side of the line-out, to intercept Moss Keane's palm-back for Ireland.*

# SCOTTISH INTERNATIONAL RECORDS

*From 1890–91, when uniform points-scoring was first adopted by International Board countries, to 30 April 1978. Both team and individual records are against International Board countries, only, except for the match against the SRU President's XV in the 1972–73 centenary season.*

## TEAM RECORDS

### Highest score
35 v Wales (35–10) 1924 Inverleith
  (Edinburgh)
*v individual countries*
28 v England (28–19) 1931 Murrayfield
29 v Ireland (29–14) 1913 Inverleith
35 v Wales (35–10) 1924 Inverleith
31 v France (31–3) 1912 Inverleith
 9 v N Zealand (9–14) 1972 Murrayfield
10 v S Africa (10–18) 1960 Port Elizabeth
12 v Australia (12–8) 1958 Murrayfield

### Biggest winning points margin
28 v France (31–3) 1912 Inverleith
*v individual countries*
20 v England (26–6) 1971 Murrayfield
19 v Ireland (19–0) 1920 Inverleith
25 v Wales (35–10) 1924 Inverleith
28 v France (31–3) 1912 Inverleith
No win v N Zealand
 6 v S Africa (6–0) 1906 Hampden Park
  (Glasgow)
 7 v Australia (10–3) 1975 Murrayfield

### Highest score by opposing team
44 S Africa (0–44) 1951 Murrayfield
*by individual countries*
27 England (14–27) 1967 Twickenham
26 Ireland (8–26) 1953 Murrayfield
35 Wales (12–35) 1972 Cardiff
23 France (3–23) 1977 Paris (Parc des
  Princes)
24 New Zealand (0–24) 1975 Auckland
44 S Africa (0–44) 1951 Murrayfield
23 Australia (3–23) 1970 Sydney

### Biggest losing points margin
44 v S Africa (0–44) 1951 Murrayfield
*v individual countries*
20 v England (6–26) 1977 Twickenham
21 v Ireland (0–21) 1950 Dublin
23 v Wales (12–35) 1972 Cardiff
20 v France (3–23) 1977 Parc des Princes
24 v New Zealand (0–24) 1975 Auckland

44 v S Africa (0–44) 1951 Murrayfield
20 v Australia (3–23) 1970 Sydney

### Most points by Scotland in International Championship in a season – 77
(in season 1924–25)

### Most tries by Scotland in International Championship in a season – 17
(in season 1924–25)

### Most tries by Scotland in an international
8 v Wales (35–10) 1924 Inverleith

*Scotland scored 12 tries v Wales at Raeburn Place in 1887, but this was before uniform scoring was adopted*

### Most tries against Scotland in an international
**9 by S Africa (0–44) 1951 Murrayfield**

## INDIVIDUAL RECORDS

### Most capped player
A B Carmichael   50   1967–78
*in individual positions*
*Full-back*
D Drysdale   25 (26)★   1923–29
K J F Scotland   25 (27)★   1957–65
*Wing*
A R Smith   33   1955–62
*Centre*
G P S Macpherson   26   1922–32
*Fly-half*
G H Waddell   18   1957–62
*Scrum-half*
J B Nelson   25   1925–31
*Prop*
A B Carmichael   50   1967–78
*Hooker*
F A L Laidlaw   32   1965–71
*Lock*
A F McHarg   39(41)‡   1968–78

*Flanker*
W I D Elliot   29   1947–54
*No 8*
J W Telfer   22 (25)†   1964–70

*One of Drysdale's caps was against New South Wales.*
*Two of Scotland's caps were at fly-half.*
*A R Irvine, 27 caps, has been chosen 4 times as a wing.*
*†Telfer won 3 caps as a flanker*
*‡McHarg has won 2 caps at No 8*

180

**Most points in internationals – 107**
A R Irvine (27 appearances) 1973–78

**Most points in an international – 13**
F H Turner v France 1912 Inverleith
P C Brown v England 1972 Murrayfield

**Most tries in internationals – 23**
I S Smith (32 appearances) 1924–33

**Most tries in an international – 4**
W A Stewart v Ireland 1913 Inverleith
I S Smith v France 1925 Inverleith
I S Smith v Wales 1925 Swansea

*G C Lindsay scored 5 tries v Wales at Raeburn Place*
*in 1887, but this was before uniform scoring was adopted*
*In 1925 I S Smith scored 6 tries in succession – the last 3*
*of the match v France, and the first 3 of the next match*
*v Wales*

**Most points in International Championship in a season – 26**
A R Irvine   1973–74 and 1975–76

**Most tries in International Championship in a season – 8**
I S Smith   1924–25

**Most points on overseas tour – 56**
W Lauder (5 appearances) Australia 1970

**Most points in any match on tour – 24**
D W Morgan v Wellington 1975 Wellington, NZ

**Most tries in any match on tour – 3**
A R Smith v Eastern Transvaal 1960 Springs, SA

*Andy Irvine, Scotland's top points-scorer in internationals, seems about to fall into the clutches of England's Billy Beaumont, while Scott (left), Colclough, Rafter, and Cotton also move in.*

# THE 1977–78 SEASON IN IRELAND

**Paul MacWeeney**

On paper Ireland made only a fractional improvement last season on their bottom-of-the-table position in 1977, nor were there any clear indications that 1979 will produce enough fresh talent to challenge the overlordship of Wales and France in the International Championship. However, the quixotic gesture of the Scottish captain, Douglas Morgan, in rejecting the probability of a draw for the remote chance of snatching a win in the first engagement of the season for the two countries, at Lansdowne Road, made an astonishing difference to everyone's outlook.

A dark cloud seemed to overhang Ireland's teams during the previous campaign, but that victory in the first encounter of 1978 bred a feeling of optimism. If, in the end, it turned out to be unfounded, the players at least acquired a spirit of determination which had been sadly lacking a year earlier. Under the ludicrous, and extremely dangerous, ground conditions at the Parc des Princes in February, the forwards refused to be overwhelmed by a more powerful, and in some positions very much heavier, French pack. This enabled the sharp-shooting out-half, Tony Ward, to give the opposition a real fright with a dropped goal attempt in the last few seconds. Ward delayed just a fraction too long and the kick, from just outside the 22, was charged down. Had it gone over to give Ireland a 12–10 margin France would, no doubt, have donned national mourning; but even such an improbable verdict could hardly have presaged a repeat performance against Wales.

Here again, forward power in the set scrums was the decisive factor. Yet Wales had to wait until the seventy-fifth minute for the try that broke a 13-all deadlock; and even then the French referee, Georges Domercq, might well have penalised Ray Gravell for obstruction in shielding Edwards and Fenwick from would-be tacklers.

With only the minor placings at stake at Twickenham, the Irish forwards seemed unable to move out of low gear in a first half of depressingly low quality on both sides. Yet once again they regained their competitive urge after the interval and it needed a really fine England try, possibly the best combined effort in any of the matches of the tournament, to give the home team third place and push Ireland down to fourth.

The difference between 1977 and 1978 was the emergence of

Ward as a goal-kicker of the highest calibre. He took every chance afforded to him except two in the first half against Wales. His timing was superb and his temperament that of a veteran rather than a debutant. If he had had the pace to make the occasional outside break he might even have been rated the outstanding back in the five countries. His hands were proof against any lapses by his scrum-half, John Moloney, and his line-kicking was of fine quality; but his attempts to create openings for his threequarters by jinking inside were seldom rewarding.

182

Although Moloney showed great defensive qualities and mature judgment, his service was too slow and too lobbed to provide Ward with anything like the space enjoyed by Phil Bennett outside Gareth Edwards for Wales. The centres, McNaughton and McKibbin, were strong defenders but showed limited attacking flair. McLennan's reputation might have been much enhanced if the ball had travelled more frequently towards the left wing. Ensor, meanwhile, made an extremely successful return at full-back.

Noel Murphy, as coach for the first time, infused the players with his famed competitive spirit for Munster and Ireland over a long career, and the one controversial issue was the shifting of Mike Gibson to the right wing. When he missed the Scottish match through injury, Gibson's hopes of beating Willie John McBride's record number of 63 caps had looked remote, so his return in a position which he had never previously occupied seemed to some an almost artificial attempt to ensure that he moved to the top of the list. In practice it turned out to be an inspired move. With Tom Grace clearly a declining force, there was no other candidate with genuine claims. From the start Gibson revelled in the greater freedom afforded to him on the wing, compared with the more congested areas of out-half and centre, and his razor-sharp reactions, acceleration over a short distance, and appetite for work produced more positive progress than in any other Irish back.

The forwards still lacked a second-row pair like McBride and Molloy, though Moss Keane showed the benefits of going on a Lions' tour and made a big advance. However, he still needs a partner of comparable physique. Spring and Steele, hard as they tried, were too lightly-framed for the full demands of the position. Duggan and Slattery maintained their reputations in rear, though a faster flanker than the long-serving and gallant McKinney may be needed this season. A new loose-head prop and a really heavy lock could be other requirements.

If Ireland's senior international performances yielded no dramatic improvement on the previous season, there were

*The Ireland team v Scotland at Lansdowne Road.*
*Back row: P E Hughes (referee), J F Slattery, J B O'Driscoll, M I Keane, D E Spring,*
*W P Duggan, P A Orr, A Welsby (touch judge), O E Doyle (touch judge). Front row:*
*A C McLennan, A R McKibbin, P P McNaughton, J F Coffey (IRU president),*
*J J Moloney (capt), P C Whelan, M P Fitzpatrick, T O Grace. On ground: A H Ensor,*
*A J P Ward.*

encouraging signs in other directions. In the schoolboy internationals, which are termed the 19 age group in the other home countries, England were beaten for the first time at the third attempt, 22–16, in a superb match at Lansdowne Road. Six days later a second successive victory was achieved over Scotland, 21–7, at Inverleith.

The win over England represented a dramatic improvement. In 1977 the English boys outclassed their Irish opponents 37–6 at Gloucester, and if Wales, in the same year, had to work harder at Lansdowne Road, they also won, 10–4. This time Ireland had lost only 10–12 to the touring Australians at Limerick just before Christmas, and if that was to be taken as a yardstick the wins over England and Scotland in April were not exactly surprising. The Australians had run rings around first Wales and then England in January. The Irish had their strongest pack of forwards since joining the international circuit in 1975, among them an outstanding line-out jumper in Moylett; a solid front row in Iveston, Douglas, and John Blair; a 17-year-old No 8 of rare potential in Andrew Blair; and a big and intelligent flanker in their captain, Philip Matthews. With good possession in both matches, McDonnell, at scrum-half, sent out a long and accurate service that enabled a talented partner, Dean, to use a wide variety of tactics. The threequarters – Nowlan, Keogh, Bauress, and Hooks – were the strongest combination in the four countries. Excellent timing of their passes by the centres gave the wings maximum space in which to show their pace and determination. The two tries against England were models of slick handling. But for the individual thrusts of the visiting scrum-half and captain, Youngs, who scored two tries, Ireland's margin would have been much more decisive.

Those victories were not the only source of satisfaction. Leinster's Under 19 team beat Lancashire Colts 15–3 in Dublin in March and, thanks to a generous sponsor, were able to go to London and beat the English Colts 20–6 at Rosslyn Park prior to Ireland's senior international match at Twickenham. The Leinster side produced attacking football of the highest quality in both their matches, and upheld expectations. Since their formation in 1968–69 they have built up a remarkable record of 27 wins in 30 matches against Welsh, English, and home opposition and have provided a dozen players to Irish international teams. Between the Leinster Under 19 team and the schoolboys, who are in the 18 age group, Ireland have a highly promising pool of future talent.

A narrow, and not altogether convincing, 7–3 win over Scotland in a 'B' international at Murrayfield early in December was an encouraging prelude to the full international programme, and four of the side – McNaughton, Ward, Spring, and Fitzpatrick – went on to gain full caps. Another who might have done so but for injury in the final trial was the Ulster scrum-half Colin Patterson, who scored a Gallion-type try against the Scots.

In the build-up to the inter-provincial tournament, Ulster started their programme on a promising note with wins over their traditional English county opponents, Cumbria and Yorkshire. Leinster again suffered defeats against Perpignan and Llanelli, but both were narrow ones and the spirit was higher than in the previous season. In their first inter-provincial match, however, against Munster in Cork, Leinster met with a sharp set-back which eventually led to a triple tie at the top of the table. They found peak form with a comfortable win over Ulster at Lansdowne Road, and after all three had overcome Connacht, Munster fell at the last hurdle against Ulster at Ravenhill.

The standard in the tournament was no higher than has been the case in recent years, but new enthusiasm could be infused into it by a big sponsorship announced in the later stages of the season. A banking company has put up £36,000 over the next three years, and this should ease financial pressure with the outside fixtures. It should ensure, in Leinster's case, the continuity of the Perpignan and Llanelli matches, or if one or other falls out, the funds to find a replacement. Ulster are no doubt very happy to go along with Cumbria and Yorkshire, but Munster break interesting new ground this season with opposition from Middlesex and an Exiles XV composed of London Irish, Welsh, and Scottish players.

There were two other sponsorships. An oil company sub-sidised the Schools internationals with a welcome £2,000, which it is hoped will be continued; and a hotel manager with a keen interest in junior sport put up £1,000 to enable the Leinster youth team to accept their London invitation.

At senior club level, Shannon were the only side to retain their provincial knockout trophy, beating Garryowen in the Munster Cup final – a repeat of the previous year when Garry-owen were also favourites. Wanderers, who bore a charmed life in the earlier rounds, survived to win against University Col-lege Dublin in the Leinster final.

In Ulster there was a big surprise when Ballymena, the Ulster League champions and strong favourites to achieve the double, were beaten in the Ulster Cup final by CIYMS. Only a short while earlier, the latter had been struggling to avoid relegation in the League. Corinthians were pre-eminent west of the Shan-non, winning both the Connacht Cup and League. University College Cork, who had gone down in the Munster Cup semi-final stage to eventual runners-up Garryowen, made things worse for the latter by beating them in the final of the Munster League.

## INTER-PROVINCIAL MATCHES
Ulster 18, Connacht 3; Munster 15, Leinster 10; Leinster 29, Ulster 18; Munster 10, Connacht 6; Leinster 30, Connacht 9; Ulster 9, Munster 6

**Provincial Champions:** Triple tie – Leinster, Ulster and Munster
**Schools Inter-Provincial Champions:** Leinster

## WINNERS OF PROVINCIAL TOURNAMENTS

### CONNACHT
**Senior Cup:** Corinthians
**Senior League:** Corinthians
**Junior Cup:** Creggs
**Senior Schools Cup:** St Joseph's, Garbally Park
**Junior Schools Cup:** St Ignatius, Galway

### LEINSTER
**Senior Cup:** Wanderers
**Senior League:** St Mary's Coll
**Metropolitan Cup:** St Mary's Coll
**Provincial Towns Cup:** Athy
**Old Belvedere Sevens:** St Mary's Coll
**Senior Schools Cup:** Clongowes Wood Coll
**Junior Schools Cup:** Terenure Coll

### ULSTER
**Senior Cup:** Church of Ireland Young Men's Society (CIYMS)
**Senior League:** Ballymena
**Senior Schools Cup:** Bangor Gram-mar
**Schools Medallion Shield:** Belfast Royal Academy

### MUNSTER
**Senior Cup:** Shannon
**Senior League:** UC Cork
**Cork Charity Cup:** UC Cork
**Limerick Charity Cup:** Garryowen
**Senior Schools Cup:** Presentation Brothers Coll, Cork
**Junior Schools Cup:** Christian Brothers Coll, Cork

# IRISH INTERNATIONAL PLAYERS
*(up to 30 April 1978)*

## ABBREVIATIONS

| | |
|---|---|
| *A* | Australia |
| *E* | England |
| *F* | France |
| *M* | Maoris |
| *NSW* | New South Wales |
| *NZ* | New Zealand |
| *S* | Scotland |
| *SA* | South Africa |
| *P* | Ireland v IRFU President's XV at Lansdowne Road in IRFU centenary season, 1974–75 |

| | |
|---|---|
| *W* | Wales |
| (R) | Replacement |
| NIFC | North of Ireland Football Club |
| CIYMS | Church of Ireland Young Men's Society |
| KCH | King's College Hospital |
| Note: | Years given for Five Nations' matches are for second half of season: eg 1972 means season 1971–72 |
| NB | One of Ireland's two matches against France in 1972 was a non–championship match |

**Abraham, M** (Bective Rangers) 1912 *E, S, W*, 1913 *SA*, 1914 *W*
**Adams, C** (Old Wesley) 1908 *E*, 1909 *E, F*, 1910 *F*, 1911 *E, S, W, F*, 1912 *S, W*, 1913 *W, F, SA*, 1914 *E, S, F*
**Agar, R D** (Malone) 1947 *E, S, W, F*, 1948 *F*, 1949 *S, W*, 1950 *E, W, F*
**Agnew, P J** (CIYMS) 1974 *F* (R), 1976 *A*
**Ahearn, T** (Queen's Coll, Cork) 1899 *E*
**Alexander, R** (NIFC, Police Union) 1936 *E, S, W*, 1937 *E, S, W*, 1938 *E, S*, 1939 *E, S, W*
**Allen, C E** (Derry, Liverpool) 1900 *E, S, W*, 1901 *E, S, W*, 1903 *S, W*, 1904 *E, S, W*, 1905 *E, S, W*, 1906 *E, S, W, NZ*, 1907 *S, W, SA*
**Allen, G G** (Derry, Liverpool) 1896 *E, S, W*, 1897 *E, S*, 1898 *E, S*, 1899 *E, W*
**Allen, T C** (NIFC) 1885 *E, S*
**Allen, W S** (Wanderers) 1875 *E*
**Allison, J B** (Edinburgh U) 1899 *E, S*, 1900 *E, S, W*, 1901 *E, S, W*, 1902 *E, S, W*, 1903 *S*
**Anderson, F E** (Queen's U, Belfast, NIFC) 1953 *E, S, W, F*, 1954 *E, S, W, F, NZ*, 1955 *E, S, W, F*
**Anderson, H J** (Old Wesley) 1903 *E, S*, 1906 *E, S*
**Andrews, G** (NIFC) 1875 *E, S*
**Andrews, H W** (NIFC) 1889 *S, W, M*
**Archer, A M** (Dublin U, NIFC) 1879 *S*
**Arigho, J E** (Lansdowne) 1928 *E, W, F*, 1929 *E, S, W, F*, 1930 *E, S, W, F*, 1931 *E, S, W, F*, 1932 *SA*
**Armstrong, W K** (NIFC) 1961 *E, SA*
**Arnott, D T** (Lansdowne) 1876 *E*
**Ash, W H** (NIFC) 1875 *E*, 1876 *E*, 1877 *S*
**Aston, H R** (Dublin U) 1908 *E, W*
**Atkins, A P** (Bective Rangers) 1924 *F*
**Atkinson, J M** (NIFC) 1927 *F*, 1928 *NSW*
**Atkinson, J R** (Dublin U) 1882 *S, W*

**Bagot, J C** (Dublin U, Lansdowne) 1879 *E, S*, 1880 *E, S*, 1881 *S*
**Bailey, A H** (UC Dublin and Lansdowne) 1934 *W*, 1935 *E, S, W*, 1936 *E, S, W, NZ*, 1937 *E, S, W*, 1938 *E, S*
**Bailey, N** (Northampton) 1952 *E*
**Bardon, M E** (Bohemian) 1934 *E*
**Barlow, M** (Wanderers) 1875 *E*
**Barnes, R J** (Dublin U, Armagh) 1933 *W*
**Barr, A** (Methodist Coll, Belfast) 1898 *W*, 1899 *S*, 1901 *E, S*
**Beamish, C E St J** (RAF, Leicester) 1933 *S, W*, 1934 *S, W*, 1935 *E, S, W*, 1936 *E, S, W, NZ*, 1938 *W*
**Beamish, G R** (RAF, Leicester) 1925 *E, S, W*, 1928 *E, S, W, F*, 1929 *E, S, W, F*, 1930 *S, W, F*, 1931 *E, S, W, F*, 1932 *E, S, W, SA*, 1933 *E, S, W*

**Beatty, W J** (NIFC, Richmond) 1910 *F*, 1912 *W, F*
**Becker, V** (Lansdowne) 1974 *F, W*
**Beckett, G G P** (Dublin U) 1908 *E, S, W*
**Bell, R J** (NIFC) 1875 *E*, 1876 *E*
**Bell, W E** (Belfast Collegians) 1953 *E, S, W, F*
**Bennett, F** (Belfast Collegians) 1913 *S*
**Bent, G C** (Dublin U) 1882 *E, W*
**Berkery, P J** (Lansdowne) 1954 *W*, 1955 *W*, 1956 *W, S*, 1957 *E, S, W, F*, 1958 *S, E, A*
**Bermingham, J J** (Blackrock Coll) 1921 *E, S, W, F*
**Blackham, J C** (Queen's Col, Cork) 1909 *S, W, F*, 1910 *E, S, W*
**Blake-Knox, S E F** (NIFC) 1976 *E, S*, 1977 *F* (R)
**Blayney, J** (Wanderers) 1950 *S*
**Bond, A T W** (Derry) 1894 *S, W*
**Bornemann, W W** (Wanderers) 1960 *E, S, W*, 1961 *SA*
**Bowen, D St J** (Cork Const) 1977 *W, E, S*
**Boyd, C A** (Dublin U) 1900 *S*, 1901 *S, W*
**Boyle, C V** (Dublin U) 1936 *E, S, W, NZ*, 1937 *E, S, W*, 1938 *W*, 1939 *W*
**Brabazon, H M** (Dublin U) 1884 *E*, 1886 *E*
**Bradley, M J** (Dolphin) 1920 *W, F*, 1922 *E, S, W, F*, 1923 *E, S, W, F*, 1925 *S, W, F*, 1926 *E, S, W, F*, 1927 *W, F*
**Bradshaw, G** (Belfast Collegians) 1903 *W*
**Bradshaw, R M** (Wanderers) 1885 *E, S*
**Brady, A M** (UC Dublin, Malone) 1966 *S*, 1968 *E, S, W*
**Brady, J A** (Wanderers) 1976 *E, S*
**Brady, J R** (CIYMS, Belfast) 1951 *S, W*, 1953 *E, S, W, F*, 1954 *W*, 1956 *W, F*, 1957 *E, S, W, F*
**Bramwell, T** (NIFC) 1928 *F*
**Brand, T N** (NIFC) 1925 *NZ*
**Brennan, J I** (CIYMS, Belfast) 1957 *S, W*
**Bresnihan, F P K** (UC Dublin, Lansdowne, London Irish) 1966 *E, W*, 1967 *E, S, W, F, A*, 1968 *E, S, W, F, A*, 1969 *E, S, W, F*, 1970 *E, S, W, F, SA*, 1971 *E, S, W, F*
**Brett, J T** (Monkstown) 1914 *W*
**Bristow, J R** (NIFC) 1879 *E*
**Brophy, N H** (Blackrock Coll, UC Dublin) 1957 *E, F*, 1959 *E, S, W, F*, 1960 *F*, 1961 *S, W, SA*, 1962 *E, S, W*, 1963 *E, W*, 1967 *E, S, W, F, A*
**Brown, E L** (Instonians) 1958 *F*
**Brown, G S** (Monkstown and United Services) 1912 *S, W*, 1913 *SA*
**Brown, H** (Windsor) 1877 *E*
**Brown, T** (Windsor) 1877 *E, S*
**Brown, W H** (Dublin U) 1899 *E*
**Brown, W J** (Malone) 1970 *S, W, F, SA*
**Brown, W S** (Dublin U) 1893 *S, W*, 1894 *E, S, W*

Doherty, A (Old Wesley) 1974 P (R)
Doherty, W D (Guy's Hospital) 1920 E, S, W, 1921 E, S, W, F
Donaldson, J A (Belfast Collegians) 1958 E, S, W, A
Donovan, T M (Queen's Coll, Cork) 1889 S
Dooley, J F (Galwegian) 1959 E, S, W
Doran, B R W (Lansdowne) 1900 S, W, 1901 E, S, W, 1902 E, S, W
Doran, E F (Lansdowne) 1890 S, W
Doran, G P (Lansdowne) 1899 S, W, 1900 E, S, 1902 S, W, 1903 W, 1904 E
Douglas, A C (Instonians) 1923 F, 1924 E, S, 1928 S, NSW
Downing, A J (Dublin U) 1882 W
Dowse, J C A (Monkstown) 1914 S, W, F
Doyle, J L (Bective Rangers) 1935 W
Doyle, M G (Blackrock Coll, UC Dublin) 1965 E, S, W, F, SA, 1966 E, S, W, F, 1967 E, S, W, F, A (2), 1968 E, S, W, F, A
Doyle, T J (Wanderers) 1968 E, S, W
Duggan, A T A (Lansdowne) 1964 F, NZ, 1966 W, 1967 S, W, A (2), 1968 E, S, W, F, 1969 E, S, W, F, 1970 E, S, W, F, SA, 1971 E, S, W, F, 1972 F
Duggan, W (UC Cork) 1920 S, W
Duggan, W P (Blackrock Coll) 1975 E, S, F, W, 1976 A, F, W, S, NZ, 1977 W, E, S, F, 1978 S, F, W, E
Dunlop, R (Dublin U) 1889 W, 1890 E, S, W, 1891 E, S, W, 1892 E, S, 1893 W, 1894 W
Dunn, P E F (Bective Rangers) 1923 S
Dunn, T B (NIFC) 1936 NZ
Dunne, M J (Lansdowne) 1929 E, S, F, 1930 E, S, W, F, 1932 E, S, W, 1933 E, S, W, 1934 E, S, W
Dwyer, P J (UC Dublin) 1962 W, 1963 F, 1964 S, W, NZ

Edwards, H G (Dublin U) 1877 E, 1878 E
Edwards, R W (Malone) 1904 W
Edwards, T (Lansdowne) 1889 M, 1890 E, S, W, 1892 W, 1893 E
Edwards, W V (Malone) 1912 E, F
Egan, J D (Bective Rangers) 1922 S
Egan, J T (Cork Constitution) 1931 E, F, 1932 SA
Egan, M S (Garryowen) 1893 E, 1895 S
Ekin, W (Queen's Coll, Belfast) 1888 S, W
English, M A F (Lansdowne, Limerick Bohemians) 1958 W, F, 1959 E, S, F, 1960 E, S, 1961 S, W, F, 1962 W, F, 1963 E, S, W, 1964 NZ
Ensor, A H (Wanderers) 1973 W, F, 1974 F, W, E, S, P, NZ, 1975 E, S, F, W, 1976 A, F, W, E, NZ, 1977 F, 1978 S, F, W, E
Entrican, J C (Queen's U, Belfast) 1931 S

Fagan, C (Wanderers) 1956 E, S, F
Fagan, G L (Kingstown School) 1878 E
Farrell, J L (Bective Rangers) 1926 E, S, W, F, 1927 E, S, W, F, 1928 E, S, W, F, NSW, 1929 E, S, W, F, 1930 E, S, W, F, 1931 E, S, W, F, 1932 E, S, W, SA
Feddis, N (Lansdowne) 1956 E
Feighery, C F P (Lansdowne) 1972 E, F (2)
Feighery, T A O (St Mary's Coll) 1977 W, E
Ferris, J H (Queen's Coll, Belfast) 1900 E, S, W, 1901 W
Finlay, J E (Queen's U, Belfast) 1913 E, S, W, 1920 E, S, W
Finlay, W (NIFC) 1876 E, 1877 E, S, 1878 E, 1879 E, S, 1880 S, 1882 S
Finn, R (UC Dublin) 1977 F
Fitzgerald, C C (Glasgow U, Dungannon) 1902 E, 1903 E, S
Fitzgerald, J (Wanderers) 1884 W
Fitzpatrick, M P (Wanderers) 1978 S
Fletcher, W W (Kingstown) 1882 S, W, 1883 E
Flood, R S (Dublin U) 1925 W
Flynn, M K (Wanderers) 1959 F, 1960 F, 1962 E, S, W, F, 1964 E, S, W, F, 1965 E, S, W, F, SA, 1966 E, S, F, 1972 E, F (2), 1973 NZ
Fogarty, T (Garryowen) 1891 W
Foley, B O (Shannon) 1976 F, E, 1977 W (R)
Forbes, R E (Malone) 1907 E
Forrest, A J (Wanderers) 1880 E, 1881 E, S, 1882 E, W, 1883 E
Forrest, E G (Wanderers) 1889 S, W, M, 1890 E, S, 1891 E, 1893 S, 1894 E, S, W, 1895 W, 1897 E, S

Forrest, H (Wanderers) 1893 S, W
Fortune, J J (Clontarf) 1964 E, NZ
Foster, A R (Derry) 1910 E, S, F, 1911 E, S, W, F, 1912 E, S, W, F, 1914 E, S, W, 1921 E, S, W
Franks, J G (Dublin U) 1898 E, S, W
Frazer, E F (Bective Rangers) 1891 S, 1892 S
Freer, A E (Lansdowne) 1901 E, S, W
Fulton, J (NIFC) 1895 S, W, 1896 S, W, 1897 E, 1898 W, 1899 E, 1900 W, 1901 E, 1902 E, S, W, 1903 E, S, 1904 E, S

Gaffikin, W (Windsor) 1875 E
Gage, J H (Queen's U, Belfast) 1926 S, W, 1927 S, W
Galbraith, E (Dublin U) 1875 E
Galbraith, H T (Belfast Acad) 1890 W
Galbraith, R (Dublin U) 1875 E, 1876 E, 1877 E
Ganly, J B (Monkstown) 1927 E, S, W, F, 1928 E, S, W, F, NSW, 1929 S, F, 1930 F
Gardiner, F (NIFC) 1900 E, S, 1901 E, W, 1902 E, S, W, 1903 E, W, 1904 E, S, W, 1906 E, S, W, 1907 S, W, 1908 S, W, 1909 E, S, F
Gardiner, J B (NIFC) 1923 E, S, W, F, 1924 E, S, W, F, 1925 E, S, W, F, NZ
Gardiner, S (Albion) 1893 E, S
Gardiner, W (NIFC) 1892 E, S, 1893 E, S, W, 1894 E, S, W, 1895 E, S, W, 1896 E, S, W, 1897 E, S, 1898 W
Garry, M G (Bective Rangers) 1909 E, S, W, F, 1911 E, S, W
Gaston, J T (Dublin U) 1954 E, S, W, F, NZ, 1955 W, 1956 E, F
Gavin, T J (Moseley, London Irish) 1949 E, F
Gibson, C M H (Cambridge U, NIFC) 1964 E, S, W, F, 1965 E, S, W, F, SA, 1966 E, S, W, F, 1967 E, S, W, F, A (2), 1968 E, S, W, A, 1969 E, S, W, 1970 E, S, W, F, SA, 1971 E, S, W, F, 1972 F (2), 1973 NZ, E, S, W, F, 1974 F, W, E, S, P, 1975 E, S, F, W, 1976 A, F, W, E, S, NZ, 1977 W, E, S, F, 1978 F, W, E
Gifford, H P (Wanderers) 1890 S
Gillespie, J C (Dublin U) 1922 W, F
Gilpin, F G (Queen's U, Belfast) 1962 E, S, F
Glass, D C (Belfast Collegians) 1958 F, 1960 W, 1961 W, SA
Godfrey, R P (UC Dublin) 1954 S, W
Goodall, K G (City of Derry and Newcastle U) 1967 E, S, W, F, A (2), 1968 E, S, W, F, A, 1969 E, S, F, 1970 E, S, W, F, SA
Gordon, A (Dublin U) 1884 S
Gordon, T G (NIFC) 1877 E, S, 1878 E
Gotto, R P C (NIFC) 1907 SA
Goulding, W J (Cork) 1879 S
Grace, T O (UC Dublin, St Mary's Coll) 1972 E, F, 1973 NZ, E, S, W, 1974 E, S, P, NZ, 1975 E, S, F, W, 1976 A, F, W, E, S, NZ, 1977 W, E, S, F, 1978 S
Graham, R I (Dublin U) 1911 F
Grant, E L (CIYMS) 1971 E, S, W, F
Grant, P J (Bective Rangers) 1894 S, W
Graves, C R A (Wanderers) 1934 E, S, W, 1935 E, S, W, 1936 E, S, W, NZ, 1937 E, S, 1938 E, S, W
Gray, R D (Old Wesley) 1923 E, S, 1925 F, 1926 F
Gregg, R J (Queen's U, Belfast) 1953 E, S, W, F, 1954 E, S, F
Greene, E H (Dublin U, Kingstown) 1882 W, 1884 W, 1885 E, S, 1886 E
Greer, R (Kingstown) 1876 E
Greeves, T J (NIFC) 1907 E, S, W, 1909 W, F
Griffin, C S (London Irish) 1951 E, F
Griffin, J L (Wanderers) 1949 S, W
Griffiths, W (Limerick) 1878 E
Grimshaw, C (Queen's U, Belfast) 1969 E (R)
Guerin, B N (Galwegian) 1956 S
Gwynn, A P (Dublin U) 1895 W
Gwynn, L H (Dublin U) 1893 S, 1894 E, S, W, 1897 S, 1898 E, S

Hakin, R F (CIYMS) 1976 W, S, NZ, 1977 W, E, F
Hall, R O N (Dublin U) 1884 W
Hall, W H (Instonians) 1923 E, S, W, F, 1924 S, F
Hallaran, C F G T (Royal Navy) 1921 E, S, W, 1922 E, S, W, 1923 E, F, 1924 E, S, W, F, 1925 F, 1926 E, F
Halpin, T (Garryowen) 1909 S, W, F, 1910 E, S, W, 1911 E, S, W, F, 1912 E, S, F
Hamilton, A J (Lansdowne) 1884 W
Hamilton, R L (NIFC) 1926 F
Hamilton, R W (Wanderers) 1893 W

188

189

Levis, F H (Wanderers) 1884 *E*
Lightfoot, E J (Lansdowne) 1931 *E, S, W, F*, 1932 *E, S, W, SA*, 1933 *E, S, W*
Lindsay, H (Dublin U and Armagh) 1893 *E, S, W*, 1894 *E, S, W*, 1895 *E*, 1896 *E, S, W*, 1898 *E, S, W*
Little, T J (Bective Rangers) 1898 *W*, 1899 *S, W*, 1900 *S, W*, 1901 *E, S*
Lloyd, R A (Dublin U and Liverpool) 1910 *E, S*, 1911 *E, S, W, F*, 1912 *E, S, W, F*, 1913 *E, S, W, F, SA*, 1914 *E, F*, 1920 *E, F*
Lydon, C (Galwegian) 1956 *S*
Lyle, R K (Dublin U) 1910 *W, F*
Lyle, T R (Dublin U) 1885 *E, S*, 1886 *E*, 1887 *E, S*
Lynch, J F (St Mary's Coll) 1971 *E, S, W, F*, 1972 *E, F* (2), 1973 *NZ, E, S, W*, 1974 *F, W, E, S, P, NZ*
Lynch, L (Lansdowne) 1956 *S*
Lytle, J H (NIFC) 1894 *E, S, W*, 1895 *S, W*, 1896 *E, S, W*, 1897 *E, S*, 1898 *E, S*, 1899 *S*
Lytle, J N (NIFC) 1889 *W, M*, 1890 *E*, 1891 *E, S*, 1894 *E, S, W*
Lyttle, V J (Collegians and Bedford) 1938 *E*, 1939 *E, S*

McAllan, G H (Dungannon) 1896 *S, W*
Macaulay, J (Limerick) 1887 *E, S*
McBride, W J (Ballymena) 1962 *E, S, W, F*, 1963 *E, S, W, F*, 1964 *E, S, F, NZ*, 1965 *E, S, W, F, SA*, 1966 *E, S, W, F*, 1967 *E, S, W, F, A* (2), 1968 *E, S, W, F, A*, 1969 *E, S, W, F*, 1970 *E, S, W, F, SA*, 1971 *E, S, W, F*, 1972 *E, F* (2), 1973 *NZ, E, S, W, F*, 1974 *F, W, E, S, P, NZ*, 1975 *E, S, F, W*
McCallan, B (Ballymena) 1960 *E, S*
McCarten, R J (London Irish) 1961 *E, W, F*
McCarthy, E A (Kingstown) 1882 *W*
McCarthy, J S (Dolphin) 1948 *E, S, W, F*, 1949 *E, S, W, F*, 1950 *W*, 1951 *E, S, W, F*, 1952 *E, S, W, F, SA*, 1953 *E, S, F*, 1954 *E, S, W, F, NZ*, 1955 *E, F*
MacCarthy, St G (Dublin U) 1882 *W*
McCarthy, T (Cork) 1898 *W*
McClelland, T A (Queen's U, Belfast) 1921 *E, S, W, F*, 1922 *E, W, F*, 1923 *E, S, W, F*, 1924 *E, S, W, F*, 1925 *NZ*
McClenahan, R O (Instonians) 1923 *E, S, W*
McClinton, A N (NIFC) 1910 *W, F*
McCombe, W McM (Dublin U, Bangor) 1968 *F*, 1975 *E, S, F, W*
McConnell, A A (Collegians) 1948 *E, S, W, F, A*, 1949 *E, F*
McConnell, G (Derry and Edinburgh U) 1912 *E, F*, 1913 *W, F*
McConnell, J W (Lansdowne) 1913 *S*
McCormac, F M (Wanderers) 1909 *W*, 1910 *W, F*
McCormick, W J (Wanderers) 1930 *E*
McCoull, H C (Belfast Albion) 1895 *E, S, W*, 1899 *E*
McCourt, D (Queen's U, Belfast) 1948 *A*
McCracken, H (NIFC) 1954 *W*
McDermott, S J (London Irish) 1955 *S, W*
Macdonald, J A (Methodist Coll, Belfast) 1875 *E*, 1876 *E*, 1877 *S*, 1878 *E*, 1879 *S*, 1880 *E*, 1881 *S*, 1882 *E, S*, 1883 *E, S*, 1884 *E, S*
McDonnell, A C (Dublin U) 1889 *W*, 1890 *S, W*, 1891 *E*
McDowell, J C (Instonians) 1924 *F*, 1925 *NZ*
McFarland, B A T (Derry) 1920 *S, W, F*, 1922 *W*
McGann, B J (Lansdowne) 1969 *E, S, W, F*, 1970 *E, S, W, F, SA*, 1971 *E, S, W, F*, 1972 *E, F* (2), 1973 *NZ, E, S, W*, 1976 *F, W, E, S, NZ*
McGown, T M W (NIFC) 1899 *E, S*, 1901 *S*
McGrath, N F (Oxford U and London Irish) 1934 *W*
McGrath, T (Garryowen) 1956 *W*, 1958 *F*, 1960 *E, S, W, F*, 1961 *SA*
McGrath, P J (UC Cork) 1965 *E, S, W, SA*, 1966 *E, S, W, F*, 1967 *A* (2)
McGrath, R J M (Wanderers) 1977 *W, E, F* (R)
McGuire, E P (UC Galway) 1963 *E, S, W*, 1964 *E, S, W, F, NZ*
MacHale, S (Lansdowne) 1965 *E, S, W, F, SA*, 1966 *E, S, W, F*, 1967 *S, W, F*
McIldowie, G (Malone) 1907 *SA*, 1910 *E, S, W*
McIlrath, J A (Ballymena) 1976 *A, F, NZ*, 1977 *W, E*
McIlwaine, E H (NIFC) 1895 *S, W*
McIlwaine, E N (NIFC) 1875 *E*, 1876 *E*
McIlwaine, J E (NIFC) 1897 *E, S*, 1898 *E, S, W*, 1899 *E, W*
McIntosh, L M (Dublin U) 1884 *S*

MacIvor, C V (Dublin U) 1912 *E, S, W, F*, 1913 *E, S, F*
McKay, J W (Queen's U, Belfast) *E, S, W, F*, 1948 *E, S, W, F, A*, 1949 *E, S, W, F*, 1950 *E, S, W, F*, 1951 *E, S, W, F*, 1952 *F, SA*
McKee, W D (NIFC) 1948 *E, S, W, F, A*, 1949 *E, S, W, F*, 1950 *E, F*, 1952 *SA*
McKelvey, J M (Queen's U, Belfast) 1956 *E, F*
McKibbin, A R (Instonians) 1977 *W, E, S*, 1978 *S, F, W, E*
McKibbin, C H (Instonians) 1976 *S* (R)
McKibbin, D (Instonians) 1950 *E, S, W, F*, 1951 *E, S, W, F*
McKibbin, H R (Queen's U, Belfast) 1938 *W*, 1939 *E, S, W*
McKinney, S A (Dungannon) 1972 *E, F* (2), 1973 *W, F*, 1974 *F, E, S, P, NZ*, 1975 *E, S*, 1976 *A, F, W, E, S, NZ*, 1977 *W, E, S*, 1978 *S* (R), *F, W, E*
McLaughlin, J H (Derry) 1887 *E, S*, 1888 *S, W*
McLean, R E (Dublin U) 1881 *S*, 1882 *E, S, W*, 1883 *E, S*, 1884 *E, S*, 1885 *E*
Maclear, B (Cork County and Monkstown) 1905 *E, S, W*, 1906 *E, S, W, NZ*, 1907 *E, S, W, SA*
McLennan, A C (Wanderers) 1977 *F*, 1978 *S, F, W, E*
McLoughlin, F M (Northern) 1976 *A*
McLoughlin, R J (Blackrock Coll) 1962 *E, S, F*, 1963 *E, S, W*, 1964 *E, S, NZ*, 1965 *E, S, W, F, SA*, 1966 *E, S, W, F*, 1971 *E, S, W, F*, 1972 *E, F* (2), 1973 *NZ, E, S, W, F*, 1974 *F, W, E, S, P, NZ*, 1975 *E, S, F, W*
McMahon, L B (Blackrock Coll and UC Dublin) 1931 *E*, 1932 *SA*, 1933 *E*, 1934 *E*, 1936 *E, S, W*, 1937 *E, S, W*, 1938 *E, S*
McMaster, A W (Ballymena) 1972 *E, F* (2), 1973 *NZ, E, S, W, F*, 1974 *F, E, S, P*, 1975 *F, W*, 1976 *A, F, W, NZ*
McMordie, J (Queen's Coll, Belfast) 1886 *S*
McMorrow, A (Garryowen) 1951 *W*
McMullen, A R (Cork) 1881 *E, S*
McNamara, V (UC Cork) 1914 *E, S, W*
McNaughton, P P (Greystones) 1978 *S, F, W, E*
MacSweeney, D A (Blackrock Coll) 1955 *S*
McVicker, H (Army, Richmond) 1927 *E, S, W*, 1928 *F, NSW*
McVicker, J (Collegians) 1924 *E, S, W, F*, 1925 *E, S, W, F, NZ*, 1926 *E, S, W, F*, 1927 *E, S, W, F*, 1928 *W, NSW*, 1930 *F*
McVicker, S (Queen's U, Belfast) 1922 *E, S, W, F*
Madden, M N (Sunday's Well) 1955 *E, S, W*
Magee, J T (Bective Rangers) 1895 *E*
Magee, L M (Bective Rangers and London Irish) 1895 *E, S, W*, 1896 *E, S, W*, 1897 *E, S*, 1898 *E, S, W*, 1899 *E, S, W*, 1900 *E, S, W*, 1901 *E, S, W*, 1902 *E, S, W*, 1903 *E, S, W*, 1904 *W*
Maginiss, R M (Dublin U) 1875 *E*, 1876 *E*
Magrath, R M (Cork Constitution) 1909 *S*
Maguire, J F (Cork) 1884 *S*
Mahony, J (Dolphin) 1923 *E*
Malcolmson, G L (RAF, NIFC) 1936 *E, S, W, NZ*, 1937 *E, S, W*
Maloney, J (UC Dublin) 1950 *S*
Marshall, B D E (Queen's U, Belfast) 1963 *E*
Massey-Westropp, R H (Limerick and Monkstown) 1886 *E*
Matier, R N (NIFC) 1878 *E*, 1879 *S*
Mattsson, J (Wanderers) 1948 *E*
Mays, K M A (UC Dublin) 1973 *NZ, E, S, W*
Mayne, R B (Queen's U, Belfast) 1937 *W*, 1938 *E, W*, 1939 *E, S, W*
Mayne, R H (Belfast Academy) 1888 *S, W*
Mayne, T (NIFC) 1921 *E, S, F*
Meares, A W D (Dublin U) 1899 *S, W*, 1900 *E, W*
Megaw, J (Richmond and Instonians) 1934 *W*, 1938 *E*
Millar, A (Kingstown) 1880 *E*, 1883 *E*
Millar, H J (Monkstown) 1904 *W*, 1905 *E, W, S*
Millar, S (Ballymena) 1958 *F*, 1959 *E, S, W, F*, 1960 *E, S, W, F*, 1961 *E, S, W, F, SA* (2), 1962 *E, S, F*, 1963 *E, S, W, F*, 1964 *F*, 1968 *E, S, W, F, A*, 1969 *E, S, W, F*, 1970 *E, S, W, F, SA*
Millar, W H J (Queen's U, Belfast) 1951 *E, S, W*, 1952 *S, W*
Miller, F H (Wanderers) 1886 *S*
Milliken, R A (Bangor) 1973 *E, S, W, F*, 1974 *F, W, E, S, P, NZ*, 1975 *E, S, F, W*
Millin, T J (Dublin U) 1925 *W*

190

**Minch, J B** (Bective Rangers) 1913 *SA, E, S*, 1914 *E, S*
**Moffat, J** (Belfast Academy) 1888 *S, W*, 1889 *S, M*, 1890 *S, W*, 1891 *S*
**Moffatt, J E** (Old Wesley) 1904 *S*, 1905 *E, S, W*
**Moffett, J W** (Ballymena) 1961 *E, S*
**Molloy, M G** (UC Galway, London Irish) 1966 *E, F*, 1967 *E, S, W, F, A* (2), 1968 *E, S, W, F, A*, 1969 *E, S, W, F*, 1970 *E, S, W, F*, 1971 *E, S, W, F*, 1973 *F*, 1976 *A*
**Moloney, J J** (St Mary's Coll) 1972 *E, F* (2), 1973 *NZ, E, S, W, F*, 1974 *E, W, E, S, P, NZ*, 1975 *E, S, F, W*, 1976 *S*, 1978 *S, F, W, E*
**Moloney, L A** (Garryowen) 1976 *W* (R), *S*, 1978 *S* (R)
**Monteith, J D E** (Queen's U, Belfast) 1947 *E, S, W*
**Montgomery, A** (NIFC) 1895 *S*
**Montgomery, F P** (Queen's U, Belfast) 1914 *E, S, W*
**Montgomery, R** (Cambridge U) 1887 *E, S, W*, 1891 *E*, 1892 *W*
**Moore, C M** (Dublin U) 1887 *S*, 1888 *S, W*
**Moore, D F** (Wanderers) 1883 *E, S*, 1884 *E, W*
**Moore, F W** (Wanderers) 1884 *W*, 1885 *E, S*, 1886 *S*
**Moore, H** (Windsor) 1876 *E*, 1877 *S*
**Moore, H** (Queen's U, Belfast) 1910 *S*, 1911 *W, F*, 1912 *E, S, W, F*, 1913 *SA*
**Moore, T A P** (Highfield) 1967 *A*, 1973 *NZ, E, S, W, F*, 1974 *F, W, E, S, P, NZ*
**Moore, W D** (Queen's Coll, Belfast) 1878 *E*
**Moran, F G** (Clontarf) 1936 *E*, 1937 *E, S, W*, 1938 *S, W*, 1939 *E, S, W*
**Morell, H B** (Dublin U) 1881 *E, S*, 1882 *E, W*
**Morgan, G J** (Clontarf) 1934 *E, S, W*, 1935 *E, S, W*, 1936 *E, S, W, NZ*, 1937 *E, S, W*, 1938 *E, S, W*, 1939 *E, S, W*
**Moriarty, C C H** (Monkstown) 1899 *W*
**Moroney, J C M** (Garryowen) 1968 *W, A*, 1969 *E, S, W, F*
**Moroney, T A** (UC, Dublin) 1964 *W*, 1967 *E, A*
**Morphy, E McG** (Dublin U) 1908 *E*
**Morris, D P** (Bective Rangers) 1931 *W*, 1932 *E*, 1935 *E, S, W*, 1936 *NZ*
**Morrow, J W R** (Queen's Coll, Belfast) 1882 *S*, 1883 *E, S*, 1884 *E, W*, 1885 *S*, 1886 *E, S*, 1888 *S*
**Mortell, M** (Dolphin) 1953 *E, S, W, F*, 1954 *E, S, W, F, NZ*
**Morton, W A** (Dublin U) 1888 *S*
**Moyers, L W** (Dublin U) 1884 *W*
**Mulcahy, W A** (Bective Rangers) 1958 *E, S, W, F, A*, 1959 *E, S, W, F*, 1960 *E, S, W*, 1961 *E, S, W, SA* (2), 1962 *E, S, W, F*, 1963 *E, S, W, F*, 1964 *E, S, W, F, NZ*, 1965 *E, S, W, F, SA*
**Mullan, B** (Clontarf) 1947 *E, S, W, F*, 1948 *E, S, W, F*
**Mullane, J P** (Limerick Bohemians) 1928 *W*, 1929 *F*
**Mullen, K D** (Old Belvedere) 1947 *E, S, W, F*, 1948 *E, S, W, F, A*, 1949 *E, S, W, F*, 1950 *E, S, W, F*, 1951 *E, S, W, F*, 1952 *S, W, F, SA*
**Mulligan, A A** (Wanderers) 1956 *E, F*, 1957 *E, S, W, F*, 1958 *E, S, F, A*, 1959 *E, S, W, F*, 1960 *E, S, W, F*, 1961 *W, F, SA* (2)
**Murphy, C J** (Lansdowne) 1939 *E, S, W*, 1947 *E, F*
**Murphy, J G M W** (London Irish) 1952 *E, S, W, SA*, 1954 *NZ*, 1958 *W*
**Murphy, N F** (Cork Constitution) 1930 *E, W*, 1931 *E, S, W, F*, 1932 *E, S, W, SA*, 1933 *E*
**Murphy, N A A** (Cork Constitution) 1958 *A, E, S, W, F*, 1959 *E, S, W, F*, 1960 *E, S, W, F*, 1961 *E, S, W, SA*, 1962 *E*, 1964 *E, S, W, F, NZ*, 1965 *E, S, W, F, SA*, 1966 *E, S, W, F*, 1967 *E, S, W, F, A*, 1969 *E, S, W, F*
**Murphy-O'Connor, J** (Bective Rangers) 1954 *E*
**Murray, H W** (Dublin U) 1877 *S*, 1878 *E*, 1879 *E*
**Murray, J B** (UC Dublin) 1963 *F*
**Murray, P F** (Wanderers) 1927 *F*, 1929 *E, S, F*, 1930 *E, S, W, F*, 1931 *E, S, W, F*, 1932 *E, S, W, SA*, 1933 *E, S, W*
**Murtagh, C W** (Portadown) 1977 *S*
**Myles, J** (Dublin U) 1875 *E*

**Nash, L C** (Queen's Coll, Cork) 1889 *S*, 1890 *E, W*, 1891 *E, S, W*
**Neely, M R** (Collegians) 1947 *E, S, W, F*
**Neill, H J** (NIFC) 1885 *E, S*, 1886 *S*, 1887 *E, S, W*, 1888 *S, W*
**Neill, J McF** (Instonians) 1926 *F*
**Nelson, J E** (Malone) 1948 *E, S, W, A*, 1949 *E, S, W, F*, 1950 *E, S, W, F*, 1951 *E, W, F*, 1954 *F*

**Nelson, R** (Queen's Coll, Belfast) 1882 *E, S*, 1883 *S*, 1886 *S*
**Nesdale, T J** (Garryowen) 1961 *F*
**Neville, W C** (Dublin U) 1879 *E, S*
**Nicholson, P C** (Dublin U) 1900 *E, S, W*
**Norton, G W** (Bective Rangers) 1949 *E, S, W, F*, 1950 *E, S, W, F*, 1951 *E, S, F*
**Notley, J R** (Wanderers) 1952 *S, F*

**O'Brien, B** (Derry) 1893 *S, W*
**O'Brien, B A P** (Shannon) 1968 *E, S, F*
**O'Brien, D J** (London Irish, Cardiff and Old Belvedere) 1948 *E, S, W*, 1949 *E, S, W, F*, 1950 *E, S, W, F*, 1951 *E, S, W, F*, 1952 *E, S, W, F, SA*
**O'Brien-Butler, P E** (Monkstown) 1897 *S*, 1898 *E, S*, 1899 *W*, 1900 *E*
**O'Callaghan, C T** (Carlow) 1910 *W, F*, 1911 *E, S, W, F*, 1912 *F*
**O'Callaghan, M P** (Sunday's Well) 1962 *W*, 1964 *E, F*
**O'Callaghan, P** (Dolphin) 1967 *E, A* (2), 1968 *E, S, W, F*, 1969 *E, S, W, F*, 1970 *E, S, W, F, SA*, 1976 *F, W, E, S, NZ*
**O'Connell, P** (Bective Rangers) 1913 *W, F*, 1914 *E, S, W, F*
**O'Connell, W J** (Lansdowne) 1955 *F*
**O'Connor, H S** (Dublin U) 1957 *E, S, W, F*
**O'Connor, J** (Garryowen) 1895 *S*
**O'Connor, J H** (Bective Rangers) 1889 *M*, 1890 *E, S, W*, 1891 *E, S*, 1892 *E, W*, 1893 *E, S*, 1894 *E, S, W*, 1895 *E*, 1896 *E, S, W*
**O'Connor, J J** (Garryowen) 1909 *F*
**O'Connor, J J** (UC Cork) 1933 *S*, 1934 *E, S, W*, 1935 *E, S, W*, 1936 *S, W, NZ*, 1938 *S*
**O'Connor, P J** (Lansdowne) 1887 *W*
**O'Donoghue, P J** (Bective Rangers) 1955 *E, S, W, F*, 1956 *W*, 1957 *E, F*, 1958 *E, S, W, A*
**Odbert, R V M** (RAF) 1928 *F*
**O'Driscoll, B J** (Manchester) 1971 *E, S, W, F* (R)
**O'Driscoll, J B** (London Irish) 1978 *S*
**O'Flanagan, K P** (London Irish) 1948 *A*
**O'Flanagan, M** (Lansdowne) 1948 *S*
**O'Hanlon, B** (Dolphin) 1947 *E, S, W*, 1948 *E, S, W, F*, 1949 *E, S, W, F*, 1950 *F*
**O'Leary, A** (Cork Constitution) 1952 *E, S, W*
**O'Loughlin, D B** (UC Cork) 1938 *E, S, W*, 1939 *E, S, W*
**O'Meara, J A** (UC Cork, Dolphin) 1951 *E, S, W, F*, 1952 *E, S, W, F, SA*, 1953 *E, S, W, F*, 1954 *E, S, F, NZ*, 1955 *E, F*, 1956 *S, W*, 1958 *W*
**O'Neill, H O'H** (Queen's U, Belfast, UC Cork) 1930 *E, S, W*, 1933 *E, S, W*
**O'Neill, J B** (Queen's U, Belfast, UC Belfast) 1920 *S*
**O'Neill, W A** (UC Dublin) 1952 *E*, 1953 *E, S, W, F*, 1954 *NZ*
**O'Reilly, A J F** (Old Belvedere, Leicester) 1955 *E, S, W, F*, 1956 *E, S, W, F*, 1957 *E, S, W, F*, 1958 *E, S, W, F, A*, 1959 *E, S, W, F*, 1960 *E, S, W, F*, 1961 *E, F, SA*, 1963 *S, W, F*, 1970 *E*
**Orr, P A** (Old Wesley) 1976 *F, W, E, S, NZ*, 1977 *W, E, S, F*, 1978 *S, F, W, E*
**O'Sullivan, A C** (Dublin U) 1882 *S*
**O'Sullivan, J M** (Limerick) 1884 *S*, 1887 *S*
**O'Sullivan, P J A** (Galwegians) 1957 *E, S, W, F*, 1959 *E, S, W, F*, 1961 *E, S, SA*, 1962 *W, F*, 1963 *F*, 1964 *NZ*
**O'Sullivan, W** (Queen's Coll, Cork) 1895 *S*
**Owens, R H** (Dublin U) 1922 *E, S*

**Parfrey, P** (UC Cork) 1974 *NZ*
**Parke, J C** (Monkstown) 1903 *W*, 1904 *E, S, W*, 1905 *W*, 1906 *E, S, W, NZ*, 1907 *E, S, W, SA*, 1908 *E, S, W*, 1909 *E, S, W, F*
**Parr, J S** (Wanderers) 1914 *E, S, W, F*
**Patterson, R d'A** (Wanderers) 1912 *S, W, F*, 1913 *E, S, W, F, SA*
**Payne, C T** (NIFC) 1926 *E*, 1927 *E, S, F*, 1928 *E, S, W, NSW*, 1929 *E, W, F*, 1930 *E, S, W, F*
**Pedlow, A C** (CIYMS) 1953 *W*, 1954 *E, F, NZ*, 1955 *E, S, W, F*, 1956 *E, S, W, F*, 1957 *E, S, W, F*, 1958 *E, S, W, F, A*, 1959 *E*, 1960 *E, S, W, F*, 1961 *S, SA*, 1962 *W*, 1963 *F*
**Pedlow, J** (Bessbrook) 1882 *S*, 1884 *W*
**Pedlow, R** (Bessbrook) 1891 *W*
**Pedlow, T B** (Queen's Coll, Belfast) 1889 *S, W*
**Peel, T** (Limerick) 1892 *E, S, W*

191

192

**Peirce, W** (Cork) 1881 *E*
**Phipps, G C** (Army) 1950 *E, W*, 1952 *E, W, F*
**Pike, T O** (Lansdowne) 1927 *E, S, W*, 1928 *E, S, W, F, NSW*
**Pike, V J** (Lansdowne) 1931 *E, S, W*, 1932 *E, S, W, SA*, 1933 *E, S, W*, 1934 *E, S, W*
**Pike, W W** (Kingstown) 1879 *E*, 1881 *E, S*, 1882 *E*, 1883 *S*
**Pinion, G** (Belfast Collegians) 1909 *E, S, W, F*
**Piper, O J S** (Cork Constitution) 1909 *E, S, W, F*, 1910 *E, S, W, F*
**Polden, S E** (Clontarf) 1913 *W, F*, 1914 *F*, 1920 *F*
**Popham, I** (Cork Constitution) 1922 *S, W, F*, 1923 *F*
**Potterton, H N** (Wanderers) 1920 *W*
**Pratt, R H** (Dublin U) 1933 *E, S, W*, 1934 *E, S*
**Price, A H** (Dublin U) 1920 *S, F*
**Pringle, J C** (NIFC) 1902 *S, W*
**Purcell, N M** (Lansdowne) 1921 *E, S, W, F*
**Purdon, H** (NIFC) 1879 *E, S*, 1880 *E*, 1881 *E, S*
**Purdon, W B** (Queen's Coll, Belfast) 1906 *E, S, W*
**Purser, F C** (Dublin U) 1898 *E, S, W*

**Quinlan, S V J** (Blackrock) 1956 *E, W, F*, 1958 *W*
**Quinn, B T** (Old Belvedere) 1947 *F*
**Quinn, J P** (Dublin U) 1910 *E, S*, 1911 *E, S, W, F*, 1912 *E, S, W*, 1913 *E, W, F*, 1914 *E, S, F*
**Quinn, K** (Old Belvedere) 1947 *F*, 1948 *A*, 1953 *E, S, F*
**Quirke, J T M** (Blackrock Coll) 1962 *E, S*, 1968 *S*
**Quinn, M A M** (Lansdowne) 1973 *F*, 1974 *F, W, E, S, P, NZ*, 1977 *S, F*

**Rambaut, D F** (Dublin U) 1887 *E, S, W*, 1888 *W*
**Rea, H H** (Edinburgh U) 1967 *A*, 1969 *F*
**Read, H M** (Dublin U) 1910 *E, S*, 1911 *E, S, W, F*, 1912 *E, S, W, F*, 1913 *E, S, SA*
**Rearden, J V** (Cork Constitution) 1934 *E, S*
**Reid, C** (NIFC) 1899 *S, W*, 1900 *E*, 1903 *W*
**Reid, J L** (Richmond) 1934 *S, W*
**Reid, P J** (Garryowen) 1948 *E, W, F, A*
**Reid, T E** (Garryowen) 1953 *E, S, W*, 1954 *F, NZ*, 1955 *E, S*, 1956 *E, F*, 1957 *E, S, W, F*
**Reidy, C J** (London Irish) 1937 *W*
**Reidy, G F** (Dolphin and Lansdowne) 1953 *W*, 1954 *E, S, W, F*
**Richey, H A** (Dublin U) 1889 *W*, 1890 *S*
**Ridgeway, E C** (Wanderers) 1932 *S, W*, 1935 *E, S, W*
**Riordan, W F** (Cork Constitution) 1910 *E*
**Ritchie, J S** (London Irish) 1956 *E, F*
**Robb, C G** (Queen's Coll, Belfast) 1904 *E, S, W*, 1906 *S, NZ*
**Robbie, J C** (Dublin U) 1976 *A, F, NZ*, 1977 *S, F*
**Robinson, T T H** (Wanderers) 1904 *E, S*, 1905 *E, S, W*, 1906 *NZ*, 1907 *E, S, W, SA*
**Roche, J** (Wanderers) 1890 *E, S, W*, 1891 *E, S, W*, 1892 *W*
**Roche, R E** (UC Galway) 1955 *E, S*, 1957 *S, W*
**Roche, W J** (UC Cork) 1920 *E, S, F*
**Roddy, P J** (Bective Rangers) 1920 *S, F*
**Roe, R** (Lansdowne) 1952 *E*, 1953 *E, S, W, F*, 1954 *E, S, W, F*, 1955 *E, S, W, F*, 1956 *E, S, W, F*, 1957 *E, S, W, F*
**Rooke, C V** (Dublin U) 1891 *E, W*, 1892 *E, S, W*, 1893 *E, S, W*, 1894 *E, S, W*, 1895 *E, S, W*, 1896 *E, S, W*, 1897 *E, S*
**Ross, D J** (Belfast Academy) 1884 *E*, 1885 *S*, 1886 *E, S*
**Ross, G R P** (CIYMS) 1955 *W*
**Ross, J F** (NIFC) 1886 *S*
**Ross, J P** (Lansdowne) 1885 *E, S*, 1886 *E, S*
**Ross, N G** (Malone) 1927 *E, F*
**Ross, W McC** (Queen's U, Belfast) 1932 *E, S, W*, 1933 *E, S, W*, 1934 *E, S*, 1936 *NZ*
**Russell, J** (UC Cork) 1931 *E, S, W, F*, 1932 *SA*, 1933 *E, S, W*, 1934 *E, S, W*, 1935 *E, S, W*, 1936 *E, S, W*, 1937 *E, S*
**Rutherford, W G** (Tipperary) 1884 *E, S*, 1885 *E*, 1886 *E*, 1888 *W*
**Ryan, E** (Dolphin) 1937 *W*, 1938 *E, S*
**Ryan, J** (Rockwell Coll) 1897 *E*, 1898 *E, S, W*, 1899 *E, S, W*, 1900 *S, W*, 1901 *E, S*, 1902 *E*, 1904 *E*
**Ryan, J G** (UC Dublin) 1939 *E, S, W*
**Ryan, M** (Rockwell Coll) 1897 *E, S*, 1898 *E, S, W*, 1899 *E, S, W*, 1900 *E, S, W*, 1901 *E, S, W*, 1903 *E*, 1904 *E, S*

**Sayers, H J M** (Lansdowne) 1935 *E, S, W*, 1936 *E, S, W*, 1938 *W*, 1939 *E, S, W*
**Schute, F** (Wanderers) 1878 *E*, 1879 *E*
**Schute, F G** (Dublin U) 1913 *E, S, SA*
**Scott, D** (Malone) 1961 *F, SA*, 1962 *S*
**Scott, R D** (Queen's U, Belfast) 1967 *E, F*, 1968 *E, F, S*
**Scovell, R H** (Kingstown) 1883 *E*, 1884 *E*
**Scriven, G** (Dublin U) 1879 *E, S*, 1880 *E, S*, 1881 *E*, 1882 *S*, 1883 *E, S*
**Sealy, J** (Dublin U) 1896 *E, S, W*, 1897 *S*, 1899 *E, S, W*, 1900 *E, S*
**Shanahan, T** (Lansdowne) 1885 *E, S*, 1886 *E*, 1888 *S, W*
**Shaw, G M** (Windsor) 1877 *S*
**Sheehan, M D** (London Irish) 1932 *E*
**Sherry, B F** (Terenure Coll) 1967 *E, S, A* (2), 1968 *E, F*
**Sherry, M J A** (Lansdowne) 1975 *F, W*
**Siggins, J A E** (Belfast Collegians) 1931 *E, S, W, F*, 1932 *E, S, W, SA*, 1933 *E, S, W*, 1934 *E, S, W*, 1935 *E, S, W*, 1936 *E, S, W, NZ*, 1937 *E, S, W*
**Slattery, J F** (UC Dublin, Blackrock Coll) 1970 *E, S, W, F, SA*, 1971 *E, S, W, F*, 1972 *E, F* (2), 1973 *NZ, E, S, W, F*, 1974 *F, W, E, S, P, NZ*, 1975 *E, S, F, W*, 1976 *A*, 1977 *S, F*, 1978 *S, F, W, E*
**Smartt, F N B** (Dublin U) 1908 *E, S*, 1909 *E*
**Smith, J H** (London Irish) 1951 *E, S, W, F*, 1952 *E, S, W, F, SA*, 1954 *W, F, NZ*
**Smith, R E** (Lansdowne) 1892 *E*
**Smithwick, F F S** (Monkstown) 1898 *S, W*
**Smyth, J T** (Queen's U, Belfast) 1920 *F*
**Smyth, P J** (Belfast Collegians) 1911 *E, S, F*
**Smyth, R S** (Dublin U) 1903 *E, S*, 1904 *E*
**Smyth, T** (Malone and Newport) 1908 *E, S, W*, 1909 *E, S, W*, 1910 *E, S, W, F*, 1911 *E, S, W*, 1912 *E*
**Smyth, W S** (Belfast Collegians) 1910 *W, F*, 1920 *E*
**Solomons, B A H** (Dublin U) 1908 *E, S, W*, 1909 *E, S, W, F*, 1910 *E, S, W*
**Spain, A W** (UC Dublin) 1925 *NZ*
**Sparrow, W** (Dublin U) 1893 *W*, 1894 *E*
**Spring, D E** (Dublin U) 1978 *S*
**Spunner, H F** (Wanderers) 1881 *E, S*, 1884 *W*
**Stack, C R R** (Dublin U) 1889 *S*
**Stack, G H** (Dublin U) 1875 *E*
**Steele, H W** (Ballymena) 1976 *E*, 1977 *F*, 1978 *F, W, E*
**Stephenson, G V** (Queen's U, Belfast) 1920 *F*, 1921 *E, S, W, F*, 1922 *E, S, W, F*, 1923 *E, S, W, F*, 1924 *E, S, W, F*, 1925 *E, S, W, F, NZ*, 1926 *E, S, W, F*, 1927 *E, S, W, F*, 1928 *E, S, W, F, NSW*, 1929 *E, W, F*, 1930 *E, S, W, F*
**Stephenson, H W V** (United Services) 1922 *S, W, F*, 1924 *E, S, W, F*, 1925 *E, S, W, F, NZ*, 1928 *E, NSW*
**Stevenson, J** (Dungannon) 1889 *M, S*
**Stevenson, J B** (Instonians) 1958 *E, S, W, F, A*
**Stevenson, R** (Dungannon) 1887 *E, S, W*, 1889 *S, W, M*, 1890 *E, S, W*, 1891 *W*, 1892 *W*, 1893 *E, S, W*
**Stevenson, T H** (Belfast Acad) 1895 *E, W*, 1896 *E, S, W*, 1897 *E, S*
**Stewart, A L** (NIFC) 1913 *W, F*, 1914 *F*
**Stewart, W J** (Preston Grasshoppers) 1922 *F*, 1924 *S*, 1928 *E, S, W, F*, 1929 *E, S, W, F*
**Stoker, E W** (Wanderers) 1888 *S, W*
**Stoker, F O** (Wanderers) 1886 *S*, 1888 *W*, 1889 *S, M*, 1891 *W*
**Stokes, O S** (Cork Bankers) 1882 *E*, 1884 *E*
**Stokes, P** (Garryowen) 1913 *E, S*, 1914 *F*, 1920 *E, S, W, F*, 1921 *E, S, F*, 1922 *W, F*
**Stokes, R D** (Queen's Coll, Cork) 1891 *S, W*
**Strathdee, E** (Queen's U, Belfast) 1947 *E, S, W*, 1948 *W, F, A*, 1949 *E, S, W*
**Stuart, C P** (Clontarf) 1913 *SA*
**Stuart, I M B** (Dublin U) 1924 *E, S*
**Sugars, H S** (Dublin U) 1905 *NZ*, 1907 *S, SA*
**Sugden, M** (Wanderers) 1925 *E, S, W, F*, 1926 *E, S, W, F*, 1927 *E, S, W*, 1928 *E, S, W, F, NSW*, 1929 *E, S, W, F*, 1930 *E, S, W, F*, 1931 *E, S, W, F*
**Sullivan, D B** (UC Dublin) 1922 *E, S, W, F*
**Sweeney, J A** (Blackrock Coll) 1907 *E, S, W*
**Symes, G R** (Monkstown) 1895 *E*
**Synge, J S** (Lansdowne) 1929 *S*

**Taggart, T** (Dublin U) 1887 *W*
**Taylor, A S** (Queen's Coll, Belfast) 1910 *E, S, W*, 1912 *F*
**Taylor, D R** (Queen's Coll, Belfast) 1903 *E*

**Taylor, J** (Belfast Collegians) 1914 *E, S, W*
**Taylor, J W** (NIFC) 1879 *S,* 1880 *E, S,* 1881 *S,* 1882 *E, S,* 1883 *E, S*
**Tector, W R** (Wanderers) 1955 *E, S, F*
**Tedford, A** (Malone) 1902 *E, S, W,* 1903 *E, S, W,* 1904 *E, S, W,* 1905 *E, S, W,* 1906 *E, S, W, NZ,* 1907 *E, S, W, SA,* 1908 *E, S, W*
**Teehan, C** (UC Cork) 1939 *E, S, W*
**Thompson, C** (Belfast Collegians) 1907 *E, S,* 1908 *E, S, W,* 1909 *E, S, W, F,* 1910 *E, S, W, F*
**Thompson, J A** (Queen's Coll, Belfast) 1885 *S*
**Thompson, J K S** (Dublin U) 1921 *W,* 1922 *E, S, F,* 1923 *E, S, W, F*
**Thompson, R G** (Lansdowne) 1882 *W*
**Thompson, R H** (Instonians) 1952 *F, SA,* 1954 *E, S, W, F, NZ,* 1955 *S, W, F,* 1956 *W*
**Thornhill, T** (Wanderers) 1892 *E, S, W,* 1893 *E*
**Thrift, H** (Dublin U) 1904 *W,* 1905 *E, S, W,* 1906 *E, W, NZ,* 1907 *E, S, W, SA,* 1908 *E, S, W,* 1909 *E, S, W, F*
**Tierney, D** (UC Cork) 1938 *S, W,* 1939 *E*
**Tillie, C R** (Dublin U) 1887 *E, S,* 1888 *S, W*
**Todd, A W P** (Dublin U) 1913 *W, F,* 1914 *F*
**Torrens, J D** (Bohemians) 1938 *W,* 1939 *E, S, W*
**Tuke, B B** (Bective Rangers) 1890 *E,* 1891 *E, S,* 1892 *E,* 1894 *E, S, W,* 1895 *E, S*
**Turley, N** (Blackrock Coll) 1962 *E*
**Tydings, J** (Young Munster) 1968 *A*
**Tyrrell, W** (Queen's U, Belfast) 1910 *F,* 1913 *E, S, W, F,* 1914 *E, S, W, F*

**Uprichard, R J H** (Harlequins and RAF) 1950 *S, W*

**Waide, S L** (Oxford U, NIFC) 1932 *E, S, W,* 1933 *E, W*
**Waites, J** (Bective Rangers) 1886 *S,* 1889 *M, W,* 1890 *E, S, W,* 1891 *E*
**Waldron, O C** (London Irish) 1966 *S, W,* 1968 *A*
**Walker, S** (Instonians) 1934 *E, S,* 1935 *E, S, W,* 1936 *E, S, W, NZ,* 1937 *E, S, W,* 1938 *E, S, W*
**Walkington, D B** (NIFC) 1887 *E, W,* 1888 *W,* 1890 *E, W,* 1891 *E, S, W*
**Walkington, R B** (NIFC) 1875 *E,* 1876 *E,* 1877 *E, S,* 1878 *E,* 1879 *S,* 1880 *E, S,* 1882 *E, S*
**Wall, H** (Dolphin) 1965 *S, W*
**Wallace, Jas** (Wanderers) 1904 *E, S*
**Wallace, Jos** (Wanderers) 1903 *S, W,* 1904 *E, S, W,* 1905 *E, S, W,* 1906 *W, NZ*
**Wallace, T H** (Cardiff) 1920 *E, S, W*
**Wallis, A K** (Wanderers) 1892 *E, S, W,* 1893 *E, W*
**Wallis, C O'N** (Old Cranleighans and Wanderers) 1936 *NZ*
**Wallis, T G** (Wanderers) 1921 *F,* 1922 *E, S, W, F*
**Wallis, W A** (Wanderers) 1880 *S,* 1881 *E, S,* 1882 *W,* 1883 *S*
**Walmsley, G** (Bective Rangers) 1894 *E*
**Walpole, A** (Dublin U) 1888 *S,* 1889 *M*
**Walsh, E J** (Lansdowne) 1887 *E, S, W,* 1892 *E, S, W,* 1893 *E*
**Walsh, H D** (Dublin U) 1875 *E,* 1876 *E*
**Walsh, J C** (UC Cork, Sunday's Well) 1960 *S,* 1961 *E, S, F, SA* (2), 1963 *E, S, W,* 1964 *E, S, W, F, NZ,* 1965 *S, W, F, SA,* 1966 *S, W, F,* 1967 *E, S, W, F, A*
**Ward, A J P** (Garryowen) 1978 *S, F, W, E*
**Warren, J P** (Kingstown) 1883 *E*
**Warren, R G** (Lansdowne) 1884 *W,* 1885 *E, S,* 1886 *E,* 1887 *E, S, W,* 1888 *S, W,* 1889 *S, M, W,* 1890 *E, S, W*
**Watson, R** (Wanderers) 1913 *SA*
**Wells, H G** (Bective Rangers) 1891 *S, W,* 1894 *E, S*
**Westby, A J** (Dublin U) 1876 *E*
**Wheeler, G H** (Queen's Coll, Belfast) 1884 *S,* 1885 *E*
**Wheeler, J R** (Queen's U, Belfast) 1922 *E, S, W, F,* 1924 *E*
**Whelan, P C** (Garryowen) 1975 *E, S,* 1976 *NZ,* 1977 *W, E, S, F,* 1978 *S, F, W, E*
**White, M** (Queen's Coll, Cork) 1906 *E, S, W,* 1907 *E, W, SA*
**Whitestone, A M** (Dublin U) 1877 *E,* 1879 *E, S,* 1880 *E,* 1883 *S*
**Wilkinson, R W** (Wanderers) 1948 *A*
**Williamson, F W** (Dolphin) 1930 *E, S, W*
**Willis, W J** (Lansdowne) 1879 *E*
**Wilson, F** (CIYMS) 1977 *W, E, S*
**Wilson, H G** (Glasgow U) 1905 *E, S, W,* 1906 *E, S, W, NZ,* 1907 *E, S, W, SA,* 1908 *E, S, W,* 1909 *E, S, W,* 1910 *W*
**Wilson, W H** (Bray) 1877 *E, S*
**Withers, H H C** (Army and Blackheath) 1931 *E, S, W, F,* 1932 *SA*
**Wolfe, E J** (Armagh) 1882 *E*
**Wood, G H** (Dublin U) 1913 *W,* 1914 *F*
**Wood, B G M** (Garryowen) 1954 *E, S,* 1956 *E, S, W, F,* 1957 *E, S, W, F,* 1958 *E, S, W, F, A,* 1959 *E, S, W, F,* 1960 *E, S, W, F,* 1961 *E, S, W, F, SA* (2)
**Woods, D C** (Bessbrook) 1889 *S, M*
**Wright, R A** (Monkstown) 1912 *S*

**Yeates, R A** (Dublin U) 1889 *S, W*
**Young, G** (UC Cork) 1913 *E*
**Young, R M** (Collegians) 1965 *E, S, W, F, SA,* 1966 *E, S, W, F,* 1967 *W, F,* 1968 *W, A,* 1969 *E, S, W, F,* 1970 *E, S, W, F, SA,* 1971 *E, S, W, F*

193

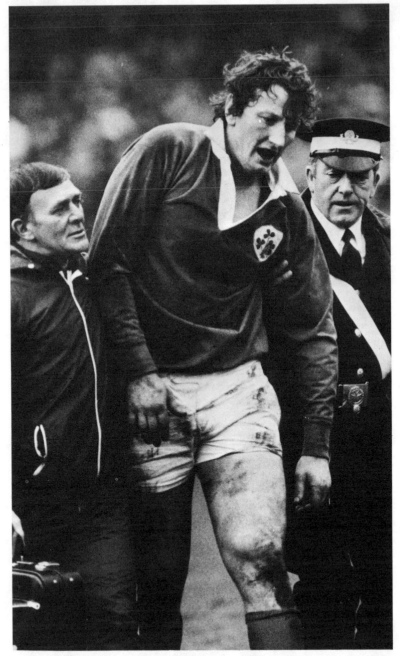

*Willie Duggan, 17 times capped at No 8 for Ireland, leaves the field for repairs against Scotland at Lansdowne Road.*

# IRISH INTERNATIONAL RECORDS

*From 1890–91, when uniform point-scoring was first adopted by International Board Countries,*
*to 30 April 1978. Both team and individual records are against International Board countries*
*only, except for the match against the IRFU President's XV in the 1974–75 centenary season.*

## TEAM RECORDS

### Highest score

26 { v Scotland (26–8) 1953 Murrayfield
{ v England (26–21) 1974 Twickenham
*v individual countries*
26 v England (26–21) 1974 Twickenham
26 v Scotland (26–8) 1953 Murrayfield
19 v Wales { (19–3) 1925 Belfast
{ (19–9) 1927 Dublin
25 v France { (25–5) 1911 Cork
{ (25–6) 1975 Dublin
10 v N Zealand (10–10) 1973 Dublin
12 v S Africa (12–15) 1906 Belfast
15 v Australia (15–8) 1967 Dublin

---

### Biggest winning points margin
24 v France (24–0) 1913 Cork
*v individual countries*
22 v England (22–0) 1947 Dublin
21 v Scotland (21–0) 1950 Dublin
16 v Wales (19–3) 1925 Belfast
24 v France (24–0) 1913 Cork
No win v N Zealand
3 v S Africa (9–6) 1965 Dublin
7 v Australia { (15–8) 1967 Dublin
{ (10–3) 1968 Dublin

---

### Highest score by opposing team
38 S Africa (0–38) 1912 Dublin
*by individual countries*
36 England (14–36) 1938 Dublin
29 Scotland (14–29) 1913 Inverleith
  (Edinburgh)
34 Wales (9–34) 1976 Dublin
27 France (6–27) 1964 Paris
17 N Zealand (9–17) 1935 Dublin
38 S Africa (0–38) 1912 Dublin
20 Australia (10–20) 1976 Dublin

---

### Biggest losing points margin
38 v S Africa (0–38) 1912 Dublin
*v individual countries*
22 v England (14–36) 1938 Dublin
19 v Scotland (0–19) 1920 Inverleith

29 v Wales (0–29) 1907 Cardiff
23 v France (3–26) 1976 Paris
15 v N Zealand (0–15) 1905 Dublin
38 v S Africa (0–38) 1912 Dublin
13 v Australia (3–16) 1947 Dublin

---

### Most points by Ireland in International Championship in a season – 61
(in season 1968–69)

---

### Most tries by Ireland in International Championship in a season – 12
(in seasons 1927–28 and 1952–53)

---

### Most tries by Ireland in an international
6 { v France (24–0) 1913 Cork
{ v Scotland (26–8) 1953 Murrayfield

---

### Most tries against Ireland in an international
10 by S Africa (0–38) 1912 Dublin

---

## INDIVIDUAL RECORDS
### Most capped player
C M H Gibson   65   1964–78
*in individual positions*
*Full-back*
T J Kiernan   54   1960–73
*Wing*
A T A Duggan } 25 { 1964–72
T O Grace   } { 1972–78
*Centre*
G V Stephenson   39 (42)*   1920–30
*Fly-half*
J W Kyle   46   1947–58
*Scrum-half*
M Sugden   27 (28)†   1925–31
*Prop*
R J McLoughlin   40   1962–75
*Hooker*
K W Kennedy   45   1965–75

196

*Fergus Slattery (left), 34 caps, and Stewart McKinney, 25, both have some way to go to equal Noel Murphy's record of 41 for an Ireland flanker.*

*Lock*
W J McBride   63   1962–75
*Flanker*
N A A Murphy   41   1958–69
*No 8*
G R Beamish   25   1925–33

*\* Stephenson played twice on the wing and once against NSW*
*N J Henderson, 40 caps, played 5 times at full-back, and 35 times at centre*
*C M H Gibson, 65 caps, has won 37 as a centre, 25 at fly-half and three as a wing*
*† Sugden played once against NSW*

**Most points in internationals – 158**
T J Kiernan (54 appearances) 1960–73

**Most points in an international – 14**
J C M Moroney v France 1969 Dublin

**Most tries in internationals – 11**
A T A Duggan (25 appearances) 1964–72

**Most tries in an international – 3**
J P Quinn v France 1913 Cork
E O'D Davy v Scotland 1930 Murrayfield
S Byrne v Scotland 1953 Murrayfield

**Most points in International Championship in a season – 38**
A J P Ward (4 appearances) 1977–78

**Most points for Ireland on overseas tour – 53**
T J Kiernan (6 matches) 1967 Australia

**Most points in any match on tour – 17**
T J Kiernan v Queensland 1967 Brisbane

**Most tries in any match on tour – 3**
A T A Duggan v Victoria 1967 Melbourne

# THE 1977–78 SEASON IN WALES

**John Billot** *Western Mail*, Cardiff

The exploits of the national team overshadowed all else on the rugby field in Wales and reflected the pride of its people in a game that means so much to them. In 10 seasons Wales have been outright champions on six occasions and twice joint-first, taking three Grand Slams and five Triple Crowns. The achievement of three Triple Crowns in three successive seasons was unique.

John Dawes, coach to the national side, thought 'this team deserves to be recognised as one of the greatest of all time'. The Prime Minister, Cardiff's own Jim Callaghan, thought similarly, and the team, WRU officials, and VIPs of Welsh connection were entertained at 10 Downing Street on 3 April 1978. It was an occasion to remember, with the Welsh anthem, 'Hen Wlad Fy Nhadau', being sung in the hallowed Pillared Room.

There were hearts in mouths more than once during the battles for the Grand Slam; notably when Hignell missed the penalty shot that would have given England a draw at Twickenham in the opening match, and frequently in Dublin, where Ireland's disrupters in the shape of a fiery pack were hard to look upon. We even saw the great J P R Williams under stress as his sliced clearance pitched over his own goal-line and gave Ireland a try. It was Fenwick who came to the rescue, and the sturdy Bridgend centre provided 16 points with four penalty goals and a try. The Welsh team readily admitted this to be their hardest match of the season. Ireland's 16 points made up their highest score against Wales for 51 years – since they won 19–9 in Dublin in 1927.

After the waterlogged match at Twickenham and the bitingly cold day at Cardiff against Scotland, it was at least pleasant to have ideal conditions in Ireland – ideal, that is, except for the ferocity of the Irish forwards. Still, the outcome was Wales's record fifteenth Triple Crown; and a record eighth Grand Slam was in the offing.

Before that, Scotland's 14 points at Cardiff were the most they had scored on a Welsh ground since their one and only Grand Slam team of 1925 won 24–14 at Swansea. The cold conditions seemed to inhibit Welsh handling and only a few hours after the match a blizzard cut off Cardiff from the west. Many of the Welsh team were snowed up in their hotel until the Monday.

*The Wales team v England at Twickenham.*
*Back row: N R Sanson (referee), S P Fenwick, G Price, J Squire, G A D Wheel, A J Martin, D L Quinnell, R W Windsor, A G Faulkner, T J Cobner. Front row: T G R Davies, J P R Williams, P Bennett (capt), G O Edwards, J J Williams, R W R Gravell.*

In the final match against France, the Grand Slam holders of the previous season dropped vital passes, missed important kicks at goal, and failed to capitalise on their early 7–0 lead. The day was one to remember for Phil Bennett, who became the first Welsh outside-half to score two tries in a match since Raymond Ralph, of Newport, 47 years earlier. Bennett, with 166 points for Wales in international matches, overtook Tom Kiernan's 158 for Ireland to set a new record for the Northern Hemisphere. When his 44 points for the Lions are also added in, Bennett, with 210, has beaten New Zealander Don Clarke's world record of 207 points.

Gareth Edwards, the master tactician at Twickenham, was at his best against France, and set up Bennett's second try with a dazzling burst, dummy, and pass out to J J Williams, who returned the ball infield brilliantly to Bennett. Edwards's dropped goal in this match was another gem. It was a keen disappointment that he could not spare the time to tour with Wales in Australia in the close season.

Wales would have used an unchanged team throughout the season, but Gerald Davies, on the verge of making his forty-fifth appearance to become his country's most-capped three-quarter, withdrew against France because of hamstring trouble and Newport's Gareth Evans took his place. One interesting fact that emerged from a newspaper investigation was the real age, 37, of 'Charlie' Faulkner, the Pontypool and Wales prop. 'It's not how old I am but how well I play on the field that matters', he insisted. By that criterion he could well go on for a few years yet.

At club level, there were many who considered Cardiff would be among the honours at the season's end; but after leading the Welsh championship race for over four months they faded into second place. They also failed in the Cup semi-final against Swansea, who went on to win the trophy as their first significant achievement in a competition since they last won the Welsh club title in 1912–13. Thanks to their superb pack the Swansea men were far too strong for Newport, the previous Cup-holders, in the final.

Pontypridd became the unofficial Welsh club champions by winning the *Western Mail* Trophy for the second time in three years. They lost only six championship matches and were unlucky to go down to Newport in the fourth round of the Cup. Cardiff were runners-up in the club table for the tenth time since rugby resumed after the war, yet they would have taken the title had they managed to win one of their two fixtures with Pontypridd. Maesteg, who finished third, had the consolation of winning the Merit Table title. They had an outstanding pack, and look likely to remain a power in Welsh rugby. Llanelli, champions of the previous season, lost much of their sparkle because their tight forwards were often in difficulty. Newport, too, lacked consistency, as did Aberavon and Bridgend; but Bridgend had great success in the Sevens, winning both major titles.

Welsh Youth lost all three games in a season for the first time. They went down 6–3 to Welsh Schools, 19–9 to French Youth, and 12–7 to England Colts, who, at Cardiff, registered their first success on Welsh soil. Welsh Schools (19 Group) were beaten 25–6 by the brilliant Australian Schoolboys at Cardiff, but recovered to account for Scotland 26–3, Yorkshire 16–3, and France 7–3. This last was a distasteful match, with an excess of French vigour being shown. Finally England recorded their fourth successive win over the Welsh boys, 21–10, at Gosforth. Welsh Schools (15 Group), in their seventy-fifth anniversary season, defeated South of Scotland 22–0 at Bridgend, but lost 10–4 against the same opponents at Hawick. The 15 Group beat Edinburgh Schools 21–8 and swamped Italy 64–0 at Cardiff.

Monmouthshire regained the Welsh Counties Cup from Glamorgan with a 13–12 win at Pontypool after being 0–12 down; Rumney (Cardiff) won the Welsh Brewers' Cup by beating Nantyglo 25–9 at the National Ground to become the champion Welsh Districts club; but the Royal Regiment of Wales lost the Army Cup 12–13 to the Duke of Wellington's Regiment in Germany. Earlier in the season the 'Royals' had defeated a Mexican Select XV 24–6 after a thousand miles coach trip from their base in the jungle territory of Belize.

## SNELLING SEVENS 1978 *(6 May, Cardiff Arms Park)*

**Preliminary round:** Cross Keys 12, Abertillery 10; Maesteg 18, Newbridge 12
**First round:** Cardiff 24, Swansea 10; Ebbw Vale 20, Glamorgan Wanderers 0; Pontypool 14, Neath 12; Moseley 20, Cross Keys 4; Llanelli 26, Penarth 0;

Bridgend 24, Aberavon 4; Newport 22, Pontypridd 0; London Welsh 18,
Maesteg 16
**Second round:** Cardiff 34, Ebbw Vale 6; Moseley 12, Pontypool 10; Bridgend 24,
Llanelli 6; Newport 22, London Welsh 18
**Semi-finals:** Cardiff 22, Moseley 10; Bridgend 24, Newport 10
**Final:** Bridgend 38, Cardiff 16
**TEAMS IN FINAL**

200

**Bridgend:** A Rose; V Jenkins; I Lewis (*capt*), Gerald Williams; Gareth Williams,
G Davies, L Davies
**Cardiff:** D Preece; P Elliott; G H Davies, J Davies (*capt*); T Charles, A Phillips,
R Dudley-Jones
**Referee** D O Hughes (Newbridge)
*Newport have won the tournament 9 times, Cardiff 6, Bridgend 4, Llanelli 3, Neath twice, and Ebbw Vale once.*

## WELSH UNOFFICIAL CLUB CHAMPIONSHIP 1977–78

| | W | D | L | F | A | Avge |
|---|---|---|---|---|---|---|
| Pontypridd | 34 | 1 | 6 | 882 | 321 | 84·14 |
| Cardiff | 30 | 1 | 7 | 860 | 428 | 80·26 |
| Maesteg | 24 | 0 | 9 | 694 | 291 | 72·72 |
| Swansea | 22 | 0 | 10 | 670 | 333 | 68·75 |
| Llanelli | 23 | 1 | 13 | 708 | 436 | 63·51 |
| Bridgend | 26 | 2 | 15 | 712 | 477 | 62·79 |
| Newport | 24 | 0 | 15 | 618 | 432 | 61·53 |
| Ebbw Vale | 23 | 3 | 14 | 593 | 451 | 61·25 |
| Aberavon | 22 | 1 | 14 | 602 | 490 | 60·81 |
| Neath | 21 | 0 | 16 | 557 | 502 | 56·75 |
| Pontypool | 19 | 1 | 15 | 641 | 412 | 55·71 |
| London Welsh | 17 | 1 | 14 | 437 | 417 | 54·68 |
| Newbridge | 17 | 2 | 22 | 431 | 486 | 43·90 |
| S W Police | 12 | 0 | 19 | 354 | 622 | 38·70 |
| Tredegar | 11 | 2 | 18 | 410 | 502 | 38·70 |
| Cross Keys | 13 | 2 | 22 | 337 | 568 | 37·83 |
| Glam Wands | 12 | 0 | 20 | 385 | 416 | 37·50 |
| Abertillery | 11. | 2 | 27 | 340 | 709 | 30·00 |
| Penarth | 8 | 0 | 26 | 294 | 941 | 23·52 |

## WHITBREAD MERIT TABLE 1977–78

*(Only matches against other teams in the table count)*

| | W | D | L | F | A | Avge |
|---|---|---|---|---|---|---|
| Maesteg | 16 | 0 | 5 | 388 | 154 | 76·19 |
| Pontypridd | 18 | 1 | 6 | 484 | 212 | 74·00 |
| Swansea | 12 | 0 | 6 | 329 | 172 | 66·66 |
| Ebbw Vale | 14 | 2 | 8 | 296 | 256 | 62·50 |
| Llanelli | 12 | 1 | 7 | 374 | 224 | 62·50 |
| Newport | 13 | 0 | 8 | 335 | 214 | 61·90 |
| Pontypool | 14 | 0 | 9 | 457 | 218 | 60·86 |
| Aberavon | 15 | 1 | 10 | 406 | 308 | 59·61 |
| Neath | 14 | 0 | 10 | 335 | 316 | 58·33 |
| Bridgend | 15 | 1 | 12 | 398 | 310 | 55·35 |
| Cross Keys | 7 | 2 | 16 | 183 | 420 | 32·00 |
| Newbridge | 7 | 1 | 16 | 216 | 339 | 31·25 |
| Glam Wands | 6 | 0 | 16 | 191 | 338 | 27·27 |
| Abertillery | 6 | 1 | 19 | 179 | 489 | 25·00 |
| Penarth | 0 | 0 | 22 | 103 | 704 | 00·00 |

## WRU NATIONAL SEVENS 1978 (*13 May, Penygraig*)

**Preliminary round:** Bridgend 12, Cardigan 0
**First round:** Cardiff 12, Bridgend Sports Club 7; Abercynon 6, Newport 4;
Maesteg 12, Wrexham 8; Carmarthen 12, Cross Keys 6; Pontypool United 16,
Abercrave 15; Gowerton 12, Cowbridge 8; Ebbw Vale 10, Pontypool 6; Bridgend
16, Llanelli 0
**Second round:** Cardiff 16, Abercynon 13; Maesteg 16, Carmarthen 12;
Pontypool United 24, Gowerton 6; Bridgend 14, Ebbw Vale 4
**Semi-finals:** Maesteg 16, Cardiff 12; Bridgend 18, Pontypool United 3
**Final:** Bridgend 22, Maesteg 18
**TEAMS IN FINAL**
**Bridgend:** F Owen; A Rose; I Lewis (*capt*), Gerald Williams; Gareth Williams,
G Davies, L Davies
**Maesteg:** C Donovan; I Hopkins (*capt*); I Hall, L O'Connor; R Lewis, I Thomas,
J Thomas
**Referee** K Rowlands (Ynysybwl)

# WELSH INTERNATIONAL PLAYERS
*(up to 30 April 1978)*

## ABBREVIATIONS

| | |
|---|---|
| A | Australia |
| E | England |
| F | France |
| I | Ireland |
| M | Maoris |
| NSW | New South Wales |

| | |
|---|---|
| NZ | New Zealand |
| NZA | New Zealand Army |
| S | Scotland |
| SA | South Africa |
| (R) | Replacement |
| Note; | Years given for Five Nations' matches are for second half of season, e.g. 1972 means season 1971–72 |

**Alexander, E P** (Llandovery Coll, Cambridge U) 1885 S, 1886 E, S, 1887 E, I
**Alexander, W H** (Llwynypia) 1898 E, I, 1899 E, I, S, 1901 I, S
**Allen, C P** (Oxford U, Beaumaris) 1884 E, S
**Andrews, F G** (Swansea) 1884 E, S
**Andrews, F** (Pontypool) 1912 SA, 1913 E, I, S
**Andrews, G** (Newport) 1926 E, S, 1927 E, F, I
**Anthony, L** (Neath) 1948 E, F, S
**Arnold, W** (Swansea) 1903 S
**Arthur, C S** (Cardiff) 1888 I, M, 1891 E
**Arthur, T** (Neath) 1927 F, I, S, 1929 E, F, I, S, 1930 E, F, I, S, 1931 E, F, I, S, SA, 1933 E, S
**Ashton, C** (Aberavon) 1959 E, I, S, 1960 E, I, S, 1962 I
**Attewell, L** (Newport) 1921 E, F, S

**Badger, O** (Llanelli) 1895 E, I, S, 1896 E
**Baker, A** (Neath) 1921 I, 1923 E, F, I, S
**Baker, A M** (Newport) 1909 F, S, 1910 S
**Bancroft, J** (Swansea) 1909 E, F, I, S, 1910 E, F, I, S, 1911 E, F, I, 1912 E, I, S, 1913 I, 1914 E, F, S
**Bancroft, W J** (Swansea) 1890 E, I, S, 1891 E, I, S, 1892 E, I, S, 1893 E, I, S, 1894 E, I, S, 1895 E, I, S, 1896 E, I, S, 1897 E, 1898 E, I, S, 1899 E, I, S, 1900 E, I, S, 1901 E, I, S
**Barlow, T M** (Cardiff) 1884 I
**Barrell, R** (Cardiff) 1929 I, F, S, 1933 I
**Bartlett, J D** (Llanelli) 1927 S, 1928 E, S
**Bassett, A** (Cardiff) 1934 I, 1935 E, I, S, 1938 E, S
**Bassett, J** (Penarth) 1929 E, F, I, S, 1930 E, I, S, 1931 E, F, I, S, SA, 1932 E, I, S
**Bayliss, G** (Pontypool) 1933 S
**Bebb, D I E** (Carmarthen TC and Swansea) 1959 E, F, I, S, 1960 E, F, I, S, SA, 1961 E, F, I, S, 1962 E, F, I, S, 1963 E, F, NZ, 1964 E, F, S, SA, 1965 E, F, I, S, 1966 A, F, 1967 E, F, I, S
**Beckingham, G** (Cardiff) 1953 E, S, 1958 F
**Bennett, I** (Aberavon) 1937 I
**Bennett, P** (Cardiff Quins) 1891 E, S, 1892 I, S
**Bennett, P** (Llanelli) 1969 F (R), 1970 SA, F, S, 1972 S (R), NZ, 1973 E, S, I, F, A, 1974 I, F, E, 1975 S (R), I, 1976 E, S, I, F, 1977 I, F, E, S, 1978 E, S, I, F
**Bergiers, R T E** (Cardiff Coll of Ed, Llanelli) 1972 E, F, S, NZ, 1973 E, S, I, F, A, 1974 E, 1975 I
**Bevan, G** (Llanelli) 1947 E
**Bevan, J A** (Cambridge U) 1881 E
**Bevan, J C** (Cardiff and Cardiff Coll of Ed) 1971 E, F, I, S, 1972 E, F, S, NZ, 1973 E, S
**Bevan, J D** (Aberavon) 1975 F, E, S, A
**Bevan, S** (Swansea) 1904 I
**Beynon, B** (Swansea) 1920 E, S
**Beynon, E** (Swansea) 1925 F, I
**Biggs, N** (Cardiff) 1888 M, 1889 I, 1892 I, 1893 E, I, S, 1894 E, I
**Biggs, S** (Cardiff) 1895 E, S, 1896 S, 1897 E, 1898 E, I, 1899 I, S, 1900 I

**Birch, J** (Neath) 1911 F, S
**Birt, F W** (Newport) 1911 E, S, 1912 E, I, S, SA, 1913 E
**Bishop, E H** (Swansea) 1889 S
**Blackmore, J** (Abertillery) 1909 E
**Blake, J** (Cardiff) 1899 E, I, S, 1900 E, I, S, 1901 E, I, S
**Blakemore, R E** (Newport) 1947 E
**Bland, A F** (Cardiff) 1887 E, I, S, 1888 I, S, M, 1890 E, I, S
**Blyth, L** (Swansea) 1951 SA, 1952 E, S
**Blyth, W R** (Swansea) 1974 E, 1975 S (R)
**Boon, R W** (Cardiff) 1930 F, S, 1931 E, F, I, S, SA, 1932 E, S, 1933 E, I
**Booth, J** (Pontymister) 1898 I
**Boots, G** (Newport) 1898 E, I, 1899 I, 1900 E, I, S, 1901 E, I, S, 1902 E, I, S, 1903 E, I, S, 1904 E
**Boucher, A W** (Newport) 1892 E, I, S, 1893 E, I, S, 1894 E, 1895 E, I, S, 1896 E, I, 1897 E
**Bowcott, H M** (Cardiff and Cambridge U) 1929 F, I, S, 1930 E, 1931 E, S, 1933 E, I
**Bowdler, F A** (Cross Keys) 1927 NSW, 1928 E, F, I, S, 1929 E, F, I, S, 1930 E, 1931 SA, 1932 E, I, S, 1933 I
**Bowen, C** (Llanelli) 1896 E, I, S, 1897 E
**Bowen, D H** (Llanelli) 1883 E, 1886 E, S, 1887 E
**Bowen, G E** (Swansea) 1887 I, S, 1888 I, S
**Bowen, W** (Swansea) 1921 F, S, 1922 E, F, I, S
**Bowen, Wm** (Swansea) 1886 E, S, 1887 E, I, S, 1888 M, 1889 I, S, 1890 E, I, S, 1891 E, S
**Brace, D O** (Llanelli and Oxford U) 1956 E, F, I, S, 1957 E, 1960 F, I, S, 1961 I
**Braddock, K J** (Newbridge) 1966 A, 1967 I, S
**Bradshaw, K** (Bridgend) 1964 E, F, I, S, SA, 1966 E, F, I, S
**Brewer, T J** (Newport) 1950 E, 1955 E, S
**Brice, A** (Aberavon) 1899 E, I, S, 1900 E, I, S, 1901 E, I, S, 1902 E, I, S, 1903 E, I, S, 1904 E, I, S
**Bridie, R H** (Newport) 1882 I
**Britton, G** (Newport) 1961 S
**Broughton, A** (Treorchy) 1927 NSW, 1929 S
**Brown, A** (Newport) 1921 I
**Brown, J** (Cardiff) 1907 E, I, S, 1908 E, F, S, 1909 E
**Brown, J** (Cardiff) 1925 I
**Burcher, D H** (Newport) 1977 I, F, E, S
**Burgess, R C** (Ebbw Vale) 1977 I, F, E, S
**Burnett, R** (Newport) 1953 E
**Burns, J** (Cardiff) 1927 I, F
**Bush, P F** (Cardiff) 1905 NZ, 1906 E, SA, 1907 I, 1908 E, S, 1910 I, S

**Cale, W R** (Newbridge and Pontypool) 1949 E, I, S, 1950 E, F, I, S
**Cattell, A** (Llanelli) 1883 E, S
**Challinor, C** (Neath) 1939 E
**Clapp, T J S** (Newport) 1882 I, 1883 E, S, 1884 E, I, S, 1885 E, S, 1886 S, 1887 E, I, S, 1888 I, S
**Clare, J** (Cardiff) 1883 E

**Clarke, S S** (Neath) 1882 *I*, 1887 *I*
**Cleaver, W B** (Cardiff) 1947 *A, E, F, I, S*, 1948 *E, F, I, S*, 1949 *I*, 1950 *E, F, I, S*
**Clement, W H** (Llanelli) 1937 *E, I, S*, 1938 *E, I, S*
**Cobner, T J** (Pontypool) 1974 *S, I, F, E*, 1975 *F, E, S, I, A*, 1976 *E, S*, 1977 *F, E, S*, 1978 *E, S, I, F*
**Coldrick, A P** (Newport) 1911 *E, I, S*, 1912 *E, F, S*
**Coleman, E** (Newport) 1949 *E, I, S*
**Coles, F C** (Pontypool) 1960 *F, I, S*
**Collins, J** (Aberavon) 1958 *A, E, F, S*, 1959 *E, F, I, S*, 1960 *E*, 1961 *F*
**Collins, T** (Mountain Ash) 1923 *I*
**Conway-Rees, J** (Llanelli) 1892 *S*, 1893 *E*, 1894 *E*
**Cook, T** (Cardiff) 1949 *I, S*
**Cope, W** (Cardiff and Blackheath) 1896 *S*
**Cornish, F H** (Cardiff) 1897 *E*, 1898 *E, I*, 1899 *I*
**Cornish, R A** (Cardiff) 1923 *E, S*, 1924 *E*, 1925 *E, F, S*, 1926 *E, F, I, S*
**Coslett, K** (Aberavon) 1962 *E, F, S*
**Cowey, B T V** (Welch Regt and Newport) 1934 *E, I, S*, 1935 *E*
**Cresswell, B** (Newport) 1960 *E, F, I, S*
**Cummins, W** (Treorchy) 1922 *E, F, I, S*
**Cunningham, L J** (Aberavon) 1960 *E, F, I, S*, 1962 *E, F, I, S*, 1963 *NZ*, 1964 *E, F, I, S, SA*

**Daniel, D J** (Llanelli) 1891 *S*, 1894 *I, S*, 1898 *E, I*, 1899 *E, I*
**Daniel, L T D** (Newport) 1970 *S*
**Darbyshire, G** (Bangor) 1881 *E*
**Dauncey, F H** (Newport) 1896 *E, I, S*
**Davey, E C** (Swansea) 1930 *F*, 1931 *E, F, I, S, SA*, 1932 *E, I, S*, 1933 *E, S*, 1934 *E, I, S*, 1935 *E, I, NZ, S*, 1936 *S*, 1937 *E, I*, 1938 *E, I*
**David, R** (Cardiff) 1907 *I*
**David, T P** (Llanelli, Pontypridd) 1973 *F, A*, 1976 *I, F*
**Davidge, G D** (Newport) 1959 *F*, 1960 *F, I, S, SA*, 1961 *E, I, S*, 1962 *F*
**Davies, A C** (London Welsh) 1889 *I*
**Davies, B** (Llanelli) 1895 *E*, 1896 *E*
**Davies, C H A** (Llanelli and Cardiff) 1957 *I*, 1958 *A, E, I, S*, 1960 *SA*, 1961 *I*
**Davies, C L** (Cardiff) 1956 *E, I, S*
**Davies, C R** (Bedford and RAF) 1934 *E*
**Davies, C** (Cardiff) 1947 *A, F, I, S*, 1948 *E, F, I, S*, 1949 *F*, 1950 *E, F, I, S*, 1951 *E, I, S*
**Davies, D** (Bridgend) 1921 *I*, 1925 *I*
**Davies, D B** (Llanelli) 1907 *E*
**Davies, D B** (Llanelli) 1962 *I*, 1963 *E, S*
**Davies, D G** (Cardiff) 1923 *E, S*
**Davies, D H** (Neath) 1904 *S*
**Davies, D H** (Aberavon) 1924 *E*
**Davies, D I** (Swansea) 1939 *E*
**Davies, D J** (Neath) 1962 *I*
**Davies, D M** (Somerset Police) 1950 *E, F, I, S*, 1951 *E, F, I, S, SA*, 1952 *E, F, I, S*, 1953 *I, F, NZ*, 1954 *E*
**Davies, E** (Aberavon) 1947 *A*, 1948 *I*
**Davies, E** (Maesteg) 1919 *NZA*
**Davies, E** (Cardiff) 1912 *E, F*
**Davies, G** (Swansea) 1900 *E, I, S*, 1901 *E, I, S*, 1905 *E, I, S*
**Davies, G** (Cambridge U and Pontypridd) 1947 *S, A*, 1948 *E, F, I, S*, 1949 *E, F, S*, 1951 *E, S*
**Davies, G** (Llanelli) 1921 *F, I*, 1925 *F*
**Davies, G** (Cardiff) 1928 *F*, 1929 *E*, 1930 *S*
**Davies, H** (Swansea) 1898 *E, I*, 1901 *I, S*
**Davies, H** (Newport) 1924 *S*
**Davies, H** (Swansea and Llanelli) 1939 *I, S*, 1947 *E, F, I, S*
**Davies, H** (Neath) 1912 *E, S*
**Davies, H J** (Cambridge U and Aberavon) 1959 *E, S*
**Davies, I T** (Llanelli) 1914 *F, I, S*
**Davies, Rev J A** (Swansea) 1913 *F, I, S*, 1914 *E, F, I, S*
**Davies, J H** (Aberavon) 1923 *I*
**Davies, L** (Llanelli) 1954 *F, S*, 1955 *I*
**Davies, L** (Swansea) 1939 *I, S*
**Davies, L** (Bridgend) 1966 *E, I, S*
**Davies, M J** (Blackheath) 1939 *I, S*
**Davies, N G** (London Welsh) 1955 *E*
**Davies, R H** (Oxford U and London Welsh) 1957 *F, I, S*, 1958 *A*, 1962 *E, S*
**Davies, S** (Treherbert) 1923 *I*

**Davies, T J** (Swansea and Llanelli) 1953 *E, F, I, S*, 1957 *E, F, I, S*, 1958 *A, E, F, S*, 1959 *E, F, I, S*, 1960 *E, SA*, 1961 *E, F, S*
**Davies, T G R** (Cardiff and London Welsh) 1966 *A*, 1967 *E, F, I, S*, 1968 *E, S*, 1969 *S, I, F, NZ* (2), *A*, 1971 *E, F, I, S*, 1972 *E, F, S, NZ*, 1973 *E, S, I, F, A*, 1974 *S, F, E*, 1975 *F, E, S, I*, 1976 *E, S, I, F*, 1977 *I, F, E, S*, 1978 *E, S, I*
**Davies, T M** (London Welsh, Swansea) 1969 *A, E, F, I, NZ* (2), *S*, 1970 *E, F, I, S, SA*, 1971 *E, F, I, S*, 1972 *E, F, S, NZ*, 1973 *E, S, I, F, A*, 1974 *S, I, F, E*, 1975 *F, E, S, I, A*, 1976 *E, S, I, F*
**Davies, W** (Cardiff) 1896 *S*
**Davies, W** (Swansea) 1931 *SA*, 1932 *E, I, S*
**Davies, W** (Aberavon) 1912 *I, S*
**Davies, W T H** (Swansea) 1936 *I*, 1937 *E, I*, 1939 *E, I, S*
**Davis, W E N** (Cardiff) 1939 *E, I, S*
**Dawes, S J** (London Welsh) 1964 *F, I, SA*, 1965 *E, F, I, S*, 1966 *A*, 1968 *F, I*, 1969 *E, A, NZ*, 1970 *E, F, I, S, SA*, 1971 *E, F, I, S*
**Day, H C** (Newport) 1930 *F*, 1931 *E, S*
**Day, H T** (Newport) 1892 *I*, 1893 *E, S*, 1894 *I, S*
**Day, T** (Swansea) 1931 *E, F, I, S, SA*, 1932 *E, I, S*, 1934 *I, S*, 1935 *E, I, S*
**Deacon, T** (Swansea) 1891 *I*, 1892 *E, I, S*
**Delahay, W J** (Bridgend) 1922 *E, F, I, S*, 1923 *E, F, I, S*, 1924 *NZ*, 1925 *E, F, I, S*, 1926 *E, F, I, S*, 1927 *S*
**Devereux, D** (Neath) 1958 *A, E, S*
**Dobson, G** (Cardiff) 1900 *S*
**Dobson, T** (Cardiff) 1898 *E, I*, 1899 *E, S*
**Douglas, W M** (Cardiff) 1886 *E, S*, 1887 *E, S*
**Dowell, W** (Newport) 1907 *E, I, S*, 1908 *E, F, I, S*
**Dyke, J C M** (Penarth) 1906 *SA*
**Dyke, L M** (Penarth and Cardiff) 1910 *I*, 1911 *F, I, S*

**Edwards, A B** (London Welsh and Army) 1955 *E, S*
**Edwards, B** (Newport) 1951 *I*
**Edwards, D** (Glynneath) 1921 *E*
**Edwards, G O** (Cardiff and Cardiff Coll of Ed) 1967 *F, E, NZ*, 1968 *E, F, I, S*, 1969 *A, E, F, I, NZ* (2), *S*, 1970 *E, F, I, S, SA*, 1971 *E, F, I, S*, 1972 *E, F, S, NZ*, 1973 *E, S, I, F, A*, 1974 *S, I, F, E*, 1975 *F, E, S, I, A*, 1976 *E, S, I, F*, 1977 *I, F, E, S*, 1978 *E, S, I, F*
**Elliott, J E** (Cardiff) 1894 *I*, 1898 *E, I*
**Elsey, W J** (Cardiff) 1895 *E*
**Evans, A C** (Pontypool) 1924 *E, F, I*
**Evans, B** (Swansea) 1933 *S*
**Evans, B** (Llanelli) 1933 *E, S*, 1936 *E, I, S*, 1937 *E*
**Evans, B E** (Llanelli) 1920 *E*, 1922 *E, F, I, S*
**Evans, C** (Pontypool) 1960 *E*
**Evans, D** (Penygraig) 1896 *I, S*, 1897 *E*, 1898 *E*
**Evans, D B** (Swansea) 1926 *E*
**Evans, D D** (Cheshire and Cardiff U) 1934 *E*
**Evans, D P** (Llanelli) 1960 *SA*
**Evans, D W** (Cardiff) 1889 *I, S*, 1890 *E, I*, 1891 *E*
**Evans, E** (Llanelli) 1937 *E*, 1939 *I, S*
**Evans, F** (Llanelli) 1921 *S*
**Evans, G** (Cardiff) 1947 *A, E, F, I, S*, 1948 *E, F, I, S*, 1949 *E, I, S*
**Evans, G L** (Newport) 1977 *F* (R), 1978 *F*
**Evans, I** (London Welsh) 1934 *I, S*
**Evans, I** (Swansea) 1922 *E, F, I, S*
**Evans, J** (Llanelli) 1896 *I, S*, 1897 *E*
**Evans, J** (Blaina) 1904 *E*
**Evans, J** (Pontypool) 1907 *E, I, S*
**Evans, J D** (Cardiff) 1958 *F, I*
**Evans, J E** (Llanelli) 1924 *S*
**Evans, J R** (Newport) 1934 *E*
**Evans, O J** (Cardiff) 1887 *E, S*, 1888 *I, S*
**Evans, P** (Llanelli) 1951 *E, F*
**Evans, R** (Cardiff) 1889 *S*
**Evans, R** (Bridgend) 1963 *F, I, S*
**Evans, R T** (Newport) 1947 *F, I*, 1950 *E, F, I, S*, 1951 *E, F, I, S*
**Evans, T** (Llanelli) 1906 *I*, 1907 *E, I, S*, 1908 *A, I*, 1909 *E, F, I, S*, 1910 *E, F, I, S*, 1911 *E, F, I, S*
**Evans, T** (Swansea) 1924 *I*
**Evans, T G** (London Welsh) 1970 *E, I, S, SA*, 1972 *E, F, S*
**Evans, T P** (Swansea) 1975 *F, E, S, I, A*, 1976 *E, S, I, F*, 1977 *I*
**Evans, V** (Neath) 1954 *F, I, S*
**Evans, W** (Llanelli) 1958 *A*

202

203

**Jenkins, V G J** (Oxford U, Bridgend, London Welsh) 1933 E, I, 1934 I, S, 1935 E, NZ, S, 1936 E, I, S, 1937 E, 1938 E, S, 1939 E
**Jenkins, W** (Cardiff) 1912 F, I, 1913 I, S
**John, A** (Llanelli) 1925 I, 1928 E, I, S
**John, B** (Llanelli and Cardiff) 1966 A, 1967 NZ, S, 1968 E, F, I, S, 1969 A, E, F, I, NZ (2), S, 1970 E, I, S, SA, 1971 E, F, I, S, 1972 E, F, S
**John, D E** (Llanelli) 1923 F, I, 1928 E, I, S
**John, E R** (Neath) 1950 E, F, I, S, 1951 E, F, I, S, SA, 1952 E, F, I, S, 1953 E, F, I, NZ, S, 1954 E
**John, G** (St Luke's Coll, Exeter) 1954 E, F
**John, J H** (Swansea) 1926 E, F, I, S, 1927 E, F, I, S
**Johnson, T** (Cardiff) 1921 E, F, I, 1923 E, F, S, 1924 E, NZ, S, 1925 E, F, S
**Johnson, W D** (Swansea) 1953 E
**Jones, A H** (Cardiff) 1933 E, S
**Jones, B** (Abertillery) 1914 E, F, I, S
**Jones, Bert** (Llanelli) 1934 I, S
**Jones, Bob** (Llwynypia) 1901 I
**Jones, B J** (Newport) 1960 F, I
**Jones, B Lewis** (Llanelli) 1950 E, F, I, S, 1951 E, S, SA, 1952 E, F, I
**Jones, C W** (Cambridge U and Cardiff) 1934 E, I, S, 1935 E, I, NZ, S, 1936 E, I, S, 1938 E, I, S
**Jones, C W** (Bridgend) 1920 E, F, S
**Jones, D** (Neath) 1927 NSW
**Jones, D** (Aberavon) 1897 E
**Jones, D** (Swansea) 1947 E, F, I, 1949 E, F, I, S
**Jones, D** (Treherbert) 1902 E, I, S, 1903 E, I, S, 1905 E, I, NZ, S, 1906 E, S, SA
**Jones, D** (Newport) 1926 E, F, I, S, 1927 E
**Jones, D** (Llanelli) 1948 E
**Jones, D K** (Llanelli and Cardiff) 1962 E, F, I, S, 1963 E, F, NZ, 1964 E, S, SA, 1966 E, F, I, S
**Jones, D P** (Pontypool) 1907 I
**Jones, E** (Llanelli) 1930 F, 1933 E, I, S, 1935 E
**Jones, Elvet** (Llanelli) 1939 S
**Jones, G** (Cardiff) 1930 S, 1933 I
**Jones, G** (Ebbw Vale) 1963 F, I, S
**Jones, H** (Penygraig) 1902 I, S
**Jones, H** (Neath) 1904 I
**Jones, H** (Neath) 1929 E, S
**Jones, H** (Swansea) 1930 F, I
**Jones, Iorwerth** (Llanelli) 1927 NSW, 1928 E, F, I, S
**Jones, Ivor** (Llanelli) 1924 E, S, 1927 F, I, NSW, S, 1928 E, F, I, S, 1929 E, F, I, S, 1930 E, S
**Jones, I C** (London Welsh) 1968 I
**Jones, J** (Aberavon) 1901 E
**Jones, J A** (Cardiff) 1883 S
**Jones, Jim** (Aberavon) 1919 NZA, 1920 E, S, 1921 F, I, S
**Jones, J** (Swansea) 1924 F
**Jones, J P** (Pontypool) 1908 A, 1909 E, F, I, S, 1910 E, F, 1912 E, F, 1913 F, I, 1920 F, I, 1921 E
**Jones, K D** (Cardiff) 1960 SA, 1961 E, S, I, 1962 E, F, 1963 E, I, S, NZ
**Jones, K J** (Newport) 1947 A, E, F, I, S, 1948 E, F, I, S, 1949 E, F, I, S, 1950 E, F, I, S, 1951 E, F, I, S, SA, 1952 E, F, I, S, 1953 E, F, I, NZ, S, 1954 E, F, I, S, 1955 E, F, I, S, 1956 E, F, I, S, 1957 E
**Jones, K W J** (Oxford U and London Welsh) 1934 E
**Jones, P B** (Newport) 1921 S
**Jones, P** (Newport) 1912 SA, 1913 E, F, S, 1914 E, F, I, S
**Jones, R** (Swansea) 1901 I, 1902 E, 1904 E, I, S, 1905 E, 1908 A, F, I, 1909 E, F, I, S, 1910 E, F
**Jones, R** (London Welsh) 1929 E
**Jones, R B** (Cambridge U) 1933 E, S
**Jones, R E** (Coventry) 1967 E, F, 1968 F, I, S
**Jones, R** (Northampton) 1926 E, F, S
**Jones, R** (Swansea) 1927 NSW, 1928 F
**Jones, T B** (Newport) 1882 I, 1883 E, S, 1884 S, 1885 E, S
**Jones, Tom** (Newport) 1922 E, F, I, S, 1924 E, S
**Jones, T** (Pontypool) 1913 S
**Jones, W** (Cardiff) 1898 E, I
**Jones, W I** (Llanelli and Cambridge U) 1925 E, F, I, S
**Jones, W J** (Llanelli) 1924 I
**Jones, W K** (Cardiff) 1967 NZ, 1968 E, F, I, S
**Jones, W** (Mountain Ash) 1905 I
**Jones-Davies, T E** (London Welsh) 1930 E, I, 1931 E, S
**Jordan, H M** (Newport) 1885 E, S, 1889 S

**Joseph, W** (Swansea) 1902 E, I, S, 1903 E, I, S, 1904 E, S, 1905 E, I, NZ, S, 1906 E, I, S, SA
**Jowett, W F** (Swansea) 1903 E
**Judd, S** (Cardiff) 1953 E, F, I, NZ, S, 1954 E, F, S, 1955 E, S
**Judson, J H** (Llanelli) 1883 E, S

**Kedzlie, Q D** (Cardiff) 1888 I, S
**Knill, F M D** (Cardiff) 1976 F (R)

**Lang, J** (Llanelli) 1931 F, I, 1934 I, S, 1935 E, I, NZ, S, 1936 E, I, S, 1937 E
**Lawrence, S** (Bridgend) 1925 I, S, 1926 F, I, S, 1927 E
**Law, V J** (Newport) 1939 I
**Legge, W G** (Newport) 1937 I, 1938 I
**Leleu, J** (London Welsh and Swansea) 1959 E, S, 1960 F, SA
**Lemon, A** (Neath) 1929 I, 1930 F, I, S, 1931 E, F, I, S, SA, 1932 E, I, S, 1933 I
**Lewis, A J** (Ebbw Vale) 1970 F, 1971 E, F, I, 1972 E, F, S, 1973 E, S, I, F
**Lewis, A R** (Abertillery) 1966 A, E, F, I, S, 1967 I
**Lewis, B** (Swansea) 1912 I, 1913 I
**Lewis, C P** (Llandovery) 1882 I, 1883 E, S, 1884 E, S
**Lewis, D H** (Cardiff) 1886 E, S
**Lewis, E J** (Llandovery) 1881 E
**Lewis, G W** (Richmond) 1960 E, S
**Lewis, H** (Swansea) 1913 F, I, S, 1914 E
**Lewis, J** (Llanelli) 1887 I
**Lewis, J M C** (Cardiff and Cambridge U) 1912 E, 1913 F, I, S, 1914 E, F, I, S, 1921 I, 1923 E, S
**Lewis, M** (Treorchy) 1913 F
**Lewis, T** (Cardiff) 1926 E, 1927 E, S
**Lewis, W H** (London Welsh and Cambridge U) 1926 I, 1927 E, F, I, NSW, 1928 F
**Lewis, W** (Llanelli) 1925 F
**Llewellyn, P D** (Swansea) 1973 I, F, A, 1974 S, E
**Llewellyn, W** (Llwynypia) 1899 E, I, S, 1900 E, I, S, 1901 E, I, S, 1902 E, I, S, 1903 I, 1904 E, I, S, 1905 E, I, NZ, S
**Llewelyn, D B** (Newport and Llanelli) 1970 E, F, I, S, SA 1971 E, F, I, S, 1972 E, F, S, NZ
**Lloyd, D J** (Bridgend) 1966 A, E, F, I, S, 1967 E, F, I, S, 1968 F, I, S, 1969 A, E, F, I, NZ, S, 1970 F, 1972 E, F, S, 1973 E, S
**Lloyd, E** (Llanelli) 1895 S
**Lloyd, G L** (Newport) 1896 I, 1899 I, S, 1900 E, S, 1901 E, S, 1902 I, S, 1903 E, I, S
**Lloyd, P** (Llanelli) 1890 E, S, 1891 E, I
**Lloyd, R** (Pontypool) 1913 F, I, S, 1914 E, F, I, S
**Lloyd, T** (Maesteg) 1953 F, I
**Lloyd, T C** (Neath) 1909 F, 1913 F, I, 1914 E, F, I, S
**Lockwood, T W** (Newport) 1887 E, S, I
**Long, E** (Swansea) 1936 E, I, S, 1937 E, S, 1939 I, S
**Lyne, H S** (Newport) 1883 S, 1884 E, I, S, 1885 E

**Maddocks, H T** (London Welsh) 1906 E, I, S, 1907 E, S, 1910 F
**Maddocks, K** (Neath) 1957 E
**Main, D R** (London Welsh) 1959 E, F, I, S
**Mainwaring, H J** (Swansea) 1961 F
**Mainwaring, W T** (Aberavon) 1967 E, F, I, NZ, S, 1968 E
**Major, W** (Maesteg) 1949 E, 1950 S
**Male, B O** (Cardiff) 1921 F, 1923 S, 1924 I, S, 1927 E, F, I, S, 1928 F, I, S
**Manfield, L** (Mountain Ash and Cardiff) 1939 I, S, 1947 A, 1948 E, F, I, S
**Mann, B B** (Cardiff) 1881 E
**Mantle, J T** (Loughborough Colls and Newport) 1964 E, SA
**Margrave, F L** (Llanelli) 1884 E, S
**Marsden-Jones, D** (Cardiff) 1921 E, 1924 NZ
**Martin, A J** (Aberavon) 1973 A, 1974 S, I, 1975 F, E, S, I, A, 1976 E, S, I, F, 1977 I, F, E, S, 1978 E, S, I, F
**Martin, W J** (Newport) 1912 F, I, 1919 NZA
**Mathias, R** (Llanelli) 1970 F
**Matthews, Rev A A** (Lampeter) 1886 S
**Matthews, C** (Bridgend) 1939 I
**Matthews, J** (Cardiff) 1947 A, E, 1948 E, F, S, 1949 E, F, I, S, 1950 E, F, I, S, 1951 E, F, I, S
**McCall, B E W** (Welch Regt and Newport) 1936 E, I, S
**McCarley, A** (Neath) 1938 E, I, S

**McCutcheon, W** (Swansea) 1891 *S*, 1892 *E*, 1893 *E*, *S*, *I*, 1894 *E*
**Meredith, A** (Devonport Services) 1949 *E*, *I*, *S*
**Meredith, B V** (St Luke's Coll, London Welsh and Newport) 1954 *F*, *I*, *S*, 1955 *E*, *F*, *I*, *S*, 1956 *E*, *F*, *I*, *S*, 1957 *E*, *F*, *I*, *S*, 1958 *A*, *E*, *I*, *S*, 1959 *E*, *F*, *I*, *S*, 1960 *E*, *F*, *S*, *SA*, 1961 *E*, *I*, *S*, 1962 *E*, *F*, *I*, *S*
**Meredith, C C** (Neath) 1953 *NZ*, *S*, 1954 *E*, *F*, *I*, *S*, 1955 *E*, *F*, *I*, *S*, 1956 *F*, *I*, 1957 *E*, *S*
**Meredith, J** (Swansea) 1888 *I*, *S*, 1890 *E*, *S*
**Merry, G E** (Pill Harriers) 1912 *F*, *I*
**Michael, G** (Swansea) 1923 *E*, *F*, *S*
**Michaelson, R C B** (Aberavon and Cambridge U) 1963 *E*
**Miller, F** (Mountain Ash) 1896 *I*, 1900 *E*, *I*, *S*, 1901 *E*, *I*, *S*
**Mills, F** (Swansea) 1892 *E*, *I*, *S*, 1893 *E*, *I*, *S*, 1894 *E*, *I*, *S*, 1895 *E*, *I*, *S*, 1896 *E*
**Moore, W J** (Bridgend) 1933 *I*
**Morgan, C H** (Llanelli) 1957 *F*, *I*
**Morgan, C I** (Cardiff) 1951 *F*, *I*, *SA*, 1952 *E*, *I*, *S*, 1953 *F*, *I*, *NZ*, *S*, 1954 *E*, *I*, *S*, 1955 *E*, *F*, *I*, *S*, 1956 *E*, *F*, *I*, *S*, 1957 *E*, *F*, *I*, *S*, 1958 *E*, *F*, *I*, *S*
**Morgan, D** (Swansea) 1885 *S*, 1886 *E*, *S*, 1887 *E*, *I*, *S*, 1889 *I*
**Morgan, D** (Llanelli) 1895 *I*, 1896 *E*
**Morgan, D R** (Llanelli) 1962 *E*, *F*, *I*, *S*, 1963 *E*, *F*, *I*, *NZ*, *S*
**Morgan, E** (Llanelli) 1920 *I*, 1921 *E*, *F*, *S*
**Morgan, E T** (London Welsh) 1902 *E*, *I*, *S*, 1903 *I*, 1904 *E*, *I*, *S*, 1905 *E*, *I*, *NZ*, *S*, 1906 *E*, *I*, *S*, *SA*, 1908 *F*
**Morgan, Edgar** (Swansea) 1914 *E*, *F*, *I*, *S*
**Morgan, F L** (Llanelli) 1938 *E*, *I*, *S*, 1939 *E*
**Morgan, H J** (Abertillery) 1958 *E*, *F*, *I*, *S*, 1959 *F*, *I*, 1960 *E*, 1961 *E*, *F*, *I*, *S*, 1962 *E*, *F*, *I*, *S*, 1963 *F*, *I*, *S*, 1965 *E*, *F*, *I*, *S*, 1966 *A*, *E*, *F*, *I*, *S*
**Morgan, H P** (Newport) 1956 *E*, *F*, *I*, *S*
**Morgan, I** (Swansea) 1908 *A*, 1909 *E*, *F*, *I*, *S*, 1910 *E*, *F*, *I*, *S*, 1911 *E*, *F*, *I*, 1912 *S*
**Morgan, J** (Llanelli) 1912 *SA*, 1913 *E*
**Morgan, M E** (Swansea) 1938 *E*, *I*, *S*, 1939 *E*
**Morgan, N** (Newport) 1960 *F*, *I*, *S*
**Morgan, P** (Aberavon) 1961 *E*, *F*, *S*
**Morgan, T** (Llanelli) 1889 *I*
**Morgan, W G** (Cambridge U) 1927 *F*, *I*, 1929 *E*, *F*, *I*, *S*, 1930 *F*, *I*
**Morgan, W L** (Cardiff) 1910 *S*
**Morley, J C** (Newport) 1929 *E*, *F*, *I*, *S*, 1930 *E*, *I*, 1931 *E*, *F*, *I*, *S*, *SA*, 1932 *E*, *I*, *S*
**Morris, G L** (Swansea) 1882 *I*, 1883 *E*, *S*, 1884 *E*, *S*
**Morris, H T** (Cardiff) 1951 *F*, 1955 *F*, *I*
**Morris, I** (Swansea) 1924 *E*, *S*
**Morris, R R** (Swansea and Bristol) 1933 *S*, 1937 *S*
**Morris, S** (Cross Keys) 1920 *E*, *F*, *I*, *S*, 1922 *E*, *F*, *I*, *S*, 1923 *E*, *F*, *I*, *S*, 1924 *E*, *F*, *NZ*, *S*, 1925 *E*, *F*, *S*
**Morris, W** (Abertillery) 1919 *NZA*, 1920 *F*, 1921 *I*
**Morris, W** (Llanelli) 1896 *I*, *S*, 1897 *E*
**Morris, W D** (Neath) 1967 *E*, *F*, 1968 *E*, *F*, *I*, *S*, 1969 *A*, *E*, *F*, *I*, *NZ* (2), *S*, 1970 *E*, *F*, *I*, *S*, *SA*, 1971 *E*, *F*, *I*, *S*, 1972 *E*, *F*, *S*, *NZ*, 1973 *E*, *S*, *I*, *A*, 1974 *S*, *I*, *F*, *E*
**Morris, W J** (Newport) 1965 *S*, 1966 *F*
**Morris, W J** (Pontypool) 1963 *I*, *S*
**Murphy, C** (Cross Keys) 1935 *E*, *I*, *S*

**Nash, D** (Ebbw Vale) 1960 *SA*, 1961 *E*, *F*, *I*, *S*, 1962 *F*
**Neil, W** (Cardiff) 1904 *I*, *S*, 1905 *E*, *I*, *S*, 1907 *E*, *I*, 1908 *E*, *F*, *I*, *S*
**Newman, C H** (Newport) 1881 *E*, 1882 *I*, 1883 *E*, *S*, 1884 *E*, *S*, 1885 *E*, *S*, 1886 *E*, 1887 *E*
**Nicholas, T J** (Cardiff) 1919 *NZA*
**Nicholl, C B** (Cambridge U and Llanelli) 1891 *I*, 1892 *E*, *I*, *S*, 1893 *E*, *I*, *S*, 1894 *E*, *S*, 1895 *E*, *I*, *S*, 1896 *E*, *I*, *S*
**Nicholls, D W** (Llanelli) 1894 *I*
**Nicholls, E G** (Cardiff) 1896 *I*, *S*, 1897 *E*, 1898 *E*, *I*, 1899 *E*, *I*, *S*, 1900 *I*, *S*, 1901 *E*, *I*, *S*, 1902 *E*, *I*, *S*, 1903 *I*, 1904 *E*, 1905 *I*, *NZ*, 1906 *E*, *I*, *S*, *SA*
**Nicholls, F E** (Cardiff and Harlequins) 1892 *I*
**Nicholls, H** (Cardiff) 1958 *I*
**Nicholls, S H** (Cardiff) 1888 *M*, 1889 *I*, *S*, 1891 *S*
**Norris, C H** (Cardiff) 1963 *F*, 1966 *F*
**Norton, W B** (Cardiff) 1882 *I*, 1883 *E*, *S*, 1884 *E*, *I*, *S*

**O'Connor, A** (Aberavon) 1960 *SA*, 1961 *E*, *S*, 1962 *F*, *I*

**O'Connor, R** (Aberavon) 1957 *E*
**O'Shea, J P** (Cardiff) 1967 *I*, *S*, 1968 *F*, *I*, *S*
**Oliver, G** (Pontypool) 1920 *E*, *F*, *I*, *S*
**Osborne, W T** (Mountain Ash) 1902 *E*, *I*, *S*, 1903 *E*, *I*, *S*
**Ould, W J** (Cardiff) 1924 *E*, *S*
**Owen, A** (Swansea) 1924 *E*
**Owen, G** (Newport) 1955 *F*, *I*, 1956 *E*, *F*, *I*, *S*
**Owen, R M** (Swansea) 1901 *I*, 1902 *E*, *I*, *S*, 1903 *E*, *I*, *S*, 1904 *E*, *I*, *S*, 1905 *E*, *I*, *NZ*, *S*, 1906 *E*, *I*, *S*, *SA*, 1907 *E*, *S*, 1908 *A*, *F*, *I*, 1909 *E*, *F*, *I*, *S*, 1910 *E*, *F*, 1911 *E*, *F*, *I*, *S*, 1912 *E*, *S*

**Packer, H** (Newport) 1891 *E*, 1895 *I*, *S*, 1896 *E*, *I*, *S*, 1897 *E*
**Palmer, F** (Swansea) 1922 *E*, *I*, *S*
**Parfitt, F C** (Newport) 1893 *E*, *I*, *S*, 1894 *E*, *I*, *S*, 1895 *S*, 1896 *I*, *S*
**Parker, D** (Swansea) 1924 *F*, *I*, *NZ*, 1925 *E*, *F*, *I*, *S*, 1929 *F*, *I*, 1930 *E*
**Parker, T** (Swansea) 1919 *NZA*, 1920 *E*, *I*, *S*, 1921 *E*, *F*, *I*, *S*, 1922 *E*, *F*, *I*, *S*, 1923 *E*, *F*, *S*
**Parker, W** (Swansea) 1899 *E*, *S*
**Parsons, G** (Newport) 1947 *E*
**Pascoe, D** (Bridgend) 1923 *F*, *I*
**Pask, A E I** (Abertillery) 1961 *F*, 1962 *E*, *F*, *I*, *S*, 1963 *E*, *F*, *I*, *NZ*, *S*, 1964 *E*, *F*, *I*, *S*, *SA*, 1965 *E*, *F*, *I*, *S*, 1966 *A*, *E*, *F*, *I*, *S*, 1967 *I*, *S*
**Payne, G W** (Army and Pontypridd) 1960 *E*, *I*, *S*
**Payne, H** (Swansea) 1935 *NZ*
**Peacock, H** (Newport) 1929 *F*, *I*, *S*, 1930 *F*, *I*, *S*
**Peake, E** (Chepstow) 1881 *E*
**Pearson, T W** (Cardiff and Newport) 1891 *E*, *I*, 1892 *E*, *S*, 1894 *I*, *S*, 1895 *E*, *I*, *S*, 1897 *E*, 1898 *E*, *I*, 1903 *E*
**Pegge, E V** (Neath) 1891 *E*
**Perrett, F** (Neath) 1912 *SA*, 1913 *E*, *F*, *I*, *S*
**Perrins, V C** (Newport) 1970 *S*, *SA*
**Perry, W** (Neath) 1911 *E*
**Phillips, B** (Aberavon) 1925 *E*, *F*, *I*, *S*, 1926 *E*
**Phillips, H** (Newport) 1927 *E*, *F*, *I*, *NSW*, *S*, 1928 *E*, , *F*, *I*, *S*
**Phillips, H** (Swansea) 1952 *F*
**Phillips, L A** (Newport) 1900 *E*, *I*, *S*, 1901 *S*
**Phillips, P** (Newport) 1892 *E*, 1893 *E*, *I*, *S*, 1894 *E*, *S*
**Phillips, W D** (Cardiff) 1881 *E*, 1882 *I*, 1884 *E*, *I*, *S*
**Plummer, R C S** (Newport) 1912 *F*, *I*, *S*, *SA*, 1913 *E*
**Pook, T** (Newport) 1895 *S*
**Powell, G** (Ebbw Vale) 1957 *F*, *I*
**Powell, J** (Cardiff) 1906 *I*
**Powell, J** (Cardiff) 1923 *I*
**Powell, R W** (Newport) 1888 *I*, *S*
**Powell, W C** (London Welsh) 1926 *F*, *I*, *S*, 1927 *E*, *F*, *I*, 1928 *F*, *I*, *S*, 1929 *E*, *F*, *I*, *S*, 1930 *F*, *I*, *S*, 1931 *E*, *F*, *I*, *S*, *SA*, 1932 *E*, *I*, *S*, 1935 *E*, *I*, *S*
**Powell, W J** (Cardiff) 1920 *E*, *F*, *I*, *S*
**Price, B** (Newport) 1961 *F*, *I*, 1962 *E*, *S*, 1963 *E*, *F*, *NZ*, *S*, 1964 *E*, *F*, *I*, *S*, *SA*, 1965 *E*, *F*, *I*, *S*, 1966 *A*, *E*, *F*, *I*, *S*, 1967 *E*, *F*, *I*, *S*, 1969 *A*, *F*, *I*, *NZ* (2), *S*
**Price, G** (Pontypool) 1975 *F*, *E*, *S*, *I*, *A*, 1976 *E*, *S*, *I*, *F*, 1977 *I*, *F*, *E*, *S*, *1978 E*, *S*, *I*, *F*
**Price, M J** (Pontypool and RAF) 1959 *E*, *F*, *I*, *S*, 1960 *E*, *F*, *I*, *S*, 1962 *E*
**Price, R E** (Weston) 1939 *I*, *S*
**Price, T G** (Llanelli) 1965 *E*, *F*, *I*, *S*, 1966 *A*, *E*, 1967 *F*, *S*
**Priday, A J** (Cardiff) 1958 *I*, 1961 *I*
**Pritchard, C** (Pontypool) 1928 *E*, *F*, *I*, *S*, 1929 *E*, *F*, *I*, *S*
**Pritchard, C C** (Newport and Pontypool) 1904 *I*, *S*, 1905 *NZ*, 1906 *E*, *S*
**Pritchard, C M** (Newport) 1904 *I*, 1905 *E*, *NZ*, *S*, 1906 *E*, *I*, *S*, *SA*, 1907 *E*, *I*, *S*, 1908 *E*, 1910 *E*, *F*
**Prosser, D R** (Cardiff) 1934 *I*, *S*
**Prosser, G** (Neath) 1934 *E*, *I*, *S*, 1935 *NZ*
**Prosser, J** (Cardiff) 1921 *I*
**Prosser, R** (Pontypool) 1956 *F*, *S*, 1957 *F*, *I*, *S*, 1958 *A*, *E*, *F*, *I*, *S*, 1959 *E*, *F*, *I*, *S*, 1960 *E*, *F*, *I*, *S*, *SA*, 1961 *F*, *I*
**Prothero, G J** (Bridgend) 1964 *F*, *I*, *S*, 1965 *E*, *F*, *I*, *S*, 1966 *E*, *F*, *I*, *S*
**Pryce-Jenkins, T J** (London Welsh) 1888 *I*, *S*
**Pugh, C** (Maesteg) 1924 *E*, *F*, *I*, *NZ*, *S*, 1925 *E*, *S*
**Pugsley, J** (Cardiff) 1910 *E*, *I*, *S*, 1911 *E*, *F*, *I*, *S*
**Pullman, J** (Neath) 1910 *F*

205

**Purdon, F** (Newport) 1881 E, 1882 I, 1883 E, S

**Quinnell, D L** (Llanelli) 1972 F (R), NZ, 1973 E, S, A, 1974 S, F, 1975 E (R), 1977 I (R), F, E, S, 1978 E, S, I, F

**Radford, W J** (Newport) 1923 I
**Ralph, A R** (Newport) 1931 F, I, SA, 1932 E, I, S
**Ramsey, S H** (Treorchy) 1896 E, 1904 E
**Randell, R** (Aberavon) 1924 F, I
**Raybould, W H** (London Welsh, Cambridge U and Newport) 1967 E, F, I, NZ, S, 1968 F, I, 1970 E, F (R), I, SA
**Rees, Aaron** (Maesteg) 1919 NZA
**Rees, Alan** (Maesteg) 1962 E, F, S
**Rees, A M** (London Welsh) 1934 E, 1935 E, I, NZ, S, 1936 E, I, S, 1937 E, I, S, 1938 E, S
**Rees, B I** (London Welsh) 1967 F, I, S
**Rees, C F W** (London Welsh) 1974 I, 1975 A
**Rees, D** (Swansea) 1968 F, I, S
**Rees, Dan** (Swansea) 1900 E, 1903 E, S, 1905 E, S
**Rees, E B** (Swansea) 1919 NZA
**Rees, H** (Cardiff) 1937 I, S, 1938 E, I, S
**Rees, J I** (Swansea) 1934 E, I, S, 1935 NZ, S, 1936 E, I, S, 1937 E, I, S, 1938 E, I, S
**Rees, J** (Swansea) 1920 E, F, I, S, 1921 E, I, S, 1922 E, 1923 E, F, I, 1924 S
**Rees, L** (Cardiff) 1933 I
**Rees, P** (Llanelli) 1947 F, I
**Rees, P M** (Newport) 1961 E, I, S, 1964 I
**Rees, T** (Newport) 1935 I, NZ, S, 1936 E, I, S, 1937 E, S
**Rees, T A** (Llandovery) 1881 E
**Rees, T E** (London Welsh) 1926 F, I, 1927 NSW, 1928 E
**Rees-Jones, G R** (Oxford U and London Welsh) 1934 E, S, 1935 I, NZ, 1936 E
**Reeves, F** (Cross Keys) 1920 F, I, 1921 E
**Rhapps, J** (Penygraig) 1897 E
**Rice-Evans, W** (Swansea) 1890 S, 1891 E, S
**Richards, B** (Swansea) 1960 F
**Richards, C** (Pontypool) 1922 E, F, I, S, 1924 I
**Richards, E S** (Swansea) 1885 E, 1887 S
**Richards, G** (Cardiff) 1927 S
**Richards, I** (Cardiff) 1925 E, F, S
**Richards, K** (Bridgend) 1960 SA, 1961 E, F, I, S
**Richards, M C R** (Cardiff) 1968 F, I, 1969 A, E, F, I, NZ (2), S
**Richards, R** (Aberavon) 1913 F, I, S
**Richards, R** (Cross Keys) 1956 F
**Richards, T L** (Maesteg) 1923 I
**Rickard, A** (Cardiff) 1924 F
**Ring, J** (Aberavon) 1921 E
**Roberts, C** (Neath) 1958 F, I
**Roberts, D E A** (London Welsh) 1930 E
**Roberts, E** (Llanelli) 1886 E, 1887 I
**Roberts, E J** (Llanelli) 1888 I, S, 1889 I
**Roberts, H M** (Cardiff) 1960 SA, 1961 E, F, I, S, 1962 F, S, 1963 I
**Roberts, J** (Cardiff) 1927 E, F, I, NSW, S, 1928 E, F, I, S, 1929 E, F, I, S
**Roberts, M G** (London Welsh) 1971 E, F, I, S, 1973 I, F, 1975 S
**Roberts, T** (Newport) 1921 F, I, S, 1922 E, F, I, S, 1923 E, S
**Roberts, W** (Cardiff) 1929 E
**Robins, J D** (Birkenhead Park) 1950 E, F, I, S, 1951 E, F, I, S, 1953 E, F, I
**Robins, R J** (Pontypridd) 1953 S, 1954 F, S, 1955 E, F, I, S, 1956 E, F, 1957 E, F, I, S
**Robinson, I R** (Cardiff) 1974 F, E
**Rocyn-Jones, D N** (Cambridge U) 1925 I
**Roderick, W B** (Llanelli) 1884 I
**Rosser, M** (Penarth) 1924 F, S
**Rowlands, C F** (Aberavon) 1926 I
**Rowlands, D C T** (Pontypool) 1963 E, F, I, NZ, S, 1964 E, F, I, S, SA, 1965 E, S, I, F
**Rowlands, G** (RAF and Cardiff) 1953 NZ, 1954 E, F, 1956 F
**Rowlands, J** (Lampeter) 1885 E
**Rowlands, K A** (Cardiff) 1962 F, I, 1963 I, 1965 F, I
**Rowles, G R** (Penarth) 1892 E

**Samuel, D** (Swansea) 1891 I, 1893 I
**Samuel, F** (Mountain Ash) 1922 F, I, S

**Samuel, J** (Swansea) 1891 I
**Scourfield, T** (Torquay) 1930 F
**Scrine, F** (Swansea) 1899 E, S, 1901 I
**Shanklin, J L** (London Welsh) 1970 F, 1972 NZ, 1973 I, F
**Shaw, G** (Neath) 1972 NZ, 1973 E, S, I, F, A, 1974 S, I, F, E, 1977 I, F
**Shea, J** (Newport) 1919 NZA, 1920 E, S, 1921 E
**Shell, R C** (Aberavon) 1973 A (R)
**Simpson, H J** (Cardiff) 1884 E, I, S
**Shrimshire, R T** (Newport) 1899 E, I, S
**Skym, A** (Llanelli) 1928 E, F, I, S, 1930 E, F, I, S, 1931 E, F, I, S, SA, 1932 E, I, S, 1933 E, I, S, 1935 E
**Smith, J S** (Cardiff) 1884 E, I, 1885 E
**Sparks, B** (Neath) 1954 I, 1955 E, F, 1956 E, I, S, 1957 S
**Spiller, W** (Cardiff) 1910 I, S, 1911 E, F, I, S, 1912 E, F, SA, 1913 E
**Squire, J** (Newport) 1977 I, F, 1978 E, S, I, F
**Stadden, W H** (Cardiff) 1884 I, 1886 E, S, 1887 I, 1888 S, M, 1890 E, S
**Stephens, G** (Neath) 1912 E, I, F, S, SA, 1913 E, F, I, S, 1919 NZA
**Stephens, Rev J G** (Llanelli) 1922 E, F, I, S
**Stephens, J R G** (Neath) 1947 E, F, I, S, 1948 I, 1949 F, I, S, 1951 F, SA, 1952 E, F, I, S, 1953 E, F, I, NZ, S, 1954 E, I, 1955 E, F, I, S, 1956 F, I, S, 1957 E, F, I, S
**Stock, A** (Newport) 1924 F, NZ, 1926 E, S
**Stone, P** (Llanelli) 1949 F
**Strand-Jones, J** (Llanelli) 1902 E, I, S, 1903 E, S
**Summers, R H B** (Haverfordwest) 1881 E
**Sweet-Escott, R B** (Cardiff) 1891 S, 1894 I, 1895 I

**Tamplin, W E** (Cardiff) 1947 A, F, I, S, 1948 E, F, S
**Tanner, H** (Swansea and Cardiff) 1935 NZ, 1936 E, I, S, 1937 E, I, S, 1938 E, I, S, 1939 E, I, S 1947 E, F, I, S, 1948 E, F, I, S, 1949 E, F, I, S
**Tarr, D J** (Swansea and Royal Navy) 1935 NZ
**Taylor, A R** (Cross Keys) 1937 I, 1938 I, 1939 E
**Taylor, C G** (Ruabon) 1884 E, I, S, 1885 E, S, 1886 E, S, 1887 E, I
**Taylor, J** (London Welsh) 1967 E, F, I, NZ, S, 1968 F, I, 1969 A, E, F, I, NZ, S, 1970 F, 1971 E, F, I, S, 1972 E, F, S, NZ, 1973 E, S
**Thomas, A** (Newport) 1963 NZ, 1964 E
**Thomas, A G** (Swansea, Cardiff) 1952 E, F, I, S, 1953 F, I, S, 1954 E, F, I, 1955 F, I, S
**Thomas, Bob** (Swansea) 1900 E, I, S, 1901 E
**Thomas, Brian** (Neath and Cambridge U) 1963 E, F, I, NZ, S, 1964 E, F, I, S, SA, 1965 E, 1966 E, I, S, 1967 NZ, 1969 E, F, I, NZ (2), S
**Thomas, C J** (Newport) 1888 I, M, 1889 I, S, 1890 E, I, S, 1891 E, I
**Thomas, C** (Bridgend) 1925 E, S
**Thomas, D** (Aberavon) 1961 I
**Thomas, D** (Swansea) 1930 I, S, 1932 E, I, S, 1933 E, S, 1934 E, 1935 E, I, S
**Thomas, D** (Llanelli) 1954 I
**Thomas, Dick** (Mountain Ash) 1906 SA, 1908 F, I, 1909 S
**Thomas, D J** (Swansea) 1904 E, 1908 A, 1910 E, I, S, 1911 E, F, I, S, 1912 E
**Thomas, D L** (Neath) 1937 E
**Thomas, E** (Newport) 1904 I, S, 1909 F, I, S, 1910 F
**Thomas, G** (Llanelli) 1923 E, F, I, S
**Thomas, G** (Newport) 1888 M, 1890 I, 1891 S
**Thomas, H** (Llanelli) 1912 F
**Thomas, H** (Neath) 1936 E, I, S, 1937 E, I, S
**Thomas, H W** (Swansea) 1912 SA, 1913 E
**Thomas, I** (Bryncethin) 1924 E
**Thomas, L C** (Cardiff) 1885 E, S
**Thomas, M C** (Newport and Devonport Services) 1949 F, 1950 E, F, I, S, 1951 E, F, I, S, SA, 1952 E, F, I, S, 1953 E, 1956 E, F, I, S, 1957 E, S, 1958 E, F, I, S, 1959 F, I
**Thomas, M** (St Bart's Hospital) 1919 NZA, 1921 F, I, S, 1923 F, 1924 E
**Thomas, R** (Pontypool) 1909 F, I, 1911 S, F, 1912 E, S, SA, 1913 S
**Thomas, R C C** (Swansea) 1949 F, 1952 F, I, 1953 F, I, NZ, S, 1954 E, F, I, S, 1955 I, S, 1956 F, I, S, 1957 E, 1958 A, E, F, I, S, 1959 E, F, I, S
**Thomas, R L** (London Welsh) 1889 I, S, 1890 I, 1891 E, I, S 1892 E

206

**Thomas, S** (Llanelli) 1890 *E, S*, 1891 *I*
**Thomas, W** (Llanelli and Swansea) 1927 *E, F, I, S*, 1929 *E*, 1931 *E, S, SA*, 1932 *E, I, S*, 1933 *E, I, S*
**Thomas, W D** (Llanelli) 1966 *A*, 1968 *F, I, S*, 1969 *A, E, NZ*, 1970 *E, F, I, S, SA*, 1971 *E, F, I, S*, 1972 *E, F, S, NZ*, 1973 *E, S, I, F*, 1974 *E*
**Thomas, W H** (Llandovery Coll, Cambridge U) 1885 *S*, 1886 *E, S*, 1887 *E, S*, 1888 *I, S*, 1890 *E, I*, 1891 *I, S*
**Thomas, W J** (Cardiff) 1961 *F*, 1963 *F*
**Thomas, W L** (Newport) 1894 *S*, 1895 *E, I*
**Thomas, W T** (Abertillery) 1930 *E*
**Thomson, J** (Cross Keys) 1923 *E*
**Towers, W H** (Swansea) 1887 *I*, 1888 *M*
**Travers, G** (Pill Harriers) 1903 *E, I, S*, 1905 *E, I, NZ, S*, 1906 *E, I, S, SA*, 1907 *E, I, S*, 1908 *A, E, F, I, S*, 1909 *E, I, S*, 1911 *F, I, S*
**Travers, W H** (Newport) 1937 *I, S*, 1938 *E, I, S*, 1939 *E, I, S*, 1949 *E, F, I, S*
**Treharne, E** (Pontypridd) 1881 *E*, 1883 *E*
**Trew, W J** (Swansea) 1900 *E, I, S*, 1901 *E, S*, 1903 *S*, 1905 *S*, 1906 *S*, 1907 *E, S*, 1908 *A, E, F, I, S*, 1909 *E, F, I, S*, 1910 *E, F, S*, 1911 *E, F, I, S*, 1912 *S*, 1913 *F, S*
**Trott, R F** (Cardiff) 1948 *E, F, I, S*, 1949 *E, F, I, S*
**Truman, H** (Llanelli) 1934 *E*, 1935 *E*
**Trump, L** (Newport) 1912 *E, F, I, S*
**Turnbull, B R** (Cardiff) 1925 *I*, 1927 *E, S*, 1928 *E, F*, 1930 *S*
**Turnbull, M J** (Cardiff) 1933 *E, I*

**Uzzell, H** (Newport) 1912 *E, F, I, S*, 1913 *F, I, S*, 1914 *E, F, I, S*, 1920 *E, F, I, S*
**Uzzell, J** (Newport) 1963 *NZ*, 1965 *E, F, I, S*

**Vickery, W** (Aberavon) 1938 *E, I, S*, 1939 *E*
**Vile, T H** (Newport) 1908 *E, S*, 1910 *I*, 1912 *F, I, SA*, 1913 *E*, 1921 *S*
**Vincent, H C** (Bangor) 1882 *I*

**Waldron, R** (Neath) 1965 *E, F, I, S*
**Waller, P D** (Newport) 1908 *A*, 1909 *E, F, I, S*, 1910 *F*
**Walters, D** (Llanelli) 1902 *E*
**Wanbon, R** (Aberavon) 1968 *E*
**Ward, W** (Cross Keys) 1934 *I, S*
**Warlow, J** (Llanelli) 1962 *I*
**Watkins, D** (Newport) 1963 *E, F, I, NZ, S*, 1964 *E, F, I, S, SA*, 1965 *E, F, I, S*, 1966 *E, F, I, S*, 1967 *E, F, I*
**Watkins, E** (Neath) 1924 *E, F, I, S*
**Watkins, E** (Blaina) 1926 *F, I, S*
**Watkins, E** (Cardiff) 1935 *NZ*, 1937 *I, S*, 1938 *E, I, S*, 1939 *E, S*
**Watkins, H** (Llanelli) 1904 *I, S*, 1905 *E, I, S*, 1906 *E*
**Watkins, L** (Oxford U and Llandaff) 1881 *E*
**Watkins, S J** (Newport and Cardiff) 1964 *F, I, S*, 1965 *E, F, I, S*, 1966 *A, E, F, I, S*, 1967 *E, F, I, NZ, S*, 1968 *E, S*, 1969 *E, F, I, NZ, S*, 1970 *E, I*
**Watkins, W** (Newport) 1959 *F*
**Watts, D** (Maesteg) 1914 *E, F, I, S*
**Watts, J** (Llanelli) 1907 *E, I, S*, 1908 *A, E, F, I, S*, 1909 *F, I, S*
**Watts, W** (Llanelli) 1914 *E*
**Watts, W H** (Newport) 1892 *E, I, S*, 1893 *E, I, S*, 1894 *E, I, S*, 1895 *E, I*, 1896 *E*
**Weaver, D** (Swansea) 1964 *E*
**Webb, J** (Abertillery) 1907 *S*, 1908 *A, E, F, I, S*, 1909 *E, F, I, S*, 1910 *E, F, I, S*, 1911 *E, F, I, S*, 1912 *E, S*
**Webb, J E** (Newport) 1888 *M*, 1889 *S*
**Wells, G** (Cardiff) 1955 *E, S*, 1957 *F, I*, 1958 *A, E, S*
**Westacott, D** (Cardiff) 1906 *I*
**Wetter, H** (Newport) 1912 *SA*, 1913 *E*
**Wetter, J** (Newport) 1914 *F, I, S*, 1920 *E, F, I, S*, 1921 *E*, 1924 *I, NZ*
**Wheel, G A D** (Swansea) 1974 *I, E* (R), 1975 *F, E, I, A*, 1976 *E, S, I, F*, 1977 *I, E, S*, 1978 *E, S, I, F*
**Wheeler, P J** (Aberavon) 1967 *NZ*, 1968 *E*
**Whitfield, J** (Newport) 1919 *NZA*, 1920 *E, F, I, S*, 1921 *E*, 1922 *E, F, I, S*, 1924 *I, S*

**Whitson, G** (Newport) 1956 *F*, 1960 *I, S*
**Williams, B** (Llanelli) 1920 *F, I, S*
**Williams, B L** (Cardiff) 1947 *A, E, F, I, S*, 1948 *E, F, I, S*, 1949 *E, I, S*, 1951 *I, SA*, 1952 *S*, 1953 *E, F, I, NZ, S*, 1954 *S*, 1955 *E*
**Williams, C** (Aberavon) 1977 *E, S*
**Williams, C** (Llanelli) 1924 *NZ*, 1925 *E*
**Williams, C D** (Cardiff and Neath) 1955 *F*, 1956 *F*
**Williams, D** (Ebbw Vale) 1963 *E, F, I, S*, 1964 *E, F, I, S, SA*, 1965 *E, F, I, S*, 1966 *A, E, I, S*, 1967 *E, F, NZ*, 1968 *E*, 1969 *A, E, F, I, NZ* (2), *S*, 1970 *E, I, S, SA*, 1971 *E, F, I, S*
**Williams, E** (Neath) 1924 *NZ*, 1925 *F*
**Williams, E** (Aberavon) 1925 *E, S*
**Williams, F L** (Cardiff) 1929 *F, I, S*, 1930 *E, F, I, S*, 1931 *F, I, SA*, 1932 *E, I, S*, 1933 *I*
**Williams, G** (London Welsh) 1950 *F, I*, 1951 *E, F, I, S, SA*, 1952 *E, F, I, S*, 1953 *NZ*, 1954 *E*
**Williams, G** (Aberavon) 1936 *E, I, S*
**Williams, J** (Blaina) 1920 *E, F, I, S*, 1921 *F, I, S*
**Williams, J F** (London Welsh) 1905 *I, NZ*, 1906 *S, SA*
**Williams, J J** (Llanelli) 1973 *F* (R), *A*, 1974 *S, I, F, E*, 1975 *F, E, S, I, A*, 1976 *E, S, I, F*, 1977 *I, F, E, S*, 1978 *E, S, I, F*
**Williams, J L** (Cardiff) 1906 *SA*, 1907 *E, I, S*, 1908 *A, E, I, S*, 1909 *E, F, I, S*, 1910 *I*, 1911 *E, F, I, S*
**Williams, J P R** (London Welsh) 1969 *A, E, F, I, NZ* (2), *S*, 1970 *E, F, I, S, SA*, 1971 *E, F, I, S*, 1972 *E, F, S*, *NZ*, 1973 *E, S, I, F, A*, 1974 *S, I, F*, 1975 *F, E, S, I, A*, 1976 *E, S, I, F*, 1977 *I, F, E, S*, 1978 *E, S, I, F*
**Williams, L** (Cardiff) 1957 *F, I, S*, 1958 *E, F, I, S*, 1959 *E, I, S*, 1961 *F*, 1962 *E, S*
**Williams, L** (Llanelli and Cardiff) 1947 *A, E, F, I, S*, 1948 *I*, 1949 *E*
**Williams, M** (Newport) 1923 *F*
**Williams, O** (Llanelli) 1947 *A, E, S*, 1948 *E, F, I, S*
**Williams, R** (Llanelli) 1954 *S*, 1957 *F*, 1958 *A*
**Williams, R D G** (Newport) 1881 *E*
**Williams, R F** (Cardiff) 1912 *SA*, 1913 *E, S*, 1914 *I*
**Williams, R H** (Llanelli) 1954 *F, I, S*, 1955 *F, I, S*, 1956 *E, I, S*, 1957 *E, F, I, S*, 1958 *A, E, F, I, S*, 1959 *E, F, I, S*, 1960 *E*
**Williams, S** (Aberavon) 1939 *E, I, S*
**Williams, S** (Llanelli) 1947 *E, F, I, S*, 1948 *F, S*
**Williams, T** (Pontypridd) 1882 *I*
**Williams, T** (Swansea) 1888 *I, S*
**Williams, T** (Swansea) 1912 *I*, 1913 *F*, 1914 *E, F, I, S*
**Williams, T** (Cross Keys) 1935 *I, NZ, S*, 1936 *E, I, S*, 1937 *I, S*
**Williams, Tudor** (Swansea) 1921 *F*
**Williams, W** (Crumlin) 1927 *E, F, I, S*
**Williams, W A** (Newport) 1952 *F, I*, 1953 *E*
**Williams, W E O** (Cardiff) 1887 *I, S*, 1889 *S*, 1890 *E, S*
**Williams, W H** (Pontymister) 1900 *E, I, S*, 1901 *E*
**Williams, W O G** (Swansea) 1951 *F, SA*, 1952 *E, F, I, S*, 1953 *E, F, I, NZ, S*, 1954 *E, F, I, S*, 1955 *E, F, I, S*, 1956 *E, I, S*
**Williams, W P J** (Neath) 1974 *I, F*
**Willis, W R** (Cardiff) 1950 *E, F, I, S*, 1951 *E, F, I, S, SA*, 1952 *E, S*, 1953 *NZ, S*, 1954 *E, F, I, S*, 1955 *E, F, I, S*
**Wiltshire, M L** (Aberavon) 1967 *NZ*, 1968 *E, F, S*
**Windsor, R W** (Pontypool) 1973 *A*, 1974 *S, I, F, E*, 1975 *F, E, S, I, A*, 1976 *E, S, I, F*, 1977 *I, F, E, S*, 1978 *E, S, I, F*
**Winfield, H B** (Cardiff) 1903 *I*, 1904 *E, I, S*, 1905 *NZ*, 1906 *E, I, S*, 1907 *I, S*, 1908 *A, E, F, I, S*
**Winmill, S** (Cross Keys) 1921 *E, F, I, S*
**Wooller, W** (Sale, Cambridge U and Cardiff) 1933 *E, I, S*, 1935 *E, I, NZ, S*, 1936 *E, I, S*, 1937 *E, I, S*, 1938 *I, S*, 1939 *E, I, S*

**Young, G A** (Cardiff) 1886 *E, S*
**Young, J** (Harrogate, RAF, London Welsh) 1968 *F, I, S*, 1969 *E, F, I, NZ, S*, 1970 *E, F, I*, 1971 *E, F, I, S*, 1972 *E, F, S, NZ*, 1973 *E, S, I, F*

207

*Steve Fenwick, here seen tackling Jean-Michel Aguirre of France at Cardiff, was winning his sixteenth cap for Wales; but Arthur Gold, with 25 appearances as a centre, is still his country's most-capped player in the position.*

# WELSH INTERNATIONAL RECORDS

*From 1890–91, when uniform points-scoring was first adopted by International Board countries, to 30 April 1978. Both team and individual records are for matches against International Board countries only.*

## TEAM RECORDS

### Highest score
49 v France (49–14) 1910 Swansea
*v individual countries*
34 v England (34–21) 1967 Cardiff
35 v Scotland (35–12) 1972 Cardiff
34 v Ireland (34–9) 1976 Dublin
49 v France (49–14) 1910 Swansea
16 v N Zealand (16–19) 1972 Cardiff
 6 v S Africa (6–6) 1970 Cardiff
28 v Australia (28–3) 1975 Cardiff

### Biggest winning points margin
42 v France (47–5) 1909 Colombes (Paris)
*v individual countries*
25 v England (25–0) 1905 Cardiff
23 v Scotland (35–12) 1972 Cardiff
29 v Ireland (29–0) 1907 Cardiff
42 v France (47–5) 1909 Colombes
 5 v N Zealand (13–8) 1953 Cardiff
No win v S Africa
25 v Australia (28–3) 1975 Cardiff

### Highest score by opposing team
35 Scotland (10–35) 1924 Inverleith
  (Edinburgh)
*by individual countries*
25 England (0–25) 1896 Blackheath
35 Scotland (10–35) 1924 Inverleith
19 Ireland $\begin{cases} (3–19) \ 1925 \ Belfast \\ (9–19) \ 1927 \ Dublin \end{cases}$
22 France (13–22) 1965 Colombes
33 N Zealand (12–33) 1969 Auckland
24 S Africa (3–24) 1964 Durban
16 Australia (19–16) 1969 Sydney

### Biggest losing points margin
25 $\begin{cases} v \ England \ (0–25) \ 1896 \ Blackheath \\ v \ Scotland \ (10–35) \ 1924 \ Inverleith \end{cases}$
*v individual countries*
25 v England (0–25) 1896 Blackheath
25 v Scotland (10–35) 1924 Inverleith
16 v Ireland (3–19) 1925 Belfast
10 v France (6–16) 1958 Cardiff

21 v N Zealand (12–33) 1969 Auckland
21 v S Africa (3–24) 1964 Durban
 3 v Australia (11–14) 1966 Cardiff

### Most points by Wales in International Championship in a season – 102
(in season 1975–76)

### Most tries by Wales in International Championship in a season – 21
(in season 1909–10)

### Most tries by Wales in an international
11 v France (47–5) 1909 Colombes

### Most tries against Wales in an international
8 by Scotland (10–35) 1924 Inverleith

*England scored 13 tries v Wales in 1881 and Scotland 12 tries in 1887, but this was before uniform scoring was adopted*

## INDIVIDUAL RECORDS

### Most capped player
G O Edwards   53   1967–78
*in individual positions*
*Full-back*
J P R Williams   45   1969–78
*Wing*
K J Jones   44*   1947–57
*Centre*
A J Gould   25 (27)**   1885–97
*Fly-half*
C I Morgan   29†   1951–58
*Scrum-half*
G O Edwards   53   1967–78
*Prop*
D Williams   36   1963–71
*Hooker*
B V Meredith   34   1954–62

*\*T G R Davies, 44 caps, has won 33 as a wing, and 11 as a centre*
*\*\*Gould won 2 caps at full-back*
*†P Bennett, 29 caps, has won one at full-back, as a replacement, one on the wing and two at centre, once as a replacement*

*Lock*
B Price   32   1961–69
*Flanker*
W D Morris   32 (34)‡   1967–74
*No 8*
T M Davies   38   1969–76
‡*Morris won his first two caps at No. 8*

210

**Most points in internationals – 166**
P Bennett (29 appearances) 1969–78

**Most points in an international – 19**
J Bancroft v France 1910 Swansea
K S Jarrett v England 1967 Cardiff
P Bennett v Ireland 1976 Dublin

**Most tries in internationals – 20**
G O Edwards (53 appearances) 1967–78

**Most tries in an international – 4**
W Llewellyn* v England 1899 Swansea
R A Gibbs v France 1908 Cardiff
M C R Richards v England 1969 Cardiff

*on first appearance*

**Most points in International
Championship in a season – 38**
P Bennett (4 appearances) 1975–76

**Most tries in International
Championship in a season – 6**
R A Gibbs   1907–08
M C R Richards   1968–69

**Most points on overseas tour – 42**
K S Jarrett (5 appearances) Australia/
New Zealand 1969

**Most points in any match on tour – 15**
K S Jarrett v Otago 1969 Dunedin, NZ

**Most tries in any match on tour – 3**
M C R Richards v Otago 1969 Dunedin,
NZ

*Phil Bennett took his
record points-total for
Wales to 166 in 1977–78.
With his 44 points for the
Lions, he becomes the
world's record-holder in
international rugby with
210 points.*

# WRU CHALLENGE CUP 1977–78

**29 April, Cardiff**
**Swansea 13** (2DG 1PG 1T)   **Newport 9** (3PG)

Swansea's predicted victory – their first – in the Schweppes
WRU Cup final, though bringing a great day in their history,
was hardly a dynamic performance against a Newport side that
had disappointingly little to offer. The losers' forwards were
badly beaten as ball-winners, and the Swansea captain, Alan
Meredith, put it in a nutshell when he said: 'I don't think either
team played at their best.'

The winners, indeed, were acutely aware that they had not
risen to the occasion in the manner hoped for by a crowd of
almost 40,000. The gate-takings were nearly £80,000, of which
the finalists received £10,000 each.

The build-up to the final generated a certain amount of con-
troversy with both teams, by resting key players, virtually
'opting out' in certain fixtures after the semi-final round. Newport, for example, made no pretence of contesting the issue in
their match at Pontypool and lost to the valley team by a record
36–7 margin. Their abashed supporters did not even have the
consolation of seeing their side score a try in the final. Swansea
sent a team to Pontypridd that did not contain a single member
of their Cup final line-up. With Pontypridd and Cardiff lying
neck-and-neck at a crucial stage in the season, such a policy
debased the value of the unofficial club championship matches.

Newport, with both their regular outside-halves, Rogers and
Keith James, on the injury list for the final, were compelled to
use Gareth Evans, the British Lion, normally a centre for his
club, in the position. He contributed a few neatly-placed punts,
but with so little worthwhile possession the Cup-holders' back
division seldom posed any threats. Their ability to absorb
pressure, however, was once again apparent and Swansea's try,
from a moment of opportunism, was only the third against
Newport in the six Cup games. Another handicap to the losers
was that David Ford, who hooked in their Cup-winning team
the previous season as a late deputy for the unfit Steve Jones, had
been sent off a week earlier at Bath and was under automatic
suspension. This time the roles were reversed, with Jones taking
Ford's place.

David Richards, the Swansea outside-half, who won the

Lloyd Lewis Memorial Trophy as the man of the match by a one-vote margin from the excellent Roger Blyth, just about deserved the decision. He gave a highly efficient display, in spite of an erratic service from his scrum-half Huw Davies, who fell a long way below his normal form. But it was the power and pressure of the Swansea pack, which included four internationals – Llewellyn, Wheel, Keyworth, and T P Evans – that finally decided the issue. For Newport, who fought back gamely, Jeff Squire, their Lions' forward, was outstanding.

212

Richards dropped a smart goal, from a pass that bounced twice, to give Swansea their first score. Gareth Jenkins then dropped another, from 35 metres, to maintain the lead after Webber had kicked a penalty goal for Newport. The only try of the match came when Herdman, the Swansea hooker, took a tap-back from Phil Llewellyn (from Newport's throw-in!) at the front of a line-out and raced 15 metres, at surprising speed, to score. The conversion attempt failed, but with Blyth kicking a penalty goal Swansea led 13–3 at half-time. After that the only scores were two penalty goals by Webber for Newport, who might have got a try in the last minute if Bale, with an overlap, had not been given an untakeable pass.

Aberavon were favourites in the semi-final tie with Newport on the Cardiff club ground, but a downpour at the start flooded the pitch extensively. This not only reduced the game to a mud-slog but also neutralised Aberavon's superior back division. An interception by Gareth Evans, who ran more than 55 metres for a 'gift' try, which was duly converted, was the turning point and the same player raced through again, after a glorious break, for a second try which sealed Newport's 10–6 victory.

Cardiff rallied superbly in the other semi-final, a magnificent match, at Aberavon, and chipped into Swansea's 15–3 lead. Their effort, however, came too late and Swansea made themselves favourites for the final with their 18–13 win.

One of the competition's most astonishing games was the third-round tie at Pontypool Park where Cardiff, with their forwards swamped, set up only five effective attacks. Yet Gerald Davies, their captain, scored four superb tries from those few chances and his side triumphed 16–11.

## TEAMS IN THE FINAL

**Swansea:** W R Blyth; H Rees, A D Meredith (*capt*), G Jenkins, A Donovan; D S Richards, H Davies; *No 8* R Moriarty; *Second Row* T P Evans, G A D Wheel, B G Clegg, M Keyworth; *Front Row* H Hopkins, J Herdman, P D Llewellyn
**Scorers** *Try:* Herdman   *Dropped Goals:* Richards, Jenkins   *Penalty Goal:* Blyth
**Newport:** C Webber; K Davies, D H Burcher (*capt*), N Brown, D Bale;

G L Evans, D B Williams; *No 8* J Squire; *Second Row* B Lease, J Watkins, A Mogridge, G Evans; *Front Row* C Smart, S Jones, R Morgan
**Scorer** *Penalty Goals:* Webber (3)
**Referee** C Norling

## RESULTS

### First round

Aberavon 16  Crumlin 6

Aberavon Quins 0  Ruthin 9

Abercrave 8  Rumney (Cardiff) 16

Abercynon 24  Bynea 3

Bargoed 0  Newbridge 6

Bonymaen 10  Porthcawl 7

Brecon 10  Narberth 10*

Bridgend 13  Maesteg 10

BSC (Port Talbot) 4  Llanelli 20

Burry Port 9  Swansea 19

Cardigan 4  Waunarlwydd 7

Croesyceiliog 9  Abercarn 10

Cross Keys 16  Gowerton 3

Cwmavon 7  Tenby 6

Cwmgwrach 18  Llantwit Major 3

Cwmllynfell 10  Cardiff Internationals AC 6

Ebbw Vale 10  Pyle 6

Garndiffaith 0  Cardiff 9

Glamorgan Wands 13  New Dock Stars 21

Llandaff 17  Morriston 3

Llandaff North 3  Bedwas 19

Neath 22  Wrexham 12

Newport 31  Llanharan 4

Oakdale 3  Brynamman 19

Pontypool 86  Ystalyfera 6

Pontypool Utd 29  Loughor 6

Pontypridd 27  Cardiff HSOB 6

Rhiwbina 9  Penygraig 3

Rhydyfelin 11  Milford Haven 3

Risca 3  Abertillery 12

Tumble 18  BP Llandarcy 9

Ystrad Rhondda 19  Penygroes 3

*Narberth won on goal-kicking elimination test.*

### Second round

Aberavon 56  Ystrad Rhondda 10

Abertillery 12  Abercynon 14

Abercarn 7  Cross Keys 9

Bedwas 20  New Dock Stars 0

Bridgend 13  Waunarlwydd 3

Brynamman 11  Bonymaen 0

Cardiff 27  Cwmavon 6

Cwmllynfell 12  Pontypool 20

Llandaff 9  Ebbw Vale 12

Llanelli 68  Narberth 3

Newbridge 26  Rhydyfelin 12

Newport 30  Rhiwbina 3

Pontypridd 34  Tumble 4

Rumney (Cardiff) 9  Neath 16

Ruthin 10  Cwmgwrach 10*

Swansea 14  Pontypool United 9

*Cwmgwrach won on 'more tries' rule.*

### Third round

Aberavon 10  Bridgend 6

Bedwas 9  Cross Keys 3

Cwmgwrach 6  Pontypridd 37
(at Glynneath)

Llanelli 34  Brynamman 7

Neath 10  Ebbw Vale 16

Newport 14  Abercynon 3

Pontypool 11  Cardiff 16

Swansea 14  Newbridge 8

### Fourth round

Aberavon 19  Llanelli 13

Bedwas 12  Swansea 20

Ebbw Vale 10  Cardiff 29

Newport 9  Pontypridd 7

### Semi-finals

Newport 10  Aberavon 6 (*at Cardiff*)

Swansea 18  Cardiff 13 (*at Aberavon*)

**Final** (*at Cardiff Arms Park*)
Swansea 13  Newport 9

### Previous finals
(*all at Cardiff Arms Park*)

### Previous finals
(*all at Cardiff Arms Park*)

| 1972 | Neath 15  Llanelli 9 |
|------|----------------------|
| 1973 | Llanelli 30  Cardiff 7 |
| 1974 | Llanelli 12  Aberavon 10 |
| 1975 | Llanelli 15  Aberavon 6 |
| 1976 | Llanelli 15  Swansea 4 |
| 1977 | Newport 16  Cardiff 15 |

213

# THE 1977–78 SEASON IN FRANCE

**Bob Donahue** *Herald Tribune*, Paris

At Twickenham in September, an all–French back row played as Barbarians against the Lions. The Jubilee Match was a stylish bracket to set before a centennial French winter, Britons first having taught rugby to Paris schoolboys *circa* 1877 in the Bois de Boulogne. In March, at the other end of the 1977–78 season, the International Board closed the brackets, no less in style, with its announcement in London that France had been accepted for membership.

To France, in October, the Home Unions sent George Burrell, John Dawes, and Peter Wheeler to lead a President's XV against Jacques Fouroux's men not far from that same Bois de Boulogne. The two All Blacks who did most to defeat the French in November, Graham Mourie and Lawrie Knight, spent the winter helping Paris University Club against the likes of Montélimar and Fumel. England borrowed locks Nigel Horton and Maurice Colclough from French clubs for the Championship campaign.

In his team talks, Frances's coach 'Toto' Desclaux was able to impress on his players the 'self control' that netted favourable penalty balances in the Championship, but what he could not quite obtain was spirit. Failures, first against New Zealand and last against Wales, did not lead to any particular despondency; neither did the intervening successes against England, Scotland, and Ireland bring any transcending joy. It was as if the 15-man Grand Slam of the previous year had burnt out enthusiasm for a time.

Half-hearted was the plan of a divided selection committee – amid public impatience with forward rugby, however powerful – to restore running attack in the show-case national side. While one faction changed the half-backs, overruling coach Desclaux, the other kept the single-minded coach and his pack. 'Evolution, not revolution' was the official line. But no definite policy seemed to emerge.

After the Grand Slam of the previous season Rumania had come to Paris in June for a charity match; Fouroux's pack won 9–6 on their knees, no try was scored, and the selectors looked ahead to Argentina. There, early in July, France needed six second-half penalty goals from Aguirre to draw a try-less second international. In November, the All Blacks took hope from an inconclusive defeat in the first international at Toulouse, where Bryan Williams scored the first try by an International Board country against France in 20 months. 'But wait', the French said, 'for the second international in Paris!' Yet there New Zealand scored another try and a decisive victory, too, by 15 to 3. It was early in France's season, and of course the injured Bastiat and Rives were missed.

Rumania came to Clermont-Ferrand in December, and, as in June, lost a try-less affair 9–6. It was the last appearance of Fouroux, the forwards' leader from scrum-half and first French captain to win seven Championship matches in two seasons. He retired that day, just in time; Jean-Pierre Romeu, the line-kicker and France's record international scorer, stayed on, only to be dropped. Bitterness was to linger inside and around the team throughout the winter.

Thus France entered the Championship in January with its fifteenth set of half-backs since Edwards and Bennett first paired for Wales in 1970. Jérôme Gallion took a try with each of his first three caps, but fly-half Bernard Viviès never received the attacking brief he had been picked to exploit. Alone among the five nations the French continued to reject squad training. Wings, of which France used five, continued to throw in at the line-out. Full-back Aguirre had an indifferent winter as a goal-kicker.

England's forwards were more incisive than France's in Paris until injuries told; Irish and Welsh Lions later looked none the worse for their 1977 trek 'down under'. Therefore it was a moot question whether the French pack had declined or the others had improved. Robert Paparemborde left Cardiff believing that Cholley, Paco, and he had still to meet their masters.

At Murrayfield, where Haget justified his recall beside Michel Palmié, the ill-starred French backs were given their head, in the rain, long enough for Scotland to lead 13–0. The damage was nobly undone, but the day had been dark for attack-minded selectors. Consequently, when Ireland goaded in Paris, blinkered bludgeoning almost lost the game. 'Rugby starts up front, but it isn't supposed to stop there!' said Jean Piqué, coach of the backs and a selector. Now all waited for the big match in Cardiff.

Like Wales, France had outscored England, Scotland, and Ireland three years in a row. This time the Grand Slam rubber went to the side that wasted fewer opportunities. No one belittled the Welsh victory. There was talk among Frenchmen of a season wasted, and an All Black lesson unlearnt; and there was sympathy with apprentice captain Jean-Pierre Bastiat, at sea between a cut-off pack and five backs only tentatively brought into play in their first Championship.

Wins over Rumania (9–6) by the senior side, over Czecho-slovakia (63–0) and Italy (31–9) by France 'B', and over Poland (26–9) and Spain (20–3) by an Extra XV won the FIRA honours for France. France 'B' also beat Wales 'B' 15–3 at Nantes and Scotland 'B' 11–3 at Le Havre. England won an Under 23 match 10–3 at Orrell. France Juniors beat Wales Youth 19–9 at Bourg-en-Bresse, won the FIRA tournament at Parma – Italy were second and the Soviet Union third – and beat England Colts 11–3 at Camborne. France Schools (19 Group) beat Scotland 8–3 at Goldenacre and England 12–0 at Chateauroux, but lost to Wales 7–3 at Neath.

The club championship was again a one-team show. Block-busters Béziers completed the league phase undefeated, and took their sixth title in eight years by beating Jean-Pierre Romeu's Montferrand in the final, at Parc des Princes, by four goals, a penalty goal, and a try (31 pts) to a goal and a dropped goal (9). Three of the winners' tries, all converted, came in the last quarter of an hour. Up to then Montferrand had done well, but the Béziers forwards had the last word. There was a capacity crown of 50,000, paying nearly £200,000, so the *'finale'*, at least, retains its appeal.

## FRENCH CLUB CHAMPIONSHIP WINNERS

(First Division)

| | | | |
|---|---|---|---|
| **1892** Racing Club de France | **1910** FC Lyon | **1935** Biarritz | **1959** Racing Club de France |
| **1893** Stade Français | **1911** Bordeaux UC | **1936** Narbonne | |
| **1894** Stade Français | **1912** Stade Toulousain | **1937** Vienne | **1960** Lourdes |
| **1895** Stade Français | **1913** Bayonne | **1938** Perpignan | **1961** Béziers |
| **1896** Olympique de Paris | **1914** Perpignan | **1939** Biarritz | **1962** Agen |
| **1897** Stade Français | **1915** *No competition* | **1940–42** *No competition* | **1963** Mont-de-Marsan |
| **1898** Stade Français | **1916–19*** | **1943** Bayonne | |
| **1899** Bordeaux UC | **1920** Tarbes | **1944** Perpignan | **1964** Pau |
| **1900** Racing Club de France | **1921** Perpignan | **1945** Agen | **1965** Agen |
| **1901** Stade Français | **1922** Stade Toulousain | **1946** Pau | **1966** Agen |
| **1902** Racing Club de France | **1923** Stade Toulousain | **1947** Stade Toulousain | **1967** Montauban |
| **1903** Stade Français | **1924** Stade Toulousain | **1948** Lourdes | **1968** Lourdes† |
| **1904** Bordeaux UC | **1925** Perpignan | **1949** Castres | **1969** Bègles |
| **1905** Bordeaux UC | **1926** Stade Toulousain | **1950** Castres | **1970** La Voulte |
| **1906** Bordeaux UC | **1927** Stade Toulousain | **1951** Carmaux | **1971** Béziers |
| **1907** Bordeaux UC | **1928** Pau | **1952** Lourdes | **1972** Béziers |
| **1908** Stade Français | **1929** Quillan | **1953** Lourdes | **1973** Tarbes |
| **1909** Bordeaux UC | **1930** Agen | **1954** Grenoble | **1974** Béziers |
| | **1931** Toulon | **1955** Perpignan | **1975** Béziers |
| | **1932** Lyon Olympique U | **1956** Lourdes | **1976** Agen |
| | **1933** Lyon Olympique U | **1957** Lourdes | **1977** Béziers |
| | **1934** Bayonne | **1958** Lourdes | **1978** Béziers |

\* *from 1916 to 1919 the Championship was replaced by the 'Coupe de L'Esperance'.*
† *Lourdes beat Toulon on tries, in a final drawn 9–9.*

# FRENCH INTERNATIONAL PLAYERS
*(up to 30 April 1978)*

## ABBREVIATIONS

| A | Australia |
|---|---|
| E | England |
| I | Ireland |
| NZ | New Zealand |
| S | Scotland |
| SA | South Africa |
| W | Wales |
| (R) | Replacement |

Note: Years given for Five Nations' matches are for second half of season, e.g. 1972 refers to season 1971–72

**Club Abbreviations** ASF–Association Sportive Française; BEC–Bordeaux Etudiants Club; CASG–Club Athletique des Sports Generaux; PUC–Paris University Club; RCF–Racing Club de France; SBUC–Stade Bordelais University Club; SCUF–Sporting Club Universitaire de France; SF–Stade Français, SOE–Stade Olympien des Etudiants

Note: *France awards 'caps' against other opponents besides the International Board countries but only matches against the latter have been included in this list*

**Abadie, A** (S Paloise) 1964 *I*
**Abadie, A** (SC Graulhet) 1967 *SA* (3), *NZ*, 1968 *S, I*
**Aguirre, J-M** (Bagnères) 1971 *A*, 1972 *S*, 1973 *W, I, 1974 I, W, SA*, 1976 *W* (R), *E, A*, 1977 *W, E, S, I, NZ* (2), 1978 *E, S, I, W*
**Albaladejo, P** (US Dacquoise) 1954 *E*, 1960 *W, I, 1961 S, SA, E, W, I, NZ* (2), *A*, 1962 *S, E, W, I*, 1963 *S, E, I, W*, 1964 *S, NZ, W, I, SA*
**Alvarez, A** (US Tyrosse) 1947 *S, I, W, E*, 1948 *I, A, S, W, E*, 1949 *I, E, W*, 1951 *S, E, W*
**Amand, H** (SF) 1906 *NZ*
**Ambert, A** (S Toulousain) 1930 *S, I, W, E*
**Amestoy, J-B** (S Montois) 1964 *NZ, E*
**André, G** (RCF) 1913 *SA, E, W, I*, 1914 *I, W, E*
**Anduran, J** (SCUF) 1910 *W*
**Arcalis, R** (CA Briviste) 1950 *S, I*, 1951 *I, E, W*
**Aristouy, P** (S Paloise) 1948 *S*, 1950 *S, I, E, W*
**Arnal, J-M** (RCF) 1914 *I, W*
**Arnaudet, M** (FC Lourdes) 1964 *I*, 1967 *W*
**Arrieta, J** (St Francais) 1953 *E, W*
**Astre, R** (Béziers) 1972 *I*, 1973 *E* (R), 1975 *E, S, I, SA* (2), 1976 *A*
**Augé, J** (US Dax) 1929 *S, W*
**Augras, L** (SU Agen) 1931 *I, S, W*
**Averous, J-L** (La Voulte) 1975 *S, I, SA*(2), 1976 *I, W, E, A* (2), 1977 *W, E, S, I*, 1978 *E, S, I*
**Azarete, J-L** (US Dacquoise, St Jean-de-Luz) 1969 *W*, 1970 *S, I, W*, 1971 *S, I, E, SA* (2), *A*, 1972 *W, E, I, A*, 1973 *NZ, W, I*, 1974 *I, SA* (2), 1975 *W*

**Bader, E** (SS Primevères) 1927 *I, S*
**Badin, C** (RC Chalon) 1973 *W, I*
**Baillette, M** (US Perpignan) 1925 *I, S, NZ*, 1926 *W*, 1927 *I, W*, 1930 *S, I, E*, 1931 *I, S, E*
**Ballarin, J** (S Tarbais) 1924 *E*, 1925 *NZ, S*
**Baquet, J** (S Toulousain) 1921 *I*
**Barrau, M** (S Beaumontois and S Toulousain) 1971 *S, E, W*, 1972 *W, E, A* (2), 1973 *S, NZ, E, I*, 1974 *I, S*
**Barrère, P** (RC Toulonnais) 1931 *W*
**Barthe, J** (FC Lourdais) 1955 *S*, 1956 *I, W, E*, 1957 *S, I, E, W*, 1958 *S, E, W, I, SA* (2), *A*, 1959 *S, E, W*
**Barthe, E** (SA Bordelais) 1925 *W, E*
**Bascou, P** (A Bayonnais) 1914 *E*
**Basquet, G** (SU Agen) 1947 *S, I, W, E*, 1948 *A, I, S, W, E*, 1949 *S, I, E, W*, 1950 *S, I, E, W*, 1951 *S, I, E, W*, 1952 *S, I, SA, W, E*
**Bastiat, J-P** (US Dax) 1970 *S, I, W*, 1971 *S, I, SA*, 1972 *A, S*, 1973 *E*, 1974 *SA*, 1975 *W*, 1976 *S, I, W, E, A* (2), 1977 *W, E, S, I*, 1978 *E, S, I, W*
**Baudry, N** (AS Montferrandaise) 1949 *S, I, W*
**Baulon, R** (CS Vienne) 1954 *S, NZ, W, E*, 1955 *I, E, W*, 1956 *S, E, I, W*, 1957 *S, I*

**Baux, J-P** (AC Lannemezan) 1968 *NZ* (2), *SA* (2)
**Bavozet, J** (FC Lyon) 1911 *S, E, W*
**Bayard, J** (S Toulousain) 1923 *S, E, W*, 1924 *W*
**Bayardon, J** (RC Chalon) 1964 *S, NZ, E*
**Beaurin, C** (SF) 1907 *E*, 1908 *E*
**Beguet, L** (RCF) 1922 *I*, 1923 *S, W, E, I*, 1924 *S, I, E*
**Behoteguy, A** (A Bayonnais) 1923 *E*, 1924 *S, I, E, W*, 1926 *E*, 1927 *E*, 1928 *I, E, W*, 1929 *S, W, E*
**Behoteguy, H** (RCF) 1923 *W*, 1928 *I, E, W*
**Belascain, C** (A Bayonnais) 1978 *E, S, I, W*
**Belletante, G** (S Nantais U) 1951 *I, E, W*
**Bénésis, R** (R C Narbonne and S U Agen) 1969 *W*, 1970 *S, I, W, E*, 1971 *S, I, E, W, A*, 1972 *W, E, S, I* (2) *A*, 1973 *NZ, E, W, I*, 1974 *I, W, E, S*
**Berejnoi, J-C** (SC Tulle) 1964 *S, W, I, SA*, 1965 *S, I, E, W*, 1966 *S, I, E, W*, 1967 *S, A, E, W, I*
**Berges, B** (S Toulousain) 1926 *I*
**Berges-Cau, R** (FC Lourdes) 1976 *E* (R)
**Bergougnan, Y** (S Toulousain) 1945 *S, I, W, E*, 1948 *S, W, E*, 1949 *S, E*
**Bernard, R** (US Bergerac) 1951 *S, I, E, W*
**Bernon, J** (FC Lourdes) 1922 *I*, 1923 *S*
**Berot, J-L** (S Toulousain) 1968 *NZ, A*, 1969 *S, I*, 1970 *E*, 1971 *S, I, E, W, SA* (2), *A* (2), 1972 *S, I, A, E, W*, 1974 *I*
**Bertrand, P** (US Bressane) 1951 *I, E, W*, 1953 *S, I, E, W*
**Bertranne, R** (S Bagnerais, RC Toulon) 1971 *E, W, SA, A* (2), 1972 *I, S*, 1973 *NZ, E*, 1974 *I, W, E, S, SA* (2), 1975 *W, E, S, I, SA* (2), 1976 *S, I, W, E, A* (2), 1977 *W, E, S, I, NZ* (2), 1978 *E, S, I, W*
**Besset, E** (FC Grenoble) 1924 *S*
**Besset, L** (SCUF) 1914 *W, E*
**Besson, R** (CASG) 1924 *I, E*, 1926 *S, W*, 1927 *I*
**Besson, P** (CA Brive) 1963 *S, I, E*, 1968 *SA*
**Bidart, L** (S Rochelais) 1953 *W*
**Biemouret, P** (SU Agen) 1969 *E, W*, 1970 *I, W, E*, 1971 *W, SA* (2), *A*, 1972 *I, E, W, A*, 1973 *S, NZ, E, W, I*
**Bienes, R** (UC Cognac) 1950 *S, I, E, W*, 1951 *S, I, E, W*, 1952 *S, I, SA, W, E*, 1953 *S, I, E*, 1954 *S, I, NZ, W, E*, 1956 *S, I, W, E*
**Bigot, C** (US Quillan) 1930 *S, E*, 1931 *I, S*
**Bilbao, L** (St Jean-de-Luz Ol) 1978 *I*
**Billac, E** (A Bayonnais) 1920 *S, E, W, I*, 1921 *S, W*, 1922 *W*, 1923 *E*
**Billière, M** (S Toulousain) 1968 *NZ*
**Bioussa, A** (S Toulousain) 1924 *W*, 1925 *I, NZ, S, E*, 1926 *S, I, E*, 1928 *E, W*, 1929 *I, E, W*, 1930 *S, I, E, W*
**Bioussa, C** (S Toulousain) 1913 *W, I*, 1914 *I*
**Biraben, M** (US Dax) 1920 *W, I*, 1921 *S, W, E, I*, 1922 *S, E, I*
**Boffelli, V** (Aurillac) 1971 *A*, 1972 *S, I*, 1974 *I, W, E, S, SA* (2), 1975 *W, S, I*

**Bonal, J-M** (S Toulousain) 1968 *E, W, NZ* (2), *SA* (2), 1969 *S, I, E,* 1970 *W, E*
**Bonamy, R** (SA Bordelais) 1928 *I*
**Boniface, A** (S Montois) 1954 *I, NZ, W, E,* 1955 *S, I,* 1956 *S, I, W,* 1957 *S, I, W,* 1958 *S, E,* 1959 *E,* 1961 *NZ* (2), *A,* 1962 *E, W, I,* 1963 *S, I, E, W,* 1964 *S, NZ, E, W,* 1965 *W,* 1966 *S, I, E, W*
**Boniface, G** (S Montois) 1960 *W, I,* 1961 *S, SA, E, W, I, NZ* (3), 1963 *S, I, E, W,* 1964 *S,* 1965 *S, I, E, W,* 1966 *S, I, E, W*
**Bonnes, E** (RC Narbonne) 1924 *W*
**Bonnus, F** (RC Toulonnais) 1950 *S, I, E, W*
**Bontemps, D** (S Rochelais) 1968 *SA*
**Borchard, G** (RCF) 1908 *E,* 1909 *E, W, I,* 1911 *I*
**Borde, F** (RCF) 1920 *I,* 1921 *S, W, E,* 1922 *S, W,* 1923 *S, I,* 1924 *E,* 1925 *I,* 1926 *E*
**Bordenave, L** (RC Toulonnais) 1948 *A, S, W, E,* 1949 *S*
**Boubee, J** (S Tarbais) 1921 *S, E, I,* 1922 *E, W,* 1923 *E, I,* 1925 *NZ, S*
**Boudreau, R** (SCUF) 1910 *W, S*
**Bouguyon, G** (FC Grenoble) 1961 *SA, E, W, I, NZ* (3), *A*
**Boujet, C** (FC Grenoble) 1968 *NZ, A* (R), *SA*
**Bouquet, J** (CS Bourgoin) 1954 *S,* 1955 *E,* 1956 *S, I, W, E,* 1957 *S, E, W,* 1958 *S, E,* 1959 *S, W, I,* 1960 *S, E, W, I,* 1961 *S, SA, E, W, I,* 1962 *S, E, W, I*
**Bourdeu, R** (FC Lourdais) 1952 *S, I, SA, W, E,* 1953 *S, I, E*
**Bourgarel, R** (S Toulousain) 1970 *S, I, E,* 1971 *W, SA* (2), 1973 *S*
**Bousquet, A** (AS Béziers) 1921 *E, I*
**Bousquet, R** (SC Albi) 1927 *I, S, W, E,* 1929 *W, E,* 1930 *W*
**Boyau, M** (SBUC) 1912 *I, S, W, E,* 1913 *W, I*
**Branca, G** (SF) 1928 *S,* 1929 *I, S*
**Branlat, A** (RCF) 1906 *NZ, E,* 1908 *W*
**Brejassou, R** (S Tarbais) 1952 *S, I, SA, W, E,* 1953 *E, W,* 1954 *S, I, NZ,* 1955 *S, I, E, W*
**Bringeon, A** (Biarritz) 1925 *W*
**Brun, G** (CS Vienne) 1950 *E, W,* 1951 *S, E, W,* 1952 *S, I, SA, W, E,* 1953 *E, W*
**Bruneau, M** (SBUC) 1910 *W, E,* 1913 *SA, E*
**Brunet, Y** (USA Perpignan) 1975 *SA*
**Buisson, H** (AS Béziers) 1931 *E*
**Buonomo, Y** (AS Béziers) 1971 *A,* 1972 *I*
**Burgun, M** (RCF) 1909 *I,* 1910 *W, S, I,* 1911 *S, E,* 1912 *I, S,* 1913 *S, E,* 1914 *E*
**Bustaffa, D** (US Carcassonnaise) 1977 *NZ* (2), 1978 *W*
**Buzy, E** (FC Lourdais) 1947 *S, I, W, E,* 1948 *I, S, A, W, E,* 1949 *S, I, E, W*

**Cabanier, J-M** (US Montauban) 1964 *S,* 1965 *S, I, W,* 1966 *S, I, E, W,* 1967 *S, A, E, W, I, SA* (2), *NZ,* 1968, *S, I*
**Cabrol, H** (AS Béziers) 1972 *A* (2[1R]), 1974 *SA*
**Cadenat, J** (SCUF) 1910 *S, E,* 1911 *W, I,* 1912 *W, E,* 1913 *I*
**Cahuc, F** (St Girons SC) 1922 *S*
**Calvo, G** (FC Lourdais) 1961 *NZ* (2)
**Camberabero, G** (La Voulte S) 1961 *NZ,* 1967 *A, E, W, I, SA* (3), 1968 *S, E, W*
**Camberabero, L** (La Voulte S) 1965 *S, I,* 1966 *E, W,* 1967 *A, E, W, I,* 1968 *S, E, W*
**Cambré, T** (FC Oloron) 1920 *E, W, I*
**Camel, A** (S Toulousain) 1928 *S, I, E, W,* 1929 *S, W, E,* 1930 *S, I, E, W*
**Camel, M** (S Toulousain) 1929 *W, E*
**Camicas, F** (S Tarbais) 1928 *S, I, E, W,* 1929 *I, S, W, E*
**Camo, E** (CA Villeneuvois) 1931 *I, S, W, E*
**Campaes, A** (FC Lourdais) 1965 *W,* 1967 *NZ,* 1968 *S, I, E, W, NZ* (2), *A,* 1969 *S, W,* 1973 *NZ*
**Cantoni, J** (AS Béziers) 1970 *W,* 1971 *S, I, E, W, SA* (2), 1972 *S, I,* 1973 *S, NZ, W, I,* 1975 *W* (R)
**Capdouze, J** (S Paloise) 1964 *SA,* 1965 *S, I, E*
**Capendeguy, J-M** (CA Béglais) 1968 *NZ*
**Capmau,** (S Toulousain) 1914 *E*
**Carabignac, J** (SU Agen) 1951 *S, I,* 1952 *SA, W, E,* 1953 *S, I*
**Carbonne, P** (US Perpignan) 1927 *W*
**Caron, L** (Lyon OU) 1947 *E,* 1948 *A, I, W, E,* 1949 *S, I, E, W*

**Carrère, C** (RC Toulonnais) 1967 *S, A, E, W, I, SA* (3), *NZ,* 1968 *S, I, E, W, NZ, A,* 1969 *S, I,* 1970 *S, I, W, E,* 1971 *E, W*
**Carrère, J** (RC Vichy) 1956 *S,* 1957 *E, W,* 1958 *S, SA* (2), 1959 *I*
**Carrère, R** (S Montois) 1953 *E*
**Casaux, L** (S Tarbais) 1959 *I,* 1962 *S*
**Cassayet, A** (S Tarbais) 1920 *S, E, W,* 1921 *W, E, I,* 1922 *S, E, W,* 1923 *S, W, I, E,* 1924 *S, E, W,* 1925 *I, NZ, S, W,* 1926 *S, I, E, W,* 1927 *I, S, W*
**Cassiède, M** (US Dax) 1961 *NZ, A*
**Castets, J** (RC Toulon) 1923 *W, E, I*
**Caujolle, J** (S Tarbais) 1909 *E,* 1913 *SA, E,* 1914 *W, E*
**Caussarieu, G** (S Paloise) 1929 *I*
**Cayrefourcq, E** (S Tarbais) 1921 *E*
**Cazals, P** (S Montois) 1961 *NZ, A*
**Cazenave, A** (S Paloise) 1927 *E,* 1928 *S*
**Cazenave, F** (RCF) 1950 *E,* 1952 *S,* 1954 *I, NZ, W, E*
**Celaya, M** (Biarritz) 1953 *E, W,* 1954 *I, E,* 1955 *S, I, E, W,* 1956 *S, I, W, E,* 1957 *S, I, E, W,* 1958 *S, E, A, W,* 1959 *S, E,* 1960 *S, E, W, I,* 1961 *S, SA, E, W, I, NZ* (3), *A*
**Cessieux, J** (FC Lyon) 1906 *NZ*
**Cester, E** (Toulouse OEC, Valence Sp) 1966 *S, I, E,* 1967 *W,* 1968 *S, I, E, W, NZ* (2), *A, SA* (2), 1969 *S, I, E, W,* 1970 *S, I, W, E,* 1971 *A,* 1973 *S, NZ, W, I,* 1974 *I, W, E, S*
**Chapuy, L** (SF) 1926 *S*
**Charpentier, G** (SF) 1911 *E,* 1912 *W, E*
**Chateau, A** (A Bayonnais) 1913 *SA*
**Chenevay, C** (FC Grenoble) 1968 *SA*
**Chevallier, B** (AS Montferrand) 1952 *S, I, SA, W, E,* 1953 *E, W,* 1954 *S, I, NZ, W,* 1955 *S, I, E, W,* 1956 *S, I, W, E,* 1957 *S*
**Chilo, A** (RCF) 1920 *S, W,* 1925 *I, NZ*
**Cholley, G** (Castres Ol) 1975 *E, S, I, SA* (2), 1976 *S, I, W, E, A* (2), 1977 *W, E, S, I, NZ* (2), 1978 *E, S, I, W*
**Choy, J** (RC Narbonne) 1930 *S, I, E, W,* 1931 *I*
**Clady, A** (FC Lézignan) 1931 *I, S, E*
**Clauzel, F** (AS Béziers) 1924 *E, W,* 1925 *W*
**Claverie, H** (FC Lourdais) 1954 *NZ, W*
**Clement, J** (RCF) 1921 *S, W, E,* 1922 *S, E, W, I,* 1923 *S, W, I*
**Clement, P** (RCF) 1931 *W*
**Cluchague, L** (Biarritz) 1924 *S,* 1925 *E*
**Colombier, J** (AS St Junien) 1952 *SA, W, E*
**Combe, J** (SF) 1910 *S, E, I,* 1911 *S*
**Communeau, M** (SF) 1906 *NZ, E,* 1907 *E,* 1908 *E, W,* 1909 *E, W, I,* 1910 *S, E, I,* 1911 *S, E, I,* 1912 *I, S, W, E,* 1913 *SA, E, W*
**Conil de Beyssac, J** (SBUC) 1912 *I, S,* 1914 *I, W, E*
**Constant, G** (US Perpignan) 1920 *W*
**Coscoll, G** (AS Béziers) 1921 *S, W*
**Coulon, J** (FC Grenoble) 1928 *S*
**Crabos, R** (RCF) 1920 *S, E, W, I,* 1921 *S, W, E, I,* 1922 *S, E, W, I,* 1923 *S, I,* 1924 *S, I*
**Crampagne, J** (CA Béglais) 1967 *SA*
**Crancee, R** (FC Lourdais) 1961 *S*
**Crauste, M** (RCF) 1958 *S, E, A, W, I,* 1959 *E, W, I,* 1960 *S, E, W, I,* 1961 *S, SA, E, W, I, NZ* (3), *A,* 1962 *S, E, W, I,* 1963 *S, I, E, W,* 1964 *S, NZ, E, W, I, SA,* 1965 *S, I, E, W,* 1966 *S, I, E, W*
**Crichton, W H** (Havre AC) 1906 *NZ, E*

**Darrieussecq, A** (Biarritz Ol) 1973 *E*
**Danion, J** (RC Toulon) 1924 *I*
**Danos, P** (AS Béziers) 1958 *S, E, W, I, SA* (2), 1959 *S, E, W, I,* 1960 *S, E*
**Darrouy, C** (S Montois) 1957 *I, E, W,* 1959 *I,* 1963 *S, I, W, E,* 1964 *NZ, E, W, I, SA,* 1965 *S, I, E,* 1966 *S, I, E, W,* 1967 *S, A, E, W, I, SA* (3)
**Daudignon, G** (SF) 1928 *S*
**Dauga, B** (S Montois) 1964 *S, NZ, E, W, I, SA,* 1965 *S, E, I, W,* 1966 *S, I, E, W,* 1967 *S, E, W, I, A, SA* (4), *NZ,* 1968 *S, I, NZ* (3), *A, SA* (2), 1969 *S, I, E,* 1970 *S, I, W, E,* 1971 *S, I, E, W, SA* (2), *A* (2), 1972 *S, I, W*
**Dauger, J** (A Bayonnais) 1953 *S*
**Decamps, P** (RCF) 1911 *S*
**Dedet, J** (SF) 1910 *S, E, I,* 1911 *W, I,* 1912 *S,* 1913 *E, I*
**Dedeyn, P** (RCF) 1906 *NZ*
**Dedieu, P** (AS Béziers) 1963 *E,* 1964 *W, I, SA,* 1965 *S, I, E, W*
**De Gregorio, J** (FC Grenoble) 1960 *S, E, W, I,* 1961 *S, SA, E, W, I,* 1962 *S, E, W,* 1963 *S, W,* 1964 *NZ, E*

218

Dehez, J-L (SU Agen) 1967 *SA*
De Jouvencel, E (SF) 1909 *W, I*
De Laborderie, M (RCF) 1921 *I*, 1922 *I*, 1925 *W, E*
De Malmann, R (RCF) 1908 *E, W*, 1909 *E, W, I*, 1910 *E, I*
De Muison, J (SF) 1910 *I*
Destarac, L (S Tarbais) 1926 *S, I, E, W*, 1927 *W, E*
Desvouges, R (SF) 1914 *W*
Dizabo, P (US Tyrosse) 1948 *S, A, E*, 1949 *S, I, E, W*, 1950 *S, I*
Domec, A (AS Carcassonne) 1929 *W*
Domec, H (FC Lourdais) 1953 *W*, 1954 *S, I, NZ, W, E*, 1955 *S, I, E, W*, 1956 *I, W*, 1958 *E, A, W, I*
Domenech, A (RC Vichy) 1954 *W, E*, 1955 *S, I, E, W*, 1956 *S, I, W, E*, 1957 *S, I, E, W*, 1958 *E, S, W*, 1960 *S, E, W, I*, 1961 *S, SA, E, W, I, NZ* (3), *A*, 1962 *S, E, W, I*, 1963 *W*
Domercq, J (A Bayonnais) 1912 *I, S*
Dourthe, C (US Dax) 1967 *S, A, E, W, I, SA* (3), NZ, 1968 *NZ, W, SA* (2), 1969 *W*, 1971 *SA* (R), 1972 *I* (2), *A* (2), 1973 *NZ, E, S*, 1974 *I, SA* (2), 1975 *W, E, S*
Droitecourt, M (AS Montferrand) 1973 *NZ* (R), *E*, 1974 *E, S, SA*, 1975 *SA* (2), 1976 *S, I, W, A*
Dubertrand, A (AS Montferrand) 1971 *A* (2), 1972 *I*, 1974 *I, W, E, SA*, 1976 *S*
Dubois, D (CA Béglais) 1971 *S*
Duclos, A (FC Lourdes) 1931 *S*
Ducousso, J (S Tarbais) 1925 *S, W, E*
Dufau, G (RCF) 1948 *I, A*, 1949 *I, W*, 1950 *S, E, W*, 1951 *S, I, E, W*, 1952 *SA, W*, 1953 *S, I, E, W*, 1954 *S, I, NZ, W, E*, 1955 *S, I, E, W*, 1956 *S, I, W*, 1957 *S, I, E, W*
Dufau, J (Biarritz) 1912 *I, S, W, E*
Duffourcq, J (SBUC) 1906 *NZ, E*, 1907 *E*, 1908 *W*
Dufour, R (S Tarbais) 1911 *W*
Duhau, J (SF) 1928 *I*, 1930 *I*, 1931 *I, S, W*
Dulaurans, C (S Toulousain) 1926 *I*, 1928 *S*, 1929 *W*
Du Manoir, Y (RCF) 1925 *I, NZ, S, W, E*, 1926 *S*, 1927 *I, S*
Dupont, C (FC Lourdes) 1923 *S, W, I*, 1924 *S, I, W*, 1925 *S*, 1927 *E*, 1928 *W*, 1929 *I*
Dupouy, A (SA Bordelais) 1924 *W*
Duprat, B (A Bayonnais) 1966 *E, W*, 1967 *S, A, E, SA* (2), 1968 *S, I*, 1972 *E, W, I, A*
Dupré, P (RCF) 1909 *W*
Dupuy, J (S Tarbais) 1956 *S, I, W, E*, 1957 *S, I, E, W*, 1958 *S, E, SA* (2), 1959 *S, E, W, I*, 1960 *W, I*, 1961 *S, SA, E, NZ*, 1962 *S, E, W, I*, 1963 *W*, 1964 *S*
Du Souich, C (SCUF) 1911 *W, I*
Dutin, B (S Montois) 1968 *NZ, A, SA*
Dutour, F (S Toulousain) 1911 *E, I*, 1912 *S, W, E*, 1913 *S*
Dutrain, H (S Toulousain) 1947 *E*, 1949 *I, E, W*
Duval, R (SF) 1908 *E, W*, 1909 *E*, 1911 *E, W, I*

Echave, L (SU Agen) 1961 *S*
Esponda, J (RCF) 1967 *SA* (2), 1968 *NZ* (2), *SA*, 1969 *S, I* (R), *E*
Estève, A (AS Béziers) 1971 *SA*, 1972 *E, W, I* (2), *A*, 1973 *S, NZ, E, I*, 1974 *I, W, E, S, SA* (2), 1975 *W, E*
Etcheberry, J (SA Rochefort) 1923 *W, I*, 1924 *S, I, E, W*, 1926 *S, I, E*, 1927 *I, S, W*
Etchenique, J-M (Biarritz) 1974 *SA*, 1975 *E*
Etchepare, J (A Bayonnais) 1922 *I*
Etcheverry, M (S Paloise) 1971 *S, I*
Eutrope, A (SCUF) 1913 *I*

Fabre, J (S Toulousain) 1963 *E, I, S, W*, 1964 *S, E, NZ*
Failliot, P (RCF) 1911 *S, W, I*, 1912 *I, S, E*, 1913 *E, W*
Fargues, H (US Dax) 1923 *I*
Faure, F (S Tarbais) 1914 *I, W, E*
Favre, M (FC Lyon) 1913 *E, W*
Ferrien, R (S Tarbais) 1950 *S, I, E, W*
Fite, R (CA Brive) 1963 *W*
Forestier, J (SCUF) 1912 *W*
Forgues, F (A Bayonnais) 1911 *S, E, W*, 1912 *I, E, W*, 1913 *S, SA, W*, 1914 *I, E*
Fort, J (SU Agen) 1967 *W, I, SA* (4)
Fourcade, G (BEC) 1909 *E, W*
Foures, H (S Toulousain) 1951 *S, I, E, W*
Fournet, F (ASM) 1950 *W*
Fouroux, J (La Voulte S, Auch) 1972 *I*, 1974 *W, E, SA* (2), 1975 *W*, 1976 *S, I, W, E, A*, 1977 *W, E, S, I, NZ* (2)
Franquenelle, A (SC Vaugirard) 1911 *S*, 1913 *W, I*
Furcade, R (US Perpignan) 1952 *S*

Gachassin, J (FC Lourdais) 1961 *I, S*, 1964 *E, I, NZ, S, SA, W*, 1965 *S, E, I, W*, 1966 *E, I, W, S*, 1967 *A, I, S, W, NZ*, 1968 *E, I*, 1969 *I, S*
Galau, H (S Toulousain) 1924 *E, I, S, W*
Galia, J (US Quillan) 1927 *E*, 1928 *E, I, W, S*, 1929 *E, I*, 1930 *E, I, S, W*, 1931 *E, S, W*
Gallion, J (RC Toulon) 1978 *E, S, I, W*
Galy, J (US Perpignan) 1953 *W*
Gasc, J (SC Graulhet) 1977 *NZ*
Gasparotto, G (Montferrand) 1976 *A*
Gaudermen, P (RCF) 1906 *E*
Gayraud, W (S Toulousain) 1920 *I*
Gensanne, R (AS Béziers) 1962 *E, I, S, W*, 1963 *S*
Gerald, G (RCF) 1927 *E*, 1928 *S*, 1929 *E, I, S, W*, 1930 *E, I, S, W*, 1931 *E, I, S*
Gerintes, G (CASG) 1925 *I*, 1926 *W*
Giaccardy, M (SBUC) 1907 *E*
Gommes, J (RCF) 1909 *I*
Gonnet, C-A (SC Albi) 1921 *E, I*, 1922 *E, W*, 1924 *E, S*, 1926 *E, I, S, W*, 1927 *E, I, S, W*
Got, R (US Perpignan) 1920 *I*, 1921 *S, W*, 1922 *E, I, S, W*, 1924 *E, I, W*
Gourdon, J-F (RCF, Bagnères) 1974 *S, SA* (2), 1975 *W, E, S, I*, 1976 *S, I, W, E*, 1978 *E, S*
Graciet, R (SA Bordelais) 1926 *I, W*, 1927 *S*, 1929 *E*, 1930 *W*
Graule, V (Arlequins Perpignanais) 1926 *E, I, W*, 1927 *S, W*
Greffe, M (FC Grenoble) 1968 *W, NZ* (2), *SA*
Gruarin, A (RC Toulon) 1964 *I, SA, W*, 1965 *E, I, S, W*, 1966 *S, I, W*, 1967 *A, E, I, S, W, NZ*, 1968 *I, S*
Guelorget, P (RCF) 1931 *E*
Guichemerre, A (US Dax) 1920 *E*, 1921 *E, I*, 1923 *S*
Guilbert, A (RC Toulonnais) 1975 *E, S, I, SA* (2), 1976 *A*, 1977 *NZ* (2)
Guillemin, P (RCF) 1908 *E, W*, 1909 *E, I*, 1910 *E, I, S, W*, 1911 *E, S, W*
Guilleux, P (SU Agen) 1952 *SA*

Haget, A (PUC) 1953 *E*, 1954 *E, I, NZ*, 1955 *E, W*, 1957 *E, I*, 1958 *SA*
Haget, F (SU Agen, Biarritz Ol) 1975 *SA*, 1976 *S*, 1978 *S, I, W*
Haget, H (CASG) 1928 *S*
Halet, AS Strasbourg) 1925 *NZ, S, W*
Harize, D (S Cahors, S Toulousain) 1975 *SA* (2), 1976 *A* (2), 1977 *W, E, S, I*
Hauc, J (RC Toulon) 1928 *E*, 1929 *I, S*
Hauser, M (FC Lourdais) 1969 *E*
Hedembaigt, M (A Bayonnais) 1913 *S, SA*, 1914 *W*
Herice, D (CA Béglais) 1950 *I*
Herrero, A (RC Toulonnais) 1964 *E, I, SA, NZ, W*, 1965 *E, I, S, W*, 1966 *W*, 1967 *A, E, I, S*
Hiquet, J-C (SU Agen) 1964 *E*
Hoche, M (PUC) 1957 *E, I, W*
Hortoland, J-P (AS Béziers) 1971 *A*
Houblain, H (SCUF) 1909 *E*, 1910 *W*
Houdet, R (SF) 1927 *S, W*, 1928 *W*, 1929 *E, I, S*, 1930 *E, S*
Hourdebaigt (SBUC) 1909 *I*, 1910 *E, I, S, W*
Hubert, A (ASF) 1906 *E*, 1907 *E*, 1908 *E, W*, 1909 *E, I, W*
Hutin, R (CASG) 1927 *I, S, W*

Icard, J (SF) 1909 *E, W*
Iguinitz, E (A Bayonnais) 1914 *E*
Ihingoue, D (BEC) 1912 *I, S*
Imbernon, J-F (US Perpignan) 1976 *I, W, E, A*, 1977 *W, E, S, I, NZ* (2), 1978 *E*
Iracabal, J (A Bayonnais) 1968 *NZ* (2), *SA*, 1969 *I, S, W*, 1970 *E, I, S, W*, 1971 *W, A, SA* (2), 1972 *I, E, W, A*, 1973 *S, NZ, E, W, I*, 1974 *I, W, E, S, SA* (R)
Isaac, H (RCF) 1907 *E*, 1908 *E*

Jardel, J (SA Bordelais) 1928 *E, I*
Jaureguy, A (RCF) 1920 *E, I, S, W*, 1922 *S, W*, 1923 *E, I, S, W*, 1924 *S, W*, 1925 *I, NZ*, 1926 *E, S, W*, 1927 *E, I*, 1928 *E, S, W*, 1929 *E, I, S*
Jaureguy, P (S Toulousain) 1913 *I, S, SA, W*
Jeangrand, H (S Tarbais) 1921 *I*
Jeanjean, P (RC Toulonnais) 1948 *I*
Jerome, G (SF) 1906 *E, NZ*
Joinel, J-L (CA Brive) 1977 *NZ*

**Pellissier, L** (RCF) 1928 *E, I, W*
**Peron, P** (RCF) 1975 *SA* (2)
**Pesteil, J-P** (AS Béziers) 1975 *SA*, 1976 *A*
**Petit, C** (SU Lorrain) 1931 *W*
**Peyroutou** (CA Périgueux) 1911 *E, S*
**Phliponneau, J-F** (AS Montferrand) 1973 *W, I*
**Piazza, A** (US Montauban) 1968 *A, NZ*
**Pierrot, G** (S Paloise) 1914 *E, I, W*
**Pilon, J** (CA Périgourdin) 1949 *E*, 1950 *E*
**Piqué, J** (S Paloise) 1961 *A, NZ* (2), 1962 *S*, 1964 *E, I, NZ, SA, W*, 1965 *E, I, S, W*
**Piquemal, M** (S Tarbais) 1927 *I, S*, 1929 *I*, 1930 *E, I, S, W*
**Piquiral, E** (RCF) 1924 *E, I, S, W*, 1925 *E*, 1926 *E, I, S, W*, 1927 *E, I, S, W*, 1928 *E*
**Piteu, R** (S Paloise) 1921 *E, I, S, W*, 1922 *E, I, S, W*, 1923 *E*, 1924 *E, I, S, W*, 1925 *E, I, NZ*, 1926 *E*
**Plantefol, A** (RCF) 1967 *SA* (3), *NZ*, 1968 *E, NZ, W*, 1969 *E, W*
**Plantey, S** (RCF) 1961 *A*
**Podevin, G** (SF) 1913 *I, W*
**Poirier, G** (SCUF) 1907 *E*
**Pomathios, M** (SU Agen) 1948 *A, E, I, S, W*, 1949 *E, I, S, W*, 1950 *I, S, W*, 1951 *E, I, S, W*, 1952 *E, W*, 1953 *I, S, W*, 1954 *S*
**Pons, P** (S Toulousain) 1920 *E, S, W*, 1921 *S, W*, 1922 *S*
**Porra, M** (FC Lyon) 1931 *I*
**Porthault, A** (RCF) 1951 *E, S, W*, 1952 *I*, 1953 *I, S*
**Poydebasque, F** (A Bayonnais) 1914 *I, W*
**Prat, J** (FC Lourdais) 1947 *E, I, S, W*, 1948 *A, E, I, S, W*, 1949 *E, I, S, W*, 1950 *E, I, S, W*, 1951 *E, S, W*, 1952 *E, I, S, SA, W*, 1953 *E, I, S, W*, 1954 *E, I, NZ, S, W*, 1955 *E, I, S, W*
**Prat, M** (FC Lourdais) 1951 *I*, 1952 *E, I, S, SA, W*, 1953 *E, I, S*, 1954 *E, I, NZ, W*, 1955 *E, I, S, W*, 1956 *I, W*, 1957 *I, S, W*, 1958 *A, I, W*
**Prevost, A** (SC Albi) 1927 *I, S, W*
**Princlary, J** (CA Brive) 1947 *I, S, W*
**Puech, L** (S Toulousain) 1920 *E, I, S*, 1921 *E, I*
**Puget, M** (CA Brive) 1966 *I, S*, 1967 *NZ, SA* (3), 1968 *NZ* (2), *SA* (2), 1969 *E*, 1970 *W*
**Puig, A** (Arlequins Perpignanais) 1926 *E, S*
**Pujol, T** (SOE Toulouse) 1906 *NZ*

**Quaglio, A** (SC Mazamétain) 1958 *A, E, I, S, SA* (2), *W*, 1959 *E, I, S, W*
**Quilis, A** (RC Narbonne) 1967 *SA* (2), *NZ*, 1971 *I*

**Ramis, R** (USA Perpignanais) 1922 *E, I*, 1923 *W*
**Rancoule, H** (FC Lourdais) 1955 *E, W*, 1958 *A, I, SA, W*, 1959 *S, W*, 1960 *I*, 1961 *NZ* (2), *SA, E, W*, 1962 *E, I, S, W*
**Raymond, F** (S Toulousain) 1925 *S*, 1927 *W*, 1928 *I*
**Razat, J-P** (SU Agen) 1963 *I, S*
**Rebujent, R** (RCF) 1963 *E*
**Revillon, J** (RCF) 1926 *E, I*, 1927 *S*
**Ribere, E** (US Perpignan) 1924 *I*, 1925 *I, NZ, S*, 1926 *I, S, W*, 1927 *E, I, S, W*, 1928 *E, I, S, W*, 1929 *E, I*, 1930 *E, I, S, W*, 1931 *E, I, S, W*
**Rives, J-P** (S Toulousain) 1975 *E, S, I*, 1976 *S, I, W, E, A* (2), 1977 *W, E, S, I*, 1978 *E, S, I, W*
**Rodrigo, M** (SA Mauléon) 1931 *I, W*
**Rogé, L** (AS Béziers) 1953 *E, W*, 1954 *S*, 1955 *I, S*, 1956 *E, W*, 1957 *S*, 1960 *E, S*
**Rollet, J** (A Bayonnais) 1961 *A, NZ*, 1963 *I*
**Romero, H** (US Montauban) 1962 *E, I, S, W*, 1963 *E*
**Romeu, J-P** (AS Montferrand) 1973 *S, NZ, E, W, I*, 1974 *W, E, S, SA* (2[1R]), 1975 *W, SA*, 1976 *S, I, W, E*, 1977 *W, E, S, I, NZ* (2)
**Roques, A** (Cadurcien) 1958 *A, I, SA* (2), *W*, 1959 *E, I, S, W*, 1960 *E, I, W, S*, 1961 *E, I, S, SA, W*, 1962 *E, I, S, W*, 1963 *S*
**Roques, J-C** (CA Briviste) 1966 *I, S*
**Rossignol, J-C** (CA Brive) 1972 *A*
**Rouan, J-C** (RC Narbonne) 1953 *I, S*
**Roucaries, G** (US Perpignan) 1956 *S*
**Rouffia, L** (US Romans) 1948 *I*
**Roujas R,** (S Tarbais) 1910 *I*
**Rousie, M** (CA Villeneuvois) 1931 *S*
**Rousset, G** (AS Béziers) 1975 *SA*
**Ruiz, A** (S Tarbais) 1968 *SA*

**Rupert, J-J** (US Tyrosse) 1964 *S*, 1965 *E, W*, 1966 *E, I, S, W*, 1968 *S*

**Sagot, R** (SF) 1906 *NZ*, 1908 *E*, 1909 *W*
**Saisset, O** (AS Béziers) 1972 *I, S, A* (2), 1973 *S, NZ, E, W, I*, 1974 *I, SA* (2), 1975 *W*
**Salinie, R** (US Perpignan) 1923 *E*
**Salut, J** (Toulouse OEC) 1967 *S*, 1968 *E, I, NZ*, 1969 *I*
**Samatan, R** (SU Agen) 1930 *E, I, S, W*, 1931 *E, I, S, W*
**Sanac, A** (US Perpignan) 1953 *I, S*, 1954 *E*, 1957 *E, I, S, W*
**Sangalli, F** (Narbonne) 1975 *I, SA* (2), 1976 *S, A* (2), 1977 *W, E, S, I, NZ* (2)
**Sarrade, R** (S Paloise) 1929 *I*
**Saux, J-P** (S Paloise) 1960 *W*, 1961 *A, E, I, NZ* (3), *SA, W*, 1962 *E, I, S, W*, 1963 *E, I, S*
**Savy, M** (AS Montferrand) 1931 *E, I, S, W*
**Sayrou, J** (US Perpignan) 1926 *W*, 1928 *E, W*, 1929 *E, S, W*
**Scohy, R** (EC Bordeaux) 1931 *E, S, W*
**Sebedio, J** (S Tarbais) 1913 *E, S*, 1914 *I*, 1920 *I, S*, 1922 *E, S*, 1923 *S*
**Semmartin, J** (SCUF) 1913 *I, W*
**Senal, G** (AS Béziers) 1974 *SA* (2), 1975 *W*
**Sentilles, J** (S Tarbais) 1912 *E, W*, 1913 *S, SA*
**Serin, L** (AS Béziers) 1928 *E*, 1929 *E, W*, 1930 *E, I, S, W*, 1931 *E, I, W*
**Serre, P** (US Perpignan) 1920 *E, S*
**Servole, L** (RC Toulon) 1931 *E, I, S, W*
**Sicart, N** (US Perpignan) 1922 *I*
**Sillières, J** (S Tarbais) 1970 *I, S*, 1971 *E, I, S*, 1972 *E, W*
**Siman, M** (AS Montferrand) 1948 *E*, 1949 *S*, 1950 *E, I, S, W*
**Sitjar, M** (SU Agen) 1964 *I, W*, 1967 *A, E, I, SA* (2), *W*
**Skréla, J-C** (S Toulousain) 1971 *SA, A* (2), 1972 *E, W, I* (2[1R]), *A*, 1973 *W*, 1974 *W, E, S*, 1975 *W* (R), *E, S, I, SA* (2), 1976 *S, I, W, E, A* (2), 1977 *W, E, S, I, NZ* (2), 1978 *E, S, I, W*
**Soro, R** (FC Lourdais, and US Romans) 1947 *E, I, S, W*, 1948 *A, E, I, S, W*, 1949 *E, I, S, W*
**Sorrondo, M** (US Montauban) 1947 *E, I, S, W*, 1948 *I*
**Soulie, E** (CASG) 1920 *E, I*, 1921 *E, I, S*, 1922 *E, I, W*
**Spanghero, C** (RC Narbonne) 1971 *E, SA* (2), *W, A,* (2), 1972 *E, S, I, W, A* (2), 1974 *I, W, E, S, SA*, 1975 *E, S, I*
**Spanghero, W** (RC Narbonne) 1964 *SA*, 1965 *E, I, S, W*, 1966 *E, I, S, W*, 1967 *A, E, S, SA* (4), *NZ*, 1968 *A, E, I, S, NZ* (3), *SA* (2), *W*, 1969 *I, S, W*, 1971 *E, SA, W*, 1972 *E, I, A* (2), 1973 *S, NZ, E, W, I*
**Stener, G** (PUC) 1956 *E, I, S*, 1958 *SA* (2)
**Struxiano, P** (S Toulousain) 1913 *I, W*, 1920 *E, I, S, W*
**Sutra, G** (RC Narbonne) 1967 *SA*, 1969 *W*, 1970 *I, S*
**Swierczinski, C** (CA Béglais) 1969 *E*

**Taffary, M** (RCF) 1975 *W, E, S, I*
**Taillantou, J** (S Paloise) 1930 *I, W*
**Tarricq, P** (FC Lourdais) 1958 *A, I, W*
**Tavernier** (S Toulousain) 1913 *I*
**Terreau, M** (US Bressane) 1947 *E, I, S, W*, 1948 *A, E, I, W*, 1949 *S*, 1951 *S*
**Theuriet, A** (SCUF) 1909 *E, W*, 1910 *S*, 1911 *W*, 1913 *E*
**Thevenot, G** (SCUF) 1910 *E, I, W*
**Thierry, R** (RCF) 1920 *E, S, W*
**Thil, P** (S Nantais UC) 1912 *E, W*, 1913 *E, S, SA, W*
**Tignol, P** (S Toulousain) 1953 *I, S*
**Torreilles, S** (US Perpignan) 1956 *S*
**Trillo, J** (CA Béglais) 1967 *SA* (2), *NZ*, 1968 *A, I, NZ* (3), *S*, 1969 *E, I, W*, 1970 *E, 1971 I, S, SA* (2), *A* (2), 1972 *S, A* (2), 1973 *S, E*
**Triviaux, R** (US Cognac) 1931 *E*

**Ugartemendia, J-L** (St Jean-De-Luz) 1975 *S, I*

**Vallot, E** (SCUF) 1912 *S*
**Vannier, M** (RCF) 1953 *W*, 1954 *I, S*, 1955 *E, I, S, W*, 1956 *E, I, S, W*, 1957 *E, I, S, W*, 1958 *A, E, I, S, W*, 1960 *E, I, S, W*, 1961 *A, E, I, NZ, SA, W*
**Vaquer, F** (US Perpignan) 1921 *S, W*, 1922 *W*
**Vaquerin, A** (AS Béziers) 1972 *S, I, A*, 1973 *S, I*, 1974 *W, E, S, SA* (2), 1975 *W, E, S, I*, 1976 *A* (2[1R])
**Vareilles, C** (SF) 1907 *E*, 1908 *E, W*, 1910 *E, S*
**Varenne, F** (RCF) 1952 *S*

221

**Varvier, T** (RCF) 1906 *E*, 1909 *E*, *W*, 1911 *E*, *W*, 1912 *I*
**Vellat, E** (FC Grenoble) 1927 *E*, *I*
**Verger, A** (SF) 1927 *E*, *W*, 1928 *E*, *I*, *W*
**Verges** (SF) 1906 *E*, *NZ*, 1907 *E*
**Viard, G** (RC Narbonne) 1969 *W*, 1970 *S*, 1971 *I*, *S*
**Vigerie, M** (SU Agen) 1931 *W*
**Vigier, R** (AS Montferrand) 1956 *E*, *S*, *W*, 1957 *E*, *S*, *W*, 1958 *A*, *E*, *I*, *S*, *SA* (2), *W*, 1959 *S*, *E*, *W*, *I*
**Vignes, C** (RCF) 1958 *E*, *S*

**Villepreux, P** (S Toulousain) 1967 *I*, *SA*, *NZ*, 1968 *I*, *NZ* (3), *A*, 1969 *E*, *I*, *S*, *W*, 1970 *E*, *I*, *S*, *W*, 1971 *E*, *I*, *S*, *W*, *A* (2), 1972 *E*, *I* (2), *S*, *W*, *A* (2)
**Viviès, B** (SU Agen) 1978 *E*, *S*, *I*, *W*

**Yachvili, M** (SC Tulle) 1968 *A*, *E*, *NZ*, *W*, 1969 *I*, *S*, 1971 *E*, *SA* (2), *A*, 1975 *SA*

**Zago, F** (US Montauban) 1963 *E*, *I*

222

*Jérôme Gallion, who ousted Jacques Fouroux at scrum-half for France, scored a try in each of his first three international appearances, but he failed on this occasion, against Wales at Cardiff. G C 'Tot' Robinson, of Percy Park, scored a try on his first five appearances for England.*

# FRENCH INTERNATIONAL RECORDS

*From 1890–91, when uniform points-scoring was first adopted by International Board countries, to 30 April 1978. Both team and individual records are against International Board countries only, unless otherwise stated.*

## TEAM RECORDS

### Highest score
37 v England (37–12) 1972 Colombes (Paris)
*v individual countries*
37 v England (37–12) 1972 Colombes
23 v Scotland (23–3) 1977 Parc des Princes (Paris)
27 v Ireland (27–6) 1964 Colombes
22 v Wales (22–13) 1965 Colombes
18 v N Zealand (18–13) 1977 Toulouse
25 v S Africa (25–38) 1975 Bloemfontein
34 v Australia (34–6) 1976 Parc des Princes

### Biggest winning points margin
28 v Australia (34–6) 1976 Parc des Princes
*v individual countries*
25 v England (37–12) 1972 Colombes
20 v Scotland (23–3) 1977 Parc des Princes
23 v Ireland (26–3) 1976 Parc des Princes
10 v Wales (16–6) 1958 Cardiff
 7 v N Zealand (13–6) 1973 Parc des Princes
 5 v S Africa (19–14) 1967 Johannesburg
28 v Australia (34–6) 1976 Parc des Princes

### Highest score by opposing team
49 Wales (14–49) 1910 Swansea

*S Africa beat 'France' 55–6 at Parc des Princes on 3 January 1907, but it is not regarded as an official international match*
*by individual countries*
41 England (13–41) 1907 Richmond
31 Scotland (3–31) 1912 Inverleith (Edinburgh)
25 Ireland $\begin{cases}(5–25) \text{ 1911 Cork} \\ (6–25) \text{ 1975 Dublin}\end{cases}$

49 Wales (14–49) 1910 Swansea
38 N Zealand (8–38) 1906 Parc des Princes
38 S Africa $\begin{cases}(5–38) \text{ 1913 Bordeaux} \\ (25–38) \text{ 1975 Bloemfontein}\end{cases}$
15 Australia $\begin{cases}(16–15) \text{ 1972 Brisbane} \\ (18–15) \text{ 1976 Bordeaux}\end{cases}$

### Biggest losing points margin
42 v Wales (5–47) 1909 Colombes

*The 6–55 defeat by S Africa in Paris in 1907 is regarded as unofficial*

*v individual countries*
37 v England (0–37) 1911 Twickenham
28 v Scotland (3–31) 1912 Inverleith
24 v Ireland (0–24) 1913 Cork
42 v Wales (5–47) 1909 Colombes
30 v N Zealand (8–38) 1906 Parc des Princes
33 v S Africa (5–38) 1913 Bordeaux
 2 v Australia (11–13) 1971 Toulouse

### Most points by France in International Championship in a season – 82
(in season 1975–76)

### Most tries by France in International Championship in a season – 13
(in season 1975–76)

### Most tries by France in an international
6 $\begin{cases} \text{v Ireland (27–6) 1964 Colombes} \\ \text{v England (35–13) 1970 Colombes} \\ \text{v England (37–12) 1972 Colombes} \\ \text{v England (30–9) 1976 Parc des} \\ \quad \text{Princes} \\ \text{v Australia (34–6) 1976 Parc des} \\ \quad \text{Princes}\end{cases}$

**Most tries against France in an international**
11 by Wales (5–47) 1909 Colombes

*S Africa's 13 tries in the 1907 match in Paris are regarded as unofficial*

**Most points on a tour (all matches)**
282 in South Africa (11 matches) 1975

# INDIVIDUAL RECORDS

## Most capped player
B Dauga   50   1964–72
*in individual positions*
*Full-back*
M Vannier   30   1953–61
*Wing*
J Dupuy   ⎰ 28   1956–64
C Darrouy  ⎱        1957–67
*Centre*
J-P Lux   32 (40)*   1967–75
*Fly-half*
P Albaladejo   23 (24)†   1954–64
*Scrum-half*
G Dufau   33   1948–57
*Prop*
A Domenech   33 (34)‡   1954–63
*Hooker*
R Bénésis   24   1969–74
*Lock*
E Cester   30   1966–74
*Flanker*
M Crauste   39 (43)§   1958–66
*No 8*
G Basquet   26   1947–52

*\*Lux played 8 times on the wing*
*R Bertranne, 37 caps, has won 24 as a centre and 13 as a wing*
*†Albaladejo won his first cap at full-back*
*‡Domenech was capped once at No 8*
*§Crauste played 4 times at No 8*
*B Dauga, 50 caps, won 29 as lock and 21 at No. 8*
*W Spanghero, 42 caps, won 21 at No 8, 16 at lock and 5 as flanker*
*M Celaya, 35 caps, won 18 as lock, 15 at No 8, and 2 as flanker*

**Most points in internationals – 139**
J-P Romeu (22 appearances) 1973–77

**Most points in an international – 17**
G Camberabero v Australia 1967
   Colombes

**Most tries in internationals – 14**
C Darrouy (28 appearances) 1957–67

**Most tries in an international – 3**
M Crauste v England 1962 Colombes
C Darrouy v Ireland 1963 Dublin

**Most points in International Championship in a season – 32**
G Camberabero (3 appearances) 1966–67

**Most tries in International Championship in a season – 4**
M Crauste (4 appearances) 1961–62
C Darrouy (3 appearances) 1964–65

**Most points on overseas tour – 71**
J-P Romeu (7 appearances) 1975 S Africa

**Most points in any match on tour – 19**
J L Dehez v SW Districts (SA) 1967
   George

**Most tries in any match on tour – 4**
R Bertranne v W Transvaal 1971
   Potchefstroom

# THE 1977 SEASON IN SOUTH AFRICA

**Reg Sweet** *The Daily News*, Durban

In November 1977, and appropriately at Cape Town's historic Newlands, a new administration emerged for rugby in South Africa. It was designated, as it has been down the years, the South African Rugby Board. But its format has been changed. It now embraces the SA Rugby Board as such, the SA Rugby Federation (Coloured), and the SA Rugby Association (Black). The decision to amalgamate was unanimous. One further step had been taken along the road which, South African rugby hopes, will lead to its acceptance again as an equal playing partner on the international scene. It was a unanimous decision, too, that the Federation and the Association will be represented on the SA Rugby Board by their respective presidents and by two additional members apiece.

The scene is changing in an atmosphere of harmony and close cooperation. The addition to the national selection panel of Mr Doug Dyers of the SARF and Mr Alfred Dwesi of SARA, and the widely scaled mixed Springbok trials in Pretoria, added materially to the year's developments. There were no discordant notes. The appearance of black and white South African players in the festival matches in Buenos Aires and in Paris was well accepted, and in several invitation sides leading non-white players performed with promise. At club level, such as in Natal where non-white sides played in the domestic leagues of Durban and Pietermaritzburg, the effect was similar. The scene has shifted smoothly.

It is to be the same at provincial level. In the Sport Pienaar competition, subsidiary of the Currie Cup, two SARF and two SARA teams were to enter the lists in 1978 with the same promotion prospects as any other. Rugby Board president Dr Danie Craven has made it clear that non-white administrators will play a steadily increasing role in control of the game in the years ahead and that integrated rugby from club to international level is assured.

These are the points of significant progress. Not yet in the fold, however, is the third non-white controlling body, the SA Rugby Union, whose president, Mr Abdul Abass of Kimberley, remains opposed to affiliation. But for the rest the progress has been marked.

Inevitably, the 1977 season's chief spectacle was the official launching of the new Loftus Versfeld stadium in Pretoria – a massive project with seating for close on 66,000, and manifold facilities which include a theatre for smaller operations and X-rays. It was a mighty project, costing more than £2 million; and it was paid for, every cent of it, before the kick-off on 27 August.

Guests of honour from nearly all the rugby–playing countries, and a 'World XV' which in fact embraced a squad of some 30 ranking players, captained by Willie John McBride and managed by Sid Millar, were hosted by the Northern Transvaal RFU. The Loftus Versfeld match against South Africa was their primary objective, but they had subsidiary games against Western Province and Northern Transvaal. With the International Board, which had held an historic first meeting at Newlands the week before, in attendance, South Africa fielded eight new caps, and in a rousing display scored six tries to four in their 45–24 victory. South Africa awarded 'caps' for this match.

The South African sides for the festival stemmed from the first mixed-racial trials, from which four non–white players made their way into the SA Gazelles and SA Country Districts sides. Two of them, Timothy Nkonki and Hennie Shields, subsequently went with Northern Transvaal skipper Thys Lourens to Argentina for the UAR celebration matches, and Nkonki later to Paris with Springbok captain Morné du Plessis for the FFR jubilee.

In their provincial games, the Invitation XV were beaten 56–26 by Western Transvaal and 41–26 by Northern Transvaal, after leading 16–6 at half-time. Their defeats had to be seen in context. What remained a matter for wonderment was how Millar and McBride got their players into the shape they did in the couple of days they had for preparation. It was a substantial achievement.

The Currie Cup front saw the return to premiership of Northern Transvaal, who beat Orange Free State 27–12 in the final at Pretoria. Free State, Western Province, and Natal took the first three placings in their section of the competition and Northerns, Rhodesia, and Transvaal (tied with Eastern Province) in theirs. For the second time in three seasons Stellenbosch University won the national inter–club championship in Durban over Easter, and for the fifth successive time the Shimlas of Free State University wound up the season with victory in the SA Sevens at Pretoria.

A sadness of the season was the sudden death of former Springbok captain Hennie Muller, who collapsed shortly after addressing a school function in Cape Town. In his 13 internationals between 1949 and 1953, Muller had restructured several aspects of back-row play.

Ken Kennedy, the former Lions' hooker, led London Irish on a short tour which showed two victories and four honourable defeats, with the following results: v Western Province Coloured League XV, W 27–10; v Boland, L 15–22; v Eastern Province, L 12–26; v SA Rugby Association XV, W 36–0; v Natal Invitation XV, L 18–23; v Northern Transvaal Invitation XV, L 16–21. The Irish, as a club team, did remarkably well against their strong provincial opponents.

Currie Cup placings for the season were:

*Section A*

| | | P | W | D | L | F | A | Pts |
|---|---|---|---|---|---|---|---|---|
| | **Free State** | 10 | 9 | 1 | 0 | 361 | 161 | 18 |
| | **W Province** | 10 | 8 | 2 | 0 | 285 | 130 | 16 |
| | **Natal** | 10 | 3 | 6 | 1 | 174 | 194 | 7 |
| | **Boland** | 10 | 3 | 7 | 0 | 155 | 216 | 6 |
| | **E Transvaal** | 10 | 1 | 9 | 0 | 159 | 378 | 2 |

*Section B*

| | | P | W | D | L | F | A | Pts |
|---|---|---|---|---|---|---|---|---|
| | **N Transvaal** | 10 | 8 | 2 | 0 | 230 | 109 | 16 |
| | **Rhodesia** | 10 | 7 | 3 | 0 | 234 | 190 | 14 |
| | **Transvaal** | 10 | 4 | 6 | 0 | 237 | 217 | 8 |
| | **E Province** | 10 | 4 | 6 | 0 | 205 | 283 | 8 |
| | **W Transvaal** | 10 | 2 | 7 | 1 | 173 | 335 | 5 |

**CURRIE CUP FINAL** (Pretoria)
Northern Transvaal 27, Free State 12

## INTERNATIONAL MATCH

### 27 August, Pretoria
### SOUTH AFRICA 45 (3G 5PG 3T)
### WORLD INVITATION XV 24 (4G)

**SOUTH AFRICA:** D S L Snyman (WP); J S Germishuys (OFS), C Wagenaar (NT), D C Froneman (OFS), H Potgieter (OFS); R Blair (WP), B J Wolmarans (OFS); *No 8* M du Plessis (WP) (*capt*); *Second Row* M T S Stofberg (OFS), L C Moolman (NT), J L van Heerden (NT), P E Veldsman (WP); *Front Row* N S E Bezuidenhout (NT), R J Cockrell (WP), D C du Plessis (NT)
**Scorers** *Tries:* Stofberg (2), Potgieter, Germishuys, Wolmarans, Strydom
*Conversions:* Blair (3) *Penalty Goals:* Blair (5)
**WORLD INVITATION XV:** J P R Williams (Wales); J-L Averous (France), W M Osborne (NZ), A Travaglini (Argentina), T G R Davies (Wales); P E McLean (Australia), G O Edwards (Wales); *No 8* A R Sutherland (NZ); *Second Row* J-P Rives (France), W J McBride (Ireland) (*capt*), A M Haden (NZ), I A Kirkpatrick (NZ); *Front Row* W K Bush (NZ), R W Norton (NZ), G Cholley (France)
**Scorers** *Tries:* Averous (2), McLean, Haden *Conversions:* McLean (4)
**Referee** G Bezuidenhout (Transvaal)

227

# SOUTH AFRICAN INTERNATIONAL PLAYERS *(up to 30 April 1978)*

**ABBREVIATIONS**

| | |
|---|---|
| *A* | Australia |
| *BI* | British Isles teams |
| *E* | England |
| *F* | France |
| *I* | Ireland |
| *NZ* | New Zealand |

| | |
|---|---|
| *S* | Scotland |
| *W* | Wales |
| Wld | World Invitation XV |
| (T) | Tour to Northern Hemisphere |
| (ST) | Short tour to Northern Hemisphere |
| (R) | Replacement – (2 [1R]) denotes two appearances, one as a replacement |

**Ackermann, D S P** (Western Province) 1955 *BI* (3), 1956 *A* (2), *NZ* (2), 1958 *F*
**Albertyn, P K** (South Western Districts) 1924 *BI* (4)
**Alexander, E** (Griqualand West) 1891 *BI* (2)
**Allen, P B** (Eastern Province) 1960 *S*
**Allport, P** (Western Province) 1910 *BI* (2)
**Anderson, J A** (Western Province) 1903 *BI*
**Anderson, J H** (Western Province) 1896 *BI* (3)
**Andrew, J B** (Transvaal) 1896 *BI*
**Antelme, M J G** (Transvaal) 1960 *NZ* (4), 1960–61 (T) *F*
**Apsey, J T** (Western Province) 1933 *A* (2), 1938 *BI*
**Ashley, S** (Western Province) 1903 *BI*
**Aston, F T D** (Transvaal) 1896 *BI* (4)
**Aucamp, J** (Western Transvaal) 1924 *BI* (2)

**Baard, A P** (Western Province) 1960–61 (T) *I*
**Babrow, L** (Western Province) 1937 *A* (2), *NZ* (3)
**Barnard, J H** (Transvaal) 1964–65 (ST) *S*, 1965 *A* (2), *NZ* (2)
**Barnard, R W** (Transvaal) 1970 *NZ* (R)
**Barnard, W H M** (Northern Transvaal) 1949 *NZ*, 1951–52 (T) *W*
**Barry, J** (Western Province) 1903 *BI* (3)
**Bastard, W E** (Natal) 1937 *A*, *NZ* (3), 1938 *BI* (2)
**Bates, A J** (Western Transvaal) 1969–70 (T) *E*, 1970 *NZ* (2), 1972 *E*
**Bayvel, P C R** (Transvaal) 1974 *BI* (2), 1974 (ST) *F* (2), 1975 *F* (2), 1976 *NZ* (4)
**Bedford, T P** (Natal) 1963 *A* (4), 1964 *W*, *F*, 1964–65 (ST) *I*, 1965 *A* (2), 1968 *BI* (4), 1968–69 (ST) *F* (2), 1969 *A* (4), 1969–70 (T) *S*, *E*, *I*, *W*, 1971 *F* (2)
**Bekker, H P J** (Northern Transvaal) 1951–52 (T) *E*, *F*, 1953 *A* (4), 1955 *BI* (3), 1956 *A* (2), *NZ* (4)
**Bekker, M J** (Northern Transvaal) 1960 *S*
**Bekker, R P** (Northern Transvaal) 1953 *A* (2)
**Bergh, W F** (South Western Districts) 1931–32 (T) *W*, *I*, *E*, *S*, 1933 *A* (5), 1937 *A* (2), *NZ* (3), 1938 *BI* (3)
**Bestbier, A** (Orange Free State) 1974 (ST) *F* (R)
**Bester, J J N** (Western Province) 1924 *BI* (2)
**Bester, J L A** (Western Province) 1938 *BI* (2)
**Beswick, A M** (Border) 1896 *BI* (2)
**Bezuidenhoudt, C E** (Northern Transvaal) 1962 *BI* (3)
**Bezuidenhoudt, N S E** (Northern Transvaal) 1972 *E* 1974 *BI* (3), 1974 (ST) *F* (2), 1975 *F* (2), 1977 Wld
**Bierman, J N** (Transvaal) 1931–32 (T) *I*
**Bisset, W M** (Western Province) 1891 *BI* (2)
**Blair, R** (Western Province) 1977 Wld
**Bosch, G R** (Transvaal) 1974 *BI*, 1974 (ST) *F* (2), 1975 *F* (2), 1976 *NZ* (4)
**Bosman, N J S** (Transvaal) 1924 *BI* (3)
**Botha, J** (Transvaal) 1903 *BI*
**Botha, J P F** (Northern Transvaal) 1962 *BI* (3)
**Botha, P H** (Transvaal) 1965 *A* (2)
**Boyes, H C** (Griqualand West) 1891 *BI* (2)
**Brand, G H** (Western Province) 1928 *NZ* (2), 1931–32 (T) *W*, *I*, *E*, *S*, 1933 *A* (5), 1937 *A* (2), *NZ* (2), 1938 *BI*

**Bredenkamp, M** (Griqualand West) 1896 *BI* (2)
**Brewis, J D** (Northern Transvaal) 1949 *NZ* (4), 1951–52 (T) *S*, *I*, *W*, *E*, *F*, 1953 *A*
**Briers, T P D** (Western Province) 1955 *BI* (4), 1956 *NZ* (3)
**Brink, D J** (Western Province) 1906–07 (T) *S*, *W*, *E*
**Brooks, D** (Border) 1906–07 (T) *S*
**Brown, C** (Western Province) 1903 *BI* (3)
**Brynard, G S** (Western Province) 1965 *A*, *NZ* (4), 1968 *BI* (2)
**Buchler, J U** (Transvaal) 1951–52 (T) *S*, *I*, *W*, *E*, *F*, 1953 *A* (4), 1956 *A*
**Burdett, A F** (Western Province) 1906–07 (T) *S*, *I*
**Burger, W A G** (Border) 1906–07 (T) *S*, *I*, *W*, 1910 *BI*

**Carelse, G** (Eastern Province) 1964 *W*, *F*, 1964–65 (ST) *I*, *S*, 1967 *F* (3), 1968–69 (ST) *F* (2), 1969 *A* (4), 1969–70 (T) *S*
**Carlson, R A** (Western Province) 1972 *E*
**Carolin, H W** (Western Province) 1903 *BI*, 1906–07 (T) *S*, *I*
**Castens, H H** (Western Province) 1891 *BI*
**Chignell, T W** (Western Province) 1891 *BI*
**Cilliers, G D** (Orange Free State) 1963 *A* (3)
**Claassen, J T** (Western Transvaal) 1955 *BI* (4). 1956 *A* (2), *NZ* (4), 1958 *F* (2), 1960 *S*, *NZ* (3), 1960–61 (T) *W*, *I*, *E*, *S*, *F*, 1961 *I*, *A* (2), 1962 *BI* (4)
**Clarke, W H** (Transvaal) 1933 *A*
**Clarkson, W A** (Natal) 1921 *NZ* (2), 1924 *BI*
**Cloete, H A** (Western Province) 1896 *BI*
**Cockrell, C H** (Western Province) 1969–70 (T) *S*, *I*, *W*
**Cockrell, R J** (Western Province) 1974 (ST) *F* (2), 1975 *F* (2), 1976 *NZ* (2), 1977 Wld
**Coetzee, J H H** (Western Province) 1974 *BI*, 1975 *F* (R), 1976 *NZ* (4)
**Cope, D** (Transvaal) 1896 *BI*
**Cotty, W** (Griqualand West) 1896 *BI*
**Crampton, G** (Griqualand West) 1903 *BI*
**Craven, D H** (Western Province) 1931–32 (T) *W*, *I*, *S*, 1933 *A* (5), 1937 *A* (2), *NZ* (3), 1938 *BI* (3)
**Cronje, P A** (Transvaal) 1971 *F* (2), *A* (3), 1974 *BI* (2)
**Crosby, J H** (Transvaal) 1896 *BI*
**Crosby, N** (Transvaal) 1910 *BI* (2)
**Currie, C** (Griqualand West) 1903 *BI*

**D'Alton, G** (Western Province) 1933 *A*
**Daneel, G M** (Western Province) 1928 *NZ* (4), 1931–32 (T) *W*, *I*, *E*, *S*
**Daneel, H J** (Western Province) 1906–07 (T) *S*, *I*, *W*, *E*
**Davidson, M** (Eastern Province) 1910 *BI*
**De Bruyn, J** (Orange Free State) 1974 *BI*
**De Jongh, H P K** (Western Province) 1928 *NZ*
**De Klerk, I J** (Transvaal) 1969–70 (T) *E*, *I*, *W*
**De Klerk, K B H** (Transvaal) 1974 *BI* (3 [1R]), 1975 *F* (2), 1976 *NZ* (3 [1R])
**De Kock, A** (Griqualand West) 1891 *BI*
**De Kock, J S** (Western Province) 1921 *NZ*, 1924 *BI*

Delport, W H (Eastern Province) 1951–52 (T) S, I, W, E, F, 1953 A (4)
De Melker, S C (Griqualand West) 1903 BI, 1906–07 (T) E
Devenish, C (Griqualand West) 1896 BI
Devenish, G St L (Transvaal) 1896 BI
Devenish, M (Transvaal) 1891 BI
De Villiers, D I (Transvaal) 1910 BI (3)
De Villiers, D J (Western Province) 1962 BI (2), 1964–65 (ST) I, 1965 NZ (3), 1967 F (4), 1968 BI (4), 1968–69 (ST) F (2), 1969 A (2), 1969–70 (T) E, I, W, 1970 NZ (4)
De Villiers, H A (Western Province) 1906–07 (T) S, W, E
De Villiers, H O (Western Province) 1967 F (4), 1968–69 (ST) F (2), 1969 A (4), 1969–70 (T) S, E, I, W
De Villiers, P du P (Western Province) 1928 NZ (3), 1931–32 (T) E, 1933 A, 1937 A (2), NZ
Devine, D (Transvaal) 1924 BI, 1928 NZ
De Vos, D J J (Western Province) 1964–65 (ST) S, 1969 A, 1969–70 (T) S
De Waal, A N (Western Province) 1967 F (4)
De Waal, P (Western Province) 1896 BI
De Wet, A E (Western Province) 1969 A (2), 1969–70 (T) E
De Wet, P (Western Province) 1938 BI (3)
Dinkelmann, E E (Northern Transvaal) 1951–52 (T) S, I, E, F, 1953 A (2)
Dirksen, C W (Northern Transvaal) 1963 A, 1964 W, 1964–65 (ST) I, S, 1967 F (4), 1968 BI (2)
Dobbin, F J (Griqualand West) 1903 BI (2), 1906–07 (T) S, W, E, 1910 BI, 1912–13 (T) S, I, W
Dobie, J A R (Transvaal) 1928 NZ
Dormehl, P J (Western Province) 1896 BI (2)
Douglass, F W (Eastern Province) 1896 BI
Dryburgh, R G (Western Province) 1955 BI (3), 1956 A, NZ (2), 1960 NZ (2)
Duff, B (Western Province) 1891 BI (3)
Duffy, B A (Border) 1928 NZ
Du Plessis, D C (Northern Transvaal) 1977 Wld
Du Plessis, F (Transvaal) 1949 NZ (3)
Du Plessis, M (Western Province) 1971 A (3), 1974 BI (2), 1974 (ST) F (2), 1975 F (2), 1976 NZ (4), 1977 Wld
Du Plessis, N J (Western Transvaal) 1921 NZ (2), 1924 BI (3)
Du Plessis, P G (Northern Transvaal) 1972 E
Du Plooy, A J J (Eastern Province) 1955 BI
Du Preez, F C H (Northern Transvaal) 1960–61 (T) E, S, 1961 A (2), 1962 BI (4), 1963 A, 1964 W, F, 1965 A (2), NZ (4), 1967 F, 1968 BI (4), 1968–69 (ST) F (2), 1969 A (2), 1969–70 (T) S, I, W, 1970 NZ (4), 1971 F (2), A (3)
Du Preez, J G H (Western Province) 1956 NZ
Du Rand, J A (Rhodesia) 1949 NZ (2), 1951–52 (T) S, I, W, E, F, 1953 A (4), 1955 BI (4), 1956 A (2), NZ (4)
Du Toit, A F (Western Province) 1928 NZ (2)
Du Toit, B A (Transvaal) 1938 BI (3)
Du Toit, P A (Northern Transvaal) 1949 NZ (3), 1951–52 (T) S, I, W, E, F
Du Toit, P S (Western Province) 1958 F (2), 1960 NZ (4), 1960–61 (T) W, I, E, S, F, 1961 I, A (2)
Duvenage, F P (Griqualand West) 1949 NZ (2)

Ellis, J H (South West Africa) 1965 NZ (4), 1967 F (4), 1968 BI (4), 1968–69 (ST) F (2), 1969 A (4), 1969–70 (T) S, I, W, 1970 NZ (4), 1971 F (2), A (3), 1972 E, 1974 BI (4), 1974 (ST) F (2), 1976 NZ
Ellis, M (Transvaal) 1921 NZ (2), 1924 BI (4)
Engelbrecht, J P (Western Province) 1960 S, 1960–61 (T) W, I, E, S, F, 1961 A (2), 1962 BI (3), 1963 A (2), 1964 W, F, 1964–65 (ST) I, S, 1965 A (2), NZ (4), 1967 F (4), 1968 BI (2), 1968–69 (ST) F (2), 1969 A (2)
Etlinger, T E (Western Province) 1896 BI

Ferris, H H (Transvaal) 1903 BI
Forbes, H H (Transvaal) 1896 BI
Fourie, C (Eastern Province) 1974 (ST) F (2), 1975 F (2)
Fourie, T T (South-East Transvaal) 1974 BI
Fourie, W L (South West Africa) 1958 F (2)
Francis, J A J (Transvaal) 1912–13 (T) S, I, W, E, F
Frederickson, D (Transvaal) 1974 BI
Frew, A (Transvaal) 1903 BI
Froneman, D C (Orange Free State) 1977 Wld

Froneman, I L (Border) 1933 A
Fry, S P (Western Province) 1951–52 (T) S, I, W, E, F, 1953 A (4), 1955 BI (4)

Gage, J H (Orange Free State) 1933 A
Gainsford, J L (Western Province) 1960 S, NZ (4), 1960–61 (T) W, I, E, S, F, 1961 A (2), 1962 BI (4), 1963 A (4), 1964 W, F, 1964–65 (ST) I, S, 1965 A (2), NZ (4), 1967 F (3)
Geel, P J (Orange Free State) 1949 NZ
Geere, V (Transvaal) 1933 A (5)
Geffin, A (Transvaal) 1949 NZ (4), 1951–52 (T) S, I, W
Gentles, T A (Western Province) 1955 BI (3), 1956 NZ (2), 1958 F
Geraghty, E M (Border) 1949 NZ
Gerber, M C (Eastern Province) 1958 F (2), 1960 S
Gericke, F W (Transvaal) 1960 S
Germishuys, J S (Orange Free State) 1974 BI, 1976 NZ (4), 1977 Wld
Gibbs, B (Griqualand West) 1903 BI
Goosen, C P (Orange Free State) 1965 NZ
Gorton, H C (Transvaal) 1896 BI
Gould, R L (Natal) 1968 BI (4)
Gray, B G (Western Province) 1931–32 (T) W, E, S, 1933 A
Greenwood, C M (Western Province) 1961 I
Greyling, P J F (Orange Free State) 1967 F (4), 1968 BI, 1968–69 (ST) F (2), 1969 A (4), 1969–70 (T) S, E, I, W, 1970 NZ (4), 1971 F (2), A (3), 1972 E
Grobler, C J (Orange Free State) 1971 BI, 1975 F (2)
Guthrie, F H (Western Province) 1891 BI (2), 1896 BI

Hahn, C H L (Transvaal) 1910 BI (3)
Hamilton, F (Eastern Province) 1891 BI
Harris, T A (Transvaal) 1937 NZ (2), 1938 BI (3)
Hartley, A J (Western Province) 1891 BI
Hattingh, L B (Orange Free State) 1933 A
Heatlie, B H (Western Province) 1891 BI (2), 1896 BI (2), 1903 BI (2)
Hepburn, T (Western Province) 1896 BI
Hill, R A (Rhodesia) 1960–61 (T) W, I, 1961 I, A (2), 1962 BI, 1963 A
Hirsch, J G (Eastern Province) 1906–07 (T) I, 1910 BI
Hobson, T E C (Western Province) 1903 BI
Hoffman, R S (Boland) 1953 A
Holton, D N (Eastern Province) 1960 S
Hopwood, D J (Western Province) 1960 S, NZ (2), 1960–61 (T) W, E, S, F, 1961 I, A (2), 1962 BI (4), 1963 A (3), 1964 W, F, 1964–65 (ST) S, 1965 NZ (2)
Howe, B F (Border) 1956 NZ (2)
Howe-Browne, N R F G (Western Province) 1910 BI (3)

Immelman, J H (Western Province) 1912–13 (T) F

Jackson, D C (Western Province) 1906–07 (T) I, W, E
Jackson, J S (Western Province) 1903 BI
Jansen, J S (Orange Free State) 1970 NZ (4), 1971 F (2), A (3), 1972 E
Jennings, C B (Border) 1937 NZ
Johnstone, P G A (Western Province) 1951–52 (T) S, I, W, E, F, 1956 A, NZ (3)
Jones, C H (Transvaal) 1903 BI (2)
Jones, P S T (Western Province) 1896 BI (3)
Jordaan, R P (Northern Transvaal) 1949 NZ (4)
Joubert, S J (Western Province) 1906–07 (T) I, W, E

Kaminer, J (Transvaal) 1958 F
Kelly, E W (Griqualand West) 1896 BI
Kenyon, B J (Border) 1949 NZ
Kipling, H G (Griqualand West) 1931–32 (T) W, I, E, S, 1933 A (5)
Kirkpatrick, A I (Griqualand West) 1953 A, 1956 NZ, 1958 F, 1960 S, NZ (4), 1960–61 (T) W, I, E, S, F
Knight, A S (Transvaal) 1912–13 (T) S, I, W, E, F
Koch, A C (Boland) 1949 NZ (3), 1951–52 (T) S, I, W, E, F, 1953 A (3), 1955 BI (4), 1956 A, NZ (2), 1958 F (2), 1960 NZ (2)
Koch, H V (Western Province) 1949 NZ (4)
Kotze, G J M (Western Province) 1967 F (4)
Krantz, E F W (Orange Free State) 1976 NZ
Krige, J D (Western Province) 1903 BI (2), 1906–07 (T) S, I, W

229

230

231

**Versfeld, C** (Western Province) 1891 *BI*
**Versfeld, M** (Western Province) 1891 *BI* (3)
**Vigne, J T** (Transvaal) 1891 *BI* (3)
**Viljoen, J F** (Griqualand West) 1971 *F* (2), *A* (3), 1972 *E*
**Viljoen, J T** (Natal) 1971 *A* (3)
**Visagie, P J** (Griqualand West) 1967 *F* (4), 1968 *BI* (4), 1968–69 (ST) *F* (2), 1969 *A* (4), 1969–70 (T) *S, E,* 1970 *NZ* (4), 1971 *F* (2), *A* (3)
**Visser, P J** (Transvaal) 1933 *A*
**Viviers, S S** (Orange Free State) 1956 *A* (2), *NZ* (3)
**Vogel, M L** (Orange Free State) 1974 *BI* (R)

**Wagenaar, C** (Northern Transvaal) 1977 Wld
**Wahl, J J** (Western Province) 1949 *NZ*
**Walker, A P** (Natal) 1921 *NZ* (2), 1924 *BI* (4)
**Walker, H N** (Orange Free State) 1953 *A,* 1956 *A, NZ* (2)
**Walker, H W** (Transvaal) 1910 *BI* (3)
**Walton, D C** (Natal) 1964 *F,* 1964–65 (ST) *I, S,* 1965 *NZ* (2), 1969 *A* (2), 1969–70 (T) *E*

**Waring, F W** (Western Province) 1931–32 (T) *I, E,* 1933 *A* (5)
**Wessels, J J** (Western Province) 1896 *BI* (3)
**Whipp, P J M** (Western Province) 1974 *BI* (2), 1975 *F,* 1976 *NZ* (3)
**White, J** (Border) 1931–32 (T) *W,* 1933 *A* (5), 1937 *A* (2), *NZ* (2)
**Williams, A E** (Griqualand West) 1910 *BI*
**Williams, D O** (Western Province) 1937 *A* (2), *NZ* (3), 1938 *BI* (3)
**Williams, J G** (Northern Transvaal) 1971 *F* (2), *A* (3), 1972 *E,* 1974 *BI* (3), 1974 (ST) *F* (2), 1976 *NZ* (2)
**Wilson, L G** (Western Province) 1960 *NZ* (2), 1960–61 (T) *W, I, E, F,* 1961 *I, A* (2), 1962 *BI* (4), 1963 *A* (4), 1964 *W, F,* 1964–65 (ST) *I, S,* 1965 *A* (2), *NZ* (4)
**Wolmarans, B J** (Orange Free State) 1977 Wld
**Wyness, M R K** (Western Province) 1962 *BI* (4), 1963 *A*

**Zeller, W C** (Natal) 1921 *NZ* (2)
**Zimerman, M** (Western Province) 1931–32 (T) *W, I, E, S*

232

*Piet Visagie, the former Griqualand West fly-half who holds the Springbok record for most points in international matches: 130 in 25 appearances.*

# SOUTH AFRICAN INTERNATIONAL RECORDS

*From 1890–91, when uniform points-scoring was first adopted by International Board countries, to 30 April 1978, except in the case of matches against British Isles. These date from 1910, when Lions' teams first became representative of the Four Home Unions. Both team and individual records are against International Board countries and British Isles only, unless otherwise stated.*

## TEAM RECORDS

### Highest score
44 v Scotland (44–0) 1951 Murrayfield

*S Africa beat France 55–6 at Parc des Princes (Paris) on 3 January 1907, but it is not regarded as an official international match*

*v individual countries*

9 v England { (9–3) 1913 Twickenham / (9–18) 1972 Johannesburg

44 v Scotland (44–0) 1951 Murrayfield
38 v Ireland (38–0) 1912 Dublin
24 v Wales (24–3) 1964 Durban

38 v France { (38–5) 1913 Bordeaux / (38–25) 1975 Bloemfontein

20 v N Zealand (20–17) 1970 Johannesburg
30 v Australia (30–11) 1969 Johannesburg
34 v B Isles (34–14) 1962 Bloemfontein

### Biggest winning points margin
44 v Scotland (44–0) 1951 Murrayfield

*v individual countries*

7 v England (7–0) 1932 Twickenham
44 v Scotland (44–0) 1951 Murrayfield
38 v Ireland (38–0) 1912 Dublin
21 v Wales (24–3) 1964 Durban
33 v France (38–5) 1913 Bordeaux
17 v N Zealand (17–0) 1928 Durban
25 v Australia (28–3) 1961 Johannesburg
20 v B Isles (34–14) 1962 Bloemfontein

### Highest score by opposing team
28 B Isles (9–28) 1974 Pretoria

*by individual countries*

18 England (9–18) 1972 Johannesburg
10 Scotland (18–10) 1960 Port Elizabeth
12 Ireland (15–12) 1906 Belfast
6 Wales (6–6) 1970 Cardiff
25 France (38–25) 1975 Bloemfontein
20 N Zealand (3–20) 1965 Auckland
21 Australia (6–21) 1933 Durban
28 B Isles (9–28) 1974 Pretoria

### Biggest losing points margin
19 v B Isles (9–28) 1974 Pretoria

*v individual countries*

9 v England (9–18) 1972 Johannesburg
6 v Scotland (0–6) 1906 Glasgow
3 v Ireland (6–9) 1965 Dublin
No defeat v Wales
5 v France (14–19) 1967 Johannesburg
17 v N Zealand (3–20) 1965 Auckland
15 v Australia (6–21) 1933 Durban
19 v B Isles (9–28) 1974 Pretoria

### Most tries by South Africa in an international
10 v Ireland (38–0) 1912 Dublin

*S Africa scored 13 tries in the 'unofficial' match v France in Paris in 1907*

### Most tries against South Africa in an international

5 { by B Isles (22–23) 1955 Johannesburg / by N Zealand (3–20) 1965 Auckland / by B Isles (9–28) 1974 Pretoria

### Most points on overseas tour (all matches)
753 in Australia/N Zealand (26 matches) 1937

### Most tries on overseas tour (all matches)
161 in Australia/N Zealand (26 matches) 1937

## INDIVIDUAL RECORDS

### Most capped player
F C H du Preez } 38 1960–71
J H Ellis } 1965–76

234

*in individual positions*
*Full-back*
L G Wilson   27   1960–65
*Wing*
J P Engelbrecht   33   1960–69
*Centre*
J L Gainsford   33   1960–67
*Fly-half*
P J Visagie   25   1967–71
*Scrum-half*
D J de Villiers   25   1962–70
*Prop*
J F K Marais   35   1963–74
*Hooker*
G F Malan   18   1958–65
*Lock*
F C H du Preez   31 (38)*   1960–71
*Flanker*
J H Ellis   38   1965–76
*No 8*
D J Hopwood   22†   1960–65

*\*du Preez won 7 caps as a flanker*
*†T P Bedford, 25 caps, won 19 at No 8 and 6 as a flanker*

**Most points in internationals – 130**
P J Visagie (25 appearances) 1967–71

**Most points in international series – 43**
P J Visagie (4 appearances) v Australia 1969

**Most points in an international – 22**
G R Bosch v France 1975 Pretoria

*D Mare scored 22 points in the 'unofficial' match v France in Paris in 1907.*

**Most tries in internationals – 8**
J L Gainsford (33 appearances) 1960–67
J P Engelbrecht (33 appearances) 1960–69

**Most tries in an international – 3**
E E McHardy v Ireland 1912 Dublin
J A Stegmann v Ireland 1912 Dublin
K T van Vollenhoven v B Isles 1955 Cape Town
H J van Zyl v Australia 1961 Johannesburg

**Most points for South Africa on overseas tour – 190**
G H Brand (20 appearances) 1937 Australia/N Zealand

**Most tries for South Africa on overseas tour – 22**
J A Loubser (20 appearances) 1906–07 B Isles/France

**Most points for South Africa in international series on tour – 24**
D F T Morkel (5 appearances) 1912–13 B Isles/France

**Most tries for South Africa in international series on tour – 6**
E E McHardy (5 appearances) 1912–13 B Isles/France

**Most points for South Africa in any match on tour – 25**
P J Visagie v South Australia 1971 Adelaide

**Most tries for South Africa in any match on tour – 6**
R G Dryburgh v Queensland 1956 Brisbane

# THE 1977 SEASON IN NEW ZEALAND

**John Brooks** *The Christchurch Press*

From the inconclusive and unsatisfactory national trials in May 1977 to the selection in the following September of an intriguingly new All Blacks' team for the tour of France, the season was one of ups and downs, comings and goings, and changes of emphasis.

Chief among these was the greatly increased participation by the backs in play at international level, a fact put into bold relief in the four-match series against the touring Lions. Except in the first international at Wellington, the Lions' pack was demonstrably superior to its New Zealand counterpart. This was especially so in the final international at Auckland. Yet in spite of this the Lions lost the series, 1–3. They might well have drawn it but for the All Blacks' involvement in the 15-man game and the splendid organisation of their defence, which nullified the Lions' advantage in possession. The man behind this quiet revolution was Jack Gleeson, who deposed John Stewart as New Zealand's chief selector and coach. He had long been an advocate of rugby for the whole team.

It was a year of hail and farewell among the top echelon of players. First Andy Leslie, captain of the All Blacks since 1974, retired from international play, and by the end of the season his successor as New Zealand's skipper, Tane Norton, had followed suit. The popular Norton went out with 27 caps as hooker to his credit – a New Zealand record in the position. The effervescent Grant Batty, after scoring the match-winning try in the first international against the Lions, hobbled into retirement. Kent Lambert, who missed two of the internationals because of an appendix operation, first announced that he could not afford time off for the tour of France and then declared that he was going over to rugby league.

When the team to tour France was announced, the biggest shock was the omission of Ian Kirkpatrick, an All Black since 1967 and New Zealand's top international try-scorer. He had played throughout the series against the Lions. Also pensioned off was scrum-half Sid Going, the delight and despair of the New Zealand rugby public for some years. He had been dropped after the second international against the Lions, and both he and his successor Lyn Davis were left out of the side for France. Both men were 34.

New heroes were quick to emerge. Lawrie Knight and Gary

Seear made notable advances as No 8s, and Bevan Wilson (full-back) and Brian Ford (left wing) were exciting newcomers to the All Blacks for the last two matches against the Lions. Graham Mourie, who had captained the New Zealand side in Argentina late in 1976, displaced Kevin Eveleigh as flanker halfway through the series. It was significant that the big three of the Argentinian tour, Ron Don (manager), Jack Gleeson (coach), and Graham Mourie (captain), occupied the same positions for the visit to France.

236

One of the most welcome sights of 1977 was the return of Andy Haden, the 6ft 7in Auckland lock, to the international arena. Haden was a junior member of the 1972–73 All Blacks in Britain and France but, along with many of his colleagues, was dropped in 1974. He played two seasons for Tarbes, in southern France, and then returned to New Zealand to become the top personality of the 1976 inter-provincial championship. His reappearance in the national team was especially welcome in view of the retirement of Peter Whiting, his Ponsonby clubmate and for so long New Zealand's chief line-out exponent.

The national first division championship, in its second year, was won by Canterbury, who put up a remarkable performance by winning all 10 games. They were excellently led by Alex Wyllie. The major surprise of the competition was the fall from grace of Bay of Plenty, the 1976 champions. In spite of having four All Blacks in their backline they won only two of their 10 matches and were relegated to the second division.

It was still being argued whether this competition was more important than the one for the Ranfurly Shield, which continued on its familiar challenge basis. It was clear, however, that the Shield whipped up more interest and fervour than the 'league', which lost a lot in public interest because of the staggered nature of its fixtures. An attempt is being made by the NZRFU to put this matter right.

Manawatu, with a strong pack of forwards and some clever backs, held the Shield throughout the season, beating back seven challenges. Two of their heroes were Mark Donaldson and Gary Knight, who were chosen for the All Blacks' tour of France.

The game maintained its strength as far as numbers of participants were concerned, and the emphasis on coaching and instruction for young players was underlined. Delegates to the Congress of Asian and Pacific Rugby Countries, held near Christchurch in July 1977, were impressed at the work being done at grassroots level, and Bob Stuart, the much-esteemed captain of the 1953–54 All Blacks in Britain, continues to play a major role in this respect.

# NEW ZEALAND INTERNATIONAL PLAYERS (*up to 30 April 1978*)

## ABBREVIATIONS

| | |
|---|---|
| *A* | Australia |
| *AW* | Anglo-Welsh |
| *BI* | British Isles teams |
| *E* | England |
| *F* | France |
| *I* | Ireland |
| *S* | Scotland |

| | |
|---|---|
| *SA* | South Africa |
| *W* | Wales |
| (T) | Tour to Northern Hemisphere |
| (ST) | Short tour to Northern Hemisphere |
| (R) | Replacement – (2 [1R]) denotes two appearances, one as a replacement |

**Abbott, H L** (Taranaki) 1905–06 (T) *F*
**Aitken, G G** (Wellington) 1921 *SA* (2)
**Allen, F R** (Auckland) 1946 *A* (2), 1947 *A* (2), 1949 *SA* (2)
**Alley, G T** (Canterbury) 1928 *SA* (3)
**Archer, W R** (Otago, Southland) 1955 *A* (2), 1956 *SA* (2)
**Argus, W G** (Canterbury) 1946 *A* (2), 1947 *A* (2)
**Arnold, D A** (Canterbury) 1963–64 (T) *I, W, E, F*
**Arnold, K D** (Waikato) 1947 *A* (2)
**Ashby, D L** (Southland) 1958 *A*
**Asher, A** (Auckland) 1903 *A*
**Atkinson, H** (West Coast) 1913 *A*
**Avery, H E** (Wellington) 1910 *A* (3)

**Badeley, C E O** (Auckland) 1921 *SA* (2)
**Baird, J** (Otago) 1913 *A*
**Ball, N** (Wellington) 1931 *A*, 1932 *A* (2), 1935–36 (T) *W, E*
**Barrett, J** (Auckland) 1913 *A* (2)
**Barry, E F** (Wellington) 1934 *A*
**Batty, G B** (Wellington, Bay of Plenty) 1972–73 (T) *W, S, E, I, F*, 1973 *E*, 1974 *A* (2), 1974 (ST) *I*, 1975 *S*, 1976 *SA* (4), 1977 *BI*
**Batty, W** (Auckland) 1930 *BI* (3), 1931 *A*
**Beatty, G E** (Taranaki) 1950 *BI*
**Bell, R H** (Otago) 1951 *A*, 1952 *A* (2)
**Belliss, E A** (Wanganui) 1921 *SA* (3)
**Bennet, R** (Otago) 1905 *A*
**Berghan, T** (Otago) 1938 *A* (3)
**Bevan, V D** (Wellington) 1949 *A* (2), 1950 *BI* (4)
**Birtwistle, W M** (Canterbury) 1965 *SA* (4), 1967–68 (T) *E, W, S*
**Black, J E** (Canterbury) 1977 (ST) *F*
**Black, N W** (Auckland) 1949 *SA*
**Black, R S** (Otago) 1914 *A*
**Blake, A W** (Wairarapa) 1949 *A*
**Boggs, E G** (Auckland) 1946 *A*, 1949 *SA*
**Bond, J G** (Canterbury) 1949 *A*
**Booth, E E** (Otago) 1905–06 (T) *F*, 1907 *A* (2)
**Bowden, N J G** (Taranaki) 1952 *A*
**Bowers, R G** (Wellington) 1953–54 (T) *I, F*
**Bowman, A W** (Hawke's Bay) 1938 *A* (3)
**Bremner, S G** (Auckland, Canterbury) 1952 *A*, 1956 *SA*
**Briscoe, K C** (Taranaki) 1959 *BI*, 1960 *SA* (4), 1963–64 (T) *I, W, E, S*
**Brown, C** (Taranaki) 1913 *A* (2)
**Brown, R H** (Taranaki) 1955 *A*, 1956 *SA* (4), 1957 *A* (2), 1958 *A* (3), 1959 *BI* (2), 1961 *F* (3), 1962 *A*
**Brownlie, C J** (Hawke's Bay) 1924–25 (T) *W, E, F*
**Brownlie, M J** (Hawke's Bay) 1924–25 (T) *I, W, E, F*, 1928 *SA* (4)
**Bruce, J A** (Auckland) 1914 *A* (2)
**Bruce, O D** (Canterbury) 1976 *SA* (3), 1977 *BI* (3), 1977 (ST) *F* (2)

**Bryers, R F** (King Country) 1949 *A*
**Budd, T A** (Southland) 1946 *A*, 1949 *A*
**Bullock-Douglas, G A H** (Wanganui) 1932 *A* (3), 1934 *A* (2)
**Burgess, G F** (Southland) 1905 *A*
**Burgess, R E** (Manawatu) 1971 *BI* (3), 1972 *A*, 1972–73 (T) *W, I, F*
**Burke, P S** (Taranaki) 1955 *A*, 1957 *A* (2)
**Burns, P J** (Canterbury) 1908 *AW*, 1910 *A* (3), 1913 *A*
**Bush, R G** (Otago) 1931 *A*
**Bush, W K** (Canterbury) 1974 *A* (2), 1975 *S*, 1976 *I*, *SA* (2), 1977 *BI* (3 [1R])
**Buxton, J B** (Canterbury) 1955 *A*, 1956 *SA*

**Cain, M J** (Taranaki) 1914 *A* (3)
**Callesen, J A** (Manawatu) 1974 *A* (3), 1975 *S*
**Cameron, D** (Taranaki) 1908 *AW* (3)
**Carleton, S R** (Canterbury) 1928 *SA* (3), 1929 *A* (3)
**Carrington, K R** (Auckland) 1971 *BI* (3)
**Casey, S T** (Otago) 1905–06 (T) *S, I, E, W*, 1907 *A* (3), 1908 *AW*
**Catley, E H** (Waikato) 1946 *A*, 1947 *A* (2), 1949 *SA* (4)
**Caughey, T H C** (Auckland) 1932 *A* (2), 1934 *A* (2), 1935–36 (T) *S, I, E*, 1936 *A*, 1937 *SA*
**Caulton, R W** (Wellington) 1959 *BI* (3), 1960 *SA* (2), 1961 *F*, 1963 *E* (2), 1963–64 (T) *I, W, E, S, F*, 1964 *A* (3)
**Cherrington, N P** (North Auckland) 1950 *BI*
**Christian, D L** (Auckland) 1949 *SA*
**Clark, D W** (Otago) 1964 *A* (2)
**Clark, W H** (Wellington) 1953–54 (T) *W, I, E, S*, 1955 *A* (2), 1956 *SA* (3)
**Clarke, A H** (Auckland) 1958 *A*, 1959 *BI*, 1960 *SA*
**Clarke, D B** (Waikato) 1956 *SA* (2), 1957 *A* (2), 1958 *A* (2), 1959 *BI* (4), 1960 *SA* (4), 1961 *F* (3), 1962 *A* (5), 1963 *E* (2), 1963–64 (T) *I, W, E, S, F*, 1964 *A* (2)
**Clarke, I J** (Waikato) 1953–54 (T) *W*, 1955 *A* (3), 1956 *SA* (4), 1957 *A* (2), 1958 *A* (2), 1959 *BI* (2), 1960 *SA* (2), 1961 *F* (3), 1962 *A* (3), 1963 *E* (2)
**Clarke, R L** (Taranaki) 1932 *A* (2)
**Cobden, D G** (Canterbury) 1937 *SA*
**Cockerill, M S** (Taranaki) 1951 *A* (3)
**Cockroft, E A** (South Canterbury) 1913 *A*, 1914 *A* (2)
**Collins, A J** (Taranaki) 1932 *A* (2), 1934 *A*
**Collins, J L** (Poverty Bay) 1964 *A*, 1965 *SA* (2)
**Colman, J D** (Taranaki) 1907 *A* (2), 1908 *AW* (2)
**Connor, D M** (Auckland) 1961 *F* (3), 1962 *A* (5), 1963 *E* (2), 1964 *A* (2)
**Conway, R J** (Otago, Bay of Plenty) 1959 *BI* (3), 1960 *SA* (3), 1965 *SA* (4)
**Cooke, A E** (Auckland, Wellington) 1924–25 (T), *I, W, E, F*, 1930 *BI* (4)
**Cooke, R J** (Canterbury) 1903 *A*
**Corner, M M N** (Auckland) 1930 *BI* (3), 1931 *A*, 1934 *A*, 1935–36 (T) *E*
**Cossey, R R** (Counties) 1958 *A*

**Cottrell, A I** (Canterbury) 1929 *A* (3), 1930 *BI* (4), 1931 *A*, 1932 *A* (3)
**Cottrell, W D** (Canterbury) 1968 *A* (2), *F* (2), 1970 *SA*, 1971 *BI* (4)
**Couch, M B R** (Wairarapa) 1947 *A*, 1949 *A*, (2)
**Coughlan, T D** (South Canterbury) 1958 *A*
**Creighton, J N** (Canterbury) 1962 *A*
**Cross, T** (Canterbury) 1904 *BI*, 1905 *A*
**Crowley, P J B** (Auckland) 1949 *SA* (2), 1950 *BI* (4)
**Cummings, W** (Canterbury) 1913 *A* (2)
**Cundy, R T** (Wairarapa) 1929 *A* (R)
**Cunningham, W** (Auckland) 1905–06 (T) *S, I, F*, 1907 *A* (3), 1908 *AW* (3)
**Cupples, L F** (Bay of Plenty) 1924–25 (T) *I, W*
**Cuthill, J E** (Otago) 1913 *A*

**Dalley, W C** (Canterbury) 1924–25 (T) *I*, 1928 *SA* (4)
**Dalton, A G** Counties) 1977 (ST) *F*
**Dalton, D** (Hawke's Bay) 1935–36 (T) *I, W*, 1936 *A* (2), 1937 *SA* (3), 1938 *A* (2)
**Dalton, R A** (Wellington) 1947 *A* (2)
**Dalzell, G N** (Canterbury) 1953–54 (T) *W, I, E, S, F*
**Davies, W A** (Auckland, Otago) 1960 *SA*, 1962 *A* (2)
**Davis, K** (Auckland) 1952 *A*, 1953–54 (T) *W, I, E, S, F*, 1955 *A*, 1958 *A* (3)
**Davis, L J** (Canterbury) 1976 *I*, 1977 *BI* (2)
**Davis, W L** (Hawke's Bay) 1967 *A*, 1967–68 (T) *E, W, F, S*, 1968 *A* (2), *F*, 1969 *W* (2), 1970 *SA*
**Deans, R G** (Canterbury) 1905–06 (T) *S, I, E, W*, 1908 *AW*
**Delamore, G W** (Wellington) 1949 *SA*
**Dewar, H** (Taranaki) 1913 *A*
**Diack, E S** (Otago) 1959 *BI*
**Dick, J** (Auckland) 1937 *SA* (2), 1938 *A*
**Dick, M J** (Auckland) 1963–64 (T) *I, W, E, S, F*, 1965 *SA*, 1966 *BI*, 1967 *A*, 1967–68 (T) *E, W, F*, 1969 *W* (2), 1970 *SA* (2)
**Dixon, M J** (Canterbury) 1953–54 (T) *I, E, S, F*, 1956 *SA* (4), 1957 *A* (2)
**Dobson, R L** (Auckland) 1949 *A*
**Dodd, E H** (Wellington) 1905 *A*
**Donald, J G** (Wairarapa) 1921 *SA* (2)
**Donald, Q** (Wairarapa) 1924–25 (T) *I, W, E, F*
**Donaldson, M W** (Manawatu) 1977 (ST) *F* (2)
**Dougan, J P** (Wellington) 1972 *A*, 1973 *E*
**Downing, A J** (Auckland) 1913 *A*, 1914 *A* (3)
**Duff, R H** (Canterbury) 1951 *A* (3), 1952 *A* (2), 1955 *A* (2), 1956 *SA* (4)
**Duncan, J** (Otago) 1903 *A*
**Duncan, M G** (Hawke's Bay) 1971 *BI* (2 [1R])
**Duncan, W D** (Otago) 1921 *SA* (3)
**Dunn, J M** (Auckland) 1946 *A*

**Eastgate, B P** (Canterbury) 1952 *A* (2), 1953–54 (T) *S*
**Elliott, K G** (Wellington) 1946 *A* (2)
**Elsom, A E G** (Canterbury) 1952 *A* (2), 1953–54 (T) *W*, 1955 *A* (3)
**Elvidge, R R** (Otago) 1946 *A* (2), 1949 *SA* (4), 1950 *BI* (3)
**Erceg, P** (Auckland) 1951 *A* (3), 1952 *A*
**Evans, D A** (Hawke's Bay) 1910 *A*
**Eveleigh, K A** (Manawatu) 1976 *SA* (2), 1977 *BI* (2)

**Fanning, A H N** (Canterbury) 1913 *A*
**Fanning, B J** (Canterbury) 1903 *A*, 1904 *BI*
**Farrell, C P** (Auckland) 1977 *BI* (2)
**Fawcett, C L** (Auckland) 1976 *SA* (2)
**Fea, W R** (Otago) 1921 *SA*
**Finlay, B E L** (Manawatu) 1959 *BI*
**Finlay, J** (Manawatu) 1946 *A*
**Finlayson, I H** (North Auckland) 1928 *SA* (4), 1930 *BI* (2)
**Fitzgerald, J T** (Wellington) 1952 *A*
**Fitzpatrick, B B J** (Wellington) 1953–54 (T) *W, I, F*
**Fletcher, C J** (North Auckland) 1921 *SA*
**Fogarty, R D** (Taranaki) 1921 *SA* (2)
**Ford, B R** (Marlborough) 1977 *BI* (2)
**Francis, A R H** (Auckland) 1905 *A*, 1907 *A* (3), 1908 *AW* (3), 1910 *A* (3)
**Francis, W** (Wellington) 1913 *A* (2), 1914 *A* (3)
**Frazer, H F** (Hawke's Bay) 1946 *A* (2), 1947 *A* (2), 1949 *SA*
**Fryer, F C** (Canterbury) 1907 *A* (3), 1908 *AW*
**Fuller, W B** (Canterbury) 1910 *A* (2)

**Furlong, B D M** (Hawke's Bay) 1970 *SA*

**Gallaher, D** (Auckland) 1903 *A*, 1904 *BI*, 1905–06 (T) *S, E, W, F*
**Gard, P C** (North Otago) 1971 *BI*
**Gardiner, A J** (Taranaki) 1974 *A*
**Geddes, J H** (Southland) 1929 *A*
**Geddes, W McK** (Auckland) 1913 *A*
**Gemmell, B McL** (Auckland) 1974 *A* (2)
**George, V L** (Southland) 1938 *A* (3)
**Gilbert, G D M** (West Coast) 1935–36 (T), *S, I, W, E*
**Gillespie, C T** (Wellington) 1913 *A*
**Gillespie, W D** (Otago) 1958 *A*
**Gillett, G A** (Canterbury, Auckland) 1905–06 (T) *S, I, E, W*, 1907 *A* (2), 1908 *AW* (2)
**Gillies, C C** (Otago) 1936 *A*
**Gilray, C M** (Otago) 1905 *A*
**Glasgow, F T** (Taranaki, Southland) 1905–06 (T) *S, I, E, W, F*, 1908 *AW*
**Glenn, W S** (Taranaki) 1904 *BI*, 1905–06 (T) *F*
**Goddard, M P** (South Canterbury) 1946 *A*, 1947 *A* (2), 1949 *SA* (2)
**Going, S M** (North Auckland) 1967 *A*, 1967–68 (T) *F*, 1968 *F*, 1969 *W* (2), 1970 *SA* (2 [1R]), 1971 *BI* (4), 1972 *A* (3), 1972–73 (T) *W, S, E, I, F*, 1973 *E*, 1974 (ST) *I*, 1975 *S*, 1976 *I* (R), *SA* (4), 1977 *BI* (2)
**Graham, D J** (Canterbury) 1958 *A* (2), 1960 *SA* (2), 1961 *F* (3), 1962 *A* (5), 1963 *E* (2), 1963–64 (T) *I, W, E, S, F*, 1964 *A* (3)
**Graham, J B** (Otago) 1914 *A* (2)
**Grant, L A** (South Canterbury) 1947 *A* (2), 1949 *SA* (2)
**Gray, D** (Canterbury) 1908 *AW*, 1913 *A*
**Gray, K F** (Wellington) 1963–64 (T) *I, W, E, S, F*, 1964 *A* (3), 1965 *SA* (4), 1966 *BI* (4), 1967–68 (T) *W, F, S*, 1968 *A, F* (2), 1969 *W* (2)
**Gray, W N** (Bay of Plenty) 1955 *A* (2), 1956 *SA* (4)
**Grenside, B A** (Hawke's Bay) 1928 *SA* (4), 1929 *A* (2)
**Griffiths, J L** (Wellington) 1934 *A*, 1935–36 (T) *S, I, W*, 1936 *A* (2), 1938 *A*
**Guy, R A** (North Auckland) 1971 *BI* (4)

**Haden, A M** (Auckland) 1977 *BI* (4), 1977 (ST) *F* (4)
**Hadley, S** (Auckland) 1928 *SA* (4)
**Hadley, W E** (Auckland) 1934 *A* (2), 1935–36 (T) *S, I, W, E*, 1936 *A* (2)
**Haig, J S** (Otago) 1946 *A* (2)
**Haig, L S** (Otago) 1950 *BI* (3), 1951 *A* (3), 1953–54 (T) *W, E, S*
**Hales, D A** (Canterbury) 1972 *A* (3), 1972–73 (T) *W*
**Hamilton, D C** (Southland) 1908 *AW*
**Hammond, I A** (Marlborough) 1952 *A*
**Harper, E T** (Canterbury) 1904 *BI*, 1905–06 (T) *F*
**Harris, P C** (Manawatu) 1976 *SA*
**Hart, A H** (Taranaki) 1924–25 (T) *I*
**Hart, G F** (Canterbury) 1930 *BI* (4), 1931 *A*, 1934 *A*, 1935–36 (T) *S, I, W*, 1936 *A* (2)
**Harvey, I H** (Wairarapa) 1928 *SA*
**Harvey, L R** (Otago) 1949 *SA* (4), 1950 *BI* (4)
**Harvey, P** (Canterbury) 1904 *BI*
**Hasell, E W** (Canterbury) 1913 *A* (2)
**Hayward, H** (Auckland) 1908 *AW*
**Hazlett, E J** (Southland) 1966 *BI* (4), 1967 *A*, 1967–68 (T) *E*
**Hazlett, W E** (Southland) 1928 *SA* (4), 1930 *BI* (4)
**Heeps, T R** (Wellington) 1962 *A* (5)
**Heke, W R** (North Auckland) 1929 *A* (3)
**Hemi, R C** (Waikato) 1953–54 (T) *W, I, E, S, F*, 1955 *A* (3), 1956 *SA* (3), 1957 *A* (2), 1959 *BI* (3)
**Henderson, P W** (Wanganui) 1949 *SA* (4), 1950 *BI* (3)
**Herewini, M A** (Auckland) 1962 *A*, 1963–64 (T) *I, S, F*, 1965 *SA*, 1966 *BI* (4), 1967 *A*
**Hill, S F** (Canterbury) 1955 *A*, 1956 *SA* (3), 1957 *A* (2), 1958 *A*, 1959 *BI* (4)
**Holder, E C** (Buller) 1934 *A*
**Hook, L S** (Auckland) 1929 *A* (3)
**Hooper, J A** (Canterbury) 1937 *SA* (3)
**Hopkinson, A E** (Canterbury) 1967–68 (T) *S*, 1968 *A, F* (3), 1969 *W*, 1970 *SA* (3)
**Hore, J** (Otago) 1930 *BI* (3), 1932 *A* (3), 1934 *A* (2), 1935–36 (T) *S, E*
**Horsley, R H** (Wellington) 1960 *SA* (3)
**Hotop, J** (Canterbury) 1952 *A* (2), 1955 *A*
**Hughes, A M** (Auckland) 1949 *A* (2), 1950 *BI* (4)

**Meates, K F** (Canterbury) 1952 *A* (2)
**Meates, W A** (Otago) 1949 *SA* (3), 1950 *BI* (4)
**Metcalfe, T C** (Southland) 1931 *A*, 1932 *A*
**Mexted, G G** (Wellington) 1950 *BI*
**Mill, J J** (Hawke's Bay, Wairarapa) 1924–25 (T) *W, E, F*, 1930 *BI*
**Milliken, H M** (Canterbury) 1938 *A* (3)
**Milner, H P** (Wanganui) 1970 *SA*
**Mitchell, N A** (Southland, Otago) 1935–36 (T) *S, I, W, E*, 1936 *A*, 1937 *SA*, 1938 *A* (2)
**Mitchell, T W** (Canterbury) 1976 *SA* (R)
**Mitchell, W J** (Canterbury) 1910 *A* (2)
**Mitchinson, F E** (Wellington) 1907 *A* (3), 1908 *AW* (3), 1910 *A* (3)
**Moffitt, J E** (Wellington) 1921 *SA* (3)
**Moore, G J T** (Otago) 1949 *A*
**Moreton, R C** (Canterbury) 1962 *A* (2), 1964 *A* (3), 1965 *SA* (2)
**Morgan, J E** (North Auckland) 1974 *A*, 1974 (ST) *I*, 1976 *SA* (3)
**Morris, T J** (Nelson Bays) 1972 *A* (3)
**Morrison, T C** (South Canterbury) 1938 *A* (3)
**Morrison, T G** (Otago) 1973 *E* (R)
**Morrissey, P J** (Canterbury) 1962 *A* (3)
**Mourie, G N K** (Taranaki) 1977 *BI* (2), 1977 (ST) *F* (2)
**Muller, B L** (Taranaki) 1967 *A*, 1967–68 (T) *E, W, F*, 1968 *A, F*, 1969 *W*, 1970 *SA* (3), 1971 *BI* (4)
**Mumm, W J** (Buller) 1949 *A*
**Murdoch, K** (Otago) 1970 *SA*, 1972 *A*, 1972–73 (T) *W*
**Murdoch, P H** (Auckland) 1964 *A* (2), 1965 *SA* (3)
**Murray, H V** (Canterbury) 1913 *A*, 1914 *A* (2)
**Murray P C** (Wanganui) 1908 *AW*
**Mynott, H J** (Taranaki) 1905–06 (T) *I, W, F*, 1907 *A* (3), 1910 *A* (2)

**Nathan, W J** (Auckland) 1962 *A* (5), 1963 *E* (2), 1963–64 (T) *W, F*, 1966 *BI* (4), 1967 *A*
**Nelson, K A** (Otago) 1962 *A* (2)
**Nepia, G** (Hawke's Bay, East Coast) 1924–25 (T) *I, W, E, F*, 1929 *A*, 1930 *BI* (4)
**Nesbit, S R** (Auckland) 1960 *SA* (2)
**Newton, F** (Canterbury) 1905–06 (T) *E, W, F*
**Nicholls, H E** (Wellington) 1921 *SA*
**Nicholls, M F** (Wellington) 1921 *SA* (3), 1924–25 (T) *I, W, E, F*, 1928 *SA*, 1930 *BI* (2)
**Nicholson, G W** (Auckland) 1903 *A*, 1904 *BI*, 1907 *A* (2)
**Norton, R W** (Canterbury) 1971 *BI* (4), 1972 *A* (3), 1972–73 (T) *W, S, E, I, F*, 1973 *E*, 1974 (ST) *I*, 1975 *S*, 1976 *I, SA* (4), 1977 *BI* (4)

**O'Brien, J G** (Auckland) 1914 *A*
**O'Callaghan, M W** (Manawatu) 1968 *F* (3)
**O'Callaghan, T R** (Wellington) 1949 *A*
**O'Donnell, D H** (Wellington) 1949 *A*
**O'Leary, M J** (Auckland) 1910 *A* (2), 1913 *A* (2)
**Oliver, C J** (Canterbury) 1929 *A* (2), 1934 *A*, 1935–36 (T) *S, I, W, E*
**Oliver, D J** (Wellington) 1930 *BI* (2)
**Oliver, F J** (Southland) 1976 *SA*, 1977 *BI* (4), 1977 (ST) *F* (2)
**Oliver, O D** (Otago) 1953–54 (T) *I, F*
**Orr, R W** (Otago) 1949 *A*
**Osborne, W M** (Wanganui) 1975 *S*, 1976 *SA* (2 [2R]), 1977 *BI* (4), 1977 (ST) *F* (2[1R])
**O'Sullivan, J M** (Taranaki) 1905–06 (T) *S, I, E, W*, 1907 *A*
**O'Sullivan, T P A** (Taranaki) 1960 *SA*, 1961 *F*, 1962 *A* (2)

**Page, J R** (Wellington) 1931 *A*, 1932 *A* (3), 1934 *A* (2)
**Palmer, B P** (Auckland) 1929 *A*, 1932 *A* (2)
**Parker, J H** (Canterbury) 1924–25 (T) *I, W, E*
**Parkhill, A A** (Otago) 1937 *SA* (3), 1938 *A* (3)
**Parkinson, R M** (Poverty Bay) 1972 *A* (3), 1972–73 (T) *W, S, E*, 1973 *E*
**Paton, H** (Otago) 1910 *A* (2)
**Patterson, A** (Otago) 1908 *AW* (2), 1910 *A* (3)
**Phillips, W J** (King Country) 1937 *SA*, 1938 *A* (2)
**Pickering, E A R** (Waikato) 1958 *A*, 1959 *BI* (2)
**Pollock, H R** (Wellington) 1932 *A* (3), 1936 *A* (2)
**Porter, C G** (Wellington) 1924–25 (T) *F*, 1929 *A* (2), 1930 *BI* (4)
**Proctor, A C** (Otago) 1932 *A*

**Purdue, C** (Southland) 1905 *A*
**Purdue, E G** (Southland) 1905 *A*
**Purdue, G B** (Southland) 1931 *A*, 1932 *A* (3)
**Purvis, N A** (Otago) 1976 *I*

**Quaid, C E** (Otago) 1938 *A* (2)

**Rangi, R E** (Auckland) 1964 *A* (2), 1965 *SA* (4), 1966 *BI* (4)
**Rankin, J G** (Canterbury) 1936 *A* (2), 1937 *SA*
**Reedy, W J** (Wellington) 1908 *AW* (2)
**Reid, A R** (Waikato) 1952 *A*, 1956 *SA* (2), 1957 *A* (2)
**Reid, K H** (Wairarapa) 1929 *A* (2)
**Reid, S T** (Hawke's Bay) 1935–36 (T) *S, I, W, E*, 1936 *A* (2), 1937 *SA* (3)
**Reside, W B** (Wairarapa) 1929 *A*
**Rhind, P K** (Canterbury) 1946 *A* (2)
**Richardson, J** (Otago, Southland) 1921 *SA* (3), 1924–25 (T) *I, W, E, F*
**Ridland, J** (Southland) 1910 *A* (3)
**Roberts, E J** (Wellington) 1914 *A* (3), 1921 *SA* (2)
**Roberts, F** (Wellington) 1905–06 (T) *S, I, E, W*, 1907 *A* (3), 1908 *AW* (2), 1910 *A* (3)
**Roberts, R W** (Taranaki) 1913 *A*, 1914 *A* (3)
**Robertson, B J** (Counties) 1972 *A* (2), 1972–73 (T) *S, E, I, F*, 1974 *A* (3), 1974 (ST) *I*, 1976 *I, SA* (4), 1977 *BI* (3), 1977 (ST) *F* (2)
**Robertson, D J** (Otago) 1974 *A* (3), 1974 (ST) *I*, 1975 *S*, 1976 *I, SA* (3), 1977 *BI*
**Robilliard, A C C** (Canterbury) 1928 *SA* (4)
**Robinson, C E** (Southland) 1951 *A* (3), 1952 *A* (2)
**Roper, R A** (Taranaki) 1949 *A*, 1950 *BI* (4)
**Rowley, H C B** (Wanganui) 1949 *A*
**Ryan, J** (Wellington) 1910 *A*, 1914 *A* (3)

**Sadler, B S** (Wellington) 1935–36 (T) *S, I, W*, 1936 *A* (2)
**Savage, L T** (Canterbury) 1949 *SA* (3)
**Saxton, C K** (South Canterbury) 1938 *A* (3)
**Scott, R W H** (Auckland) 1946 *A* (2), 1947 *A* (2), 1949 *SA* (4), 1950 *BI* (4), 1953–54 (T) *W, I, E, S, F*
**Scown, A I** (Taranaki) 1972 *A* (3), 1972–73 (T) *W* (R), *S*
**Scrimshaw, G** (Canterbury) 1928 *SA*
**Seear, G A** (Otago) 1977 (ST) *F* (2)
**Seeling, C E** (Auckland) 1904 *BI*, 1905–06 (T) *S, I, E, W, F*, 1907 *A* (2), 1908 *AW* (3)
**Sellars, G M V** (Auckland) 1913 *A*
**Siddells, S K** (Wellington) 1921 *SA*
**Simon, H J** (Otago) 1937 *SA* (3)
**Simpson, J G** (Auckland) 1947 *A* (2), 1949 *SA* (4), 1950 *BI* (3)
**Sims, G S** (Otago) 1972 *A*
**Skeen, J R** (Auckland) 1952 *A*
**Skinner, K L** (Otago, Counties) 1949 *SA* (4), 1950 *BI* (4), 1951 *A* (3), 1952 *A* (2), 1953–54 (T) *W, I, E, S, F*, 1956 *SA* (2)
**Skudder, G R** (Waikato) 1969 *W*
**Smith, A E** (Taranaki) 1969 *W* (2), 1970 *SA*
**Smith, G W** (Auckland) 1905–06 (T) *S, I*
**Smith, I S T** (Otago, North Otago) 1964 *A* (3), 1965 *SA* (3) 1966 *BI* (3)
**Smith, J B** (North Auckland) 1946 *A*, 1947 *A*, 1949 *A* (2)
**Smith, R M** (Canterbury) 1955 *A*
**Smith, W E** (Nelson) 1905 *A*
**Snow, E M** (Nelson) 1929 *A* (3)
**Solomon, F** (Auckland) 1931 *A*, 1932 *A* (3)
**Sonntag, W T C** (Otago) 1929 *A* (3)
**Spencer, J C** (Wellington) 1905 *A*, 1907 *A* (R)
**Spillane, A** (South Canterbury) 1913 *A* (2)
**Stead, J W** (Southland) 1904 *BI*, 1905–06 (T) *S, I, E, F*, 1908 *AW* (2)
**Steel, A G** (Canterbury) 1966 *BI* (4), 1967 *A*, 1967–68 (T) *F, S*, 1968 *A* (2)
**Steel, J** (West Coast) 1921 *SA* (3), 1924–25 (T) *W, E, F*
**Steele, L B** (Wellington) 1951 *A* (3)
**Steere, E R G** (Hawke's Bay) 1930 *BI* (4), 1931 *A*, 1932 *A*
**Stephens, O G** (Wellington) 1968 *F*
**Stevens, I N** (Wellington) 1972–73 (T) *S, E*, 1974 *A*
**Stewart, A J** (Canterbury, South Canterbury) 1963 *E* (2), 1963–64 (T) *I, W, E, S, F*, 1964 *A*
**Stewart, J D** (Auckland) 1913 *A* (2)

**Stewart, K W** (Southland) 1973 *E*, 1974 *A* (3), 1974 (ST) *I*, 1975 *S*, 1976 *I*, *SA* (2)
**Stewart, R T** (South Canterbury, Canterbury) 1928 *SA* (4) 1930 *BI*
**Stohr, L B** (Taranaki) 1910 *A* (3)
**Storey, P W** (South Canterbury) 1921 *SA* (2)
**Strahan, S C** (Manawatu) 1967 *A*, 1967–68 (T) *E*, *W*, *F*, *S*, 1968 *A* (2), *F* (3), 1970 *SA* (3), 1972 *A* (3), 1973 *E*
**Strang, W A** (South Canterbury) 1928 *SA* (2), 1930 *BI* (2), 1931 *A*
**Stringfellow, J C** (Wairarapa) 1929 *A* (2[1R])
**Stuart, K C** (Canterbury) 1955 *A*
**Stuart, R C** (Canterbury) 1949 *A* (2), 1953–54 (T) *W*, *I*, *E*, *S*, *F*
**Stuart, R L** (Hawke's Bay) 1977 (ST) *F* (R)
**Sullivan, J L** (Taranaki) 1937 *SA* (3), 1938 *A* (3)
**Sutherland, A R** (Marlborough) 1970 *SA* (2), 1971 *BI*, 1972 *A* (3), 1972–73 (T) *W*, *E*, *I*, *F*
**Svenson, K S** (Wellington) 1924–25 (T) *I*, *W*, *E*, *F*
**Swain, J P** (Hawke's Bay) 1928 *SA* (4)

**Tanner, J M** (Auckland) 1950 *BI*, 1951 *A* (3), 1953–54 (T) *W*
**Tanner, K J** (Canterbury) 1974 *A* (3), 1974 (ST) *I*, 1975 *S*, 1976 *I*, *SA*
**Taylor, H M** (Canterbury) 1913 *A*, 1914 *A* (3)
**Taylor, J M** (Otago) 1937 *SA* (3), 1938 *A* (3)
**Taylor, N M** (Bay of Plenty) 1977 *BI* (2 [1R]), 1977 (ST) *F* (2)
**Taylor, R** (Taranaki) 1913 *A* (2)
**Tetzlaff, P L** (Auckland) 1947 *A* (2)
**Thimbleby, N W** (Hawke's Bay) 1970 *SA*
**Thomas, B T** (Auckland, Wellington) 1962 *A*, 1964 *A* (3)
**Thomson, H D** (Wellington) 1908 *AW*
**Thorne, G S** (Auckland) 1968 *A* (2), *F* (3), 1969 *W*, 1970 *SA* (4)
**Thornton, N H** (Auckland) 1947 *A* (2), 1949 *SA*
**Tilyard, J T** (Wellington) 1913 *A*
**Tindill, E W T** (Wellington) 1935–36 (T) *E*
**Townsend, L J** (Otago) 1955 *A* (2)
**Tremain, K R** (Canterbury, Hawke's Bay) 1959 *BI* (3), 1960 *SA* (4), 1961 *F* (2), 1962 *A* (3), 1963 *E* (2), 1963–64 (T) *I*, *W*, *E*, *S*, *F*, 1964 *A* (3), 1965 *SA* (4), 1966 *BI* (4), 1967 *A*, 1967–68 (T) *E*, *W*, *S*, 1968 *A*, *F* (3)
**Trevathan, D** (Otago) 1937 *SA* (3)
**Tuck, J M** (Waikato) 1929 *A* (3)
**Turtill, H S** (Canterbury) 1905 *A*
**Tyler, G A** (Auckland) 1903 *A*, 1904 *BI*, 1905–06 (T) *S*, *I*, *E*, *W*, *F*

**Udy, D K** (Wairarapa) 1903 *A*
**Urlich, R A** (Auckland) 1970 *SA* (2)
**Urbahn, R J** (Taranaki) 1959 *BI* (3)
**Uttley, I N** (Wellington) 1963 *E* (2)

**Vincent, P B** (Canterbury) 1956 *SA* (2)
**Vodanovich, I M H** (Wellington) 1955 *A* (3)

**Wallace, W J** (Wellington) 1903 *A*, 1904 *BI*, 1905–06 (T) *S*, *I*, *E*, *W*, *F*, 1907 *A* (3), 1908 *AW*
**Walsh, P T** (Counties) 1955 *A* (3), 1956 *SA* (3), 1957 *A* (2), 1958 *A* (3), 1959 *BI*, 1963 *E*
**Ward, R H** (Southland) 1936 *A*, 1937 *SA* (2)
**Waterman, A C** (North Auckland) 1929 *A* (2)
**Watkins, E L** (Wellington) 1905 *A*
**Watt, B A** (Canterbury) 1962 *A* (2), 1963 *E* (2), 1963–64 (T) *W*, *E*, *S*, 1964 *A*
**Watt, J M** (Otago) 1936 *A* (2)
**Watt, J R** (Wellington) 1958 *A*, 1960 *SA* (4), 1961 *F* (2), 1962 *A* (2)
**Webb, D S** (North Auckland) 1959 *BI*
**Wells, J** (Wellington) 1936 *A* (2)
**West, A H** (Taranaki) 1921 *SA* (2)
**Whineray, W J** (Canterbury, Waikato, Auckland) 1957 *A* (2), 1958 *A* (3), 1959 *BI* (4), 1960 *SA* (4), 1961 *F* (3), 1962 *A* (5), 1963 *E* (2), 1963–64 (T) *I*, *W*, *E*, *S*, *F*, 1965 *SA* (4)
**White, A** (Southland) 1921 *SA*, 1924–25 (T) *I*, *E*, *F*
**White, H L** (Auckland) 1953–54 (T) *I*, *E*, *F*, 1955 *A*
**White, R A** (Poverty Bay) 1949 *A* (2), 1950 *BI* (4), 1951 *A* (3), 1952 *A* (2), 1953–54 (T) *W*, *I*, *E*, *S*, *F*, 1955 *A* (3), 1956 *SA* (4)
**White, R M** (Wellington) 1946 *A* (2), 1947 *A* (2)
**Whiting, G J** (King Country) 1972 *A* (2), 1972–73 (T) *S*, *E*, *I*, *F*
**Whiting, P J** (Auckland) 1971 *BI* (3), 1972 *A* (3), 1972–73 (T) *W*, *S*, *E*, *I*, *F*, 1974 *A* (3), 1974 (ST) *I*, 1976 *I*, *SA* (4)
**Williams, B G** (Auckland) 1970 *SA* (4), 1971 *BI* (3), 1972 *A* (3), 1972–73 (T) *W*, *S*, *E*, *I*, *F*, 1973 *E*, 1974 *A* (3), 1974 (ST) *I*, 1975 *S*, 1976 *I*, *SA* (4), 1977 *BI* (4), 1977 (ST) *F*
**Williams, G C** (Wellington) 1967–68 (T) *E*, *W*, *F*, *S*, 1968 *A*
**Williams, P** (Otago) 1913 *A*
**Williment, M** (Wellington) 1964 *A*, 1965 *SA* (3), 1966 *BI* (4), 1967 *A*
**Willocks, C** (Otago) 1946 *A* (2), 1949 *SA* (3)
**Wilson, A** (Wellington) 1908 *AW* (2), 1910 *A* (3), 1913 *A* (2), 1914 *A* (3)
**Wilson, B W** (Otago) 1977 *BI* (2)
**Wilson, D D** (Canterbury) 1953–54 (T) *E*, *S*
**Wilson, H W** (Otago) 1949 *A*, 1950 *BI*, 1951 *A* (3)
**Wilson, N L** (Otago) 1951 *A* (3)
**Wilson, S S** (Wellington) 1977 (ST) *F* (2)
**Wolfe, T N** (Wellington, Taranaki) 1961 *F* (3), 1962 *A* (2), 1963 *E*
**Wood, M E** (Canterbury, Auckland) 1903 *A*, 1904 *BI*
**Wrigley, E** (Wairarapa) 1905 *A*
**Wylie, J T** (Auckland) 1913 *A*
**Wyllie, A J** (Canterbury) 1970 *SA* (2), 1971 *BI* (3), 1972–73 (T) *W*, *S*, *E*, *I*, *F*, 1973 *E*

**Yates, V M** (North Auckland) 1961 *F* (3)
**Young, D** (Canterbury) 1956 *SA*, 1958 *A* (3), 1960 *SA* (4), 1961 *F* (3), 1962 *A* (4), 1963 *E* (2), 1963–64 (T) *I*, *W*, *E*, *S*, *F*

241

# NEW ZEALAND INTERNATIONAL RECORDS

*From 1890–91, when uniform points-scoring was first adopted by International Board countries, to 30 April 1978, except in the case of matches against British Isles. These date from 1910, when British Isles teams first became representative of the Four Home Unions. Both team and individual records are against International Board countries and British Isles only, unless otherwise stated.*

## TEAM RECORDS

### Highest score

38 { v France (38–8) 1906 Parc des Princes (Paris) / v Australia (38–13) 1936 Dunedin / v Australia (38–3) 1972 Auckland

*v individual countries*
23 v England (23–11) 1967 Twickenham
24 v Scotland (24–0) 1975 Auckland
17 v Ireland (17–9) 1935 Dublin
33 v Wales (33–12) 1969 Auckland
38 v France (38–8) 1906 Parc des Princes
20 v S Africa (20–3) 1965 Auckland
38 v Australia { (38–13) 1936 Dunedin / (38–3) 1972 Auckland
24 v B Isles (24–11) 1966 Auckland

### Biggest winning points margin
35 v Australia (38–3) 1972 Auckland
*v individual countries*
15 v England (15–0) 1905 Crystal Palace (London)
24 v Scotland (24–0) 1975 Auckland
15 v Ireland (15–0) 1905 Dublin
21 v Wales (33–12) 1969 Auckland
30 v France (38–8) 1906 Parc des Princes
17 v S Africa (20–3) 1965 Auckland
35 v Australia (38–3) 1972 Auckland
17 v B Isles (20–3) 1966 Dunedin

### Highest score by opposing team
25 Australia (11–25) 1934 Sydney
*by individual countries*
16 England (10–16) 1973 Auckland
 9 Scotland (14–9) 1972 Murrayfield
10 Ireland (10–10) 1973 Dublin
16 Wales (19–16) 1972 Cardiff
18 France (13–18) 1977 Toulouse
20 S Africa (17–20) 1970 Johannesburg
25 Australia (11–25) 1934 Sydney
17 B Isles (18–17) 1959 Dunedin

### Biggest losing points margin
17 v South Africa (0–17) 1928 Durban
*v individual countries*
13 v England (0–13) 1936 Twickenham
No defeat v Scotland
No defeat v Ireland
 5 v Wales (8–13) 1953 Cardiff
 7 v France (6–13) 1973 Parc des Princes
17 v S Africa (0–17) 1928 Durban
15 v Australia (5–20) 1964 Wellington
10 v B Isles (3–13) 1971 Wellington

### Most tries by New Zealand in an international
10 v France (38–8) 1906 Parc des Princes

### Most tries against New Zealand in an international
 5 by S Africa (6–17) 1937 Auckland

### Most points on overseas tour (all matches)
868 in B Isles/France (33 matches) 1905–06

### Most tries on overseas tour (all matches)
215 in B Isles/France (33 matches) 1905–06

## INDIVIDUAL RECORDS

### Most capped player
C E Meads   55   1957–71
*in individual positions*
*Full-back*
D B Clarke   31   1956–64
*Wing*
B G Williams   29 (31)**   1970–77
*Centre (includes 2nd five–eighth)*
B J Robertson   20   1972–77

*1st five–eighth*
E W Kirton   13   1967–70
*Scrum-half*
S M Going   29   1967–77
*Prop*
W J Whineray   32   1957–65
*Hooker*
R W Norton   27   1971–77
*Lock*
C E Meads   48 (55)*   1957–71
*Flanker*
K R Tremain   36 (38)†   1959–68
I A Kirkpatrick   36(39)††   1967–77
*No 8*
B J Lochore   24 (25)‡   1963–71

*Meads won 5 caps as a flanker, 2 as a No 8*
**Williams has won 2 caps as a centre*
†*Tremain won 2 caps as a No 8*
††*Kirkpatrick has won 3 caps as a No 8*
‡*Lochore won 1 cap as a lock*

**Most points in internationals – 207**
D B Clarke (31 appearances) 1956–64

**Most points in an international – 24**
W F McCormick v Wales 1969 Auckland

**Most tries in internationals – 16**
I A Kirkpatrick (39 appearances) 1967–77

**Most tries in an international – 4**
D McGregor v England 1905 Crystal
   Palace

**Most points for New Zealand on overseas tour – 230**
W J Wallace (25 appearances) 1905–06
   B Isles/France

**Most tries for New Zealand on overseas tour – 42**
J Hunter (23 appearances) 1905–06
   B Isles/France

243

**Most points for New Zealand in international series on tour – 32**
W F McCormick (4 appearances) 1967
   B Isles/France

**Most tries for New Zealand in international series on tour – 5**
K S Svenson (4 appearances) 1924–25
   B Isles/France

**Most points for New Zealand in any match on tour – 41**
J F Karam v South Australia 1974
   Adelaide

**Most tries for New Zealand in any match on tour – 8**
T R Heeps v Northern NSW 1962
   Quirindi

# THE 1977 SEASON IN AUSTRALIA

**Don Wilkey** Canberra

244 Australia, most unusually, had no rugby international matches in 1977. The breathing space, however, was not altogether a bad thing. It led to important administrative advances, not least the decision to pursue an international programme aimed ultimately at providing the Wallabies with at least three international matches every year. Annual meetings with New Zealand have already been arranged until 1983, with more, no doubt, to follow. For the first time sponsorship became an integral part of the game and without it some of the season's major fixtures would not have taken place.

In the absence of international matches, teams representing Sydney, Queensland, and New South Wales Country all made sizeable tours abroad. Sydney won six of their eight matches in Japan, Canada, the UK, and Russia, but in what they regarded as the most important fixture of all, against Cardiff, they lost 7–23. Queensland crossed the Tasman for three matches in New Zealand. After losing the first, 7–19 against Otago, they easily accounted for Mid-Canterbury, 28–3, and then excelled themselves by beating Canterbury, with their liberal sprinkling of All Blacks, 19–15. It was the second year in succession that they had won against these formidable opponents. At the end of the season New South Wales Country, always ready to tour, visited Fiji, the USA, Canada, and New Zealand, winning seven of their 12 matches.

Finally, the outstandingly successful tour of Britain by the Australian 19 Group Schoolboys, and an undefeated tour of New Zealand by their counterparts in the 16 Group, were most encouraging signs for the future.

In Australia itself the season began with a flourish with a visit from the New Zealand Barbarians, who were guests for the twenty-first anniversary of Barbarian rugby in Australia and won both their matches in Sydney. One of these was the principal object of their visit, against the Australian Barbarians, whom they beat 24–10. They also accounted for Sydney, 35–12, yet lost to Queensland, 9–14, in their opening game.

Queensland dominated the season's domestic programme. Their all-important interstate matches against New South Wales were played in an atmosphere of unprecedented rivalry, and the supremely confident Queenslanders won both games convincingly, 23–16 and 18–6.

# AUSTRALIAN INTERNATIONAL
# PLAYERS *(up to 30 April 1978)*

## ABBREVIATIONS

| | |
|---|---|
| *Am* | America |
| *BI* | British Isles teams |
| *E* | England |
| *F* | France |
| *Fj* | Fiji |
| *I* | Ireland |
| *J* | Japan |
| *M* | Maoris |
| *NZ* | New Zealand |
| *S* | Scotland |
| *SA* | South Africa |
| *TG* | Tonga |
| *W* | Wales |
| (R) | Replacement – (2[1R]) denotes two appearances, one of them as a replacement |
| (T) | Tour to Northern Hemisphere |
| (ST) | Short tour to Northern Hemisphere |
| *NB* | *Australia awards 'caps' for matches against Fiji, the Maoris, Tonga, Japan, and America, in addition to the International Board countries and the British Isles* |

**Abrahams, A M F** (New South Wales) 1967 *NZ*, 1968 *NZ*, 1969 *W*
**Adams, N J** (New South Wales) 1955 *NZ*
**Adamson, R W** (New South Wales) 1912 *Am*
**Allan, T** (New South Wales) 1946 *NZ* (2), *M*, 1947 *NZ*, 1947–48 (T) *S, I, W, E, F*, 1949 *M* (3), *NZ* (2)
**Anlezark, E A** (New South Wales) 1905 *NZ*
**Austin, L R** (New South Wales) 1963 *E*

**Baker, R L (** (New South Wales) 1904 *BI* (2)
**Baker, W H** (New South Wales) 1914 *NZ* (3)
**Ballesty, J P** (New South Wales) 1968 *NZ* (2), *F*, 1968–69 (ST) *I, S*, 1969 *W, SA* (3)
**Bannon, D P** (New South Wales) 1946 *M ,*
**Barker, H S** (New South Wales) 1952 *Fj* (2), *NZ* (2), 1953 *SA*, 1954 *Fj* (2)
**Barnett, J T** (New South Wales) 1907 *NZ* (3), 1908–09 (T), *W, E*
**Barry, M J** (Queensland) 1971 *SA*
**Barton, R F D** (New South Wales) 1899 *BI*
**Batch, P G** (Queensland) 1975–76 (T), *S, W, E*, 1976 *Fj* (3), 1976–77 (ST) *F* (2)
**Batterham, R P** (New South Wales) 1967 *NZ*, 1970 *S*
**Battishall, B R** (New South Wales) 1973–74 (ST) *E*
**Baxter, A J** (New South Wales) 1949 *M* (3), *NZ* (2), 1951 *NZ* (2), 1952 *NZ* (2)
**Baxter, T J** (Queensland) 1958 *NZ*
**Beith, B McN** (New South Wales) 1914 *NZ*
**Bell, K R** (Queensland) 1968–69 (ST) *S*
**Bennett, W G** (Queensland) 1931 *M*, 1933 *SA* (3)
**Bermingham, J V** (Queensland) 1934 *NZ* (2), 1937 *SA*
**Berne, J E** (New South Wales) 1975–76 (T) *S*
**Betts, T N** (Queensland) 1951 *NZ* (2), 1954 *Fj*
**Biilmann, R R** (New South Wales) 1933 *SA* (4)
**Birt, R** (Queensland) 1914 *NZ*
**Blair, M R** (New South Wales) 1931 *M, NZ*
**Bland, G V** (New South Wales) 1932 *NZ* (3), 1933 *SA* (4)
**Blomley, J** (New South Wales) 1949 *M* (3), *NZ* (2), 1950 *BI* (2)
**Boland, S B** (Queensland) 1899 *BI* (2), 1903 *NZ*
**Bonis, E T** (Queensland) 1929 *NZ* (3), 1930 *BI*, 1931 *M, NZ*, 1932 *NZ* (3), 1933 *SA* (5), 1934 *NZ* (2), 1936 *NZ* (2), *M*, 1937 *SA*, 1938 *NZ*
**Bosler, J M** (New South Wales) 1953 *SA*
**Bouffler, R F** (New South Wales) 1899 *BI*
**Bourke, T K** (Queensland) 1947 *NZ*
**Boyce, E S** (New South Wales) 1962 *NZ* (2), 1964 *NZ* (3), 1965 *SA* (2), 1966–67 (T) *W, S, E, I, F*, 1967 *I*
**Boyce, J S** (New South Wales) 1962 *NZ* (3), 1963 *E*, *SA* (4), 1964 *NZ* (2), 1965 *SA* (2)

**Boyd, A** (New South Wales) 1899 *BI*
**Boyd, A F McC** (Queensland) 1958 *M*
**Brass, J E** (New South Wales) 1966 *BI*, 1966–67 (T) *W, S, E, I, F*, 1967 *I, NZ* 1968 *NZ, F*, 1968–69 (ST) *I, S*
**Breckenridge, J W** (New South Wales) 1929 *NZ* (3), 1930 *BI*
**Bridle, O L** (Victoria) 1931 *M*, 1932 *NZ* (3), 1933 *SA* (3), 1934 *NZ* (2), 1936 *NZ* (2), *M*
**Broad, E G** (Queensland) 1949 *M*
**Brockhoff, J D** (New South Wales) 1949 *M (2)*, *NZ* (2), 1950 *BI* (2), 1951 *NZ* (2)
**Brown, B R** (Queensland) 1972 *NZ* (2)
**Brown, J V** (New South Wales) 1956 *SA* (2), 1957 *NZ* (2), 1957–58 (T) *W, I, E, S, F*
**Brown, R C** (New South Wales) 1975 *E* (2)
**Brown, S W** (New South Wales) 1953 *SA* (3)
**Buchan, A J** (New South Wales) 1946 *NZ* (2), 1947 *NZ* (2), 1947–48 (T) *S, I, W, E, F*, 1949 *M*
**Burdon, A** (New South Wales) 1903 *NZ*, 1904 *BI* (2), 1905 *NZ*
**Burge, A B** (New South Wales) 1907 *NZ*, 1908–09 (T) *W*
**Burge, P H** (New South Wales) 1907 *NZ* (3)
**Burke, C T** (New South Wales) 1946 *NZ*, 1947 *NZ* (2), 1947–48 (T), *S, I, W, E, F*, 1949 *M* (2), *NZ* (2), 1950 *BI* (2), 1951 *NZ* (3), 1953 *SA* (3), 1954 *Fj*, 1955 *NZ* (3), 1956 *SA* (2)
**Burnet, D R** (New South Wales) 1972 *F* (2), *NZ* (3), *Fj*
**Butler, O F** (New South Wales) 1969 *SA* (2), 1970 *S*, 1971 *SA* (2), 1971–72 (ST) *F* (2)

**Cameron, A S** (New South Wales) 1951 *NZ* (3), 1952 *Fj* (2), *NZ* (2), 1953 *SA* (4), 1954 *Fj* (2), 1955 *NZ* (3), 1956 *SA* (2), 1957 *NZ*, 1957–58 (T) *I*
**Campbell, J D** (New South Wales) 1910 *NZ* (3)
**Canniffe, W D** (Queensland) 1907 *NZ*
**Carberry, C M** (New South Wales) 1973 *Tg*, 1973–74 (ST) *E*, 1975–76 (T) *I, Am*, 1976 *Fj* (3)
**Cardy, A M** (New South Wales) 1966 *BI* (2), 1966–67 (T) *W, S, E, I, F*, 1968 *NZ* (2)
**Carew, P J** (Queensland) 1899 *BI* (4)
**Carmichael, P P** (Queensland) 1904 *BI*, 1907 *NZ*, 1908–09 (T) *W, E*
**Carpenter, M G** (Victoria) 1938 *NZ* (2)
**Carr, E T A** (New South Wales) 1913 *NZ* (3), 1914 *NZ* (3)
**Carroll, D B** (New South Wales) 1908–09 (T) *W*, 1912 *Am*
**Carroll, J C** (New South Wales) 1953 *SA*
**Carroll, J H** (New South Wales) 1958 *M* (2), *NZ* (3), 1959 *BI* (2)

*Paul McLean of Queensland, a member of the famous Australian rugby family and scorer of the record number of points, 154, by a Wallaby player on tour.*

**Macdougall, S G** (New South Wales and Australian Capital Territory) 1971 *SA*, 1973–74 (ST) *E*, 1974 *NZ* (3), 1975 *E* (2), 1975–76 (T) *E*
**McGhie, G H** (Queensland) 1929 *NZ* (2), 1930 *BI*
**McGill, A N** (New South Wales) 1968 *NZ* (2), *F*, 1969 *W, SA* (4), 1970 *S*, 1971 *SA* (3), 1971–72 (ST) *F* (2), 1972 *F* (2), *NZ* (3), 1973 *Tg* (2)
**McKid, W A** (New South Wales) 1975–76 (T) *E*, 1976 *Fj*
**McKinnon, A** (Queensland) 1904 *BI*
**McKivat, C H** (New South Wales) 1907 *NZ* (2), 1908–09 (T) *W, E*
**McLaughlin, R E M** (New South Wales) 1936 *NZ* (2)
**McLean, A D** (Queensland) 1933 *SA* (5), 1934 *NZ* (2), 1936 *NZ* (2), *M*
**McLean, J D** (Queensland) 1904 *BI* (2), 1905 *NZ*
**McLean, J J** (Queensland) 1971 *SA* (2), 1971–72 (ST) *F* (2), 1972 *F* (2), *NZ* (3), *Fj*, 1973–74 (ST) *W, E*, 1974 *NZ*
**McLean, P E** (Queensland) 1974 *NZ* (3), 1975 *J* (2), 1975–76 (T) *S, W, E, I*, 1976 *Fj* (3), 1976–77 (ST) *F* (2)
**McLean, R A** (New South Wales) 1971 *SA* (3), 1971–72 (ST) *F* (2)
**McLean, W M** (Queensland) 1946 *NZ* (2), *M*, 1947 *NZ* (2)
**McMahon, M J** (Queensland) 1913 *NZ*
**McMaster, R E** (Queensland) 1946 *NZ* (2), *M*, 1947 *NZ* (2), 1947–48 (T) *I, W*
**MacMillan, D I** (Queensland) 1950 *BI* (2)
**McMullen, K V** (New South Wales) 1962 *NZ* (2), 1963 *E, SA*
**McShane, J M S** (New South Wales) 1937 *SA* (2)
**Mackney, W A R** (New South Wales) 1933 *SA* (2), 1934 *NZ* (2)
**Magrath, E** (New South Wales) 1961 *Fj, SA, F*
**Malcolm, S J** (New South Wales) 1929 *NZ* (3), 1930 *BI*, 1931 *NZ*, 1932 *NZ* (3), 1933 *SA* (2), 1934 *NZ* (2)
**Malone, J H** (New South Wales) 1936 *NZ* (2), *M*, 1937 *SA*
**Mandible, E F** (New South Wales) 1907 *NZ* (2), 1908–09 (T) *W*
**Manning, J** (New South Wales) 1904 *BI*
**Manning, R C S** (Queensland) 1967 *NZ*
**Mansfield, B W** (New South Wales) 1975 *J*
**Marks, H** (New South Wales) 1899 *BI* (2)
**Marks, R J P** (Queensland) 1962 *NZ* (2), 1963 *E, SA* (3), 1964 *NZ* (3), 1965 *SA* (2), 1966–67 (T) *W, S, E, I, F*, 1967 *I*

**Marshall, J S** (New South Wales) 1949 *M*
**Massey-Westropp, M** (New South Wales) 1914 *NZ*
**Maund, J W** (New South Wales) 1903 *NZ*
**Meadows, J E C** (Victoria) 1974 *NZ*, 1975–76 (T) *S, W, I, Am*, 1976 *Fj* (2), 1976–77 (ST) *F* (2)
**Meadows, R W** (New South Wales) 1958 *M* (3), *NZ* (3)
**Meibusch, J H** (Queensland) 1904 *BI*
**Meibusch, L S** (Queensland) 1912 *Am*
**Messenger, H H** (New South Wales) 1907 *NZ* (2)
**Middleton, S A** (New South Wales) 1908–09 (T) *E*, 1910 *NZ* (3)
**Miller, A R** (New South Wales) 1952 *Fj* (2), *NZ* (2), 1953 *SA* (4), 1954 *Fj* (2) 1955 *NZ* (3), 1956 *SA* (2), 1957 *NZ* (2), 1957–58 (T) *W, E, S, F*, 1958 *M* (3), 1959 *BI* (2), 1961 *Fj* (3), *SA, F*, 1962 *NZ* (2), 1966 *BI* (2), 1966–67 (T) *W, S, I, F*, 1967 *I, NZ*
**Miller, J M** (New South Wales) 1962 *NZ*, 1963 *E, SA* 1966–67 (T) *W, S, E*
**Miller, S W J** (New South Wales) 1899 *BI*
**Monaghan, L E** (New South Wales) 1973–74 (ST) *E*, 1974 *NZ* (3), 1975 *E* (2), 1975–76 (T) *S, W, E, I, Am*, 1976–77 (ST) *F*
**Monti, C I A** (Queensland) 1938 *NZ*
**Mooney, T P** (Queensland) 1954 *Fj* (2)
**Moran, H M** (New South Wales) 1908–09 (T) *W*
**Morrissey, W** (Queensland) 1914 *NZ*
**Morton, A R** (New South Wales) 1957 *NZ* (2), 1957–58 (T) *F*, 1958 *M* (3), *NZ* (3), 1959 *BI* (2)
**Mossop, R P** (New South Wales) 1949 *NZ* (2), 1950 *BI* (2), 1951 *NZ*
**Moutray, I E** (New South Wales) 1963 *SA*
**Murphy, P J** (Queensland) 1910 *NZ* (3), 1913 *NZ* (3), 1914 *NZ* (3)
**Murphy, W** (Queensland) 1912 *Am*

**Nicholson, F C** (Queensland) 1904 *BI*
**Nicholson, F V** (Queensland) 1903 *NZ*, 1904 *BI*

**O'Brien, F W H** (New South Wales) 1937 *SA*, 1938 *NZ*
**O'Donnell, C** (New South Wales) 1913 *NZ* (2)
**O'Donnell, I C** (New South Wales) 1899 *BI* (2)
**O'Donnell, J M** (New South Wales) 1899 *BI*
**O'Gorman, J F** (New South Wales) 1961 *Fj, SA* (2), *F*, 1962 *NZ*, 1963 *E, SA* (4), 1965 *SA* (2), 1966–67 (T) *W, S, E, I, F*, 1967 *I*
**O'Neill, D J** (Queensland) 1964 *NZ* (2)

O'Neill, J M (Queensland) 1952 NZ (2), 1956 SA (2)
Osborne, D H (Victoria) 1975 E (2), J
Outterside, R (New South Wales) 1959 BI (2)
Oxenham, A McE (Queensland) 1904 BI, 1907 NZ
Oxlade, A M (Queensland) 1904 BI (2), 1905 NZ, 1907 NZ
Oxlade, B D (Queensland) 1938 NZ (3)

Palfreyman, J R L (New South Wales) 1929 NZ, 1930 BI, 1931 NZ, 1932 NZ
Parkinson, C E (Queensland) 1907 NZ
Pashley, J J (New South Wales) 1954 Fj (2), 1958 M (3)
Pauling, T P (New South Wales) 1936 NZ, 1937 SA
Pearse, G K (New South Wales) 1975–76 (T) W (R), I, Am, 1976 Fj (3)
Penman, A P (New South Wales) 1905 NZ
Perrin, P D (Queensland) 1962 NZ
Perrin, T D (New South Wales) 1931 M, NZ
Phelps, R (New South Wales) 1955 NZ (2), 1956 SA (2), 1957 NZ (2), 1957–58 (T) W, I, E, S, F, 1958 M, NZ (3), 1961 Fj (3), SA (2), F, 1962 NZ (2)
Phipps, J A (New South Wales) 1953 SA (4), 1954 Fj (2), 1955 NZ (2), 1956 SA (2)
Phipps, P J (New South Wales) 1955 NZ
Piper, B J C (New South Wales) 1946 NZ (2), M, 1947 NZ, 1947–48 (T) S, I, W, E, F, 1949 M (3)
Potter, R T (Queensland) 1961 Fj
Pope, A M (Queensland) 1968 NZ (R)
Potts, J M (New South Wales) 1957 NZ (2), 1957–58 (T) W, I, 1959 BI
Prentice, C W (New South Wales) 1914 NZ
Prentice, W S (New South Wales) 1908–09 (T) W, E, 1910 NZ (3), 1912 Am
Price, R A (New South Wales) 1974 NZ (3), 1975 E (2), J (2), 1975–76 (T) Am
Primmer, C J (Queensland) 1951 NZ (2)
Procter, I J (New South Wales) 1967 NZ
Prosser, R B (New South Wales) 1966–67 (T) E, I, 1967 I, NZ, 1968 NZ (2), F, 1968–69 (ST) I, S, 1969 W, SA (4), 1971 SA (3), 1971–72 (ST) F (2), 1972 F (2), NZ (3), Fj
Pugh, G H (New South Wales) 1912 Am
Purcell, M P (Queensland) 1966–67 (T) W, S, 1967 I
Purkis, E M (New South Wales) 1957–58 (T) S, 1958 M

Ramalli, C (New South Wales) 1938 NZ (2)
Ramsay, K M (New South Wales) 1936 M, 1937 SA, 1938 NZ (2)
Rankin, R (New South Wales) 1936 NZ (2), M, 1937 SA (2), 1938 NZ (2)
Rathie, D S (Queensland) 1972 F (2)
Redwood, C (Queensland) 1903 NZ, 1904 BI (3)
Reid, T W (New South Wales) 1961 Fj (3), SA, 1962 NZ
Reilly, N P (Queensland) 1968 NZ (2), F, 1968–69 (ST) I, S, 1969 W, SA (4)
Reynolds, L J (New South Wales) 1910 NZ (2[1R])
Richards, E W (Queensland) 1904 BI (2), 1905 NZ, 1907 NZ
Richards, T J (Queensland) 1908–09 (T) W, E, 1912 Am
Richards, V S (New South Wales) 1936 NZ (2[1R]), M, 1937 SA, 1938 NZ
Richardson, G C (Queensland) 1971 SA (3), 1972 NZ (2), Fj, 1973 Tg (2), 1973–74 (ST) W
Riley, S A (New South Wales) 1903 NZ
Roberts, B T (New South Wales) 1956 SA
Roberts, H F (Queensland) 1961 Fj (2), SA, F
Robertson, I J (New South Wales) 1975 J (2)
Rose, H A (New South Wales) 1967 I, NZ, 1968 NZ (2), F, 1968–69 (ST) I, S, 1969 W, SA (4), 1970 S
Rosenblum, R G (New South Wales) 1969 SA (2), 1970 S
Rosewell, J S H (New South Wales) 1907 NZ (2)
Ross, A W (New South Wales) 1929 NZ, 1930 BI, 1931 M, NZ, 1932 NZ (2), 1933 SA, 1934 NZ (2)
Rothwell, P R (New South Wales) 1951 NZ (3), 1952 Fj
Row, F L (New South Wales) 1899 BI (3)
Row, N E (New South Wales) 1907 NZ (2), 1908–09 (T) E, 1910 NZ (3)
Rowles, P G (New South Wales) 1972 Fj, 1973–74 (ST) E

Roxburgh, J R (New South Wales) 1968 NZ (2), F, 1969 W, SA (4), 1970 S
Ruebner, G (New South Wales) 1966 BI (2)
Russell, C J (New South Wales) 1907 NZ (3), 1908–09 (T) W, E
Ryan, J R (New South Wales) 1975 J, 1975–76 (T) I, Am, 1976 Fj (3)
Ryan, K J (Queensland) 1957–58 (T) E, 1958 M, NZ (3)
Ryan, P F (New South Wales) 1963 E, SA 1966 BI (2)

Sampson, J H (New South Wales) 1899 BI
Sayle, J L (New South Wales) 1967 NZ
Schulte, B G (Queensland) 1946 NZ, M
Scott, P R I (New South Wales) 1962 NZ (2)
Shambrook, G G (Queensland) 1976 Fj (2)
Shaw, A A (Queensland) 1973–74 (ST) W, E, 1975 E (2), J, 1975–76 (T) S, W, E, I, Am, 1976 Fj (3), 1976–77 (ST) F (2)
Shaw, G A (New South Wales) 1969 W, SA (R), 1970 S, 1971 SA (3), 1971–72 (ST) F (2), 1973–74 (ST) W, E, 1974 NZ (3), 1975 E (2), J (2), 1975–76 (T) W, E, I, Am, 1976 Fj (3), 1976–77 (ST) F (2)
Shehadie, N M (New South Wales) 1947 NZ, 1947–48 (T) E, F, 1949 M (3), NZ (2), 1950 BI (2), 1951 NZ (3), 1952 Fj (2), NZ, 1953 SA (4), 1954 Fj (2), 1955 NZ (3), 1956 SA (2), 1957 NZ, 1957–58 (T) W, I
Sheil, A G R (Queensland) 1956 SA
Shepherd, D J (Victoria) 1964 NZ, 1965 SA (2), 1966 BI (2)
Simpson, R J (New South Wales) 1913 NZ
Skinner, A J (New South Wales) 1969 W, SA, 1970 S
Slater, S H (New South Wales) 1910 NZ
Smith, F B (New South Wales) 1905 NZ, 1907 NZ (3)
Smith, L M (New South Wales) 1905 NZ
Smith, P V (New South Wales) 1967 NZ, 1968 NZ (2), F, 1968–69 (ST) I, S, 1969 W, SA
Smith, R A (New South Wales) 1971 SA (2), 1972 F (2), NZ (3[1R]), Fj, 1975 E (2), J (2), 1975–76 (T) S, W, E, I, Am, 1976 Fj (3), 1976–77 (ST) F (2)
Solomon, H J (New South Wales) 1949 M, NZ, 1950 BI (2), 1951 NZ (2), 1952 Fj (2), NZ (2), 1953 SA (3), 1955 NZ
Spragg, S A (New South Wales) 1899 BI (4)
Stapleton, E T (New South Wales) 1951 NZ (3), 1952 Fj (2), NZ (2), 1953 SA (4), 1954 Fj, 1955 NZ (3), 1958 NZ
Steggall, J C (Queensland) 1931 M, NZ, 1932 NZ (3), 1933 SA (5)
Stegman, T R (New South Wales) 1973 Tg (2)
Stephens, O G (New South Wales) 1973 Tg (2), 1973–74 (ST) W, 1974 NZ (2)
Stone, A H (New South Wales) 1937 SA, 1938 NZ (2)
Stone, C G (New South Wales) 1938 NZ
Stone, J M (New South Wales) 1946 M, NZ
Storey, G P (New South Wales) 1929 NZ (R), 1930 BI
Storey, K P (New South Wales) 1936 NZ
Storey, N J D (New South Wales) 1962 NZ
Strachan, D J (New South Wales) 1955 NZ (2)
Street, N O (New South Wales) 1899 BI
Stuart, R (New South Wales) 1910 NZ (2)
Stumbles, B D (New South Wales) 1972 NZ (3[1R]), Fj
Sturtridge, G S (Victoria) 1929 NZ, 1932 NZ (3), 1933 SA (5)
Sullivan, P D (New South Wales) 1971 SA (3), 1971–72 (ST) F (2), 1972 F (2), NZ (2), Fj, 1973 Tg (2), 1973–74 (ST) W
Summons, A J (New South Wales) 1957–58 (T) W, I, E, S, 1958 M, NZ (3), 1959 BI (2)
Suttor, D C (New South Wales) 1913 NZ (3)
Swannell, B I (New South Wales) 1905 NZ
Sweeney, T L (Queensland) 1953 SA

Taafe, B S (New South Wales) 1969 SA, 1972 F (2)
Tanner, W H (Queensland) 1899 BI (2)
Tasker, W G (New South Wales) 1913 NZ (3), 1914 NZ (3)
Tate, M J (New South Wales) 1951 NZ, 1952 Fj (2), NZ (2), 1953 SA, 1954 Fj (2)
Taylor, D A (Queensland) 1968 NZ (2), F, 1968–69 (ST) I, S
Taylor, J I (New South Wales) 1971 SA, 1972 F (2), Fj

**Teitzel, R G** (Queensland) 1966–67 (T) *W, S, E, I, F,* 1967 *I, NZ*
**Thompson, E G** (Queensland) 1929 *NZ* (3), 1930 *BI*
**Thompson, F** (New South Wales) 1913 *NZ* (3), 1914 *NZ* (2)
**Thompson, J** (Queensland) 1914 *NZ* (2)
**Thompson, P D** (Queensland) 1950 *BI*
**Thompson, R J** (Western Australia) 1971 *SA,* 1971–72 (ST) *F* (R), 1972 *Fj*
**Thornett, J E** (New South Wales) 1955 *NZ* (3), 1956 *SA* (2), 1957–58 (T) *W, I, S, F,* 1958 *M* (2), *NZ* (2), 1959 *BI* (2), 1961 *Fj* (2), *SA* (2), *F,* 1962 *NZ* (4), 1963 *E, SA* (4), 1964 *NZ* (3), 1965 *SA* (2), 1966 *BI* (2), 1966–67 (T) *F*
**Thornett, R N** (New South Wales) 1961 *Fj* (3), *SA* (2), *F,* 1962 *NZ* (5)
**Thorpe, A C** (New South Wales) 1929 *NZ* (R)
**Timbury, F R V** (Queensland) 1910 *NZ* (2)
**Tindall, E N** (New South Wales) 1973 *Tg*
**Tolhurst, H A** (New South Wales) 1931 *M, NZ*
**Tonkin, A E J** (New South Wales) 1947–48 (T) *S, I, W, E, F,* 1950 *BI*
**Tooth, R M** (New South Wales) 1951 *NZ* (3), 1954 *Fj* (2), 1955 *NZ* (3), 1957 *NZ* (2)
**Towers, C H T** (New South Wales) 1929 *NZ* (2), 1930 *BI,* 1931 *M, NZ,* 1934 *NZ* (2), 1937 *SA* (2)
**Trivett, R K** (Queensland) 1966 *BI* (2)
**Turnbull, A** (Victoria) 1961 *Fj*
**Turnbull, R V** (New South Wales) 1968–69 (ST) *I*
**Tweedale, E** (New South Wales) 1946 *NZ* (2), 1947 *NZ,* 1947–48 (T) *S, I, E, F,* 1949 *M* (3)

**Vaughan, G N** (Victoria) 1957–58 (T) *E, S, F,* 1958 *M* (3)
**Verge, A** (New South Wales) 1904 *BI* (2)

**Walden, R J** (New South Wales) 1934 *NZ,* 1936 *NZ* (2), *M*
**Walker, A K** (New South Wales) 1947 *NZ,* 1947–48 (T) *E, F,* 1950 *BI* (2)
**Walker, A S B** (New South Wales) 1912 *Am*
**Wallach, C** (New South Wales) 1913 *NZ* (2), 1914 *NZ* (3)
**Walsh, J J** (New South Wales) 1953 *SA* (4)
**Walsh, P B** (New South Wales) 1904 *BI* (3)
**Walsham, K P** (New South Wales) 1962 *NZ,* 1963 *E*

**Ward, P G** (New South Wales) 1899 *BI* (4)
**Ward, T** (Queensland) 1899 *BI*
**Watson, G W** (Queensland) 1907 *NZ*
**Watson, W T** (New South Wales) 1912 *Am,* 1913 *NZ* (3), 1914 *NZ*
**Weatherstone, L J** (Australian Capital Territory) 1975 *E* (2), *J* (2), 1975–76 (T) *S* (R), *E, I*
**Webb, W** (New South Wales) 1899 *BI* (2)
**Wells, B G** (New South Wales) 1958 *M*
**Westfield, R E** (New South Wales) 1929 *NZ* (2)
**White, C J B** (New South Wales) 1899 *BI,* 1903 *NZ,* 1904 *BI*
**White, J M** (New South Wales) 1904 *BI*
**White, J P L** (New South Wales) 1958 *NZ* (3), 1961 *Fj* (3), *SA* (2), *F,* 1962 *NZ* (5), 1963 *E, SA* (4), 1964 *NZ* (3), 1965 *SA* (2)
**White, M C** (Queensland) 1931 *M, NZ,* 1932 *NZ* (2), 1933 *SA* (5)
**White, S W** (New South Wales) 1956 *SA* (2), 1957–58 (T) *I, E, S,* 1958 *M* (2)
**White, W G S** (Queensland) 1933 *SA* (5), 1934 *NZ* (2), 1936 *NZ* (2), *M*
**White, W J** (New South Wales) 1932 *NZ*
**Wickham, S M** (New South Wales) 1903 *NZ,* 1904 *BI* (3), 1905 *NZ*
**Williams, D** (Queensland) 1913 *NZ,* 1914 *NZ* (3)
**Williams, J L** (New South Wales) 1963 *SA* (3)
**Wilson, B J** (New South Wales) 1949 *NZ* (2)
**Wilson, C R** (Queensland) 1957 *NZ,* 1958 *NZ* (3)
**Wilson, V W** (Queensland) 1937 *SA* (2), 1938 *NZ* (3)
**Windon, C J** (New South Wales) 1946 *NZ* (2), 1947 *NZ,* 1947–48 (T) *S, I, W, E, F,* 1949 *M* (3), *NZ* (2), 1951 *NZ* (3), 1952 *Fj* (2), *NZ* (2)
**Windon, K S** (New South Wales) 1937 *SA* (2), 1946 *M*
**Windsor, J C** (Queensland) 1947 *NZ*
**Winning, K C** (Queensland) 1951 *NZ*
**Wogan, L W** (New South Wales) 1913 *NZ* (3), 1914 *NZ* (3)
**Wood, F** (New South Wales) 1907 *NZ* (3), 1910 *NZ* (3), 1913 *NZ* (3), 1914 *NZ* (3)
**Wood, R N** (Queensland) 1972 *Fj*
**Wright, K J** (New South Wales) 1975 *E* (2), *J,* 1975–76 (T) *Am,* 1976–77 (ST) *F* (2)

**Yanz, K** (New South Wales) 1957–58 (T) *F*

# AUSTRALIAN INTERNATIONAL RECORDS

*From 1890–91, when uniform points-scoring was first adopted by International Board countries, to 30 April 1978, except in the case of matches against British Isles. These date from 1910, when British Isles teams first became officially representative of the Four Home Unions. Both team and individual records are against International Board countries and British Isles only, unless otherwise stated.*

## TEAM RECORDS
### Highest score
30 v England (30–21) 1975 Brisbane
*v individual countries*
30 v England (30–21) 1975 Brisbane
23 v Scotland (23–3) 1970 Sydney
20 v Ireland (20–10) 1976 Dublin
16 v Wales (16–19) 1969 Sydney
15 v France $\left\{ \begin{array}{l} (15–16) \text{ 1972 Brisbane} \\ (15–18) \text{ 1976 Bordeaux} \end{array} \right.$
25 v N Zealand (25–11) 1934 Sydney
21 v S Africa (21–6) 1933 Durban
 8 v B Isles (8–11) 1966 Sydney

### Biggest winning points margin
20 v Scotland (23–3) 1970 Sydney
*v individual countries*
12 v England (23–11) 1967 Twickenham
20 v Scotland (23–3) 1970 Sydney
13 v Ireland (16–3) 1947 Dublin
 3 v Wales (14–11) 1966 Cardiff
 2 v France (13–11) 1971 Toulouse
15 v N Zealand (20–5) 1964 Wellington
15 v S Africa (21–6) 1933 Durban
 1 v B Isles (6–5) 1930 Sydney

### Highest score by opposing team
38 $\left\{ \begin{array}{l} \text{N Zealand (13–38) 1936 Dunedin} \\ \text{N Zealand (3–38) 1972 Auckland} \end{array} \right.$
*by individual countries*
23 England (6–23) 1976 Twickenham
12 Scotland (8–12) 1958 Murrayfield
15 Ireland (8–15) 1967 Dublin
28 Wales (3–28) 1975 Cardiff
34 France (6–34) 1976 Paris (Parc des Princes)
38 $\left\{ \begin{array}{l} \text{N Zealand (13–38) 1936 Dunedin} \\ \text{N Zealand (3–38) 1972 Auckland} \end{array} \right.$
30 S Africa (11–30) 1969 Johannesburg
31 B Isles (0–31) 1966 Brisbane

### Biggest losing points margin
35 v N Zealand (3–38) 1972 Auckland
*v individual countries*
17 v England $\left\{ \begin{array}{l} (3–20) \text{ 1973 Twickenham} \\ (6–23) \text{ 1976 Twickenham} \end{array} \right.$
 7 v Scotland (3–10) 1975 Murrayfield
 7 v Ireland $\left\{ \begin{array}{l} (8–15) \text{ 1967 Dublin} \\ (3–10) \text{ 1968 Dublin} \end{array} \right.$
25 v Wales (3–28) 1975 Cardiff
28 v France (6–34) 1976 Parc des Princes
35 v N Zealand (3–38) 1972 Auckland
25 v S Africa (3–28) 1961 Johannesburg
31 v B Isles (0–31) 1966 Brisbane

### Most tries by Australia in an international
 6 v Scotland (23–3) 1970 Sydney

### Most tries against Australia in an international
8 by South Africa (3–28) 1961 Johannesburg

### Most points on overseas tour (all matches)
500 in B Isles/France (35 matches) 1947–48

### Most tries on overseas tour (all matches)
115 in B Isles/France (35 matches) 1947–48

## INDIVIDUAL RECORDS
### Most capped players
P G Johnson   39   1959–71
G V Davis   39   1963–72

252

*in individual positions*
*Full-back*
A N McGill   19   1968–72
*Wing*
J W Cole   22   1968–74
*Centre*
G A Shaw   20   1969–76
*Fly-half*
P F Hawthorne   21   1962–67
*Scrum-half*
J N B Hipwell   26   1968–76
*Prop*
R B Prosser   24   1967–72
*Hooker*
P G Johnson   39   1959–71
*Lock*
A R Miller   19(31)†   1952–67
*Flanker*
G V Davis   39   1963–72
*No 8*
J F O'Gorman   13(17)‡   1961–67

†*Miller won 12 caps as a prop*
‡*O'Gorman won 4 caps as a flanker*

**Most points in internationals – 65**
A N McGill (19 appearances)* 1968–72

*excludes 2 appearances against Tonga*

**Most points in an international – 15**
A N McGill v N Zealand 1968 Brisbane
R L Fairfax v France 1972 Brisbane
P E McLean v France 1976 Bordeaux

**Most tries in internationals – 7**
C J Windon (15 appearances)* 1946–52
*excludes 5 appearances against Maoris and Fiji*

**Most points on overseas tour – 154**
P E McLean (18 appearances) B Isles
1975–76

**Most tries on overseas tour – 23**
C J Russell B Isles 1908–09

**Most points in international series on tour – 28**
P F Hawthorne (4 appearances) 1966–67
B Isles/France

**Most points in any match on tour – 23**
J C Hindmarsh v Glamorgan 1975 Neath

**Most tries in any match on tour – 6**
J S Boyce v Wairarapa (NZ) 1962
Masterton

*Terry Cobner, of Pontypool and Wales, caught with his pants nearly, but not quite, down. He was one of the 15 Lions who gave such a scintillating display for an International Invitation XV against Moseley in the Sam Doble Memorial Match at The Reddings.*

# LEADING CAP WINNERS

*(up to 30 April 1978)*

## ENGLAND

| | |
|---|---|
| J V Pullin | 42 |
| D J Duckham | 36 |
| D P Rogers | 34 |
| A Neary | 34 |
| W W Wakefield | 31 |
| E Evans | 30 |
| R Cove-Smith | 29 |
| C R Jacobs | 29 |
| M P Weston | 29 |
| J Butterfield | 28 |
| A T Voyce | 27 |
| J S Tucker | 27 |
| C N Lowe | 25 |
| J D Currie | 25 |
| M S Phillips | 25 |
| C B Stevens | 25 |
| F E Cotton | 25 |
| R E G Jeeps | 24 |
| P J Larter | 24 |
| A G Ripley | 24 |
| P J Squires | 24 |
| J MacG K Kendall-Carpenter | 23 |
| R W D Marques | 23 |
| W J A Davies | 22 |
| P E Judd | 22 |
| C W Ralston | 22 |
| J G G Birkett | 21 |
| H G Periton | 21 |
| P J Dixon | 21 |
| P B Jackson | 20 |

## SCOTLAND

| | |
|---|---|
| A B Carmichael | 50 |
| A F McHarg | 41 |
| H F McLeod | 40 |
| D M D Rollo | 40 |
| J MacD Bannerman | 37 |
| J McLauchlan | 37 |
| A R Smith | 33 |
| I S Smith | 32 |
| F A L Laidlaw | 32 |
| N S Bruce | 31 |
| I H P Laughland | 31 |
| G L Brown | 30 |
| W I D Elliot | 29 |
| W M Simmers | 28 |
| P K Stagg | 28 |
| J W Y Kemp | 27 |
| K J F Scotland | 27 |
| P C Brown | 27 |
| A R Irvine | 27 |
| I R McGeechan | 27 |
| D Drysdale | 26 |
| J C McCallum | 26 |
| G P S Macpherson | 26 |
| W E Maclagan | 25 |
| J B Nelson | 25 |
| J P Fisher | 25 |
| J W Telfer | 25 |
| J M Renwick | 25 |
| G D Stevenson | 24 |
| M C Morrison | 23 |
| J A Beattie | 23 |
| M J Campbell-Lamerton | 23 |
| J N M Frame | 23 |
| W C C Steele | 23 |
| D R Bedell-Sivright | 22 |
| A Robson | 22 |
| S Wilson | 22 |
| R J Arneil | 22 |
| R G MacMillan | 21 |
| W P Scott | 21 |
| W E Kyle | 21 |
| J M B Scott | 21 |
| J R Paterson | 21 |
| W B Welsh | 21 |
| P W Kininmonth | 21 |

| | |
|---|---|
| A J W Hinshelwood | 21 |
| D W Morgan | 21 |
| C Reid | 20 |
| D S Davies | 20 |
| J C Dykes | 20 |
| W R Logan | 20 |
| J C Dawson | 20 |
| J T Greenwood | 20 |
| J W C Turner | 20 |
| N A MacEwan | 20 |

## IRELAND

| | |
|---|---|
| C M H Gibson | 65 |
| W J McBride | 63 |
| T J Kiernan | 54 |
| J W Kyle | 46 |
| K W Kennedy | 45 |
| G V Stephenson | 42 |
| N A A Murphy | 41 |
| N J Henderson | 40 |
| R J McLoughlin | 40 |
| S Millar | 37 |
| J R Kavanagh | 35 |
| W A Mulcahy | 35 |
| E O'D Davy | 34 |
| J F Slattery | 34 |
| A C Pedlow | 30 |
| G T Hamlet | 30 |
| W E Crawford | 30 |
| J D Clinch | 30 |
| J L Farrell | 29 |
| B G M Wood | 29 |
| A J F O'Reilly | 29 |
| M Sugden | 28 |
| J S McCarthy | 28 |
| L M Magee | 27 |
| A R Dawson | 27 |
| M G Molloy | 27 |
| R M Young | 26 |
| G R Beamish | 25 |
| K D Mullen | 25 |
| J C Walsh | 25 |
| R P K Bresnihan | 25 |
| A T A Duggan | 25 |
| B J McGann | 25 |

| | |
|---|---|
| T O Grace | 25 |
| S A McKinney | 25 |
| J A E Siggins | 24 |
| M I Keane | 24 |
| A Tedford | 23 |
| J W McKay | 23 |
| J J Moloney | 23 |
| F Gardiner | 22 |
| J A O'Meara | 22 |
| A A Mulligan | 22 |
| M K Flynn | 22 |
| A H Ensor | 22 |
| C E Allen | 21 |
| R Roe | 21 |
| P O'Callaghan | 21 |
| J C Parke | 20 |
| J McVicker | 20 |
| C J Hanrahan | 20 |
| D J O'Brien | 20 |
| N H Brophy | 20 |
| M G Doyle | 20 |

## WALES

| | |
|---|---|
| G O Edwards | 53 |
| J P R Williams | 45 |
| K J Jones | 44 |
| T G R Davies | 44 |
| T M Davies | 38 |
| D Williams | 36 |
| R M Owen | 35 |
| B V Meredith | 34 |
| D I E Bebb | 34 |
| W D Morris | 34 |
| W J Bancroft | 33 |
| B Price | 32 |
| J R G Stephens | 32 |
| W J Trew | 29 |
| C I Morgan | 29 |
| P Bennett | 29 |
| A J Gould | 27 |
| W C Powell | 27 |
| M C Thomas | 27 |
| H J Morgan | 27 |
| R C C Thomas | 26 |
| A E I Pask | 26 |

256

| | |
|---|---|
| S J Watkins | 26 |
| J Taylor | 26 |
| G Travers | 25 |
| H Tanner | 25 |
| B John | 25 |
| N R Gale | 25 |
| W D Thomas | 25 |
| E Gwyn Nicholls | 24 |
| R T Gabe | 24 |
| D J Lloyd | 24 |
| J J Hodges | 23 |
| E C Davey | 23 |
| J A Gwilliam | 23 |
| R H Williams | 23 |
| J Young | 23 |
| J J Williams | 23 |
| T R Prosser | 22 |
| B L Williams | 22 |
| W O G Williams | 22 |
| S J Dawes | 22 |
| R W Windsor | 22 |
| T J Davies | 21 |
| E M Jenkins | 21 |
| B Thomas | 21 |
| W R Willis | 21 |
| D Watkins | 21 |
| W Llewellyn | 20 |
| A F Harding | 20 |
| J Webb | 20 |
| A Skym | 20 |
| A J Martin | 20 |

## FRANCE

*NB Matches against International Board countries only*

| | |
|---|---|
| B Dauga | 50 |
| M Crauste | 43 |
| W Spanghero | 42 |
| J-P Lux | 40 |
| J Prat | 38 |
| R Bertranne | 37 |
| M Celaya | 35 |
| A Boniface | 34 |
| A Domenech | 34 |
| J-C Skréla | 34 |

| | |
|---|---|
| G Dufau | 33 |
| M Vannier | 30 |
| E Cester | 30 |
| P Villepreux | 29 |
| C Darrouy | 28 |
| J Dupuy | 28 |
| C Dourthe | 28 |
| J Iraçabal | 28 |
| A Cassayet | 27 |
| J Bouquet | 27 |
| G Basquet | 26 |
| A Jauréguy | 25 |
| R Biénès | 25 |
| E Ribère | 25 |
| M Prat | 25 |
| L Mias | 25 |
| J Gachassin | 25 |
| J-P Bastiat | 25 |
| P Albaladejo | 24 |
| C Lacaze | 24 |
| R Bénésis | 24 |
| J Trillo | 24 |
| A Roques | 23 |
| G Boniface | 23 |
| C Carrère | 23 |
| M Pomathios | 22 |
| J-P Romeu | 22 |
| M Communeau | 21 |
| F Moncla | 21 |
| J-L Azarète | 21 |
| G Cholley | 21 |
| B Chevallier | 20 |
| P Lacroix | 20 |
| C Spanghero | 20 |
| J-M Aguirre | 20 |
| A Paco | 20 |

## SOUTH AFRICA

| | |
|---|---|
| F C H Du Preez | 38 |
| J H Ellis | 38 |
| J F K Marais | 35 |
| J P Engelbrecht | 33 |
| J L Gainsford | 33 |
| J T Claassen | 28 |

| | |
|---|---|
| F du T Roux | 27 |
| L G Wilson | 27 |
| T P Bedford | 25 |
| D J de Villiers | 25 |
| P J F Greyling | 25 |
| S H Nomis | 25 |
| P J Visagie | 25 |
| D J Hopwood | 22 |
| A C Koch | 22 |
| J A du Rand | 21 |

## NEW ZEALAND

| | |
|---|---|
| C E Meads | 55 |
| I A Kirkpatrick | 39 |
| K R Tremain | 38 |
| W J Whineray | 32 |
| D B Clarke | 31 |
| B G Williams | 31 |
| S M Going | 29 |
| R W Norton | 27 |
| B J Lochore | 25 |
| B E McLeod | 24 |
| K F Gray | 24 |
| I J Clarke | 24 |
| R A White | 23 |
| D J Graham | 22 |
| D Young | 22 |
| K L Skinner | 20 |

| | |
|---|---|
| C R Laidlaw | 20 |
| I N MacEwan | 20 |
| P J Whiting | 20 |
| B J Robertson | 20 |

## AUSTRALIA

| | |
|---|---|
| P G Johnson | 42 |
| A R Miller | 41 |
| G V Davis | 39 |
| J E Thornett | 37 |
| N M Shehadie | 30 |
| J N B Hipwell | 28 |
| K W Catchpole | 27 |
| C T Burke | 26 |
| G A Shaw | 26 |
| R B Prosser | 25 |
| J K Lenehan | 24 |
| J P L White | 24 |
| J W Cole | 24 |
| R Phelps | 23 |
| R A Smith | 22 |
| E T Bonis | 21 |
| P F Hawthorne | 21 |
| R J Heming | 21 |
| A N McGill | 21 |
| A S Cameron | 20 |
| B J Ellwood | 20 |
| C J Windon | 20 |

## WORLD'S LEADING CAP–WINNERS
*(up to 30 April 1978)*

For purposes of comparison, the following list includes only caps won for individual countries against the International Board countries and the British Isles, and in special centenary or celebration matches. Where additional caps have been given for other matches, the player's total number of caps is shown in brackets.

| | | | | |
|---|---|---|---|---|
| C M H Gibson (Ireland) | 65 | | J W Kyle (Ireland) | 46 |
| W J McBride (Ireland) | 63 | | K W Kennedy (Ireland) | 45 |
| C E Meads (New Zealand) | 55 | | J P R Williams (Wales) | 45 |
| T J Kiernan (Ireland) | 54 | | K J Jones (Wales) | 44 |
| G O Edwards (Wales) | 53 | | T G R Davies (Wales) | 44 |
| B Dauga (France) | 50 (63) | | M Crauste (France) | 43 (62) |
| A B Carmichael (Scotland) | 50 | | W Spanghero (France) | 42 (51) |

| | | | |
|---|---|---|---|
| **J V Pullin** (England) | 42 | **H F McLeod** (Scotland) | 40 |
| **G V Stephenson** (Ireland) | 41 (42) | **D M D Rollo** (Scotland) | 40 |
| **N A A Murphy** (Ireland) | 41 | **R J McLoughlin** (Ireland) | 40 |
| **A F McHarg** (Scotland) | 41 | **J-P Lux** (France) | 40 (47) |
| **N J Henderson** (Ireland) | 40 | | |

258

Australia's leading cap–winners, on the same basis, are P G Johnson 39 (42) and G V Davis 39. A R Miller has 41 Australian caps, but only 31 against the International Board countries and the British Isles.

The following list incorporates appearances by home countries' players for British Isles teams (the Lions) in international matches against New Zealand, Australia, and South Africa (*up to 30 April 1978*). The number of Lions' appearances is shown in brackets.

| | | | |
|---|---|---|---|
| **W J McBride** (Ireland) | 80 (17) | **H F McLeod** (Scotland) | 46 (6) |
| **C M H Gibson** (Ireland) | 77 (12) | **T M Davies** (Wales) | 46 (8) |
| **G O Edwards** (Wales) | 63 (10) | **J McLauchlan** (Scotland) | 45 (8) |
| **T J Kiernan** (Ireland) | 59 (5) | **M Crauste** (France) | 43 |
| **C E Meads** (New Zealand) | 55 | **R J McLoughlin** (Ireland) | 43 (3) |
| **J P R Williams** (Wales) | 53 (8) | **B V Meredith** (Wales) | 42 (8) |
| **J W Kyle** (Ireland) | 52 (6) | **D I E Bebb** (Wales) | 42 (8) |
| **B Dauga** (France) | 50 | **W Spanghero** (France) | 42 |
| **A B Carmichael** (Scotland) | 50 | **G V Stephenson** (Ireland) | 41 |
| **N A A Murphy** (Ireland) | 49 (8) | **N J Henderson** (Ireland) | 41 (1) |
| **K W Kennedy** (Ireland) | 49 (4) | **W A Mulcahy** (Ireland) | 41 (6) |
| **J V Pullin** (England) | 49 (7) | **D Williams** (Wales) | 41 (5) |
| **T G R Davies** (Wales) | 49 (5) | **A F McHarg** (Scotland) | 41 |
| **K J Jones** (Wales) | 47 (3) | **D M D Rollo** (Scotland) | 40 |
| **S Millar** (Ireland) | 46 (9) | **J-P Lux** (France) | 40 |

Most appearances for the Lions are by W J McBride, 17, R E G Jeeps (England) 13, C M H Gibson 12, and A J F O'Reilly (Ireland), R H Williams (Wales), and G O Edwards 10 each, up to 30 April 1978.

# INTERNATIONAL REFEREES AND OFFICIALS 1977–78

*(up to 30 April 1978, in matches between International Board countries, v British Isles and in special centenary or celebration matches for which caps were awarded)*

## Leading Referees
*10 or more Internationals*

| | | | | | |
|---|---|---|---|---|---|
| **K D Kelleher** | Ireland | 21 | **J P Murphy** | N Zealand | 13 |
| **D G Walters** | Wales | 21 | **T H Vile** | Wales | 12 |
| **R C Williams** | Ireland | 20 | **M A Allan** | Scotland | 11 |
| **M Joseph** | Wales | 19 | **A I Dickie** | Scotland | 11 |
| **M J Dowling** | Ireland | 18 | **N H Lambert** | Ireland | 11 |
| **B S Cumberlege** | England | 16 | **R F Johnson** | England | 11 |
| **A E Freethy** | Wales | 16 | **T N Pearce** | England | 10 |
| **I David** | Wales | 14 | **Air Cdre G C Lamb** | England | 10 |
| **D P D'Arcy** | Ireland | 14 | **Dr I R Vanderfield** | Australia | 10 |
| **C H Gadney** | England | 13 | **N R Sanson** | Scotland | 10 |

## Referees – International Match Appearances 1977–78
*Figures in brackets indicate number of games controlled*

**England**
P E Hughes (1), A Welsby (1)
**Scotland**
N R Sanson (2)
**Ireland**
J R West (3)
**Wales**
C G P Thomas (3)

**France**
G Domercq (1), F Palmade (1)
**New Zealand**
P A McDavitt (1), B Duffy (1), D H Millar (2)
**South Africa**
G P Bezuidenhout (1)
**Australia**

## Rugby Union Officials 1977–78

**ENGLAND**
President **Sir Anthony Wharton CBE**
Hon Treasurer **B F Boyden**
Secretary
**Air Cdre R H G Weighill CBE DFC**

**SCOTLAND**
President **Brig F H Coutts CBE**
Sec/Treasurer **J Law OBE**

**IRELAND**
President **J F Coffey**
Hon Treasurer **J E Nelson**
Sec/Treasurer **R FitzGerald**

**WALES**
President **T Rowley Jones**
Hon Treasurer **K M Harris CBE**
Secretary **W H Clement MC**

**FRANCE**
President **A J R Ferrasse**
Treasurer General **A Cazaux**
Secretary **J-C Bourrier**

**SOUTH AFRICA**
President **Dr D H Craven**
Sec/Treasurer **A Kellermann**

**NEW ZEALAND**
President **J G Galvin**
Chairman **C A Blazey OBE**
Sec/Treasurer **J M Jeffs**

**AUSTRALIA**
President **R E M McLaughlin MBE**
Hon Treasurer **L J Howard**
Secretary **J D Dedrick**

# INTERNATIONAL REFEREES
## (from the 1919–20 season onwards, up to 30 April 1978)

*Details of the Northern Hemisphere referees were initially supplied by Mr C H Gadney, to whom we owe our thanks. The list is confined to matches between the International Board countries, v British Isles and to special centenary or celebration matches for which caps were awarded. Where referees have officiated at five or more international matches the totals are shown in brackets.*

### ABBREVIATIONS

| | | | |
|---|---|---|---|
| A | Australia | S | Scotland |
| BI | British Isles | SA | South Africa |
| E | England | W | Wales |
| F | France | Wld | World Invitation XV |
| I | Ireland | (C) | Centenary |
| NZ | New Zealand | (R) | Replacement |

*Pres XV* President's XV

**Ackermann, C J** (South Africa) 1953 *SA v A* (2), 1955 *SA v BI*, 1958 *SA v F*
**Acton, W H** (Ireland) 1926 *W v E, E v S*
**Allan, M A** (Scotland) 1931 *I v W, I v SA*, 1933 *E v I, I v W*, 1934 *I v E*, 1935 *E v I, I v W*, 1936 *I v E*, 1937 *I v W*, 1947 *I v E*, 1948 *I v W* **(11)**
**Anderson, C** (Scotland) 1928 *I v F*
**Angus, A W** (Scotland) 1924 *W v E*
**Austin, A W C** (Scotland) 1952 *W v F*, 1953 *I v E*, 1954 *I v W*
**Austry, R** (France) 1972 *E v I*

**Baise, M** (South Africa) 1967 *SA v F* (2), 1968 *SA v BI* (2), 1969 *SA v A*, 1974 *SA v BI* (2) **(7)**
**Baise, S** (South Africa) 1969 *SA v A*
**Barnes, P** (Australia) 1938 *A v NZ*
**Baxter, J** (England) 1920 *S v I*, 1921 *W v S, I v S*, 1923 *W v S*, 1925 *W v S, I v W* **(6)**
**Bean, A S** (England) 1939 *W v S*, 1947 *F v W, W v A*, 1948 *S v F, W v F*, 1949 *F v S, S v I* **(7)**
**Beattie, R A** (Scotland) 1937 *E v W*, 1938 *W v E*, 1947 *W v E, I v A*, 1948 *I v W*, 1949 *I v E*, 1950 *E v I, I v W* **(8)**
**Bell, T** (Ireland) 1932 *S v W*, 1933 *E v W*
**Bezuidenhout, G P** (South Africa) 1976 *SA v NZ* (3), 1977 *SA v Wld*
**Bott, J G** (England) 1931 *W v S*, 1933 *W v S*
**Boundy, L M** (England) 1955 *S v I*, 1956 *W v S*, 1957 *F v S, I v F, S v I*, 1958 *S v F*, 1959 *S v I, S v SA* **(8)**
**Brook, P G** (England) 1963 *F v W*, 1964 *W v S*, 1965 *W v I, I v SA*, 1966 *F v I* **(5)**
**Brown, D A** (England) 1960 *I v W*
**Brunton, J** (England) 1924 *W v NZ*
**Burmeister, R D** (South Africa) 1949 *SA v NZ* (2), 1953 *SA v A*, 1955 *SA v BI* (2), 1960 *SA v NZ* (2), 1961 *SA v A* **(8)**
**Burnett, D I H** (Ireland) 1977 *W v E*
**Burnett, R T** (Australia) 1974 *A v NZ*, 1975 *A v E*
**Burnett, W** (Scotland) 1932 *I v E*, 1934 *W v I*
**Burrell, G** (Scotland) 1958 *E v I*, 1959 *W v I*
**Burrell, R P** (Scotland) 1966 *I v W*, 1967 *I v F, F v NZ*, 1969 *I v E, F v W* **(5)**

**Calitz, M** (South Africa) 1961 *SA v I*
**Calmet, R** (France) 1970 *E v W*
**Carlson, K R V** (South Africa) 1962 *SA v BI*
**Chapman, W S** (Australia) 1938 *A v NZ* (2)
**Clark, K H** (Ireland) 1973 *E v F*, 1974 *S v F*, 1976 *F v E*

**Cooney, R C** (Australia) 1929 *A v NZ*, 1930 *A v BI*, 1932 *A v NZ*, 1934 *A v NZ*
**Cooney, W M** (Australia) 1972 *A v F*, 1975 *A v E*
**Cooper, Dr P F** (England) 1952 *I v W*, 1953 *S v W, W v I, W v NZ*, 1954 *I v NZ, W v S*, 1956 *F v I, W v F*, 1957 *F v W* **(9)**
**Craven, W S D** (England) 1920 *F v W*
**Crawford, S H** (Ireland) 1920 *S v W*, 1921 *S v E*
**Crowe, K J** (Australia) 1965 *A v SA*, 1966 *A v BI*, 1968 *A v NZ*
**Cumberlege, B S** (England) 1926 *S v I, W v I*, 1927 *S v F, I v S, I v W*, 1928 *S v I*, 1929 *F v I, S v F, I v S*, 1930 *I v F, S v I*, 1931 *I v S*, 1932 *S v SA, S v I*, 1933 *I v S*, 1934 *S v I* **(16)**
**Cunningham, J G** (Scotland) 1921 *F v I*
**Cuny, Dr A** (France) 1976 *W v S*

**D'Arcy, D P** (Ireland) 1967 *E v F, E v S,* F v W, 1968 *E v W,* S v E, *F v SA*, 1969 *E v F, W v E*, 1970 *W v S*, 1971 *W v E*, 1973 *F v NZ, F v W*, 1975 *E v S, W v A* **(14)**
**David, I** (Wales) 1938 *E v S*, 1939 *S v E*, 1947 *E v S*, 1952 *S v F, I v S, E v I*, 1953 *S v I*, 1954 *S v F, E v NZ, S v NZ, F v NZ, F v E*, 1955 *I v F*, 1956 *F v E* **(14)**
**Day, H L V** (England) 1934 *S v W*
**De Bruyn, C J** (South Africa) 1969 *SA v A*, 1974 *SA v BI* (2)
**Dickie, A I** (Scotland) 1954 *F v I, E v I, W v F*, 1955 *I v E, W v I*, 1956 *E v I, I v W*, 1957 *W v E, I v E*, 1958 *W v A, W v F* **(11)**
**Domercq, G** (France) 1972 *S v NZ*, 1973 *W v E*, 1976 *E v W*, 1977 *S v W*, 1978 *I v W* **(5)**
**Donaldson, S** (Ireland) 1937 *S v E*
**Doocey, T F** (New Zealand) 1976 *NZ v I*
**Dowling, M J** (Ireland) 1947 *S v W*, 1950 *W v S, S v E, W v F*, 1951 *W v E, S v W, F v W, E v S, S v SA*, 1952 *W v S, F v SA, S v E*, 1953 *W v E, E v S*, 1954 *E v W*, 1955 *S v W*, 1956 *S v F, S v E* **(18)**
**Duffy, B** (New Zealand) 1977 *NZ v BI*
**Durand, C** (France) 1969 *E v S*, 1970 *I v S*, 1971 *E v S*

**Elliott, H B** (England) 1955 *F v S*, 1956 *I v S*
**Engelbrecht, Dr G K** (South Africa) 1964 *SA v W*
**Evans, W J** (Wales) 1958 *F v E, I v A*

**Farquhar, A B** (New Zealand) 1961 *NZ v F* (3), 1962 *NZ v A* (2), 1964 *NZ v A* **(6)**
**Faull, J W** (Wales) 1936 *S v I, E v NZ*, 1937 *E v I*

**Pretorius, N F** (South Africa) 1938 *SA v BI*
**Price, F G** (Wales) 1963 *I v F*
**Priest, T E** (England) 1953 *I v F*
**Pring, J P G** (New Zealand) 1966 *NZ v BI*, 1967 *NZ v A*, 1968 *NZ v F*, 1971 *NZ v BI* (4), 1972 *NZ v A* **(8)**
**Purcell, N** (Ireland) 1927 *S v E*

**Reilly, J R** (Australia) 1972 *A v F*
**Robbertse, P** (South Africa) 1967 *SA v F*, 1969 *SA v A*, 1970 *SA v NZ* (2)
**Roberts, E** (Wales) 1924 *F v S*
**Roberts, R A** (England) 1924 *F v W*
**Robertson, W A** (Scotland) 1920 *I v E, E v F*
**Robson, C F** New Zealand) 1963 *NZ v E*
**Royds, P M R** (England) 1921 *W v F*, 1923 *F v I*

**St Guilhem, J** (France) 1974 *S v E*, 1975 *W v I*
**Sanson, N R** (Scotland) 1974 *W v F, F v SA*, 1975 *I v Pres XV* (C), *SA v F* (2), 1976 *I v A, I v W*, 1977 *W v I*, 1978 *F v E, E v W* **(10)**
**Schoeman, J P J** (South Africa) 1968 *SA v BI*
**Schofield, T D** (Wales) 1920 *E v S*, 1921 *E v I*, 1922 *S v I*
**Scott, J M B** (Scotland) 1923 *E v W*
**Scott, R L** (Scotland) 1927 *F v I, E v W*
**Slabber, M J** (South Africa) 1955 *A v BI*, 1960 *SA v NZ*
**Strasheim, Dr E A** (South Africa) 1958 *SA v F*, 1960 *SA v S, SA v NZ*, 1962 *SA v BI* (2), 1964 *SA v F*, 1967 *SA v F*, 1968 *SA v BI* **(8)**
**Strasheim, Dr J J** (South Africa) 1938 *SA v BI*
**Sturrock, J C** (Scotland) 1921 *E v W, F v E*, 1922 *W v I*
**Sullivan, G** (New Zealand) 1950 *NZ v BI*
**Sutherland, F E** (New Zealand) 1930 *NZ v BI*

**Taylor, A R** (New Zealand) 1965 *NZ v SA* (R), 1972 *NZ v A*
**Taylor, J A S** (Scotland) 1957 *W v I*, 1960 *E v W, F v E, W v SA*, 1962 *E v W, F v I, I v W* **(7)**
**Tennant, J M** (Scotland) 1920 *I v F*, 1921 *I v W*, 1922 *W v E, E v F, I v F, I v E*, 1923 *I v W* **(7)**
**Thomas, C G P** (Wales) 1977 *F v NZ*, 1978 *S v F, F v I*

**Tierney, A T** (Australia) 1957 *A v NZ*, 1959 *A v BI*
**Tindill, E W T** (New Zealand) 1950 *NZ v BI* (2), 1955 *NZ v A*
**Titcomb, M H** (England) 1966 *W v S*, 1967 *W v I, W v NZ*, 1968 *I v W, S v A*, 1971 *S v W, E v Pres XV* (C), 1972 *W v F* **(8)**
**Tolhurst, H A** (Australia) 1951 *A v NZ* (2)
**Tomalin, L C** (Australia) 1947 *A v NZ*, 1950 *A v BI*
**Treharne, G J** (Wales) 1960 *I v SA*, 1961 *E v SA, I v E, I v F*, 1963 *S v I* **(5)**
**Tulloch, J L** (Scotland) 1920 *W v E*, 1924 *W v I*

**Vanderfield, Dr I R** (Australia) 1956 *A v SA*, 1961 *A v F*, 1962 *A v NZ*, 1966 *A v BI*, 1967 *A v I*, 1968 *A v NZ*, 1970 *A v S*, 1971 *A v SA*, 1974 *A v NZ* (2) **(10)**
**Van der Horst, A W** (South Africa) 1933 *SA v A*
**Vile, T H** (Wales) 1923 *S v F, E v I, I v S, S v E, F v E*, 1924 *I v E, S v I, E v S*, 1925 *E v I*, 1927 *E v I*, 1928 *E v S*, 1931 *F v I* **(12)**

**Walsh, L** (New Zealand) 1949 *NZ v A*
**Walters, D G** (Wales) 1959 *F v S, I v E, E v S, I v F*, 1960 *S v F, E v I, I v S, F v I*, 1961 *F v SA, E v F*, 1962 *E v I, F v E*, 1963 *E v S*, 1964 *E v I, F v E, F v I*, 1965 *I v F, S v I, E v S, S v SA*, 1966 *F v E* **(21)**
**Warren, T H H** (Scotland) 1928 *W v I*
**Welsby, A** (England) 1976 *F v I*, 1978 *W v F*
**West, J R** (Ireland) 1974 *E v W*, 1975 *S v W*, 1976 *W v F*, 1977 *F v NZ*, 1978 *W v S, S v E* **(6)**
**Wheeler, Dr E de C** (Ireland) 1925 *S v F*
**Wheeler, Dr J R** (Ireland) 1929 *S v E*, 1930 *S v W*, 1931 *E v W, S v E*, 1932 *E v S*, 1933 *S v E* **(6)**
**Whittaker, J B G** (England) 1947 *I v F, W v I*
**Wilkins, H E B** (England) 1925 *F v NZ*, 1929 *W v F*
**Williams, R C** (Ireland) 1957 *S v W, E v F*, 1958 *E v W, E v A, S v A, S v E*, 1959 *W v E, S v W, E v F*, 1960 *S v E*, 1961 *F v S, S v W*, 1962 *S v F*, 1963 *F v S, S v W, W v NZ*, 1964 *S v F, S v NZ, F v NZ, S v E* **(20)**
**Wolstenholme, B H** (New Zealand) 1955 *NZ v A*
**Woolley, A** (South Africa) 1970 *SA v NZ*

**Young, J** (Scotland) 1971 *F v W*, 1972 *E v W*, 1973 *E v NZ*

262

# INTERNATIONAL MATCH APPEARANCES FOR BRITISH ISLES TEAMS (*up to 30 April 1978*)

*From 1910 onwards, when British Isles teams first became officially representative of the Four Home Unions.*

## ABBREVIATIONS

| | |
|---|---|
| *A* | Australia |
| *NZ* | New Zealand |
| *SA* | South Africa |
| (R) | Replacement (2 [1R]) denotes two appearances, one of them as a replacement |

## CLUB ABBREVIATIONS

| | |
|---|---|
| NIFC | North of Ireland Football Club |
| CIYMS | Church of Ireland Young Men's Society |

**Aarvold, C D** (Cambridge U, Blackheath and England) 1930 *NZ* (4), *A*
**Alexander, R** (NIFC and Ireland) 1938 *SA* (3)
**Arneil, R J** (Edinburgh Acads and Scotland) 1968 *SA* (4)
**Ashcroft, A** (Waterloo and England) 1959 *A*, *NZ*

**Baker, D G S** (Old Merchant Taylors and England) 1955 *SA* (2)
**Bassett, J** (Penarth and Wales) 1930 *NZ* (4), *A*
**Beamish, G R** (Leicester, RAF and Ireland) 1930 *NZ* (4), *A*
**Beaumont, W B** (Fylde and England) 1977 *NZ* (3)
**Bebb, D I E** (Swansea and Wales) 1962 *SA* (2), 1966 *A* (2), *NZ* (4)
**Bennett, P** (Llanelli and Wales) 1974 *SA* (4), 1977 *NZ* (4)
**Bevan, J C** (Cardiff Coll of Ed, Cardiff and Wales) 1971 *NZ*
**Black, A W** (Edinburgh U and Scotland) 1950 *NZ* (2)
**Black, B H** (Oxford U, Blackheath and England) 1930 *NZ* (4), *A*
**Blakiston, A F** (Northampton and England) 1924 *SA* (4)
**Bowcott, H M** (Cambridge U, Cardiff and Wales) 1930 *NZ* (4), *A*
**Boyle, C V** (Dublin U and Ireland) 1938 *SA* (2)
**Brand, T N** (NIFC and Ireland) 1924 *SA* (2)
**Bresnihan, F P K** (UC Dublin and Ireland) 1968 *SA* (3)
**Brophy, N H** (UC Dublin and Ireland) 1962 *SA* (2)
**Brown, G L** (W of Scotland and Scotland) 1971 *NZ* (2), 1974 *SA* (3), 1977 *NZ* (3)
**Budge, G M** (Edinburgh Wands and Scotland) 1950 *NZ*
**Burcher, D H** (Newport and Wales) 1977 *NZ*
**Butterfield, J** (Northampton and England) 1955 *SA* (4)

**Cameron, A** (Glasgow HSFP and Scotland) 1955 *SA* (2)
**Campbell-Lamerton, M J** (Halifax, Army and Scotland) 1962 *SA* (4), 1966 *A* (2), *NZ* (2)
**Cleaver, W B** (Cardiff and Wales) 1950 *NZ* (3)
**Clifford, T** (Young Munster and Ireland) 1950 *NZ* (3), *A* (2)
**Cobner, T J** (Pontypool and Wales) 1977 *NZ* (2)
**Connell, G C** (Trinity Acads and Scotland) 1968 *SA*
**Cotton, F E** (Loughborough Colls, Coventry, and England) 1974 *SA* (4), 1977 *NZ* (3)
**Coulman, M J** (Moseley and England) 1968 *SA*
**Cove-Smith, R** (Old Merchant Taylors and England) 1924 *SA* (4)
**Cowan, R C** (Selkirk and Scotland) 1962 *SA*
**Cromey, G E** (Queen's U, Belfast and Ireland) 1938 *SA*

**Cunningham, W A** (Lansdowne and Ireland) 1924 *SA*
**Dancer, G T** (Bedford) 1938 *SA* (3)
**Davies, C** (Cardiff and Wales) 1950 *NZ*

**Davies, D M** (Somerset Police and Wales) 1950 *NZ* (2), *A*
**Davies, D S** (Hawick and Scotland) 1924 *SA* (4)
**Davies, H J** (Newport and Wales) 1924 *SA*
**Davies, T G R** (Cardiff, London Welsh and Wales) 1968 *SA*, 1971 *NZ* (4)
**Davies, T J** (Llanelli and Wales) 1959 *NZ* (2)
**Davies, T M** (London Welsh, Swansea and Wales) 1971 *NZ* (4), 1974 *SA* (4)
**Davies, W P C** (Harlequins and England) 1955 *SA* (3)
**Dawes, S J** (London Welsh and Wales) 1971 *NZ* (4)
**Dawson, A R** (Wanderers and Ireland) 1959 *A* (2), *NZ* (4)
**Dixon, P J** (Harlequins and England) 1971 *NZ* (3)
**Doyle, M G** (Blackrock Coll and Ireland) 1968 *SA*
**Drysdale, D** (Heriot's FP and Scotland) 1924 *SA* (4)
**Duckham, D J** (Coventry and England) 1971 *NZ* (3)
**Duggan, W P** (Blackrock Coll and Ireland) 1977 *NZ* (4)
**Duff, P L** (Glasgow Acads and Scotland) 1938 *SA* (2)

**Edwards, G O** (Cardiff and Wales) 1968 *SA* (2), 1971 *NZ* (4), 1974 *SA* (4)
**Evans, G L** (Newport and Wales) 1977 *NZ* (3)
**Evans, R T** (Newport and Wales) 1950 *NZ* (4), *A* (2)
**Evans, T P** (Swansea and Wales) 1977 *NZ*
**Evans, W R** (Cardiff and Wales) 1959 *A*, *NZ* (3)

**Farrell, J L** (Bective Rangers and Ireland) 1930 *NZ* (4), *A*
**Faull, J** (Swansea and Wales) 1959 *A*, *NZ* (3)
**Fenwick, S P** (Bridgend and Wales) 1977 *NZ* (4)
**Foster, A R** (Queen's Univ, Belfast and Ireland) 1910 *SA* (3)

**Gibson, C M H** (Cambridge U, NIFC and Ireland) 1966 *NZ* (4), 1968 *SA* (4[1R]), 1971 *NZ* (4)
**Giles, J L** (Coventry and England) 1938 *SA* (2)
**Graves, C R A** (Wanderers and Ireland) 1938 *SA* (2)
**Greenwood, J T** (Dunfermline and Scotland) 1955 *SA* (4)
**Grieve, C F** (Oxford U and Scotland) 1938 *SA* (2)
**Griffiths, G M** (Cardiff and Wales) 1955 *SA* (3)
**Griffiths, V M** (Newport and Wales) 1924 *SA* (2)

**Handford, F G** (Manchester and England) 1910 *SA* (3)
**Harding, W Rowe** (Cambridge U, Swansea and Wales) 1924 *SA* (3)
**Harris, S W** (Blackheath and England) 1924 *SA* (2)
**Hayward, D J** (Newbridge and Wales) 1950 *NZ* (3)
**Henderson, N J** (Queen's U, Belfast, NIFC and Ireland) 1950 *NZ*
**Henderson, R G** (Northern and Scotland) 1924 *SA* (2)
**Hendrie, K G P** (Heriot's FP and Scotland) 1924 *SA*
**Hewitt, D** (Queen's U, Belfast, Instonians and Ireland) 1959 *A* (2), *NZ* (3), 1962 *SA*
**Higgins, R** (Liverpool and England) 1955 *SA*
**Hinshelwood, A J W** (London Scottish and Scotland) 1966 *NZ* (2), 1968 *SA*
**Hodgson, J McD** (Northern and England) 1930 *NZ* (2)

**Hopkins, R** (Maesteg and Wales) 1971 *NZ* (R)
**Horrocks-Taylor, J P** (Leicester and England) 1959 *NZ*
**Horton, A L** (Blackheath and England) 1968 *SA* (3)
**Howard, W G** (Old Birkonians) 1938 *SA*
**Howie, R A** (Kirkcaldy and Scotland) 1924 *SA* (4)

**Irvine, A R** (Heriot's FP and Scotland) 1974 *SA* (2), 1977 *NZ* (4)
**Isherwood, G A M** (Old Alleynians and Sale) 1910 *SA* (3)

**Jackson, P B** (Coventry and England) 1959 *A* (2), *NZ* (3)
**Jarman, H** (Newport and Wales) 1910 *SA* (3)
**Jeeps, R E G** (Northampton and England) 1955 *SA* (4), 1959 *A* (2), *NZ* (3), 1962 *SA* (4)
**Jenkins, V G J** (Oxford U, London Welsh and Wales) 1938 *SA*
**John, B** (Cardiff and Wales) 1968 *SA*, 1971 *NZ* (4)
**John, E R** (Neath and Wales) 1950 *NZ* (4), *A* (2)
**Jones, B L** (Llanelli and Wales) 1950 *NZ*, *A* (2)
**Jones, D K** (Llanelli, Cardiff, and Wales) 1962 *SA* (3), 1966 *A* (2), *NZ*
**Jones, E L** (Llanelli and Wales) 1938 *SA* (2)
**Jones, Ivor** (Llanelli and Wales) 1930 *NZ* (4), *A*
**Jones, K D** (Cardiff and Wales) 1962 *SA* (4)
**Jones, K J** (Newport and Wales) 1950 *NZ* (2)
**Jones, J P** (Pontypool, Newport and Wales) 1910 *SA* (3)

**Keane, M I** (Lansdowne and Ireland) 1977 *NZ*
**Kennedy, K W** (CIYMS, London Irish and Ireland) 1966 *A* (2), *NZ* (2)
**Kiernan, T J** (Cork Const and Ireland) 1962 *SA*, 1968 *SA* (4)
**Kinnear, R M** (Heriot's FP and Scotland) 1924 *SA* (4)
**Kininmonth, P W** (Oxford U, Richmond and Scotland) 1950 *NZ* (3)
**Kyle, J W** (Queen's U Belfast, NIFC and Ireland) 1950 *NZ* (4), *A* (2)

**Laidlaw, F A L** (Melrose and Scotland) 1966 *NZ* (2)
**Lamont, R A** (Instonians and Ireland) 1966 *NZ* (4)
**Lane, M F** (UC Cork and Ireland) 1950 *NZ*, *A*
**Larter, P J** (Northampton, RAF and England) 1968 *SA*
**Lewis, A R** (Abertillery and Wales) 1966 *NZ* (3)
**Lynch, J F** (St Mary's Coll and Ireland) 1971 *NZ* (4)

**McBride, W J** (Ballymena and Ireland) 1962 *SA* (2), 1966 *NZ* (3), 1968 *SA* (4), 1971 *NZ* (4), 1974 *SA* (4)
**Macdonald, R** (Edinburgh U and Scotland) 1950 *NZ*, *A*
**McFadyean, C W** (Moseley and England) 1966 *NZ* (4)
**McGeechan, I R** (Headingley and Scotland) 1974 *SA* (4), 1977 *NZ* (4 [1R])
**McKay, J W** (Queen's U, Belfast and Ireland) 1950 *NZ* (4), *A* (2)
**McKibbin, H R** (Queen's U, Belfast and Ireland) 1938 *SA* (3)
**McLauchlan, J** (Jordanhill and Scotland) 1971 *NZ* (4), 1974 *SA* (4)
**McLeod, H F** (Hawick and Scotland) 1959 *A* (2), *NZ* (4)
**McLoughlin, R J** (Gosforth, Blackrock Coll and Ireland) 1966 *A* (2), *NZ*
**Macpherson, N C** (Newport and Scotland) 1924 *SA* (4)
**Macrae, D J** (St Andrew's U and Scotland) 1938 *SA*
**McVicker, J** (Collegians and Ireland) 1924 *SA* (3)
**Martindale, S A** (Kendal and England) 1930 *A*
**Marsden-Jones, D** (London Welsh and Wales) 1924 *SA* (2)
**Marques, R W D** (Harlequins and England) 1959 *A*, *NZ*
**Martin, A J** (Aberavon and Wales) 1977 *NZ*
**Matthews, J** (Cardiff and Wales) 1950 *NZ* (4), *A* (2)
**Maxwell, R B** (Birkenhead Park) 1924 *SA*
**Mayne, R B** (Queen's U, Belfast and Ireland) 1938 *SA* (3)
**Meredith, B V** (Newport and Wales) 1955 *SA* (4), 1962 *SA* (4)
**Meredith, C C** (Neath and Wales) 1955 *SA* (4)

**Millar, S** (Ballymena and Ireland) 1959 *A* (2), *NZ*, 1962 *SA* (4), 1968 *SA* (2)
**Milliken, R A** (Bangor and Ireland) 1974 *SA* (4)
**Morgan, C I** (Cardiff and Wales) 1955 *SA* (4)
**Morgan, D W** (Stewart's Melville FP and Scotland) 1977 *NZ* (2 [1R])
**Morgan, G J** (Clontarf and Ireland) 1938 *SA*
**Morgan, H J** (Abertillery and Wales) 1959 *NZ* (2), 1962 *SA* (4)
**Morgan, M E** (Swansea and Wales) 1938 *SA* (2)
**Morley, J C** (Newport and Wales) 1930 *NZ* (3)
**Mulcahy, W A** (UC Dublin and Ireland) 1959 *A*, *NZ*, 1962 *SA* (4)
**Mullen, K D** (Old Belvedere and Ireland) 1950 *NZ* (2), *A*
**Mulligan, A A** (Wanderers, London Irish and Ireland) 1959 *NZ*
**Murphy, N A A** (Cork Const and Ireland) 1959 *A*, *NZ* (3), 1966 *A* (2), *NZ* (2)
**Murray, P F** (Wanderers and Ireland) 1930 *NZ* (3), *A*

**Neale, M E** (Bristol) 1910 *SA* (3)
**Neary, A** (Broughton Park and England) 1977 *NZ*
**Nelson, J E** (Malone and Ireland) 1950 *NZ* (2), *A* (2)
**Nicholson, B E** (Harlequins and England) 1938 *SA*
**Norris, C H** (Cardiff and Wales) 1966 *NZ* (3)
**Novis, A L** (Blackheath and England) 1930 *NZ* (2), *A*

**O'Neill, H O'H** (Queen's U, Belfast and Ireland) 1930 *NZ* (4), *A*
**O'Reilly, A J F** (Old Belvedere and Ireland) 1955 *SA* (4), 1959 *A* (2), *NZ* (4)
**Orr, P A** (Old Wesley and Ireland) 1977 *NZ*
**O'Shea, J P** (Cardiff and Wales) 1968 *SA*

**Parker, D** (Swansea and Wales) 1930 *NZ* (4), *A*
**Pask, A E I** (Abertillery and Wales) 1962 *SA* (3), 1966 *A* (2), *NZ* (3)
**Patterson, W M** (Sale and England) 1959 *NZ*
**Pedlow, A C** (CIYMS and Ireland) 1955 *SA* (2)
**Pillman, C H** (Blackheath and England) 1910 *SA* (2)
**Piper, O J S** (Cork Const and Ireland) 1910 *SA*
**Poole, H** (Cardiff) 1930 *NZ*
**Preece, I** (Coventry and England) 1950 *NZ*
**Prentice, F D** (Leicester and England) 1930 *NZ*, *A*
**Price, B** (Newport and Wales) 1966 *A* (2), *NZ* (2)
**Price, G** (Pontypool and Wales) 1977 *NZ* (4)
**Price, M J** (Pontypool and Wales) 1959 *A* (2), *NZ* (3)
**Prosser, T R** (Pontypool and Wales) 1959 *NZ*
**Pullin, J V** (Bristol and England) 1968 *SA* (3), 1971 *NZ* (4)

**Quinnell, D L** (Llanelli and Wales) 1971 *NZ*, 1977 *NZ* (2)

**Ralston, C W** (Richmond and England) 1974 *SA*
**Rees, H E** (Neath and Wales 'B') 1977 *NZ*
**Reeve, J S R** (Harlequins and England) 1930 *NZ* (3), *A*
**Reid, T E** (Garryowen and Ireland) 1955 *SA* (2)
**Rew, H** (Blackheath, Army and England) 1930 *NZ* (4)
**Reynolds, F J** (Old Cranleighans and England) 1938 *SA* (2)
**Richards, M C R** (Cardiff and Wales) 1968 *SA* (3)
**Richards, T J** (Bristol) 1910 *SA* (3)
**Rimmer, G** (Waterloo and England) 1950 *NZ*
**Risman, A B W** (Loughborough Colls and England) 1959 *A* (2), *NZ* (2)
**Robins, J D** (Birkenhead Park and Wales) 1950 *NZ* (3), *A* (2)
**Robins, R J** (Pontypridd and Wales) 1955 *SA* (4)
**Rogers, D P** (Bedford and England) 1962 *SA* (2)
**Rowlands, K A** (Cardiff and Wales) 1962 *SA* (3)
**Rutherford, D** (Gloucester and England) 1966 *A*

**Savage, K F** (Northampton and England) 1968 *SA* (4)
**Scotland, K J F** (Cambridge U, Heriot's FP and Scotland) 1959 *A* (2), *NZ* (3)
**Sharp, R A W** (Oxford U, Redruth and England) 1962 *SA* (2)
**Slattery, J F** (Blackrock Coll and Ireland) 1974 *SA* (4)
**Smith, A R** (Edinburgh Wands, London Scottish and Scotland) 1962 *SA* (3)
**Smith, D F** (Richmond and England) 1910 *SA* (3)
**Smith, D W C** (London Scottish and Scotland) 1950 *A*

**Smith, G K** (Kelso and Scotland) 1959 *A* (2), *NZ* (2)
**Smith, I S** (Oxford U, London Scottish and Scotland) 1924 *SA* (2)
**Smyth, T** (Malone, Newport and Ireland) 1910 *SA* (2)
**Spong, R S** (Old Millhillians and England) 1930 *NZ* (4), *A*
**Spoors, J A** (Bristol) 1910 *SA* (3)
**Squire, J** (Newport and Wales) 1977 *NZ*
**Squires, P J** (Harrogate and England) 1977 *NZ*
**Stagg, P K** (Oxford U, Sale and Scotland) 1968 *SA* (3)
**Steele, W C C** (Bedford, RAF and Scotland) 1974 *SA* (2)
**Stephens, J R G** (Neath and Wales) 1950 *A* (2)
**Stevenson, R C** (St Andrew's Univ and Scotland) 1910 *SA* (3)

**Tanner, H** (Swansea and Wales) 1938 *SA*
**Taylor, A R** (Cross Keys and Wales) 1938 *SA* (2)
**Taylor, J** (London Welsh and Wales) 1971 *NZ* (4)
**Taylor, R B** (Northampton and England) 1968 *SA* (4)
**Telfer, J W** (Melrose and Scotland) 1966 *A* (2), *NZ* (3), 1968 *SA* (3)
**Thomas, M C** (Newport and Wales) 1950 *NZ* (2), *A*, 1959 *NZ*
**Thomas, R C C** (Swansea and Wales) 1955 *SA* (2)
**Thomas, W D** (Llanelli and Wales) 1966 *NZ* (2), 1968 *SA* (2[1R]), 1971 *NZ* (2)
**Thompson, R H** (Instonians, London Irish and Ireland) 1955 *SA* (3)
**Travers, W H** (Newport and Wales) 1938 *SA* (2)
**Turner, J W C** (Gala and Scotland) 1968 *SA* (4)

**Unwin, E J** (Rosslyn Park, Army and England) 1938 *SA* (2)
**Uttley, R M** (Gosforth and England) 1974 *SA* (4)

**Voyce, A T** (Gloucester and England) 1924 *SA* (2)

**Waddell, G H** (Cambridge U, London Scottish and Scotland) 1962 *SA* (2)
**Waddell, H** (Glasgow Acads and Scotland) 1924 *SA* (3)

**Walker, S** (Instonians and Ireland) 1938 *SA* (3)
**Wallace, W** (Percy Park) 1924 *SA*
**Waller, P D** (Newport and Wales) 1910 *SA* (3)
**Waters, J A** (Selkirk and Scotland) 1938 *SA*
**Watkins, D** (Newport and Wales) 1966 *A* (2), *NZ* (4)
**Watkins, S J** (Newport and Wales) 1966 *A* (2), *NZ*
**Webb, J** (Abertillery and Wales) 1910 *SA* (3)
**Welsh, W B** (Hawick and Scotland) 1930 *NZ*
**Weston, M P** (Richmond, Durham City and England) 1962 *SA* (4), 1966 *A* (2)
**Wheeler, P J** (Leicester and England) 1977 *NZ* (3)
**Whitley, H** (Northern and England) 1924 *SA* (3) ·
**Willcox, J G** (Oxford U, Harlequins and England) 1962 *SA* (3)
**Williams, B L** (Cardiff and Wales) 1950 *A* (2), *NZ* (3)
**Williams, D** (Ebbw Vale and Wales) 1966 *A* (2), *NZ* (3)
**Williams, D B** (Cardiff and Wales 'B') 1977 *NZ* (3)
**Williams, J J** (Llanelli and Wales) 1974 *SA* (4), 1977 *NZ* (3)
**Williams, J P R** (London Welsh and Wales) 1971 *NZ* (4), 1974 *SA* (4)
**Williams, R H** (Llanelli and Wales) 1955 *SA* (4), 1959 *A* (2), *NZ* (4)
**Williams, S H** (Newport and England) 1910 *SA* (3)
**Williams, W O G** (Swansea and Wales) 1955 *SA* (4)
**Willis, W R** (Cardiff and Wales) 1950 *NZ*, *A* (2)
**Windsor, R W** (Pontypool and Wales) 1974 *SA* (4), 1977 *NZ*
**Wilson, S** (London Scottish and Scotland)) 1966 *A*, *NZ* (4)
**Wood, B G M** (Garryowen and Ireland) 1959 *NZ* (2)
**Wood, K B** (Leicester) 1910 *SA*

**Young, A T** (Cambridge U, Blackheath and England) 1924 *SA*
**Young, J** (Harrogate, RAF and Wales) 1968 *SA*
**Young, J R C** (Oxford U, Harlequins and England) 1959 *NZ*
**Young, R M** (Queen's U, Belfast, Collegians and Ireland) 1966 *A* (2), *NZ*, 1968 *SA*

# RESULTS OF BRITISH ISLES MATCHES
## (up to 30 April 1978)

*From 1910 onwards – the tour to South Africa in that year was the first fully representative one in which the Four Home Unions cooperated.*

## v SOUTH AFRICA

**Played 26   British Isles won 7, South Africa won 15,  Drawn 4**

1910 *1* Johannesburg
**South Africa** 1G 3T (14)
to 1DG 2T (10)

*2* Port Elizabeth
**British Isles** 1G 1T (8) to 1Г (3)

*3* Cape Town
**South Africa** 3G 1PG 1T (21) to 1G (5)
*South Africa won series 2–1*

1924 *1* Durban
**South Africa** 1DG 1T (7) to 1T (3)

*2* Johannesburg
**South Africa** 1G 1PG 3T (17) to 0

*3* Port Elizabeth
**Drawn** 1T (3) each

*4* Cape Town
**South Africa** 1DG 4T (16)
to 1PG 2T (9)
*South Africa won series 3–0, with 1 draw*

1938 *1* Johannesburg
**South Africa** 4G 2PG (26)
to 4PG (12)

*2* Port Elizabeth
**South Africa** 2G 2PG 1T (19)
to 1T (3)

*3* Cape Town
**British Isles** 1G 1PG 1DG 3T (21)
to 2G 1PG 1T (16)
*South Africa won series 2–1*

1955 *1* Johannesburg
**British Isles** 4G 1T (23) to 2G 2PG 2T (22)

*2* Cape Town
**South Africa** 2G 5T (25)
to 1PG 2T (9)

*3* Pretoria
**British Isles** 1PG 1DG 1T (9)
to 2PG (6)

*4* Port Elizabeth
**South Africa** 2G 1DG 3T (22)
to 1G 1T (8)
*Series drawn 2–2*

1962 *1* Johannesburg
**Drawn** 1T (3) each

*2* Durban
**South Africa** 1PG (3) to 0

*3* Cape Town
**South Africa** 1G 1PG (8) to 1DG (3)

*4* Bloemfontein
**South Africa** 5G 2PG 1T (34)
to 1G 1PG 2T (14)
*South Africa won series 3–0, with 1 draw*

1968 *1* Pretoria
**South Africa** 2G 4PG 1T (25)
to 1G 5PG (20)

*2* Port Elizabeth
**Drawn** 2PG (6) each

*3* Cape Town
**South Africa** 1G 2PG (11) to 2PG (6)

*4* Johannesburg
**South Africa** 2G 1DG 2T (19) to 2PG (6)
*South Africa won series 3–0, with 1 draw*

1974 *1* Cape Town
**British Isles** 3PG 1DG (12) to 1DG (3)

*2* Pretoria
**British Isles** 1G 1PG 1DG 4T (28) to 2PG 1DG (9)

*3* Port Elizabeth
**British Isles** 1G 2PG 2DG 2T (26)
to 3PG (9)

*4* Johannesburg
**Drawn** British Isles 1G 1PG 1T (13)
South Africa 3PG 1T (13)
*British Isles won series 3–0, with 1 draw*

## v NEW ZEALAND
**Played 24   British Isles won 5, New Zealand won 17,  Drawn 2**

1930 *1* Dunedin
**British Isles** 2T (6) to 1T (3)

*2* Christchurch
**New Zealand** 2G 1GM (13) to 2G (10)

*3* Auckland
**New Zealand** 1G 1DG 2T (15)
to 2G (10)

*4* Wellington
**New Zealand** 2G 4T (22)
to 1G 1PG (8)
*New Zealand won series 3–1*

1950 *1* Dunedin
**Drawn** 2T 1PG (9) each

*2* Christchurch
**New Zealand** 1G 1T (8) to 0

*3* Wellington
**New Zealand** 1PG 1T (6) to 1PG (3)

*4* Auckland
**New Zealand** 1G 1DG 1T (11)
to 1G 1PG (8)
*New Zealand won series 3–0, with 1 draw*

1959 *1* Dunedin
**New Zealand** 6PG (18)
to 1G 1PG 3T (17)

*2* Wellington
**New Zealand** 1G 2T (11)
to 1G 1PG (8)

*3* Christchurch
**New Zealand** 2G 1PG 1DG 2T (22)
to 1G 1PG (8)

*4* Auckland
**British Isles** 3T (9) to 2PG (6)
*New Zealand won series 3–1*

1966 *1* Dunedin
**New Zealand** 1G 2PG 1DG 2T (20)
to 1PG (3)

*2* Wellington
**New Zealand** 2G 1PG 1T (16)
to 3PG 1DG (12)

*3* Christchurch
**New Zealand** 2G 2PG 1T (19)
to 2T (6)

*4* Auckland
**New Zealand** 3G 1PG 1DG 1T (24)
to 1G 1PG 1T (11)
*New Zealand won series 4–0*

1971 *1* Dunedin
**British Isles** 2PG 1T (9) to 1PG (3)

*2* Christchurch
**New Zealand** 2G 1PG 3T (22)
to 1PG 1DG 2T (12)

*3* Wellington
**British Isles** 2G 1DG (13) to 1T (3)

*4* Auckland
**Drawn** British Isles 1G 2PG 1DG (14)
New Zealand 1G 2PG 1T (14)
*British Isles won series 2–1, with 1 draw*

1977 *1* Wellington
**New Zealand** 2G 1T (16) to 4PG (12)

*2* Christchurch
**British Isles** 3PG 1T (13) to 3PG (9)

*3* Dunedin
**New Zealand** 1G 2PG 1DG 1T (19)
to 1PG 1T (7)

*4* Auckland
**New Zealand** 2PG 1T (10)
to 1G 1PG (9)
*New Zealand won series 3–1*

## v AUSTRALIA

**Played 7   British Isles won 6, Australia won 1, Drawn 0**

1930 Sydney
**Australia** 2T (6) to 1G (5)

1950 *1* Brisbane
**British Isles** 2G 2PG 1DG (19)
to 2PG (6)

*2* Sydney
**British Isles** 3G 1PG 2T (24) to 1T (3)
*British Isles won series 2–0*

1959 *1* Brisbane
**British Isles** 1G 2PG 1DG 1T (17)
to 2PG (6)

*2* Sydney
**British Isles** 3G 1PG 2T (24) to 1PG (3)
*British Isles won series 2–0*

1966 *1* Sydney
**British Isles** 1G 1PG 1T (11) to 1G 1PG (8)

*2* Brisbane
**British Isles** 5G 1PG 1DG (31) to 0
*British Isles won series 2–0*

267

# BRITISH ISLES RECORDS
*(up to 30 April 1978)*

*From 1910 onwards – the tour to South Africa in that year was the first fully representative one in which the Four Home Unions cooperated.*

## TEAM RECORDS

**Highest score**
31 v Australia (31–0) 1966 Brisbane
*v individual countries*
28 v S Africa (28–9) 1974 Pretoria

17 v N Zealand (17–18) 1959 Dunedin
31 v Australia (31–0) 1966 Brisbane

**Biggest winning points margin**
31 v Australia (31–0) 1966 Brisbane
*v individual countries*
19 v S Africa (28–9) 1974 Pretoria
10 v N Zealand (13–3) 1971 Wellington
31 v Australia (31–0) 1966 Brisbane

**Highest score by opposing team**
34 S Africa (14–34) 1962 Bloemfontein
*by individual countries*
34 S Africa (14–34) 1962 Bloemfontein
24 N Zealand (11–24) 1966 Auckland
 8 Australia (11–8) 1966 Sydney

**Biggest losing points margin**
20 v S Africa (14–34) 1962 Bloemfontein
*v individual countries*
20 v S Africa (14–34) 1962 Bloemfontein
17 v N Zealand (3–20) 1966 Dunedin
 1 v Australia (5–6) 1930 Sydney

**Most tries by B Isles in an international**
| | v Australia (24–3) 1950 Sydney |
| | v S Africa (23–22) 1955 Johannesburg |
| 5 | v Australia (24–3) 1959 Sydney |
| | v Australia (31–0) 1966 Brisbane |
| | v S Africa (28–9) 1974 Pretoria |

**Most tries against B Isles in an international**
7 by S Africa (9–25) 1955 Cape Town

**Most points on overseas tour (all matches)**
842 In Australia, New Zealand and
 Canada (33 matches) 1959
(includes 582 points in 25 matches in
New Zealand)

**Most tries on overseas tour (all matches)**
165 In Australia, New Zealand and
 Canada (33 matches) 1959
(includes 113 tries in 25 matches in New
Zealand)

# INDIVIDUAL RECORDS

**Most capped player**
W J McBride   17   1962–74

**Most points in internationals – 44**
P Bennett (8 appearances) 1974–77

**Most points in an international – 17**
T J Kiernan v S Africa 1968 Pretoria

**Most tries in internationals – 6**
A J F O'Reilly (10 appearances) 1955–59

**Most tries in an international – 2**
C D Aarvold v N Zealand 1930
 Christchurch
J E Nelson v Australia 1950 Sydney
M J Price v Australia 1959 Sydney
M J Price v N Zealand 1959 Dunedin
D K Jones v Australia 1966 Brisbane
T G R Davies v N Zealand 1971
 Christchurch
J J Williams v S Africa 1974 Pretoria
J J Williams v S Africa 1974 Port
 Elizabeth

**Most points for B Isles on overseas tour – 188**
B John (17 appearances) 1971 Australia /
 N Zealand
(includes 180 points in 16 appearances
in N Zealand)

**Most tries for B Isles on overseas tour – 22***
A J F O'Reilly (23 appearances) 1959
 Australia/N Zealand/Canada
(includes 17* tries in 17 appearances in
N Zealand)
*\* Includes one penalty try*

**Most points for B Isles in international series – 35**
T J Kiernan (4 appearances) 1968
 S Africa

**Most tries for B Isles in international series – 4**
J J Williams (4 appearances) 1974 S Africa

**Most points for B Isles in any match on tour – 37**
A G B Old v South Western Districts
 1974 Mossel Bay, SA

**Most tries for B Isles in any match on tour – 6**
D J Duckham v West Coast-Buller 1971
 Greymouth, NZ
J J Williams v South Western Districts
 1974 Mossel Bay, SA
(A R Irvine scored 5 tries from full-back
 v King Country–Wanganui 1977
 Taumarunui, NZ)

# WORLD INTERNATIONAL RECORDS

*From 1890–91, when uniform points-scoring was first adopted by International Board countries, to 30 April 1978. Both team and individual records are for matches between International Board countries, matches for and against British Isles, and for special centenary or other celebration matches for which caps were awarded.*

## TEAM RECORDS

**Highest score – 49**
Wales (49–14) v France 1910 Swansea

---

**Biggest winning margin – 44**
South Africa (44–0) v Scotland 1951 Murrayfield

---

**Most tries in an international – 11**
Wales (47–5) v France 1909 Paris (Colombes)

---

**Most points on an overseas tour (all matches) – 868**
New Zealand to B Isles/France (33 matches) 1905–06

---

**Most tries on an overseas tour (all matches) – 215**
New Zealand to B Isles/France 33 matches) 1905–06

---

**Most points in an international series – 97**
New Zealand v Australia (3 matches) 1972 in NZ

---

**Most tries in an international series – 16**
South Africa v B Isles (4 matches) 1955 in SA
New Zealand v Australia (3 matches) 1972 in NZ

---

**Most points in Five Nations Championship in a season – 102**
Wales 1975–76

---

**Most tries in Five Nations Championship in a season – 21**
Wales 1909–10

---

**Biggest win on a major tour (all matches)**
117–6 New Zealand v S Australia 1974 Adelaide

## INDIVIDUAL RECORDS
(including appearances for British Isles, shown in brackets)

**Most capped player**
W J McBride (Ireland)   80 (17)*
   1962–75
*in individual positions*
*Full-back*
T J Kiernan (Ireland)   59 (5)   1960–73
*Wing*
K J Jones (Wales)   47 (3)*   1947–57
*Centre (includes 2nd five-eighth)*
C M H Gibson (Ireland)   45 [77 (12)]**   1964–78
*Fly-half (includes 1st five-eighth)*
J W Kyle (Ireland)   52 (6)   1947–58
*Scrum-half*
G O Edwards (Wales)   63 (10)   1967–78
*Prop*
A B Carmichael (Scotland)   50   1967–78
*Hooker*
K W Kennedy (Ireland)   49 (4)   1965–75
J V Pullin (England) 49 (7) 1966–76
*Lock*
W J McBride (Ireland)   80 (17)   1962–75
*Flanker*
N A A Murphy (Ireland)   49 (8)   1958–69
*No 8*
T M Davies (Wales)   46 (8)†   1969–76

---

\* *T G R Davies (Wales), 49 (5), has won 37 caps as a wing and 12 as a centre, one of them for the Lions*
\*\**Gibson has made 37 appearances for Ireland as a centre and 8 for the Lions, making 45 at centre in all. As a fly-half he has made 25 appearances for Ireland and 4 for the Lions, making 29 in all. He has also made three appearances for Ireland on the wing. His 65 caps for Ireland are the record for an individual country*
† *B Dauga (France), 50 caps, won 21 at No 8 and 29 at lock*

---

**Most points in internationals – 210**
P Bennett (Wales) [37 (8) appearances] 1969–78

**Most points in an international –24**
W F McCormick (NZ) v Wales 1969
  Auckland

**Most tries in internationals – 23**
I S Smith (Scotland) (32 appearances)
  1924–33

270

**Most tries in an international – 5**
D Lambert (England) v France 1907
  London (Richmond)

**Most penalty goals in an
international – 6**
D B Clarke (NZ) v B Isles 1959 Dunedin
G R Bosch (SA) v France 1975 Pretoria

**Most dropped goals in an
international – 3**
P Albaladejo (France) v Ireland 1960
  Paris (Colombes)
P F Hawthorne (Australia) v England
  1967 Twickenham

**Most points in an international
season – 49**
G Camberabero (France) (4 appearances)
  1966–67
*(includes match v Australia)*

**Most points in Five Nations
Championship in a season – 38**
R W Hosen (England) (4 appearances)
  1966–67
P Bennett (Wales) (4 appearances)
  1975–76
A J P Ward (Ireland) (4 appearances)
  1977–78

**Most tries in Five Nations
Championship in a season – 8**
C N Lowe (England) (4 appearances)
  1913–14
I S Smith (Scotland) (4 appearances)
  1924–25

**Most points on an overseas tour – 230**
W J Wallace (NZ) (25 appearances) in
  B Isles/France 1905–06

**Most tries on an overseas tour – 42**
J Hunter (NZ) (23 appearances) in
  B Isles/France 1905–06

**Most points in any match on tour – 41**
J F Karam (NZ) v South Australia 1974
  Adelaide

**Most tries in any match on tour – 8**
T R Heeps (NZ) v Northern NSW 1962
  Quirindi

# INTERNATIONAL TOURS
*Indicates replacement during tour, throughout this section*

## BRITISH ISLES TEAMS TO AUSTRALIA AND NEW ZEALAND

### 1888

**Full record**
in Australia       Played 16   Won 14   Lost 0   Drawn 2   Points for 210   Against 65
in New Zealand Played 19   Won 13   Lost 2   Drawn 4   Points for   82   Against 33

**Players**
*Full-backs:* J T Haslam (Batley), A G Paul (Swinton)
*Threequarters:* H C Speakman (Runcorn), Dr H Brooks (Edinburgh U, Durham),
J Anderton (Salford), A E Stoddart (Blackheath)
*Half-backs:* W Bumby (Swinton), J Nolan (Rochdale Hornets), W Burnett (Hawick)
*Forwards:* C Mathers (Bramley), S Williams (Salford), T Banks (Swinton),
R L Seddon (Swinton), H Eagles (Swinton), A J Stuart (Dewsbury),
W H Thomas (Cambridge U), T Kent (Salford), A P Penketh (Douglas, IOM),
R Burnett (Hawick), A J Laing (Hawick), Dr J Smith (Edinburgh U),
J P Clowes (Halifax)
**Captains** †R L Seddon, A E Stoddart   **Managers** A Shaw, A Shrewsbury

†*Stoddart took over as captain after Seddon had been drowned in Australia*

### 1899 (Australia only)

**Full record**       Played 21   Won 18   Lost 3   Drawn 0   Points for 333   Against 90
**International record**   Played 4    Won 3    Lost 1
**International details**   British Isles   3    Australia 13
                      British Isles 11    Australia   0
                      British Isles 11    Australia 10
                      British Isles 13    Australia   0

**Players**
*Full-backs:* E Martelli (Dublin U), C E K Thompson (Lancashire)
*Threequarters:* A B Timms (Edinburgh U), E T Nicholson (Birkenhead Park),
A M Bucher (Edinburgh Acads), E G Nicholls (Cardiff), G P Doran (Lansdowne)
*Half-backs:* Rev M Mullineux (Blackheath), G Cookson (Manchester),
C Y Adamson (Durham)
*Forwards:* F M Stout (Gloucester), J W Jarman (Bristol), H G S Gray (Scottish Trials),
G R Gibson (Northern), W Judkins (Coventry), F C Belson (Bath),
J S Francombe (Manchester), B I Swannell (Northampton), G V Evers (Moseley),
T M W McGown (N of Ireland), A Ayre-Smith (Guy's Hospital)
**Captain and Manager** Rev M Mullineux

### 1904

**Full record**
in Australia       Played 14   Won 14   Lost 0   Drawn 0   Points for 265   Against 51
in New Zealand Played   5   Won   2   Lost 2   Drawn 1   Points for   22   Against 33
**International record**
v Australia      Played 3    Won 3
v New Zealand Played 1    Lost 1

**International details**

| v Australia | British Isles 17 | Australia | 0 |
| | British Isles 17 | Australia | 3 |
| | British Isles 16 | Australia | 0 |
| v New Zealand | British Isles 3 | New Zealand 9 | |

**Players**

*Full-back:* C F Stanger-Leathes (Northern)

*Threequarters:* J L Fisher (Hull and E Riding), R T Gabe (Cardiff), W F Jowett (Swansea), W Llewellyn (Llwynypia and Newport), E T Morgan (London Welsh and Guy's Hospital), P F McEvedy (Guy's Hospital), A B O'Brien (Guy's Hospital)

*Half-backs:* P F Bush (Cardiff), F C Hulme (Birkenhead Park), T H Vile (Newport)

*Forwards:* D R Bedell-Sivright (Cambridge U), T S Bevan (Swansea), S N Crowther (Lennox), J T Sharland (Streatham), D D Dobson (Oxford U), C D Patterson (Malone), R W Edwards (Malone), A F Harding (Cardiff, London Welsh), B S Massey (Hull and E Riding), R J Rogers (Bath), F McK Saunders (Guy's Hospital), D H Traill (Guy's Hospital), B I Swannell (Northampton)

**Captain** D R Bedell-Sivright **Manager** A B O'Brien

## 1908 (Anglo–Welsh)

**Full record**

 in Australia Played 9 Won 7 Lost 2 Drawn 0 Points for 139 Against 48
 in New Zealand Played 17 Won 9 Lost 7 Drawn 1 Points for 184 Against 153

**International record**

 v New Zealand Played 3 Lost 2 Drawn 1

**International details** British Isles 5 New Zealand 32
 British Isles 3 New Zealand 3
 British Isles 0 New Zealand 29

**Players**

*Full-backs:* J C M Dyke (Cardiff), E J Jackett (Falmouth, Leicester)

*Threequarters:* F E Chapman (Westoe, West Hartlepool), R A Gibbs (Cardiff), J L Williams (Cardiff), R B Griffiths (Newport), J P 'Ponty' Jones (Pontypool, London Welsh), J P 'Tuan' Jones (Guy's Hospital), Dr P F McEvedy (Guy's Hospital), H H Vassall (Oxford U, Blackheath)

*Half-backs:* J Davey (Redruth), H Laxon (Cambridge U), W L Morgan (Cardiff), G L Williams (Liverpool)

*Forwards:* H Archer (Guy's Hospital), R Dibble (Bridgwater and Albion), P J Down (Bristol), G V Kyrke (Marlborough Nomads), R K Green (Neath), E Morgan (Swansea), L S Thomas (Penarth), A F Harding (Cardiff, London Welsh), J F Williams (London Welsh), G R Hind (Guy's Hospital), F S Jackson (Leicester), W L Oldham (Coventry), J A S Ritson (Northern), T W Smith (Leicester)

**Captain** A F Harding **Manager** G H Harnett

## 1930

**Full record**

 in New Zealand Played 21 Won 15 Lost 6 Drawn 0 Points for 420 Against 205
 in Australia Played 7 Won 5 Lost 2 Drawn 0 Points for 204 Against 113

**International record**

 v New Zealand Played 4 Won 1 Lost 3
 v Australia Played 1 Won 0 Lost 1

**International details**

| v New Zealand | British Isles 6 | New Zealand 3 |
| | British Isles 10 | New Zealand 13 |
| | British Isles 10 | New Zealand 15 |
| | British Isles 8 | New Zealand 22 |
| v Australia | British Isles 5 | Australia 6 |

**Players**
*Full-backs:* J Bassett (Penarth), W G McG Bonner (Bradford)
*Threequarters:* C D Aarvold (Cambridge U and Blackheath), J S R Reeve
(Harlequins), J C Morley (Newport), A L Novis (Blackheath and Army),
R Jennings (Redruth), H M Bowcott (Cambridge U and Cardiff),
T E Jones-Davies (London Welsh), P F Murray (Wanderers)
*Half-backs:* R S Spong (Old Millhillians), W H Sobey (Old Millhillians),
T C Knowles (Birkenhead Park), H Poole (Cardiff)
*Forwards:* F D Prentice (Leicester), H Rew (Blackheath and Army), D Parker
(Swansea), W B Welsh (Hawick), B H Black (Oxford U and Blackheath),
M J Dunne (Lansdowne), G R Beamish (Leicester and RAF), J L Farrell (Bective
Rangers), J McD Hodgson (Northern), H O'H O'Neill (Queen's U, Belfast)
Ivor Jones (Llanelli), H Wilkinson (Halifax), S A Martindale (Kendall),
D A Kendrew (Woodford, Leicester, and Army), H C S Jones (Manchester)
**Captain** F D Prentice   **Manager** J Baxter

## 1950

**Full record**
   in New Zealand Played 23 Won 17 Lost 5 Drawn 1 Points for 420 Against 162
   in Australia      Played  6 Won  5 Lost 1 Drawn 0 Points for 150 Against  52
**International record**
   v New Zealand Played 4   Won 0   Lost 3   Drawn 1
   v Australia      Played 2   Won 2   Lost 0   Drawn 0
**International details**

| | | | |
|---|---|---|---|
| v New Zealand | British Isles | 9 | New Zealand  9 |
| | British Isles | 0 | New Zealand  8 |
| | British Isles | 3 | New Zealand  6 |
| | British Isles | 8 | New Zealand 11 |
| v Australia | British Isles 19 | Australia |  6 |
| | British Isles 24 | Australia |  3 |

**Players**
*Full-backs:* G W Norton (Bective Rangers), W B Cleaver (Cardiff),
B Lewis Jones* (Devonport Services and Llanelli)
*Threequarters:* D W C Smith (London Scottish), M F Lane (UC Cork),
K J Jones (Newport), M C Thomas (Devonport Services and Newport),
B L Williams (Cardiff), J Matthews (Cardiff), N J Henderson (Queen's U, Belfast),
R Macdonald (Edinburgh U)
*Half-backs:* J W Kyle (Queen's U, Belfast), I Preece (Coventry), W R Willis (Cardiff),
G Rimmer (Waterloo), A W Black (Edinburgh U)
*Forwards:* V G Roberts (Penryn), J S McCarthy (Dolphin), R T Evans (Newport),
J W McKay (Queen's U, Belfast), J R G Stephens (Neath), E R John (Neath),
P W Kininmonth (Oxford U and Richmond), J E Nelson (Malone),
D J Hayward (Newbridge), J D Robins (Birkenhead Park), T Clifford (Young
Munster), C Davies (Cardiff), G M Budge (Edinburgh Wanderers), D M Davies
(Somerset Police), Dr K D Mullen (Old Belvedere)
**Captain** Dr K D Mullen   **Manager** Surgeon-Captain (D) L B Osborne (RN)
**Assistant Manager** E L Savage

## 1959

**Full record**
   in Australia      Played  6 Won  5 Lost 1 Drawn 0 Points for 174 Against  70
   in New Zealand Played 25 Won 20 Lost 5 Drawn 0 Points for 582 Against 266
**International record**
   v Australia      Played 2   Won 2   Lost 0
   v New Zealand Played 4   Won 1   Lost 3

**International details**

| v Australia | British Isles 17 | Australia | 6 |
| | British Isles 24 | Australia | 3 |
| v New Zealand | British Isles 17 | New Zealand 18 |
| | British Isles 8 | New Zealand 11 |
| | British Isles 8 | New Zealand 22 |
| | British Isles 9 | New Zealand 6 |

274

**Players**

*Full-backs:* T J Davies (Llanelli), K J F Scotland (Cambridge U)
*Threequarters:* J R C Young (Oxford U), P B Jackson (Coventry),
A J F O'Reilly (Old Belvedere), N H Brophy (UC Dublin), M J Price (Pontypool),
W M Patterson* (Sale), D Hewitt (Queen's U, Belfast), J Butterfield (Northampton),
M C Thomas (Newport), G H Waddell (Cambridge U)
*Half-backs:* J P Horrocks-Taylor* (Leicester), A B W Risman (Manchester U),
M A F English (Limerick Bohemians), R E G Jeeps (Northampton),
S Coughtrie (Edinburgh Acads), A A Mulligan* (Wanderers, London Irish)
*Forwards:* B V Meredith (Newport), R Prosser (Pontypool), A R Dawson (Wanderers),
H F McLeod (Hawick), G K Smith (Kelso), S Millar (Ballymena),
B G M Wood (Garryowen), R H Williams (Llanelli), W A Mulcahy (UC Dublin),
W R Evans (Cardiff), R W D Marques (Harlequins), A Ashcroft (Waterloo),
N A A Murphy (Cork Constitution), H J Morgan (Abertillery), J Faull (Swansea)
**Captain** A R Dawson    **Manager** A W Wilson    **Assistant Manager** O B Glasgow

---

**1966**

**Full record**

| in Australia | Played 8 Won 7 Lost 0 Drawn 1 Points for 202 Against 48 |
| in New Zealand | Played 25 Won 15 Lost 8 Drawn 2 Points for 300 Against 281 |

**International record**

| v Australia | Played 2 | Won 2 | Lost 0 |
| v New Zealand | Played 4 | Won 0 | Lost 4 |

**International details**

| v Australia | British Isles 11 | Australia | 8 |
| | British Isles 31 | Australia | 0 |
| v New Zealand | British Isles 3 | New Zealand 20 |
| | British Isles 12 | New Zealand 16 |
| | British Isles 6 | New Zealand 19 |
| | British Isles 11 | New Zealand 24 |

**Players**

*Full-backs:* D Rutherford (Gloucester), S Wilson (London Scottish), T G Price* (Llanelli)
*Threequarters:* D I E Bebb (Swansea), A J W Hinshelwood (London Scottish),
K F Savage (Northampton), S J Watkins (Newport), D K Jones (Cardiff)
F P K Bresnihan* (UC Dublin), M P Weston (Durham City),
C W McFadyean (Moseley), J C Walsh (Sunday's Well)
*Half-backs:* C M H Gibson (Cambridge U), D Watkins (Newport),
A R Lewis (Abertillery), R M Young (Queen's U, Belfast)
*Forwards:* R A Lamont (Instonians), A E I Pask (Abertillery),
N A A Murphy (Cork Constitution), D Grant (Hawick), G J Prothero (Bridgend),
J W Telfer (Melrose), W J McBride (Ballymena), M J Campbell-Lamerton (London Scottish), W D Thomas (Llanelli), B Price (Newport), R J McLoughlin (Gosforth),
D L Powell (Northampton), C H Norris (Cardiff), D Williams (Ebbw Vale),
K W Kennedy (CIYMS), F A L Laidlaw (Melrose)
**Captain** M J Campbell-Lamerton    **Manager** D J O'Brien
**Assistant Manager** J D Robins

## 1971

**Full record**

   in Australia     Played  2  Won  1  Lost 1  Drawn 0  Points for  25  Against  27

   in New Zealand Played 24  Won 22  Lost 1  Drawn 1  Points for 555  Against 204

**International record**

   v New Zealand  Played 4    Won 2    Lost 1    Drawn 1

**International details**

   v New Zealand  British Isles  9   New Zealand  3

               British Isles 12   New Zealand 22

               British Isles 13   New Zealand  3

               British Isles 14   New Zealand 14

## Players

*Full-backs:* R Hiller (Harlequins), J P R Williams (London Welsh)

*Threequarters:* D J Duckham (Coventry), A G Biggar (London Scottish), T G R Davies (London Welsh), J C Bevan (Cardiff Coll of Education), A J Lewis (Ebbw Vale), J S Spencer (Headingley), S J Dawes (London Welsh), C W W Rea (Headingley)

*Half-backs:* C M H Gibson (North of Ireland), B John (Cardiff), G O Edwards (Cardiff), R Hopkins (Maesteg)

*Forwards:* T M Davies (London Welsh), P J Dixon (Harlequins), J Taylor (London Welsh), J F Slattery (UC Dublin), M L Hipwell (Terenure Coll), D L Quinnell (Llanelli), R J Arneil* (Leicester), W D Thomas (Llanelli), W J McBride (Ballymena), M G Roberts (London Welsh), G L Brown (West of Scotland), T G Evans* (London Welsh), A B Carmichael (West of Scotland), R J McLoughlin (Blackrock Coll), J McLauchlan (Jordanhill Coll), J F Lynch (St Mary's Coll), C B Stevens* (Harlequins and Penzance–Newlyn), J V Pullin (Bristol), F A L Laidlaw (Melrose)

**Captain** S J Dawes   **Manager** Dr D W C Smith   **Assistant Manager** C R James

## 1977 (New Zealand and Fiji only)

**Full record**        Played 26  Won 21  Lost 4  Drawn 1  Points for 607  Against 320

   in New Zealand Played 25  Won 21  Lost 3  Drawn 1  Points for 586  Against 295

   in Fiji         Played 1  Lost 1  Points for 21  Against 25

**International record**

   v New Zealand  Played 4    Won 1    Lost 3

**International details**

   v New Zealand  British Isles 12   New Zealand 16

               British Isles 13   New Zealand  9

               British Isles  7   New Zealand 19

               British Isles  9   New Zealand 10

## Players

*Full-backs:* A R Irvine (Heriot's FP), B H Hay (Boroughmuir)

*Threequarters:* P J Squires (Harrogate), H E Rees (Neath), J J Williams (Llanelli), G L Evans (Newport), C M H Gibson (North of Ireland FC), S P Fenwick (Bridgend), D H Burcher (Newport), I R McGeechan (Headingley)

*Half-backs:* P Bennett (Llanelli), J D Bevan (Aberavon), D W Morgan (Stewart's Melville FP), D B Williams (Cardiff), A D Lewis* (Cambridge U & London Welsh)

*Forwards:* W P Duggan (Blackrock Coll), J Squire (Newport), T J Cobner (Pontypool), T P Evans (Swansea), A Neary (Broughton Park), D L Quinnell (Llanelli), G L Brown (West of Scotland), N E Horton (Moseley), A J Martin (Aberavon), M I Keane (Lansdowne), W B Beaumont* (Fylde), F E Cotton (Sale), P A Orr (Old Wesley), G Price (Pontypool), C Williams (Aberavon), A G Faulkner* (Pontypool), R W Windsor (Pontypool), P J Wheeler (Leicester)

**Captain** P Bennett   **Manager** G Burrell

**Assistant Manager** S J Dawes

## BRITISH ISLES TEAMS TO SOUTH AFRICA

### 1891

**Full record**    Played 19 Won 19 Lost 0 Drawn 0 Points for 224 Against 1
**International record** Played 3 Won 3
**International details** British Isles 4 South Africa 0
                        British Isles 3 South Africa 0
                        British Isles 4 South Africa 0

**Players**
*Full-backs:* W G Mitchell (Cambridge U and Richmond), E Bromet (Cambridge U)
*Threequarters:* P R Clauss (Oxford U), R L Aston (Cambridge U),
W E Maclagan (London Scottish)
*Half-backs:* H Marshall (Blackheath), B G Roscoe (Lancashire),
A Rotherham (Cambridge U), W Wotherspoon (Cambridge U)
*Forwards:* W E Bromet (Oxford U), J H Gould (Old Leysians),
J Hammond (Cambridge U), P F Hancock (Somerset), W J Jackson (Gloucester),
R G MacMillan (London Scottish), E Mayfield (Cambridge U),
C P Simpson (Cambridge U), A A Surtees (Cambridge U),
R Thompson (Cambridge U), W H Thorman (Cambridge U), T Whittaker
(Lancashire)
**Captain** W E Maclagan  **Manager** E H Ash

### 1896

**Full record**    Played 21 Won 19 Lost 1 Drawn 1 Points for 310 Against 45
**International record** Played 4 Won 3 Lost 1
**International details** British Isles 8 South Africa 0
                        British Isles 17 South Africa 8
                        British Isles 9 South Africa 3
                        British Isles 0 South Africa 5

**Players**
*Full-back:* J F Byrne (Moseley)
*Threequarters:* C A Boyd (Dublin U), J T Magee (Bective Rangers),
L Q Bulger (Dublin U and Lansdowne), C O Robinson (Northumberland),
O G Mackie (Cambridge U and Wakefield Trinity)
*Half-backs:* Rev M Mullineux (Blackheath), S P Bell (Cambridge U),
L M Magee (Bective Rangers and London Irish)
*Forwards:* J Hammond (Blackheath and Cambridge U), T J Crean (Dublin Wands),
A W D Meares (Dublin U), R Johnston (Dublin Wands), A D Clinch (Dublin U),
J Sealy (Dublin U), W J Carey (Oxford U), P F Hancock (Blackheath and Somerset),
W Mortimer (Marlborough Nomads), A F Todd (Blackheath),
R C Mullins (Oxford U), G W Lee* (Rockcliff)
**Captain** J Hammond  **Manager** R Walker

### 1903

**Full record**    Played 22 Won 11 Lost 8 Drawn 3 Points for 231 Against 138
**International record** Played 3 Won 0 Lost 1 Drawn 2
**International details** British Isles 10 South Africa 10
                        British Isles 0 South Africa 0
                        British Isles 0 South Africa 8

**Players**
*Full-back:* E M Harrison (Guy's Hospital)
*Threequarters:* A E Hind (Cambridge U), I G Davidson (North of Ireland),
G F Collett (Gloucestershire), R T Skrimshire (Newport and Blackheath),
E F Walker (Lennox)

*Half-backs:* L L Greig (United Services), J I Gillespie (Edinburgh Acads),
R M Neill (Edinburgh Acads), P S Hancock (Richmond)
*Forwards:* M C Morrison (Royal HSFP), W P Scott (West of Scotland),
D R Bedell-Sivright (Cambridge U), W T C Cave (Cambridge U),
J C Hosack (Edinburgh Wands), A Tedford (Malone), R S Smyth (Dublin U),
Joseph Wallace (Dublin Wands), James Wallace (Dublin Wands),
F M Stout (Richmond), T A Gibson (Cambridge U)
**Captain** M C Morrison  **Manager** J Hammond

## 1910

**Full record**  Played 24 Won 13 Lost 8 Drawn 3 Points for 290 Against 236
**International record**  Played 3  Won 1  Lost 2
**International details**  British Isles 10  South Africa 14
British Isles  8  South Africa  3
British Isles  5  South Africa 21

### Players

*Full-back:* S H Williams (Newport)
*Threequarters:* A Melville Baker (Newport), R C S Plummer (Newport),
M E Neale (Bristol), A R Foster (Derry), C G Timms (Edinburgh U),
J P Jones (Pontypool and Newport), J A Spoors (Bristol), K B Wood (Leicester)
*Half-backs:* N F Humphreys (Tynedale), A N McClinton (North of Ireland),
G A M Isherwood (Cheshire, Sale and Old Alleynians), E Milroy* (Watsonians)
*Forwards:* Dr T Smyth (Newport), W Tyrrell (Queen's U, Belfast),
D F Smith (Richmond), P D Waller (Newport), J Reid-Kerr (Greenock Wands),
R Stevenson (St Andrew's U), L M Speirs (Watsonians), E O'D Crean (Liverpool),
H Jarman (Newport), O J S Piper (Cork Constitution),
Dr W A Robertson (Edinburgh U and Hartlepool Rovers), C H Pillman (Blackheath),
W J Ashby (Queen's Coll, Cork), F G Handford* (Kersal), T J Richards* (Bristol),
J Webb* (Abertillery)
**Captain** Dr T Smyth  **Managers** W Cail and Walter E Rees

## 1924

**Full record**  Played 21 Won 9 Lost 9 Drawn 3 Points for 175 Against 155
**International record**  Played 4  Lost 3  Drawn 1
**International details**  British Isles 3  South Africa  7
British Isles 0  South Africa 17
British Isles 3  South Africa  3
British Isles 9  South Africa 16

### Players

*Full-backs:* D Drysdale (Heriots FP), W F Gaisford (St Bart's Hospital),
T E Holliday (Aspatria)
*Threequarters:* R Harding (Swansea), I S Smith (Oxford U), S W Harris (Blackheath),
W Wallace (Percy Park), R M Kinnear (Heriots FP), J H Bordass (Cambridge U),
R B Maxwell (Birkenhead Park)
*Half-backs:* H J Davies* (Newport), V M Griffiths (Newport), H Waddell (Glasgow
Acads), W A Cunningham* (Lansdowne), A T Young (Blackheath),
H Whitley (Northern)
*Forwards:* Dr R Cove-Smith (Old Merchant Taylors), A F Blakiston (Blackheath),
A T Voyce (Gloucester), N C Macpherson (Newport), R G Henderson (Northern),
K G P Hendrie (Heriots FP), D S Davies (Hawick), R A Howie (Kirkcaldy),
A Ross (Kilmarnock), J D Clinch (Dublin U), Dr W J Roche (UC Cork, Newport),
J McVicker (Belfast Collegians), D Marsden-Jones (Cardiff and London Welsh),
M J Bradley (Dolphin), T N Brand (North of Ireland)
**Captain** Dr R Cove-Smith  **Manager** H Packer

## 1938

**Full record**      Played 23  Won 17  Lost 6  Drawn 0  Points for 407  Against 272
**International record**  Played 3  Won 1  Lost 2
**International details**   British Isles 12   South Africa 26
                          British Isles  3   South Africa 19
                          British Isles 21   South Africa 16

**Players**

278   *Full-backs:* V G J Jenkins (London Welsh), C F Grieve (Oxford U)
*Threequarters:* E J Unwin (Rosslyn Park), W H Clement (Llanelli), E L Jones (Llanelli),
C V Boyle (Dublin U), R Leyland (Waterloo), D J Macrae (St Andrews U),
H R McKibbin (Queen's U, Belfast), B E Nicholson (Old Whitgiftians and Harlequins)
*Half-backs:* F J Reynolds (Old Cranleighans), G E Cromey (Queen's U, Belfast),
J L Giles (Coventry), H Tanner (Swansea), G J Morgan (Clontarf)
*Forwards:* S Walker (Belfast Instonians) M E Morgan (Swansea),
W G Howard (Old Birkonians), W H Travers (Newport), C R A Graves (Dublin
Wands), R B Mayne (Queen's U), G T Dancer (Bedford), S R Couchman (Old
Cranleighans), A G Purchas (Coventry), J A Waters (Selkirk), P L Duff (Glasgow
Acads), I Williams (Cardiff), A R Taylor (Cross Keys), R Alexander (North of Ireland)
**Captain** S Walker   **Manager** B C Hartley   **Assistant Manager** H A Haigh-Smith

## 1955

**Full record**      Played 24  Won 18  Lost 5  Drawn 1  Points for 418  Against 271
**International record**  Played 4  Won 2  Lost 2
**International details**   British Isles 23   South Africa 22
                          British Isles  9   South Africa 25
                          British Isles  9   South Africa  6
                          British Isles  8   South Africa 22

**Players**

*Full-backs:* A Cameron (Glasgow HSFP), A G Thomas (Llanelli)
*Threequarters:* A R Smith (Cambridge U), F D Sykes (Northampton),
H Morris (Cardiff), A C Pedlow (Queen's U, Belfast), J Butterfield (Northampton),
W P C Davies (Harlequins), A J F O'Reilly (Old Belvedere), J P Quinn (New Brighton),
G Griffiths* (Cardiff)
*Half-backs:* C I Morgan (Cardiff), D G S Baker (Old Merchant Taylors),
J E Williams (Old Millhillians), R E G Jeeps (Northampton), T Lloyd (Maesteg)
*Forwards:* R H Thompson (Instonians), C C Meredith (Neath),
B V Meredith (Newport), H F McLeod (Hawick), W O Williams (Swansea),
R Roe (Lansdowne), T Elliot (Gala), E J S Michie (Aberdeen U),
T E Reid (Garryowen), R H Williams (Llanelli), J T Greenwood (Dunfermline),
R J Robins (Pontypridd), R Higgins (Liverpool), D S Wilson (Metropolitan Police),
R C C Thomas (Swansea)
**Captain** R H Thompson   **Manager** J A E Siggins   **Assistant Manager** D E Davies

## 1962

**Full record**      Played 24  Won 15  Lost 5  Drawn 4  Points for 351  Against 208
**International record**  Played 4  Won 0  Lost 3  Drawn 1
**International details**   British Isles  3   South Africa  3
                          British Isles  0   South Africa  3
                          British Isles  3   South Africa  8
                          British Isles 14   South Africa 34

**Players**

*Full-backs:* T J Kiernan (UC Cork), J G Willcox (Oxford U)

*Threequarters:* N H Brophy (Blackrock), D I E Bebb (Swansea), R C Cowan (Selkirk),
A R Smith (Edinburgh Wands), J M Dee (Hartlepool Rovers), W R Hunter (CIYMS),
M P Weston (Durham City), D K Jones (Llanelli), D Hewitt (Queen's U, Belfast)

*Half-backs:* R A W Sharp (Oxford U), R E G Jeeps (Northampton),
G H Waddell (London Scottish), A O'Connor (Aberavon),
H J C Brown* (RAF, Blackheath)

*Forwards:* S Millar (Ballymena), K D Jones (Cardiff), D M D Rollo (Howe of Fife),
T P Wright (Blackheath), B V Meredith (Newport), A E I Pask (Abertillery),
S A M Hodgson (Durham City), M J Campbell-Lamerton (Army, Halifax),
W J McBride (Ballymena), W A Mulcahy (Bohemians), K A Rowlands (Cardiff),
H J Morgan (Abertillery), D P Rogers (Bedford), J Douglas (Stewart's Coll FP),
D Nash (Ebbw Vale), H O Godwin* (Coventry), G D Davidge* (Newport)

**Captain** A R Smith   **Manager** Instructor-Commander D B Vaughan RN
**Assistant Manager** H R McKibbin

## 1968

| | |
|---|---|
| **Full record** | Played 20 Won 15 Lost 4 Drawn 1 Points for 377 Against 181 |
| **International record** | Played 4 Won 0 Lost 3 Drawn 1 |
| **International details** | British Isles 20 South Africa 25 |
| | British Isles 6 South Africa 6 |
| | British Isles 6 South Africa 11 |
| | British Isles 6 South Africa 19 |

**Players**

*Full-backs:* T J Kiernan (Cork Constitution), R Hiller (Harlequins)

*Threequarters:* A J W Hinshelwood (London Scottish), W K Jones (Cardiff),
M C R Richards (Cardiff), K F Savage (Northampton), F P K Bresnihan (UC Dublin),
T G R Davies (Cardiff), K S Jarrett (Newport), W H Raybould (London Welsh),
J W C Turner (Gala)

*Half-backs:* C M H Gibson (N of Ireland), B John (Cardiff), G O Edwards (Cardiff),
R M Young (Queen's U, Belfast), G C Connell* (London Scottish)

*Forwards:* A L Horton (Blackheath), M J Coulman (Moseley), S Millar (Ballymena),
J P O'Shea (Cardiff), P J Larter (Northampton), W J McBride (Ballymena)
P K Stagg (Sale), W D Thomas (Llanelli), J V Pullin (Bristol), J Young (Harrogate),
M G Doyle (Blackrock Coll), J Taylor (London Welsh), K G Goodall* (City of Derry),
R J Arneil (Edinburgh Acads), R B Taylor (Northampton), J W Telfer (Melrose),
B R West* (Northampton)

**Captain** T J Kiernan   **Manager** D K Brooks   **Assistant Manager** A R Dawson

## 1974

| | |
|---|---|
| **Full record** | Played 22 Won 21 Drawn 1 Points for 729 Against 207 |
| **International record** | Played 4 Won 3 Drawn 1 |
| **International details** | British Isles 12 South Africa 3 |
| | British Isles 28 South Africa 9 |
| | British Isles 26 South Africa 9 |
| | British Isles 13 South Africa 13 |

**Players**

*Full-backs:* A R Irvine (Heriot's FP), J P R Williams (London Welsh)

*Threequarters:* T O Grace (St Mary's Coll, Dublin), C F W Rees (London Welsh),
W C C Steele (Bedford and RAF), J J Williams (Llanelli), A J Morley* (Bristol)
R T E Bergiers (Llanelli), G W Evans (Coventry), I R McGeechan (Headingley),
R A Milliken (Bangor, N Ireland)

*Half-backs:* P Bennett (Llanelli), A G B Old (Leicester),
C M H Gibson* (North of Ireland FC), G O Edwards (Cardiff),
J J Moloney (St Mary's Coll, Dublin)
*Forwards:* T M Davies (Swansea), A G Ripley (Rosslyn Park), T P David (Llanelli),
S A McKinney (Dungannon), A Neary (Broughton Park), J F Slattery (Blackrock Coll),
G L Brown (West of Scotland), W J McBride (Ballymena), C W Ralston (Richmond),
R M Uttley (Gosforth), M A Burton (Gloucester), A B Carmichael (West of Scotland),
F E Cotton (Coventry), J McLauchlan (Jordanhill), K W Kennedy (London Irish),
R W Windsor (Pontypool)
**Captain** W J McBride  **Manager** A G Thomas  **Assistant Manager** S Millar

280

## NEW ZEALAND TO BRITISH ISLES AND FRANCE

**1888–89** (The Maoris)

**Full record**　　　Played 74　Won 49　Lost 20　Drawn 5　Points for 394　Against 188
**International record**　Played 3　Won 1　Lost 2
**International details**　Maoris 13　Ireland　4
　　　　　　　　　　　　Maoris　0　Wales　　5
　　　　　　　　　　　　Maoris　0　England 7
**Players**
*Backs:* W Elliot (Grafton), D R Gage (Poneke), C Goldsmith (Te Aute Coll),
E Ihimaira (Te Aute Coll), P Keogh (Kaikorai), H H Lee (Riverton),
C Madigan (Grafton), E McCausland (Gordon), F Warbrick (Tauranga),
J A Warbrick (Hawke's Bay), W Warbrick (Matata), H J Wynyard (North Shore),
W T Wynyard (North Shore)
*Forwards:* W Anderson (Hokianga), T R Ellison (Poneke), Wi Karauria (Nelson),
R Maynard (North Shore), Wiri Nehua (Te Aute Coll), T Rene (Nelson),
D Stewart (Thames), R G Taiaroa (Dunedin), Alfred Warbrick (Matata),
Arthur Warbrick (Matata), A Webster (Hokianga), G A Williams (Poneke),
G Wynyard (North Shore)
**Captain** J A Warbrick  **Managers** J R Scott and T Eyton

**1905–06**

**Full record**　　　　Played 33　Won 32　Lost 1　Drawn 0　Points for 868　Against 47
　in B Isles　　　　Played 32　Won 31　Lost 1　Drawn 0　Points for 830　Against 39
　in France　　　　Played　1　Won　1　Lost 0　Drawn 0　Points for　38　Against　8
**International record**　Played 5　Won 4　Lost 1　Drawn 0
**International details**　New Zealand 12　Scotland 7
　　　　　　　　　　　　New Zealand 15　Ireland　0
　　　　　　　　　　　　New Zealand 15　England 0
　　　　　　　　　　　　New Zealand　0　Wales　3
　　　　　　　　　　　　New Zealand 38　France　8
**Players**
*Full-backs:* G A Gillett (Canterbury), W J Wallace (Wellington)
*Threequarters:* H L Abbott (Taranaki), E E Booth (Otago), R G Deans (Canterbury),
E T Harper (Canterbury), D McGregor (Wellington), G W Smith (Auckland),
H D Thomson (Wanganui)
*Five-eighths:* J Hunter (Taranaki), H J Mynott (Taranaki), J W Stead (Southland)
*Scrum-half:* F Roberts (Wellington)
*Forwards:* S Casey (Otago), J Corbett (West Coast), W Cunningham (Auckland),
D Gallaher (Auckland), F T Glasgow (Taranaki), W S Glenn (Taranaki),
W Johnston (Otago), W H Mackrell (Auckland), A McDonald (Otago),
F Newton (Canterbury), G W Nicholson (Auckland), J M O'Sullivan (Taranaki),
C E Seeling (Auckland), G A Tyler (Auckland)
**Captain** D Gallaher  **Manager** G H Dixon

## 1924–25

| Full record | Played 30 Won 30 Lost 0 Drawn 0 Points for 721 Against 112 |
|---|---|
| in B Isles | Played 28 Won 28 Lost 0 Drawn 0 Points for 654 Against 98 |
| in France | Played 2 Won 2 Lost 0 Drawn 0 Points for 67 Against 14 |

**International record** Played 4 Won 4

**International details**

| New Zealand | 6 | Ireland | 0 |
|---|---|---|---|
| New Zealand | 19 | Wales | 0 |
| New Zealand | 17 | England | 11 |
| New Zealand | 30 | France | 6 |

**Players**

*Full-back:* G Nepia (Hawke's Bay)
*Threequarters:* H W Brown (Taranaki), A H Hart (Taranaki), F W Lucas (Auckland),
A C C Robilliard (Canterbury), J Steel (West Coast), K S Svenson (Wellington)
*Five-eighths:* C E O Badeley (Auckland), A E Cooke (Auckland),
N P McGregor (Canterbury), M F Nicholls (Wellington), L Paewai (Hawke's Bay)
*Scrum-halves:* W C Dalley (Canterbury), J J Mill (Hawke's Bay)
*Forwards:* C J Brownlie (Hawke's Bay), M J Brownlie (Hawke's Bay),
L F Cupples (Bay of Plenty), Q Donald (Wairarapa), I H Harvey (Wairarapa),
W R Irvine (Hawke's Bay), R R Masters (Canterbury), B V McCleary (Canterbury),
H G Munro (Otago), J H Parker (Canterbury), C G Porter (Wellington)
J Richardson (Southland), R T Stewart (South Canterbury), A H West (Taranaki),
A White (Southland)
**Captain** C G Porter   **Manager** S S M Dean


## 1926–27 (The Maoris)

| Full record | Played 31 Won 22 Lost 7 Drawn 2 Points for 459 Against 194 |
|---|---|
| in England and Wales | Played 16 Won 8 Lost 6 Drawn 2 Points for 126 Against 113 |
| in France | Played 15 Won 14 Lost 1 Drawn 0 Points for 333 Against 81 |

**International record** Played 1 Won 1

**International details** Maoris 12  France 3

**Players**

*Full-backs:* R Pelham (Auckland), H Phillips (Marlborough)
*Threequarters:* W P Barclay (Hawke's Bay), A C Falwasser (Taranaki),
L R Grace (Hawke's Bay), W Lockwood (East Coast), E Love (Wellington),
W Potaka (Wanganui), T P Robinson (Canterbury)
*Five-eighths:* J R Bell (Southland), J H MacDonald (Marlborough),
M Mete (Manawhenua), D Wi Neera (Wellington)
*Scrum-halves:* H Kingi (Wanganui), W H Shortland (Hawke's Bay)
*Forwards:* A Crawford (East Coast), T Dennis (Poverty Bay), J Gemmell
(Hawke's Bay), S W Gemmell (Hawke's Bay), P Haupapa (Bay of Plenty), J Manihera
(Canterbury), T Manning (South Canterbury), Rev P Matene (North Auckland),
O S Olsen (North Auckland), W Rika (North Auckland), J Stewart (Otago),
D Tatana (Manawhenua), W H Wilson (Hawke's Bay)
**Captain** W P Barclay   **Managers** W T Parata and H Harris


## 1935–36 (British Isles only)

| Full record | Played 28 Won 24 Lost 3 Drawn 1 Points for 431 Against 180 |
|---|---|

**International record** Played 4 Won 2 Lost 2

**International details**

| New Zealand | 18 | Scotland | 8 |
|---|---|---|---|
| New Zealand | 17 | Ireland | 9 |
| New Zealand | 12 | Wales | 13 |
| New Zealand | 0 | England | 13 |

**Players**

*Full-back:* G D M Gilbert (West Coast)
*Threequarters:* N Ball (Wellington), H M Brown (Auckland),
T H C Caughey (Auckland), G F Hart (Canterbury), N A Mitchell (Southland),
C J Oliver (Canterbury)
*Five-eighths:* J L Griffiths (Wellington), J R Page (Wellington), D Solomon (Auckland),
E W T Tindill (Wellington)
*Scrum-halves:* M M N Corner (Auckland), B S Sadler (Wellington)
*Forwards:* G T Adkins (South Canterbury), J J Best (Marlborough),
W R Collins (Hawke's Bay), D Dalton (Hawke's Bay), W E Hadley (Auckland),
J Hore (Otago), R R King (West Coast), A Lambourn (Wellington),
A Mahoney (Bush), J E Manchester (Canterbury), R M McKenzie (Manawatu),
H F McLean (Auckland), C S Pepper (Auckland), S T Reid (Hawke's Bay),
F H Vorrath (Otago), J G Wynyard (Waikato)
**Captain** J E Manchester  **Manager** V R S Meredith

282

---

**1953–54**

| Full record | Played 31 Won 25 Lost 4 Drawn 2 Points for 446 Against 129 |
| in B Isles | Played 29 Won 25 Lost 2 Drawn 2 Points for 438 Against 115 |
| in France | Played 2 Won 0 Lost 2 Drawn 0 Points for 8 Against 14 |
| **International record** | Played 5 Won 3 Lost 2 |
| **International details** | New Zealand 8 Wales 13 |
| | New Zealand 14 Ireland 3 |
| | New Zealand 5 England 0 |
| | New Zealand 3 Scotland 0 |
| | New Zealand 0 France 3 |

**Players**

*Full-backs:* J W Kelly (Auckland), R W H Scott (Auckland)
*Threequarters:* M J Dixon (Canterbury), A E G Elsom (Canterbury),
W S S Freebairn (Manawatu), R A Jarden (Wellington), J T Fitzgerald (Wellington),
J M Tanner (Auckland)
*Five-eighths:* B B J Fitzpatrick (Wellington), C J Loader (Wellington),
D D Wilson (Canterbury), R G Bowers (Wellington), L S Haig (Otago)
*Scrum-halves:* V D Bevan (Wellington), K Davis (Auckland)
*Forwards:* W A McCaw (Southland), R C Stuart (Canterbury),
W H Clark (Wellington), P F Jones (North Auckland), R J O'Dea (Thames Valley)
O D Oliver (Otago), K P Bagley (Manawatu), G N Dalzell (Canterbury),
R A White (Poverty Bay), I J Clarke (Waikato), B P Eastgate (Canterbury),
K L Skinner (Otago), H L White (Auckland), R C Hemi (Waikato),
C A Woods (Southland)
**Captain** R C Stuart  **Manager** N Millard  **Assistant Manager** A E Marslin

---

**1963–64**

| Full record | Played 34 Won 32 Lost 1 Drawn 1 Points for 568 Against 153 |
| in B Isles | Played 30 Won 28 Lost 1 Drawn 1 Points for 508 Against 137 |
| in France | Played 4 Won 4 Lost 0 Drawn 0 Points for 60 Against 16 |
| **International record** | Played 5 Won 4 Lost 0 Drawn 1 |
| **International details** | New Zealand 6 Ireland 5 |
| | New Zealand 6 Wales 0 |
| | New Zealand 14 England 0 |
| | New Zealand 0 Scotland 0 |
| | New Zealand 12 France 3 |

**Players**
*Full-back:* D B Clarke (Waikato)
*Threequarters:* R W Caulton (Wellington), W L Davis (Hawke's Bay),
M J Dick (Auckland), I S T Smith (Otago), P F Little (Auckland),
I R MacRae (Hawke's Bay)
*Five-eighths:* D A Arnold (Canterbury), P T Walsh (Counties),
M A Herewini (Auckland), E W Kirton (Otago), B A Watt (Canterbury)
*Scrum-halves:* K C Briscoe (Taranaki), C R Laidlaw (Otago)
*Forwards:* I J Clarke (Waikato), K F Gray (Wellington), J M Le Lievre (Canterbury),
W J Whineray (Auckland), D Young (Canterbury), J Major (Taranaki),
R H Horsley (Manawatu), C E Meads (King Country), A J Stewart (Canterbury),
S T Meads (King Country), K E Barry (Thames Valley), D J Graham (Canterbury),
W J Nathan (Auckland), K R Tremain (Hawke's Bay), B J Lochore (Wairarapa),
K A Nelson (Otago)
**Captain** W J Whineray **Manager** F D Kilby **Assistant Manager** N J McPhail

## 1967

| Full record | Played 15 Won 14 Lost 0 Drawn 1 Points for 294 Against 129 |
| in B Isles | Played 11 Won 10 Lost 0 Drawn 1 Points for 207 Against 78 |
| in France | Played 4 Won 4 Lost 0 Drawn 0 Points for 87 Against 51 |
| **International record** | Played 4 Won 4 Lost 0 |
| **International details** | New Zealand 23 England 11 |
| | New Zealand 13 Wales 6 |
| | New Zealand 21 France 15 |
| | New Zealand 14 Scotland 3 |

**Players**
*Full-back:* W F McCormick (Canterbury)
*Threequarters:* M J Dick (Auckland), W M Birtwistle (Waikato), A G Steel
(Canterbury), P H Clarke (Marlborough), G S Thorne (Auckland), W L Davis
(Hawke's Bay)
*Five-eighths:* I R MacRae (Hawke's Bay), G F Kember (Wellington),
W D Cottrell (Canterbury), E W Kirton (Otago), M A Herewini (Auckland)
*Scrum-halves:* C R Laidlaw (Otago), S M Going (North Auckland)
*Forwards:* B J Lochore (Wairarapa), I A Kirkpatrick (Canterbury),
W J Nathan (Auckland), K R Tremain (Hawke's Bay), G C Williams (Wellington),
M C Wills (Taranaki), C E Meads (King Country), A G Jennings (Bay of Plenty),
S C Strahan (Manawatu), A E Smith (Taranaki), A E Hopkinson (Canterbury),
E J Hazlett (Southland), B L Muller (Taranaki), K F Gray (Wellington),
B E McLeod (Counties), J Major (Taranaki)
**Captain** B J Lochore **Manager** C K Saxton **Assistant Manager** F R Allen

## 1972–73

| Full record | Played 30 Won 23 Lost 5 Drawn 2 Points for 568 Against 254 |
| in Britain and | |
| Ireland | Played 26 Won 20 Lost 4 Drawn 2 Points for 521 Against 227 |
| in France | Played 4 Won 3 Lost 1 Drawn 0 Points for 47 Against 27 |
| **International record** | Played 5 Won 3 Lost 1 Drawn 1 |
| **International details** | New Zealand 19 Wales 16 |
| | New Zealand 14 Scotland 9 |
| | New Zealand 9 England 0 |
| | New Zealand 10 Ireland 10 |
| | New Zealand 6 France 13 |

**Players**
*Full-backs:* J F Karam (Wellington), T J Morris (Nelson–Bays)
*Threequarters:* B G Williams (Auckland), G B Batty (Wellington),
D A Hales (Canterbury), G R Skudder (Waikato), B J Robertson (Counties),
I A Hurst (Canterbury)
*Five-eighths:* R M Parkinson (Poverty Bay), M Sayers (Wellington),
R E Burgess (Manawatu), I N Stevens (Wellington)
*Scrum-halves:* S M Going (North Auckland), G L Colling (Otago)
*Forwards:* A R Sutherland (Marlborough), A J Wyllie (Canterbury),
B Holmes (North Auckland), I A Kirkpatrick (Poverty Bay), K W Stewart (Southland),
A I Scown (Taranaki), H H Macdonald (Canterbury), I M Eliason (Taranaki),
A M Haden (Auckland), P J Whiting (Auckland), K Murdoch (Otago),
J D Matheson (Otago), K K Lambert (Manawatu), G J Whiting (King Country),
R A Urlich (Auckland), R W Norton (Canterbury), L A Clark* (Otago),
A L R McNicol* (Wanganui)
**Captain** I A Kirkpatrick   **Manager** F L Todd   **Assistant Manager** R H Duff

**1974** (to Ireland, and UK)

| **Full Record** | Played 8  Won 7  Lost 0  Drawn 1  Points for 127  Against 50 |
|---|---|
| in Ireland | Played 6  Won 6  Lost 0  Drawn 0  Points for 102  Against 34 |
| **International record** | Played 1    Won 1 |
| **International details** | New Zealand 15    Ireland 6 |

**Players**
*Full-backs:* J F Karam (Wellington), K T Going (North Auckland)
*Threequarters:* T W Mitchell (Canterbury), B G Williams (Auckland),
G B Batty (Wellington), B J Robertson (Counties), I A Hurst (Canterbury),
J E Morgan (North Auckland), G M Kane (Waikato)
*Half-backs:* D J Robertson (Otago), O D Bruce (Canterbury),
S M Going (North Auckland), I N Stevens (Wellington)
*Forwards:* A R Leslie (Wellington), L G Knight (Auckland),
I A Kirkpatrick (Poverty Bay), K W Stewart (Southland), K A Eveleigh (Manawatu),
P J Whiting (Auckland), H H Macdonald (Canterbury), J A Callesen (Manawatu), K J
Tanner (Canterbury), A J Gardiner (Taranaki), W K Bush (Canterbury),
K K Lambert (Manawatu), R W Norton (Canterbury), G M Crossman (Bay of Plenty)
**Captain** A R Leslie   **Manager** N H Stanley   **Assistant Manager** J J Stewart

**1977** (France only, except for one match in Italy)

| **Full record** | Played 9  Won 8  Lost 1  Points for 216  Against 86 |
|---|---|
| in Italy | Played 1  Won 1  Points for 17  Against 9 |
| in France | Played 8  Won 7  Lost 1  Points for 199  Against 77 |
| **International record** | Played 2  Won 1  Lost 1  Points for 28  Against 21 |
| **International details** | New Zealand 13    France 18 |
| | New Zealand 15    France  3 |

**Players**
*Full-back:* B W Wilson (Otago)
*Threequarters:* B G Williams (Auckland), B R Ford (Marlborough), B J Robertson
(Counties), S S Wilson (Wellington), N M Taylor (Bay of Plenty), W M Osborne
(Wanganui), B Hegarty* (Wellington & Biarritz)
*Half-backs:* O D Bruce (Canterbury), B J McKechnie (Southland), M W Donaldson
(Manawatu), K M Greene (Waikato)
*Forwards;* G N K Mourie (Taranaki), K A Eveleigh (Manawatu), L G Knight
(Poverty Bay), G A Seear (Otago), R G Myers (Waikato), R L Stuart (Hawke's
Bay), F J Oliver (Southland), A M Haden (Auckland), G A Knight (Manawatu),
B R Johnstone (Auckland), J C Ashworth (Canterbury), J T McEldowney
(Taranaki), A G Dalton (Counties), J E Black (Canterbury)
**Captain** G N K Mourie   **Manager** R M Don   **Assistant Manager** J Gleeson

# NEW ZEALAND TO SOUTH AFRICA

## 1928

**Full record**        Played 22 Won 16 Lost 5 Drawn 1 Points for 339 Against 144
**International record**   Played 4   Won 2   Lost 2
**International details**   New Zealand   0   South Africa 17
                                       New Zealand   7   South Africa   6
                                       New Zealand   6   South Africa 11
                                       New Zealand 13   South Africa   5

285

### Players

*Full-back:* H T Lilburne (Canterbury)
*Threequarters:* S R Carleton (Canterbury), B A Grenside (Hawke's Bay),
D F Lindsay (Otago), F W Lucas (Auckland), A C C Robilliard (Canterbury),
C A Rushbrook (Wellington), T R Sheen (Auckland)
*Five-eighths:* L M Johnson (Wellington), N P McGregor (Canterbury),
M F Nicholls (Wellington), W A Strang (South Canterbury)
*Scrum-halves:* W C Dalley (Canterbury), F D Kilby (Wellington)
*Forwards:* G T Alley (Canterbury), C J Brownlie (Hawke's Bay),
M J Brownlie (Hawke's Bay), J T Burrows (Canterbury),
I H Finlayson (North Auckland), S Hadley (Auckland), I H Harvey (Wairarapa),
W E Hazlett (Southland), J Hore (Otago), R G McWilliams (Auckland),
G Scrimshaw (Canterbury), E M Snow (Nelson), R T Stewart (South Canterbury),
J P Swain (Hawke's Bay), E P Ward (Taranaki)
**Captain** M J Brownlie   **Manager** W F Hornig

## 1949

**Full record**        Played 24 Won 14 Lost 7 Drawn 3 Points for 230 Against 146
**International record**   Played 4   Lost 4
**International details**   New Zealand 11   South Africa 15
                                       New Zealand   6   South Africa 12
                                       New Zealand   3   South Africa   9
                                       New Zealand   8   South Africa 11

### Players

*Full-backs:* J W Goddard (South Canterbury), R W H Scott (Auckland)
*Threequarters:* E G Boggs (Auckland), I J Botting (Otago), P Henderson (Wanganui),
W A Meates (Otago), Dr R R Elvidge (Otago), M P Goddard (South Canterbury)
*Five-eighths:* F R Allen (Auckland), K E Gudsell (Wanganui), N W Black (Auckland),
G W Delamore (Wellington), J C Kearney (Otago)
*Scrum-halves:* W J Conrad (Waikato), L T Savage (Canterbury)
*Forwards:* L A Grant (South Canterbury), N H Thornton (Auckland),
P J B Crowley (Auckland), P Johnstone (Otago), J R McNab (Otago),
H F Frazer (Hawke's Bay), L R Harvey (Otago), M J McHugh (Auckland),
C Willocks (Otago), D L Christian (Auckland), R A Dalton (Otago),
J G Simpson (Auckland), K L Skinner (Otago), E H Catley (Waikato),
N L Wilson (Otago)
**Captain** F R Allen   **Manager** J H Parker   **Assistant Manager** A McDonald

## 1960

**Full record**        Played 26 Won 20 Lost 4 Drawn 2 Points for 441 Against 164
**International record**   Played 4   Won 1   Lost 2   Drawn 1
**International details**   New Zealand   0   South Africa 13
                                       New Zealand 11   South Africa   3
                                       New Zealand 11   South Africa 11
                                       New Zealand   3   South Africa   8

**Players**
*Full-backs:* D B Clarke (Waikato), W A Davies (Auckland)
*Threequarters:* D H Cameron (Mid-Canterbury), R W Caulton (Wellington),
K F Laidlaw (Southland), R F McMullen (Auckland), T P A O'Sullivan (Taranaki),
J R Watt (Wellington)
*Five-eighths:* S G Bremner (Canterbury), A H Clarke (Auckland),
T R Lineen (Auckland), S R Nesbit (Auckland)
*Scrum-halves:* K C Briscoe (Taranaki), R J Urbahn (Taranaki)
*Forwards:* E J Anderson (Bay of Plenty), R J Boon* (Taranaki),
Dr H C Burry (Canterbury), I J Clarke (Waikato), R J Conway (Otago),
W D Gillespie (Otago), D J Graham (Canterbury), R C Hemi (Waikato),
R H Horsley (Wellington), M W Irwin (Otago), P F Jones (North Auckland),
I N MacEwan (Wellington), C E Meads (King Country), E A R Pickering (Waikato),
K R Tremain (Canterbury), W J Whineray (Auckland), D Young (Canterbury)
**Captain** W J Whineray  **Manager** T H Pearce  **Assistant Manager** J L Sullivan

---

**1970**

**Full record**　　Played 24 Won 21 Lost 3 Drawn 0 Points for 687 Against 228
**International record** Played 4 Won 1 Lost 3 Drawn 0
**International details** New Zealand　6　South Africa 17
　　　　　　　　　　　New Zealand　9　South Africa　8
　　　　　　　　　　　New Zealand　3　South Africa 14
　　　　　　　　　　　New Zealand 17　South Africa 20

**Players**
*Full-back:* W F McCormick (Canterbury)
*Threequarters:* M J Dick (Auckland), B A Hunter (Otago) B G Williams (Auckland),
G S Thorne (Auckland), W L Davis (Hawke's Bay), H P Milner (Wanganui)
*Five-eighths:* I R MacRae (Hawke's Bay), W D Cottrell (Canterbury),
E W Kirton (Otago), B D M Furlong (Hawke's Bay), G F Kember (Wellington)
*Scrum-halves:* C R Laidlaw (Otago), S M Going (North Auckland)
*Forwards:* B J Lochore (Wairarapa), A R Sutherland (Marlborough),
I A Kirkpatrick (Poverty Bay), A J Wyllie (Canterbury),
T N Lister (South Canterbury), B Holmes (North Auckland), C E Meads (King
Country), S C Strahan (Manawatu), A E Smith (Taranaki), J F Burns (Canterbury),
B L Muller (Taranaki), K Murdoch (Otago), A E Hopkinson (Canterbury),
N W Thimbleby (Hawke's Bay), B E McLeod (Counties), R A Urlich (Auckland)
**Captain** B J Lochore  **Manager** R L Burk  **Assistant Manager** I M H Vodanovich

---

**1976**

**Full record**　　Played 24 Won 18 Lost 6 Drawn 0 Points for 610 Against 291
**International record** Played 4 Won 1 Lost 3
**International details** New Zealand　7　South Africa 16
　　　　　　　　　　　New Zealand 15　South Africa　9
　　　　　　　　　　　New Zealand 10　South Africa 15
　　　　　　　　　　　New Zealand 14　South Africa 15

**Players**
*Full-backs:* L W Mains (Otago), C L Fawcett (Auckland)
*Threequarters:* B G Williams (Auckland), N A Purvis (Otago),
B J Robertson (Counties), W M Osborne (Wanganui), G B Batty (Bay of Plenty),
T W Mitchell (Canterbury)
*Five-eighths:* J E Morgan (N Auckland), J L Jaffray (Otago), D J Robertson (Otago),
O D Bruce (Canterbury)
*Scrum-halves:* L J Davis (Canterbury), S M Going (N Auckland)

*Forwards:* A R Leslie (Wellington), A R Sutherland (Marlborough),
K A Eveleigh (Manawatu), L G Knight (Poverty Bay) I A Kirkpatrick (Poverty Bay),
K W Stewart (Southland), P J Whiting (Auckland), G A Seear (Otago),
F J Oliver (Southland), H H Macdonald (N Auckland), K K Lambert (Manawatu),
W K Bush (Canterbury), K J Tanner (Canterbury), B R Johnstone (Auckland),
P C Harris* (Manawatu), R W Norton (Canterbury), G M Crossman (Bay of Plenty)
**Captain** A R Leslie   **Manager** N H Stanley   **Assistant Manager** J J Stewart

## SOUTH AFRICA TO BRITISH ISLES AND FRANCE

**1906–07** (British Isles only)

| | |
|---|---|
| **Full record** | Played 28  Won 25  Lost 2  Drawn 1  Points for 553  Against 79 |
| **International record** | Played 4   Won 2   Lost 1   Drawn 1 |
| **International details** | South Africa  0   Scotland  6 |
| | South Africa 15   Ireland  12 |
| | South Africa 11   Wales    0 |
| | South Africa  3   England  3 |

**Players**
*Full-backs:* A R Burmeister (WP), A F Marsberg (GW), S Joubert* (WP)
*Threequarters:* A C Stegmann (WP), J A Loubser (WP), J le Roux (WP),
A Morkel (TVL), J D Krige (WP), H A de Villiers (WP), J G Hirsch (EP),
S C de Melker (GW)
*Half-backs:* H W Carolin (WP), F J Dobbin (GW), D C Jackson (WP), D Mare (WP)
*Forwards:* P J Roos (WP), W A Burger (B), D Brooks (B), W A Neill (B),
H J Daneel (WP), P A le Roux (WP), D J Brink (WP), W C Martheze (GW),
J W E Raaff (GW), W S Morkel (TVL), D F T Morkel (TVL), H G Reid (TVL),
W A Millar (WP), A F Burdett (WP)
**Captain** P J Roos   **Manager** J C Carden

**1912–13**

| | |
|---|---|
| **Full record** | Played 27  Won 24  Lost 3  Drawn 0  Points for 441  Against 101 |
| in B Isles | Played 26  Won 23  Lost 3  Drawn 0  Points for 403  Against  96 |
| in France | Played  1  Won  1  Lost 0  Drawn 0  Points for  38  Against   5 |
| **International record** | Played 5   Won 5   Lost 0 |
| **International details** | South Africa 16   Scotland 0 |
| | South Africa 38   Ireland  0 |
| | South Africa  3   Wales    0 |
| | South Africa  9   England 3 |
| | South Africa 38   France  5 |

**Players**
*Full-backs:* P G Morkel (WP), J J Meintjies (GW)
*Threequarters:* J Stegmann (WP), A van der Hoff (TVL), E E McHardy (OFS),
W J Mills (WP), R R Luyt (WP), G M Wrentmore (WP), W A Krige (WP),
J Morkel (WP)
*Half-backs:* J D McCulloch (GW), F P Luyt (WP), J Immelman (WP), F J Dobbin (GW)
*Forwards:* E H Shum (TVL), D F T Morkel (TVL), T F van Vuuren (EP),
G Thompson (WP), A S Knight (TVL), S N Cronje (TVL), E T Delaney (GW),
W H Morkel (WP), S H Ledger (GW), L H Louw (WP) J A J Francis (TVL),
J S Braine (GW), W A Millar (WP), J D Luyt (EP)
**Captain** W A Millar   **Manager** M Honnet

**1931–32** (British Isles only)

| | |
|---|---|
| **Full record** | Played 26 Won 23 Lost 1 Drawn 2 Points for 407 Against 124 |
| **International record** | Played 4 Won 4 |
| **International details** | South Africa 8 Wales 3 |
| | South Africa 8 Ireland 3 |
| | South Africa 7 England 0 |
| | South Africa 6 Scotland 3 |

288 **Players**

*Full-backs:* J C Tindall (WP), G H Brand (WP)
*Threequarters:* J van Niekerk (WP), M Zimerman (WP), J H van der Westhuizen (WP), F D Venter (TVL), J C van der Westhuizen (WP), B G Gray (WP), F W Waring (WP), J White (B), D O Williams* (Villagers)
*Half-backs:* B L Osler (WP), M G Francis (OFS), P de Villiers (WP), D H Craven (Stellenbosch U)
*Forwards:* M M Louw (WP), S R du Toit (WP), A van der Merwe (Worcester), S C Louw (WP), P J Mostert (WP), A J McDonald (WP), L C Strachan (TVL), J N Bierman (TVL), H G Kipling (GW), G M Daneel (TVL), V Geere (TVL), P J Nel (N), W F Bergh (SWD), H M Forrest (TVL), J B Dold (EP)
**Captain** B L Osler  **Manager** T B Pienaar

**1951–52**

| | |
|---|---|
| **Full record** | Played 31 Won 30 Lost 1 Drawn 0 Points for 562 Against 167 |
| in B Isles | Played 27 Won 26 Lost 1 Drawn 0 Points for 499 Against 143 |
| in France | Played 4 Won 4 Lost 0 Drawn 0 Points for 63 Against 24 |
| **International record** | Played 5 Won 5 |
| **International details** | South Africa 44 Scotland 0 |
| | South Africa 17 Ireland 5 |
| | South Africa 6 Wales 3 |
| | South Africa 8 England 3 |
| | South Africa 25 France 3 |

**Players**

*Full-backs:* J Buchler (TVL), A C Keevy (E TVL)
*Threequarters:* J K Ochse (WP), F P Marais (Boland), M J Saunders (B), P Johnstone (WP), M T Lategan (WP), R A M van Schoor (R), D J Sinclair (TVL), S S Viviers (OFS)
*Half-backs:* J D Brewis (N TVL), D J Fry (WP), J S Oelofse (TVL), P A du Toit (N TVL)
*Forwards:* P W Wessels (OFS), W H Delport (EP), A C Koch (Boland), A Geffin (TVL), H P J Bekker (N TVL), F E van der Ryst (TVL), E E Dinkelmann (N TVL), J A Pickard (WP), G Dannhauser (TVL), W H M Barnard (GW), S P Fry (WP), C J van Wyk (TVL), B Myburgh (E TVL), J A du Rand (R), B J Kenyon (B), H S Muller (TVL)
**Captain** B J Kenyon  **Manager** F W Mellish  **Assistant Manager** Dr D H Craven

**1960–61**

| | |
|---|---|
| **Full record** | Played 34 Won 31 Lost 1 Drawn 2 Points for 567 Against 132 |
| in B Isles | Played 30 Won 28 Lost 1 Drawn 1 Points for 476 Against 110 |
| in France | Played 4 Won 3 Lost 0 Drawn 1 Points for 91 Against 22 |
| **International record** | Played 5 Won 4 Lost 0 Drawn 1 |
| **International details** | South Africa 3 Wales 0 |
| | South Africa 8 Ireland 3 |
| | South Africa 5 England 0 |
| | South Africa 12 Scotland 5 |
| | South Africa 0 France 0 |

**Players**

*Full-backs:* L G Wilson (WP), G J Wentzel (EP)
*Threequarters:* H J van Zyl (TVL), M J G Antelme (TVL), J P Engelbrecht (WP),
F du T Roux (WP), B P van Zyl* (WP), A I Kirkpatrick (GW), J L Gainsford
(WP), D A Stewart (WP), B B van Niekerk (OFS)
*Half-backs:* K Oxlee (N), C F Nimb (WP), R J Lockyear (GW), P de W Uys (N TVL)
*Forwards:* P S du Toit (WP), S P Kuhn (TVL), J L Myburgh (N TVL),
D N Holton (EP), G F Malan (WP), R A Hill (R), R G Johns* (WP),
A S Malan (TVL), J T Claassen (W TVL), H S van der Merwe (N TVL),
P J van Zyl (Boland), H J M Pelser (TVL), G H van Zyl (WP), J P F Botha
(N TVL), F C H du Preez (N TVL), D J Hopwood (WP), A P Baard (WP)
**Captain** A S Malan  **Manager** W F Bergh  **Assistant Manager** M M ('Boy') Louw

289

**1965** (Ireland and Scotland only)

**Full record**        Played 5  Won 0  Lost 4  Drawn 1  Points for 37  Against 53
**International record**  Played 2   Won 0   Lost 2   Drawn 0
**International details**  South Africa 6   Ireland   9
                          South Africa 5   Scotland 8

**Players**

*Full-back:* L G Wilson (WP)
*Threequarters:* G D Cilliers (OFS), C W Dirksen (N TVL), J P Engelbrecht (WP),
J L Gainsford (WP), W J Mans (WP), D A Stewart (WP)
*Half-backs:* J H Barnard (TVL), K Oxlee (N), S C Conradie* (WP),
D J de Villiers (WP), D J J de Vos (WP)
*Forwards:* S P Kuhn (TVL), J F K Marais (WP), J B Neethling (WP), D C Walton
(N), J W Wessels (OFS), G Carelse (EP), F C H du Preez (N TVL), A S Malan
(TVL), J Schoeman (WP), M R Suter (N), T P Bedford (N), D J Hopwood (WP)
**Captain** A S Malan  **Manager** B M Medway  **Assistant Manager** M M Louw

**1968** (France only)

**Full record**        Played 6  Won 5  Lost 1  Drawn 0  Points for 84   Against 43
**International record**  Played 2   Won 2
**International details**  South Africa 12   France   9
                          South Africa 16   France  11

**Players**

*Full-backs:* H O de Villiers (WP), R L Gould (N)
*Threequarters:* J P Engelbrecht (WP), S H Nomis (TVL), E Olivier (WP),
F du T Roux (WP), O A Roux (N TVL)
*Half-backs:* P J Visagie (GW), M A Menter (N TVL), D J de Villiers (WP),
P de W Uys (N TVL)
*Forwards:* J F K Marais (WP), J L Myburgh (N TVL), J B Neethling (WP),
G Pitzer (N TVL), D C Walton (N), F C H du Preez (N TVL), J P Naude (WP),
G Carelse (EP), J H Ellis (SWA), P J F Greyling (OFS), M J Lourens (N TVL),
T P Bedford (N)
**Captain** D J de Villiers  **Manager** F C Eloff  **Assistant Manager** J T Claassen

**1969–70** (British Isles only)

**Full record**        Played 24  Won 15  Lost 5  Drawn 4  Points for 323  Against 157
**International record**  Played 4   Lost 2   Drawn 2
**International details**  South Africa 3   Scotland  6
                          South Africa 8   England 11
                          South Africa 8   Ireland   8
                          South Africa 6   Wales     6

**Players**
*Full-backs:* H O de Villiers (WP), P J Durand (WP)
*Threequarters:* R N Grobler (N TVL), G H Muller (WP), S H Nomis (TVL),
A E van der Watt (WP), E Olivier (WP), O A Roux (N TVL),
J P van der Merwe (WP), P J van der Schyff (W TVL), F du T Roux* (GW)
*Half-backs:* M J Lawless (WP), P J Visagie (GW), D J de Villiers (Boland),
D J J de Vos (W TVL)
*Forwards:* J L Myburgh (N TVL), J B Neethling (WP), J F K Marais (EP),
R Potgieter (N TVL), G Carelse (EP), A E de Wet (WP), F C H du Preez
(N TVL), G Pitzer (N TVL), D C Walton (N), M C J van Rensburg (N),
A J Bates (W TVL), J H Ellis (SWA), P J F Greyling (TVL), P I van Deventer
(GW), T P Bedford (N), M W Jennings (Boland), I J de Klerk* (TVL),
C H Cockrell* (WP), R Barnard* (TVL)
**Captain** D J de Villiers **Manager** C A J Bornman **Assistant Manager** A S Malan

**1974** (France only)

**Full record**        Played 9  Won 8  Lost 1  Drawn 0  Points for 170  Against 74
**International record**  Played 2   Won 2
**International details**  South Africa 13   France 4
                          South Africa 10   France 8

**Players**
*Full-backs:* I W Robertson (R), D S L Snyman (WP)
*Threequarters:* C Fourie (EP), W P Stapelberg (N TVL), C F Pope (WP),
P J M Whipp (WP), J J Oosthuizen (WP), J A van Staden (N TVL)
*Half-backs:* J C P Snyman (OFS), G R Bosch (TVL), P C R Bayvel (TVL),
R J McCallum (WP)
*Forwards:* M du Plessis (WP), J L Kritzinger (TVL), J H Ellis (SWA),
T T Fourie (SE TVL), C J Grobler (OFS), J L Van Heerden (N TVL),
J G Williams (N TVL), K B H De Klerk (TVL), J De Bruyn (OFS), J F K Marais
(EP), N S E Bezuidenhoudt (N TVL), J C J Stander (OFS),
D S Van Den Berg (N), A Bestbier (OFS), R J Cockrell (WP)
**Captain** J F K Marais **Manager** J Z Le Roux
**Assistant Managers** J T Claassen and A I Kirkpatrick*

# SOUTH AFRICA TO AUSTRALIA AND NEW ZEALAND

## 1921

**Full record**
  in Australia        Played  4  Won  4  Lost 0  Drawn 0  Points for  83  Against 38
  in New Zealand  Played 19  Won 15  Lost 2  Drawn 2  Points for 244  Against 81
**International record**
  v New Zealand  Played 3   Won 1   Lost 1   Drawn 1
**International details**  South Africa 5   New Zealand 13
                          South Africa 9   New Zealand  5
                          South Africa 0   New Zealand  0

**Players**
*Full-backs:* P G Morkel (WP), I B de Villiers (TVL)
*Threequarters:* A J van Heerden (TVL), W C Zeller (N), J S Weepner (WP),
Henry Morkel (WP), W D Sendin (GW), W A Clarkson (N), S S Strauss (GW),
C du P Meyer (WP)
*Half-backs:* J S de Kock (WP), J C Tindall (WP), J P Michau (WP),
W H Townsend (N)

*Forwards:* T B Pienaar (WP), W H (Boy) Morkel (WP), M Ellis (TVL),
N J du Plessis (W TVL), G W van Rooyen (TVL), J M Michau (TVL),
T L Kruger (TVL), A P Walker (N), Royal Morkel (WP), F W Mellish (WP),
Harry Morkel (WP), J S Olivier (WP), L B Siedle (N), P J Mostert (WP),
H H Scholtz (WP)
**Captain** T B Pienaar  **Manager** H C Bennett

## 1937

**Full record**
  in Australia     Played  9 Won  8 Lost 1 Drawn 0 Points for 342 Against  65
  in New Zealand Played 17 Won 16 Lost 1 Drawn 0 Points for 411 Against 104
**International record**
  in Australia     Played 2  Won 2
  in New Zealand Played 3  Won 2  Lost 1
**International details**
  v Australia       South Africa  9   Australia        5
                    South Africa 26   Australia      17
  v New Zealand South Africa  7   New Zealand 13
                    South Africa 13   New Zealand  6
                    South Africa 17   New Zealand  6

**Players**
*Full-backs:* G H Brand (WP), F G Turner (TVL)
*Threequarters:* D O Williams (WP), P J Lyster (N), J A Broodryk (TVL),
A D Lawton (WP), L Babrow (WP), J L A Bester (Gardens), S R Hofmeyr (WP),
J White (B), G P Lochner (EP)
*Half-backs:* D F van de Vyver (WP), T A Harris (TVL), D H Craven (EP),
P du P de Villiers (WP)
*Forwards:* W E Bastard (N), W F Bergh (TVL), B A du Toit (TVL), C B Jennings
(B), J W Lotz (TVL), M M Louw (WP), S C Louw (TVL), H J Martin (TVL),
P J Nel (N), A R Sheriff (TVL), L C Strachan (TVL), M A van den Berg (WP),
G L van Reenen (WP) H H Watt (WP)
**Captain** P J Nel  **Manager** P W Day  **Assistant Manager** A de Villiers

## 1956

**Full record**
  in Australia     Played  6 Won  6 Lost 0 Drawn 0 Points for 150 Against  26
  in New Zealand Played 23 Won 16 Lost 6 Drawn 1 Points for 370 Against 177
**International record**
  v Australia       Played 2  Won 2
  v New Zealand Played 4  Won 1  Lost 3
**International details**
  v Australia       South Africa  9   Australia        0
                    South Africa  9   Australia        0
  v New Zealand South Africa  6   New Zealand 10
                    South Africa  8   New Zealand  3
                    South Africa 10   New Zealand 17
                    South Africa  5   New Zealand 11

**Players**
*Full-backs:* J U Buchler (TVL), S S Viviers (OFS)
*Threequarters:* K T van Vollenhoven (N TVL), P G Johnstone (TVL),
R G Dryburgh (N), J du Preez (WP), T P Briers* (WP), W Rosenberg (TVL),
P E Montini (WP), A I Kirkpatrick (GW), J J Nel (WP)

*Half-backs:* C A Ulyate (TVL), B F Howe (B), B D Pfaff (WP), T A Gentles (WP), C F Strydom (OFS)
*Forwards:* H P J Bekker (N TVL), A C Koch (Boland), P S du Toit (WP), H N Walker (W TVL), A J van der Merwe (Boland), M Hanekom (Boland), J A du Rand (N TVL), J T Claassen (W TVL), C J de Nysschen (N), J A J Pickard (WP), C J van Wyk (TVL), D S P Ackermann (WP), C J de Wilzem (OFS), G P Lochner (WP), D F Retief (N TVL), J Starke* (Stellenbosch)
**Captain** S S Viviers  **Manager** Dr D H Craven  **Assistant Manager** D J de Villiers

292

## 1965

**Full record**
in Australia      Played  6  Won  3  Lost 3  Drawn 0  Points for 184  Against  53
in New Zealand  Played 24  Won 19  Lost 5  Drawn 0  Points for 485  Against 232
**International record**
v Australia      Played 2   Lost 2
v New Zealand  Played 4   Won 1   Lost 3
**International details**
v Australia       South Africa 11   Australia       18
                South Africa  8   Australia       12
v New Zealand  South Africa  3   New Zealand  6
                South Africa  0   New Zealand 13
                South Africa 19   New Zealand 16
                South Africa  3   New Zealand 20

### Players
*Full-backs:* L G Wilson (WP), C G Mulder (E TVL)
*Threequarters:* J P Engelbrecht (WP), F du T Roux (GW), J L Gainsford (WP), E Olivier* (WP), G Brynard (WP), J T Truter (N), S H Nomis (TVL), W J Mans (WP), C J C Cronje (E TVL)
*Half-backs:* K Oxlee (N), J H Barnard (TVL), D J de Villiers (WP), C M Smith (OFS)
*Forwards:* D J Hopwood (WP), J A Nel (W TVL), J Schoeman (WP), F C H du Preez (N TVL), J P Naude (WP), J H Ellis (SWA), A W MacDonald (Rho), G F Malan (TVL), C P van Zyl (OFS), D C Walton (N), C P Goosen (OFS), T P Bedford (N), L J Slabber* (OFS), P H Botha (TVL), A Janson (WP), W H Parker (EP), J F Marais (EP)
**Captain** D J de Villiers  **Manager** J F Louw  **Assistant Manager** H S (Hennie) Muller

## 1971 (Australia only)

**Full record**      Played 13  Won 13  Lost 0  Drawn 0  Points for 396  Against 102
**International record**  Played 3   Won 3
**International details**  South Africa 19   Australia 11
                    South Africa 14   Australia  6
                    South Africa 18   Australia  6

### Players
*Full-backs:* I D McCallum (WP), O A Roux (N TVL)
*Threequarters:* G H Muller (WP), S H Nomis (TVL), J T Viljoen (N), P A Cronje (TVL), J S Jansen (OFS), P S Swanson (TVL), A E van der Watt* (WP)
*Half-backs:* P J Visagie (GW), D S L Snyman (WP), J F Viljoen (GW), D J J de Vos (W TVL)
*Forwards:* J F K Marais (EP), M J Louw (TVL), J T Sauermann (TVL), J F B van Wyk (N TVL), R W Barnard (TVL), F C H du Preez (N TVL), J J Spies (N TVL), J G Williams (N TVL), J H Ellis (SWA), P J F Greyling (TVL), M J Lourens (N TVL), T P Bedford (N), M du Plessis (WP), A J Bates* (W TVL)
**Captain** J F K Marais  **Manager** G P Lochner  **Assistant Manager** J T Claassen

# AUSTRALIA TO BRITISH ISLES AND FRANCE

**1908–09** (England and Wales only)

**Full record**  Played 31 Won 25 Lost 5 Drawn 1 Points for 438 Against 149
**International record**  Played 2  Won 1  Lost 1
**International details**  Australia 6  Wales  9
Australia 9  England 3

**Players**

*Full-backs:* P P Carmichael (Queensland), W Dix (Armidale)
*Threequarters:* C Russell (Newtown), F B Smith (Central West), H Daly (Central West),
D B Carroll (St George), J Hickey (Glebe), E Mandible (Sydney),
E Parkinson (Queensland)
*Five-eighths:* W Prentice (West Suburbs), A J McCabe (S Sydney),
J M Stevenson (Northern)
*Scrum-halves:* F Wood (Glebe), C H McKivat (Glebe)
*Forwards:* Dr H M Moran (Newcastle), T S Griffen (Glebe), S A Middleton (Glebe),
E McIntyre (Central West), K Gavin* (Central West), P A McCue (Newtown),
J T Barnett (Newtown), P H Burge (S Sydney), A B Burge* (S Sydney),
C E Murnin (Eastern Suburbs), N E Row (Eastern Suburbs),
M McArthur (Eastern Suburbs), P Flanagan (Queensland), T J Richards (Queensland),
C H McMurtrie (Orange), R R Craig (Balmain), C A Hammand (University)
**Captain** Dr H M Moran  **Manager** J McMahon  **Assistant Manager** S Wickham

**1927–28** (New South Wales, 'The Waratahs')

**Full Record**  Played 31 Won 24 Lost 5 Drawn 2 Points for 432 Against 207
in B Isles  Played 28 Won 22 Lost 4 Drawn 2 Points for 400 Against 177
in France  Played 3 Won 2 Lost 1 Drawn 0 Points for 32 Against 30
**International record**  Played 5  Won 3  Lost 2
**International details**  New South Wales  5  Ireland  3
New South Wales 18  Wales  8
New South Wales  8  Scotland 10
New South Wales 11  England 18
New South Wales 11  France  8

**Players**

*Full-back:* A W Ross (Sydney U)
*Threequarters:* E E Ford (Glebe-Balmain), A C Wallace (University and
Glebe-Balmain), A J A Bowers (Randwick), G C Gordon (YMCA), W H Mann
(University), C H T Towers (Randwick), W B J Sheehan (University),
S C King (Western Suburbs), J B Egan (Eastern Suburbs)
*Half-backs:* T Lawton (Western Suburbs), S J Malcolm (Newcastle),
F W Meagher (Randwick), J L Duncan (Randwick)
*Forwards:* J A Ford (Glebe-Balmain), A J Tancred (Glebe-Balmain),
J W Breckenridge (Glebe-Balmain), E N Greatorex (YMCA), A N Finlay (University),
G P Storey (Western Suburbs), G Bland (Manly), E J Thorn (Manly),
C L Fox (North Sydney), B Judd (Randwick), M R Blair (Western Suburbs),
J G Blackwood (Eastern Suburbs), H F Woods (YMCA), K Tarleton (YMCA),
J L Tancred (Glebe-Balmain)
**Captain** A C Wallace  **Manager** E Gordon Shaw

**1947–48**

**Full record**  Played 35 Won 29 Lost 6 Drawn 0 Points for 500 Against 243
in B Isles  Played 30 Won 25 Lost 5 Drawn 0 Points for 429 Against 197
in France  Played 5 Won 4 Lost 1 Drawn 0 Points for 71 Against 46
**International record**  Played 5  Won 3  Lost 2

**International details**

| | | |
|---|---|---|
| Australia | 16 | Scotland 7 |
| Australia | 16 | Ireland 3 |
| Australia | 0 | Wales 6 |
| Australia | 11 | England 0 |
| Australia | 6 | France 13 |

### Players

*Full-backs:* B J C Piper (NSW), C J Windsor (Queensland)
*Threequarters:* C C Eastes (NSW), A E J Tonkin (NSW), J W T MacBride (NSW),
T K Bourke (Queensland), T Allan (NSW), M L Howell (NSW), A K Walker (NSW)
*Five-eighths:* J F Cremin (NSW), N A Emery (NSW), E G Broad (Queensland)
*Scrum-halves:* C T Burke (NSW), R M Cawsey (NSW)
*Forwards:* W M McLean (Queensland), A J Buchan (NSW), C J Windon (NSW),
J O Stenmark (NSW), K C Winning (Queensland), J G Fuller (NSW),
G M Cooke (Queensland), P A Hardcastle (NSW), D F Kraefft (NSW),
N Shehadie (NSW), R E McMaster (Queensland), E Tweedale (NSW),
D H Keller (NSW), E H Davis (Victoria), K H Kearney (NSW), W L Dawson (NSW)
**Captain** W M McLean  **Manager** A J Tancred  **Assistant Manager** J Noseda

---

### 1957–58

| | | |
|---|---|---|
| **Full record** | Played 34 Won 16 Lost 15 Drawn 3 Points for 285 Against 244 | |
| in B Isles | Played 30 Won 14 Lost 13 Drawn 3 Points for 248 Against 203 | |
| in France | Played 4 Won 2 Lost 2 Drawn 0 Points for 37 Against 41 | |

**International record** Played 5 Lost 5

**International details**

| | | |
|---|---|---|
| Australia | 3 | Wales 9 |
| Australia | 6 | Ireland 9 |
| Australia | 6 | England 9 |
| Australia | 8 | Scotland 12 |
| Australia | 0 | France 19 |

### Players

*Full-backs:* T G Curley (NSW), J K Lenehan (NSW)
*Threequarters:* K J Donald (Queensland), R Phelps (NSW), A R Morton (NSW),
O G Fox (NSW), J A Phipps (NSW), G D Bailey (NSW), J M Potts (NSW),
S W White (NSW)
*Half-backs:* R Harvey (NSW), A Summons (NSW), D Logan (NSW),
D M Connor (Queensland)
*Forwards:* R A L Davidson (NSW), P T Fenwicke (NSW), N M Hughes (NSW),
W J Gunther (NSW), J E Thornett (NSW), K Yanz (NSW), E M Purkis (NSW),
A R Miller (NSW), A S Cameron (NSW), D M Emanuel (NSW), S Scotts (NSW),
N Shehadie (NSW), G N Vaughan (Victoria), K J Ryan (Queensland),
J V Brown (NSW), R Meadows (NSW)
**Captain** R A L Davidson  **Manager** T H McClenaughan
**Assistant Manager** D L Cowper

---

### 1966–67

| | | |
|---|---|---|
| **Full record** | Played 34 Won 17 Lost 14 Drawn 3 Points for 348 Against 322 | |
| in B Isles | Played 30 Won 15 Lost 13 Drawn 2 Points for 303 Against 280 | |
| in France | Played 4 Won 2 Lost 1 Drawn 1 Points for 45 Against 42 | |

**International record** Played 5 Won 2 Lost 3

**International details**

| | | |
|---|---|---|
| Australia | 14 | Wales 11 |
| Australia | 5 | Scotland 11 |
| Australia | 23 | England 11 |
| Australia | 8 | Ireland 15 |
| Australia | 14 | France 20 |

**Players**
*Full-backs:* J K Lenehan (NSW), P F Ryan (NSW)
*Threequarters:* E S Boyce (NSW), P V Smith (NSW), R Webb (Victoria),
R J Marks (Queensland), J E Brass (NSW), A M Cardy (NSW), J A Francis (NSW)
*Five-eighths:* P R Gibbs (Victoria), A M C Moore (NSW), P F Hawthorne (NSW)
*Scrum-halves:* J N B Hipwell (NSW), K W Catchpole (NSW)
*Forwards:* J E Thornett (NSW), R Cullen (Queensland), R B Prosser (NSW),
R G Teitzel (Queensland), R J Heming (NSW), R D Tulloch (Victoria),
J O'Gorman (NSW), G V Davis (NSW), C P Crittle (NSW), P G Johnson (NSW),
A R Miller (NSW), J M Miller (NSW), D A O'Callaghan (NSW),
D A Taylor (Queensland), M P Purcell (Queensland), J Guerassimoff (Queensland),
R Taylor* (NSW)
**Captain** J E Thornett  **Manager** R E M McLaughlin  **Assistant Manager** A S Roper

295

**1968** (Ireland and Scotland only)

| | |
|---|---|
| **Full record** | Played 5 Won 2 Lost 3 Drawn 0 Points for 38 Against 40 |
| **International record** | Played 2 Lost 2 |
| **International details** | Australia 3 Ireland 10 |
| | Australia 3 Scotland 9 |

**Players**
*Full-back:* A N McGill (NSW)
*Threequarters:* T R Forman (NSW), R P Batterham (NSW), J W Cole (NSW),
B D Honan (Queensland), A M Pope (Queensland), P V Smith (NSW),
J E Brass (NSW)
*Five-eighth:* J P Ballesty (NSW)
*Scrum-halves:* M J Barry (Queensland), J N B Hipwell (NSW)
*Forwards:* P G Johnson (NSW), P Darveniza (NSW), R B Prosser (NSW),
R V Turnbull (NSW), N P Reilly (Queensland), S C Gregory (Queensland),
K R Bell (Queensland), A J Skinner (NSW), D A Taylor (Queensland),
H A Rose (NSW), G V Davis (NSW)
**Captain** P G Johnson  **Manager** J H Lord  **Assistant Manager** D M Connor

**1971** (France only)

| | |
|---|---|
| **Full record** | Played 8 Won 4 Lost 4 Drawn 0 Points for 110 Against 101 |
| **International record** | Played 2 Won 1 Lost 1 |
| **International details** | Australia 13 France 11 |
| | Australia 9 France 18 |

**Players**
*Full-back:* A N McGill (NSW)
*Threequarters:* J W Cole (NSW), R P Batterham (NSW), L Monaghan (NSW),
J J McLean (Queensland), D L'Estrange (Queensland), D Rathie (Queensland),
G A Shaw (NSW)
*Half-backs:* G C Richardson (Queensland), R L Fairfax (NSW), J N B Hipwell (NSW),
G Grey (NSW)
*Forwards:* G V Davis (NSW), M Flynn (Queensland), P D Sullivan (NSW),
R McLean (NSW), O Butler (NSW), S Gregory (Queensland), B Stumbles (NSW),
R Smith (NSW), D Dunworth (Queensland), R B Prosser (NSW),
B Brown (Queensland), P G Johnson (NSW), R Thompson (WA)
**Captain** G V Davis  **Manager** J French  **Assistant Manager** R I Templeton

**1973** (England and Wales only)

| | |
|---|---|
| **Full record** | Played 8 Won 2 Lost 5 Drawn 1 Points for 85 Against 131 |

**International record** Played 2   Lost 2
**International details** Australia 0   Wales   24
Australia 3   England 20

**Players**
*Full-backs:* A N McGill (NSW), R L Fairfax (NSW) (utility back)
*Threequarters:* L E Monaghan (NSW), O Stephens (NSW), J J McLean (Queensland),
D R Burnet (NSW), R D L'Estrange (Queensland), G A Shaw (NSW)
*Half-backs:* G C Richardson (Queensland), P G Rowles (NSW), J N B Hipwell (NSW),
R G Hauser (South Australia)
*Forwards:* K G McCurrach (NSW), A A Shaw (Queensland), P D Sullivan (NSW),
B R Battishall (NSW), M R Cocks (Queensland), G Fay (NSW), R A Smith (NSW),
S C Gregory (NSW), J L Howard (NSW), R Graham (NSW), S G Macdougall
(NSW), M E Freney (Queensland), C M Carberry (NSW)
**Captain** P D Sullivan   **Manager** J E Freedman   **Assistant Manager** R I Templeton

296

---

**1975–76** (including one match in USA)

| | |
|---|---|
| **Full record** | Played 26  Won 19  Lost 6  Drawn 1  Points for 496  Against 349 |
| in B Isles | Played 25  Won 18  Lost 6  Drawn 1  Points for 472  Against 337 |
| in USA | Played  1  Won  1  Points for 24  Against 12 |

**International record** Played 5   Won 2   Lost 3
**International details** Australia 3   Scotland 10
Australia 3   Wales   28
Australia 6   England 23
Australia 20   Ireland   10
Australia 24   USA     12

**Players**
*Full-back:* M A Fitzgerald (NSW)
*Threequarters:* J R Ryan (NSW), L E Monaghan (NSW), P G Batch (Queensland),
L J Weatherstone (ACT), G A Shaw (NSW), W A McKid (NSW),
R D L'Estrange (Queensland), J Berne (NSW)
*Half-backs:* K J Wright (NSW), P E McLean (Queensland), J C Hindmarsh (NSW),
J N B Hipwell (NSW), R G Hauser (Queensland), G O Grey* (NSW)
*Forwards:* A A Shaw (Queensland), M E Loane (Queensland), R A Price (NSW),
G K Pearse (NSW), J K Lambie (NSW), G Cornelsen (NSW), R A Smith (NSW),
B W Mansfield (NSW), D W Hillhouse (Queensland), G S Eisenhauer (NSW[C]),
G Fay* (NSW), J E C Meadows (Victoria), S G Macdougall (ACT),
S C Finnane (NSW), R Graham (NSW), P A Horton (NSW), C M Carberry (NSW)
**Captain** J N B Hipwell   **Manager** R V Turnbull   **Assistant Manager** J D Brockhoff

---

**1976** (France only, except for one match in Italy)

| | |
|---|---|
| **Full record** | Played 10  Won 4  Lost 6  Drawn 0  Points for 114  Against 163 |
| in France | Played  9  Won 3  Lost 6  Drawn 0  Points for  98  Against 148 |
| in Italy | Played  1  Won 1  Lost 0  Drawn 0  Points for  16  Against  15 |

**International record** Played 2   Lost 2
**International details** Australia 15   France 18
Australia 6   France 34

**Players**
*Full-back:* P E McLean (Queensland)
*Threequarters:* P G Batch (Queensland), L E Monaghan (NSW), J R Ryan (NSW),
P J Crowe (NSW), G A Shaw (NSW), W A McKid (NSW),
G G Shambrook (Queensland)
*Half-backs:* K J Wright (NSW), J C Hindmarsh (NSW), R G Hauser (Queensland),
G O Grey (NSW)

*Forwards:* M E Loane (Queensland), A A Shaw (Queensland),
G Cornelsen (NSW), G K Pearse (NSW), B R Battishall (NSW), R A Smith (NSW),
D W Hillhouse (Queensland), G S Eisenhauer (NSW), K S Besomo (NSW),
R Graham (NSW), S C Finnane (NSW), J E C Meadows (Victoria),
D A Dunworth (Queensland), C M Carberry (NSW), P A Horton (NSW),
A M Gelling* (NSW)
**Captain** G A Shaw   **Manager** J G Bain   **Assistant Manager** R I Templeton

## AUSTRALIA TO SOUTH AFRICA

### 1933

| **Full record** | Played 23   Won 12 Lost 10 Drawn 1 Points for 299 Against 195 |
|---|---|
| **International record** | Played 5   Won 2   Lost 3 |
| **International details** | Australia  3   South Africa 17 |
| | Australia 21   South Africa  6 |
| | Australia  3   South Africa 12 |
| | Australia  0   South Africa 11 |
| | Australia 15   South Africa  4 |

**Players**
*Full-backs:* Dr A W Ross (NSW), F G McPhillips (NSW)
*Threequarters:* W J Warlow (Queensland), B A Grace (NSW), A D McLean
(Queensland), J Kelaher (NSW), J B Young (NSW), Dr G S Sturtridge (Victoria),
D L Cowper (Victoria), J C Steggall (Queensland)
*Half-backs:* R R Biilmann (NSW), C N Campbell (NSW), S J Malcolm (NSW),
W G Bennett (Queensland)
*Forwards:* O L Bridle (Victoria), J B T Doneley (Queensland),
G M Cooke (Queensland), W A Mackney (NSW), W Ritter (Queensland), W G S White
(Queensland), A J Hodgson (NSW), E Love (NSW), J G Clark (Queensland),
G Bland (NSW), R B Loudon (NSW), M C White (Queensland), M F Morton
(NSW) W H Cerutti (NSW), E T Bonis (Queensland)
**Captain** A W Ross   **Manager** Dr W F Mathews

### 1953

| **Full record** | Played 27   Won 16 Lost 10 Drawn 1 Points for 450 Against 413 |
|---|---|
| **International record** | Played 4   Won 1   Lost 3 |
| **International details** | Australia  3   South Africa 25 |
| | Australia 18   South Africa 14 |
| | Australia  8   South Africa 18 |
| | Australia  9   South Africa 22 |

**Players**
*Full-backs:* T Sweeney (Queensland), R Colbert (NSW)
*Threequarters:* E Stapleton (NSW), G Jones (Queensland), S W White (NSW),
G Horsley (Queensland), H S Barker (NSW), J Blomley (NSW), H J Solomon (NSW),
J A Phipps (NSW)
*Half-backs:* S W Brown (NSW), M Tate (NSW), C T Burke (NSW), J Bosler (NSW)
*Forwards:* N Shehadie (NSW), E Morey (NSW), A S Cameron (NSW),
A R Miller (NSW), C F Forbes (Queensland), R A L Davidson (NSW),
J C Carroll (NSW), F-M Elliott (NSW), J J Walsh (NSW), J Bain (NSW),
K A Cross (NSW), R Outterside (NSW), C Windon (NSW), D Brockhoff (NSW),
B B Johnson (NSW), N McL Hughes (NSW)
**Captain** H J Solomon   **Manager** J W Breckenridge   **Assistant Manager** A C Wallace

**1961** (Short)

| | |
|---|---|
| **Full record** | Played 6 Won 3 Lost 2 Drawn 1 Points for 90 Against 80 |
| **International record** | Played 2 Lost 2 |
| **International details** | Australia 3 South Africa 28 |
| | Australia 11 South Africa 23 |

### Players
*Full-back:* J Lenehan (NSW)
*Threequarters:* M Cleary (NSW), F Magrath (NSW), R Phelps (NSW),
B Ellwood (NSW), J Lisle (NSW)
*Half-backs:* J Dowse (NSW), H Roberts (Queensland), O Edwards (Queensland),
K Catchpole (NSW)
*Forwards:* T Reid (NSW), E Heinrich (NSW), J O'Gorman (NSW), R Heming (NSW),
J Thornett (NSW), R Thornett (NSW), G Macdougall (NSW), A Miller (NSW),
J White (NSW), D McDeed (NSW), P Johnson (NSW)
**Captain** K Catchpole **Manager** B J Halvorsen

**1963**

| | |
|---|---|
| **Full record** | Played 24 Won 15 Lost 8 Drawn 1 Points for 303 Against 233 |
| **International record** | Played 4 Won 2 Lost 2 |
| **International details** | Australia 3 South Africa 14 |
| | Australia 9 South Africa 5 |
| | Australia 11 South Africa 9 |
| | Australia 6 South Africa 22 |

### Players
*Full-backs:* T Casey (NSW), P Ryan (NSW)
*Threequarters:* K Walsham (NSW), J Williams (NSW), J Boyce (NSW),
J Wolfe (Queensland), R Marks (Queensland), I Moutray (NSW), P Jones (NSW),
B Ellwood (NSW)
*Half-backs:* P Hawthorne (NSW), J Klem (NSW), K Catchpole (NSW),
K McMullen (NSW)
*Forwards:* J Guerassimoff (Queensland), D O'Neill (Queensland), G Davis (NSW),
D Shepherd (Victoria), E Heinrich (NSW), J O'Gorman (NSW), R Heming (NSW),
J M Miller (NSW), P Crittle (NSW), J Thornett (NSW), J White (NSW),
L Austin (NSW), J Freedman (NSW), B Bailey (NSW), P Johnson (NSW),
M Jenkinson (NSW)
**Captain** J Thornett **Manager** R E M McLaughlin **Assistant Manager** A S Roper

**1969**

| | |
|---|---|
| **Full record** | Played 26 Won 15 Lost 11 Drawn 0 Points for 465 Against 353 |
| **International record** | Played 4 Won 0 Lost 4 Drawn 0 |
| **International details** | Australia 11 South Africa 30 |
| | Australia 9 South Africa 16 |
| | Australia 3 South Africa 11 |
| | Australia 8 South Africa 19 |

### Players
*Full-backs:* A N McGill (NSW), B A Weir (NSW)
*Threequarters:* T R Forman (NSW), R P Batterham (NSW), J W Cole (NSW),
P D Moore (Queensland), S O Knight (NSW), P V Smith (NSW),
B D Honan (Queensland), G A Shaw (NSW)
*Half-backs:* J P Ballesty (NSW), R G Rosenblum (NSW), J N B Hipwell (NSW),
M J Barry (Queensland)
*Forwards:* J R Roxburgh (NSW), J L Howard (NSW), R B Prosser (NSW),
S S Sullivan (Queensland), B S Taafe (NSW), P Darveniza (NSW),

S C Gregory (Queensland), A M Abrahams (NSW), N P Reilly (Queensland),
O F Butler (NSW), G V Davis (NSW), M R Cocks (NSW), B McDonald (NSW),
R J Kelleher (Queensland), H A Rose (NSW), A J Skinner (NSW),
R Wood* (Queensland)
**Captain** G V Davis    **Manager** C C Eastes    **Assistant Manager** D M Connor


# ENGLAND TO AUSTRALIA, NEW ZEALAND AND FIJI

**1963** (New Zealand and Australia only)

**Full record**
  in New Zealand Played 5  Won 1  Lost 4  Drawn 0  Points for 45  Against 73
  in Australia       Played 1  Won 0  Lost 1  Drawn 0  Points for  9  Against 18
**International record**
  v New Zealand  Played 2   Lost 2
  v Australia       Played 1   Lost 1
**International details**   England 11   New Zealand 21
                          England  6   New Zealand  9
                          England  9   Australia      18

**Players**
*Full-back:* R W Hosen (Northampton)
*Threequarters:* M S Phillips (Fylde), F D Sykes (Northampton),
M P Weston (Durham City), J C Gibson (United Services), J M Ranson (Rosslyn Park),
J M Dee (Hartlepool Rovers)
*Half-backs:* R F Read (Harlequins), J P Horrocks-Taylor (Leicester),
T C Wintle (St Mary's Hospital), S J S Clarke (Cambridge U)
*Forwards:* P E Judd (Coventry), J E Highton (United Services),
C R Jacobs (Northampton), H O Godwin (Coventry), J D Thorne (Bristol),
J E Owen (Coventry), T A Pargetter (Coventry),
A M Davis (Torquay Athletic), D P Rogers (Bedford), D G Perry (Bedford),
B J Wightman (Coventry), V R Marriott (Harlequins)
**Captain** M P Weston    **Manager** J T W Berry
**Assistant Manager** M R Steele-Bodger


**1973** (Fiji and New Zealand only)

**Full record**
  in Fiji           Played 1  Won 1  Lost 0  Drawn 0  Points for 13  Against 12
  in New Zealand Played 4  Won 1  Lost 3  Drawn 0  Points for 47  Against 60
**International record**
  v New Zealand  Played 1   Won 1
**International details**   England 16   New Zealand 10
**Players**
*Full-backs:* P A Rossborough (Coventry), A M Jorden (Blackheath)
*Threequarters:* D J Duckham (Coventry), P M Knight (Bristol), P J Squires (Harrogate),
J P A G Janion (Richmond), G W Evans (Coventry), P S Preece (Coventry)
*Half-backs:* A G B Old (Leicester), M J Cooper (Moseley), S J Smith (Sale),
J G Webster (Moseley)
*Forwards:* M A Burton (Gloucester), C B Stevens (Penzance-Newlyn),
F E Cotton (Loughborough Colls and Coventry), J V Pullin (Bristol), J White (Bristol),
C W Ralston (Richmond), N O Martin (Bedford), R M Uttley (Gosforth),
R M Wilkinson (Cambridge U and Bedford), P J Hendy (St Ives),
A Neary (Broughton Park), J A Watkins (Gloucester), A G Ripley (Rosslyn Park)
**Captain** J V Pullin    **Manager** D L Sanders    **Assistant Manager** J Elders

**1975** (Australia only)

**Full record**        Played 8  Won 4  Lost 4  Drawn 0  Points for 217  Against 110
**International record**  Played 2   Lost 2
**International details**  England  9   Australia 16
                            England 21   Australia 30

**Players**

*Full-backs:* P E Butler (Gloucester), A J Hignell (Cambridge U)

300    *Threequarters:* P J Squires (Harrogate), A J Morley (Bristol), D M Wyatt (Bedford),
P S Preece (Coventry), K Smith (Roundhay), A W Maxwell (New Brighton),
J P A G Janion* (Richmond)

*Half-backs:* W N Bennett (Bedford), A J Wordsworth (Cambridge U),
A G B Old* (Middlesbrough), W B Ashton (Orrell), P Kingston (Gloucester),
I N Orum* (Roundhay)

*Forwards:* A G Ripley (Rosslyn Park), D M Rollitt (Bristol), A Neary (Broughton Park),
S R Callum (Upper Clapton), P J Dixon* (Gosforth), R M Uttley (Gosforth),
W B Beaumont (Fylde), R M Wilkinson (Bedford), N D Mantell (Rosslyn Park),
F E Cotton (Coventry), M A Burton (Gloucester), P J Blakeway (Gloucester),
B G Nelmes* (Cardiff), J V Pullin (Bristol), J A G D Raphael (Northampton)

**Captain** A Neary   **Manager** A O Lewis   **Assistant Manager** J Burgess


# ENGLAND TO SOUTH AFRICA

### 1972

**Full record**        Played 7  Won 6  Lost 0  Drawn 1  Points for 166  Against 58
**International record**  Played 1   Won 1
**International details**  England 18   South Africa 9

**Players**

*Full-backs:* S A Doble (Moseley), D F Whibley (Leicester)

*Threequarters:* P M Knight (Bristol), A A Richards (Fylde), J P A G Janion (Bedford),
A J Morley (Bristol), J S Spencer (Headingley), P S Preece (Coventry)

*Half-backs:* A G B Old (Middlesbrough), T Palmer (Gloucester),
L E Weston (West of Scotland), J G Webster (Moseley),
S Smith* (Loughborough Colls)

*Forwards:* M A Burton (Gloucester), F E Cotton (Loughborough Colls),
C B Stevens (Harlequins and Penzance-Newlyn), J V Pullin (Bristol),
A V Boddy (Metropolitan Police), P J Larter (RAF and Northampton),
C W Ralston (Richmond), D E J Watt (Bristol), T A Cowell (Rugby),
A Neary (Broughton Park), J A Watkins (Gloucester), J Barton (Coventry),
A G Ripley (Rosslyn Park)

**Captain** J V Pullin   **Manager** A O Lewis   **Assistant Manager** J Elders


# SCOTLAND TO SOUTH AFRICA

### 1960

**Full record**        Played 3  Won 2  Lost 1  Drawn 0  Points for 61  Against 45
**International record**  Played 1   Lost 1
**International details**  Scotland 10   South Africa 18

**Players**

*Full-back:* R W T Chisholm (Melrose)

*Threequarters:* A R Smith (Cambridge U, Edinburgh Wands),
R H Thomson (London Scottish), R C Cowan (Selkirk), G D Stevenson (Hawick),
T McClung (Edinburgh Acads), P J Burnet (London Scottish)

*Half-backs:* G H Waddell (London Scottish), R B Shillinglaw (Gala and Army),
A J Hastie (Melrose)

*Forwards:* H F McLeod (Hawick), J B Neill (Edinburgh Acads),
D M D Rollo (Howe of Fife), N S Bruce (Blackheath), T O Grant (Hawick),
J W Y Kemp (Glasgow HSFP), F H ten Bos (Oxford U, London Scottish),
W Hart (Melrose), D B Edwards (Heriot's FP), R M Tollervey (Heriot's FP),
C E B Stewart (Kelso)
**Captain** G H Waddell   **Managers** R W Shaw and C W Drummond

## SCOTLAND TO AUSTRALIA

### 1970

**Full record**       Played 6  Won 3  Lost 3  Drawn 0  Points for 109  Against 94
**International record**  Played 1   Lost 1
**International details**  Scotland 3   Australia 23
**Players**
*Full-back:* I S G Smith (London Scottish)
*Threequarters:* M A Smith (London Scottish), J N M Frame (Gala), J W C Turner (Gala),
C W Rea (W of Scotland), A G Biggar (London Scottish), A D Gill (Gala)
*Half-backs:* I Robertson (Watsonians), C M Telfer (Hawick, D S Paterson (Gala),
G C Connell (London Scottish)
*Forwards:* F A L Laidlaw (Melrose), D T Deans (Hawick), N Suddon (Hawick),
J McLauchlan (Jordanhill Coll), A B Carmichael (W of Scotland), P K Stagg (Sale),
G L Brown (W of Scotland), P C Brown (Gala), T G Elliot (Langholm),
W Lauder (Neath), G K Oliver (Gala), R J Arneil (Leicester)
**Captain** F A L Laidlaw   **Managers** H S P Monro and G Burrell

## SCOTLAND TO NEW ZEALAND

### 1975

**Full record**       Played 7  Won 4  Lost 3  Drawn 0  Points for 157  Against 104
**International record**  Played 1   Lost 1
**International details**  Scotland 0   New Zealand 24
**Players**
*Full-backs:* A R Irvine (Heriot's FP), B H Hay (Boroughmuir)
*Threequarters:* W C C Steele (RAF and London Scottish), L G Dick (Jordanhill),
J N M Frame (Gala), D L Bell (Watsonians), G A Birkett (Harlequins),
J M Renwick (Hawick)
*Half-backs:* I R McGeechan (Headingley), C M Telfer (Hawick),
A J M Lawson (London Scottish), D W Morgan (Stewart's Melville FP)
*Forwards:* D G Leslie (Dundee HSFP), G Y Mackie (Highland),
W S Watson (Boroughmuir), W Lauder (Neath), M A Biggar (London
Scottish),
A J Tomes (Hawick), I A Barnes (Hawick), A F McHarg (London Scottish),
N A K Pender (Hawick), A B Carmichael (West of Scotland).
J McLauchlan (Jordanhill), D F Madsen (Gosforth), C D Fisher (Waterloo)
**Captain** J McLauchlan   **Manager** G Burrell   **Assistant Manager** W Dickinson

## IRELAND TO SOUTH AFRICA

### 1961

**Full record**       Played 4  Won 3  Lost 1  Drawn 0  Points for 59  Against 36
**International record**  Played 1   Lost 1
**International details**  Ireland 8   South Africa 24
**Players**
*Full-back:* T J Kiernan (UC Cork, Cork Constitution)

*Threequarters:* A J F O'Reilly (Old Belvedere, Leicester), N H Brophy (UC Dublin),
J C Walsh (UC Cork, Sunday's Well), K J Houston (London Irish, Oxford U),
W J Hewitt (Instonians), J F Dooley (Galwegians)
*Half-backs:* W G Tormey (UC Dublin), D C Glass (Belfast Collegians),
A A Mulligan (Cambridge U, London Irish), T J Cleary (Limerick)
*Forwards:* S Millar (Ballymena), B G M Wood (Garryowen), J N Thomas (Blackrock),
A R Dawson (Wanderers), J S Dick (Queen's U, Belfast).
W A Mulcahy (UC Dublin, Bective Rangers), M G Culliton (Wanderers),
C J Dick (Ballymena), N A A Murphy (Cork Constitution), D Scott (Malone),
J R Kavanagh (UC Dublin, Wanderers), T McGrath (Garryowen)
**Captain** A R Dawson    **Manager** N F Murphy    **Assistant Manager** T A O'Reilly

302

# IRELAND TO AUSTRALIA

**1967**

**Full record**        Played 6  Won 4  Lost 2  Drawn 0  Points for 119  Against 80
**International record**  Played 1    Won 1
**International details**  Ireland 11    Australia 5
**Players**
*Full-back:* T J Kiernan (Cork Constitution)
*Threequarters:* A T A Duggan (Lansdowne), F P K Bresnihan (UC Dublin),
J C Walsh (UC Cork), N H Brophy (UC Dublin), P J McGrath (UC Cork),
J B Murray (UC Dublin)
*Half-backs:* C M H Gibson (NIFC), B F Sherry (Terenure), L Hall (UC Cork)
*Forwards:* S A Hutton (Malone), K W Kennedy (London Irish), S MacHale
(Lansdowne), P O'Callaghan (Dolphin), W J McBride (Ballymena), M G Molloy
(UC Galway), K G Goodall (City of Derry), T A Moore (Highfield),
M G Doyle (UC Dublin), L G Butler (Blackrock), J M Flynn
(Wanderers), D J Hickie (St Mary's College)
**Captain** T J Kiernan    **Manager** E O'D Davy    **Assistant Manager** D McKibbin

# IRELAND TO NEW ZEALAND AND FIJI

**1976**

**Full record**        Played 8  Won 5  Lost 3  Points for 96  Against 68
        in New Zealand Played 7  Won 4  Lost 3  Points for 88  Against 68
        in Fiji        Played 1  Won 1  Lost 0  Points for  8  Against  0
**International record**  Played 1    Lost 1
**International details**  Ireland 3    New Zealand 11
**Players**
*Full-backs:* A H Ensor (Wanderers), L A Moloney (Garryowen)
*Threequarters:* T O Grace (St Mary's Coll), A W McMaster (Ballymena),
J A Brady (Wanderers), C M H Gibson (North of Ireland FC), J A McIlrath
(Ballymena)
*Half-backs:* B J McGann (Cork Const), M A Quinn (Lansdowne),
D M Canniffe (Lansdowne), J C Robbie (Dublin U), R J M McGrath* (Wanderers)
*Forwards:* W P Duggan (Blackrock Coll), H W Steele (Ballymena),
S A McKinney (Dungannon), S M Deering (Garryowen), J C Davidson*
(Dungannon), R F Hakin (CIYMS), M I Keane (Lansdowne), B O Foley
(Shannon), E J O'Rafferty (Wanderers), T A O Feighery (St Mary's Coll),
P O'Callaghan (Dolphin), P A Orr (Old Wesley), R J Clegg (Bangor),
J L Cantrell (UC Dublin), P C Whelan (Garryowen)
**Captain** T O Grace  **Manager** K J Quilligan  **Assistant Manager** T W Meates

# WALES TO SOUTH AFRICA

**1964**

**Full record**     Played 4  Won 2  Lost 2  Drawn 0  Points for 43  Against 58
**International record**  Played 1  Lost 1
**International details**  Wales 3   South Africa 24
**Players**
*Full-backs:* G T R Hodgson (Neath), H J Davies (London Welsh)
*Threequarters:* D I Bebb (Carmarthen TC, Swansea), S J Watkins (Newport),
P M Rees (Newport), K Bradshaw (Bridgend), D K Jones (London Welsh,
Cardiff), S J Dawes (London Welsh)
*Half-backs:* D Watkins (Newport), M Young (Bridgend),
D C T Rowlands (Pontypool), A R Lewis (Abertillery)
*Forwards:* L J Cunningham (Aberavon), D Williams (Ebbw Vale), R G Waldron
(Neath), N R Gale (Llanelli), J Isaacs (Swansea), B E Thomas (Neath), B Price
(Newport), J T Mantle (Loughborough Colls), D J Hayward (Cardiff),
H J Morgan (Abertillery), G J Prothero (Bridgend), A E I Pask (Abertillery)
**Captain** D C T Rowlands   **Manager** D J Phillips
**Assistant Manager** Alun G Thomas

# WALES TO AUSTRALIA, NEW ZEALAND AND FIJI

**1969**

**Full record**
  in New Zealand Played 5  Won 2  Lost 2  Drawn 1  Points for 62  Against 76
  in Australia      Played 1  Won 1  Lost 0  Drawn 0  Points for 19  Against 16
  in Fiji           Played 1  Won 1  Lost 0  Drawn 0  Points for 31  Against 11
**International record**
  v New Zealand  Played 2   Lost 2
  v Australia    Played 1   Won 1
**International details**
  v New Zealand  Wales  0   New Zealand 19
                 Wales 12   New Zealand 33
  v Australia    Wales 19   Australia    16
**Players**
*Full-back:* J P R Williams (London Welsh)
*Threequarters:* S J Watkins (Newport), A P Skirving (Newport),
M C R Richards (Cardiff), S J Dawes (London Welsh), T G R Davies (Cardiff),
K S Jarrett (Newport)
*Half-backs:* B John (Cardiff), P Bennett (Llanelli), G O Edwards (Cardiff),
R Hopkins (Maesteg)
*Forwards:* T M Davies (London Welsh), D Hughes (Newbridge), W D Morris (Neath),
J Taylor (London Welsh), B Price (Newport), B E Thomas (Neath),
W D Thomas (Llanelli), D B Llewelyn (Newport), D J Lloyd (Bridgend),
D Williams (Ebbw Vale), N R Gale (Llanelli), J Young (Harrogate),
V C Perrins* (Newport)
**Captain** B Price  **Manager** H C Rogers  **Assistant Manager** D C T Rowlands

# FRANCE TO SOUTH AFRICA

**1958**

**Full record**     Played 10  Won 5  Lost 3  Drawn 2  Points for 137  Against 124
**International record**  Played 2  Won 1  Drawn 1
**International details**  France 3   South Africa 3
                          France 9   South Africa 5

**Players**

*Full-backs:* M Vannier (Racing Club de France), P Lacaze (FC Lourdais)
*Threequarters:* J Dupuy (S Tarbais), H Rancoule (FC Lourdais), J Lepatey (SC Mazamet),
L Rogé (AS Béziers), A Marquesuzaa (Racing Club de France), G Stener (Paris U),
L Casaux (S Tarbais)
*Half-backs:* R Martine (FC Lourdais), A Haget (Paris UC), P Danos (AS Béziers),
P Lacroix (S Montois)
*Forwards:* J Barthe (FC Lourdais), M Celaya (Biarritz), J Carrère (RC Toulonnais),
L Mias (SC Mazamet), B Mommejat (S Cadurcien), R Baulon (A Bayonnais),
F Moncla (Racing Club de France), L Echavé (SU Agen), A Roques (S Cadurcien),
R Barrière (AS Béziers), A Quaglio (SC Mazamet), R Vigier (AS Montferrand),
A Fremaux (Paris U), J de Gregorio (FC Grenoble)
**Captain** M Celaya  **Manager** S Saulnier  **Assistant Manager** M Laurent

## 1964

**Full record**     Played 6 Won 5 Lost 1 Drawn 0 Points for 117 Against 55
**International record**  Played 1   Won 1
**International details**  France 8   South Africa 6
**Players**
*Full-back:* P Dedieu (AS Béziers)
*Threequarters:* J Gachassin (FC Lourdais), C Darrouy (S Montois),
M Arnaudet (FC Lourdais), R Halçaren (FC Lourdais), J Dupuy (S Tarbais),
J Piqué (S Paloise)
*Half-backs:* P Albaladejo (US Dacquoise), J Capdouze (S Paloise),
J-C Hiquet (SU Agen), J-C Lasserre (US Dax), C Laborde (RCF)
*Forwards:* W Spanghero (RC Narbonne), M Crauste (FC Lourdais),
M Lira (La Voulte S), M Sitjar (SU Agen), J-J Rupert (US Tyrosse),
B Dauga (S Montois), E Cester (Toulouse OEC), A Herrero (RC Toulonnais),
A Gruarin (RC Toulonnais), J C Berejnoi (SC Tulle), M Etcheverry (S Paloise),
Y Menthiller (US Romans), J M Cabanier (US Montauban)
**Captain** M Crauste  **Manager** S Saulnier  **Assistant Manager** J Prat

## 1967

**Full record**     Played 13 Won 8 Lost 4 Drawn 1 Points for 209 Against 161
**International record**  Played 4   Won 1   Lost 2   Drawn 1
**International details**  France  3   South Africa 26
                          France  3   South Africa 16
                          France 19   South Africa 14
                          France  6   South Africa  6

**Players**
*Full-backs:* C Lacaze (SC Angoulême), P Villepreux (S Toulousain),
J Crampagne (CA Beglais)
*Threequarters:* C Darrouy (S Montois), J Londios (US Montauban),
B Duprat (A Bayonnais), J-P Lux (US Tyrosse), C Dourthe (US Dax),
J Trillo (CA Beglais), J Saby (SC Graulhet), J-P Mir (FC Lourdais)
*Half-backs:* G Camberabero (La Voulte S), J-L Dehez (SU Agen),
J-C Roques (CA Brive), M Puget (CA Brive), G Sutra (R C Narbonne)
*Forwards:* A Abadie (SC Graulhet), J-M Esponda (Racing Club de France),
M Lasserre (SU Agen), B Cardebat (US Montauban), J-M Cabanier (US Montauban),
J-C Malbet (SU Agen), B Dauga (S Montois), W Spanghero (RC Narbonne),
J Fort (SU Agen), A Plantefol (Racing Club de France), C Carrère (RC Toulonnais),
M Sitjar (SU Agen), A Quilis (RC Narbonne), G Viard (RC Narbonne)
**Captain** C Darrouy  **Manager** M Laurent  **Assistant Manager** A Garrigues

## 1971

| Full record | Played 9 Won 7 Lost 1 Drawn 1 Points for 228 Against 92 |
|---|---|
| **International record** | Played 2 Lost 1 Drawn 1 |
| **International details** | France 9 South Africa 22 |
| | France 8 South Africa 8 |

**Players**

*Full-back:* P Villepreux (S Toulousain)

*Threequarters:* R Bertranne (S Bagnerais), R Bourgarel (S Toulousain), J Cantoni (AS Béziers), C Dourthe (US Dax), A Marot (CA Brive), J Maso (R C Narbonne), J Sillières (S Tarbais), J Trillo (CA Beglais)

*Half-backs:* M Barrau (S Beaumontois), J-L Berot (S Toulousain), G Pardiès* (SU Agen), M Pebeyre (AS Montferrand)

*Forwards:* J-L Azarète (St Jean-de-Luz Ol), J-P Bastiat (US Dax), P Biemouret (SU Agen), C Carrère (RC Toulonnais), B Dauga (S Montois), A Estève (AS Béziers), M Etcheverry (S Paloise), J Iraçabal (A Bayonnais), M Lasserre (SU Agen), J le Droff (FC Auch), J-C Skrela (S Toulousain), C Spanghero (RC Narbonne), W Spanghero (RC Narbonne), C Swierczinski (CA Beglais), M Yachvili (CA Brive)

**Captain** C Carrère  **Manager** E Pebeyre

**Assistant Managers** F Cazenave and M Celaya

305

## 1975

| Full record | Played 11 Won 6 Lost 4 Drawn 1 Points for 282 Against 190 |
|---|---|
| **International record** | Played 2 Lost 2 |
| **International details** | France 25 South Africa 38 |
| | France 18 South Africa 33 |

**Players**

*Full-backs:* J M Aguirre (S Bagnerais), M Droitecourt (AS Montferrand)

*Threequarters:* J-C Amade (Biarritz Ol), J-L Averous (La Voulte Sp), D Harize (S Cahors), M Dupey (FC Auch), C Badin (CA Brive), R Bertranne (S Bagnerais), J-M Etchenique (Biarritz Ol), F Sangalli (RC Narbonne)

*Half-backs:* J-P Romeu (AS Montferrand), J P Pesteil (AS Béziers), R Astre (AS Béziers), J Fouroux (La Voulte Sp)

*Forwards:* Y Brunet (USA Perpignan), J Costantino (AS Montferrand), D Revallier (UA Gaillac), R Paparemborde (S Paloise), B Forestier (CA Beglais), G Cholley (Castres Ol), J-P Decrae (Racing Club de France), F Haget (SU Agen), A Guilbert (RC Toulon), M Julian (Castres Ol), M Yachvili (CA Brive), J-C Skréla (S Toulousain), P Peron (Racing Club de France), S Lassoujade (SU Agen), G Rousset (AS Béziers), J-L Joinel (CA Brive), M Palmie* (AS Béziers)

**Captains (joint)** R Astre and J Fouroux  **Manager** M Batigne

**Assistant Managers** M Celaya and F Cazenave

# FRANCE TO AUSTRALIA AND NEW ZEALAND

## 1961

| Full record | | |
|---|---|---|
| in New Zealand | Played 13 Won 6 Lost 7 Drawn 0 Points for 150 Against 149 |
| in Australia | Played 2 Won 2 Lost 0 Drawn 0 Points for 30 Against 20 |
| **International record** | | |
| v New Zealand | Played 3 Lost 3 |
| v Australia | Played 1 Won 1 |

**International details**

| v New Zealand | France | 6 | New Zealand | 13 |
|---|---|---|---|---|
| | France | 3 | New Zealand | 5 |
| | France | 3 | New Zealand | 32 |
| v Australia | France | 15 | Australia | 8 |

**Players**

*Full-backs:* M Vannier (RC Chalon), J Meynard (US Cognac)

*Threequarters:* S Plantey (Racing Club de France), G Boniface (S Montois), H Rancoule (RC Toulon), J Dupuy (S Tarbais), G Calvo (FC Lourdais), J Piqué (S Paloise), J Bouquet (CS Vienne), A Boniface (S Montois)

*Half-backs:* C Lacaze (FC Lourdais), G Camberabero (La Voulte S), P Albaladejo (US Dacquoise), P Lacroix (SU Agen), L Camberabero (La Voulte S), J Serin (SC Mazamet)

*Forwards:* M Celaya (S Bordelais), S Meyer (CA Perigueux), R Lefèvre (CA Brive), M Crauste (FC Lourdais), F Moncla (S Paloise), C Vidal (SC Mazamet), M Cassiede (US Dax), J P Saux (S Paloise), A Domenech (CA Brive), A Bianco (FC Auch), G Bouguyon (FC Grenoble), P Cazals (S Montois), J Laudouar (AS Soustons), J Rollet (A Bayonnais)

**Captain** F Moncla   **Manager** M Laurent   **Assistant Manager** G Basquet

---

**1968**

**Full record**

| | | | | | | | |
|---|---|---|---|---|---|---|---|
| in New Zealand | Played 12 | Won 8 | Lost 4 | Drawn 0 | Points for 154 | Against 120 |
| in Australia | Played 2 | Won 1 | Lost 1 | Drawn 0 | Points for 41 | Against 22 |

**International record**

| v New Zealand | Played 3 | Lost 3 |
|---|---|---|
| v Australia | Played 1 | Lost 1 |

**International details**

| v New Zealand | France | 9 | New Zealand | 12 |
|---|---|---|---|---|
| | France | 3 | New Zealand | 9 |
| | France | 12 | New Zealand | 19 |
| v Australia | France | 10 | Australia | 11 |

**Players**

*Full-backs:* P Villepreux (S Toulousain), C Lacaze (Angoulême)

*Threequarters:* A Campaes (FC Lourdais), J M Bonal (S Toulousain), P Besson (CA Brive), A Piazza (US Montauban), J-P Lux (US Tyrosse), C Dourthe (US Dax), J Trillo (CA Beglais), J Maso (US Perpignan)

*Half-backs:* J Andrieu (SC Graulhet), C Boujet (Grenoble), J-L Berot (S Toulousain), M Puget (CA Brive)

*Forwards:* M Greffe (Grenoble), W Spanghero (RC Narbonne), M Billiere (S Toulousain), J Salut (Toulouse OEC), C Carrère (RC Toulonnais), B Dutin (Mont de Marsan), C Chenevay (Grenoble), B Dauga (Mont de Marsan), A Plantefol (SU Agen), E Cester (Toulouse OEC), J-M Esponda (US Perpignan), M Lasserre (SU Agen), J-C Noble (La Voulte S), J Iraçabal (A Bayonnais), M Yachvili (SC Tulle), J-P Baux (CA Lannemezan)

**Captain** C Carrère   **Manager** J-C Bourrier   **Assistant Manager** A Garrigues

---

**1972** (Australia only)

| **Full record** | Played 9 | Won 8 | Lost 0 | Drawn 1 | Points for 254 | Against 122 |
|---|---|---|---|---|---|---|
| **International record** | Played 2 | Won 1 | Drawn 1 | | | |
| **International details** | France 14 | Australia 14 | | | | |
| | France 16 | Australia 15 | | | | |

306

**Players**

*Full-backs:* P Villepreux (S Toulousain), H Cabrol (AS Béziers)
*Threequarters:* B Duprat (A Bayonnais), J Cantoni (AS Béziers),
G Lavagne (AS Béziers), J Trillo (CA Beglais), C Dourthe (US Dax),
J-P Lux (US Dax), J Maso (RC Narbonne)
*Half-backs:* J-L Berot (S Toulousain), A Marot (CA Briviste),
M Barrau (S Beaumontois), J Fouroux (La Voulte Sp)
*Forwards:* J-C Skrela (S Toulousain), P Biemouret (SU Agen), O Saisset (AS Béziers),
W Spanghero (RC Narbonne), B Vinsonneau (US Dax),
C Spanghero (RC Narbonne), J-P Bastiat (US Dax), A Estève (AS Béziers),
J Iraçabal (A Bayonnais), J-L Azarète (St Jean de Luz), A Vaquerin (AS Béziers),
J-C Rossignol (CA Briviste), A Lubrano (AS Béziers), R Bénésis (SU Agen)
**Captain** W Spanghero    **Manager** R Dasse
**Assistant Managers** M Celaya and F Cazenave

307

# MEMORIES OF THE ALL BLACKS – AND A PIOUS HOPE

**Christopher Wordsworth** *The Observer*

308   Nostalgia, which is half the life-blood of cricket, is not a very highly rated commodity in rugby. Rather the cry is always for noses to the grindstone of the present, and coaches and managers, as was demonstrated (and perhaps misinterpreted) on the latest Lions' tour to New Zealand, are not visibly overjoyed when famous figures from the recent past drop in as distractions from the job in hand. But a little nostalgia might not be out of place with another visitation by the All Blacks impending this autumn. We shall be seeing a lot more of them in the near future with two further tours, albeit short ones, soon to come – to Scotland and England in 1979–80 and to Wales, to honour the WRU centenary, in 1980–81. All this should be unusually useful as a yardstick to the state of our own game.

After the All Blacks' mortifications in South Africa, where they had to rely on two 'Sunday' goal-kickers in Williams and Going, the men from New Zealand were said to be in a state of dissolution, and to have mislaid some old skills while still groping for others. Another theory has it that in the present decline of their forward play they will even be forced to rely on their backs. The truth of all this will soon be made plain.

A whiff of the same nostalgia may even help to brace us for the encounter if it reminds us of some of the lessons they have taught us and reminds us too – an occasional haymaker on the blind side notwithstanding – that sportsmanship was the name of the game in all our yesterdays.

The All Blacks at least come with the certainty that this will be one occasion when familiarity does not breed contempt. The question is, after the souring of the last Lions' tour, what else will it breed in terms of dissension if a few shrill familiar voices cry havoc from the fringes of the battlefield and the bones of old disputes and controversies are industriously polished? The pot-stirrers are only a handful and unfortunately it is not their function to understand the elements of a game that has been evolved and preserved – sometimes with more hope than wisdom from its legislators – to accommodate a fair measure of high temper and low cunning, but never viciousness. Another rumpus is what the sideline agitators crave, and they will not be happy until they get it. In the case of New Zealand, from whom the game has derived so much, it seems a particularly squalid and inept approach. War on the field certainly, within the Hague

*Ian Kirkpatrick, New Zealand's most-capped flanker, exhibits the 'looming presence' referred to by Christopher Wordsworth in his article. 'Kirkie' has now played 39 times for his country and scored 16 tries, another All Black record.*

Convention, but peace for Heaven's sake off it. A whiff of sulphur is one thing, the stink of old linen another.

Maybe it is no good sighing for the simple days of 'first up, first down' when Englishmen assumed that all rugby men were decent types, though reserving the right to comment, as the now-defunct Rugby *Wisden* once did, more in sorrow than in anger, that 'the New Zealanders, strangely enough, did not always play the game in the right spirit'. This was naturally interpreted by the winners as meaning the spirit which would have suited the losers!

The clocks will not go back to the days of the slow boat and the get-together of the Second All Blacks at the Globe at Newton Abbot in 1924, though an analysis of the effect of travel then and now on performance might be revealing. If nostalgia means the legends and the shared good things, there is, for instance, the New Zealand wing Ball ruefully saluting Obolensky's two tries – 'I would have needed a shotgun to stop him'; or Whineray selling that last immortal dummy in the Barbarians match at Cardiff in 1964 and being hailed in song by the multitude. Not a bad way to remind ourselves that the game was not bred on carping and sensationalism, and that once at least even the Welsh did not see the men from the 'Land of the Long White Cloud' through a red mist.

There may, no doubt, be incidents, and if there are none be sure there will be those to invent them, like the frustrated war correspondent in Evelyn Waugh's *Scoop*. He, it may be remembered, closed the shutters and settled down with typewriter and bottle until his despatches from the imaginary front had a genuine war nicely under way. There will be trouble, I dare say, in the line-out, that permanent *casus belli* until some genius sorts it out, and friction over the interpretation of ruck, maul and tackle and what constitutes legitimate 'impetus' in a sliding tackle to the goal-line. Depending on whether they win or lose the tourists can reckon on being condemned for their grim lack of enterprise or being slated for irresponsibility. If they dominate forward they will be ogres; if they fail to they will be cast as feckless weaklings. Yet despite recent evidence no one in his heart of hearts really believes that any home-grown pack can match the All Blacks in the basics, if the latter are true to their heritage.

There is always the risk, again, that crowd manners will plumb a new low, if that were possible. Remorseless schedules and the prying spotlight may begin to have a fraying effect on normal patience and politeness in the tourists. A hooker (of the non-rugby species) could be persuaded to bare her soul about the shortcomings of Southern Hemisphere types in bed. Half-way through the tour management will no doubt be goaded into some brusque ripostes that will catch the headlines. The Common Market butter tariff, Bob Deans's 'try' against Wales in 1905 and two famous sendings-off may not actually be mentioned, but they will be hovering in the air when the brickbats start to fly. These things can happen, as we know, in the toil and moil of any tour. Perhaps some of them will this time, to make a splash at many a breakfast table.

In the days of my youth, at Rugby School, we were made powerfully aware of the All Blacks as a looming presence, huge men as terrible as an army with banners. Yet in fact the original 1905–06 team were only welterweights by modern standards. George Nepia, again, because he had played throughout the 1924–25 tour without missing a single match, of 30, was always being held up as an example to slackers. Links with the New Zealand connection seemed all around one in those days; Hamilton-Wickes, who had played against the All Blacks for England in 1925, turning out for Harlequins 'A' against the School, his silhouette drastically altered since his forked lightning days; that fiery particle Tommy Vile refereeing (he had toured New Zealand with a British Isles team in 1904) and I can still see Micky Walford floating past the Uppingham full-back; the halves being lectured by the immaculate Harold

Kittermaster, who everyone knew had scored England's second try against Porter's All Blacks from half-way.

Perhaps it was not quite from half-way. Memory magnifies and distorts. Were the two most famous dropped goals of the 1930s, by Wooller for Cambridge and the Springbok full-back Brand against England, as vast as they seem in the mind's eye? Did Geoffrey Rees-Jones really sprout as quickly as all that, from college Second Fifteen to Wales in a flash and the last hand in two tries that beat the 1935 All Blacks at Cardiff? Memories, myths, legends: we are only a loose federation of fluids and gases without these things to hold us together, and the same applies to the game itself. By now the Dutch Disease has got at the elms on Bigside, where it all started. Beware of small grubs!

With luck and good husbandry on both sides, however, the following quotation foraged from Kenneth Pelmear's *Anthology of Rugby Football* could yet be the epilogue to the coming tour:

> 'You fhall fee gamefters retorne home from this playe with broken heades, black faces, brufed bodies, and lame legges, yet laugheinge and merylie jeftinge at theire harmes, tellinge theire adverfaries how he brake his heade to an other that he ftrake him on the face, and howe he repaied him the fame to him againe, and all this is good mirthe, without grudge or hatred, and if anye be in arrerages to the other they fkore it upp till the next plaie, and in the meane tyme will contynue loveinge frindes.'
>
> *(George Owen of Henllys, 1603; on the subject of the ancient game of Knappan)*

'Twere better so, this winter, than just another slanging match!

# ENGLISH COUNTY CHAMPIONS 1889–1978

*For details of the 1977–78 English County Championship, please see page 120.*

## FIRST SYSTEM

| | | | |
|---|---|---|---|
| 1889 | **Yorkshire,** undefeated, declared champions by RU (scored 18G 17T to 1G 3T) | 1890 | **Yorkshire,** undefeated, declared champions (scored 10G 16T to 2G 4T) |

## SECOND SYSTEM

| | | |
|---|---|---|
| 1891 | **Lancashire** champions. | Group Winners – Yorkshire, Surrey, Gloucestershire. |
| 1892 | **Yorkshire** champions. | Group Winners – Lancashire, Kent, Midlands. |
| 1893 | **Yorkshire** champions. | Group Winners – Cumberland, Devon, Middlesex. |
| 1894 | **Yorkshire** champions. | Group Winners – Lancashire, Gloucestershire, Midlands. |
| 1895 | **Yorkshire** champions. | Group Winners – Cumberland, Devon, Midlands. |

## THIRD SYSTEM

| | *Champions* | *Runners-up* | *Played at* |
|---|---|---|---|
| 1896 | **Yorkshire** | Surrey | Richmond |
| 1897 | **Kent** | Cumberland | Carlisle |
| 1898 | **Northumberland** | Midlands | Coventry |
| 1899 | **Devon** | Northumberland | Newcastle |
| 1900 | **Durham** | Devon | Exeter |
| 1901 | **Devon** | Durham | W Hartlepool |
| 1902 | **Durham** | Gloucestershire | Gloucester |
| 1903 | **Durham** | Kent | W Hartlepool |
| 1904 | **Kent** | Durham | Blackheath (2nd meeting) |
| 1905 | **Durham** | Middlesex | W Hartlepool |
| 1906 | **Devon** | Durham | Exeter |
| 1907 | **Devon** and **Durham** joint champions after drawn games at W Hartlepool and Exeter | | |
| 1908 | **Cornwall** | Durham | Redruth |
| 1909 | **Durham** | Cornwall | W Hartlepool |
| 1910 | **Gloucestershire** | Yorkshire | Gloucester |
| 1911 | **Devon** | Yorkshire | Headingley |
| 1912 | **Devon** | Northumberland | Devonport |
| 1913 | **Gloucestershire** | Cumberland | Carlisle |
| 1914 | **Midlands** | Durham | Leicester |
| 1920 | **Gloucestershire** | Yorkshire | Bradford |

## FOURTH SYSTEM

| | *Champions* | *Runners-up* | *Played at* |
|---|---|---|---|
| 1921 | **Gloucestershire (31)** | Leicestershire (4) | Gloucester |
| 1922 | **Gloucestershire (19)** | N Midlands (0) | Birmingham |
| 1923 | **Somerset (8)** | Leicestershire (6) | Bridgwater |
| 1924 | **Cumberland (14)** | Kent (3) | Carlisle |
| 1925 | **Leicestershire (14)** | Gloucestershire (6) | Bristol |
| 1926 | **Yorkshire (15)** | Hampshire (14) | Bradford |
| 1927 | **Kent (22)** | Leicestershire (12) | Blackheath |
| 1928 | **Yorkshire (12)** | Cornwall (8) | Bradford |
| 1929 | *****Middlesex (9)** | Lancashire (8) | Blundellsands |

| 1930 | **Gloucestershire (13)** | Lancashire (7) | Blundellsands |
|------|--------------------------|----------------|---------------|
| 1931 | **Gloucestershire (10)** | Warwickshire (9) | Gloucester |
| 1932 | **Gloucestershire (9)** | Durham (3) | Blaydon |
| 1933 | **Hampshire (18)** | Lancashire (7) | Boscombe |
| 1934 | **E Midlands (10)** | Gloucestershire (0) | Northampton |
| 1935 | **Lancashire (14)** | Somerset (0) | Bath |
| 1936 | **Hampshire (13)** | Northumberland (6) | Gosforth |
| 1937 | **Gloucestershire (5)** | E Midlands (0) | Bristol |
| 1938 | **Lancashire (24)** | Surrey (12) | Blundellsands |
| 1939 | **Warwickshire (8)** | Somerset (3) | Weston |
| 1947 | †**Lancashire (14)** | Gloucestershire (3) | Gloucester |
| 1948 | **Lancashire (5)** | E Counties (0) | Cambridge |
| 1949 | **Lancashire (9)** | Gloucestershire (3) | Blundellsands |
| 1950 | **Cheshire (5)** | E Midlands (0) | Birkenhead Park |
| 1951 | **E Midlands (10)** | Middlesex (0) | Northampton |
| 1952 | **Middlesex (9)** | Lancashire (6) | Twickenham |
| 1953 | **Yorkshire (11)** | E Midlands (3) | Bradford |
| 1954 | **Middlesex (24)** | Lancashire (6) | Blundellsands |
| 1955 | **Lancashire (14)** | Middlesex (8) | Twickenham |
| 1956 | **Middlesex (13)** | Devon (9) | Twickenham |
| 1957 | **Devon (12)** | Yorkshire (3) | Plymouth |
| 1958 | **Warwickshire (16)** | Cornwall (8) | Coventry |
| 1959 | **Warwickshire (14)** | Gloucestershire (9) | Bristol |
| 1960 | **Warwickshire (9)** | Surrey (6) | Coventry |
| 1961 | †**Cheshire (5)** | Devon (3) | Birkenhead Park |
| 1962 | **Warwickshire (11)** | Hampshire (6) | Twickenham |
| 1963 | **Warwickshire (13)** | Yorkshire (10) | Coventry |
| 1964 | **Warwickshire (8)** | Lancashire (6) | Coventry |
| 1965 | **Warwickshire (15)** | Durham (9) | Hartlepool |
| 1966 | **Middlesex (6)** | Lancashire (0) | Blundellsands |
| 1967 | ††**Surrey** and **Durham** | | |
| 1968 | **Middlesex (9)** | Warwickshire (6) | Twickenham |
| 1969 | **Lancashire (11)** | Cornwall (9) | Redruth |
| 1970 | **Staffordshire (11)** | Gloucestershire (9) | Burton-on-Trent |
| 1971 | **Surrey (14)** | Gloucestershire (3) | Gloucester |
| 1972 | **Gloucestershire (11)** | Warwickshire (6) | Coventry |
| 1973 | **Lancashire (17)** | Gloucestershire (12) | Bristol |
| 1974 | **Gloucestershire (22)** | Lancashire (12) | Blundellsands |
| 1975 | **Gloucestershire (13)** | E Counties (9) | Gloucester |
| 1976 | **Gloucestershire (24)** | Middlesex (9) | Richmond |
| 1977 | **Lancashire (17)** | Middlesex (6) | Blundellsands |
| 1978 | **N Midlands (10)** | Gloucestershire (7) | Moseley |

*After a draw at Twickenham.   †After a draw, 8–8, at Blundellsands.   ‡After a draw 0–0, at Plymouth.   ††Surrey and Durham drew 14 each at Twickenham and no score at Hartlepool and thus became joint champions.*

*Above: Jubilation for Gloucester; despondency for Harlequins. The referee awards Bob Clewes his try in the John Player Cup semi-final. Gloucester won 12–6 and went on to take the trophy. Below: John Horton, Bath's mercurial fly-half, found favour with the England selectors in 1977–78.*

# CLUB SECTION

## ENGLAND
## Bath

**Year of formation** 1865
**Grounds** Recreation Ground, Bath   **Tel** Bath 25192;   Horse Show Ground, London Road, Bath   **Tel** Bath 310548
**Colours** Blue, white, and black
**Most capped player** R A Gerrard (England) 14 caps
**Captain 1977–78** J S Waterman
**First XV 1977–78** P 49   W 28   D 1   L 20   F 984   A 746
**Review of the season** Bath, with two of England's best fly-halves, John Horton and John Palmer, played attractive if erratic rugby and were rewarded with a club-record 984 pts (John Davies 349), 146 tries (Mike Beese and Davies both 21, Palmer 16), and 25 dropped goals (Horton 15). They suffered spectacular defeats, too, notably at London Welsh (0–46), Swansea (7–45), and 6–20 at Exeter in the first round of the John Player Cup. Roger Hill (12 tries) from Newbridge and regional trialist Gary Parsons (Somerset and Avon Police) were acquisitions in the pack.

## Bedford

**Year of formation** 1886
**Ground** Goldington Road, Bedford   **Tel** Bedford 59160
**Colours** Wide hoops Oxford and Cambridge blues
**Most capped player** D P Rogers (England) 34 caps
**Captain 1977–78** R M Wilkinson
**1st XV 1977–78** P 39   W 18   L 21   F 752   A 633
**Review of the season** Bedford headed the Midland merit table, yet finished with more defeats than victories for only the second season since 1946. Inconsistency was summed up by the 65–15 win over Cambridge Univ and 9–53 defeat at Llanelli three days later. Topped 35 points seven times and totalled 128 tries, Derek Wyatt scoring 16; the other wing, Bob Demming, played in the final England trial. Tony Jorden scored 142 pts. New £90,000 clubhouse officially opened. David Jackson took over the captaincy when Bob Wilkinson stepped down for business reasons.

## Birkenhead Park

**Year of formation** 1871
**Ground** Upper Park, Park Road North, Birkenhead Merseyside.   **Tel** 051–652 4646
**Colours** Red, white, and navy blue hoops
**Most capped player** J R Paterson (Scotland) 21 caps
**Captain 1977–78** A Collett
**1st XV 1977–78** P 40   W 13   D 2   L 25   F 424   A 651
**Review of the season** Despite their poorest overall record in years, they won enough vital matches to press for re-inclusion in Northern merit table, having finished bottom the previous season. Reached Cheshire Cup final, and though losing to Sale earned a John Player Cup place as Sale qualified via the merit table. Best wins over Rugby (39–12) and at Gosforth (4–0) in a highly-successful September and October. Geoff Lee-Gallon top try-scorer for fifth consecutive season.

September and October. Geoff Lee-Gallon top try-scorer for fifth consecutive season.

## Birmingham

**Year of formation** 1911
**Ground** Forshaw Heath Lane, Portway, Solihull, Warwickshire   **Tel** 0564 82 2955
**Colours** Red jerseys, white shorts, red stockings
**Captain 1977–78** D Fourness
**1st XV 1977–78** P 36   W 19   D 3   L 14   F 527   A 440
**Review of the season** After only two defeats in their first 13 matches,
Birmingham failed to score a try in eight games between January and late April.
Hit by departure of scrum-half Peter Bullock to London. Best victory was 22–7
over Pontypool; big ones over Tredegar, Abertillery, and Penarth. Wing Dermot
O'Brien was top try-scorer with 12; Phil Tuck scored 286 pts.

## Blackheath

**Year of formation** 1858
**Ground** Rectory Field, Blackheath, London SE3   **Tel** 01–858 1578/3677
**Colours** Red and black hoops
**Most capped player** C N Lowe (England) 25 caps.
**Captain 1977–78** I Williamson
**1st XV 1977–78** P 36   W 16   D 3   L 17   F 549   A 501
**Review of the season** Blackheath provided the nucleus of Kent's County
Championship semi-finalists but had a frustrating club season, notably being
thrashed at Moseley in the John Player Cup but winning there in a friendly.
Seventh in London merit table but still qualified for this season's John Player Cup
via county cup play-off. Ian Williamson (134 pts) inspired at full-back and
newcomer Eric Bignell, never sure of a place when with Rosslyn Park, had a final
England trial as No 8. Don Sibley scored 12 tries.

## Bradford

**Year of formation** 1866
**Ground** Dracup Avenue, Lidget Green, Bradford, West Yorkshire BD7 2RJ
**Tel** Bradford 71049
**Colours** Red, amber, and black hoops, dark blue shorts, black stockings with red
and amber tops
**Most capped player** E Myers (England) 18 caps
**Captain 1977–78** R Davenport
**1st XV 1977–78** P 38   W 12   D 1   L 25   F 392   A 565
**Review of the season** Bradford, relegated from the Northern merit table in 1977,
reckoned to have won enough matches that matter to bounce straight back. Useful
acquisitions included fly-half Trevor Clark (ex-Halifax), goal-kicking centre Alan
Davidson, and No 8s Richard Dixon and Paul Savage. David Preston made a
successful return after a season's absence with a broken leg. Jeff Greenwood retired
after 30 years as match secretary, but will keep an active connection with club.
Mini-rugby instituted.

## Bristol

**Year of formation** 1888
**Ground** Memorial Ground, Filton Avenue, Horfield, Bristol BS7 0AG
**Tel** Bristol 48360
**Colours** Blue and white

**Most capped player** J V Pullin (England) 42 caps
**Captain 1977–78** K C Plummer
**1st XV 1977–78** P 47   W 30   D 1   L 16   F 767   A 512
**Review of the season** Bristol's season was overshadowed by finishing only fifth in South and South-West merit table and thus failing to qualify for the 1978–79 John Player Cup. Shoulder injury forced skipper Ken Plummer into retirement, and Alan Morley missed many matches. On the brighter side, Mike Rafter continued as an England regular, Nigel Pomphrey and Malcolm Baker were chosen for international 'B' squad, and David Sorrell, Peter Polledri, and Steve Gorvett for Under 23s. Mike Fry played his 300th game for the club and Alan Pearn scored 157 pts to pass 2,000; new wing John Lane scored 14 tries.

317

# Broughton Park

**Year of formation** 1882
**Ground** Chelsfield Grove, Chorlton, Manchester 21   **Tel** 061–881 2481
**Colours** White jerseys, black shorts
**Most capped player** A Neary (England) 34 caps
**Captain 1977–78** K O'Brien
**1st XV 1977–78** P 42   W 32   D 2   L 8   F 926   A 376
**Review of the season** Broughton Park's finest run in years included a 15-match unbeaten sequence in the autumn, a late-season win at Bedford, and qualification via merit table for the John Player Cup. Full-back Kevin O'Brien again topped 300 pts and newcomer Peter Robinson (ex-Davenport and Harrogate) was a prolific try-scorer. England Under 23 centre Tony Bond was lost to Sale, but Cumbria's Ken Moss boosted the pack.

# Camborne

**Year of formation** 1878
**Ground** Recreation Ground, Camborne   **Tel** Camborne 713227; clubhouse 712684
**Colours** Cherry and white
**Most capped player** J Collins (England) 3 caps
**Captain 1977–78** C Durant
**1st XV 1977–78** P 51   W 37   D 2   L 11   F 996   A 440
**Review of the season** Camborne celebrated their centenary with the Cornwall Cup and championship double, and now succeed Falmouth in RFU South and South-West merit table. Obvious strength was at lock, where 6ft 4in Paul Ranford with 16 tries challenged wing-threequarter David Edwards, 17, while fellow-lock Chris Durant totalled 183 pts, including five tries. Bob Lees scored 15 tries, reserve wing Chris Nicholas 14, and Durant and prop Bob Tonkin played in the County Championship.

# Cambridge University

**Year of formation** 1872
**Ground** Grange Road, Cambridge   **Tel** Cambridge 54131
**Colours** Light blue and white hoops
**Most capped player** C M H Gibson (Ireland) 65 caps
**Captains 1977** A J Hignell   **1978** J C Robbie
**1st XV 1977–78** P 26   W 13   D 1   L 12   F 492   A 537
**Review of the season** Cambridge University, disrupted throughout by injuries – notably to Alastair Hignell and Paul Parker – conceded 65 pts to Bedford, 50 to London Scottish, 46 to Cardiff, and 37 to Leicester. Even so, good wins over Gloucester, Harlequins, and Steele-Bodger's XV made defeat by Oxford a shock. Irish international scrum-half John Robbie finished top scorer with 114 pts, All

Black wing Mike O'Callaghan scored 12 tries. Wales 'B' No 8 Eddie Butler was outstanding in the pack.

## Coventry

**Year of formation** 1874
**Ground** Coundon Road, Coventry   **Tel** Coventry 591274
**Colours** Navy and white hoops, navy shorts
**Most capped player** D J Duckham (England) 36 caps
**Captain 1977–78** P A Rossborough
**1st XV 1977–78** P 45   W 24   D 5   L 16   F 840   A 619
**Review of the season** Coventry showed improvement over the previous season, reaching the John Player Cup semi-finals for fifth time in seven years, and retaining Midlands Clubs Sevens title. Lost only 2 of 13 games in late-season spell and supplied Jon Shipsides, Ian Darnell, and Paul Knee to Midlands XV. Knee reached 50 tries for club in 54th appearance, quicker than any previous player, and finished top try-scorer with 18. Peter Rossborough totalled club record 297 pts. Simon Gregory (ex-England Schools No 8) made a successful start at senior level for club, who initiated a youth XV.

## Exeter

**Year of formation** 1872
**Ground** The County Ground, St Thomas, Exeter, Devon
**Tel** Exeter 5954/78759
**Colours** Black
**Most capped player** J C R Buchanan (Scotland) 16 caps
**Captain 1977–78** P Baxter
**1st XV 1977–78** P 46   W 38   L 8   F 988   A 434
**Review of the season** A fine season, though a 0–34 defeat by Coventry was poor reward for becoming the first Devon team to reach the second round of the national cup. That defeat ended a run of 16 wins, including Bath in the first round, but a later run of 13 wins included 28–13 v Sidmouth in Devon Cup final, and 76–0 v Falmouth and 15–12 v Bristol in regional merit table. Also won the Devon Sevens. Individual honours to Bob Staddon (196 pts including 12 dropped goals), Steve Webb (157 pts), and Phil Arbourne (16 tries).

## Falmouth

**Year of formation** 1873
**Ground** Falmouth Recreation Ground, Falmouth   **Tel** Falmouth 311304
**Colours** Black and white hoops
**Captain 1977–78** G Thomas
**1st XV 1977–78** P 48   W 22   D 2   L 24   F 510   A 591
**Review of the season** Falmouth's second attempt as Cornwall's representatives in the RFU regional merit table was no luckier than their first. Though they fitted in six merit matches, four were in the space of 18 days, and scrum-half Gordon Thomas was out injured for five. They now hand over to Camborne, having played nine merit matches in two seasons and lost the lot. Highlight of season was their 6–3 win over Plymouth Albion in the John Player Cup preliminary. Individual honours to Trevor Hewitt (74 pts), Nigel Maddern (69) and Barry Trevaskis (64, including 13 tries).

## Fylde

**Year of formation** 1919

**Ground** The Woodlands Memorial Ground, Blackpool Road, Ansdell, Lytham St Annes    **Tel** Lytham 734733
**Colours** Claret, gold, and white
**Most capped player** M S Phillips (England) 25 caps
**Captain 1977–78** M J Weir
**1st XV 1977–78** P 41    W 23    L 18    F 589    A 470
**Review of the season** Fylde improved after an early run of defeats and elimination from the Lancashire Cup by Sedgley Park. England captain Bill Beaumont boosted the pack when available; Chris Bailward, from Bedford, added to the forward strength and Wayne Isherwood (ex-Sale and Kendal) solved the fly-half problem. Young players to shine included backs David Stephenson, David Shorrock, and Tony Swift and flanker Neil Leeming (20). Topped 30 points in successive late-season games against Hull, Halifax, and New Brighton.

## Gloucester

**Year of formation** 1873
**Ground** Kingsholm, Kingsholm Road, Gloucester GL1 3AX
**Tel** Gloucester 20901 (office)/28385 (club)
**Colours** Cherry and white
**Most capped player** A T Voyce (England) 27 caps
**Captain 1977–78** J A Watkins
**1st XV 1977–78** P 49    W 38    L 11    F 993    A 501
**Review of the season** Gloucester's forward power, backed up by Peter Butler – Britain's leading scorer with 451 pts – rolled them to the John Player Cup and enabled Bob Clewes (24 tries in all matches) and Richard Mogg (20 incl 3 for Gloucestershire v Cornwall) to be two of England's top-scoring wings. They lost only once in 1978 and again finished top of regional merit table. Though only Mike Burton was capped, fellow forwards Gordon Sargent, Steve Mills, Steve Boyle, and John Fidler, plus Mogg, were in England 'B' squad in Rumania. Burton retired at end of season.

## Gosforth

**Year of formation** 1877
**Ground** New Ground, Great North Road, Gosforth, Newcastle upon Tyne NE3 2DT    **Tel** Newcastle 856915
**Colours** Green and white hoops, white shorts, green and white hooped stockings
**Most capped player** R J McLoughlin (Ireland) 40 caps
**Captain 1977–78** M Young
**1st XV 1977–78** P 39    W 31    L 8    F 867    A 288
**Review of the season** Although Gosforth's two-year reign in the John Player Cup ended at Gloucester, they easily retained the Northumberland Cup and were close second to Liverpool in the North merit table. Malcolm Young and Peter Dixon played for England and Richard Breakey for Scotland, but back injury ruled out former England captain Roger Uttley. The club had 19 players in the County Championship, supplying captains for Northumberland (Colin White), Durham (John Hedley), and Cumbria (David Robinson). Best wins were over USA, Orrell (46–6 in first meeting), Richmond, and Headingley.

## Halifax

**Year of formation** 1873
**Ground** Ovenden Park, Halifax    **Tel** Halifax 65926
**Colours** Dark blue, light blue, and white narrow hoops
**Most capped players** J P Horrocks-Taylor (England) and G T Thomson (England) 9 caps each

**Captain 1977–78** R J Leathley
**1st XV 1977–78** P 40   W 22   D 1   L 17   F 436   A 469
**Review of the season** Halifax, inaugural winners of the Yorkshire Cup, reached the semi-final in the competition's centenary season before losing to Middlesbrough. Gates improved, and there were fine wins over Gosforth, Headingley, Liverpool, and Orrell. Fly-half Roger Horner, from Old Brodleians, and full-back Ron Myers, from Ripon, were good acquisitions. Centre Alan Crawshaw (broken arm) and Andrew Smith, who scored 10 tries before his cartilage operation, were ruled out for long spells.

# Harlequins

**Year of formation** 1866
**Grounds** Stoop Memorial Ground, Craneford Way, Twickenham, Middlesex and RFU Ground, Twickenham   **Tel** 01–892 3080 (Stoop)
**Colours** Light blue, magenta, chocolate, French grey, black and light green
**Most capped player** W W Wakefield (England) 31 caps
**Captain 1977–78** D A Cooke
**1st XV 1977–78** P 34   W 17   D 3   L 14   F 511   A 479
**Review of the season** Harlequins reached the semi-finals of the John Player Cup, won the Middlesex Sevens, and had a run of eight victories in an anticipated season of rebuilding. All Black Peter Whiting strengthened the pack till retiring after the Cup run; Claxton brothers Terry and Mickey were durable props; Adrian Alexander, Steve Edlmann and England Under 23 selection Paul Jackson were also lively forwards. Wings Colin Lambert (18 tries) and Gordon Wood (11) and Bill Bushell (186 pts), England 'B' selection full-back, kept the scoreboard ticking over.

# Harrogate

**Year of formation** 1871
**Ground** Claro Road, Harrogate   **Tel** Harrogate 66966/64933
**Colours** Red, amber, and black
**Most capped player** P J Squires (England) 24 caps
**Captain 1977–78** Peter Clegg
**1st XV 1977–78** P 38   W 15   L 23   F 397   A 537
**Review of the season** Harrogate continued their rebuilding programme despite a constant battle against relegation from the North merit table – a struggle they lost in 10–12 defeat at Morley in mid-April. Had talented newcomers in full-back Mike Cowling, from York, utility back Colin Simmonds, from Ripon, and forward Alf Abbott (ex-Whitby). Eleven players received first XV tie for 25 appearances in season or 35 in career. Best wins over Nuneaton (38–0), New Brighton, and at Bradford.

# Hartlepool Rovers

**Year of formation** 1879
**Ground** The Friarage, West View Road, Hartlepool   **Tel** Hartlepool 67741
**Colours** White jerseys, black shorts, red stockings
**Most capped player** G S Conway (England) 18 caps
**Captain 1977–78** J Moore
**1st XV 1977–78** P 36   W 23   D 2   L 11   F 588   A 357
**Review of the season** Hartlepool Rovers won the Durham Cup for the sixth successive time (ninth in 11 years) and also claimed to have qualified for 1978–79 North merit table in the new season after their controversial omission last time. Half-backs Alan Calvert and Kevin Wood, both 21, were among six players who appeared for Durham. Fine 25–9 win over Edinburgh Wanderers; lost only 3–9 at

Leicester in John Player Cup. Planning centenary match against Barbarians in October 1979.

## Headingley

**Year of formation** 1878
**Ground** Bridge Road, Kirkstall, Leeds 5    **Tel** Leeds 755029
**Colours** Green, black, and white jerseys, blue shorts
**Most capped player** I R McGeechan (Scotland) 27 caps
**Captain 1977–78** T Donovan
**1st XV 1977–78** P 38   W 12   D 4   L 22   F 438   A 529
**Review of the season** Headingley, with a stronger fixture list, had their worst playing record for 30 years. Andy Maxwell, injured in France v England match, was forced to retire, but full-back David Caplan became international and Barbarian in a five-day spell. Ian McGeechan continued to appear for Scotland. Recruits to the club were David Norton (ex-Nottingham) and Jim Panter (ex-Northern). Don Chappell retired after making more than 400 first-team appearances. Best wins were over Hawick, Richmond, and Northampton.

## Huddersfield

**Year of formation** 1909
**Ground** Tandem, Waterloo, Huddersfield   **Tel** Huddersfield 23864
**Colours** White, claret, and gold
**Most capped player** F D Sykes (England) 4 caps
**Captain 1977–78** J Billington
**1st XV 1977–78** P 33   W 16   D 2   L 15   F 489   A 448
**Review of the season** Huddersfield, another club surprised at omission from the North merit table, recovered from a poor start to claim a place again. Highlight was a 16–11 win at Sale; biggest victory 48–3 over Rugby. England colts forward Gary Van Bellen left to join Wakefield, but team effort compensated for the absence of outstanding individuals.

## Hull and East Riding

**Year of formation** 1901
**Ground** The Circle, Anlaby Road, Kingston-upon-Hull, North Humberside
**Tel** Hull 507918
**Colours** Cherry and white hoops, navy shorts
**Most capped player** R D Sangwin (England) 2 caps
**Captain 1977–78** R G Wigham
**1st XV 1977–78** P 35   W 13   D 1   L 21   F 401   A 512
**Review of the season** Hull and ER, new to the Northern merit table, were relegated after a bad run with four players breaking legs and four turning professional. However, the club had good service from forwards John Zgoda, England Schools player Ian Furlong, and hooker Roger Middleton. Wing Trevor Clarke reached 20 tries. Best wins were over Sheffield (30–3) and at Broughton Park (12–9).

## Leicester

**Year of formation** 1880
**Ground** The Clubhouse, Aylestone Road, Leicester LE2 7LF
**Tel** Leicester 540276
**Colours** Scarlet, green, and white
**Most capped player** W W Wakefield (England) 31 caps

**Captain 1977–78** B Hall
**1st XV 1977–78** P 41   W 17   D 2   L 12   F 849   A 573
**Review of the season** Leicester, John Player Cup finalists, provided three players to the same England XV for the first time since 1935 when Peter Wheeler, Robin Cowling, and Dusty Hare played against France. Paul Dodge was capped later. Bob Barker, top try-scorer with 27, and Gary Adey both reached 300 senior appearances. Hare top points-scorer with 305. Chalky White was an inspiring coach. Leicester beat Moseley for the first time in six years and lost only twice at home.

# Liverpool

**Year of formation** 1857
**Ground** St Michael's, Church Road, Liverpool L17 7BD   **Tel** 051–727 6330
**Colours** Red, blue, black horizontal stripes, white shorts
**Most capped player** C E Allen (Ireland) 21 caps
**Captain 1977–78** T Morris
**1st XV 1977–78** P 42   W 27   D 3   L 12   F 587   A 448
**Review of the season** Liverpool won the Northern merit table, had an outstanding John Player Cup win at London Welsh, also beat Gosforth and Sale and drew with Bristol, and were runners–up to Orrell in the Lancashire Cup. Mike Slemen played in all England's matches; lock Jim McKeon joined England Under 23 squad. Scrum-half Terry Morris made a successful switch to wing-forward, and John Hennigan was consistent at full-back.

# London Irish

**Year of formation** 1898
**Ground** The Avenue, Sunbury-on-Thames, Middlesex   **Tel** Sunbury 83034
**Colours** Emerald green jerseys, white shorts
**Most capped player** K W Kennedy (Ireland) 45 caps
**Captain 1977–78** K W Kennedy
**1st XV 1977–78** P 36   W 25   D 2   L 9   F 578   A 261
**Review of the season** London Irish were a very awkward side to play against, conceding only seven tries up to New Year. The McKibbin brothers, international Alistair and Roger from Instonians, strengthened the threequarter line, while Duncan Leopold (8 tries) was a fine attacking full-back. John Casalaspro scored 17 tries on wing, but neither Alistair McKibbin (41 pts) nor Pat Parfrey (99) entirely solved the goal-kicking problem. John O'Driscoll (8 tries) earned his first cap at flank; veterans Ken Kennedy and Mick Molloy still went well in the pack.

# London Scottish

**Year of formation** 1878
**Ground** Richmond Athletic Ground, Richmond, Surrey   **Tel** 01–940 0397
**Colours** Blue jerseys, red lion on left breast, white shorts, red stockings
**Most capped player** A F McHarg (Scotland) 41 caps
**Captain 1977–78** J A Fraser
**1st XV 1977–78** P 29   W 20   D 4   L 5   F 701   A 381
**Review of the season** London Scottish, eighth in the London merit table in 1976–77, celebrated their centenary in style, being the only side with an unbeaten record in the national merit structure and beating an SRU President's XV 37–19. Alan Lawson, ignored internationally, and Ron Wilson, dropped after two internationals, were inspiring club halves; David Gillespie totalled club record 284 pts and Tom Macnab scored 23 tries on wing. Outstanding in the pack were internationals Alastair McHarg and Mike Biggar, and Sandy Pratt (17 tries).

# London Welsh

**Year of formation** 1885
**Ground** Old Deer Park, Kew Road, Richmond, Surrey **Tel** 01–940 2520/0706
**Colours** Scarlet jerseys and white shorts
**Most capped player** J P R Williams (Wales) 45 caps
**Captain 1977–78** J Taylor
**1st XV 1977–78** P 34  W 18  D 1  L 15  F 460  A 433
**Review of the season** London Welsh were one of the strongest sides in English
rugby, yet won only three of 13 matches against Welsh opposition. John Taylor
was as enthusiastic as ever in his final season, but English international Neil
Bennett (171 pts), though well served by his old Bedford partner Alun Lewis, often
lacked confidence in Welshmen around him and overdid the kicking. Bill Davey,
from Pontypridd, was a notable gain at prop. Rhodri Ellis-Jones top try-scorer
with 11.

# Manchester

**Year of formation** 1860
**Ground** Grove Park, Grove Lane, Cheadle Hume, Cheshire
**Tel** 061–485 1115
**Colours** Red and white hooped jerseys, white shorts, red stockings
**Most capped player** G S Conway (England) 18 caps
**Captain 1977–78** P Jarvie
**1st XV 1977–78** P 41  W 16  D 1  L 24  F 437  A 530
**Review of the season** Manchester, newly promoted into the North merit table,
lost the first eight matches that counted, and even a late flourish, when they
profited from the recall of experienced players, could not avert relegation. Wing
David Grimshaw was again top scorer. Achieved a fine away win at Boroughmuir
and a double over Birkenhead Park.

# Metropolitan Police

**Year of formation** 1923
**Ground** Police Sports Club, Imber Court, Embercourt Road, East Molesey,
Surrey
**Tel** 01–398 1267
**Colours** Dark blue jerseys, white shorts (alt. sky blue jerseys)
**Most capped player** A M Rees (Wales) 13 caps
**Captain 1977–78** A V Boddy
**1st XV 1977–78** P 38  W 15  D 1  L 22  F 446  A 582
**Review of the season** Metropolitan Police struggled throughout, though veteran
scrum-half John Montgomery still proved to be one of London's rugby characters
and Tony Boddy one of London's best hookers. The side was otherwise plagued
by inexperience and injury, the early loss of Ian Burrell (broken arm) being a
crucial blow. Full-back Steve Day returned to Police after trying his luck with
Rosslyn Park and Richmond.

# Middlesbrough

**Year of formation** 1872
**Ground** Acklam Park, Green Lane, Acklam, Middlesbrough, Cleveland
**Tel** Middlesbrough 88567
**Colours** Maroon jerseys, white shorts, maroon stockings
**Most capped player** A G B Old (England) 16 caps
**Captain 1977–78** M Wright
**1st XV 1977–78** P 39  W 25  D 3  L 11  F 608  A 318

**Review of the season** Middlesbrough, another club shocked by omission from the North merit table, also reckoned to have made sure of a place in the new season. In addition they reached the Yorkshire Cup final for the second time in three years. Had half a pack of county forwards and Paul Wood was a free-scoring goal-kicker.

## Morley

324

**Year of formation** 1878
**Ground** Scatcherd Lane, Morley, Leeds   **Tel** 0532 533487
**Colours** Maroon
**Most capped player** G H Marsden (England) 3 caps
**Captain 1977–78** R D Binks
**1st XV 1977–78** P 38   W 24   L 14   F 586   A 328
**Review of the season** Morley, only one of four promoted sides to retain their place in the North merit table, were beaten at Wakefield in the second round of the Yorkshire Cup – after winning the trophy four times in six previous seasons. Yorkshire forward Alex Scotter, top points-scorer in 1976–77, missed three months injured and club record try-scorer David Hoyland moved to Sale. Promising youngsters emerged in the final weeks. New terracing completed, increasing ground capacity to 7,000.

## Moseley

**Year of formation** 1873
**Ground** The Reddings, Reddings Road, Moseley, Birmingham 13
**Tel** Birmingham 449 2149
**Colours** Black and red
**Most capped players** J Finlan (England) and N E Horton (England) 13 caps each
**Captain 1977–78** D G Warren
**1st XV 1977–78** P 40   W 28   D 1   L 11   F 861   A 450
**Review of the season** Moseley lost their edge after reaching New Year with only three defeats, the first on 27 November by an Invitation XV composed entirely of British Lions in the memorial match for Moseley's former England full-back, Sam Doble, who died at age 33. Club topped 130 tries, spread among 34 players. Scrum-half Chris Gifford, picked for England 'B', scored 12 tries; full-back Clive Meanwell scored 162 pts and fly-half Les Cusworth 111, including 7 dropped goals. Centre Barrie Corless played in all England's matches and lock Russ Field had a final trial.

## New Brighton

**Year of formation** 1875
**Ground** Reeds Lane, Leasowe Road, Moreton, Wirral L46 3RH
**Tel** 051 677 1873
**Colours** Navy blue jersey, white shorts
**Most capped player** J P Quinn (England) 5 caps
**Captain 1977–78** S J Miles
**1st XV 1977–78** P 37   W 18   L 19   F 636   A 586
**Review of the season** New Brighton, with improved fortunes and good wins over Liverpool, Manchester, Halifax, and Waterloo, expected a place in the Northern merit table in the new season. Wing John Bassnet, a product of club's colts system, played for England Under 23 and was leading try-scorer for second season. Flanker Dennis Morgan and fly-half Gordon Fair also among tries. Barry Jones again top points-scorer.

## Northampton

**Year of formation** 1880
**Ground** Franklins Gardens, Northampton  **Tel** Northampton 51543
**Colours** Black, green, and gold
**Most capped player** C R Jacobs (England) 29 caps
**Captain 1977–78** J J Page
**1st XV 1977–78** P 39  W 23  D 1  L 15  F 556  A 525

**Review of the season** Northampton, beaten at home only by Bristol, Llanelli, and London Welsh, managed only three away wins in a season still falling short of expectations. Former England flanker Bob Taylor retired aged 35 after making 300 appearances for the club; he scored a try in the final two minutes of his last home appearance, against Waterloo. The side conceded 18 tries on successive October Saturdays, at Cardiff and London Scottish, but reached the John Player Cup quarter-finals. Winger Paul McGuckian, in his first season of senior rugby, scored 17 tries and full-back Phil Raybould 104 pts.

## Northern

**Year of formation** 1876
**Ground** McCracken Park, Great North Road, Newcastle upon Tyne 3
**Tel** Wideopen 3369
**Colours** White jerseys, navy blue shorts, red stockings
**Most capped player** J D Currie (England) 25 caps
**Captain 1977–78** C E C Goatman
**1st XV 1977–78** P 40  W 19  D 2  L 19  F 545  A 468
**Review of the season** Northern, whose outstanding win was 37–9 at Bedford, fielded a young side, including Nigel Wright (fly-half), Jim Pollock (utility back), Simon Daniels (full-back), Nigel Bates (wing), and 21-year-old former Scottish Schools centre, Martin Woll. Lost 6–14 in first meeting with London Welsh and beaten by Alnwick in Northumberland Cup quarter-finals. Good wins over Harrogate (29–4) and at Birmingham (16–6), and drew with Headingley at Kirkstall.

## Nottingham

**Year of formation** 1877
**Ground** Ireland Avenue, Beeston, Nottingham  **Tel** Nottingham 254238
**Colours** Green and white jerseys, white shorts
**Most capped player** V H Cartwright (England) 14 caps
**Captain 1977–78** C J Baynes
**1st XV 1977–78** P 38  W 15  D 2  L 21  F 473  A 555
**Review of the season** Nottingham beat Bristol in the clubs' first meeting, but were badly hit by losing coach Dai Roberts to Canadian RU, England Under 23 fly-half Nick Preston to Richmond, and full-back David Norton to Headingley. Only four wins in first 20 matches. Full-back Greg Colebourne, from London Welsh, proved a useful acquisition, scoring 25 pts in 37–20 win over Rugby and 93 in all. Martin Northard scored 92 pts, and flanker David Robertson 9 tries, but the team did not reach 50 tries until mid-April.

## Nuneaton

**Year of formation** 1879
**Ground** Harry Cleaver Ground, Attleborough Road, Nuneaton
**Tel** Nuneaton 383206
**Colours** Black, red, white hoops, black shorts

**Most capped player** W A Holmes (England) 16 caps
**Captain 1977–78** R McAlpine
**1st XV 1977–78** P 38   W 9   L 29   F 328   A 946
**Review of the season** Nuneaton had their worst defensive record in the club's history and were threatened with conceding 1,000 points for the first time. Their line was crossed 26 times in Easter defeats at Pontypool and Bedford, but there were good wins at New Brighton and Bradford and over Nottingham. No 8 John Spencer (ex-West Hartlepool and England Colts) played well. Top try-scorer Terry McCarthy (8); vice-captain Andy Hudson scored 111 pts.

326

# Orrell

**Year of formation** 1927
**Ground** Edgerhall Road, Orrell, near Wigan, Greater Manchester, Lancs WN5 8TL   **Tel** Upholland 623193
**Colours** Amber and black hoops, black shorts and stockings
**Most capped player** W F Anderson (England) 1 cap
**Captain 1977–78** P Phillips
**1st XV 1977–78** P 39   W 29   D 1   L 9   F 829   A 350
**Review of the season** Orrell maintained progress and beat Liverpool in the Lancashire Cup final, avenging defeat of a fortnight earlier. Winger John Carleton played for England against The Rest and narrowly failed to become the club's second international. Good wins were scored over London Scottish, Hawick, and Sale, and Orrell were leading Pontypool 16–4 when the match was abandoned because of hail. Lost 22–30 in a memorable game at Cardiff. Home ground used for Under 23 international between England and France.

# Oxford University

**Year of formation** 1869
**Ground** University Rugby Ground, Iffley Road, Oxford   **Tel** Oxford 42017
**Colours** Dark blue
**Most capped player** J MacD Bannerman (Scotland) 37 caps
**Captains 1977** T A Bryan   **1978** A F Watkinson
**1st XV 1977–78** P 18   W 8   D 1   L 9   F 259   A 294
**Review of the season** Oxford University lost eight successive matches on their run-up to Twickenham but still won the one that mattered – for the first time in six years. After Christmas, they beat all three Services sides. Cardiff fly-half Gareth Davies made a timely recovery from knee ligament injury, and Tony Watkinson took over the goal-kicking in Stanley's match to finish top scorer (84 pts) from Tim Bryan (51). Wing Ray Hoolahan was top try-scorer with 8. Old Blues Ed Horne and Tim Enevoldson were strong props to lively hooker Byron Light.

# Plymouth Albion

**Year of formation** 1876
**Ground** Beacon Park, Plymouth   **Tel** Plymouth 772924
**Colours** Cherry, white, and green
**Most capped player** E Stanbury (England) 16 caps
**Captain 1977–78** L Ware
**1st XV 1977–78** P 50   W 32   D 2   L 16   F 762   A 555
**Review of the season** Plymouth Albion, narrowly beaten at Falmouth in the John Player Cup preliminary, had double revenge in merit matches and a notable win at Gloucester to help qualify for next season's Cup. Les Ware was one of Britain's top scorers with 362 pts in all matches, 321 for the club; flanker Richard Catchpole led

the try-scorers with 14, including 4 in home match with Falmouth. Former England Under 23 scrum-half Nigel Coombes is now settled in Plymouth after making 150-mile round-trips from Cornwall for matches and training.

# Richmond

**Year of formation** 1861
**Ground** Athletic Ground, Richmond, Surrey   **Tel** 01–940 0397
**Colours** Old gold, red, and black
**Most capped player** C W Ralston (England) 22 caps
**Captain 1977–78** I R Shackleton
**1st XV 1977–78** P 32   W 18   D 2   L 12   F 420   A 365
**Review of the season** Richmond were unlucky to 'lose' to Wasps as the home side in their drawn John Player Cup tie, but they made a quick exit from the Middlesex Sevens, which they had won three times in four seasons. Otherwise they played attractive and effective rugby, with David Rollitt, from Bristol, proving a great acquisition in the pack and Roger Shackleton generalling proceedings outside. Alan Mort scored 11 tries on the right wing, American Boyd Morrison showed promise on the left, and full-back David Whibley scored 140 pts.

# Rosslyn Park

**Year of formation** 1879
**Ground** Priory Lane, Upper Richmond Road, Roehampton, London SW15
**Tel** 01–876 1879
**Colours** Red and white hoops
**Most capped player** A G Ripley (England) 24 caps
**Captain 1977–78** P d'A Keith-Roach
**1st XV 1977–78** P 36   W 24   D 3   L 9   F 837   A 394
**Review of the season** Few sides could boast the forward riches of Rosslyn Park: British Lion Andy Ripley was ignored by England after first regional trial; John Scott, hitherto a club lock, became England No 8; Bob Mordell earned a cap against Wales at flank. Ian Wright returned from Northampton to spearhead a strong attack in which Peter Warfield, recovered from serious injuries, impressed at centre. Versatile Charles Ralston, fitting in where he could, still contributed 184 pts, while Richard Sainter scored 20 tries.

# Roundhay

**Year of formation** 1924
**Ground** Chandos Park, Chandos Avenue, Lidgett Lane, Leeds LS8 1QX
**Tel** Leeds 661815
**Colours** Emerald, scarlet, and white, white shorts
**Most capped player** D T Wilkins (England) 13 caps
**Captain 1977–78** R N Peycke
**1st XV 1977–78** P 42   W 33   L 9   F 826   A 428
**Review of the season** Roundhay suffered only one defeat – by Scottish champions Hawick – in a 20-match run, and would have had a John Player Cup place for this season had they beaten Broughton Park in last match. Beaten in Yorkshire Cup semi-finals by eventual winners, Wakefield. Top try-scorers were centre Richard Cardus, wing Mike Shearey, and forward Chris Holley. Tony Page again headed points list. Club steward John Wood was presented with a tankard to mark 20 years' service.

## Rugby

**Year of formation** 1873
**Ground** Webb Ellis Road (off Bilton Road), Rugby   **Tel** Rugby 4907
**Colours** White jerseys, navy shorts, red and white stockings
**Most capped player** G S Conway (England) 18 caps
**Captain 1977–78** T Roberts
**1st XV 1977–78** P 41   W 14   D 1   L 26   F 558   A 885
**Review of the season** Rugby's compensation for a disappointing run was qualifying for the next John Player Cup after a seven-year absence. Drew with Coventry and had their best wins over Leicester (9–7), Halifax (36–10), Tredegar (42–3), and Sale (4–3); lost 4–9 in first meeting with Oxford University. Fred Melvin and Keith Tysall played for Warwickshire; Melvin for Anglo-Scots. Charles Bend scored 10 tries; Tysall finished with nine tries and 247 pts in all. New stand officially opened.

328

## Sale

**Year of formation** 1861
**Ground** Heywood Road, Brooklands, Sale   **Tel** 061–973 6348
**Colours** Blue and white hoops, blue shorts, blue stockings
**Most capped player** E Evans (England) 30 caps
**Captain 1977–78** R N Creed
**1st XV 1977–78** P 40   W 26   D 2   L 12   F 614   A 471
**Review of the season** Sale continued their run of Cheshire Cup success and slipped from the top of the Northern merit table only in the season's final fortnight. Bolstered by the acquisition of centre Tony Bond (ex-Broughton Park), fly-half Andy Phillips (ex-Loughborough Students), and wing David Hoyland (ex-Morley), they beat London Welsh, Bedford, Neath, and Northampton. With vice-captain Steve Rule joining Salford (rugby league), Steve Midgelow took over as top points-scorer.

## Saracens

**Year of formation** 1876
**Ground** Bramley Sports Ground, Green Road, Southgate, London N14
**Tel** 01–449 3770
**Colours** Black jerseys with red star and crescent, black shorts, red stockings
**Most capped player** V S J Harding (England) 6 caps
**Captain 1977–78** D Harrigan
**1st XV 1977–78** P 38   W 17   D 2   L 19   F 638   A 486
**Review of the season** Saracens, John Player Cup semi-finalists in 1976–77, had a disappointing season and failed to qualify for 1978–79. Old firm of David Croydon (103 pts) and Peter Cadle (15 tries) as prominent as ever in threequarter line, but the frequent absence of Malcolm Phillips, who still managed 144 pts, was a blow. Clint McGregor and Andy Jaszczak were prominent in the pack, and Dennis Sanders made a successful switch from centre to flank.

## Sheffield

**Year of formation** 1902
**Ground** Abbeydale Park, Toltery Rise, Sheffield
**Tel** 362040 (steward)/360992 (groundsman)

**Colours** Blue and white bands, red stockings
**Most capped player** A G B Old (England) 16 caps
**Captain 1977–78** A G B Old
**1st XV 1977–78** P 39   W 19   D 3   L 17   F 577   A 642
**Review of the season** Sheffield, with Alan Old becoming their first international while with the club, celebrated their 75th season by claiming a place in 1978–79 North merit table. Fixture list was the strongest for 10 years; drew with Liverpool and Wilmslow and beat Halifax. They lost centre Bill Reichwald and lock Steve Newsome to Leicester, but centre Simon Mugford emerged as an outstanding prospect.

# Wakefield

**Year of formation** 1901
**Ground** College Grove, Wakefield, West Yorks   **Tel** Wakefield 72038/63431
**Colours** Black and gold
**Captain 1977–78** M Shuttleworth
**1st XV 1977–78** P 39   W 31   D 1   L 7   F 861   A 347
**Review of the season** Wakefield, winners of the Yorkshire Cup in the competition's centenary season, had a double distinction at representative level. Jeff Dowson, a new Barbarian, led Yorkshire and full-back Martin Shuttleworth skippered Yorkshire 'B'. Club celebrated 25 years of Easter visits to Wales with a win at Pontypool; Yorkshire flanker Ken Higgins scored five consecutive tries in the win over Ripon. The loose forward trio of Higgins, Dowson, and Ian Hill contributed more than 30 tries. Only home defeat was by Pontypridd.

# Wasps

**Year of formation** 1867
**Ground** Repton Avenue (off Rugby Avenue), Sudbury (Wembley), Middlesex
**Tel** 01–902 4220
**Colours** Black jerseys with golden wasp on left breast and 3 gold stripes down the sleeves, black shorts, black stockings with 3 gold hoops on turnover
**Most capped player** J E Woodward (England) 15 caps
**Captain 1977–78** A Richards
**1st XV 1977–78** P 42   W 23   D 3   L 16   F 672   A 491
**Review of the season** Wasps won a national Cup tie for the first time, Ian Bell scoring their first-ever try in the competition; they went on to the last eight, and though ninth in London merit table re-qualified for national event by retaining Middlesex Cup. Ian Ball, England Under 23 fly-half from Waterloo, had an outstanding season with 275 pts in all matches, Andy Rayner 98 pts, and Tony Richards 11 tries on wing. Veteran Alan Black, captain in leaner years, still played a notable part up front.

# Waterloo

**Year of formation** 1883
**Ground** St Anthony's Road, Blundellsands, Liverpool 23   **Tel** 051–924 4552
**Colours** Green, red, and white hoops
**Most capped player** H G Periton (England) 21 caps
**Captain 1977–78** S G Tickle
**1st XV 1977–78** P 41   W 28   D 2   L 11   F 784   A 309
**Review of the season** Waterloo, undeterred by loss of 1976–77 captain Colin

Fisher to West of Scotland and England Under 23 fly-half Ian Ball to Wasps, enjoyed another good season under new coach Charlie Hanley. Best wins were over Rosslyn Park, Bedford, North of Ireland, and Wilmslow. Scrum-half David Carfoot played for England XV against USA; lock Mal Billingham completed 400 appearances in 6–6 draw at Coventry.

## West Hartlepool

**Year of formation** 1881
**Ground** Brierton Lane, Hartlepool   **Tel** Hartlepool 72640
**Colours** Green jerseys, white shorts, green and red stockings
**Most capped player** C D Aarvold (England) 16 caps
**Captain 1977–78** D Stubbs
**1st XV 1977–78** P 38   W 19   D 2   L 17   F 452   A 501
**Review of the season** West Hartlepool, although relegated from the Northern merit table after one year's inclusion, had a club record of seven players appearing in the County Championship. John Deller, Derek Boyd, Paul Stacey, Ken Horseman, Derek Bousfield, and Peter Robinson played for Durham; David Peart for Cumbria. Boyd was also in the England Under 23 side before his long absence through knee injury. Only merit table wins were over Roundhay and Wilmslow in first and last games; beaten in Durham Cup semi-final by Blaydon.

## Wilmslow

**Year of formation** 1886   **Re-formed** 1923
**Ground** Memorial Ground, Pownall Park, Wilmslow, Cheshire
**Tel** Wilmslow 22274/24148
**Colours** Sky blue, maroon, and white jerseys, white shorts, maroon stockings
**Captain 1977–78** G W M Jones
**1st XV 1977–78** P 40   W 21   D 1   L 18   F 612   A 494
**Review of the season** Wilmslow, regularly supplying at least seven players to counties, had a successful season and headed North merit table for a time before falling away in final months. Beat Wakefield, won at Langholm and Richmond, and lost by only one point in John Player Cup at Coventry. Young flanker David Partington had another outstanding campaign.

# SCOTLAND

## Ayr

**Year of formation** 1897
**Ground** Millbrae, Alloway, Ayr   **Tel** Alloway 41944
**Colours** Pink and black
**Captain 1977–78** Q Dunlop
**1st XV 1977–78** P 33   W 19   L 14   F 460   A 412
**Review of the season** Ayr had their best season so far in the national
championship. They only just missed promotion from Division 2, being beaten on
points-difference by Haddington for the runners-up spot. John Brown, Scotland's
top scorer in 1976–77 with 307, led the club list again with 188, despite missing
two months injured. Steve Munro led the try-scorers with 10.

## Boroughmuir

**Year of formation** 1919 ('Boroughmuir FP' till 1974)
**Ground** Meggetland, Colinton Road, Edinburgh EH14 1AS   **Tel** 031–443 7571
**Colours** Navy blue and emerald green
**Most capped player** K I Ross (Scotland) 11 caps
**Captain 1977–78** C G Hogg
**1st XV 1977–78** P 27   W 23   D 1   L 3   F 657   A 233
**Review of the season** Boroughmuir's most successful since they won the last
unofficial club championship in 1973. Were only two points behind Hawick at the
top of the league, and with just three defeats in 27 matches had the best overall
record of any Scottish senior club. Won two of the Border Sevens at Hawick and
Langholm. Stand-off Duncan Wilson was top scorer with 174 pts; wing Bill
McNicoll had most tries (14), one more than international full-back Bruce Hay.

## Clarkston

**Year of formation** 1937
**Ground** Braidholm, Giffnock, Glasgow   **Tel** 041–637 5850
**Colours** Scarlet, white, and green
**Captain 1977–78** P J Jackson
**1st XV 1977–78** P 26   W 15   L 11   F 379   A 332
**Review of the season** Clarkston survived their first season in Division 2, and also
finished runners-up to Kilmarnock in Glasgow and District Cup. Stand-off Mike
Robin was top scorer with 183 pts; wing Gavin Borland scored 14 tries.

## Dunfermline

**Year of formation** 1904
**Ground** McKane Park, Dunfermline   **Tel** Dunfermline 21279
**Colours** Royal blue and white
**Most capped player** J T Greenwood (Scotland) 20 caps
**Captain 1977–78** R Young

**1st XV 1977–78** P 26   W 8   L 18   F 278   A 503
**Review of the season** Dunfermline, relegated from the national league's first division in 1975, slipped farther back, though dropping to Division 3 only on points-difference behind Edinburgh Wanderers. North-Midlands stand-off Dougie Arneil headed points-scorers with 115, but top try-scorer Mike Paul notched only 4.

332

# Edinburgh Academicals

**Year of formation** 1857
**Ground** Raeburn Place, Edinburgh   **Tel** 031–332 1070
**Colours** Blue and white stripes
**Most capped player** W I D Elliot (Scotland) 29 caps
**Captain 1977–78** R L A Blair
**1st XV 1977–78** P 25   W 10   D 1   L 14   F 281   A 333
**Review of the season** Edinburgh Academicals had the satisfaction of inflicting the only league defeat on Division 2 champions Kelso in what was otherwise a middling season. Lock forward David Loudon topped the points with 65 and Willie Henderson the try-scorers with 8.

# Edinburgh Wanderers

**Year of formation** 1868
**Ground** Murrayfield, Edinburgh EH12 5PJ   **Tel** 031–337 2196
**Colours** Red and black
**Most capped player** A R Smith (Scotland) 33 caps
**Captain 1977–78** D H Borrowman
**1st XV 1977–78** P 27   W 9   L 18   F 290   A 416
**Review of the season** Edinburgh Wanderers, relegated from Division 1 in 1977, only just escaped a further drop, finishing ahead of second-bottom Dunfermline on points-difference. Top scorers were centres David Tweedie (103 pts) and John Hume (7 tries).

# Gala

**Year of formation** 1875
**Ground** Netherdale, Galashiels   **Tel** Galashiels 3811
**Colours** Maroon jerseys, white shorts
**Most capped player** P C Brown (Scotland) 27 caps
**Captain 1977–78** R F Cunningham
**1st XV 1977–78** P 33   W 20   L 13   F 657   A 471
**Review of the season** Gala, having run Hawick to a play-off for the national title in 1977, were heavily hit by the loss of key players and had their worst season in the five years of championship, winning only four of 11 games. Stand-off Colin Gass was only one short of a century of points; wing Vic Chlebowski scored 20 tries.

# Glasgow High

**Year of formation** 1895
**Ground** Old Anniesland, Crow Road, Glasgow G12   **Tel** 041–959 1154
**Colours** Chocolate and gold

**Most capped player** J M Bannerman (Scotland) 37 caps
**Captain 1977–78** D Jerdan
**1st XV 1977–78** P 32   W 12   D 2   L 18   F 474   A 384
**Review of the season** Glasgow High, who escaped relegation only narrowly in 1977, did much better and a few more points in narrow defeats would have put them in a challenging position for promotion to Division 1. Top scorers were full-back John Hodgkinson (218 pts) and wing Forbes Leslie (11 tries).

# Gordonians

**Year of formation** 1903
**Ground** Seafield, Thorngrove Avenue, Aberdeen   **Tel** Aberdeen 37027
**Colours** Blue jerseys with gold hoop, blue shorts
**Most capped player** I G McCrae (Scotland) 6 caps
**Captain 1977–78** G L Slater
**1st XV 1977–78** P 24   W 13   D 1   L 10   F 391   A 244
**Review of the season** Gordonians won all six Division 2 league matches at home but did not travel well, picking up only one point from five away games. Stuart Irvine, 178, had most points and Peter Robertson, 20, most tries.

# Haddington

**Year of formation** 1911
**Ground** Neilson Park, Haddington   **Tel** Haddington 3702
**Colours** Scarlet jerseys and stockings, black shorts
**Captain 1977–78** I Rennie
**1st XV 1977–78** P 31   W 17   D 1   L 13   F 405   A 359
**Review of the season** Haddington, the most successful of Edinburgh area's emerging clubs, followed Highland up from national league's fourth division to first. They gained promotion as runners-up to Kelso, though edging out Ayr only on a points-difference of four. Top scorers were Gordon Smith (92 pts) and Colin Young, whose 20 tries included two in victory against Glasgow High that sealed promotion.

# Hawick

**Year of formation** 1873
**Ground** Mansfield Park, Mansfield Road, Hawick   **Tel** Hawick 4291
**Colours** Green jerseys, white shorts
**Most capped player** H F McLeod (Scotland) 40 caps
**Captain 1977–78** C B Hegarty
**1st XV 1977–78** P 30   W 23   D 1   L 6   F 665   A 229
**Review of the season** Hawick won the national championship for the fifth successive season (unbeaten for the second time in the five years of the competition) and also topped the Border League. They contributed six players to the Scotland team – Jim Renwick, Alastair Cranston, Colin Deans, Norman Pender, Alan Tomes, and club captain Brian Hegarty. Renwick was leading scorer with 171 pts; wing Ken McCartney scored 30 tries.

# Heriot's FP

**Year of formation** 1890
**Ground** Goldenacre, Ferry Road, Edinburgh
**Tel** 031–552 5925 (pavilion)/031–552 4097 (groundsman)

**Colours** Blue and white horizontal stripes
**Most capped player** K J F Scotland and A R Irvine (both Scotland) 27 caps
**Captain 1977–78** A R Irvine
**1st XV 1977–78** P 30   W 22   L 8   F 518   A 331
**Review of the season** Heriot's FP, inspired by British Lion full-back Andy Irvine, had their best championship season, finishing fourth. Their overall record, in all matches, was surpassed only by those of Boroughmuir and Hawick. Irvine again top scorer (135 pts); former Cambridge University wing Steve Page got 14 tries.

# Highland

**Year of formation** 1922
**Ground** Northern Meeting Park, Inverness. Clubhouse at Canal Park
**Tel** Inverness 38644
**Colours** Green jerseys with red band, red and green hooped stockings, black shorts
**Most capped player** N A MacEwan (Scotland) 20 caps
**Captain 1977–78** J S P Gaffney
**1st XV 1977–78** P 20   W 8   L 12   F 273   A 327
**Review of the season** Highland sorely missed Nairn MacEwan as, having run from Division 4 to 1 in minimum time, they dropped down to the second after two seasons among the élite 12. Opened their league programme with two wins, but lost the remaining matches. Former Scotland 'B' full-back David Aitchison scored most points, 75, and Ian Sutherland most tries, 5.

# Jedforest

**Year of formation** 1885
**Ground** Riverside Park, Jedburgh   **Tel** Jedburgh 2232 and 2486
**Colours** Royal blue jerseys and stockings, white shorts
**Most capped player** D M Rose (Scotland) 7 caps
**Captain 1977–78** J Brown
**1st XV 1977–78** P 32   W 16   L 16   F 443   A 475
**Review of the season** Jedforest remain the only Border League club never to have played in the national first division. They finished fourth in Division 2, but scored more points (207) than any other club in that division. Also notched a Border League win against Hawick for the second successive year. Cameron Thompson was top scorer on two counts; 91 pts including 10 tries.

# Jordanhill

**Year of formation** 1972 (on amalgamation of College and School FP clubs)
**Ground** Kilmardinny Playing Fields, Milngavie Road, Bearsden, Glasgow G61 3TB   **Tel** 041–942 8980
**Colours** Green and red
**Most capped player** J (Ian) McLauchlan (Scotland) 37 caps
**Captain 1977–78** J McLauchlan
**1st XV 1977–78** P 28   W 13   D 4   L 11   F 407   A 304
**Review of the season** Jordanhill had a better record outside the league, in which they struggled before avoiding relegation from Division 1. They were helped by four vital points, from Melrose and Langholm, in November games against Border

opposition. Full-back Myles Erskine missed his points century by one; former Scottish Schools cap Malcolm Hurst scored 10 tries.

# Kelso

**Year of formation** 1876
**Ground** Poynder Park, Kelso, Roxburghshire   **Tel** Kelso 2300
**Colours** Black and white
**Most capped player** G K Smith (Scotland) 18 caps
**Captain 1977–78** R E Paxton
**1st XV 1977–78** P 35   W 23   D 1   L 11   F 521   A 456
**Review of the season** Kelso won promotion to Division 1 for a second time, their only championship defeat being against Edinburgh Academicals in their opening game. Also annexed two Border Sevens trophies, at Melrose and Jedforest. Full-back Dave Cowe had 127 pts; wing Jimmy Fleming topped the try list with 13 – two more than flanker-captain Eric Paxton. Junior and semi-junior teams won their own Border titles.

# Kilmarnock

**Year of formation** 1868
**Ground** Bellsland, Queens Drive, Kilmarnock   **Tel** Kilmarnock 22314
**Colours** White with red hoop surmounted by white Maltese cross
**Most capped player** A Ross (Scotland) 2 caps
**Captain 1977–78** H R McHardy
**1st XV 1977–78** P 42   W 32   L 10   F 886   A 435
**Review of the season** Kilmarnock, who began the league in Division 3 in 1973, continued their regular annual improvement by finishing third in Division 1. Also won Glasgow and District Cup for the first time, and retained Ayrshire Cup. Derek Martin was Scotland's leading scorer with 302 pts (279 for club) and wing John Robertson, with 30 tries, shared top place in the national list with Hawick's Ken McCartney.

# Langholm

**Year of formation** 1872
**Ground** Milntown, Langholm, Dumfriesshire   **Tel** Langholm 386
**Colours** Crimson jerseys and blue shorts
**Most capped player** C Elliot (Scotland) 12 caps
**Captain 1977–78** C B Muir
**1st XV 1977–78** P 28   W 17   L 11   F 448   A 354
**Review of the season** Langholm, threatened by relegation in 1977, recovered to their 1976 position, fifth in Division 1. They broke exactly even in the 10 games played and finished with three successive wins. Leading scorers were Chic Muir (75 pts) and Irving Davidson (8 tries).

# Leith Academicals

**Year of formation** 1922
**Ground** Hawkhill, Lochend Road, Edinburgh 7   **Tel** 031–554 1111
**Colours** Royal blue and white hooped jerseys, white shorts
**Captain 1977–78** D G B Main

**1st XV 1977–78** P 28   W 16   D 1   L 11   F 353   A 268
**Review of the season** Leith Academicals, promoted in 1976 but relegated in 1977, returned to Division 2 by winning the third with 100% record. This achievement was equalled only by Glenrothes in Division 7.

## Madras College FP

**Year of formation** 1960
**Ground** Station Park, St Andrews, Fife   **Tel** St Andrews 3933
**Colours** Navy blue jerseys and stockings, white shorts
**Captain 1977–78** J Scott
**1st XV 1977–78** P 30   W 23   L 7   F 565   A 284
**Review of the season** Madras won promotion for the second successive season, this time as runners–up to Leith Academicals in Division 3. But the run-in was close, Madras winning their last two games 6–3 against Marr and 19–18 against promotion rivals Glasgow Academicals. Beaten by Glenrothes in Midlands Cup final.

## Melrose

**Year of formation** 1877
**Ground** Greenyards, Melrose   **Tel** Melrose 2559
**Colours** Yellow and black
**Most capped player** F A L Laidlaw (Scotland) 32 caps
**Captain 1977–78** W Mitchelhill
**1st XV 1977–78** P 28   W 15   L 13   F 410   A 368
**Review of the season** Melrose, Division 2 champions the previous season, were relegated from Division 1 for second time in three years. They never recovered from losing their first four championship matches. Robin Wood was leading scorer with 114 pts; Greg Jackson and Rob Moffat scored 9 tries apiece.

## Preston Lodge FP

**Year of formation** 1929
**Ground** Pennypit Park, Prestonpans   **Tel** Prestonpans 810309
**Colours** Black, maroon and white
**Captain 1977–78** J C Reynolds
**1st XV 1977–78** P 28   W 14   L 14   F 363   A 437
**Review of the season** Preston Lodge, Division 3 champions in 1977, broke even in all games in 1977–78 but won only two of 11 in the league and were relegated. John Forsyth topped both scoring lists – 67 pts including 9 tries.

## Selkirk

**Year of formation** 1907
**Ground** Philiphaugh, Selkirk   **Tel** Selkirk 20403
**Colours** Navy blue jerseys, white shorts
**Most capped player** J A Waters (Scotland) 16 caps
**Captain 1977–78** J Y Rutherford
**1st XV 1977–78** P 33   W 21   L 12   F 608   A 347
**Review of the season** Selkirk, relegated from Division 1 in 1977, made a poor challenge for promotion, losing four of their first seven championship matches.

The Rutherford brothers headed the try-scoring, Bill with 16 and John 12 despite absence on injured list. Keith Hendrie totalled 113 pts. The club suffered serious flood damage to its premises in late autumn.

## Stewart's Melville FP

**Year of formation** 1973 (on amalgamation of Daniel Stewart's College FP and Melville College FP)
**Grounds** Inverleith and Ferryfield, Ferry Road, Edinburgh EH5 2DW
**Tel** Edinburgh (031) 552 3004 and 552 2112
**Colours** Scarlet jerseys with broad black band divided by narrow gold band, white shorts, black stockings
**Most capped player** D W Morgan (Scotland) 21 caps
**Captain 1977–78** D W Morgan
**1st XV 1977–78** P 28    W 17    L 11    F 503    A 387
**Review of the season** Stewart's Melville FP, led by international captain Douglas Morgan, made sure of an extension to their first season in Division 1 by winning three of their opening four league matches, but they had only one more win, against bottom-of-table Highland. Morgan scored most points, 181 (including 79 of their 127 in the league); Edinburgh wing Andy Blackwood headed the tries with 15.

## Watsonians

**Year of formation** 1875
**Ground** Myreside, Edinburgh    **Tel** 031–447 1395
**Colours** Maroon and white
**Most capped player** J C McCallum (Scotland) 26 caps
**Captain 1977–78** D H F Forrest
**1st XV 1977–78** P 26    W 10    D 2    L 14    F 310    A 348
**Review of the season** Watsonians avoided relegation to Division 2 thanks to a last-minute try by Kenny Ross which forced a 7–7 draw with Jordanhill in the final league game. The club had struggled after losing their first four matches in the championship. Ross was leading try-scorer with 11; Euan Kennedy topped points with 82.

## West of Scotland

**Year of formation** 1865
**Ground** Burnbrae, Glasgow Road, Milngavie, Glasgow G62 6HX
**Tel** 041–956 2891
**Colours** Red and yellow hooped jerseys, navy blue shorts
**Most capped player** A B Carmichael (Scotland) 50 caps
**Captain 1977–78** A B Carmichael
**1st XV 1977–78** P 30    W 16    D 1    L 13    F 453    A 319
**Review of the season** West of Scotland, led by Scottish record cap-winner Sandy Carmichael, maintained their championship challenge until mid-November but then fell away, losing their last four matches. They also lost their two-year hold on Glasgow and District Cup. Stand-off Bryan Gossman failed by one point to reach three figures; wing Mike Nellany headed the try tally with 14.

J P R Williams (Wales and Bridgend) keeps the Baa-Baas' attack flowing in the Jubilee Match between the Barbarians and the 1977 Lions. Ian McGeechan (Scotland and Headingley) (left) and Tony Neary (Broughton Park) hurry back to cover for the Lions.

# WALES

## Aberavon

**Year of formation** 1876
**Ground** Talbot Athletic Ground, Manor Street, Port Talbot, Glamorgan
**Tel** Port Talbot 2427
**Colours** Red and black hoops, white shorts, red stockings
**Most capped player** E M Jenkins (Wales) 21 caps
**Captain 1977–78** R C Shell
**1st XV 1977–78** P 48   W 31   D 1   L 16   F 921   A 610
**Review of the season** Aberavon, favourites to beat Newport in the Schweppes WRU Cup semi-final, suffered a shock defeat that caused an unexpected slump in which they won just one of their last seven fixtures. Ian Hall and Morton Howells retired, but veteran Billy Mainwaring cancelled his retirement to play again excellently. British Lion prop Clive Williams, injured in New Zealand, missed the whole season. Keri Coslett joined from Llanelli to make outstanding contribution as versatile back and goalkicker, scoring 264 pts. New centre Neil Hutchings also impressed, scoring 25 tries; Greg Rees scored 18.

## Abertillery

**Year of formation** 1883
**Ground** The Park, Abertillery, Gwent   **Tel** Abertillery 2226
**Colours** Green and white hooped jerseys, white shorts
**Most capped player** H J Morgan (Wales) 27 caps
**Captain 1977–78** M Cairns
**1st XV 1977–78** P 50   W 16   D 2   L 32   F 501   A 821
**Review of the season** Although Abertillery continued in the doldrums and were beaten by Abercynon in the Cup, home victories over Neath, Aberavon, and Gloucester were encouraging and recruitment of players gives hope for a brighter future. Robert Norster developed as line-out specialist; John Dixon was an outstanding tight-head; Stuart Griffin impressed in the back row; John Derrick joined from Cross Keys to strengthen centre play; Nigel Paul and Gordon Thomas shared scrum-half duties effectively; and Steve Rogers proved a useful new full-back. Martin Brickell became first player to pass 1,000 pts for the club.

## Bridgend

**Year of formation** 1878
**Ground** Brewery Field, Tondu Road, Bridgend, Glamorgan
**Tel** Bridgend 2707/59032
**Colours** Blue and white stripes
**Most capped player** J P R Williams (Wales) 45 caps
**Captain 1977–78** Lyndon Thomas
**1st XV 1977–78** P 50   W 32   D 2   L 16   F 914   A 519
**Review of the season** Bridgend recruited Alan Rose and Roy Evans from Neath, and Alan Evans from Llanelli, but the retirement of prop John Lloyd because of back trouble was a considerable blow. He joined the coaching staff. Injuries to

Lyndon Thomas and Ian Lewis upset the back division's rhythm. They defeated all four Cup semi-finalists – Aberavon, Cardiff, Newport and Swansea – after being put out of the Cup at Aberavon, and ended the season with a Snelling and Welsh National sevens double. Flanker Gareth Williams broke the forward try-scoring records with five in the 74–9 victory over Penarth and a total of 21. Rose scored 22 tries, Ian Lewis 124 pts, and Gerald Williams 122. J P R Williams was appointed captain for centenary season in 1978–79.

# Cardiff

**Year of formation** 1876
**Ground** Cardiff Arms Park, Westgate Street, Cardiff **Tel** Cardiff 23546
**Colours** Cambridge blue and black
**Most capped player** G O Edwards (Wales) 53 caps
**Captain 1977–78** T G R Davies
**1st XV 1977–78** P 43 W 34 D 1 L 8 F 954 A 473
**Review of the season** Cardiff would have become Welsh champions for the first time for 20 years had they won either fixture with Pontypridd. Another disappointment was the Cup semi-final defeat by Swansea. Much satisfaction, however, in the progress of young stars Terry Holmes, Pat Daniels (top try-scorer with 21 in his first season after joining from Glamorgan Wands), and Terry Charles, son of soccer's famous John Charles. Gerald Davies, in third successive season as captain, scored 17 tries and David Barry 175 pts.

# Cross Keys

**Year of formation** 1885
**Ground** Pandy Park, Cross Keys, Gwent **Tel** Cross Keys 270289
**Colours** Black and white hoops
**Most capped player** S Morris (Wales) 19 caps
**Captain 1977–78** David Thomas
**1st XV 1977–78** P 47 W 21 D 2 L 24 F 524 A 643
**Review of the season** Cross Keys appointed former hooker Alan Talbot as new coach and were rebuilding extensively. Goalkicking wing Keith Jefferson joined from Cross Keys United (for whom he scored 33 tries in previous season and 44 points in one match) but he transferred to Newport. Geoff Hughes, another wing, left for Pontypool and injuries dogged re-elected skipper David Thomas. New fly-half Phil Watkins impressed and scrum-half Gary Davies always contributed positively. Lost to surprise-packet Bedwas in the Cup, but defeated Bridgend, Neath, and Swansea.

# Ebbw Vale

**Year of formation** 1880
**Ground** Eugene Cross Park, Ebbw Vale **Tel** Ebbw Vale 302157
**Colours** Red, white, and green hoops
**Most capped player** Denzil Williams (Wales) 36 caps
**Captain 1977–78** G Howls
**1st XV 1977–78** P 44 W 26 D 3 L 15 F 641 A 505
**Review of the season** Ebbw Vale's high hopes dissolved after a successful start. Restructuring was necessary behind the scrum, where committee-man Mike Grindle, aged 33, returned as emergency out-half, though Mike Edwards and Alan Rainbow showed promise in the position after Lyndon Miles rejoined Tredegar.

Leg injuries handicapped 1977 international Clive Burgess. Five successive home defeats included the heaviest home reverse since World War II – 6–32 by Llanelli. England trialist Steve Lewis contributed 223 pts, aggregating 1,106 in 146 games for Vale.

## Glamorgan Wanderers

342

**Year of formation** 1893
**Ground** The Memorial Ground, Stirling Road, Ely, Cardiff   **Tel** Cardiff 591039
**Colours** Cambridge blue, black, and white
**Captain 1977–78** W James
**1st XV 1977–78** P 41   W 20   L 21   F 604   A 482
**Review of the season** Glamorgan Wanderers lost centre Pat Daniels to Cardiff in September, Gren Suchecki, to Pontypridd, full-back Gareth Price, who went to London, and Paddy Keepings, a lively flanker who retired because of persistent leg injury. Robin Havard, sharp attacker at full-back or wing, scored 5 tries against Oxford playing on the wing and totalled 136 pts. David Mullins, a promising new fly-half, played for Glamorgan; lock Mike Thomas set a high work-rate. Notable victories were scored over Pontypool and at Neath.

## Llanelli

**Year of formation** 1872
**Ground** Stradey Park, Llanelli, Dyfed   **Tel** Llanelli 4060
**Colours** Scarlet jerseys with white collars, club crest on left breast
**Most capped player** Phil Bennett (Wales) 29 caps
**Captain 1977–78** Phil Bennett
**1st XV 1977–78** P 44   W 29   D 1   L 14   F 903   A 497
**Review of the season** Llanelli's brightest aspect was the installation of a new £41,000 floodlighting system – best in Wales. Otherwise there were numerous disappointments, topped by the fourth round Cup defeat at Aberavon. Roy Bergiers broke a leg in the Cup first round and Barry Llewelyn retired. Bernard Thomas returned from Italy and flanker Keith Williams made a big impact, but the pack was not strong enough and there were six home defeats. Vernon Richards, outstanding youth international scrum-half, joined late in season. Phil Bennett scored 206 pts for the club; Andy Hill 114 including 22 tries.

## Maesteg

**Year of formation** 1882
**Ground** Llynvi Road, Maesteg, Mid-Glamorgan   **Tel** Maesteg 732283
**Colours** Black and amber
**Most capped player** C Pugh (Wales) 7 caps
**Captain 1977–78** W Pole
**1st XV 1977–78** P 45   W 35   L 10   F 1078   A 354
**Review of the season** Maesteg enjoyed their most successful season since 1950, winning merit table title and defeating Welsh champions Pontypridd, Bridgend (twice), Aberavon, Swansea, and Pontypool (twice). Wing Colin Donovan scored 37 tries in his first season to break the record of Norman Davies (36). Gwyn Evans, capped by Wales 'B', scored 229 pts and emphasised his potential at fly-half. John Morgan, new No 8 John Thomas, Brian Morris, and David Williams were notable forwards under Billy Pole's command. Scrum-half Adrian Jones joined from Cardiff to share duties with Alan Thomas.

*There was good reason for singing all the way home to Llanelli after Wales's victory over Scotland. Two sons of Stradey Park, Derek Quinnell (above, handing off Mike Biggar) and Ray Gravell (below), both scored tries in the Welsh victory.*

# Neath

**Year of formation** 1871
**Ground** The Gnoll, Gnoll Park Road, Neath, West Glamorgan   **Tel** Neath 4420
**Colours** Black with white Maltese cross
**Most capped player** W D Morris (Wales) 34 caps
**Captains 1977–78** Glyn Shaw/Peter Davies
**1st XV 1977–78** P 44   W 27   L 17   F 749   A 554
**Review of the season** Neath had a disappointing season on the whole, despite a record 31–13 victory over Cardiff. Home record satisfactory but frequently dismal away. Glyn Shaw turned professional with Widnes in November, so Peter Davies took over the captaincy. Record scorer and vice-captain John Poole transferred to Pontypridd in October and injuries, notably to new scrum-half Huw Morgan, also disrupted the team. David Cole, always reliable at centre, was top scorer with 202 pts, while Mike Jenkins scored 16 tries, and Elgan Rees 15 in limited appearances.

344

# Newbridge

**Year of formation** 1890
**Ground** Welfare Ground, Bridge Street, Newbridge, Gwent
**Tel** Newbridge 243247
**Colours** Blue and black hoops
**Most capped player** D Hayward (Wales) 15 caps
**Captains 1977–78** Howard Evans/Malcolm Lewis
**1st XV 1977–78** P 50   W 23   D 2   L 25   F 567   A 544
**Review of the season** Newbridge again disappointed despite a marginally better record. Howard Evans moved from outside-half to centre, then left for London in December and veteran flanker Malcolm Lewis assumed command. Keith Westwood and Alan Williams formed a new coaching unit in succession to David Harries. Return of scrum-half Terry Evans and centre David George helped morale. Highlight was Clive Davis's Wales 'B' cap and selection for Wales's tour to Australia. Tony Browning, wing turned full-back, was outstanding, while schools cap Justin Robinson looked a polished out-half.

# Newport

**Year of formation** 1874
**Ground** Rodney Parade, Newport, Gwent   **Tel** Newport 58193
**Colours** Black and amber
**Most capped player** K J Jones (Wales) 44 caps
**Captain 1977–78** D H Burcher
**1st XV 1977–78** P 45   W 29   L 16   F 721   A 468
**Review of the season** Newport only just failed to retain the Welsh Cup, losing to Swansea in the final, but their playing record declined sharply as their back play deteriorated and pack lacked customary authority. British Lion Brynmor Williams joined from Cardiff in December to bring flair to scrum-half, and flanker Keith Poole, aged 34, passed Ian Ford's record 482 appearances for the club. Keith James returned after five years with other clubs and dropped 12 goals. Leighton Davies scored 157 pts, Chris Webber 106.

# Penarth

**Year of formation** 1880
**Ground** Athletic Grounds, Lavernock Road, Penarth, South Glamorgan

**Tel** Penarth 708402
**Colours** Royal blue (alternative with white hoops)
**Most capped player** J Bassett (Wales) 15 caps
**Captain 1977–78** A T J Hodge
**1st XV 1977–78** P 43   W 13   D 1   L 29   F 414   A 1,021
**Review of the season** Penarth struggled again; hardly a novel situation but nonetheless frustrating. Player/coach Dennis John left in December, new captain Tony Hodge missed a long spell injured, and another experienced loose forward, John James, faded from the scene. Finding a replacement scrum-half for Dennis John proved a major problem, though brothers Gareth and Phil Davies looked promising halves late in the season. Veteran Wally Carter eventually returned at No 8: he had helped Penarth beat Barbarians in 1971, but this time the Baa-Baas scored a record 84–12 win.

345

# Pontypool

**Year of formation** 1901
**Ground** Pontypool Park, Pontypool   **Tel** Pontypool 3492 (ground)/2524 (HQ)
**Colours** Red, white, and black hoops
**Most capped player** T R Prosser (Wales) and R Windsor (Wales) 22 caps
**Captain 1977–78** T J Cobner
**1st XV 1977–78** P 46   W 28   D 1   L 17   F 1,052   A 501
**Review of the season** Pontypool, when at full strength, re-affirmed that they possessed the best pack in Wales, while improving backs shared 123 tries, a club record. Goff Davies scored 34, schoolboy Gareth Davies 9 in 10 matches on the other wing, and excellent full-back Peter Lewis totalled 330 pts to be top scorer in Wales. No 8 Paul Clark scored 3 tries in 11 minutes against Cross Keys. Took the ground record of Newport (17 months' standing) and Ebbw Vale (12 months') in 10 days.

# Pontypridd

**Year of formation** 1876
**Ground** Sardis Road Ground, Pwllgwaun, Pontypridd   **Tel** Pontypridd 405006
**Colours** Black and white hoops
**Most capped player** R J Robins (Wales) 13 caps
**Captain 1977–78** T P David
**1st XV 1977–78** P 56   W 47   D 1   L 8   F 1,306   A 482
**Review of the season** Pontypridd became Welsh champions for the second time in three years, defeating Cardiff twice in crucial matches, and were unlucky to lose their Cup quarter-final at Newport. Improved all-round power despite injuries, among them one that put Tom David out for a long spell. John Poole, recruited from Neath, scored 94 pts, and other high scorers were Jeff Hazzard (213), Karl Swain (162 including 39 tries), Adrian Barwood (140 from 35 tries), and Ian Walsh (109). Bob Dyer joined from Swansea to share scrum-half duties with the excellent Robin Morgan.

# South Wales Police

**Year of formation** 1969
**Ground** Police Recreation Ground, Waterton Cross, Bridgend, Mid-Glamorgan
**Tel** Bridgend 55555 ext 218/Bridgend 4481
**Colours** Red jerseys, white shorts, royal blue stockings

**Most capped player** I Hall (Wales) 8 caps
**Captain 1977–78** P Noble
**1st XV 1977–78** P 44   W 19   L 25   F 594   A 750
**Review of the season** South Wales Police lost their first eight games, but with
ex-Wales threequarter Ian Hall returning from Aberavon as player/coach they
turned in some encouraging performances. Ended season with tour victories over
Plymouth Albion, Falmouth, and Camborne. Prop Alan Davies was in Wales 'B'
squad, and with his brothers Jeff and John formed a one-family front row. Alan
King, consistent full-back, scored 178 pts and skipper Phil Noble, playing in 43 of
the 44 games, 15 tries. Haydn Morgan was an inventive attacker.

## Swansea

**Year of formation** 1874
**Ground** St Helen's Ground, Swansea, West Glamorgan   **Tel** Swansea 57572/57318
**Colours** All white
**Most capped player** T M Davies (Wales) 38 caps
**Captain 1977–78** Alan Meredith
**1st XV 1977–78** P 40   W 30   L 10   F 828   A 435
**Review of the season** Swansea, after a first round scare when taken to extra time
at Burry Port, defeated Newport in the Schweppes WRU Cup final. Maesteg and
Cardiff were the only visitors to win at St Helen's. Powerful pack included
internationals Geoff Wheel, Trevor Evans, Phil Llewellyn, and Mark Keyworth,
Wales 'B' cap Barry Clegg, and outstanding newcomers Richard Moriarty and
Gareth Roberts. Backline flair came from scrum-half Huw Davies, fly-half David
Richards, Alan Meredith, and Alun Donovan, a surprise choice for Welsh tour of
Australia.

## Tredegar

**Year of formation** 1899
**Ground** Tredegar Recreation Ground, Park Hill, Tredegar, Gwent
**Tel** Tredegar 2879
**Colours** Red, black, and white
**Captain 1977–78** Royston Williams
**1st XV 1977–78** P 43   W 18   D 2   L 23   F 565   A 648
**Review of the season** Tredegar recruited valuable men in Cardiff centres Paul
Evans and Peter Bolland (79 pts), excellent fly-half Lyndon Miles, from Ebbw
Vale, and his brother Philip at full-back; also David Harries (ex-Newbridge) who
took over coaching. Injuries upset rebuilding plans, but prop David Leetham, lock
J L Brown, skipper Royston Williams (despite injuries), and veteran Colin James set
fine examples. First win over Maesteg for five years and home draw with Ebbw
Vale were notable feats.

# IRELAND

## Academy

**Year of formation** 1975 (formerly Belfast Royal Academy FP)
**Ground** Hydepark, Mallusk, Co. Antrim, N. Ireland   **Tel** Glengormley 3085
**Colours** Maroon jerseys, navy shorts, maroon and white stockings
**Most capped player** K J Houston (Ireland) 6 caps
**Captain 1977–78** J Morgan
**1st XV 1977–78** P 25   W 14   D 1   L 10   F 301   A 231
**Review of the season** Academy disappointed. They were knocked out of the
Ulster Senior Cup in the third round by Instonians and finished second from
bottom of the league. Forwards were reasonably consistent but the backs were not
so good. Useful foundations for future in Ricky Huddleston (scrum-half), Gordon
Henderson (flanker), Robin Hawe (prop), and Ulster flanker David Nash.

## Ballymena

**Year of formation** 1922
**Ground** Eaton Park, Ballymena   **Tel** Ballymena 6746
**Colours** Black jerseys, white shorts, black stockings with white turnover
**Most capped player** W J McBride (Ireland) 63 caps
**Captain 1977–78** A W McMaster
**1st XV 1977–78** P 23   W 17   L 6   F 535   A 282
**Review of the season** Ballymena swept majestically to the Ulster Senior League
title with skipper Wallace McMaster, the former international wing, playing very
well at centre. Willie John McBride, Ian McIlrath, Harry Steele, and Alan McLean
were other notable names in Ulster's strongest club side. They were surprisingly
beaten at the last hurdle in the Senior Cup final – by CIYMS.

## Bangor

**Year of formation** 1886
**Ground** Upritchard Park, Bloomfield Road South, Bangor, Co. Down, N. Ireland
**Colours** Old gold, royal blue and black
**Most capped player** R A Milliken (Ireland) 14 caps
**Captain 1977–78** N Scott
**1st XV 1977–78** P 35   W 23   D 4   L 8   F 613   A 310
**Review of the season** Bangor made a poor start when hit by injuries, but they
recovered dramatically and scored 142 pts in their last four matches. Had a
powerful pack, with an exciting discovery in No 8 Davy Morrow, and fast backs,
particularly Kenny Strutt on the left wing. Former international Willie McCombe
was as consistent as ever.

## Bective Rangers

**Year of formation** 1881
**Ground** Donnybrook, Dublin 4   **Tel** Dublin 693894

**Colours** Red, green, and white striped jerseys, white shorts
**Most capped player** J L Farrell (Ireland) 29 caps
**Captain 1977–78** A Anderson
**1st XV 1977–78** P 32   W 16   D 1   L 15   F 396   A 395
**Review of the season** Bective disappointed in scoring only one more win, and
point, than they conceded. A strong pack included Jon Raphael, England reserve
hooker, and John Power and Cormac O'Carroll on the flanks. Half-backs Aidan
Anderson and former Schools international Brendan Murphy also impressed, but
the team generally failed to show real potential.

# Blackrock College

**Year of formation** 1882
**Ground** Stradbrook Road, Blackrock    **Tel** Dublin 805967
**Colours** Narrow royal blue and white striped jerseys, navy shorts, navy stockings
**Most capped player** R J McLoughlin (Ireland) 40 caps
**Captain 1977–78** A Forte
**1st XV 1977–78** P 30   W 20   D 1   L 9   F 406   A 254
**Review of the season** Blackrock College fielded a powerful side with such
stalwarts as Fergus Slattery, Ned Byrne, and Willie Duggan in the pack. For the
second successive season they were long-range favourites for the Leinster Senior
Cup but played badly in their semi-final and were eliminated by UCD. Injury to
captain Tony Forte was a blow, but the future is bright with a host of talented
young backs available, among them the highly promising left wing, Mark Keogh.

# Bohemian

**Year of formation** 1922
**Ground** Thomond Park, Limerick (Junior ground/Annacotty, Co Limerick)
**Tel** Limerick 46649
**Colours** Red and white
**Most capped player** M A F English (Ireland) 16 caps
**Captain 1977–78** M Goggin
**1st XV 1977–78** P 24   W 9   D 2   L 13   F 208   A 230
**Review of the season** Bohemians had a modest season at senior level despite the
consistent goal-kicking of Brendan Moran, who also impressed as a versatile
threequarter. Portents bright following the victory of the Under 20 team in
Limerick City tournament.

# CIYMS

**Year of formation** 1922
**Ground** Circular Road, Belfast    **Tel** Belfast 768225/760120
**Colours** Black and white hooped jerseys, black shorts, blue stockings
**Most capped player** A C Pedlow (Ireland) 30 caps
**Captain 1977–78** Frank Wilson
**1st XV 1977–78** P 31   W 18   D 1   L 12   F 480   A 288
**Review of the season** CIYMS were shaping for their worst season for a decade,
having a tough battle to avoid relegation in the Ulster League. Yet they recovered
in the Ulster Cup and, to the surprise of all – and the consternation of their
opponents – beat Ballymena 14–12 in the final. Much of their earlier trouble
resulted from niggling injuries, but international lock Ronnie Hakin, out for much
of season, returned in time for the Cup.

# Clontarf

**Year of formation** 1876
**Ground** Castle Avenue, Clontarf, Dublin   **Tel** Dublin 336214
**Colours** Red and blue striped jersey, white shorts, red and blue striped stockings
**Most capped player** G J Morgan (Ireland) 19 caps
**Captain 1977–78** G Howard
**1st XV 1977–78** P 28   W 13   D 2   L 13   F 311   A 315
**Review of the season** Clontarf improved slightly on their record of the previous
season but seldom rose above a modest level. Their main weakness again was too
light a pack. The return of full-back Frank Ennis from Dublin University
strengthened the defence and he was a prolific goal-kicker, earning deserved
selection for Ireland 'B' against Scotland 'B'. Veteran scrum-half Ollie Byrne
continued to give good service.

# Collegians

**Year of formation** 1890
**Ground** Deramore Park, Belfast, N. Ireland   **Tel** Belfast 665943
**Colours** White and maroon, navy stockings with maroon tops
**Most capped player** J McVicker (Ireland) 20 caps
**Captain 1977–78** A Campbell
**1st XV 1977–78** P 25   W 12   D 5   L 8   F 186   A 229
**Review of the season** Collegians finished runners-up to Ballymena in the Ulster
League, making few changes during a good run. Arthur Campbell was an inspiring
captain, and Ashley Armstrong proved a superb asset following his transfer from
Bangor.

# Cork Constitution

**Year of formation** 1892
**Ground** Temple Hill, Ballintemple, Cork   **Tel** Cork 32563
**Colours** White, black, and blue
**Most capped player** T J Kiernan (Ireland) 54 caps
**Captain 1977–78** B Smith
**1st XV 1977–78** P 25   W 7   D 2   L 16   F 227   A 302
**Review of the season** Cork Constitution had their most indifferent season for
years, and were ousted from the Munster Cup in first round by eventual winners
Shannon. Too many experienced players had retired or were past best, while severe
leg injury kept fly-half Barry McGann out till after Christmas.

# Dolphin

**Year of formation** 1902
**Ground** Musgrave Park, Cork   **Tel** Cork 22069
**Colours** Navy blue
**Most capped player** J S McCarthy (Ireland) 28 caps
**Captain 1977–78** O Healy
**1st XV 1977–78** P 22   W 12   D 1   L 9   F 276   A 218
**Review of the season** Dolphin missed the steadying influence of former Ireland
prop Phil O'Callaghan, who played infrequently. However, the advance of young
players augurs well for the club's future. Donal Daly did well at fly-half, as did Joe
Harvey at threequarter.

## Dublin University

**Year of formation** 1854
**Ground** College Park, Trinity College, Dublin 2   **Tel** Dublin 778423
**Colours** White jerseys and shorts, black stockings with red bands at top
**Most capped player** J D Clinch (Ireland) 30 caps
**Captain 1977–78** W Ryan
**1st XV 1977–78** P 22   W 9   D 1   L 12   F 249   A 265

350

**Review of the season** Dublin University had the satisfaction of beating UCD against the odds in the annual Colours match, but otherwise they had undistinguished season. The Colours match in fact, was soured by outbreaks of fighting that led to the IRFU banning the match from Lansdowne Road in 1978–79. No 8 forward Donal Spring was capped at lock against Scotland, but injury soon afterwards kept him out for the rest of the season. His absence no doubt contributed to the Leinster Senior Cup defeat by Blackrock College. Fly-half and captain Willie Ryan was outstanding behind the scrum; Job Langbroek and Michael Gibson were leading forwards.

## Dungannon

**Year of formation** 1873
**Ground** Stevenson Park, Dungannon, N. Ireland   **Tel** Dungannon 2387
**Colours** Royal blue and white hoops, white shorts
**Most capped player** S A McKinney (Ireland) 25 caps
**Captain 1977–78** S A McKinney
**1st XV 1977–78** P 32   W 17   D 2   L 13   F 403   A 353
**Review of the season** Dungannon's highlight was provided by Stewart McKinney's coming on as a replacement for Ireland against Scotland at Lansdowne Road and scoring a dramatic try. The club's form was erratic, but the return of Alan Kempton to scrum-half and the arrival of Keith Gilpin from Malone improved the half-back sector substantially.

## Galwegian

**Year of formation** 1922
**Ground** Glenina, Galway, Co Galway   **Tel** Galway 62484
**Colours** Sky blue jerseys, white shorts
**Most capped player** P J A O'Sullivan (Ireland) 15 caps
**Captain 1977–78** W Quinn
**1st XV 1977–78** P 30   W 11   L 19   F 272   A 444
**Review of the season** Galwegians, so long the leading side in Connacht, were going through a transition period, and a poor season culminated in their comprehensive defeat by Athlone in the cup semi-final. Jack Mannion, flanker, was one of their more promising up-and-coming players.

## Garryowen

**Year of formation** 1884
**Ground** Dooradoyle, Limerick   **Tel** Limerick 46094
**Colours** Light blue jerseys with white star on breast
**Most capped player** B G M Wood (Ireland) 29 caps
**Captain 1977–78** P Whelan
**1st XV 1977–78** P 30   W 18   D 4   L 8   F 393   A 233

**Review of the season** Garryowen's star was undoubtedly Tony Ward, Ireland's discovery at fly-half. His 277 pts for the club improved Munster records he had set himself in two previous seasons. Generally a good season for the club, but little luck in premier competitions. For the second season running they were beaten in the Munster Senior Cup final by Shannon, and then by UC Cork in the Senior League final.

# Instonians

**Year of formation** 1919
**Ground** Shane Park, Stockmans Lane, Belfast BT9 7JD    **Tel** Belfast 660629
**Colours** Yellow, black and purple
**Most capped player** D Hewitt (Ireland) 18 caps
**Captain 1977–78** C H McKibbin
**1st XV 1977–78** P 30   W 16   D 4   L 10   F 266   A 173
**Review of the season** Instonians' loss of international centre Alistair McKibbin and his brother Roger to London Irish was a big blow. After an indifferent start they eventually found their feet and came back strongly, though were knocked out of the Ulster Cup by old rivals Collegians.

# Lansdowne

**Year of formation** 1872
**Ground** Lansdowne Road, Dublin 4    **Tel** Dublin 689292/689300
**Colours** Red, yellow and black
**Most capped player** E O'D Davy (Ireland) 34 caps
**Captain 1977–78** P Gahan
**1st XV 1977–78** P 27   W 12   D 3   L 12   F 329   A 298
**Review of the season** Lansdowne had a disappointing season, being beaten in their section of the Leinster Senior League, of which they were reigning champions, and going out unexpectedly in the second round of the senior cup to dark horses Terenure College. Injuries were a contributory factor, with international scrum-half Donal Canniffe out for the whole season and Moss Keane, ill following the Lions tour, not resuming till after Christmas. Keane still earned four more caps to total 24. Mick Quinn was reserve out-half for Ireland, but otherwise the backs were moderate and the pack was not quite up to usual standards.

# Malone

**Year of formation** 1892
**Ground** Gibson Park Avenue, Cregagh Road, Belfast BT6 9GL
**Tel** Belfast 57819/51312 (sec)
**Colours** White shirt, blue shorts, red stockings
**Most capped player** W E Crawford (Ireland) 30 caps
**Captain 1977–78** J Anderson
**1st XV 1977–78** P 24   W 15   L 9   F 232   A 215
**Review of the season** Though they faded from the race for Ulster League honours, Malone had a large influx of new players so their future looks bright. Forwards played well, with Dermot Dalton, Willie Duncan, and Andy McCann prominent.

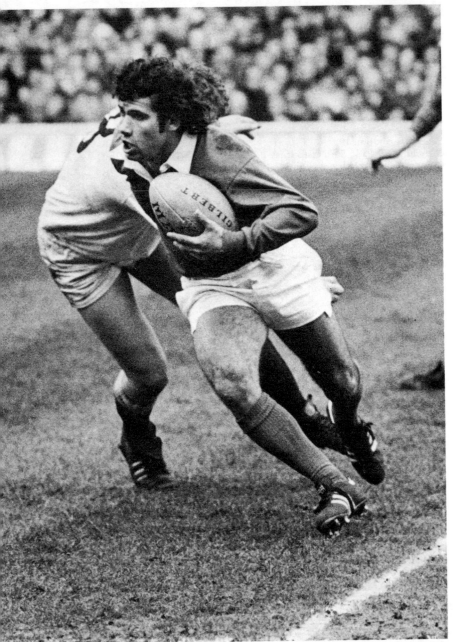

*Tony Ward, Ireland's exciting discovery at fly-half in 1978, was also a prolific scorer for his club Garryowen.*

# Monkstown

**Year of formation** 1883
**Ground** Sydney Parade, Dublin 4    **Tel** Dublin 691794
**Colours** Royal blue and gold
**Most capped player** J C Parke (Ireland) 20 caps
**Captain 1977–78** T Odbert
**1st XV 1977–78** P 31    W 14    L 17    F 377    A 433

**Review of the season** Monkstown started poorly, had a useful mid-season spell, but finished on a disappointing note. Best performances were victories over Wanderers, Old Wesley, CIYMS, and overseas visitors Chicago Lions and Montreal Irish. Centres Jack Donnelly and John McLoughlin gave many good displays; Alo Munnelly was steady full-back; Ernie McKay was a young forward of real potential.

# North of Ireland (NIFC)

**Year of formation** 1859
**Ground** Shaftesbury Avenue, Belfast BT7 2ES    **Tel** Belfast 21096/23342
**Colours** Red, black, and blue jerseys, navy shorts, black stockings with red, black, and blue turnover
**Most capped player** C M H Gibson (Ireland) 65 caps
**Captain 1977–78** S G G McComish
**1st XV 1977–78** P 30    W 17    D 3    L 10    F 208    A 145

**Review of the season** 'North's' problem, in a season in which they finished in the top half of the Ulster League, was their inability to field a settled team. Mike Gibson played as well as ever but was often absent due to representative demands. A big shock was their defeat by Rainey Old Boys in the Ulster Cup.

# Old Belvedere

**Year of formation** 1930
**Ground** Anglesea Road, Ballsbridge, Dublin 4    **Tel** Dublin 689748
**Colours** Black and white hooped jerseys, black shorts
**Most capped player** A J F O'Reilly (Ireland) 29 caps
**Captain 1977–78** D Forbes
**1st XV 1977–78** P 34    W 17    D 2    L 15    F 367    A 362

**Review of the season** Old Belvedere won their section of the Leinster Senior League for the first time, before narrowly losing to Old Wesley in the semi-final, and they enjoyed an unexpectedly good run in the Cup, going out to Wanderers only with the last kick of a semi-final replay. Dermot Forbes set a splendid captain's example in the pack; fly-half Ollie Campbell was their key back.

# Old Wesley

**Year of formation** 1891
**Ground** Donnybrook, Dublin 4    **Tel** Dublin 689149
**Colours** White jerseys with red and white band, white shorts
**Most capped player** G T Hamlet (Ireland) 30 caps
**Captain 1977–78** G Wallace
**1st XV 1977–78** P 27    W 15    D 1    L 11    F 313    A 338

**Review of the season** Old Wesley promised well, winning their section of the Leinster Senior League before Christmas and beating Old Belvedere in the semi–final. However, they then lost to St Mary's College in the final and went down rather tamely to Blackrock in the quarter-final of the Cup. Their big, strong pack, in which international prop Philip Orr and the Wallace brothers, George and Bob, were outstanding, was never adequately supported by the backs. Fly-half Douglas McCoy was a prolific goalkicker. In May 1977, the club made first overseas tour, to California.

354

## Palmerston

**Year of formation** 1899
**Ground** Milltown Road, Clonskeagh, Dublin 6  **Tel** Dublin 973126
**Colours** Black, green and white jerseys, black shorts
**Captain 1977–78** S Harte
**1st XV 1977–78** P 30  W 18  D 2  L 10  F 291  A 249
**Review of the season** Palmerston's highlight was a fine run in the Leinster Senior Cup, beating Clontarf in the second round and drawing with holders UCD in the quarter-final. They were eliminated in a tight replay. Again they had one of the heaviest and most effective packs in Leinster, and an inspiring captain, Stephen Harte, was well supported by a progressive loose trio in Colman O'Donoghue, Dick Whealens, and Paul Prett. The backs were short of pace, but Barry O'Connor was the province's No 2 scrum-half to international John Moloney.

## Queen's University, Belfast

**Year of formation** 1869
**Ground** Upper Malone Playing Fields, Upper Malone Road, Belfast
**Tel** Belfast 611662
**Colours** Royal blue jerseys, white shorts, green, blue, and black stockings
**Most capped player** J W Kyle (Ireland) 46 caps
**Captain 1977–78** C Gardner
**1st XV 1977–78** P 26  W 17  D 1  L 8  F 422  A 170
**Review of the season** Queen's, in doldrums a few years ago, continued to improve and had another good season, although they were out of luck in the Dudley Cup, the Irish Universities' championship. Outstanding players in a young team were captain and wing Chris Gardner and centre Alan Irwin, who won an Ireland 'B' cap against Scotland 'B' at Murrayfield.

## St Mary's College

**Year of formation** 1900
**Ground** Templeville Road, Dublin 6  **Tel** Dublin 900440
**Colours** Royal blue jerseys with white star, white shorts, royal blue stockings
**Most capped player** T O Grace (Ireland) 25 caps
**Captain 1977–78** J J Moloney
**1st XV 1977–78** P 27  W 19  L 8  F 365  A 290
**Review of the season** St Mary's, who had won the Leinster Senior League in January, looked to be heading for the best record of any Leinster club until unexpectedly eliminated by young and lively UC Dublin side in the second round of the Senior Cup. Captain John Moloney made a triumphant return after a season's absence to regain his place at scrum-half in the Ireland team and captain his country for the first time. In contrast, club-mate Tom Grace, whom he succeeded in the captaincy, lost his Irish team place after the opening match against Scotland.

# Sunday's Well

**Year of formation** 1924
**Ground** Musgrave Park, Cork   **Tel** Cork 25926
**Colours** Red, white and green
**Most capped player** J C Walsh (Ireland) 25 caps
**Captain 1977–78** B Cahill
**1st XV 1977–78** P 23   W 11   D 3   L 9   F 246   A 244
**Review of the season** Sunday's Well had a reasonably satisfactory season, but
suffered a big disappointment by losing to Highfield in the first round of the
Munster Senior Cup. Outstanding player was fly-half Tony Steen, who scored
93 pts, including 10 dropped goals.

# Terenure College

**Year of formation** 1941
**Ground** Lakelands Park, Terenure, Dublin 6   **Tel** Dublin 907572
**Colours** Purple, black and white
**Most capped player** M L Hipwell (Ireland) 12 caps
**Captain 1977–78** B Lynham
**1st XV 1977–78** P 32   W 11   D 1   L 20   F 344   A 450
**Review of the season** Terenure College pulled themselves together after a
near-disastrous start to the season, and it was only in a replay that Wanderers,
eventual Leinster Cup winners, beat them in the quarter-finals. Outstanding players
were captain and scrum-half Brendan Lynham, full-back John Cronin, and the
speedy Flannery brothers, Ray and Gerry, on the wings.

# University College, Cork

**Year of formation** 1872
**Ground** Mardyke, Western Road, Cork   **Tel** Cork 45772
**Colours** Red jersey with black bar, white skull-and-crossbones on chest
**Most capped player** J Russell (Ireland) 19 caps
**Captain 1977–78** C Cantillon
**1st XV 1977–78** P 28   W 18   D 5   L 5   F 350   A 162
**Review of the season** UCC proved to be the outstanding university side in
Ireland, winning not only the Dudley Cup but also the Munster Senior League and
Cork Charity Cup in a fine season. Outstanding players were scrum-half Alex
O'Regan, fly-half Moss Finn, and full-back John Barry, who totalled 129 pts.
Gerry Holland, at lock, looked an excellent prospect.

# University College, Dublin

**Year of formation** 1910
**Ground** University College Dublin, Belfield, Dublin 4   **Tel** Dublin 693616
**Colours** St Patrick's blue jerseys, white shorts, navy blue stockings with St
Patrick's blue tops
**Most capped player** R J McLoughlin (Ireland) 40 caps
**Captain 1977–78** S R Hall
**1st XV 1977–78** P 31   W 14   D 3   L 14   F 332   A 320
**Review of the season** UCD's season was punctuated by disappointments. Slow to
settle down, they were surprisingly beaten by Dublin University in the
controversial Colours match. In addition, they lost their Irish Universities title, and

were beaten 9–4 by Wanderers in the final of the Leinster Senior Cup, for which they were favourites. Fly-half Daragh Coakley was always prominent.

## University College, Galway

**Year of formation** 1874
**Ground** College Road and Renmore Road, Galway
**Colours** Maroon jerseys, white shorts, maroon stockings with white turnover
**Most capped player** M G Molloy (Ireland) 27 caps
**Captain 1977–78** P Flynn
**1st XV 1977–78** P 19   W 7   D 1   L 11   F 225   A 220
**Review of the season** UCG had an indifferent season, despite the efforts of Owen Lysaght and Paul O'Byrne, both of whom played senior inter-provincial rugby for Connacht. Hugh Maguire looked a prop forward with a future.

## Wanderers

**Year of formation** 1870
**Ground** Lansdowne Road, Dublin 4   **Tel** Dublin 689277
**Junior ground** Merrion Road, Dublin   **Tel** Dublin 693227/695272
**Colours** Blue, black, and white hooped jerseys, navy shorts, black stockings with blue and white turnover.
**Most capped player** A R Dawson (Ireland) 27 caps
**Captain 1977–78** R Gordon
**1st XV 1977–78** P 35   W 21   D 5   L 9   F 458   A 331
**Review of the season** Wanderers produced an all-representative back division, including current internationals in full-back Tony Ensor and left wing Freddie McLennan. In addition they fielded a skilful and heavy pack in which tight-head prop Mick Fitzpatrick gained international honours and lock Emmet O'Rafferty was picked against France – but had to withdraw injured. Yet despite so much talent, the season's record was patchy until the club 'came good' at the end to win the Leinster Senior Cup for the 10th time.

# FIXTURES 1978–79

*All fixtures understood to be correct at time of going to press, but subject to re-arrangement or change of date or venue.*

*English County Championship fixtures.*

## Saturday, 26 August 1978

Kelvinside Sevens
Selkirk Sevens

## Friday, 1 September

Bridgwater & Albion v Met Police

## Saturday, 2 September

**Surrey Centenary XV v International XV** (Twickenham)
Bridgend Sevens
Collegians tournament
Earlston Sevens

Aberavon v Glamorgan Wands
Abertillery v Neath
Bective Rangers v Skerries
Birmingham v Hull and ER
Bradford v Saracens
Bristol v Northampton
Burton v Nuneaton
Cardiff v East District
Chester v New Brighton
Clarkston v Preston Lodge
Clontarf v Dungannon
Coleraine v NIFC
Cork Const v Galwegians
Dolphin v Young Munster
Edinburgh Wands v Gosforth
Falmouth v Clifton
Fylde v Hartlepool Rovers
Glenrothes v Gordonians
Gloucester v Broughton Park
Haddington v Heriot's FP
Harrogate v Percy Park
Heaton Moor v Monkstown
Highfield v Sunday's Well
Highland v Boroughmuir
Jordanhill v Portadown
Kilmarnock v Ayr
Leicester v Bedford
Llanelli v Pontypridd
Manchester v Waterloo
Moseley v Nottingham
Newbridge v Ebbw Vale
Newport v Coventry
Northern v Middlesbrough
Old Alleynians v London Irish
Old Belvedere v Shannon
Palmerston v Garryowen
Plymouth Albion v London Scottish
Pontypool v Bath
Preston Grasshoppers v Richmond
Roundhay v West Hartlepool
Roundhegians v Wakefield
Rugby v Birkenhead Park
St Helens v Huddersfield
Sale v Morley
Sidcup v Blackheath
S Wales Police v Maesteg
Swansea v Cross Keys
Tredegar v Penarth
Trinity Acads v Stewart's Melville FP
Tynedale v Halifax
Wasps v Liverpool
West of Scotland v Orrell
Wilmslow v Sheffield

## Sunday, 3 September

Torquay Ath v London Scottish
Vale of Lune v Richmond
Weston-super-Mare v Met Police

## Monday, 4 September

**Plymouth Albion v Crawshay's Welsh**
Camborne v Combined Birmingham OB

## Tuesday, 5 September

Cardiff HSOB v Pontypridd
Exeter v Dallas, Texas
Harlequins v Woodford
Instonians v Bayonne
Melrose v Royal High
Nuneaton v Leicester
Old Thornensians v Huddersfield
St Helens v Halifax
Stewart's Melville FP v Edinburgh Borderers Select
Tredegar v Bridgend
Wakefield v Sandal
Wilmslow v Monkstown

## Wednesday, 6 September

**Cornwall v Crawshay's Welsh** (Camborne)
Abertillery v S Wales Police
Birmingham v Worcester
Cardiff v Glamorgan Wands
Crynant v Swansea
Galwegians v Old Crescent
Heaton Moor v Manchester
High Wycombe v Bucks
London Irish v Saracens

358

Newport v Bath
Old Wesley v Old Belvedere
Palmerston v Lansdowne
Plymouth Albion v Public School
  Wands
Pontypool v Pontypool Junior RU
Roundhay v Old Crossleyans
Rugby v Bedford
Sheffield v Headingley
Stroud v Gloucester
Tynedale v Gosforth
Wanderers v Clontarf
Westoe v Northern
Wasps v Hendon

### Thursday, 7 September

Clarkston v Skerries

### Saturday, 9 September

Kelso Sevens
Abertillery v Penarth
Ayr v Perthshire
Ballymena v Instonians
Ballynahinch v NIFC
Bangor v Jordanhill
Bath v Leicester
Bedford v London Irish
Blackheath v S Wales Police
Bridgend v Newbridge
Civil Service v Academy
Clarkston v Morpeth
Coleraine v CIYMS
Coventry v Gloucester
Derry v Collegians
Dungannon v Portadown
Edinburgh Wands v Hartlepool Rovers
Exeter v Esher
Falmouth v Devonport Services
Galwegians v Edmonton Leprechauns
Glasgow High v Northern
Gordonians v Musselburgh
Gosforth v Liverpool
Haddington v Boroughmuir
Harlequins v Northampton
Headingley v Birmingham
Heriot's FP v Lansdowne
Huddersfield v Sheffield
Kilmarnock v Sunderland
Llanelli v Aberavon
London Scottish v Orrell
London Welsh v Saracens
Manchester v Sale
Neath v Cardiff
New Brighton v Birkenhead Park
Newport v Bristol
Nottingham v Rugby
Nuneaton v Hull and ER
Plymouth Albion v Halifax
Pontypool v Tredegar
Pontypridd v Glamorgan Wands
Rosslyn Park v Met Police

Roundhay v Blaydon
Royal High v Stewart's Melville FP
Swansea v Moseley
Wakefield v Broughton Park
Wanderers v Dolphin
Wasps v Richmond
Waterloo v Glasgow Acads
West of Scotland v Alnwick
Wilmslow v Harrogate

### Sunday, 2 September

Blackrock Festival
Sunday's Well v Purple Cross
Torquay Athletic v Halifax

### Monday 11 September

Gala v Howe of Fife

### Tuesday, 12 September

Clarkston v Paisley Grammarians
Exeter v Calgary Saints
Gordonians v Aberdeen GSFP
Kelso v Berwick
Hawick v Selkirk
Sunday's Well v Concord

### Wednesday, 13 September

**Royal Navy v Hampshire**
  (Portsmouth)
Amman United v Swansea
Ards v Dungannon
Blaydon v Melrose
Bristol v Cardiff
Broughton Park v Sale
Chester v Manchester
Clifton v Bath
Ebbw Vale v Glamorgan Wands
Gloucester v Cheltenham
Heriot's FP v Leith Acads
Leicester v Birmingham
Liverpool v New Brighton
Llanelli v Bridgend
Monkstown v Bective Rangers
Moseley v Nuneaton
Newquay Hornets v Camborne
Northampton v Nottingham
Old Belvedere v Skerries
Palmerston v Blackrock Coll
Penarth v Pontypridd
Pontypool v Newport
Rugby v Coventry
Saracens v St Mary's Hospital
S Wales Police v Pembrokeshire
Wasps v Old Gaytonians

### Saturday, 16 September

**Cornwall v South of Scotland**
  (Redruth)

Aberavon v Newbridge
Bective Rangers v Athlone
Birkenhead Park v Sale
Blackrock Coll v Dungannon
Blaydon v Gala
Bristol v Swansea
Broughton Park v Cheltenham
Camborne v Teignmouth
Cardiff v Coventry
Cross Keys v Nuneaton
Derry v Academy
Ebbw Vale v Pontypridd
Exeter v Torquay Ath
Falmouth v Weston-super-Mare
Fylde v Edinburgh Wands
Galwegians v Ballymena
Glasgow High v West of Scotland
Gosforth v Rosslyn Park
Guy's Hospital v Blackheath
Halifax v Bradford
Harlequins v Llanelli
Harrogate v Rugby
Highland v Gordonians
Huddersfield v Orrell
Hull and ER v St Helens
Hutchesons' v Clarkston
Jedforest v Langholm
Jordanhill v Roundhay
Leicester v London Welsh
Liverpool v Sheffield
London Irish v US Portsmouth
London Scottish v Headingley
Maesteg v Plymouth Albion
Malone v Collegians
Melrose v Kelso
Met Police v Birmingham
Morpeth v Boroughmuir
Moseley v Bath
New Brighton v Heriot's FP
Newport v Neath
Northampton v Richmond
Northern v Wakefield
NIFC v Lisburn
Nottingham v Bedford
Old Belvedere v Bangor
Penarth v Esher
Perthshire v Kilmarnock
Pontypool v Abertillery
Portadown v Palmerston
Ryton v Haddington
Saracens v Bridgend
Shannon v Monkstown
Stewart's Melville FP v Selkirk
Sunday's Well v CIYMS
Taunton v Glamorgan Wands
Terenure Coll v Wanderers
Tredegar v West Park
Tynedale v Ayr
UC Cork v Dolphin
Vale of Lune v Instonians
Wasps v Streatham-Croydon
Waterloo v Gloucester
Wilmslow v Manchester

**Sunday, 17 September**

**London Exiles v Surrey** (Sunbury)

**Monday, 18 September**

Kelso v Preston Lodge
Selkirk v Boroughmuir

**Tuesday, 19 September**

Bridgend v Wolfhounds
Hawick v Melrose
Huddersfield v Halifax
Kilmarnock v Glasgow Acads
Newbridge v Newport

**Wednesday, 20 September**

**Cornwall v Royal Navy** (Redruth)
**Sussex v Bosuns** (Haywards Heath)
Armagh v Instonians
Bath v Cheltenham
Cardiff v Penarth
Chester v Birkenhead Park
Coventry v Birmingham
Ebbw Vale v Gloucester
Gala v Ryton
Glamorgan Wands v Tredegar
Langholm v Carlisle
London Welsh v Met Police
Rugby v Northampton
S Wales Police v Pontypool
Swansea v Penarth

**Thursday, 21 September**

Truro v Camborne

**Friday, 22 September**

Falmouth v Bridgwater & Albion
Plymouth Albion v Cheltenham

**Saturday, 23 September**

**JAPAN v FRANCE** (Tokyo)
Aberavon v Cardiff
Athlone v Sunday's Well
Ayr v Sunderland
Ballymena v Coleraine
Bath v Exeter
Bedford v Richmond
Blackheath v Northampton
Blaydon v Jordanhill
Bridgend v Pontypool
Broughton Park v Gosforth
Camborne v Paignton
Clontarf v West of Scotland
Collegians v Portadown
Cross Keys v Glamorgan Wands
Dolphin v Blackrock Coll
Dungannon v Galwegians

360

Durham City v Hull and ER
Edinburgh Univ v Edinburgh Wands
Falmouth v Newquay Hornets
Fylde v Waterloo
Gala v Glasgow High
Garryowen v Bangor
Gloucester v Bristol
Haddington v Alnwick
Harlequins v Leicester
Headingley v Wasps
Heriot's FP v Hawick
Huddersfield v Roundhay
Instonians v Bective Rangers
Jedforest v Glasgow Acads
Kelso v Clarkston
Kilmarnock v Morpeth
Leith Acads v Boroughmuir
Llanelli v Moseley
London Irish v Rosslyn Park
London Scottish v London Welsh
Maesteg v Abertillery
Manchester v Birkenhead Park
Melrose v Harrogate
Met Police v Newbridge
Middlesbrough v Rugby
Monkstown v Malone
Northern v Percy Park
Old Belvedere v Terenure Coll
Old Wesley v CIYMS
Orrell v Halifax
Otley v New Brighton
Palmerston v Greystones
Pontypridd v Newport
Sale v Coventry
Saracens v Nottingham
Selkirk v Queen's Univ
Stewart's Melville FP v Hartlepool
   Rovers
Stroud v Nuneaton
Swansea v Newport
Taunton v Tredegar
Trinity Acads v Gordonians
Vale of Lune v Oxford Univ
Wakefield v Liverpool
Wanderers v NIFC
Widnes v Sheffield
Wilmslow v Langholm

## Sunday, 24 September

**Irish Exiles v Munster** (Sunbury)
Plymouth Albion v Camborne
St Mary's Coll v West of Scotland

## Monday, 25 September

Anti-Assassins v Oxford Univ
   (Wilmslow)
Gala v Northern
Kelso v Glasgow High
Selkirk v Allan Glen's

## Tuesday, 26 September

**Herts v Eastern Counties** (Hertford)
**Notts, Lincs & Derbys v Greater
   Birmingham** (Newark)
**Somerset v Monmouthshire**
   (Weston-super-Mare)
**Bridgend v WRU President's XV**
   (*Centenary match*)
Newbridge v Tredegar

## Wednesday, 27 September

**Southern Counties v Argentinians**
   (Oxford)
**Devon v Royal Navy** (Rectory,
   Plymouth)
**Northumberland v Edinburgh and
   Dist** (Gosforth)
**Sussex v Combined London OB** (East
   Grinstead)
Aberavon v Penarth
Abertillery v Llanelli
Crediton v Exeter
Glamorgan Wands v Neath
Nuneaton v Birmingham
Pontypool v Blaenavon
Pontypridd v Cardiff

## Friday, 29 September

Dolphin v Brixham

## Saturday, 30 September

**CANADA v FRANCE** (Calgary)
**London v Argentinians**
   (Twickenham)
Aberavon v Bucharest
Academy v Portadown
Alnwick v Ayr
Ballymena v Palmerston
Bective Rangers v Shannon
Birkenhead Park v Wakefield
Birmingham v Maesteg
Boroughmuir v Northern
Bridgend v Glamorgan Wands
Bristol v Nottingham
CIYMS v Cooke
Clarkston v Kelvinside Acads
Collegians v Dungannon
Coventry v Blackheath
Ebbw Vale v S Wales Police
Edinburgh Wands v Heriot's FP
Esher v Nuneaton
Exeter v Camborne
Fylde v Bradford
Gala v Northampton
Glasgow High v Instonians
Gloucester v Bedford
Gordonians v Howe of Fife
Haddington v Selkirk
Halifax v Liverpool

Harlequins v London Welsh
Harrogate v Kelso
Hawick v Jedforest
Huddersfield v Old Edwardians
Hull and ER v Vale of Lune
Kilmarnock v Haddington
Lansdowne v Blackrock Coll
Leicester v Saracens
Leith Acads v Stewart's Melville FP
Llanelli v Newport
London Scottish v London Irish
Lydney v Pontypridd
Maesteg v Pontypool
Melrose v Langholm
Met Police v Arras, France
Middlesbrough v Roundhay
Morley v Broughton Park
Moseley v Cardiff
Neath v Bath
Newbridge v Pontypool
New Brighton v Orrell
NIFC v City of Derry
Penarth v Cross Keys
Rosslyn Park v Richmond
Rugby v Waterloo
St Austell v Falmouth
Sale v Kendal
Skerries v Dublin Univ
Sunday's Well v Corinthians
Swansea v Abertillery
Tredegar v Cardiff Coll of Ed
UC Cork v Highfield
UC Dublin v Old Belvedere
US Portsmouth v Plymouth Albion
Wanderers v Monkstown
Wasps v Manchester
West of Scotland v Gosforth
Wilmslow v Jordanhill

## Sunday, 1 October

Bective Rangers v Clontarf
Dolphin v Highfield
Kelso v Royal High

## Monday, 2 October

Selkirk v Gala
Swansea v Bucharest

## Tuesday, 3 October

South of Scotland v Durham
Aberdeen Univ v Gordonians
Nottingham v Coventry
S Wales Police v Neath

## Wednesday, 4 October

**North of England v Argentinians**
(Headingley)
*Dorset & Wilts v Bucks (Salisbury)
*Hampshire v Sussex (Portsmouth)

*Herts v Surrey (Croxley Green)
*Leicestershire v East Midlands
*Middlesex v Kent (Sudbury)
*Oxfordshire v Berkshire (Banbury)
Abertillery v Glamorgan Wands
Bath v Bucharest
Bridgend v Cross Keys
Cambridge Univ v Cambridge City
Ebbw Vale v Aberavon
Newbridge v Bristol
Newport v Abertillery
Pontypool v Gloucester
Pontypridd v S Wales Police
Wharfedale v Harrogate

361

## Saturday, 7 October

**North Midlands v Argentinians**
(Moseley)
**Ulster v Yorkshire**
Abertillery v Plymouth Albion
Academy v Queen's Univ
Bath v Aberavon
Bective Rangers v Lansdowne
Bangor v Collegians
Bedford v Exeter
Birkenhead Park v Torquay Athletic
Birmingham v Huddersfield
Blackheath v Wasps
Bristol v London Irish
Cardiff v Newport
Clifton v Glamorgan Wands
Coventry v Leicester
Cross Keys v Penarth
Dublin Univ v Terenure Coll
Dungannon v Ballymena
Ebbw Vale v Bridgend
Garryowen v Blackrock Coll
Gloucester v Bucharest
Gosforth v Fylde
Halifax v West Hartlepool
Harrogate v Middlesbrough
Harlequins v Swansea
Hartlepool Rovers v Wilmslow
Highfield v Old Belvedere
Instonians v Bohemians
Liverpool v Broughton Park
Malone v NIFC
Manchester v New Brighton
Met Police v Lydney
Monkstown v Old Wesley
Moseley v Sale
Neath v Llanelli
Newbridge v Saracens
Nuneaton v Rugby
Northampton v London Scottish
Nottingham v Northern
Orrell v Hull and ER
Oxford Univ v Henley
Penzance-Newlyn v Falmouth
Pontypool v Maesteg
Pontypridd v Wakefield
Portadown v CIYMS

Redruth v Camborne
Richmond v London Welsh
Rosslyn Park v Headingley
St Mary's Coll v Palmerston
Sheffield v Bradford
S Wales Police v Cardiff Coll of Ed
Sunday's Well v Dolphin
Wanderers v Waterloo
Weston–super–Mare v Tredegar
Young Munster v UC Cork

362

*SRU Championship: Division 1*

Boroughmuir v Kelso
Haddington v Jordanhill
Kilmarnock v Gala
Stewart's Melville FP v Heriot's
  FP
Watsonians v Langholm
West of Scotland v Hawick

*SRU Championship: Division 2*

Ayr v Edinburgh Wands
Clarkston v Highland
Gordonians v Glasgow High
Jedforest v Melrose
Madras FP v Edinburgh Acads
Selkirk v Leith Acads

**Sunday, 8 October**

Corinthians v Galwegians
St Mary's Coll v Waterloo

**Monday, 9 October**

Bristol v Bucharest

**Tuesday, 10 October**

**England Students v Argentinians**
  (Gloucester)
Oxford v Oxford Univ
Plymouth Albion v Bath

**Wednesday, 11 October**

*****North Midlands v Staffordshire**
  (Moseley)
*****Notts, Lincs & Derbys v
  Leicestershire** (Beeston)
Abertillery v Glamorgan Wands
Cambridge Univ v Northampton
Llanelli v Leinster
London Scottish v Bucharest

**Saturday, 14 October**

**ENGLAND XV v ARGENTINA**
  (Twickenham)
*****Cheshire v Durham** (Birkenhead
  Park)

*****Cornwall v Somerset** (Redruth)
*****Devon v Gloucestershire** (Exeter)
*****Northumberland v Lancashire**
  (Gosforth)
*****Yorkshire v Cumberland** (Otley)
Athlone v Academy
Bath v London Irish
Bedford v Pontypool
Blackrock Coll v Bective Rangers
Bradford v Birkenhead Park
Broughton Park v Manchester
Cambridge Univ v Guy's Hospital
CIYMS v Civil Service
Clifton v Bucharest
Clontarf v Old Belvedere
Coventry v Wanderers
Dungannon v Monkstown
Durham City v Roundhay
Fylde v Nottingham
Galwegians v Shannon
Gloucester v Harlequins
Halifax v Otley
Huddersfield v Headingley
Instonians v Collegians
Leicester v Richmond
Liverpool v Moseley
Llanelli v Swansea
London Scottish v Rosslyn Park
London Welsh v Bridgend
Malone v Ballymena
Maesteg v Newbridge
Neath v Sale
New Brighton v Loughborough
  Students
Newport v Blackheath
Northampton v Cardiff
Northern v Hartlepool Rovers
NIFC v Queen's Univ
Nuneaton v Pontypridd
Oxford v Glamorgan Wands
Palmerston v Dublin Univ
Penarth v Cardiff Coll of Ed
Rugby v Cross Keys
Sheffield v Morley
Sidmouth v Exeter
Streatham–Croydon v Saracens
Taunton v Falmouth
Tredegar v Abertillery
Tynedale v Hull and ER
US Portsmouth v Birmingham
Vale of Lune v Harrogate
Wakefield v Wilmslow
Wasps v Bristol
Waterloo v Orrell

*SRU Championship: Division 1*

Gala v Haddington
Hawick v Stewart's Melville FP
Heriot's FP v Langholm
Jordanhill v Boroughmuir
Kelso v West of Scotland
Watsonians v Kilmarnock

*SRU Championship: Division 2*

Edinburgh Wands v Jedforest
Glasgow High v Clarkston
Highland v Selkirk
Leith Acads v Ayr
Madras FP v Gordonians
Melrose v Edinburgh Acads

## Sunday, 15 October

**Connacht v Army**
Garryowen v Corinthians
Sunday's Well v Old Crescent
Waterpark v UC Cork

## Monday, 16 October

Invitation XV v Bucharest (Newport)

## Tuesday, 17 October

**Wales 'B' v Argentina** (Llanelli)
**South of Scotland v Anglo-Scots**
  (Kelso)
Neath v Maesteg
Swansea v Randwick, Sydney

## Wednesday, 18 October

**Cambridge Univ v New Zealanders**
*Berkshire v Dorset & Wilts**
  (Maidenhead)
*Buckinghamshire v Oxfordshire**
  (Bletchley)
*Eastern Counties v Middlesex**
  (Fairlop)
*Hampshire v Surrey** (Basingstoke)
*Staffordshire v Warwickshire**
  (Burton)
*Sussex v Herts** (Horsdean,
  Brighton)
Aberavon v Abertillery
Bristol v Met Police
Newport v Newbridge
Plymouth Albion v Exeter Univ
Pontypool v Ebbw Vale
Swansea v Penarth

## Saturday, 21 October

**Cardiff v New Zealanders**
**Leinster v Argentinians** (Lansdowne
  Road)
*Cumbria v Cheshire**
*Lancashire v Yorkshire** (Fylde)
*Northumberland v Durham**
  (Gosforth)
Academy v CIYMS
Ballymena v Collegians
Birkenhead Park v Gosforth
Birmingham v Plymouth Albion
Blackheath v London Scottish

Blaydon v Northern
Bradford v Huddersfield
Bridgend v Coventry
Bristol v Bath
Broughton Park v Headingley
Camborne v Newton Abbot
Davenport v Sheffield
Dolphin v Palmerston
Dublin Univ v Old Wesley
Dungannon v Instonians
Ebbw Vale v Bedford
Falmouth v Avon/Somerset Police
Garryowen v Sunday's Well
Harlequins v Rosslyn Park
Highfield v UC Cork
Hull and ER v Harrogate
Leicester v Northampton
Liverpool v Fylde
Liverpool Univ v New Brighton
London Irish v Wasps
London Welsh v Llanelli
Maesteg v Tredegar
Manchester v Manchester Univ
Met Police v Walsall
Middlesbrough v Halifax
Moseley v Aberavon
Newbridge v S Wales Police
Newport v Gloucester
NIFC v Cork Const
Nottingham v Waterloo
Orrell v Chester
Penarth v Lydney
Pontypridd v Rugby
Richmond v Oxford Univ
Roundhay v Vale of Lune
Sale v Pontypool
Saracens v Exeter
Streatham–Croydon v Nuneaton
Swansea v Neath
Wakefield v Preston Grasshoppers
Weston-super-Mare v Glamorgan
  Wands
Wilmslow v Abertillery

*SRU Championship: Division 2*

Ayr v Highland
Clarkston v Madras FP
Edinburgh Acads v Gordonians
Jedforest v Leith Acads
Melrose v Edinburgh Wands
Selkirk v Glasgow High

*SRU Championship: Division 2*

Ayr v Highland
Clarkston v Madras FP
Edinburgh Acads v Gordonians
Jedforest v Leith Acads
Melrose v Edinburgh Wands
Selkirk v Glasgow High

**Sunday, 22 October**

Bective Rangers v Wanderers
Blackrock Coll v Greystones
Galwegians v Athlone
Monkstown v Skerries
St Mary's Coll v Old Belvedere

**Tuesday, 24 October**

Neath v Cross Keys
Plymouth Albion v Devonport
  Services
Rosslyn Park v Loughborough Students
Roundhay v Carnegie Coll

**Wednesday, 25 October**

**West Wales v New Zealanders**
  (Swansea)
\***East Midlands v Notts, Lincs &**
  **Derbys** (Bedford or Northampton)
\***Warwickshire v North Midlands**
  (Coventry)
Bridgend v Cardiff
Cambridge Univ v Bedford
Ebbw Vale v Penarth
Gloucester v S Wales Police
Leicester v Oxford Univ
Pontypridd v Cardiff Coll of Ed

**Saturday, 28 October**

**London Counties v New Zealanders**
  (Twickenham)
\***Cheshire v Lancashire** (Sale)
\***Cornwall v Devon** (Camborne)
\***Durham v Cumbria** (Darlington)
\***Gloucestershire v Somerset**
  (Gloucester)
\***Yorkshire v Northumberland**
  (Morley)
 Ulster v Connacht (Ravenhill)
 Aberavon v Bridgend
 Abertillery v Weston
 Academy v Highfield
 Ballymena v Lansdowne
 Bath v St Mary's Hospital
 Birkenhead Park v Durham City
 Blackrock Coll v Bangor
 Birmingham v Exeter
 Bradford v Wilmslow
 Civil Service v NIFC
 Collegians v Palmerston
 Dublin Univ v St Mary's Coll
 Esher v Met Police
 Fylde v London Scottish
 Glamorgan Wands v Maesteg
 Gosforth v Wakefield
 Greystones v Bective Rangers
 Halifax v New Brighton
 Harlequins v Cardiff
 Huddersfield v Tynedale

Instonians v Skerries
Llanelli v Bedford
London Irish v Malone
London Welsh v Neath
Manchester v Harrogate
Morley v Hull and ER
Moseley v Coventry
Newbridge v Pontypridd
Northern v Alnwick
Nottingham v Gloucester
Nuneaton v Liverpool
Old Belvedere v Clontarf
Old Crescent v Dungannon
Old Wesley v Wanderers
Oxford Univ v Northampton
Penarth v Stroud
Pontypool v Oxford
Richmond v Cambridge Univ
Rosslyn Park v Blackheath
Roundhay v Sheffield
Rugby v Tredegar
Saracens v Bristol
Sunday's Well v UC Cork
Swansea v Leicester
Tredegar v Rugby
UC Dublin v CIYMS
Wasps v Newport
Waterloo v Chester
Waterpark v Dublin
West Hartlepool v Sale

*SRU Championship: Division 1*

Gala v West of Scotland
Hawick v Langholm
Jordanhill v Stewart's Melville FP
Kelso v Heriot's FP
Kilmarnock v Haddington
Watsonians v Boroughmuir

*SRU Championship: Division 2*

Edinburgh Wands v Edinburgh Acads
Glasgow High v Ayr
Gordonians v Clarkston
Highland v Jedforest
Leith Acads v Melrose
Madras FP v Selkirk

**Sunday, 29 October**

Crediton v Plymouth Albion
Falmouth v Camborne
Garryowen v Galwegians
UC Galway v Monkstown

**Monday, 30 October**

Dublin Univ v Greystones

**Tuesday, 31 October**

**Munster v New Zealanders**
  (Limerick)
Cross Keys v Aberavon

**Wednesday, 1 November**

*Berkshire v Bucks** (Abbey,
  Reading)
*Herts v Hampshire** (Croxley Green)
*Kent v Eastern Counties**
  (Blackheath)
*Oxfordshire v Dorset & Wilts**
  (Oxford RFC)
*Surrey v Sussex** (Rosslyn Park)
 Bristol v Exeter Univ
 Cardiff v Pontypool
 Clifton v Gloucester
 Newport v Ebbw Vale
 Pontypridd v Bridgend

**Saturday, 4 November**

**IRELAND v NEW ZEALAND**
  (Lansdowne Road)
*Lancashire v Durham** (Broughton
 Park)
*Northumberland v Cumbria**
  (Gosforth)
*Yorkshire v Cheshire** (Headingley)
 Abertillery v Pontypridd
 Bedford v Birmingham
 Blackheath v Swansea
 Blackrock Coll v NIFC
 Bradford v Nottingham
 Bridgend v Bristol
 Broughton Park v Huddersfield
 Cardiff v Maesteg
 Cambridge Univ v London Scottish
 Clontarf v Sunday's Well
 Cross Keys v Newbridge
 Dublin Univ v Collegians
 Exeter v Wasps
 Falmouth v Hayle
 Gloucester v Leicester
 Harlequins v Bath
 Harrogate v Sale
 Hull and ER v Headingley
 London Welsh v Coventry
 Maesteg v Penarth
 Morley v Roundhay
 Moseley v Newport
 Neath v Pontypool
 Northampton v Aberavon
 Nuneaton v Manchester
 Otley v Fylde
 Plymouth Albion v Met Police
 Richmond v Llanelli
 Rosslyn Park v Oxford Univ
 Rugby v New Brighton
 Saracens v London Irish
 Sheffield v Middlesbrough

Sunderland v Gosforth
Tredegar v Stroud
Tynedale v Northern
Wakefield v Halifax
Walsall v Glamorgan Wands
Waterloo v Liverpool
West Hartlepool v Orrell
Wilmslow v Birkenhead Park

*SRU Championship: Division 1*

Boroughmuir v Kilmarnock
Haddington v Langholm
Hawick v Kelso
Heriot's FP v Jordanhill
Stewart's Melville FP v Gala
West of Scotland v Watsonians

*SRU Championship: Division 2*

Ayr v Madras FP
Clarkston v Edinburgh Acads
Edinburgh Wands v Leith Acads
Jedforest v Glasgow High
Melrose v Highland
Selkirk v Gordonians

**Sunday, 5 November**

Bective Rangers v Garryowen
Dolphin v Old Crescent
Falmouth v St Barts Hospital
Galwegians v Sligo
Monkstown v Lansdowne
Skerries v Wanderers
Terenure Coll v Palmerston
Torquay Athletic v Met Police
UC Dublin v Old Belvedere

**Tuesday, 7 November**

**Ulster v New Zealanders** (Ravenhill)
Aberavon v Bristol
Oxford Univ v Oxford Univ
  Greyhounds

**Wednesday, 8 November**

**London Div County Championship
  play-off**
**Midland Div County Championship
  play-off**
Abertillery v Tredegar
Gloucester v Cambridge Univ
Llanelli v Ebbw Vale

**Friday, 10 November**

Bridgend v Neath

**Saturday, 11 November**

**WALES v NEW ZEALAND** (Cardiff)

365

*__Cheshire v Northumberland__
*__Cumbria v Lancashire__ (Chester)
*__Durham v Yorkshire__ (Hartlepool R)
*__Gloucestershire v Cornwall__
  (Bristol)
*__Somerset v Devon__ (Taunton)
Bath v Newbridge
Bedford v Aberavon
Birkenhead Park v Orrell
Birmingham v Nottingham
Bohemians v Galwegians
Bristol v Lydney
Broughton Park v Manchester Univ
Camborne v St Austell
CIYMS v Collegians
Cork Const v UC Cork
Coventry v Northampton
Dungannon v Greystones
Ebbw Vale v Cardiff
Garryowen v Old Crescent
Gloucester v Exeter
Harlequins v Richmond
Highfield v Monkstown
Huddersfield v Sale
Hull and ER v Wakefield
Instonians v NIFC
Lansdowne v Dublin Univ
Leicester v Cambridge Univ
Liverpool v Liverpool Univ
London Welsh v Moseley
Maesteg v Penarth
Malone v Academy
Manchester v Preston Grasshoppers
Morpeth v Gosforth
Northern v West Hartlepool
Nuneaton v Glamorgan Wands
Old Belvedere v Dolphin
Old Wesley v Bective Rangers
Oxford Univ v Blackheath
Paignton v Falmouth
Pontypridd v Cheltenham
Queen's Univ v Ballymena
Roundhay v Halifax
Rugby v Met Police
St Mary's Coll v Wanderers
Saracens v Wasps
Sheffield v Harrogate
Streatham–Croydon v London Irish
Sunday's Well v Waterpark
Swansea v Llanelli
UC Galway v Palmerston
US Portsmouth v London Scottish
Waterloo v New Brighton
Wilmslow v Loughborough Students

*SRU Championship: Division 1*

Gala v Heriot's FP
Haddington v Boroughmuir
Jordanhill v Hawick
Kilmarnock v West of Scotland
Langholm v Kelso
Watsonians v Stewart's Melville FP

*SRU Championship: Division 2*

Clarkston v Selkirk
Edinburgh Acads v Leith Acads
Glasgow High v Melrose
Gordonians v Ayr
Highland v Edinburgh Wands
Madras FP v Jedforest

**Sunday, 12 November**

**Connacht v Combined Irish Univs**
Newport v Rosslyn Park
Terenure Coll v Blackrock Coll

**Monday, 13 November**

Abertillery v Bristol
Pontypool v Cross Keys

**Tuesday, 14 November**

**Scottish North and Midlands v
  Anglo-Scots** (Meadowbank)
Nottingham v Leicester

**Wednesday, 15 November**

**South and South West v New
  Zealanders** (Bristol)
Coventry v Nuneaton
Gloucester v Exeter Univ
Maesteg v Cardiff College of Ed
Plymouth Albion v Bridgwater &
  Albion
UC Dublin v Palmerston

**Thursday, 16 November**

**Oxford Univ v Stanley's XV**

**Saturday, 18 November**

**Midlands v New Zealanders**
  (Leicester)
**Munster v Connacht** (Limerick)
**Schweppes WRU Cup – 1st Round**
  (*Welsh fixtures subject to re-arrangement*)
Abertillery v Maesteg
Academy v Dungannon
Bath v Coventry
Birkenhead Park v Birmingham
Blackrock Coll v Cork Const
Bristol v London Welsh
Cambridge Univ v Blackheath
Cheltenham v Rugby
CIYMS v Malone
Clontarf v Collegians
Dublin Univ v Bective Rangers
Esher v Plymouth Albion
Exeter v Devonport Services
Falmouth v Bideford
Gloucester v Camborne

Gosforth v Percy Park
Halifax v Headingley
Harlequins v Oxford Univ
Harrogate v Huddersfield
Hull and ER v Wilmslow
Instonians v Ballymena
Liverpool v West Hartlepool
London Scottish v Richmond
Loughborough Students v Fylde
Manchester Univ v Manchester
Moseley v Rosslyn Park
New Brighton v Broughton Park
Northampton v Bedford
Northern v Durham Univ
NIFC v Portadown
Nuneaton v S Wales Police
Old Millhillians v Saracens
Orrell v Roundhay
Otley v Sheffield
Palmerston v Monkstown
Sale v Nottingham
Streatham-Croydon v Met Police
Tredegar v Lydney
Wakefield v Morley
Wanderers v Old Belvedere
Wasps v Leicester
Waterloo v London Irish

*SRU Championship: Division 1*

Hawick v Gala
Heriot's FP v Watsonians
Kelso v Jordanhill
Langholm v Boroughmuir
Stewart's Melville FP v Kilmarnock
West of Scotland v Haddington

*SRU Championship: Division 2*

Ayr v Clarkston
Edinburgh Acads v Selkirk
Edinburgh Wands v Glasgow High
Jedforest v Gordonians
Leith Acads v Highland
Melrose v Madras FP

**Sunday, 19 November**

Old Crescent v UC Cork
UC Galway v Galwegians

**Tuesday, 21 November**

**Combined Services v New
 Zealanders** (Aldershot)
Gloucester v Aberavon

**Wednesday, 22 November**

**Cambridge Univ v
 M R Steele-Bodger's XV**
Neath v Maesteg
Pontypridd v Pontypool

**Friday, 24 November**

Queen's Univ v UC Cork

**Saturday, 25 November**

**ENGLAND v NEW ZEALAND**
 (Twickenham)
**English County Championship
 semi-finals** (*provisional*)
**Ulster v Leinster** (Ravenhill)
Aberavon v Pontypool
Armagh v Collegians
Bath v US Portsmouth
Bedford v Coventry
Birkenhead Park v Morley
Blackheath v Neath
Blackrock Coll v UC Dublin
Broughton Park v Nuneaton
Cardiff v Llanelli
Chester v Wilmslow
Civil Service v Palmerston
CIYMS v Derry
Clontarf v Wanderers
Cross Keys v Maesteg
Dolphin v Bohemians
Ebbw Vale v Nuneaton
Exeter v Cheltenham
Galwegians v Bective Rangers
Glamorgan Wands v S Wales Police
Gosforth v Otley
Harlequins v Cambridge Univ
Hayle v Camborne
Headingley v Harrogate
Huddersfield v St Helens
Hull and ER v Hartlepool Rovers
Instonians v UC Cork
King's Scholars v Dungannon
Leicester v Moseley
London Irish v Gloucester
London Scottish v Oxford Univ
London Welsh v Newport
Manchester v Bradford
Monkstown v Dublin Univ
Newbridge v Bridgend
New Brighton v St Mary's Coll
NIFC v Old Belvedere
Nottingham v Halifax
Oxford v Tredegar
Plymouth Albion v Barnstaple
Pontypridd v Birmingham
Rosslyn Park v Waterloo
Roundhay v Northern
Rugby v Liverpool
Saracens v Abertillery
Sheffield v Orrell
Swansea v Richmond
Terenure Coll v Ballymena
UC Galway v Academy
Wakefield v Durham City
Wasps v Met Police
Waterpark v Garryowen
Weston-super-Mare v Bristol

367

Young Munster v Sunday's Well

*SRU Championship: Division 1*

Boroughmuir v West of Scotland
Gala v Kelso
Haddington v Stewart's Melville FP
Jordanhill v Langholm
Kilmarnock v Heriot's FP
Watsonians v Hawick

*SRU Championship: Division 2*

Clarkston v Jedforest
Glasgow High v Leith Acads
Gordonians v Melrose
Highland v Edinburgh Acads
Madras FP v Edinburgh Wands
Selkirk v Ayr

**Sunday, 26 November**

Galwegians v Bective Rangers
Old Belvedere v Greystones

**Wednesday, 29 November**

**Monmouthshire v New Zealanders**
  (Newport)
Bridgend v Swansea
Cardiff v Oxford Univ
Llanelli v Bath

**Saturday, 2 December**

**Wales 'B' v France 'B'** (Aberavon)
**North of England v New Zealanders**
  (Birkenhead Park)
**South of Scotland v Glasgow**
Ulster Under 23 v Munster Under 23
1 Academy v Ballymena
Ards v Collegians
Birkenhead Park v Sunday's Well
Blackheath v Harlequins
Bridgend v Abertillery
Bristol v Newport
Burton v Sheffield
Cambridge Univ v Birmingham
Carlow-Kilkenny v Bective Rangers
CIYMS v Blackrock Coll
Coventry v Richmond
Dolphin v Shannon
Fylde v New Brighton
Gala v Gosforth
Gloucester v Moseley
Halifax v Rugby
Harrogate v Loughborough Students
Headingley v Roundhay
Instonians v Derry
Jedforest v Wilmslow
Jordanhill v Glasgow High
Kelso v Ayr
Kilmarnock v Trinity Acads

Langholm v Edinburgh Wands
Launceston v Falmouth
Liverpool v Saracens
London Irish v Plymouth Albion
London Scottish v Bath
London Welsh v Aberavon
Maesteg v Ebbw Vale
Malone v Heriot's FP
Manchester v Wakefield
Met Police v Nuneaton
Monkstown v Civil Service
Neath v Bedford
Newbridge v Cross Keys
NIFC v Lansdowne
Northampton v Llanelli
Northern v Orrell
Nottingham v UAU
Old Belvedere v Queen's Univ
Oxford Univ v Gloucester
Palmerston v Bangor
Penzance-Newlyn v Camborne
Pontypool v Glamorgan Wands
Rosslyn Park v Wasps
St Ives v Exeter
Sale v Pontypridd
S Wales Police v Widnes
Stewart's Melville FP v Clarkston
Swansea v Cardiff
Tredegar v Penarth
UC Cork v Garryowen
Vale of Lune v Broughton Park
Wanderers v Greystones
Waterloo v Leicester
Watsonians v Selkirk
West Hartlepool v Hull and ER
West of Scotland v Gordonians
Widnes v Huddersfield

**Sunday, 3 December**

Galwegians v Terenure Coll
Monkstown v Athlone

**Tuesday, 5 December**

**North and Midlands (Scotland) v
  New Zealanders** (Aberdeen)

**Wednesday, 6 December**

**Dublin Univ v UC Dublin**
Pontypridd v Cross Keys
Rosslyn Park v Exeter Univ
Sale v Manchester Univ

**Thursday, 7 December**

Gloucester v Loughborough Students

**Saturday, 9 December**

**SCOTLAND v NEW ZEALAND**
  (Murrayfield)

**Munster v Ulster** (Cork)
Abertillery v Birmingham
Ballymena v Ards
Bangor v Monkstown
Barnstaple v Exeter
Bath v Gloucester
Bective Rangers v Northampton
Birkenhead Park v Headingley
Blackrock Coll v Wanderers
Boroughmuir v Orrell
Broughton Park v Bradford
Camborne v Truro
CIYMS v Terenure
Collegians v Old Belvedere
Coventry v Llanelli
Dunfermline v West of Scotland
Dungannon v Armagh
Edinburgh Wands v Percy Park
Falmouth v Redruth
Gala v Ayr
Glamorgan Wands v Penarth
Glasgow Acads v Palmerston
Gosforth v Harrogate
Haddington v Howe of Fife
Halifax v Wilmslow
Harlequins v Bedford
Huddersfield v Hull and ER
Jedforest v Blaydon
Jordanhill v Morpeth
Kelso v Langholm
Leicester v Blackheath
Loughborough Students v Roundhay
London Welsh v Cardiff
Maesteg v Pontypridd
Manchester v Fylde
Melrose v Tynedale
Met Police v London Irish
Moseley v Bristol
Neath v Bridgend
Newbridge v Swansea
New Brighton v West Hartlepool
Newport v Aberavon
Northern v Chester
Nottingham v Liverpool
Nuneaton v Pontypool
Plymouth Albion v S Wales Police
Portadown v Academy
Preston Lodge FP v Gordonians
Richmond v Rosslyn Park
Royal High v Clarkston
Rugby v Streatham-Croydon
Sale v Waterloo
Saracens v Cheltenham
Selkirk v Kilmarnock
Skerries v NIFC
Stewart's Melville FP v Perthshire
Trinity Acads v Heriot's FP
Wakefield v Middlesbrough
Wasps v London Scottish

**Sunday, 10 December**

**Connacht v Leinster** (Galway)

Cork Const v Garryowen
UC Cork v Sunday's Well
Young Munster v Dolphin

**Tuesday, 12 December**

**Oxford Univ v Cambridge Univ**
(Twickenham)
Hillhead v Kilmarnock
Howe of Fife v Clarkston

**Wednesday, 13 December**

**Bridgend v New Zealanders**

**Friday, 15 December**

Clifton v Tredegar
Old Belvedere v Blackrock Coll

**Saturday, 16 December**

**Barbarians v New Zealanders**
(Cardiff)
**Edinburgh v Glasgow**
**Scottish North and Midlands v**
**South**
Academy v NIFC
Ballymena v Malone
Bath v Harlequins
Bective Rangers v Old Wesley
Birkenhead Park v London Scottish
Birmingham v Oxford
Blackrock Coll v Skerries
Boroughmuir v Jedforest
Bradford v Waterloo
Bristol v Leicester
Broughton Park v Halifax
Camborne v St Ives
CIYMS v Bangor
Clarkston v Trinity Acads
Dublin Univ v Sunday's Well
Dungannon v Wanderers
Ebbw Vale v Neath
Edinburgh Acads v West of Scotland
Edinburgh Univ v Haddington
Exeter v Glamorgan Wands
Falmouth v Penzance-Newlyn
Gala v Langholm
Garryowen v UC Dublin
Gloucester v Coventry
Gordonians v Stewart's Melville FP
Harrogate v Hartlepool Rovers
Heriot's FP v Glasgow Acads
Hull and ER v Roundhay
Jordanhill v Dunfermline
Kilmarnock v Edinburgh Wands
Langholm v Gala
Liverpool v Manchester
London Irish v London Welsh
Middlesbrough v Kelso
Monkstown v Cork Const
Morley v Wilmslow

Moseley v Bedford
Northampton v Wasps
Northern v Melrose
Nottingham v Gosforth
Nuneaton v New Brighton
Orrell v Wakefield
Palmerston v Young Munster
Portadown v Instonians
Preston Grasshoppers v Huddersfield
Queen's Univ v Collegians
Richmond v Blackheath
Rosslyn Park v Plymouth Albion
Sale v Headingley
Saracens v Rugby
St Mary's Coll v Dolphin
Selkirk v Hawick
Sheffield v Solihull
Taunton v Penarth
UC Cork v Galwegians
Vale of Lune v Fylde
Watsonians v Ayr

### Sunday, 17 December

**Leinster v Munster** (Lansdowne Road)

### Wednesday, 20 December

Cross Keys v Pontypool
Old Belvedere v Monkstown

### Saturday, 23 December

**Glasgow v North and Midlands** (Hughenden)
**South of Scotland v Edinburgh**
**Schweppes WRU Cup – 2nd Round**
*(Welsh fixtures subject to re-arrangement)*
Alnwick v Kelso
Ayr v Jordanhill
Ballymena v CIYMS
Bangor v Instonians
Bedford v Waterloo
Blackheath v Nottingham
Blackrock Coll v Skerries
Bradford v Orrell
Bristol v Exeter
Cardiff v Bridgend
Cheltenham v Northampton
CIYMS v Ballymena
Collegians v Academy
Coventry v Rosslyn Park
Dolphin v Cork Const
Dunfermline v Clarkston
Edinburgh Wands v Trinity Acads
Gala v Glasgow Acads
Glasgow High v Boroughmuir
Gloucester v Newport
Hartlepool Rovers v Sheffield
Headingley v Wakefield
Highland v Stewart's Melville FP

Huddersfield v Morley
Hull and ER v Davenport
Langholm v Hawick
Liverpool v Birkenhead Park
London Welsh v Leicester
Maesteg v Aberavon
Melrose v Jedforest
Middlesbrough v Gosforth
Morpeth v Northern
Moseley v Birmingham
Neath v Pontypridd
Newbridge v Abertillery
New Brighton v Waterloo
Nuneaton v Halifax
Queen's Univ v Dungannon
Penarth v S Wales Police
Plymouth Albion v Clifton
Richmond v Harlequins
Roundhay v Harrogate
Rugby v Bath
St Austell v Camborne
Selkirk v Heriot's FP
Tredegar v Weston-super-Mare
Vale of Lune v Wilmslow
Wanderers v Terenure Coll
Wasps v Saracens
West of Scotland v Broughton Park

### Sunday, 24 December

Sunday's Well v Highfield

### Tuesday, 26 December

Aberavon v Neath
Abertillery v Ebbw Vale
Bath v Clifton
Ballymena v Dungannon
Bedford v Old Paulines
Bridgend v Maesteg
Bristol v Newbridge
Campbellians v Instonians
Cardiff v Pontypridd
Clanwilliam v Dolphin
Coventry v Moseley
Cross Keys v Tredegar
Exeter v Exmouth
Falmouth v Penryn
Fylde v Preston Grasshoppers
Gloucester v Lydney
Harrogate v Bradford
Heriot's FP v Royal High
Jedforest v Hawick
Lansdowne v Wanderers
Llanelli v London Welsh
Manchester v Wilmslow
Melrose v Gala
New Brighton v Old Birkonians
Newport v Watsonians
Northampton v Harlequins
Northern v Gosforth
Old Millhillians v London Irish
Redruth v Camborne

Rugby v Nuneaton
Sale v Broughton Park
Selkirk v Dunfermline
Swansea v Glamorgan Wands
UC Cork v Cork Const
Waterloo v Birkenhead Park

## Wednesday, 27 December

**Leicester v Barbarians**
Swansea v London Welsh

## Saturday, 30 December

### English County Championship Final
### Scottish North and Midlands v Edinburgh
Aberavon v Pontypridd
Alnwick v Gala
Ayr v Glasgow Acads
Bangor v Ballymena
Bective Rangers v Old Belvedere
Bedford v Rosslyn Park
Birkenhead Park v Nuneaton
Blackheath v Birmingham
Blaydon v Selkirk
Bradford v Hull and ER
Camborne v Penryn
Clarkston v Ardrossan Acads
Coventry v Cardiff
Dunfermline v Heriot's FP
Edinburgh Univ v Boroughmuir
Falmouth v Teignmouth
Fylde v Sale
Galwegians v Athlone
Garryowen v Bohemians
Glamorgan Wands v Abertillery
Gloucester v Bridgend
Haddington v Perthshire
Harris FP v Gordonians
Harrogate v Wakefield
Hawick v Gosforth
Headingley v Leicester
Hillhead v Jordanhill
Huddersfield v Wharfedale
Instonians v Academy
Jedforest v West of Scotland
Kelso v Melrose
Lansdowne v CIYMS
Llanelli v Bristol
London Irish v Esher
London Scottish v Harlequins
Maesteg v Swansea
Manchester v Liverpool
Met Police v Saracens
Monkstown v Clontarf
Newbridge v Neath
Newport v Exeter Univ
NIFC v Collegians
Northampton v Bath
Northern v Sunderland
Orrell v Rugby
Palmerston v Corinthians

Plymouth Albion v Exeter
Pontypool v S Wales Police
Portadown v Dungannon
Preston Grasshoppers v Halifax
Roundhay v New Brighton
Sheffield v Ruthin
Stewart's Melville FP v Glasgow
  High
Sunday's Well v Terenure Coll
Tynedale v Langholm
UC Dublin v Wanderers
Wasps v Nottingham
Waterloo v Moseley
Wilmslow v Richmond

## Monday, 1 January 1979

**Bridgend v Crawshay's Welsh**
Bristol v Clifton
Cardiff v Bath
Carlisle v Langholm
Collegians v CIYMS
Ebbw Vale v Tredegar
Fylde v St Helens
Gala v Royal High
Gosforth v Novocastrians
Halifax v Sheffield
Huddersfield v Wakefield
Llanelli v Penarth
London Welsh v Bedford
Moseley v Gloucester
Newport v Cardiff Coll of Ed
Otley v Wilmslow
Pontypridd v Cilfynydd
Preston Grasshoppers v Birkenhead
  Park
Roundhay v Roundhegians
Sale v Manchester
Saracens v Blackheath
Wasps v Rosslyn Park
Wilmslow v Broughton Park

## Tuesday, 2 January

Camborne v Cornwall Under 23
Clarkston v Kilmarnock
Greenock Wanderers v Ayr
Hawick v Heriot's FP
Melrose v Glasgow High

## Wednesday, 3 January

Pontypool v Pontypridd

## Saturday, 6 January

**Ireland Trial** (Lansdowne Road)
**Scotland Trial** (Murrayfield)
**Wales Schools v Scotland
  (19 Gp)** (Newport)
Abertillery v Cheltenham
Academy v Malone

Birkenhead Park v Gala
Blackheath v Rosslyn Park
Boroughmuir v Gordonians
Bridgend v Newport
Bristol v Bedford
Broughton v Clarkston
Broughton Park v St Helens
Camborne v Plymouth Albion
Cardiff v Moseley
Collegians v Bangor
Edinburgh Acads v Kilmarnock
Ebbw Vale v Saracens
Fylde v Liverpool
Galwegians v Dolphin
Glasgow Acads v Stewart's Melville
  FP
Gloucester v London Scottish
Halifax v Harrogate
Harlequins v Army
Hillhead v Ayr
Hull and ER v Gosforth
Instonians v Blackrock Coll
Jordanhill v Alnwick
Kelso v Hawick
Langholm v Jedforest
Leicester v Bath
London Irish v Rugby
London Welsh v Northampton
Maesteg v S Wales Police
Met Police v Cross Keys
Melrose v Selkirk
Monkstown v CIYMS
Neath v Coventry
Newbridge v Glamorgan Wands
New Brighton v Sale
NIFC v Dublin Univ
Northern v Carlisle
Nottingham v US Portsmouth
Nuneaton v Roundhay
Old Belvedere v Lansdowne
Palmerston v Wanderers
Penarth v Pontypool
Richmond v Wasps
Royal High v Haddington
St Ives v Falmouth
St Mary's Coll v Ballymena
Sheffield v Huddersfield
Swansea v Aberavon
Taunton v Exeter
Tredegar v Birmingham
UC Dublin v Dungannon
Wakefield v Bradford
Waterloo v Manchester
Watsonians v Heriot's FP
West of Scotland v Edinburgh Wands
Wilmslow v Orrell

## Sunday, 7 January

Bective Rangers v Waterpark
Highfield v Garryowen
Palmerston v Wanderers
Sunday's Well v Cork Const

Terenure Coll v UC Cork

## Wednesday, 10 January

Bath v Royal Navy
Roundhay v N East Universities

## Friday, 12 January

## Welsh Schools (19 Gp) v Yorkshire Schools (Penarth)

## Saturday, 13 January

## Schweppes WRU Cup – 3rd Round
*(Welsh fixtures subject to re-arrangement)*
**Connacht U23 v Ulster U23**
Ballymena v NIFC
Bath v London Welsh
Bedford v Sale
Birkenhead Park v Nottingham
Birmingham v Newbridge
Bohemians v Palmerston
Boroughmuir v Clarkston
Bradford v Halifax
Bristol v Coventry
Chester v Huddersfield
CIYMS v Clontarf
Clifton v Exeter
Cork Const v Bective Rangers
Dublin Univ v Garryowen
Dungannon v St Mary's Coll
Fylde v Nuneaton
Gala v Orrell
Gosforth v Glasgow Acads
Harlequins v Blackheath
Headingley v Manchester
Heriot's FP v Hillhead
Highfield v Dolphin
Hull and ER v Westoe
Jedforest v Kelso
Jordanhill v Leith Acads
Kilmarnock v Highland
Langholm v Ayr
Leicester v Gloucester
Liverpool v Harrogate
London Irish v RAF
Malone v Instonians
Melrose v Hawick
Morley v Selkirk
Neath v Ebbw Vale
Newquay Hornets v Falmouth
Northampton v Moseley
Northern v West of Scotland
Old Belvedere v Wanderers
Penarth v Abertillery
Penzance-Newlyn v Plymouth Albion
Richmond v Saracens
Rosslyn Park v London Scottish
Roundhay v Otley
St Ives v Camborne
Sheffield v Wakefield
S Wales Police v Cross Keys

Stewart's Melville FP v Edinburgh
Wands
Sunday's Well v Greystones
Terenure Coll v Academy
Tredegar v Maesteg
Trinity Acads v Haddington
UC Cork v Blackrock Coll
UC Dublin v Monkstown
Wasps v Exeter Univ
Waterloo v Broughton Park
Wilmslow v New Brighton

## Sunday, 14 January

Ballinasloe v Galwegians
Clanwilliam v Palmerston

## Wednesday, 17 January

Newport v Swansea

## Thursday, 18 January

Cheltenham v Met Police

## Friday, 19 January

Abertillery v Aberavon
Haddington v Kenfig Hill
Old Belvedere v Instonians
Palmerston v Cork Const

## Saturday, 20 January

**SCOTLAND v WALES** (Murrayfield)
**IRELAND v FRANCE** (Lansdowne
Road)
Bath v Met Police
Bedford v Leicester
Birmingham v Rugby
Boroughmuir v Selkirk
Bridgwater & Albion v Exeter
Broughton Park v Preston
Grasshoppers
Cambridge Univ v Edinburgh Univ
Clarkston v Hillhead
Cooke v NIFC
Dublin Univ v Bangor
Edinburgh Wands v Kelso
Glamorgan Wands v Pontypool
Gordonians v Alnwick
Gosforth v Richmond
Halifax v Hartlepool Rovers
Harlequins v Birkenhead Park
Harrogate v Orrell
Heaton Moor v Hull and ER
Headingley v Waterloo
Heriot's FP v Cardiff
Langholm v Glasgow High
Liverpool v Bristol
London Irish v Northampton
London Scottish v Blackheath

London Welsh v Sale
Monkstown v Ballymena
New Brighton v Coventry
Nottingham v Nuneaton
Old Edwardians v Manchester
Penarth v Newbridge
Penryn v Camborne
Plymouth Albion v Weston-super-
Mare
Portadown v Collegians
Redruth v Falmouth
Royal High v West of Scotland
Saracens v Moseley
Sheffield Univ v Sheffield
Skerries v Dungannon
S Wales Police v Cheltenham
Stewart's Melville FP v Melrose
Vale of Lune v Northern
Wakefield v Roundhay
Wasps v Gloucester
Watsonians v Jedforest
West Hartlepool v Huddersfield
Wilmslow v Fylde

373

## Sunday, 21 January

Bective Rangers v Corinthians
Blackrock Coll v Old Wesley
Bohemians v UC Cork
Dolphin v Sunday's Well
Terenure Coll v Garryowen
Wanderers v St Mary's Coll
Young Munster v Galwegians

## Monday, 22 January

Cross Keys v Newport
Edinburgh Univ v Oxford Univ

## Tuesday, 23 January

Bristol v Royal Navy

## Wednesday, 24 January

Abertillery v Tredegar
Army v Oxford Univ
Bridgend v S Wales Police
Cambridge Univ v RAF
Kilmarnock v Kelvinside Acads

## Saturday, 27 January

**John Player Cup – 1st Round**
(*English fixtures subject to
re-arrangement*)
Leinster Under 23 v Ulster Under 23
Abertillery v Bridgend
Bath v Saracens
Birkenhead Park v Cambridge Univ
Blackheath v Royal Navy
Bohemians v Bective Rangers
Bradford v New Brighton
Bristol v S Wales Police

374

Broughton Park v Wilmslow
Cardiff v Aberavon
Clarkston v Haddington
Clifton v Penarth
Collegians v Instonians
Clontarf v Blackrock Coll
Coventry v Swansea
Cross Keys v Neath
Dolphin v Lansdowne
Dungannon v CIYMS
Durham City v Halifax
Fylde v Cheltenham
Garryowen v Old Wesley
Glamorgan Wands v Ebbw Vale
Gordonians v Greenock Wands
Gosforth v Manchester
Greystones v Monkstown
Hawick v Roundhay
Huddersfield v Blaydon
Hull and ER v Liverpool
Jordanhill v Haddington
Kelso v Jedforest
Kilmarnock v Royal High
Leicester v Rosslyn Park
London Welsh v London Scottish
Melrose v Watsonians
Middlesbrough v Gala
Moseley v Gloucester
Newbridge v Maesteg
Newport v Llanelli
Northern v Headingley
Nottingham v RAF
Old Crescent v Old Belvedere
Orrell v Pontypool
Otley v Harrogate
Palmerston v Academy
Pontypridd v Plymouth Albion
Portadown v Ballymena
Queen's Univ v NIFC
Richmond v Waterloo
St Mary's Hosp v Met Police
Selkirk v Langholm
Sheffield v Heaton Moor
Skerries v Sunday's Well
Stewart's Melville FP v Ayr
Torquay Ath v Camborne
Tredegar v Bridgwater & Albion
Truro v Falmouth
UC Cork v Dublin Univ
Wakefield v Hartlepool Rovers
Wanderers v Army
Wasps v Sale
West of Scotland v Boroughmuir
Weston-super-Mare v Nuneaton
West Hartlepool v Edinburgh Univ

## Sunday, 28 January

Galwegians v Westport

## Tuesday, 30 January

Kelso v Selkirk

## Wednesday, 31 January

Cambridge Univ v Royal Navy
Plymouth Albion v Exeter Univ
Rosslyn Park v Army

## Friday, 2 February

Abertillery v Old Belvedere
Bedford v London Welsh
Bridgend v Palmerston
Bristol v Gloucester
Pontypridd v Lansdowne
Rosslyn Park v Bath
Tredegar v Pontypridd

## Saturday, 3 February

**ENGLAND v SCOTLAND**
 (Twickenham)
**WALES v IRELAND** (Cardiff)
Academy v Instonians
Ayr v Hutchesons'
Birkenhead Park v Moseley
Boroughmuir v Trinity Acads
Cambridge Univ v Army
Clarkston v Jordanhill
Dungannon v Athlone
Durham Univ v Selkirk
Exeter v Exeter Univ
Gala v West Hartlepool
Garryowen v Dolphin
Glamorgan Wands v Aberavon
Gordonians v Perthshire
Halifax v Morley
Harrogate v Fylde
Hartlepool Rovers v Roundhay
Headingley v Richmond
Heaton Moor v Huddersfield
Highfield v Galwegians
Hillhead v Haddington
Hull and ER v Middlesbrough
Jedforest v Heriot's FP
Kelso v Leith Acads
Kilmarnock v Melrose
Liverpool v Sale
London Scottish v Leicester
Loughborough Students v Manchester
Met Police v Nottingham
New Brighton v Gosforth
NIFC v St Mary's Coll
Nuneaton v Bradford
Old Wesley v Collegians
Orrell v Broughton Park
Oxford Univ v RAF
Penarth v Neath
Preston Lodge FP v Edinburgh Wands
Queen's Univ v CIYMS
Rugby v Cheltenham
St Helens v Sheffield
Stewart's Melville FP v Edinburgh
 Acads
Sunday's Well v Bohemians

Wakefield v Birmingham
Wanderers v Dublin Univ
Wasps v Harlequins
Waterloo v Coventry
West of Scotland v Glasgow Acads

## Sunday, 4 February

Bective Rangers v Terenure
Bristol v Camborne
Garryowen v Dolphin
London Irish v Blackheath
Monkstown v Blackrock Coll
Saracens v Northampton

## Monday, 5 February

Newport v Bridgend
Pontypool v Newbridge

## Wednesday, 7 February

Cambridge Univ v Rosslyn Park
Oxford Univ v Royal Navy
Swansea v Pontypridd
Tredegar v Glamorgan Wands

## Saturday, 10 February

Aberavon v Cross Keys
Abertillery v Broughton Park
Academy v Collegians
Ballymena v Blackrock Coll
Bangor v NIFC
Bedford v Headingley
Birmingham v Wilmslow
Blackheath v Richmond
Bridgend v London Welsh
Camborne v Hayle
Cambridge Univ v Wasps
Cardiff v Bristol
Dublin Univ v Cork Const
Dungannon v Terenure Coll
Glamorgan Wands v Clifton
Gloucester v Bath
Gosforth v Waterloo
Halifax v Birkenhead Park
Harrogate v W Hartlepool
Huddersfield v Hartlepool Rovers
Instonians v CIYMS
Leicester v Newport
Llanelli v Harlequins
London Irish v Liverpool
London Scottish v Coventry
Loughborough Students v Wakefield
Maesteg v Met Police
Manchester v Rugby
Moseley v Northampton
Neath v Swansea
Northern v New Brighton
Nottingham v Pontypridd
Nuneaton v Edwardians
Old Belvedere v Galwegians

Orrell v Fylde
Palmerston v Clontarf
Penarth v Ebbw Vale
Rugby v Manchester
Sale v Rosslyn Park
Saracens v Pontypool
Sheffield v Hull and ER
Sidmouth v Falmouth
Streatham-Croydon v Plymouth
   Albion
S Wales Police v Newbridge
Stroud v Tredegar
Sunday's Well v Bective Rangers
UC Cork v UC Dublin
Weston-super-Mare v Exeter
Young Munster v Monkstown

*SRU Championship: Division 1*

Hawick v Kilmarnock
Heriot's FP v Haddington
Jordanhill v Gala
Kelso v Watsonians
Stewart's Melville FP v
   Boroughmuir
West of Scotland v Langholm

*SRU Championship: Division 2*

Ayr v Edinburgh Acads
Edinburgh Wands v Gordonians
Highland v Glasgow High
Jedforest v Selkirk
Leith Acads v Madras FP
Melrose v Clarkston

## Sunday, 11 February

Dolphin v Curragh
Old Belvedere v Garryowen
Wanderers v Lansdowne

## Tuesday, 13 February

Plymouth Albion v Torquay Ath

## Wednesday, 14 February

Llanelli v Glamorgan Wands
Moseley v Loughborough Students
Queen's Univ v Dublin Univ

## Friday, 16 February

Aberavon v Ebbw Vale
Bridgend v Bath
Old Belvedere v London Irish
Palmerston v Malone
Swansea v Gloucester
Tredegar v S Wales Police

375

## Saturday, 17 February

**IRELAND v ENGLAND**
(Lansdowne Road)
**FRANCE v WALES** (Paris)
**Scotland 'B' v France 'B'** (Ayr)
**Royal Navy v RAF** (Twickenham)
Abertillery v Moseley
Bangor v Sunday's Well
Birkenhead Park v Broughton Park
Birmingham v Manchester
Bradford v Sale
Boroughmuir v Edinburgh Acads
Bristol v Richmond
Dublin Univ v Instonians
Dungannon v Collegians
Edinburgh Wands v Hawick
Exeter v Barnstaple
Glamorgan Wands v Bridgend
Gordonians v Watsonians
Gosforth v Wilmslow
Greystones v NIFC
Haddington v Penicuik
Halifax v Huddersfield
Headingley v Harlequins
Heriot's FP v Clarkston
Hull and ER v Northern
Jedforest v Gala
Jordanhill v Trinity Acads
Kilmarnock v Leith Acads
Launceston v Camborne
Leicester v Fylde
London Scottish v Bedford
Loughborough Students v Liverpool
Lydney v Penarth
Marr v Ayr
Melrose v West of Scotland
New Brighton v Wakefield
Northampton v Coventry
Nottingham v Neath
Nuneaton v Oxford
Old Merchant Taylors v Oxford Univ
Orrell v Pontypridd
Penryn v Falmouth
Percy Park v Roundhay
Redruth v Plymouth Albion
Rosslyn Park v Saracens
Rugby v Cambridge Univ
Selkirk v Kelso
Sheffield v Walsall
Sidcup v Met Police
Stewart's Melville FP v Dunfermline
Wasps v London Welsh
Waterloo v Harrogate
Weston-super-Mare v Maesteg

## Sunday, 18 February

Bective Rangers v St Mary's Coll
Blackheath v Torquay Ath
Blackrock Coll v Lansdowne
Clontarf v London Irish
Dolphin v UC Galway

Garryowen v Young Munster
Monkstown v Galwegians
UC Cork v Shannon
Wanderers v Old Wesley

## Monday, 19 February

Cross Keys v Newport
Pontypool v S Wales Police

## Wednesday, 21 February

Bath v Exeter Univ
Cambridge Univ v Anti-Assassins
London Univ v Saracens
Rosslyn Park v London Irish

## Friday, 23 February

**Welsh Schools (19 Gp) v Welsh Youth**
(Bridgend)

## Saturday, 24 February

**John Player Cup – 2nd Round**
**Schweppes WRU Cup – 4th Round**
*(scheduled fixtures subject to
re-arrangement)*
Aberavon v Gloucester
Abertillery v Newport
Ballymena v Queen's Univ
Bangor v Academy
Bath v Wasps
Birkenhead Park v Waterloo
Birmingham v Taunton
Blackheath v Army
Bradford v Liverpool
Bridgend v Bedford
Camborne v Penzance-Newlyn
Cambridge Univ v Saracens
Cardiff Coll of Ed v Penarth
Coventry v Fylde
Cork Const v Wanderers
Dolphin v Old Wesley
Dublin Univ v Young Munster
Exeter v Guy's Hospital
Falmouth v St Ives
Galway Corinthians v Monkstown
Galwegians v Blackrock Coll
Harrogate v Broughton Park
Hull and ER v Preston Grasshoppers
Instonians v Armagh
Lansdowne v Garryowen
London Irish v Richmond
London Scottish v Met Police
Lydney v Tredegar
Maesteg v Cross Keys
Moseley v Gosforth
Neath v London Welsh
Newbridge v Exeter Univ
New Brighton v Cheltenham
Northampton v Leicester
Northern v Halifax

Nottingham v Oxford Univ
Old Belvedere v Waterpark
Orrell v Middlesbrough
Otley v Huddersfield
Plymouth Albion v Rugby
Royal Navy v Harlequins
  (Portsmouth)
St Helens v Wakefield  ·
Sale v Roundhay
Shannon v Sunday's Well
Skerries v Palmerston
S Wales Police v Glamorgan Wands
Stafford v Sheffield
UC Dublin v Bective Rangers
West Hartlepool v Manchester
Wilmslow v Davenport

*SRU Championship: Division 1*

Boroughmuir v Heriot's FP
Haddington v Hawick
Langholm v Gala
Kilmarnock v Kelso
Watsonians v Jordanhill
West of Scotland v Stewart's
  Melville FP

*SRU Championship: Division 2*

Ayr v Jedforest
Clarkston v Edinburgh Wands
Edinburgh Acads v Glasgow High
Gordonians v Leith Acads
Madras FP v Highland
Selkirk v Melrose

**Sunday, 25 February**

UC Galway v UC Cork

**Wednesday, 28 February**

Coventry v Met Police
Gloucester v Abertillery
Gordonians v Aberdeen Univ
Hillhead v West of Scotland
Leicester v Royal Navy
Llanelli v Cardiff
Palmerston v Old Belvedere
Roundhay v Leeds Univ

**Friday, 2 March**

Bath v Bristol
Bedford v RAF
Gloucester v Northampton
Kelso v Gala
Pontypool v Neath
Pontypridd v Newbridge
Swansea v Bridgend

**Saturday, 3 March**

**ENGLAND v FRANCE**
  (Twickenham)
**SCOTLAND v IRELAND**
  (Murrayfield)
Athlone v Garryowen
Ballymena v Old Wesley
Barnstaple v Falmouth
Birmingham v Roundhay
Blackheath v Moseley
Boroughmuir v Ayr
Broughton Park v Loughborough
  Students
Cardiff v Ebbw Vale
Cheltenham v Harrogate
Chester v Hull and ER
CIYMS v Palmerston
Cork Const v Old Belvedere
Dolphin v Waterpark
Dunfermline v Gordonians
Durham City v Sheffield
Ebbw Vale v Newport
Edinburgh Wands v Jordanhill
Exeter v Plymouth Albion
Fylde v Langholm
Glasgow Acads v Clarkston
Haddington v Melrose
Headingley v Nottingham
Heriot's FP v Edinburgh Wands
Highfield v Dungannon
Instonians v Lansdowne
Kilmarnock v Bangor
Leicester v Harlequins
Leith Acads v West of Scotland
Liverpool v Northern
Llanelli v Orrell
London Irish v St Mary's Hosp
London Welsh v Rosslyn Park
Maesteg v Glamorgan Wands
Manchester v Morley
Met Police v Birkenhead Park
Nuneaton v Saracens
New Brighton v Halifax
NIFC v Academy
Penarth v Tredegar
Queen's Univ v Bective Rangers
Richmond v London Scottish
Rugby v Oxford Univ
Sale v Gosforth
Stewart's Melville FP v Hawick
S Wales Police v Abertillery
Sunderland v Jedforest
Wakefield v Huddersfield
Wanderers v Collegians
Wasps v Coventry
Widnes v Waterloo

**Sunday, 4 March**

Clanwilliam v Blackrock Coll
Galwegians v Corinthians
Monkstown v St Mary's Coll

Sunday's Well v Old Crescent

**Wednesday, 7 March**

**East Midlands v Barbarians**
(Northampton)
**UAU Final** (Twickenham)
Bristol v Army
Cross Keys v Newbridge
Lydney v Glamorgan Wands
Nottingham v Nuneaton
Pontypool v Aberavon
Swansea v S Wales Police

**Thursday, 8 March**

Oxford Univ v Oxfordshire

**Saturday, 10 March**

**John Player Cup quarter-finals**
(*English fixtures subject to
re-arrangement*)
**Royal Navy v Army** (Twickenham)
**Welsh Youth v French Youth**
(Ebbw Vale)
Bath v Swansea
Bedford v Harlequins
Birmingham v Orrell
Birkenhead Park v Manchester
Blackrock Coll v Dublin Univ
Bradford v Gosforth
Bridgend v Aberavon
Bristol v London Scottish
Broughton Park v Fylde
Camborne v Falmouth
Civil Service v Garryowen
CIYMS v Academy
Collegians v Queen's Univ
Cross Keys v Abertillery
Edinburgh Acads v Jedforest
Exeter v Nottingham
Galwegians v St Mary's Coll
Guy's Hospital v Nuneaton
Halifax v Sale
Huddersfield v Northern
Leicester v Coventry
London Irish v Loughborough
  Students
London Welsh v Blackheath
Maesteg v Llanelli
Met Police v Stroud
Moseley v Ebbw Vale
Newbridge v Cheltenham
New Brighton v Halifax
Newton Abbot v Tredegar
Old Belvedere v Corinthians
Old Millhillians v Wasps
Palmerston v Bective Rangers
Pontypool v Cardiff
Pontypridd v Ebbw Vale
Portadown v NIFC
Richmond v Gloucester

378

Rosslyn Park v Northampton
Roundhay v Wilmslow
Rugby v Nottingham
Saracens v Neath
Sheffield v West Hartlepool
S Wales Police v Plymouth Albion
Sunday's Well v Monkstown
Wakefield v Hull and ER
Wanderers v Ballymena
Waterloo v Headingley
Young Munster v UC Cork

*SRU Championship: Division 1*

Gala v Watsonians
Hawick v Boroughmuir
Heriot's FP v West of Scotland
Jordanhill v Kilmarnock
Kelso v Haddington
Langholm v Stewart's Melville FP

*SRU Championship: Division 2*

Edinburgh Acads v Jedforest
Edinburgh Wands v Selkirk
Glasgow High v Madras FP
Highland v Gordonians
Leith Acads v Clarkston
Melrose v Ayr

**Sunday, 11 March**

Dolphin v Cork Const

**Tuesday, 13 March**

Leicester v Loughborough Students

**Wednesday, 14 March**

Cheltenham v Gloucester
Coventry v London Irish
Llanelli v S Wales Police
Newport v Glamorgan Wands
RAF v Rugby

**Friday, 16 March**

Cardiff v London Welsh
Ebbw Vale v Maesteg
Leicester v RAF
Neath v Newbridge
Old Belvedere v Dublin Univ
Palmerston v Old Wesley
Pontypridd v Abertillery
Tredegar v Cross Keys

**Saturday, 17 March**

**WALES v ENGLAND** (Cardiff)
**FRANCE v SCOTLAND** (Paris)
Academy v Bangor
Bective Rangers v Wanderers

Bedford v Saracens
Birmingham v Loughborough Students
Blaydon v Edinburgh Wands
Bohemians v Collegians
Boroughmuir v Tynedale
Bradford v Rugby
Camborne v Exeter
CIYMS v NIFC
Dalziel HSFP v Clarkston
Derry v Ballymena
Dungannon v Malone
Ebbw Vale v Bath
Fylde v Gala
Glamorgan Wands v Weston-super-
  Mare
Glasgow Acads v Melrose
Gosforth v Halifax
Haddington v Harris Acads
Harlequins v Coventry
Harrogate v Birkenhead Park
Hawick v Orrell
Headingley v Liverpool
Heriot's FP v Glasgow High
Huddersfield v Vale of Lune
Hull and ER v Broughton Park
Instonians v Queen's Univ
Jedforest v Stewart's Melville FP
Kelso v Sunderland
Kilmarnock v Bradford
Kircaldy v Gordonians
Langholm v Selkirk
Manchester v Davenport
Met Police v New Brighton
Moseley v Richmond
Northampton v Sale
Northern v Jordanhill
Nottingham v Rosslyn Park
Penarth v Askeans
Plymouth Albion v Bristol
Pontypridd v Roundhay
Sheffield v Preston Grasshoppers
US Portsmouth v Wasps
West Hartlepool v Wakefield
West of Scotland v Ayr
Wilmslow v Waterloo

## Sunday, 18 March

Bective Rangers v Wanderers
London Irish v Nuneaton
Met Police v Blackheath
Monkstown v Terenure Coll

## Monday, 19 March

Aberavon v Newport
Maesteg v Pontypool
Melrose v Edinburgh Univ

## Tuesday, 20 March

Glamorgan Wands v Pontypridd

## Wednesday, 21 March

Abertillery v Cardiff Coll of Ed
Clifton v Bristol
Cross Keys v Llanelli

## Saturday, 24 March

**Army v RAF** (Twickenham)       379
**France Colts v England Colts**
Abertillery v Nottingham
Academy v Greystones
Bangor v CIYMS
Bath v Richmond
Blackheath v Bedford
Boroughmuir v Melrose
Bradford v Wasps
Bridgend v Ebbw Vale
Broughton Park v Chester
Camborne v Launceston
Civil Service v Collegians
Clarkston v Greenock Wands
Derry v Dungannon
Edinburgh Wands v Birkenhead Park
Exeter v Cross Keys
Falmouth v Truro
Fylde v West of Scotland
Gala v Hawick
Gordonians v Kilmarnock
Gosforth v Watsonians
Headingley v New Brighton
Heriot's FP v Stewart's Melville
  FP
Huddersfield v Durham City
Hull and ER v Halifax
Jordanhill v Glasgow Acads
Kelvinside Acads v Ayr
Liverpool v Roundhay
Llanelli v Neath
London Irish v Birmingham
London Scottish v Moseley
London Welsh v Harlequins
Manchester v Orrell
Met Police v S Wales Police
Newbridge v Aberavon
Newport v Cardiff
Northern v Met Police
NIFC v Instonians
Nuneaton v Harrogate
Old Millhillians v Glamorgan Wands
Otley v Wakefield
Plymouth Albion v Maesteg
Pontypool v Penarth
Pontypridd v Weston-super-Mare
Rosslyn Park v Bristol
Rugby v West Hartlepool
Sale v Leicester
Saracens v Gloucester
Selkirk v Jedforest
Sunderland v Haddington
Tredegar v Taunton
Tynedale v Kelso
Vale of Lune v Sheffield

Waterloo v Northampton
Wilmslow v Middlesbrough

## Monday, 26 March to Thursday, 29 March

Rosslyn Park Schools Sevens

## Tuesday, 27 March

British Post Office v Scottish
  Select (Kelso)
Aberdeen GSFP v Gordonians
Haddington v North Berwick

## Wednesday, 28 March

Bristol v Aberavon
Cheltenham v Bath
Ebbw Vale v Pontypool
Gala v Melrose
Glamorgan Wands v Newbridge
Maesteg v Neath
Paignton v Exeter
Penarth v Newport
Royal High v Boroughmuir

## Saturday, 31 March

**Schweppes WRU Cup semi-finals**
  (*Welsh fixtures subject to re-arrangement*)
**England Colts v Welsh Youth** (Hull)
**Rosslyn Park Centenary Schools
  International Sevens**
Ayr v Preston Lodge FP
Ballymena v Academy
Bedford v Northampton
Birmingham v London Scottish
Boroughmuir v Sale
Bristol v Blackheath
Camborne v Newquay Hornets
Cardiff v Swansea
Cardiff Coll of Ed v Tredegar
CIYMS v Queen's Univ
Collegians v Malone
Cork Const v Instonians
Coventry v Saracens
Dungannon v Bangor
East Kilbride v Clarkston
Ebbw Vale v Llanelli
Edinburgh Wands v Glasgow Acads
Exeter v Sidcup
Fylde v Birkenhead Park
Galwegians v Skerries
Garryowen v Greystones
Glasgow High v Kilmarnock
Haddington v Watsonians
Harlequins v Royal Navy

Hawick v Abertillery
Hayle v Falmouth
Hillhead v Gordonians
Hull and ER v Blaydon
Jedforest v Otley
Kelso v Edinburgh Acads
Kendal v Roundhay
Langholm v Melrose
Leicester v Rugby
Liverpool v Orrell
Morpeth v Selkirk
Neath v Newport
Newbridge v London Welsh
New Brighton v London Irish
Northern v Morley
Nottingham v Bath
Nuneaton v Cross Keys
Penarth v Glamorgan Wands
Percy Park v Huddersfield
Plymouth Albion v Gloucester
Pontypool v Bridgend
Pontypridd v Aberavon
Richmond v Met Police
Stewart's Melville FP v NIFC
Tynedale v Gala
Wakefield v Sheffield
Wasps v Gosforth
Waterloo v St Helens
West of Scotland v Hartlepool
  Rovers
Wigton v Jordanhill
Wilmslow v Clifton

## Sunday, 1 April

All-England Under 16 Sevens
  (Sunbury)

## Monday, 2 April

Gala v Selkirk
Jedforest v Abertillery

## Wednesday, 4 April

Amman Utd v Neath
Birkenhead Park v Liverpool
Cross Keys v Swansea
Manchester v Macclesfield
Nuneaton v Coventry
Pontypridd v Penarth

## Saturday, 7 April

**John Player Cup semi-finals**
  (*English fixtures subject to
  re-arrangement*)
**Wales Schools (19 Gp) v Ireland Schools**
  (Cardiff)
Aberavon v Llanelli
Abertillery v Pontypool
Bath v Newport
Bedford v Wasps

Birkenhead Park v Leicester
Bridgend v Rosslyn Park
Bristol v Harlequins
Brixham v Falmouth
Camborne v Devonport Services
Chester v Sheffield
Civil Service v Ballymena
Clifton v Birmingham
Collegians v CIYMS
Coventry v Ebbw Vale
Cross Keys v Plymouth Albion
Esher v Pontypridd
Exeter v Streatham-Croydon
Gloucester v Cardiff
Halifax v Manchester
Harrogate v Nottingham
London Irish v Moseley
London Scottish v Saracens
London Welsh v Swansea
Maesteg v Neath
Met Police v St Helens
Middlesbrough v Huddersfield
Neath v Richmond
NIFC v Dungannon
New Brighton v Liverpool
Northampton v Headingley
Queen's Univ v Academy
Roundhay v Gosforth
Rugby v Broughton Park
Sale v Wakefield
S Wales Police v Penarth
Sunderland v Hull and ER
US Portsmouth v Blackheath
Waterloo v Northern
Wilmslow v Nuneaton

**Sunday, 8 April**

Surrey Sevens
Monkstown v Greystones

**Wednesday, 11 April**

**Scotland Schools v England
(19 Gp)** (Gala)
London Floodlit Sevens (Rosslyn
Park)
Bath v Pontypridd
Bridgend v Llanelli
Coventry v Rugby
Glamorgan Wands v Cross Keys
Liverpool v Waterloo
Maesteg v Maesteg Celtic
New Brighton v Manchester
S Wales Police v Ebbw Vale

**Thursday, 12 April**

Lydney v Gloucester

**Friday, 13 April**

**Penarth v Barbarians**
Aberavon v Northampton

Blaydon v Gordonians
Camborne v Wasps
Falmouth v Woodford
Nottingham v Hartlepool Rovers
Pontypool v Birmingham
Pontypridd v Tredegar
Rugby v Wilmslow
Saracens v Broughton Park

**Saturday, 14 April** 381

**Cardiff v Barbarians**
**Ireland Schools v Scotland (19 Gp)**
**France Schools v Wales (19 Gp)**
(Nice)
**Melrose Sevens**
Aberavon v London Welsh
Ayr v City of Derry
Bath v West Hartlepool
Birkenhead Park v Royal Navy
Bohemians v Ballymena
Bridgwater & Albion v Birmingham
Bristol v Liverpool
Camborne v Woodford
Collegians v NIFC
Cross Keys v S Wales Police
Ebbw Vale v Abertillery
Exeter v UAU
Falmouth v Old Dunstonians
Gloucester v New Brighton
Gosforth v Coventry
Halifax v Fylde
Harrogate v Bedford
Huddersfield v Wilmslow
Hull and ER v Otley
Leicester v Neath
Llanelli v Northampton
Maesteg v Bridgend
Met Police v Esher
Morley v Orrell
Newbridge v Wakefield
Northern v Sale
Nottingham v Plymouth Albion
Penzance-Newlyn v Wasps
Percy Park v Gordonians
Pontypool v Nuneaton
Pontypridd v Oxford
Roundhay v Bradford
Rugby v Headingley
Saracens v Manchester
Selkirk v Instonians
Swansea v Harlequins
Waterloo v Glasgow High
West Park v Glamorgan Wands

**Monday, 16 April**

**Swansea v Barbarians**
Bath v S Wales Police
Bedford v Nuneaton
Birkenhead Park v Glasgow High
Bridgend v Pontypridd
Bristol v Abertillery
Camborne v Streatham-Croydon

Cardiff v Harlequins
Ebbw Vale v Wakefield
Gloucester v Fylde
Harrogate v Northern
Headingley v Coventry
Leicester v Maesteg
Llanelli v Exeter Univ
Manchester v Boroughmuir
382  Neath v Aberavon
New Brighton v Morley
Newport v London Welsh
Northampton v Met Police
Penarth v Wrexham
Plymouth Albion v UAU
Pontypool v Orrell
Preston Grasshoppers v Roundhay
Redruth v Wasps
Rugby v Nottingham
Saracens v Halifax
Tredegar v Ebbw Vale
Waterloo v Royal Navy
West Hartlepool v Broughton Park
Weston-super-Mare v Birmingham
Widnes v Glamorgan Wands

**Tuesday, 17 April**

**Newport v Barbarians**
**England 19 Gp v France Schools**
  (Otley)

**Wednesday, 18 April**

Newbridge v Gloucester
Penarth v Bridgend
Pontypridd v Llanelli

**Thursday, 19 April**

Glamorgan Wands v Lydney

**Saturday, 21 April**

**John Player Cup Final**
  (Twickenham)
**Wales Schools v England 19 Gp**
  (Swansea)
Aberavon v Swansea
Abertillery v Newbridge
Bath v Llanelli
Blaydon v Sheffield
Bradford v Northern
Broughton Park v Liverpool
Burton v Hull and ER
Camborne v Redruth
Cardiff v Neath
Cheltenham v Wasps
Coventry v Bedford
Cross Keys v Pontypridd
Esher v Exeter
Falmouth v Newton Abbot
Glamorgan Wands v Penarth
Gloucester v Sale
Halifax v Waterloo

Harrogate v Morley
Headingley v Gosforth
Leicester v Bristol
Manchester v Vale of Lune
Moseley v Bridgend
New Brighton v Fylde
Newport v Pontypool
Nottingham v Richmond
Plymouth Albion v Nuneaton
Rosslyn Park v Harlequins
Roundhay v Birkenhead Park
Rugby v Huddersfield
Stroud v Birmingham
Torquay Ath v Tredegar
Wilmslow v West Hartlepool

**Tuesday, 24 April**

Falmouth v Penryn

**Wednesday, 25 April**

Birkenhead Park v New Brighton
Birmingham v Cheltenham
Bristol v Pontypool

**Friday, 27 April**

Abertillery v Cross Keys
Newbridge v Penarth
Penzance–Newlyn v Tredegar

**Saturday, 28 April**

**Schweppes WRU Cup Final** (Cardiff)
**Middlesex Sevens preliminaries**
Bedford v Bath
Birkenhead Park v Bradford
Broughton Park v Northern
Camborne v Tredegar
Cheltenham v Nottingham
Clifton v Plymouth Albion
Coventry v Bristol
Davenport v Wakefield
Exeter v Gloucester
Falmouth v Launceston
Fylde v Headingley
Glamorgan Wands v Taunton
Hartlepool Rovers v Gosforth
Huddersfield v Burton
Ilkley v Sheffield
Liverpool v Wilmslow
Manchester v Roundhay
Moseley v Leicester
New Brighton v Kendal
Northampton v Birmingham
Percy Park v Hull and ER
Pontypridd v Maesteg
Rugby v Lydney
Sale v Orrell
Vale of Lune v Halifax
Waterloo v Morley

**Sunday, 29 April**

Manchester Sevens

**Monday, 30 April**

Falmouth v St Austell
St Ives v Tredegar
S Wales Police v Pontypridd
Talywain v Pontypool

**Saturday, 5 May**

**Middlesex Sevens Finals**
(Twickenham)
**Welsh Snelling Sevens** (Cardiff)

**Saturday, 12 May**

**WRU National Sevens**                383

# MAJOR FIXTURES IN BRITAIN, IRELAND AND FRANCE 1978–79

October 1978

14  **ENGLAND XV v ARGENTINA** (Twickenham)
17  **Wales 'B' v Argentina** (Llanelli)

November

4   **IRELAND v NEW ZEALAND** (Dublin)
11  **WALES v NEW ZEALAND** (Cardiff)
25  **ENGLAND v NEW ZEALAND** (Twickenham)

December

2   **Wales 'B' v France 'B'** (Aberavon)
9   **SCOTLAND v NEW ZEALAND** (Murrayfield)
12  **Oxford Univ v Cambridge Univ** (Twickenham)
16  **BARBARIANS v NEW ZEALANDERS** (Cardiff)
30  **English County Championship Final**

January 1979

6   **Ireland Trial** (Dublin)
    **Scotland Trial** (Murrayfield)
20  **SCOTLAND v WALES** (Murrayfield)
    **IRELAND v FRANCE** (Dublin)

February

3   **ENGLAND v SCOTLAND** (Twickenham)
    **WALES v IRELAND** (Cardiff)

17  **FRANCE v WALES** (Paris)
    **IRELAND v ENGLAND** (Dublin)
    **Scotland 'B' v France 'B'** (Ayr)
    **Royal Navy v RAF** (Twickenham)

March

3   **ENGLAND v FRANCE** (Twickenham)
    **SCOTLAND v IRELAND** (Murrayfield)
7   **UAU Final** (Twickenham)
10  **Royal Navy v Army** (Twickenham)
    **Scottish Club Championship concludes**
17  **WALES v ENGLAND** (Cardiff)
    **FRANCE v SCOTLAND** (Paris)
24  **Army v RAF** (Twickenham)
31  **Schweppes WRU Cup Semi–Finals**

April

7   **John Player Cup Semi-Finals**
21  **John Player Cup Final** (Twickenham)
28  **Schweppes WRU Cup Final** (Cardiff)

May

5   **Middlesex Sevens Finals** (Twickenham)
    **Welsh Snelling Sevens** (Cardiff)
12  **WRU National Sevens**

## NEW ZEALAND TO BRITAIN AND IRELAND 1978

October

18 **Cambridge University**
21 **Cardiff**
25 **West Wales**
   (Swansea)
28 **London Counties**
   (Twickenham)

November

4  **IRELAND**
   (Dublin)
7  **Ulster**
   (Ravenhill, Belfast)
11 **WALES**
   (Cardiff)
15 **South and South West**
   (Bristol)
18 **Midlands**
   (Leicester)
21 **Combined Services**
   (Aldershot)
25 **ENGLAND**
   (Twickenham)
29 **Monmouthshire**
   (Newport)

December

2  **North of England**
   (Birkenhead Park)

5  **Scottish North and Midlands**
   (Aberdeen)
9  **SCOTLAND**
   (Murrayfield)
13 **Bridgend**
16 **Barbarians**
   (Cardiff)

## ARGENTINA TO BRITAIN AND IRELAND 1978

September

27 **Southern Counties**
   (Oxford)
30 **London**
   (Twickenham)

October

4  **North of England**
   (Headingley)
7  **North Midlands**
   (Moseley)
10 **England Students**
   (Gloucester)
14 **ENGLAND XV**
   (Twickenham)
17 **Wales 'B'**
   (Llanelli)
21 **Leinster**
   (Dublin)